7-26-65

POLITICS IN THE CONGO

POLITICS
IN THE
CONGO

DECOLONIZATION
AND INDEPENDENCE

BY CRAWFORD YOUNG

1965

PRINCETON • NEW JERSEY

PRINCETON UNIVERSITY PRESS

Printed in the United States of America
THE WILLIAM BYRD PRESS, INC.
Richmond, Virginia

Acknowledgments 1316077

THIS study is a collective enterprise. Perhaps the most difficult task in writing it is to distill from the almost endless list of persons and institutions who have helped to make the final product possible a few to whom my deep gratitude should be formally recorded.

The list must start with the professor from whom I received my first encouragement, Rupert Emerson. I join the generations of students who have deeply appreciated the sense of modesty mingled with wisdom which infuses Professor Emerson's approach to scholarship.

Two of my contemporaries working in the same field, René Lemarchand and Herbert Weiss, will perhaps recognize here and there traces of the many hours of fruitful debate I have shared with them.

No one can study the Congo without being impressed by the scope and quality of the documentary record which Belgium has produced. This tradition is now, happily, being carried on by the *Centre de Recherche et d'Information Socio-Politiques* (CRISP) and its sister institution in the Congo, the *Institut National d'Etudes Politiques* (INEP). I would like to cite specifically Benoit Verhaegen, a prime mover in both bodies, whose extraordinary scholarly productivity is not achieved through any rationing of his time, for his generous advice and counsel go my warmest thanks. To INEP's able secretary, Louis Mandala, and to his colleague David McAdams, I would like to add my expression of appreciation.

Another constant friend was Professor A. A. J. Van Bilsen, whom Belgium is fortunate to have at the head of its technical assistance program. Among his most noteworthy services was introducing me to one of his former students, Dominique Ryelandt, whom I accompanied on an administrative inquiry through most of Leopoldville province—a very valuable experience.

Traditionally, the University of Louvain has played a pioneering role in Congo research. Guy Malengreau was generous both in counsel and in making available to me some of his personal archives. No acknowledgment would be complete without mention of his assistant, Aimé Lecointre, an inexhaustible source of insight and background.

The hospitality of the *Musée Royal d'Afrique Centrale* at Tervuren was greatly appreciated. I should like to pay particular tribute to the Museum's dedicated bibliographer, Mlle. Olga Boone, its historian, Luwel, and its anthropologist, Maessen, for their unstinting cooperation. The finest Congo library in Belgium is that of the former Colonial Ministry; my thanks go to its staff, especially to Jean Berlage for his frequent bibliographic assistance. At the *Institut de Sociologie* (ex-Solvay), the Secretary, Henri Rosy, was generous in his help.

Another institution which is a great credit to Belgium and the Congo is the *Université Lovanium*. To its energetic rector, Monsignor Luc Gillon, go my thanks for making fully available both the scholarly and residential facilities of the *colline inspirée*. Among the many outstanding members of its academic staff who helped me in my work, I would like to express my special thanks to E. de Bethune, Hugues Leclercq, and Antoine Wembi.

I cannot begin to name the hundreds of Congolese officials, priests, and students who have contributed to this study during my visits to that country in 1958, 1962, and 1963. The Congo has a hidden capital of dedication to duty and professional competence of many of its officials that is too little recognized.

For offering exhaustive criticism to the entire manuscript, I am particularly grateful to Professors Verhaegen, Lemarchand, and Edouard Bustin, who are obviously exonerated from responsibility for any errors of fact or judgment which may remain.

This study was made possible by a generous grant from the Ford Foundation in support of the field research and the drafting. As always, the Foundation takes no responsibility for the presentation or the conclusions.

The University of Wisconsin Cartographic Laboratory, under the able direction of Randall Sale, gave invaluable assistance in the preparation of the maps. The University also contributed to the completion of this work through a generous grant of research leave.

Finally, a special word is in order to mark my most profound appreciation to my wife, who has so fully shared in every stage of the preparation of this study. Scarcely a page does not bear the mark of her lucid criticism. To her this study is respectfully dedicated.

Contents

Acknowledgments   v
List of Tables   x
List of Maps   xii

I. Introduction   3
II. Behemoth: A Brief Portrait   10
III. Decolonization: The Belgian Vision   33
IV. Paternalism   59
V. Desegregating Colonial Society   73
VI. From the Ground Up: The Communes   106
VII. Disintegration of the System   140
VIII. A Structure for Independence   162
IX. Elites: Chiefs, Clerks and Traders   184
X. The Mass: Workers and Peasants   204
XI. The Politics of Ethnicity   232
XII. The Rise of Nationalism: From Primary
Resistance to Political Parties   273
XIII. A Profile of Independence: 1960-1963   307
XIV. The Political Sector: Parliament, Parties
and Politicians   358
XV. The Administration and Judiciary:
Resurgent Bureaucracy   398
XVI. The Politics of Force: Army and Police   438
XVII. Federalism: The Quest for a Constitution   475
XVIII. Fragmentation: The New Provinces   533
XIX. Conclusions   572
XX. Epilogue   582

Appendix: Note on Methodological
Assumptions
Bibliography
Index

ix

Tables

1. *Conseil Colonial* Members and Background, 1958   25
2. Legislative History, Decree of March 26, 1957
   (*Statut des Villes*)   109
3. Leopoldville Election Results According to Region
   of Origin   119
4. Postwar Election Results in Belgium   142
5. Brussels and Leopoldville since World War II   149
6. Plan for New Institutions, Governmental Declaration, January 13, 1959   168
7. Six Chiefs   192
8. Prestige Scale in Elisabethville   195
9. The Modern Elite—Background of the First Congolese Government   198
10. African School Attendance in 1959   200
11. Self-Employed Africans, 1959   202
12. Growth of Wage-Earning Population   206
13. Percentage Living Outside Traditional Milieu, by
    Province   206
14. Growth in Proportion of Population Living in
    Towns   206
15. Growth of Major Congolese Cities   207
16. Origins of Population of Nine Largest Cities   207
17. Level of Education by Ethnic Group, Luluabourg   264
18. Seats Won, May, 1960, Election   302
19. Summary of Ten Major Parties   304
20. Ministries of Central Government since Independ-
    ence   346-348
21. Chronology of Major Events, 1960-1963   350
22. Agricultural Production, 1959-1962   356
23. Mineral Production, 1959-1962   357
24. *Statut Unique*   402

25. Composition of Civil Service, 1960   402
26. Table of Organization, Ministerial Cabinets (Provincial and Central)   409
27. Civil Service Reform   414
28. Judicial Organization, June 30, 1960   420
29. Fragmentation from Tananarive to Formation of New Provinces   548
30. Profile of New Provinces   552-553
31. Provincial Governments, 1960-1962   567
32. Leadership and Stability in the New Provinces   568-570

Maps

1. Free State Crisis Areas   218
2. Labor Intensive Centers, 1920's   221
3. Cotton Zones   225
4. Ethnic Map   233
5. Primary Resistance Movements   283
6. May, 1960, Elections, Ten Major Parties   303
7. Fragmentation and Disorder, 1960-1962   333
8. New Provinces   534

POLITICS IN THE CONGO

CHAPTER I

XXXXXXXXXXXXXXXXXXXXXXXXXXXXXXXXXXXXXXXXXXXXX

Introduction

XXXXXXXXXXXXXXXXXXXXXXXXXXXXXXXXXXXXXXXXXXXXX

The Voice of Jeremiah

IN 1926, a distinguished Belgian colonial magistrate, Paul Salkin, took a gloomy look forward into what the twenty-first century might hold in store for Africa.[1] Only Algeria remained a colony. The Congo was tenuously held on a trusteeship; its European tutors, however, were engulfed in a wave of disaffection and revolt. "The Negroes," sadly remarked the Governor-General to the King of the Belgians, then retired to a university professorship, "are becoming ungovernable. University graduates, worker agitators, American Negroes incite them to disobedience and suspicion. . . . Those who struggle most ardently against us are the university graduates, who owe us everything. For them, higher education means simply 'Africa for the Africans.'"[2]

Education and modernization, according to this forecast, had produced a virulent, reactive nationalism, catalyzed by a messianic, syncretic religion, "Ngoism," led by an American Negro.[3] "There is no greater race than ours," mourned the pensioned monarch. "But the working of the human spirit is beyond its ken. This is why its achievements contain the germ of their own destruction."[4] The prophecy ends in a vision of holocaust: "On the given signal, the *Force Publique*, for a long time subverted by Ngoist Christianity, rose

[1] Paul Salkin, *L'Afrique centrale dans cent ans* (Paris: Payot, 1926).

[2] *Ibid.*, p. 20.

[3] Belgian colonial thinking had been shaken by the appearance of the first messianic religious movements, with Kimbanguism sweeping a large part of the Bakongo areas, in Leopoldville province, in 1921, and the Mwana Lesa movement penetrating southern Katanga in 1925. It was widely feared that the Garveyite movement in the United States would contaminate the Congo; on the latter phenomenon, see Ch. de Bus de Warnaffe, "Le mouvement pan-nègre aux Etats-Unis et ailleurs," *Congo*, I, No. 5 (May 1922), 713-27.

[4] Salkin, *op. cit.*, p. 58.

3

and imprisoned European officers and functionaries."[5]

History and African nationalism did not grant European rule the century reprieve that Salkin predicted; they did not even concede the thirty years which another prophet, A. A. J. Van Bilsen, three decades later thought conceivable to engineer a decolonization.[6] The colonial edifice was shaken to its foundations by the unexpected and bloody riots in Leopoldville, January 4 through 6, 1959; this explosion occurred at a historic moment when the foundations of the colonizers' self-confidence had been invisibly sapped and when unarticulated misgivings and insecurity lay close to the surface, needing only the external catalyst.

In eighteen months, the Congo surged to independence on a tide over which neither colonizer nor colonized had much control. A series of improvisations followed, each tailored to yesterday's crises and perspectives, and already obsolete and even anomalous by the time of their application. Belgium, confronted with a narrow range of policy alternatives, all of which involved heavy risks, committed itself in January 1960, to *"le pari congolais"* (literally, the Congo gamble). The Congolese, leaders and led, desperately sought to adjust themselves to and to profit from the new possibilities suddenly opened to them. They were embarked on what has been aptly described as "the most radical decolonization plan ever applied in a colony."[7] The ful-

[5] *Ibid.*, p. 189. The Salkin essay created in its day a considerable stir; the outspoken Apostolic Vicar of Elisabethville, Mgr. Jean de Hemptinne, described it as *"tout à fait inopportun."*

[6] A. A. J. Van Bilsen, *Vers l'indépendance du Congo et du Ruanda-Urundi* (Brussels: 1956).

[7] J. Gérard-Libois and Benoit Verhaegen, *Congo 1960* (Brussels: Centre de Recherche et d'Information Socio-Politiques, 1961), p. 5. The *Centre de Recherche et d'Information Socio-Politiques,* hereafter referred to by its more familiar initials, CRISP, has made available to posterity an outstanding documentation on Congo politics since 1959 through its various publications. Its several collaborators, and above all Verhaegen, have shown exceptional zeal in amassing materials and acumen in their analysis. Any student of Congo politics incurs a heavy debt to CRISP and to its sister institution in the Congo,

fillment of Salkin's curiously accurate prophecy of mutiny of the *Force Publique* followed hard on the heels of independence ceremonies, and a telescoped transition in power transfer was compounded by Africa's most spectacular Africanization of the entire administration and army. In less than two years the profile of Congolese politics had altered from being tropical Africa's most completely European-dominated power structure to a degree of Africanization that only Guinea could match. This revolutionary transformation has few historic parallels.

Aims and Objects

The object of this study is to analyze an African political system that slowly emerged out of the rubble of a decolonization which went awry. It aims at contributing in a small way to a comparative politics of African independence. It is concerned with the challenge of nation-building in Africa, the strains upon the polity today growing from the arbitrary entities that empire-builders of the imperial age carved out in Africa. The bold pencil strokes on the maps at the Berlin Conference have left a latent fragmenting and secessionist potential in most tropical African states. The option of the African leadership to retain the colonial entities as separate, sovereign states poses for nearly all the new states (except Rwanda, Burundi, Somalia, Basutoland, and Swaziland) the difficult task of giving moral content and legitimation to the state by creating a sense of nation.

The requirements of nation-building involve finding a stable reconciliation of the incipient nation as a focus of identity with the pre-existing matrix of loyalties centered on the ethnic group. This means that leaders and led must stand in some relationship whereby communication between them may occur, acceptable mechanisms for conflict resolution exist, and collective action by the community in

---

the *Institut National d'Etudes Politiques* (ex-*Institut Politique Congolais*).

the interest of development may be undertaken without constant invocation of force. Further, there must be within the polity the organizational capacity to give effect to decisions made.

The Congo must be seen first against the backdrop of certain recurrent patterns in independent Africa. These include the transfer of the mobilized energies of the nationalist movement from the negative purpose of destroying the colonial government to the positive goal of nation-building and social progress, and the adaptation of the Western-style parliamentary systems which were the constitutional legacy of colonial rule to meet the requirements of unity and authority of the new state.[8] Emergent trends now becoming clear are a shift to authoritarian methods of government and an unequal distribution of the fruits of independence between the rulers and ruled.[9]

The Congo's pre-colonial history, however, did not parallel exactly that of other tropical African states, and certainly the nature of "culture contact" under Belgian rule differed in a number of significant ways from the experience of African states formerly under British or French rule or the present Portuguese colonies. The direction of decolonization, especially in the earlier phases when its plodding pace was still under the control of the Belgian administration, conformed to the unfolding Belgian vision of the future of the Congo. Thus the contours of Congolese nationalism when it finally emerged did not entirely correspond to the pattern set elsewhere on the African scene. And it is unnecessary to reiterate the special factors growing out of the drastically compressed transition period and post-independence breakdown.

[8] On this subject, on a continental scale, see Immanuel Wallerstein, *Africa, The Politics of Independence* (New York: Vintage Books, 1961); Guy Hunter, *The New Societies of Tropical Africa* (London: Oxford University Press, 1962).

[9] Martin Kilson, "Authoritarianism and Single-Party Tendencies in African Politics," *World Politics*, XV, 262-94.

It is not the purpose of this study to unravel the intricate web of causality in Congo political history since World War II, but only to examine certain aspects insofar as they illuminate the nature of the Congo political system since 1960. An effort has been made to avoid unnecessary duplication of other scholarly work on the Congo; therefore, the sections dealing with the roots of nationalism and the growth of political parties will be somewhat compressed in favor of fuller treatment of themes less well elucidated elsewhere.[10]

The role of the United Nations in the post-independence period is dealt with here only occasionally and in peripheral fashion. This is admittedly misleading in some senses; the role of the UN in the dénouement of the Congo crisis has been of enormous importance. Other external forces have played their part both through the UN and directly. This, however, is another tale, which bears its own telling. Both analytically and practically, it is possible to accept the UN and foreign influences as given constants in the political equation. This is not to suggest that the Congo situation today would be the same without the UN; rather it is quite possible that the Katanga secession would have succeeded and the former Belgian Congo would have splintered into half a dozen petty states. Further, the UN directly or indirectly has an important role in some important phases of policy-making, especially in the financial and monetary fields. (It should be added immediately that expatriate influences are very strong in these areas in most of the new African states.) The UN exerted a major influence in resolving the constitutional crisis which began September 5, 1960, with the mutual revocations by President Joseph Kasavubu and Prime Minister Patrice Lumumba, which were compounded by the neutralization of all parties by then-Colonel

[10] Herbert Weiss will shortly publish an outstanding study of the *Parti Solidaire Africain* (PSA), and eventually will produce a larger work on Congolese political parties. René Lemarchand will publish in 1964 a study on the origins of Congolese political parties. Both of these are based on extensive field work in the Congo.

Joseph Mobutu nine days later. This part of the UN role ended with the unanimous investiture of Cyrille Adoula as Prime Minister on August 2, 1961. It is arguable that the presence of UN forces has, in some areas, prevented a complete deterioration of law and order. Be this as it may, the UN's interventions have mainly been operative at the summit level; only in this sense is it accurate to suggest the epigram that the UN was "a colonial surrogate without colonial authority."[11] Our assumption here is that political forces present in the situation have moved toward an equilibrium starting from this given exogenous factor.

The Katanga phenomenon also has been relegated to a secondary position in this study.[12] Again this should not be construed as a downgrading of the significance of the Katanga secession as a pivotal issue in the political process. Rather it is argued that the Katanga secession, like the UN factor, may be taken in the present analysis as a given element in the environment within which the political system is evolving.

It would be rash indeed to claim that an analysis of decolonization processes in the Congo, no matter how careful, had laid bare the essential motor elements in the political system and to presume to predict their direction. As one of America's shrewdest students of African politics has remarked, there is at the moment an important random element in the political equation, a factor which will probably slowly contract as a more or less durable post-colonial equilibrium emerges.[13]

This study will consist of three principal sections. The first will deal with the Belgian effort to engineer the Congo-

[11] This statement was put forward for discussion at a panel discussion on the Congo organized at the African Studies Association annual meeting for 1962, held in Washington, D.C., October 11-13.

[12] This has now been the subject of an excellent study by J. Gérard-Libois, *Sécession au Katanga* (Brussels: CRISP, 1963).

[13] Suggested by Ruth Schachter-Morgenthau in a lecture on "Europeans and the Shaping of African Cultures in Independent African Countries," Harvard University, February 19, 1963.

8

lese polity. This will treat the evolving vision of the future terminal goal of colonial policy and the successive policies adopted to give effect to these objectives, culminating in the *"pari congolais."* Secondly, the particular nature of the Congolese response to colonialism will be analyzed. This will include a portrait of the Congolese elite, an evaluation of the nature of the impact of Belgian colonial policy on both rural and urban patterns, the political role of ethnicity, and the particular organizational form taken by the nationalist movement. The concluding section will be devoted to trends and forces growing out of the 1960 calamity. These include fragmentation and the groping for institutional structures; the social and economic impact of breakdown; and the roles of the political, bureaucratic, and military sectors of the power structure. Our purpose is to suggest a first approximation of the nature of the emerging political system in the independent Republic of the Congo.

CHAPTER II

Behemoth: A Brief Portrait

Platonism and the Colonial Trinity

THE Belgian colonial edifice at its height was a remarkably solid structure. A masterful summary of the precepts of the system has been put forward by Thomas Hodgkin, who suggests the term "Platonism" to epitomize Belgian colonial rule:

"Platonism is implicit in the sharp distinction, social and legal, between Belgian philosopher-kings and the mass of African producers; in the conception of education as primarily concerned with the transmission of certain unquestioned and unquestionable moral values, and intimately related to status and function; in the belief that the thought and behavior of the mass is plastic, and can be refashioned by a benevolent, wise and highly trained elite; that the prime interest of the mass is in welfare and consumer goods—football and bicycles—not liberty; and in the conviction that it is possible, by expert administration, to arrest social and political change."[1]

It is traditional to analyze the colonial power structure in the Belgian Congo in terms of a trinity composed of the administration, Church, and large enterprises. It is important to recognize that not only was this triple alliance a virtually seamless web but each component, in its area of activity, was without peer in tropical Africa in the magnitude of its impact.

THE ADMINISTRATION

On the administration side, Buell has observed that as early as the 1920's the density of administration in the Congo was unequalled in Africa, with the insignificant

[1] Thomas Hodgkin, *Nationalism in Colonial Africa* (London: Frederick Muller, 1956), p. 52.

exceptions of Mauretania and Dahomey.[2] By the time of independence, there were 10,000 Belgian civil servants and officers in the administration, magistrature, and army.[3] No Congolese, rural or urban, could have failed to perceive that he was being administered. In the urban centers this is hardly surprising, but what differentiated the Belgian system from others in Africa was the extent of its occupation and organization of the countryside. Most familiar, and most unpopular, was the agricultural officer, of which there was at least one per territory, seconded by several African agricultural assistants and a network of *moniteurs* with rudimentary training to bring the administrative system in contact with virtually all the population. Legislation permitting 60 days per year (45 after 1955) of compulsory cultivation (or other public works) was generally applied until 1957 and was still legally authorized, although largely abandoned, in 1960.[4] The most active enforcement was in the cotton zones, which covered vast sections, mainly in the eastern half of the country, and in the rural hinterland adjacent to urban centers and mining camps to supply the African population with the staple elements in its diet. As early as 1937, it was estimated that 700,000 heads of family were covered by the compulsory system.[5] Between the European agricultural agents of the administration, and those in the employ of the cotton companies, the objective was to have one for each 2,000-3,000 planters.[6]

[2] Raymond Leslie Buell, *The Native Problem in Africa,* II (New York: Macmillan Company, 1928), 466.

[3] J. Gérard-Libois, "L'assistance technique belge et la République du Congo," *Etudes Congolaises,* II, No. 3 (1962), 2.

[4] Decree of December 5, 1933. This was reduced from 60 to 45 days by the decree of December 29, 1955, and maintained after long debate and considerable opposition in the decree of May 10, 1957, reforming the *circonscriptions indigènes.*

[5] Edmond Leplae, "Résultats obtenus au Congo Belge par les cultures obligatoires alimentaires et industrielles," *Zaïre,* I (February 1947), 137.

[6] A. Brixhe, *Le coton au Congo Belge* (3rd ed.; Brussels: Ministère du Congo Belge et du Ruanda-Urundi, 1958), p. 51.

The administration made its presence felt in many other ways. The relatively dense network of secondary roads had to be maintained by the villages. Until recent years and the more general use of the automobile and truck, portage levees were a frequent element in village life. In many areas, villages had been required by the administration to relocate themselves alongside the roadways. In an earlier day, recruitment pressures for service in the mines, plantations, and army had been intense, although in the postwar years the problem had been to halt the rural exodus rather than to use administrative pressure in recruitment. The Congo's excellent medical services likewise made themselves felt; large-scale immunization campaigns were conducted to locate and eliminate epidemic diseases, especially sleeping sickness. According to official figures, in 1930, 2,780,000 Africans received medical examinations; in 1955, the figure was 6,550,000.[7] Administrative officers serving in the territorial service were required to spend twenty days per month in the bush;[8] the instructions to territorial agents underlined this point: "The Government attaches the greatest importance to *territorial functionaries' visiting frequently the diverse parts of the territory under their authority,* and entering each time into contact with the natives."[9]

THE MISSIONS

One cannot fail to be impressed by the scope of the evangelical effort in the Congo. In 1958, it was estimated that the Congo counted 5,371,785 Christians, 80 percent of whom were Roman Catholics. At the end of the colonial era, the Catholics maintained 669 mission posts, manned by nearly 6,000 European missionaries. These were aided by nearly

[7] *Le Congo Belge* (Brussels: Inforcongo, 1958), I, 404.

[8] Lord Hailey, *An African Survey* (rev. ed.; London: Oxford University Press, 1957), p. 377.

[9] *Recueil à l'usage des fonctionnaires et des agents du service territorial au Congo Belge* (5th ed.; Brussels: Ministère des colonies, 1930), p. 100. Author's emphasis. Hereafter referred to as *Receuil.*

500 African priests, with new ones being confirmed at the rate of 35-40 a year. The clergy was in turn seconded by 25,566 catechists, offering rudimentary religious instruction in the villages. In the teaching and charitable orders, there were an additional 386 Congolese brothers and 745 nuns.[10] Not only was each village in regular contact with the administration but there were few which did not receive at least occasional visits from a missionary. Further, in no other African state, with the minor exceptions of Basutoland and Burundi, was university education launched by the Church.

The Protestants were always outsiders, because with the exception of one small Belgian group, the missionary force was composed of British, American, and Scandinavian nationals, whose loyalty to the Belgian colonial enterprise was somewhat suspect. But Leopold II had been in fact equally suspicious of the political designs of non-Belgian Catholic missions, especially Cardinal Lavigerie's White Fathers. A 1906 concordat was negotiated with the Vatican which set forth the salient principle which remained in force until 1960: the missionary effort was to be essentially Belgian.

The 1906 concordat then provided a framework through which a system of cooperation could be developed between missions and administration. The state not only subsidized the Catholic mission schools but paid for the maintenance of the missionaries. An important indirect material aid was in the legal provision authorizing a land grant of 200 hectares for each mission station established, which could be used not only to help sustain the mission station with provisions but for commercial exploitation. Missionary orders such as the Trappists, Franciscans, or Capucins, which had taken vows of poverty, did not use this method of underwriting their operating costs, but others, especially the largest Congo order, the Scheutists, did so on a consid-

[10] Chambre des Représentants, session de 1959-1960, *Rapport sur l'administration du Congo Belge pendant l'année 1958*, p. 165.

13

erable scale. The result was that the missions possessed relatively substantial resources with which to carry out their task in the Congo.

The Belgian administration itself was far more committed to evangelization as an integral part of its objective than were the British or French, who were confronted with the responsibility of ruling large Muslim populations. Functionaries were reminded by the government: "Government servants are not working alone in the task of civilization. The religious orders are participating in at least equal measure. . . . Civil servants, whatever their own religious views are under a strict obligation to aid the Christian missionaries."[11]

Belgian administrators were, of course, far from unanimous in their own religious attitudes. Although very few were Protestants, many were indifferent or frankly anticlerical. However, until the last years nearly all could agree that Christianity, especially its Catholic version, was a healthy doctrine for the African mass. The first Liberal Colonial Minister, Louis Franck, in his summary of the Congo in 1930, notes with approval that there were as many Catholic missionaries as functionaries (1,800) and describes their role as most useful. He quotes with apparent endorsement the views of one of the leading Catholic figures of the period, Monsignor Roelens: "What gives us especial hope, is to note that the entire colonial elite, no matter what their own opinion may be, is today persuaded that only the Christian-Catholic religion, based on authority, is capable of changing native mentality, of giving to our Africans a clear and intimate consciousness of their duties, of inspiring in them respect for authority and a spirit of loyalty toward Belgium."[12]

THE CORPORATIONS

The final element in the trinity of power, the large com-

[11] *Receuil*, pp. 57-58.

[12] Louis Franck, *Le Congo Belge* (Brussels: La Renaissance du Livre, 1930), I, 311; II, 208-09.

14

panies, was no less remarkable in the scale of its operation. In part these companies were a survival of the concessionary regime by which Leopold sought quickly to make effective the occupation of the country by the Free State or by its surrogates. (There was little continuity, however, between the Free State economy and that later built up. The former reposed essentially on wild rubber and ivory; these accounted for nearly all exports in the 1890's, and as late as 1908 accounted for 36.7 million francs of an export total of 43.4 million.[13]) The equatorial forest zone of the central basin became the site of the immense plantations of oil palm and rubber of companies of the Lever group and the *Société Générale* (*Compagnie de Kasai,* Busira-Lomami, etc.). Large-scale mining operations really only got underway on a large scale in the 1920's, but these, once started, operated on a labor-intensive basis which made their impact enormous. The mining operations were largely concentrated in the eastern half of the country; copper and allied metals were found in southern Katanga, tin in north Ka-

[13] A. J. Wauters, *Histoire politique du Congo Belge* (Brussels: Pierre Van Fleteren, 1911), p. 164; Georges Hostelet, *L'oeuvre civilisatrice de la Belgique au Congo de 1885 à 1953* (Brussels: ARSOM, Sci. Mor. et Pol., T. XXXVII, fasc. 2, 1954), I, 467. The *Institut Royal Colonial Belge,* founded in 1929, has published three major series, one a "Classe des Sciences Morales et Politiques," a second "Classe des Sciences Naturelles et Médicales," and the transactions of its formal sessions, the "Bulletin des Séances." In 1954, a "New Series" was initiated in both the first two categories, and the *Institut* was rebaptized the *Académie Royale des Sciences Coloniales.* Finally, in 1959, it brought itself into line with contemporary polite vocabulary in renaming itself the *Académie Royale des Sciences d'Outre-Mer.* As frequent references will be made to a number of works in this important collection, some liberty will be taken with strict historic bibliographic accuracy in order to reduce confusion, and the *Académie* will be referred to by its most recent title, abbreviated ARSOM. The series will be listed respectively as "Sci. Mor. et Pol.," "Sci. Nat. et Med.," and "Bull. Séances." "N.S." will distinguish those volumes whose numbering falls into the new series initiated in 1954.

The present Belgian franc is worth only 3% of the 1914 gold franc, in which these figures are expressed.

tanga and Maniema, diamonds in two major deposits at opposite ends of Kasai, and gold in the northeastern part of Orientale and south Kivu. Rare were the areas, such as the Kwango district, where there was not at least one major enterprise, either plantation or mining, which dominated the zone around it.

As with the missions, the colonial administration was expected to give full support to the companies in recruiting labor and seeing that food was produced for the labor camps. Investment was attracted to the Congo in part because the administration was prepared to go to unusual lengths both in making available the necessary land in the case of agricultural enterprises and in supporting recruiters with whatever administrative pressure was necessary. Government policy was set forth in a 1922 circular: "It is a mistake to believe . . . that once taxes are paid and other legal obligations met, the native may remain inactive. Under no circumstances may magistrates or officials express this opinion. In every case, I should consider this to be a lack of discipline violating the recommendations of the government and our most positive duties toward our black subjects."

Later that same year, Governor-General Maurice Lippens added that every government official should be "penetrated with the idea that his reason for existence is to favor and develop our occupation and that this duty consists of supporting every enterprise."[14]

Another factor operating in this direction was the career structure of the colonial service. After twenty-three years of service, when many were still at the peak of their vigor, colonial civil servants were retired. The pension was not spectacular, and many sought further employment. Since the large companies frequently recruited such persons, it was inevitable that many functionaries would define their

[14] Buell, *op. cit.*, II, 539. Lippens, it should be added, was more inclined to act in the interests of the business community than most of his successors, who probably would not have worded the circular quite so strongly.

administrative role with some view of their own future prospects of obtaining responsible, well-remunerated employment in the private sector upon retirement. The liberal[15] PSC Minister of Congo Affairs, Maurice Van Hemelrijck, was shocked on attaining office in December 1958 to discover how many of the top functionaries at the Ministry were drawing handsome salaries from colonial companies for sitting on boards of directors, with bonuses for "services rendered"; they were allegedly representing the interests of the state, which was part owner of many of the companies. By making a serious effort to remove these men, he made a number of enemies who later took part in his defenestration in September 1959.[16]

The potential for policy influence of the private sector was vastly increased by the very high degree of concentration of ownership. The overwhelming majority of large-scale enterprises are subsidiaries of a handful of giant holding companies; the best-known and largest is the *Société Générale de Belgique*. *"La Générale"* has controlling interests in *Union Minière du Haut-Katanga, Forminière* (dia-

[15] Some terminological confusion grows out of the fact that the Belgian Liberal Party is no longer a "liberal" group in the normal American usage of the word as "progressive," or in contrast to "conservative." Belgian Liberals are so in the 19th-century sense; historically, before the introduction of universal suffrage transformed Belgian politics by giving representation to the working class through the *Parti Socialist Belge* (PSB), the Liberals were to the left of the conservative Catholic Party and, in fact, led the fight to extend suffrage. However, especially since World War II, most of the former Catholic Party, now renamed the *Parti Social Chrétien* (PSC), influenced by the progressive social doctrines which have been an important theme in the regenerated Christian Democratic movement throughout Europe, has moved clearly to the left of the Liberal Party, which has become increasingly the organ of business and professional classes and the exponent of conservative policies. The party was rebaptized as the *Parti de Liberté et du Progrès* (PLP) in late 1961; the only important doctrinal change, however, has been an effort to drop anti-clericalism as a central theme. Thus *liberal* is to be distinguished in this study from *Liberal*.

[16] Jacques Marres and Pierre de Vos, *L'équinoxe de janvier* (Brussels: Editions Euraforient, 1959), pp. 202-03.

monds), BCK railroad, *Compagnie du Congo pour le Commerce et l'Industrie* (various agricultural and trading enterprises), *Compagnie Cotonnière Congolaise* (Cotonco), *Géomines* (tin), *Compagnie Pastorale du Lomami* (cattle), and a host of lesser companies.[17] This was a truly formidable aggregation of economic power. That the private sector should seek to influence policy formulation on its own behalf was natural enough; what was unusual in the colonial situation of the Congo was the relative absence of "countervailing" influence putting forward a fundamentally different view of the public interest. The colonial trusts had easy access to policy-making organs at all levels both through membership in formal consultative institutions and informal channels.

Cracks in the Monolith

Although the tripartite alliance tended to display a monolithic face to the external world and to the Congolese, it would be misleading to underestimate the continual dialogue that went on among them. Their interests were not in fact entirely the same: the administration was, in the final

[17] There is remarkably thorough documentation available on the economic structure of the Congo. For a penetrating and detailed study of the Belgian groups involved, see *Morphologie des groupes financiers* (Brussels: CRISP, 1962). A high official of the Belgian Communist Party, Pierre Joye, in collaboration with Rosine Lewin, has produced a detailed and useful catalogue of Congo companies, *Les trusts au Congo* (Brussels: Société Populaire d'Editions, 1961). The book is the result of thorough, although not disinterested, research, and the facts in it are generally conceded to be with minor exceptions accurate. The selection of information the authors made and the interpretations they chose to place upon it derived, of course, from their ideological options. See also Joye's *Les trusts en Belgique* (3rd ed.; Brussels: Société Populaire d'Edition, 1961). For another treatment, likewise the result of careful research but starting from similar premises, see Michel Merlier, *Le Congo de la colonisation belge à l'indépendance* (Paris: François Maspero, 1962). For a less thorough, but still useful survey in English, see Herbert Solow, "The Congo is in Business," *Fortune* (November 1952).

analysis, most concerned with an effective scheme for governing the country, the missions in evangelical work, and the companies in expanding their enterprises. A classic example of this occasional tension arose over the pace of economic development in the 1920's. The competition for labor was reaching a point where widespread abuses were committed in forced recruitment, and large areas of the countryside were being literally stripped of their adult males. The Catholic missions and many individuals in the administration began to rebel at a policy which seemed to reach a point where there had to be a choice between limiting expansion by the companies or compromising permanently the essential tasks of missions and administration. The Apostolic Prefect of Ubangi district, in the north of Equateur province, declared, "The territory of Ubangi is emptied of every able-bodied man. The majority of the young men, the hope of the future, are taken from their district of origin and transplanted in the country from which they will return, if ever they do, corrupted and contaminated by every kind of subversive idea which they will spread upon returning here."

And one territorial administrator, in a Lever plantation recruiting area, wrote in September 1925, "The territorial administrators . . . are in a position to know that the exactions are becoming more numerous every day in every realm, and that they no longer leave to the populations respite or liberty. . . . Perhaps one may pardon the functionary who gives way to sentiments of bitterness when he believes himself daily becoming more and more a veritable merchant of men, when his villages empty at his approach, as at the approach of a slave-trader."[18]

In this instance, the companies were obliged to undertake a major revision of their entire labor-intensive, short-contract mode of operation and to embark, led by *Union*

[18] Buell, *op. cit.*, II, 505, 542.

Minière, on a policy of stabilization of the working force and mechanization which proved remarkably satisfactory.[19]

Censorial Organs

Mention should also be made of a group of what might be termed colonial elder statesmen who functioned as the conscience of the system. Many served on the *Conseil Colonial,* an advisory body in Belgium to whom all measures classified in terms of Belgian administrative law as legislation[20] had to be submitted. Some of these men, drawn mainly from the missions and the magistrature, took seriously their role as custodians of African welfare, although obviously within a paternal framework. On issues such as land grants and labor rights, the Van Wings and Sohiers had a definite impact.

But an important contrast with British and French environment was the virtual absence of any controls external to the colonial system itself. It was often said that metropolitan Belgium was not interested in its giant colony. This is true only in the sense of the relative lack of objective debate about its future; the Belgian public drew substantial vicarious satisfaction from the success image of the Congo and basked in the complacent glow of its own myths about imposing achievements in Africa. It is also true that the Congo, more than French and Portuguese colonies, was mainly accessible to the middle and upper classes. Corporate managerial personnel were primarily recruited from these social milieux. On the administration side, a university degree was theoretically required after World War II for entry into the colonial civil service. All elements of the

[19] L. Moutoulle, *Politique sociale du l'Union Minière du Haut Katanga* (Brussels: ARSOM, Sci. Mor. et Pol., T. XIV, fasc. 3, 1946).

[20] A "decree" was a legislative act, and required the advice, although not necessarily the consent, of the *Conseil Colonial.* No intervention of Belgian Parliament was necessary except for budgetary items. Matters which could be classed as executive acts, although at times of great importance, such as administrative structure or status of the civil service, could be decided by an "Arrêté" of the King.

colonial structure shared an aversion to "poor whites" in the Congo. Only the missions drew any significant number of their personnel from the humbler strata of Belgian society; the Catholic clergy includes many sons of the Flemish countryside.

The Belgian Parliament was required to vote on the Congo budget, but this became a strictly *pro forma* ritual. Not only did the administration have authorization to transfer items from one budget category to another but the budget itself frequently was not submitted for parliamentary discussion until six months after the start of the fiscal year.[21] Until the appearance of nationalist stirrings, the Congo was only a matter of concern to Parliament when it required a Belgian subsidy.[22] Debates were brief and perfunctory; the large portion of public investment which went through the sundry important parastatal organizations entirely escaped scrutiny.

In Britain and France, the Left maintained a barrage of criticism of colonial policy and practice. In Belgium, however, the PSB (*Parti Socialiste Belge*) until 1956 paid very little attention to Congo affairs. In its "White Book," published after the catastrophe of 1960 under the dubious slogan "The PSB was right!", a summary of Socialist stands on

[21] Hailey, *op. cit.*, p. 348.

[22] Subsidies were paid from 1921-1925 to help underwrite the massive development program of Colonial Minister Franck, then were cut off when a major crisis hit Belgian public finances in 1926. Forced to take on a heavy debt load and pay itself for a program conceived on the assumption of external assistance, the Congo literally was bankrupted by the depression beginning in 1929. Subsidies were resumed in 1931, reached a level of 150 million francs annually through 1936, and continued on a much reduced scale until 1940. It should be added that most of the latter payments went to reimburse Belgian stockholders in a number of enterprises, especially railroads, where the colony had guaranteed a minimum dividend return; from 1932-1935, these payments cost the Congo 403 million francs. Jean Stengers, *Combien le Congo a-t-il couté à la Belgique?* (Brussels: ARSOM, Sci. Mor. et Pol., N.S., T. XI, fasc. 1, 1957), pp. 318-21; Pierre Ryckmans, *Dominer pour servir* (Brussels: L'Edition Universelle, 1948), p. 201.

colonial policy from 1885-1960 devoted only 29 of some 381 pages to the period before 1956.[23] The PSB was heavily oriented to domestic policy and to advancing the cause of the working class in Belgium. In the debates on the "reprise" by Belgium in 1908, one Socialist leader commented caustically that he was more interested in stopping the treatment of Europeans like Africans in Belgium than in seeing extended to Africa the conditions of the Belgian working class. Although the PSB participated regularly in coalition governments after 1918, it only held the colonial portfolio for one period of a few days during a protracted government crisis in 1946. The Socialists always attached priority in the negotiations over distribution of ministries to obtaining key posts in formulation of labor and welfare policy. The party was further handicapped by lack of easy access to information on the Congo, since Socialists obviously were rarely to be found in the clergy or upper reaches of the private sector. The number of Socialists in the colonial administration was not very large, since for the most part recruitment did not take place from those elements of Belgian society from which the PSB drew its support.

Belgium also lacked a tradition of critical appraisal of its colonial effort from its scholarly community. Van Bilsen became a veritable pariah after publishing his moderate proposals for a thirty-year plan in 1955. Research was oriented toward social, economic, or anthropological problems, and political study was nearly exclusively restricted to improving the techniques of colonial administration, on the assumption of the permanence of the system. There was criticism, often trenchant, on aspects of colonial policy, such as paternalism,[24] labor policy,[25] racial discrimination,[26]

[23] *Congo 1885-1960, Positions Socialistes* (Brussels: Institut Vandervelde, n.d.).

[24] Guy Malengreau, "Le Congo à la croisée des chemins," *Revue Nouvelle,* V (January 1947), 3-18; V (February 1947), 95-108.

[25] Arthur Doucy and Pierre Feldheim, *Problèmes du travail et politique sociale au Congo Belge* (Brussels: Les Editions de la Li-

excessive land concessions,[27] and the delegation to private interests of land concessions in the eastern Congo (*Comité National du Kivu, Comité Spécial du Katanga*).[28] But Van Bilsen remained a solitary phenomenon; when he and some of his collaborators set up a new Congo study group in 1957, the *"groupe Marzorati,"* its claim to originality rested on its being the only research group operating within the perspective of political emancipation.[29]

Not only did the Belgian colonial system enjoy relative immunity from outside criticism but it was remarkably free from restraints from within. There were organized occasions for debate on colonial policy by those closely associated with it; an example was the National Colonial Congress, held every five years from 1920 and annually after World War II. There was also, beginning in 1929, an active *Académie Royale des Sciences d'Outre-Mer* (to use its most recent name), which published a great deal of valuable work on the Congo in nearly all fields of inquiry. Although the discourse in these bodies was at time heated, again it was focused largely on details of "native policy," especially the perennial question of "indirect rule," rather than on terminal goals.

At a more institutional level, censorial and consultative responsibilities were vested in the *Conseil Colonial*, the *Conseil du Gouvernement* and its provincial counterparts, and the Commission for the Protection of Natives. Although all

---

brairie Encyclopédique, 1952).

[26] J. Van Wing, "Le Congo déraille," ARSOM, *Bull. Séances,* 1951, pp. 609-26; A. Rubbens, "Le colour-bar au Congo belge," *Zaïre* (May 1949), pp. 503-14.

[27] E. Boelaert, "Les trois fictions du droit foncier congolais," *Zaïre,* XI (April 1957), 399-427.

[28] Edouard Mendiaux, "Le Comité National du Kivu," *Zaïre,* X (October 1956), 803-13; X (November 1956), 927-64; the government interrupted its subsidy to *Zaïre* as a result of publication of this article.

[29] A. A. J. Van Bilsen, *Vers l'indépendance du Congo et du Ruanda-Urundi* (Brussels: 1958), pp. 16-18.

of these bodies had a certain importance, none of them could be said to have played a central role. Buell remarked more than three decades ago that one of the most striking features of the Belgian colonial system was its lack of any real consultative machinery.[30] The disparity between the Congo and British and French colonies became even sharper as diverse legislative councils in the latter areas acquired both growing powers and significant African representation. Coleman's perceptive characterization of a colonial system as a classic model of pure bureaucratic government, where the "political process and the administrative process are synonymous,"[31] was nowhere more applicable than in the Congo.

The *Conseil Colonial* had fourteen members, six elected by Parliament and eight nominated by the King. Tradition provided that among the Parliamentary members the three major parties of Belgium were represented.[32] Among the eight named by the King, usage also prescribed that major interests, such as the missions and the companies, be represented. To provide for diversity of kinds of expertise, there would normally be members who had served in the colonial administration, magistrature, and agricultural service. Because of the *Conseil's* important role in approving land and mining concessions, persons with specialized knowledge in these domains would always be included. Key regions, such as the Katanga, likewise were felt entitled to a voice. The *Conseil* was thus a carefully balanced group, with considerable prestige.[33] However, efforts to formalize

[30] Buell, *op. cit.*, II, 460.

[31] Gabriel A. Almond and James S. Coleman, *The Politics of the Developing Areas* (Princeton, N. J.: Princeton University Press, 1950), p. 315.

[32] For example, in the *Conseil Colonial* of 1958, Le Roye and Waleffe were PSB representatives, Laude and De Cleene from the PSC, and Van der Linden and Van de Putte Liberals.

[33] The author is endebted to the late A. Sohier, a long-standing member of the *Conseil Colonial* and first magistrate of the *Cour de Cassation* in Belgium, for his assistance in explaning the nature and

the de facto interest representation, and in so doing to give to the interests the right to control rather than to influence the selection of its spokesmen on the *Conseil,* were always resisted.[34] Still there can be no question but what the *Conseil* exercised a generally liberalizing influence; this can be seen in the frequent bitter criticisms of it in settler organs.

TABLE 1

CONSEIL COLONIAL, 1958

Members	Named by	Background
O. Louwers	King	Magistrate
P. Orban	King	Business
M. Maquet	King	Administration
M. Robert	King	Geologist; business; Katanga
A. Sohier	King	Magistrate; Katanga
J. Van Wing	King	Missionary; ethnologist; Bas-Congo
L. O. J. De Wilde	King	Agriculture, land problems
F. Poigneux	King	Administration
N. Laude	Senate	Catholic
F. Van der Linden	Senate	Liberal; business
L. Le Roye	Senate	Socialist
N. De Cleene	Chamber of Representatives	Catholic; ethnology
M. Van de Putte	Chamber of Representatives	Liberal
F. Waleffe	Chamber of Representatives	Socialist

The basic limitation of the *Conseil* was that it could debate only legislative proposals submitted to it and could criticize only the detail, not the principle. In legal terms, since it was not "responsible" in a constitutional sense, the *Conseil* accepted this definition of its role.[35] Its relations

---

functioning of the *Conseil.* Although his *optique* may have been paternal, one cannot fail to be impressed with the genuine sense of generosity and defense of African interests as he saw them which underlay his interventions in the debates of the *Conseil Colonial.*

[34] *Compte rendu des Journées Interuniversitaires d'Etudes Coloniales* (Brussels: Institut de Sociologie Solvay, 1952), p. 70.

[35] Interview with A. Sohier, Brussels, March 6, 1962.

25

with some ministers were better than with others; not only did the Minister have the power to decide what to submit to it but the *Conseil* had no independent sources of information and had to depend upon the Minister to define what material should be adjudged "compatible" with the role" of the *Conseil* and transmitted.[36] The Minister could also decide that a matter was "urgent" and thus bypass the *Conseil;* this was done four times between 1919 and 1933.[37] The Minister had the formal right to disregard the advice of the *Conseil* by submitting a written justification to the King. In fact, however, this procedure was only resorted to once.[38] Thus, although the *Conseil Colonial* did play a role of some significance in the governing process, the nature of its representation and the limitations on its activity meant that it operated entirely within the framework of the precepts of the colonial system.

A unique feature of the Belgian system was the Commission for the Protection of Natives. This body was designed to be a sort of moral ombudsman, to maintain surveillance on the administration and companies and to expose and denounce any exploitation of the African population. Historically, the Commission was a maneuver of Leopold II to appease international opinion aroused by the first disclosures of the Congo reform movement in 1896. As its official historian concedes, "In reality, its birth was provoked by a passing campaign unleashed against the Congo Free State." The agreement of the distinguished leader of the Baptist Missionary Society, George Grenfell, to serve on the Commission was a considerable triumph for Leopold in outwitting his reform adversaries. After two

[36] Th. Heyse, *Congo Belge et Ruanda-Urundi: Notes de Droit Public et Commentaires de la Charte Coloniale* (Brussels: C. Van Campenhout, 1952-1954), I, 53.

[37] *Ibid.,* p. 47.

[38] *Ibid.,* pp. 50-54. The occasion for bypassing the *Conseil* was in the grant of a mining concession in Maniema in 1940.

years, the Commission lapsed into inactivity; "The storm passed, there seemed no need to recall it to life."[39]

With the "reprise," the Commission was revived and written into the Colonial Charter, the Congo's fundamental law during the colonial era. It was largely dominated by the Catholic missions and was one of the agencies through which the latter made known their concern regarding recruiting abuses in the 1920's. In 1919, the Commission caused a veritable scandal by stating flatly, "Since the beginning of European occupation, the population has been in a continuous decline owing to a high mortality rate . . . to a point where it is not exaggerating to say that, as a whole, the population has been reduced by half."[40]

In the interwar period, the Commission also served as an organ by which a considerable part of the Catholic missions, led by the indomitable Apostolic Vicar of Elisabethville, Monsignor de Hemptinne, fought against the indirect rule principles which became the official policy of the government. "Respectable institutions," declared the Commission in 1923, are extremely rare in Congolese traditional society; "native institutions which are merely excusable or tolerable cannot claim a protection which would assure their perpetuation. They are destined to disappear."[41] In 1936, the Commission launched a campaign for an immatriculation procedure which would assimilate to European status the educated Congolese who were just beginning to appear, especially in the clergy.[42]

[39] L. Guebels, *Rélation complète des travaux de la Commission Permanente pour la Protection des indigènes au Congo Belge* (Elisabethville: CEPSI, n.d. [1952?]), p. 28.

[40] *Ibid.*, p. 197. This probably is exaggerated; the early estimates of population are generally believed to have been greatly in excess of reality and were based on primitive statistical methods. It remains beyond doubt that large zones did experience depopulation.

[41] *Ibid.*, pp. 249-50.

[42] Ironically, by the time the immatriculation decree finally appeared, Monsignor de Hemptinne had changed his mind and opposed it as categorically as he had earlier endorsed it.

In sum, although the Commission in its early days did make some important contributions, it never served as an important control on the colonial administration. In all its history it met ten times, and only five times during the last thirty years of Belgian rule in the Congo. It became a captive to a particular approach to colonial administration, and in so doing compromised a good part of what potential it might have had as an ethical comptroller to the system.

Consultative Machinery

The other consultative set of structures was the *Conseil de Gouvernement* and its provincial replicas. Before World War II, this body, which dates back to 1914, was largely composed of functionaries and played only a small role. In 1947, however, it and its provincial counterparts were reorganized to include a substantial majority of unofficial representatives, broken down into interest categories (corporations, commercial and professional groups, labor, notables, rural and extra-rural milieux). The latter category, although intended to represent African interests, was at first only partly selected from the Congolese population. Only two Africans were named to the *Conseil de Gouvernement* in 1947, and the number was enlarged to eight in 1951. Until 1951, there were six Europeans "representing" Congolese interests, and the labor category was interpreted to mean European subaltern employees. At first the Africans selected were chiefs or notables who in some cases spoke no French and could not follow the debates. Patrice Lumumba, in his very moderate 1957 book, *Le Congo, terre d'avenir est-il menacé?*, remarked, "Certain chiefs who are now members of the provincial and government councils are only there for decoration; they must be replaced."[43] Malen-

---

[43] Patrice Lumumba, *Le Congo, terre d'avenir est-il menacé?* (Brussels: Office de Publicité, 1961), p. 45. This manuscript was written by Lumumba in 1956 in Stanleyville; its timidity was perhaps partly explicable by a desire to insure publication in Belgium, although there can be little doubt that Lumumba's thinking had changed con-

greau stated bluntly in 1952 that everyone knew the expansion of African representation in 1951 was mainly for international consumption.[44]

Ironically, the main effect of the postwar *Conseil de Gouvernement* reforms was to strengthen the voice of European pressure groups in the Congo. Nomination of the European members was made from candidates put forward by groups such as settler associations, chambers of commerce, and associations of enterprises. They were thus given an effective institutional channel for making their views known and were even stimulated to discuss a broad range of policy issues which had been left untouched before, in order to mandate their representatives at the councils. The European interest group delegates provided a significant functional representation to the permanent European community in the Congo. They arrived at meetings with a very definite set of objectives. Although the consultative nature of the councils limited somewhat their impact, European interest groups made real use of this platform to exert pressure on the colonial administration.

On the African side, the situation was entirely different. The African community was still inert and inchoate; no organizations represented any significant part of the African community which could put forward nominations—in part because of the sharp restrictions on African associations. Even those alumni associations or unions which did exist were not consulted. The administration itself selected the African members, presumably on the basis of their suitability from the administration's point of view. Thus, there were African members, but no real African representation— in contrast to the very real representation afforded the European community.

---

siderably by the time he arrived in power. For one reason or another, the publishers chose not to publish it at the time it was submitted, but pulled it out of their files in 1961 when it had become a historical document of no small importance.

[44] *Compte rendu des Journées Interuniversitaires,* p. 30.

In 1957, a final reform of the councils defined representational criteria which were not, at least on the surface, racial; Africans could theoretically be selected from any category. Nominations began to be made from the modern elite, who were better able to articulate African grievances and to defend African interests in this type of body. However, as late as 1956, six of the eight Congolese members of the *Conseil de Gouvernement* were from traditional milieux. In all but one of the provincial councils, at least half of the six Congolese members were chiefs. The striking exception was Kasai, where five of the six were from the modern elite.[45]

Until 1957, council powers were strictly consultative, although decrees had to be submitted for their discussion, except in cases of urgency. There was a *Députation Permanente* after 1947, which was composed of three functionaries and six persons from the unofficial membership, with each category naming its own delegate. This met quarterly and had the task of maintaining more continuous control of the administration. The councils were entitled to express *voeux*, which were, of course, not binding on the administration.

Accordingly, one may conclude that the bureaucracy in the Congo, although subject to a certain amount of harassment by the various consultative and censorial bodies, did not operate under any very important restraints. The nature of the bodies was such that they made little positive contribution to the problem of formulating terminal goals; in the particular instance of the *Conseil de Gouvernement*, its role, on the contrary, would by and large generate European pressures which increased the difficulties of developing timely reform policies.

Structural Immobilisme

Another striking characteristic of the Belgian adminis-

[45] Georges Brausch, *Belgian Administration in the Congo* (London: Oxford University Press, 1961), p. 50.

trative system was its extraordinarily cumbersome policy-making procedure. A draft project had first to be prepared, often by a special commission. Interested departments of the Ministry, often more than one, then had to have an opportunity to study and propose changes. When this was completed, the draft was sent to Leopoldville, with an explanatory memorandum. The services of the Governor-General then studied the project. It next had to be sent to the provincial councils, which met only once a year. The next stage was submission to the *Conseil de Gouvernement*. Finally, there followed a reexamination by the Governor-General, an expression of his definitive opinion, and retransmission to Brussels. There the draft returned to the relevant departments, was filtered through the Minister's cabinet,[46] and put before the Minister for his decision. It had then to be submitted to the *Conseil Colonial*, which often, if the problem was important, designated an ad hoc subcommittee to give it thorough study. At each step in the process, progress of the decree was at the mercy of vacations, absences in Africa, changes of ministers; not only that, but the whole process had to take place in two languages.[47] Even when the decree was published, the battle was not yet over, since it was not put into effect until the Governor-General issued an ordinance of execution. In many cases, delay at this point could be many months.

The Belgian pattern of colonial rule, then, had a number of special characteristics which are important to an under-

[46] In Belgium, as in most continental systems, the minister has the right to a politically appointed cabinet, which has the theoretical function of providing him "political" information and advice, as opposed to the purely "administrative" views which reach him through the civil service. In fact, in the case of the Congo Ministry where Catholic ministers have been the most frequent incumbents, a considerable majority of the permanent functionaries are of a Catholic political coloration. Liberal Minister Auguste Buisseret in 1954 made great use of the device of the cabinet, staffed with anti-clerical elements, to bypass the civil service.

[47] This summary was offered by A. Sohier, "La politique d'intégration," *Zaïre*, V (November 1951), 902.

standing of both the processes of decolonization and the political system which has succeeded the colonial bureaucracy. Through the combined efforts of bureaucracy, capital, and Church, each of which fashioned a formidable organizational structure in its own sector of activity, a remarkable colonial system was constructed, unparalleled in the depth of its penetration into the African societies upon which it was superimposed and in the breadth of its control of nearly the whole spectrum of human activity. The bureaucracy numbered among its successes nearly complete exemption from serious accountability to metropolitan society. There was no effective gadfly element on the left fringes of public opinion, nor was close surveillance imposed by Belgian Parliament. The advisory organs operating within the system itself were not devoid of significance, but the restraints they constituted were in the main either paternal admonition to better colonial behavior or pressures from European interest groups in the Congo. African opinion was virtually unarticulated until 1956.

The colonial behemoth, fixed on a given course by a ponderous set of procedures, was incapable of altering its direction even when it perceived that it was lumbering toward the precipice.

CHAPTER III

Decolonization: The Belgian Vision

Perspectives on Decolonization: Departure with Honor

"Les jours du colonialisme sont révolus," declared Belgium's greatest colonial pro-consul, Pierre Ryckmans, in 1946 in his last address as Governor-General of the Congo, which he chose to title "Vers l'avenir."[1] This statement hardly seems spectacular today, but, when delivered, the Ryckmans speech created a sensation in Belgian colonial circles. It articulated a general feeling of uneasiness, a realization that the colonial system was beginning to be on the defensive, that World War II had entirely changed the international environment. Other authoritative voices began to echo this sentiment; Guy Malengreau, an influential figure in liberal Catholic circles, warned in 1947 that political education must replace paternalism.[2] The Belgian Senate dispatched in 1947 the first parliamentary mission ever sent to study political development in the Congo; the senators remarked upon a pessimism concerning the future by certain elements who "think that our African territories will one day wish to break all political links with us." These fears, concluded the mission, would be groundless if reforms similar to those in neighboring territories were undertaken forthwith.[3] The Liberal Colonial Minister, Robert Godding, noted that the period of colonial exploitation was over and that the principles of the UN Charter were now applicable.[4]

[1] The title had some pungency for colonials, as this was also the title of the anthem of the Belgian Congo. Ryckman's annual addresses as Governor-General are reprinted in *Etapes et jalons* (Brussels: Maison Larcier, 1946).

[2] "Le Congo à la croisée des chemins," *Revue Nouvelle*, V, No. 1, (January 1947), 3-18; No. 2, (February 1947), 95-108.

[3] Sénat de Belgique, *Rapport de la Mission Sénatoriale au Congo et dans les territoires sous tutelle belge* (1947), p. 12.

[4] Quoted in *ibid.*, p. 10.

The San Francisco Conference to draft the United Nations Charter was a shock to the Belgian delegation. The inclusion of Article 73 concerning non-self-governing territories was seen as a distinct menace, although the ratification of the Charter by the Belgian Parliament was unanimous.[5] Belgium was a small country which had a historic fear of external interference in her colonial stewardship, but also a strong sense of respect for international obligation.[6] Article 73 was harmless enough if Belgium could apply her own interpretation. However, there were ominous forebodings that the UN would itself define the content of this provision.[7] Asia was in the process of winning its independence; in Africa itself, France was according representation in the National Assembly to the African populations it ruled, while a Labour government in Britain was introducing significant reforms in a number of its African dependencies, especially in West Africa. It was obvious that juridical arguments posited upon the permanent validity of the nineteenth-century European partition of Africa, reinforced by the vague assertion of a civilizing mission and the rights of the industrial world to develop untapped natural resources were no longer an adequate defense for the colonial system. What was required was both a refurbished justification for the Belgian colonial mission and the beginnings of a formulation of a terminal goal.

Belgium, unlike the other major colonial occupants in Africa, was a latecomer to the game of overseas expansion.

[5] A forward-looking man such as Ryckmans described the inclusion of this clause as a defeat for the colonial powers. *Dominer pour servir* (Brussels: L'Edition Universelle, 1948), p. 20.

[6] Reflective of this is the inclusion of the relevant extracts from the UN Charter at the beginning of the official set of legal codes. Pierre Piron and Jacques Devos, *Codes et Lois du Congo Belge* (8th ed.; Brussels: Maison Ferdinand Larcier, 1959-1960), I, 34-37.

[7] These forebodings and their partial fulfillment are described in O. Louwers, *L'article 73 de la Charte et l'anticolonialisme de l'Organisation des Nations Unies* (Brussels: ARSOM, Sci. Mor. & Pol., T. XXIX, fasc. 2, 1952).

Britain, France, and Portugal had behind them centuries of colonial history. In the case of Britain and France, there was a long experience of trying to cope—albeit unsuccessfully at times—with emerging nationalist movements. Programs for the future were available, at least in broad outline. Self-government was clearly to be the outcome of British stewardship in Africa, despite the chasm between British and African assumptions as to the time schedule involved, and in the case of settler territories the only recently resolved issue as to whom the self-government was for. And even though the goals defined at Brazzaville in 1944 have required complete change, the assimilation-association themes in French policy provided a framework within which development of a modern elite was encouraged and political experience could be acquired. Thus when the Algerian war, Guinean "non," and other events demanded a redefinition of objectives, independence with stability was possible.

Decolonization as a political phenomenon is inevitably marked by the necessity that the colonizer's voluntary deprivation appear tolerable. This has a dual aspect: on the one hand, the post-independence period must seem to hold the promise of a special relationship with the former colony, which makes the change seem not a humiliating rupture, but rather a dignified and proper consecration of the former colony as an adult member of the family. The existence of the Commonwealth has thus been an invaluable psychological satisfaction to Britain; to a lesser extent, the same could be said of the French Community. Secondly, the nature of the political institutions created to assume the sovereignty abandoned by the colonizer is determined to an important degree by the requirement that they be consistent with the political values of metropolitan powers. As W. J. M. Mackenzie has perceptively observed:

"[There is] a sentiment among Europeans that if they are to go, it must be with honour, honour defined by European

1316077

standards of good government and democracy. The with-drawing powers and their administrators wish to leave be-hind democratic government and decent administration. Perhaps the administrators on the spot care most for the latter, and are not much impressed by the value of party politics, at home or in Africa. But political opinion at home demands democracy."[8]

This chapter will examine the assumptions and values intermingling in successive formulations of a terminal ob-jective for Belgium in the Congo which could seem ac-ceptable both to the colonial structure and to metropolitan Belgium.

The Premise of Controlled Gradualism

The fundamental assumption in the decolonization proc-ess was that there was still plenty of time. Before World War II, there is no evidence that any real thought was given to a future outside the colonial framework; Ryck-mans in his 1937 address referred to the Congo as a "tenth province."[9] In 1946, G. Caprasse, in the *Courrier d'Afrique*, Catholic daily in Leopoldville, suggested that the centen-nial of the establishment of the Congo Free State in 1985 might be an appropriate target for termination of colonial status; but this had little echo.[10] In 1952, Petillon, in his first speech as Governor-General, declared that the time had come to begin preparing for eventual "emancipation"; and, in 1954, the newly installed Liberal-Socialist coalition gov-ernment used the word "independence" in a vague way, but with no indication as to how far off this might be.[11] Few in 1956 found Van Bilsen's thirty-year plan anything other

[8] W. J. M. Mackenzie and Kenneth Robinson, *Five Elections in Africa* (Oxford: Clarendon Press, 1960), p. 465.
[9] Ryckmans, *Etapes et jalons*, p. 84.
[10] Van Bilsen, *Vers l'indépendance*, p. 228.
[11] Brausch, *Belgian Administration in the Congo*, p. 69.

than the naïve dream of a soft-headed *"indigèniste."* Beginning in 1957, however, there was a gradual realization that
the sands were running out, and, by 1958, responsible officials were thinking in terms of ten years. But until virtually
the last minute, the colonial system approached the problem of adaptation with the assumption that several decades
would be available to carry it out. Ironically, the Achilles'
heel of the Belgian rule in Africa was always felt to be
Ruanda-Urundi, where, through the embarrassing entan-
glement of trusteeship obligation, growing pressure from
the UN was being felt for the establishment of a deadline
for independence.[12]

Linked with the belief that there was no urgency to begin the process was the assumption that decolonization
would remain under full Belgian control. Hodgkin's philos-
opher-king in his wisdom, after seeking what advice he
felt appropriate to solicit, would create by decree the Congolese state. This premise permeates official declarations
from the moment that Petillon announced the emancipation goal in 1952. It appears in both the Royal Message and
Government Declaration of January 13, 1959; Baudouin declared, "We are today resolved to lead without fatal delays,
but also without precipitate haste, the Congolese populations to independence in prosperity and peace." The Colonial Minister added, "Belgium intends to organize in the
Congo a democracy capable of exercising the prerogatives
of sovereignty and of deciding on its independence."[13] Another revealing symptom was the designation of an all-
European *Groupe de Travail* in August 1958 to undertake a
fact-finding inquiry on the basis of which to announce a
new government policy for the Congo. The technical explanation for this was that it was to be a "national" mission
reporting to the Belgian government. The mission made

[12] Jean Labrique, *Congo politique* (Leopoldville: Editions de
l'Avenir, 1957), p. 43; Van Bilsen, *Vers l'indépendance,* pp. 41, 186-
87.
[13] *Congo 1959* (2d ed.; Brussels: CRISP, 1962), pp. 44-45.

certain colossal misjudgments of the temper of Congolese opinion; an example of this is the following observation: "A large number of Congolese interlocutors asked immediate independence. . . . [On the basis of their explanations], the *Groupe de Travail* concluded that its interlocutors meant by immediate independence the immediate liberation of the individual."[14]

This approach, in addition, made the conclusions and the resulting new policy suspect to large sectors of Congolese opinion. The first act of the group of Congolese in Leopold-ville who, in October 1958, formed the *Mouvement National Congolais* (MNC) was to submit a letter to Minister (and ex-Governor-General) Petillon, declaring: "The undersigned . . . deeply regret that the Minister did not include any Congolese members in the *Groupe de Travail;* . . . fear that, without the participation of the latter, the conclusions which will emerge . . . will reflect too unilateral a viewpoint, inspired by a certain conservatism attached to the colonialist spirit . . . and formulate as of now reservations concerning the final decisions which Parliament will be led to take, following on these conclusions."[15]

The related assumption of the pliable mass, remarked in Hodgkin's Platonian metaphor, can be uncovered on both sides of the protracted debate on indirect versus direct rule. Franck, the architect of indirect rule, stated, "We are not obstinately trying to train an imitation European, a black Belgian, but rather a better Congolese, *c'est-à-dire un nègre robuste, bien portant et travailleur.*"[16] The Commission for the Protection of Natives, an adversary of indirect rule, retorted, "Colonization consists in the final analysis in causing to participate in European civilization a backward population . . . that this participation must be pushed as far as pos-

[14] *Rapport du Groupe de Travail pour l'étude du problème politique au Congo Belge* (Brussels: Inforcongo, 1959), p. 16.

[15] *Congo 1959,* p. 27.

[16] Louis Franck, *Le Congo Belge* (Brussels: La Renaissance du Livre, 1930), I, 282.

sible, so that assimilation should be the final end of all colonization . . . [and] that the more backward the population and the more radical the reforms which its accession to our civilization necessitates, the stronger, more general, and more constant our intervention in native life must be."[17] During World War II, one of the young Catholic intellectuals grouped around the progressive Elisabethville lawyer Antoine Rubbens added in the same vein: "The issue is, during the coming years, to show that we are capable of transforming this country and grouping these fragments of clans, of groups, of races in a living unit. . . . We have made this country, we have conquered it and we have grouped it, we have liberated it from the slave trade and from its internal struggles."[18]

This motif can be found, implicitly or explicitly, in most of the colonial literature and official pronouncements. Its longevity is reflected in the efforts of the three major Belgian parties, beginning especially in 1956 with congresses to define their respective approaches to the challenge of decolonization, to extend their activities to the Congo— each hoping to insure that the future Congolese state would be erected upon the basis of its particular precepts of social and political organization.

An important corollary of controlled gradualism is the pervasive legalism which characterizes much of Belgian political thought. The study of government still takes place within the walls of the faculties of law. The basic texts in political science are written in the form and spirit of a handbook in constitutional law. Many of the senior policy-making officials had been trained as magistrates. One cannot help being struck by how much of the scholarly and official discourse on political adaptation took place in the idiom of the jurist, and how little was informed by any ap-

[17] Guebels, *op. cit.*, pp. 253-54.
[18] L. Ballegeer in *Dettes de guerre* (Elisabethville: Editions de l'Essor du Congo, 1945), pp. 142-43.

parent sociological perceptions. The deeply-ingrained respect for law in Belgium is no doubt a national virtue; the arid legalism of much of the debate on colonial policy, however, partially explains its frequent lack of reality.[19]

In retrospect, the assumptions of abundant time, controlled development, and pliable subjects seem to betray a naïveté unusual to a normally practical and hard-headed nation such as Belgium. It is true that the Belgians failed as prophets and that they insufficiently extrapolated from trends elsewhere in Africa and Asia the implications for the Congo. But it is vital to recall that the colonial establishment was not subjected to serious African challenge until after the Leopoldville riots in 1959. Until about 1954, articulated African grievances related almost entirely to African status within the colonial society.[20] In the following years, the harbingers of a nationalist awakening appeared with growing frequency, but African impact on colonial decision-making processes was minuscule.

There was simply no comparison with most British and French territories, especially those in West Africa, where the colonial establishment was under constant African pressure and a broad range of policy was formulated in reaction to (although not always affording satisfaction to) nationalist demands. Until about 1957, the policy of subordinating political development to economic and social advances had the appearance of success from the Belgian point of view. Critics such as Van Bilsen had little Congolese evidence to prove that this success was more apparent than real; their

[19] Classic examples of this are two works appearing on the eve of power transfer: André Durieux, *Nationalité et citoyenneté* (Brussels: ARSOM, Sci. Mor. et Pol., N. S., T. XXIII, fasc. 2, 1959); and W. J. Ganshof van der Meersch, *Le droit électoral au Congo Belge* (Brussels: Etablissements Emile Bruylant, 1958).

[20] James Coleman, in one of the earliest surveys of African nationalism, in 1954 rated the Congo as devoid of overt nationalism—a status it shared only with Portuguese territories. "Nationalism in Tropical Africa," *American Political Science Review,* XLVIII, No. 2 (June 1954), 404-26.

arguments were based on the inevitability of emergent trends visible elsewhere in the Congo. Accurate as this reasoning was, it lacked compelling urgency to the colonial trinity.

Building from the Ground Up

A universally shared belief was that political construction should take place from the ground up. The mystical value attached to local institutions has deep roots in Belgian history. The British also gave considerable emphasis to the question of workable and effective local governmental institutions, but never with such single-minded devotion to a "build-from-the-ground-up" theory. The centralized French political tradition placed very little value on local government. In neither case was the mystique of the communes as repositories of the civic virtues of the people so embedded as it was in Belgian political culture. Belgian medieval history is dominated by the rise of the commune, not the rise of a centralizing monarchy. The great Belgian national heroes were the communal leaders, who defended the people against the exactions of the succession of alien rulers who laid claim to Belgium. Pirenne in his classic *Histoire de Belgique* lays great stress on their role.[21] In the words of another recent summary of Belgian history:

"The communes, although of different degrees of development in different parts of Belgium, were for the country an essential factor of unity, by the similarity of their development and interests, both in Flanders and in Wallony. . . . The repercussions of their victorious struggles against the feudal chiefs, led to the emancipation of the rural populations, thus striking a decisive blow against feudalism."[22]

The medieval city thus was the engine of progress, the

[21] H. Pirenne, *Histoire de Belgique,* 7 vols. (Brussels: Lamertin, 1909-1932).
[22] Louis Pierard, *Histoire de la Belgique* (Paris: Presses Universitaires de France, 1948), pp. 34, 46.

architect of unity, and the agent of liberation. This took on particular meaning from the fact that the overlords were foreign; Belgium, from 1383 until 1830, lived under Burgundian, Spanish, Austrian, French, and Dutch rule. Accordingly, when the moment came to begin shaping a Congolese state, it was fully consistent with the Belgian historic myth as well as colonial convenience that the first meaningful institution to create would be communes.

When the debate began over means of political training and the nature of the new institutions to be created, all agree that the grass roots approach was the only feasible solution.[23] Petillon in his 1952 annual declaration as Governor-General declared that the Congolese would be more closely associated with the administration of the Congo through beginning with the base. Responsibility could only be learned, it was felt, by immersion in the problems of building sewers and paving roads which are the warp and woof of urban administration. "The only effective training," wrote one authority in 1953, "is that achieved through contact with the immediate and daily needs of the population."[24] The only level of political institutions in the independent Congo which was really the product of careful study and even loving nurture was that of the urban and rural *circonscription,* each reformed in 1957 by the important decrees of March 26 (urban) and May 10 (rural). A CEPSI study in 1951, urging that priority be given to these reforms, declared: "As it happened in Belgium, the commune, progressively becoming aware of its interests and those of its inhabitants, will furnish to all an effective protection. It will be the natural framework in which the rules of a new life will be forged, in order and liberty."[25]

[23] See, for example, the special issue of *Problèmes d'Afrique Centrale,* No. 15 (1951).
[24] A. Gille, "La politique indigène au Congo Belge et au Ruanda Urundi," *Encyclopédie du Congo Belge* (Brussels: Editions Bieleveld, 1953), III, 737.
[25] Fedacol, *L'opinion publique coloniale devant l'assimilation des*

A Black Bourgeoisie

Another persistent theme with evident origins in Belgian political and social values was the interest in creating an African middle class. This object was not in fact consistently pursued in policy, because its premises were clearly open to question and because, though many would join in willing the end, few were prepared to will the means. But it is logical that to the European the Congo would seem to be a stage for the reenactment of Belgian history, whose fulfillment called for the creation of a strong middle class which would be motivated by the same impulses to stability and material progress as the artisan-merchant group who are the Belgian social heroes. An outstanding spokesman for this view was Henri Depage, who argued that building universities and granting political rights without first making it possible for Africans to attain the same economic level as Europeans "was to favor the formation of malcontents and agitators."[26] The influential *Centre d'Etudes des Problèmes Sociaux Indigènes* (CEPSI) in Elisabethville declared in 1951:

"The colonial experience of European nations must incite us to avoid creating hastily a class of highly privileged natives from whom would spring probably the elements seeking to win over the ignorant mass to accede to power and deprive it of the still indispensable assistance of the coloniser. It is, on the contrary, appropriate to favor above all and by all means the creation of middle classes. The middle classes will be finally composed of blacks and whites and will constitute the foundation upon which future elites can solidly base themselves."[27]

---

indigènes (Brussels: 1951, mimeographed), p. 33.

[26] Henri Depage, *Contribution à l'élaboration d'une doctrine visant à la promotion des indigènes du Congo Belge* (Brussels: ARSOM, Sci. Mor. et Pol., N. S., T.V, fasc. 2, 1955), p. 19.

[27] Fedacol, *op. cit.*, p. 233.

The European settler organization, Fedacol, in a confidential note to Colonial Minister Buisseret in 1955, articulated this idea even more explicitly:

"We must organize a class of *évolué* natives, who will declare their acceptance of the ideals and the principles of our Western civilization, and who will be, if on an equal standing, our equals in rights and duties, less numerous than the native mass, but powerful and influential, they will be the allies it is indispensable for us to find in the native communities. These middle classes will be the black bourgeoisie which is beginning to develop everywhere, which we must help to enrich itself and organize itself and which, like all the bourgeois of the world, will be opposed to any disruption, internal or external."[28]

And the Luluabourg paper, *Kasai*, added, "We have produced *'plumitifs,'* but not artisans, forgetting in the process that our Belgium was born from the guilds and the artisanry."[29]

Shortly after Buisseret took office in 1954, the *Association des Classes Moyennes Africaines* (ACMAF) was launched, with considerable assistance from European settler groups in many places. Buisseret as a Liberal was particularly susceptible to this line of reasoning and gave substantial encouragement through facilitating study trips to Belgium, participation in seminars, and the like.[30] A key to applying such a policy would have been a willingness to allow Africans to own land. Although a theoretical legal right to own land existed from the Congo Free State days, it was not applied, even after more specific permissive legislation was adopted in 1953. In 1960, a bare handful of landowners

[28] "Organisation et action des colons au Congo: La Fédération Congolaise des Classes Moyennes (Fedacol)," *Courrier Africaine* (CRISP) No. 35 (July 1959).

[29] Fedacol, *op. cit.*, p. 131.

[30] As is pointed out by his equally Liberal former aide, Georges Brausch, *op. cit.*, pp. 4-5.

could be found among the Africans.[31] For the most part, they were recipients of land from the *Comité Spécial du Katanga* rather than the domain lands of the government.

The Postulate of Eurafrica

Another important assumption in Belgian policy which sharply distinguishes the Congo from West Africa was that the European community was destined to play an important role not only as technicians but as participants jointly with the Congolese in the political institutions of the new state. Impossible contradictions arose between this goal and the requirement that Belgium as a constitutional democracy based on universal suffrage should bequeath to the Congo a similar set of institutions. The conundrums growing from this dilemma were a crucial factor in understanding the *immobilisme* in Belgian postwar policy.

A Eurafrican state was assumed by both European and Congolese in the early postwar years. Belgium had always resisted settler demands for the exercise of political rights on the grounds that these could only be extended when the African population was in a position to share in them. European agitation for political rights dates back, especially in the Katanga, almost to the first arrival of permanent settlers about 1911. Close contact with the Rhodesias and South Africa whetted their appetites; as early as 1920, a group of leading clerics, businessmen, and settlers in Elisabethville published a plan for reorganizing the Congo, which included a demand for elected European urban councils.[32] These European demands became more insistent after World War II, and at the same time the emerging Congolese elite began for the first time to ask that African leadership be consulted before decisions affecting them

[31] Heyse, *op. cit.*, I, 23; Aimé Lecointre, "Evolution des relations raciales et culturelles au Congo Belge de 1947 à 1957," (Louvain: typescript, n.d.) pp. 21-23.
[32] J. de Hemptinne, *Le gouvernement du Congo Belge. Projet de réorganisation administrative* (Brussels: Librairie Dewit, 1920).

were taken. As a leading missionary remarked in 1951: "Powerful forces seem to be at work, propagating feverishly new ideas: the Congolese nation is formed by the settlers and the natives; legislative power belongs to that nation; and especially to the elite of that nation which will for a long time be composed chiefly of whites."[33]

The difficulty came to a head between 1948 and 1957, in the effort to define a new regime for governing urban areas. For a time, paritary institutions seemed to offer a solution, but writing this into the statutes implied making a clear distinction between the European and African communities, and offered the latter a second-class form of representation. A temporary solution was found by adding enough interest-group representation, so defined as to be largely European, to achieve a de facto parity, without making it a formal legislative principle. The *Groupe de Travail* in 1958 found that the Europeans were still strongly attached to the parity notion as the only way in which they could be guaranteed a permanent role in Congo political institutions. They justified this on the grounds that the two races were at different stages of evolution and that a role out of proportion to that nose-counting would have provided was necessary for the European community. In its report, the *Groupe de Travail* assumed European participation at all levels; the only question really raised was whether Europeans should be integrated into the rural *circonscriptions* at the lowest level, or only at the level of the territorial council.[34]

Until 1959, the notion of a Congo state in which Europeans played a large role was generally accepted by African opinion as well. The 1956 Manifesto of *Conscience Africaine* talks of a community built together by Europeans

[33] Father Boelaert in Fedacol, *op. cit.*, p. 78. Father Boelaert has been a student of Mongo linguistics and ethnology for many years, and was an outspoken defender of African rights, especially those of rural Africans in issues such as land alienation to European firms.

[34] *Rapport du Groupe de Travail*, pp. 34-35.

and Africans, although it warns that many Belgians will have to alter their attitudes.[35] Lumumba, in 1956, wrote: "The new Eurafrican society which we are building today must be administered and directed *jointly* by Belgians and Congolese. Neither of the two fractions of the Belgo-Congolese community should dominate or oppress the other. One will find in each service or department, African and European civil servants working side by side in the direction of their country."[36]

Five years earlier, Joseph Okito, *Mouvement National Congolais-Lumumba* (MNC/L) leader who was assassinated with Lumumba in the Katanga in early 1961, had written in terms that would have warmed a Mississippian heart: "We must collaborate modestly with our civilizers in the evolution and well-being of our country, but in realizing that only the Belgians have been able to create the impulsion and maintain the direction. . . . We must remain in our place."[37]

African statements at this stage must be placed in the context of the severe restraints on free expression of political opinion and the exigencies of "tactical action." On the other hand, political perspectives for change have as their starting point the existing situation. A Congo as radically Africanized as that of 1960 would have been literally unimaginable in 1956, and it seems fair to conclude that at that time most of the Congolese leadership was prepared, or resigned, to accept substantial European participation.

The Shadow of Leopold

A final significant assumption was that the King of the Belgians would remain as the personal and institutional link binding Belgium to the Congo. Again there is no real parallel in colonial history for the vital role the royal family

[35] *Congo 1959*, p. 14.
[36] Lumumba, *Le Congo terre d'avenir, est-il menacé?* p. 201. Emphasis added.
[37] Fedacol, *op. cit.*, pp. 50-51.

has played in the Congo. Leopold II became convinced in his youthful travels that Belgium absolutely needed a colony to expand the narrow horizons of the country, to capture its imagination and embark it upon a grandiose adventure. Without the extraordinary tenacity of Leopold, the Congo Free State would never have been created. Leopold then "bequeathed" the Congo to Belgium, which took over administration of the giant royal domain with enthusiasm limited to a very narrow circle of missionaries, adventurers, and students of the reports of the geological missions to Katanga. But the royal family always retained a special interest in the Congo and a powerful conviction that tradition called for the King to take an active part in the formulation of Congo policy.

King Albert and King Leopold each visited the Congo as Crown Prince; the latter in 1933, shortly before succeeding to the throne, made a dramatic speech proposing important innovations in the field of African agriculture. It was here that the *paysannat indigène* was first formally suggested, and some grumblings were caused by the clear option expressed in favor of African agriculture instead of large-scale European settlement. As part of the campaign to gain psychological acceptance for the Belgo-Congolese community idea, Baudouin paid a royal visit to the Congo in 1955, which proved to be a spectacular success.

As the moment approached to redefine Belgian relations with the Congo, the Palace played a very active role. When a new government was formed in July 1958, the dynasty openly used its influence to achieve the designation of a "technician" Colonial Minister rather than a "politician." Petillon, as Governor-General, had won the confidence of the young King during the royal tour in 1955 and the choice of the Palace. He became marked as the "King's Minister."[38] In April 1959, after Petillon had fallen by the wayside in a December cabinet reshuffle, his successor, Van Hemelrijck,

[38] Marres and De Vos, *op. cit.*, pp. 40-42.

sought to replace the Governor-General, Henri Cornélis, whom he deemed weak and inadequate in his behavior during the Leopoldville riots. In February, after returning from a rapid tour of the Congo to win support for the January 13 message, the Minister proposed this to the Council of Ministers, who approved unanimously. An impasse developed between the Palace and the Ministry, however; Raymond Scheyven, later to become Minister of Congo Economic Affairs, was acceptable to both, but he at first refused the position. Van Hemelrijck refused to accept the magistrate Ganshof van der Meersch or General Arthéon; the King was opposed to PSC deputies Dequae (a former Colonial Minister) and Delport. Finally, on April 13, Scheyven relented and indicated he would accept the nomination. The Council of Ministers immediately met and unanimously approved the nomination. The following morning, Prime Minister Eyskens was apparently informed by the King that the Palace would refuse to endorse the proposal; after a bitter cabinet meeting, the government, over Van Hemelrijck's opposition, decided to reconcile itself to Baudouin's veto, and Eyskens announced to the press that, as Cornélis had not resigned, he continued in office.[39]

The royal message of January 13 was another striking example of the royal family's sense of responsibility for defining Congo policy. The King recorded this message, to be broadcast in advance of the governmental declaration announced for the same day. Only the Prime Minister and Van Hemelrijck had any advance knowledge that the King planned to make this statement;[40] the constitutional requirements of ministerial responsibility were thus only just barely observed.[41] Clearly the King desired to be the first to announce to the Congo the promise of independence. "I believe," he said in his address, "that I owe it to the memory of my illus-

[39] *Congo 1959*, pp. 151-52.
[40] Marres and De Vos, *op. cit.*, p. 96.
[41] Jean Stengers, "Notre nouvelle politique congolaise," *Le Flambeau*, 42d yr., No. 7-8 (September-October, 1959), p. 470.

trious predecessors, founders and consolidators of our mission in Africa, to announce to you myself the character and spirit [of the new government program]."[42]

Some Palace involvement was also apparent in the events leading to the resignation of Congo Affairs Minister Van Hemelrijck in September 1959. The latter had made many enemies in colonial circles by his blunt manner and by his determination to accelerate the pace of decolonization in order to regain the confidence of the Congolese leadership. Count d'Aspremont-Lynden, nephew of the Grand Marshal of the royal court and closely associated with the royal family, was designated by the Prime Minister to undertake a secret fact-finding mission to the Congo at the end of August; Van Hemelrijck was not informed. His resignation followed immediately.[43]

Baudouin made two more trips to the Congo, one in December 1959, and then another for the independence ceremonies. The former constituted a desperate effort to restore a deteriorating situation through a spectacular initiative; the King's plane was in the air for Stanleyville before his sudden trip was announced. In Stanleyville, the rumor spread rapidly that the King had come to liberate Lumumba, who was awaiting trial on charges of having provoked the riots of October 30 and 31;[44] in Katanga, Baudouin stifled a scheme to announce immediate secession.[45] *Force Publique* commander Janssens tried to persuade the King to proclaim independence on his own responsibility under the Crown for July 1, 1960.[46] And on independence day, the young sovereign declared, "The independence of the Congo is the crowning achievement of

[42] *Congo 1959*, p. 44.
[43] *Ibid.*, pp. 176-86.
[44] Pierre De Vos, *Vie et mort de Lumumba* (Paris: Calmann-Levy, 1961), pp. 168-71.
[45] Pierre Davister, *Katanga enjeu du monde*, pp. 51-57.
[46] E. Janssens, *J'étais le général Janssens* (Brussels: Charles Dessart, 1961), p. 153.

the mission conceived by the genius of King Leopold II, undertaken by him with a tenacious courage . . . not as a conqueror, but as a civilizer."[47]

Until virtually the last minute, it had been assumed that the King would continue to be sovereign of the Congo as well as Belgium. The duality between the Chief of State and Prime Minister, one of the key institutional factors in the Congo crisis, can only be understood in the context of Belgian hopes, which still lingered at the time of the elaboration of the *Loi Fondamentale,* that Baudouin would be chosen as head of state. Of the twelve Congolese delegations represented at the Brussels Round Table in January-February 1960, only three were opposed to the King's serving in this role at least provisionally until a definitive Congolese constitution had been drawn up by the Congolese Parliament sitting as a Constituent Assembly.[48]

It has sometimes been alleged, without much supporting evidence, that the dynasty's concern with Congo affairs has been related to financial interests in colonial companies. There is strong reason to suppose that the royal family has significant holdings in the *Société Générale.* This enormous financial empire was founded in 1822 on the initiative of King William of the Netherlands (under the influence of Saint-Simon). When the company was reorganized after Belgium broke away from the Netherlands in 1830, Leopold I apparently obtained a substantial participation. Three of the twelve current members of the Board of Directors bear the title of "Grand Marshal of the Court," and are generally recognized to represent the dynasty. However, there is no evidence that they play an important role in the management of *"La Générale".*[49]

Rather, the role of the dynasty should be related to the

[47] *Congo 1960* (Brussels: CRISP, 1961), I, 318-19.

[48] *Ibid.,* p. 48. These were, however, three of the most important, the Cartel of Abako, PSA, MNC/K, Parti du Peuple; CEREA; and MNC/L.

[49] *La Morphologie des groupes financiers,* pp. 63-64, 78-82.

complex of historic myths which have grown out of Leopold II's foundation of the Congo Free State. The behavior of the monarchy is most comprehensible in recent years as a conscious effort to fulfill a role believed to be historically prescribed. This brief recapitulation does not fully capture the important network of influence radiating from the Palace. The royal family and its entourage sought to remain closely informed on Congo developments; they were in touch with all important milieux of colonial society. Most Belgian academic specialists concerned with the problem of political adaptation in the Congo have been invited to visit the royal residence at Laeken. The annals of Belgian political gossip and *petite histoire* are replete with tales relating the current Palace standing of the various well-known colonial authorities.

Decline and Fall of the Belgo-Congolese Community

Since Ryckmans first called for an end to classic patterns of colonial rule in 1946, Belgium moved slowly, at first imperceptibly, toward a definition of its terminal objectives. The first moves were in the direction of giving body to the traditional doctrine of paternalism. Judgment day was to be postponed and the new exigencies of international accountability satisfied by redoubling efforts in the economic and social realm. Coupled with this were efforts to head off nationalist aspirations among the emerging modern elite by insuring that special status satisfaction was accorded through the badge of "civilization" of an immatriculation decree and a campaign against racial discrimination. The illusion that the crux of the difficulties lay in race relations was particularly resilient. After the royal visit in 1955, Baudouin pointed to "human relations" as the basic problem confronting the Congo. The *Groupe de Travail* could conclude that by "immediate independence" their Congolese interlocutors merely were asking to end racial discrimination. The parliamentary commission dispatched to inquire into the causes of the Leopoldville riots in 1959 placed frustration over continued racial disabilities as the central factor.[50]

Beginning with Petillon's speech in 1952, the idea of the Belgo-Congolese community served as a transitional goal between the intolerable prospect of total rupture and the impossibility of maintaining colonial domination as an end unto itself. Like the Commonwealth and the French Community, it was a vague and somewhat formless idea, capable of a variety of interpretations. In itself, it was a hopelessly inadequate program; Van Bilsen accurately points out, "It expressed beyond any doubt the desire to find new forms of hegemony or a prolonged Belgian tutelage."[51] But it did at least give formal recognition to the need for a concrete goal. To an extent, it provided the liberal with a framework within which to urge change and adaptation, and the conservative a way of accepting it. Not even progressive Belgians could be expected to desire an independence which involved a sharp break in Belgium's special relationship with the Congo; as Van Bilsen observed, all secretly hoped for some form of Belgo-Congolese union.[52]

The content of the Belgo-Congolese community idea gradually was transformed, even while the slogan continued to be employed. In 1955, Baudouin declared that Belgium and the Congo formed a single nation. Former Colonial Minister Wigny held that the objective was "permanent maintenance of an enlarged Belgium."[53] Although never fully articulated as government policy, the accent

[50] Chambre des Représentants, Session 1958-1959: Document Parlementaire 100/3, March 27, 1959. Commission parlementaire chargée de faire une enquête sur les événements qui se sont produits à Léopoldville en janvier, 1959. *Rapport.*

[51] A. A. J. Van Bilsen, *L'indépendance du Congo* (Tournai, Belgium: Casterman, 1962), p. 42.

[52] Van Bilsen, *Vers l'indépendance,* p. 177.

[53] Stengers, "Notre nouvelle politique," pp. 453-54.

seemed to be placed upon some sort of integration of the Congo with Belgium.[54] Thereafter, the Belgo-Congolese Community hypothesis was altered to assume that the Congo would possess full internal autonomy, and that the community would be a paritary association between the two states, linked by the Crown, with the unspoken assumption that, as the older partner, Belgium would enjoy seniority rights in the partnership. It will be recalled that at this point it was also assumed that the Congo would have its internal institutions built upon the parity principle.

The premise of internal autonomy and a community linking two separate states had a major shortcoming: logic and the postulates of democracy required that this community could not be imposed by one of the partners, but rather had to be freely negotiated by both. Its creation therefore supposed the erection of a Congolese state whose structures were legitimated by some organization of the consent of the population compatible with Belgian democratic precepts. It was on this assumption that Lumumba wrote in favor of the Belgo-Congolese community in 1956;[55] the authors of the *Conscience Africaine* Manifesto set forth this idea explicitly:

"To speak clearly, the Congolese who reflect on these problems fear that certain persons may deform the idea of a Belgo-Congolese Community, to make it a brake on the total emancipation of the Congolese people, a means also for indefinitely perpetuating the domination of at least the preponderate influence of the Europeans, forming a privileged caste. In the sense which we give the idea, such a Community, far from being an obstacle, must be the means for realizing our total emancipation."[56]

[54] See Arthur Doucy's introductory speech at the colloquium organized by the *Institut de Sociologie Solvay*, November 22, 1958, reprinted as *L'avenir politique du Congo Belge* (Brussels: Les Editions de la Librairie Encyclopédique, 1959), p. 25.

[55] Lumumba, *op. cit.*, p. 201.

[56] *Congo 1959*, p. 11.

In 1957, publicist Jean Labrique, a press attaché of the Governor-General who had extensive Congolese contacts, found in a series of interviews with Congolese leaders a belief that the construction of a democratic Congolese polity was a prerequisite to the definition of any Eurafrican formulas.[57] Cynicism about this formula grew as the years passed without any clear definition of its content. The influential Katanga editor Jean Sépulchre denounced it as "*fantomale*" and a pretext for *immobilisme*.[58] And the brilliant son of the Congo's ablest Governor-General, André Ryckmans, wrote in a letter in early 1957: "As for the Belgo-Congolese Community, I sincerely wonder if there is a single African who believes in it; the Africans are psychologists enough to recognize the enormous ingredient of hypocrisy there is in the present declarations. . . . There again I agree with Van Bilsen that we were wrong to trumpet this theme at every turn, rendering it thus suspect; there is nothing so ridiculous as an all-purpose slogan."[59]

As Belgian rule in the Congo neared its close, however, the community slogan gradually faded away. The *Groupe de Travail* affirmed that the great majority of persons testifying expressed the desire to see Belgium lead the Congo to full internal autonomy, and that at this time the two parties would freely negotiate the new links of association; the two

[57] Jean Labrique, *Congo politique* (Leopoldville: Editions de l'Avenir, 1957), pp. 176-96. Labrique was shortly thereafter expelled from the Congo, apparently for having become too involved in stimulating the establishment of the first independent Congolese journals, *Quinze* and *Congo*.

[58] Jean Sépulchre, *Propos sur le Congo politique de demain: autonomie et fédéralisme* (Elisabethville: Editions de l'Essor du Congo, 1958), p. 7.

[59] J. K. (Van der Dussen), *André Ryckmans* (Brussels: Charles Dessart, 1961), p. 196. The younger Ryckmans came to a tragic end near Thysville in July 1960, assassinated by a band of mutinous soldiers while on a rescue mission. This collection of diary notes and letters is one of the best records available of events of the last decade in the Bayaka and Bakongo areas of Leopoldville Province. "J. K." is Jean de Kestergat Van der Dussen, Congo correspondent of *La Libre Belgique*.

aspects were said to be indissolubly interrelated.[60] Count d'Aspremont-Lynden, in a memorandum on the special fact-finding mission to the Congo to which he was assigned, still maintained, in August 1959, "It goes without saying that the authorities of the Congo have never envisaged any other final objective than the creation of a community between Belgium and the Congo."[61] Belgian expectations in this regard then rapidly dwindled to a meager Treaty of Friendship and Technical Assistance, signed on June 29, 1960, but not ratified by either Parliament.

Finally, when the time came to give a political superstructure to the bureaucratic colonial system, the norms of representative democracy in Belgium necessarily came into play. All agreed in principle that institutions should be "adapted," but in the final analysis the only familiar standard of reference for Belgians and Congolese was the Belgian constitution. "Far from imposing purely European solutions, we intend to favor original adaptations, based upon African characteristics and cherished traditions," stated the royal message.[62] Yet, when work was completed on the provisional constitution, the *Loi Fondamentale*, it was virtually a replica of the Belgian constitution, even down to the maverick features, such as coopted Senators. The self-respect of both departing Belgian rulers and succeeding Congolese elite required that the regime they defined pass scrutiny as "democratic." The *Groupe de Travail* suggested that one criterion was universal suffrage, "which alone gives to the representation of the people an unquestioned legitimacy,"[63] and another the application of the UN Universal Declaration of Human Rights. In virtually improvising from scratch a political system, the metropolitan model became even more important than in most

[60] *Rapport du Groupe de Travail,* p. 16.
[61] *Congo 1959,* p. 176.
[62] *Ibid,* p. 45.
[63] *Rapport du Groupe de Travail,* p. 30.

former British and French territories, where a certain amount of experience in the functioning of representative political institutions before transfer of power was permitted.

Although Belgian postwar colonial perspective slowly changed beneath a façade of policy immobility, the stubborn attachment to outworn shibboleths has proved costly. A number of the key assumptions underlying the first approaches to the decolonization problem were increasingly out of joint with the times. It became clear that time was not going to be limitless, that the "empire of silence" would dissolve under the gradual coagulation of latent nationalist forces, that African society was ceasing to be malleable clay in the hands of the colonizer, that a handful of African barkeepers could not be a black bourgeoisie vigilant to defend the colonial order. The tides of nationalism would not be reversed simply by building more schools and hospitals, issuing a few immatriculation cards to the prominent members of the modern elite, or admitting a few wellgroomed Congolese to European restaurants. However vague and unrealistic it was, the Belgo-Congolese community slogan had some value as a transitional idea, which by its very existence forced some debate on adaptation. This, in turn, clearly revealed a number of the contradictions in the Belgian view of the future. Paritary institutions in the Congo could not be reconciled with democracy; a Belgo-Congolese community which was in fact initally thought of as an association between a horse and a rider could hardly be viable if both were to be given a chance to consent freely to the relationship.

In the long run, the very posing of these problems provided the answer. It was inevitable that the democratic values of metropolitan Belgium would triumph over the desires of Europeans in the Congo to build a paritary wall around their privileges. And subordinating the construction

57

of the Belgo-Congolese community to the free consent of both parties meant necessarily abandoning the kind of relationship implied in the first formulations.

Until 1959, the debate on terminal objectives took place virtually in a vacuum, within the walls of the European community. After the Leopoldville riots, there was for the first time a real effort to negotiate the future with African leadership; this profoundly transformed the nature of the dialogue. The pattern of events elsewhere in Afro-Asia and the increasingly apparent inconsistency and impracticality of schemes which sought attenuated hegemony under the guise of autonomy and a Belgo-Congolese community had invisibly transformed Belgian perspectives. In 1955-1956, Van Bilsen's proposals were indignantly repudiated by nearly all sectors of metropolitan and colonial opinion. Only three years later, the promise of independence "without fatal delays" from Baudouin found unanimous acceptance.

CHAPTER IV

※※※

Paternalism

※※※

The Paternal Metaphor

IN ANNOUNCING that a Round Table Conference would be organized to negotiate the problems of political transition in January 1960, Congo Minister De Schrijver permitted himself a small digression on the subject of the rural populations: "I see these simple populations outside the large urban centers, and I feel myself more than ever the father of a family. And if I have ten children, that has prepared me to better understand these peoples. . . . We know that all the children of a family must work together to achieve the big goals. And these children are like the ten fingers of my two hands. When I am in the Congo, I listen to all the voices. . . . I say to those who only represent two fingers, 'You don't have the right to ask me not to take account of the eight others.'"[1]

It is at first view surprising that a member of the PSC's liberal wing and an architect of radical decolonization should fall back on this imagery seven months before independence. And yet this metaphor is one of the most familiar in the colonial lexicon.

"You are my father and my mother," the rural African told the administrator or missionary, who nodded approvingly. "Africans are like big children," echoed the colonial literature. And certainly these statements describe an important aspect of the psychology of the colonial situation. There was a pervasive sense of dependence imposed on the colonized by his subjugation. It is the same phenomenon that Mannoni describes in Madagascar by means of a somewhat different metaphor;[2] what distinguishes the

---

[1] *Congo 1959*, p. 251.

[2] O. Mannoni, *Prospero and Caliban* (New York: Frederick Praeger, 1956).

Congo is that this image was dignified as a systematic guide to action by the colonizer.

The antecedents of paternalism as a guide to policy can be traced back to the founding of the Free State. However, until World War II, it was more an implicit assumption than an explicit political theory. Before the war, the social and political immaturity of Congolese populations was so self-evident to the colonizer that no elaboration was required. But in the changed international environment of the postwar years, colonialism was on the defensive, and explicit justifications for its prolongation were necessary. It was in response to this need that paternalism as an ideology of colonial administration became articulated.

In its broadest sense, the doctrine was summed up by Ryckmans in his famous epigram, *"dominer pour servir. . . .* This is the sole excuse for colonial conquest; it is also its complete justification."[3] More specifically, it meant a particular solicitude for the welfare of the child, assuring that his illnesses were tended, his education provided, and his physical comfort guaranteed. It meant that a proper parental concern needed to be shown for his moral upbringing. It meant that the adolescent frequently had to be protected against himself, responsibility was accorded parsimoniously and under close supervision. It meant that it was frequently necessary to take harsh measures and impose some duties whose value was beyond the child's immature scope of understanding.

In policy terms, reduced to its simplest expression, paternalism required an aggressive expansion in social and economic fields, with political advance postponed until some undefined threshold of maturity had been reached. Few would dispute the proposition that there is some correlation between the level of economic and social well-being

[3] Pierre Ryckmans, *Dominer pour servir* (Brussels: L'Edition Universelle, 1948).

and the prospects for stable, democratic government. The fallacy here lay in the assumption that the colonizer could methodically impose and carry out an economic and social development program until he was satisfied that the requisites for political advance existed. But as long as criticisms of the system were mainly external, it was easy to dismiss them as misguided. A crucial dimension of paternalism was its persuasiveness to responsible levels of colonial officialdom. Paternalism was an important guide to action because it carried conviction to its practitioners, however much it may smack of humbug to later critics.

Economic and Social Development

There were impressive achievements in the rapid expansion of the economic and social infrastructure after World War II. Industrial paternalism had been pioneered by the large companies to stabilize their working force—beginning about 1926 when the labor shortage reached crisis proportions—and had proved a spectacular success. Decent housing was provided; family allowances were paid to the workers, schools built for the children and *foyers sociaux* established for the women. One of the best statements of the paternalist philosophy is contained in a 1946 memorandum of *Union Minière*, setting forth the principles of its social policy:

"The colonizer must never lose sight of the fact that the Negroes have the souls of children, souls which mold themselves to the methods of the educator; they watch, listen, feel, and imitate. The European must, in all circumstances, show himself a chief without weakness, good-willed without familiarity, active in method and especially just in the punishment of misbehavior, as in the reward of good deed. . . . (The European camp head) must interest himself constantly in the life of the natives, in their well-being;

must guide them, examine their complaints; punish them when necessary with the tact, the calm and the firmness which are required."[4]

In the urban areas, this policy was manifested by an active policy of promoting African housing, especially through the *Office des Cités Africaines*, and the rapid expansion of schools and hospitals. According to a European Common Market survey, the Congo's medical infrastructure in 1958 was the best in tropical Africa.[5] A network of social centers was established to help train women for family responsibility in the urban environment. Tropical Africa's first generalized social security program was established by the decree of June 6, 1956. In 1946, legislation had been adopted requiring the establishment of paritary *Conseils d'enterprise*, with half of the worker members elected; these were similar to company unions and were a forum for labor-management discussion of worker grievances. They are generally believed by employers to be a useful mechanism; in preempting the role of the unions in this area, the *conseils* no doubt were one factor in the very slow growth of African labor organizations.

In the countryside, the *Fonds du Bien-Etre Indigène* operated in a wide spectrum of welfare enterprises. In zones selected for their relative poverty, sanitary campaigns were undertaken, food storage facilities built, livestock provided, vocational schools constructed; it is claimed that three million peasants were provided with drinking water through a string of village wells.[6] The FBI was created in 1947, with the two-billion-franc payment Belgium made in settlement of wartime expenses incurred by the Congo essen-

[4] L. Moutoulle, *Politique sociale de l'Union Minière du Haut Katanga* (Brussels: ARSOM, Sci. Mor. et Pol., T. XIV, fasc. 3, 1946) pp. 5-6, 15.
[5] Brausch, *Belgian Administration in the Congo*, p. 8.
[6] *Le Congo Belge*, 2 vols. (Brussels: Inforcongo, 1958), I, 473.

tially on behalf of the colonizer.[7] The annual resources were substantial, averaging six million dollars.[8]

It is unnecessary to undertake a complete catalogue of the economic and social programs which were the armature of paternalism. There can be no doubt that the achievements were impressive, that the independent Congo inherited an economic and social infrastructure of premier quality. The colonial tasks to which Belgium set itself with clarity of purpose were competently accomplished. Hailey is quite right to add that the "concern of the Administration has not in fact been merely material; there has been a real element of good will toward the African population and its welfare."[9] Good will is implicit in the paternal metaphor. The fatal flaw lay not simply in the predominance of material objectives, but in the failure to involve the beneficiaries in any way other than as passive recipients of the largesse.

An important aspect of the institutional structuring of paternalism was the Belgian practice of setting up a series of "parastatal" organizations to implement a good part of the policy. "Parastatal" in Belgian usage has been defined by one writer as "a national public service . . . legally granted a juridical personality distinct from the state and a varying degree of autonomy with relation to the central authority."[10] However, one should add that in Belgium itself this type of body is a de facto growth whose precise constitutional position has never been fully determined. The very ambiguity of their status has in a number of cases facilitated the development of these organisms into shadowy empires

[7] Stengers, *Combien le Congo a-t-il coûté à la Belgique,* pp. 133-43.

[8] Henri Beckers, "Le Fonds du Bien-Etre Indigène," *Zaïre,* V (October 1951), 788.

[9] Hailey, *An African Survey,* p. 218.

[10] Prosper Madrandele, *Les Parastataux au Congo,* Mémoire en Sciences Politiques et Administratives, Université Lovanium, 1960, p. 26.

whose actions had vital implications in broad areas of social and economic policy, but were not subject to any responsible public control. In the Congo, the parastatal sector ranged from the giant *pouvoirs concédants, Comité Spécial du Katanga* (CSK) and the *Comité National du Kivu* (CNKi), which were autonomous, semi-private states-within-the-state, to institutions in the social field such as the FBI. They included much of the transport system, public utilities, national parks, the social security funds, housing, scientific research institutions,[11] the central bank, and marketing boards. It can be seen that they covered a large range of the economic and social activity of the government; their autonomy was considerable, and in a number of cases they developed into veritable feudal fiefdoms. In many instances, they had their headquarters in expensive new buildings in Brussels. An important part of the public investment in the Congo passed through these bodies; very large sums were controlled by them.[12] The colonial pension fund, in 1960, contained ten billion francs and had available for investment each year approximately one billion.[13] Liquidation or transfer of these bodies was one of the most perplexing institutional problems of decolonization, and it is still far from solved with more than one major scandal in evaporation of parastatal assets likely to result.[14] In all, some forty parastatal bodies of varying descriptions were established.

The postwar economic boom in the Congo played its part in making financially possible this enormous effort without requiring Belgian participation. There is room for

[11] Such as the outstanding *Institut National Pour l'Etude Agronomique au Congo Belge* (INEAC) and the *Institut pour la Recherche Scientifique en Afrique Centrale* (IRSAC).

[12] Van Bilsen, *Vers l'indépendance,* pp. 67-69. The CSK paid out 459 million francs in dividends alone in 1954.

[13] Document 93, Conférence de la Table Ronde Economique Belgo-Congolaise, Brussels, May 1960.

[14] "Quelques notes sur le Contentieux Belgo-Congolais," *Etudes Congolaises,* III, No. 4 (1962), 30-36.

serious doubt as to whether the Congo can afford the generous social welfare policy bequeathed by Belgium. There was great indignation in Belgium when the World Health Organization suggested in a 1961 report that the country could not continue to support the pre-independence level of medical services; but objectively the point is hard to gainsay. Had this infrastructure required Belgian subsidy, as did similar undertakings in former British or especially French Africa, one may well wonder whether a harder look would not have been taken at many projects. The economic and social infrastructure was also financed in part by external borrowing; while it is true that Belgium guaranteed most of the Congo loans, the public debt in 1960, especially the external repayments due in hard currency, was generally conceded to be excessive. Service of the debt was 24 percent of the 1960 budget.

The Constraints of Paternalism

Paternalism had its constraints as well as its welfare aspects. Colonial policy was riddled with regulations and requirements predicated upon the social and economic as well as the political "immaturity" of the colonial charges. The African was bound to his employer by a *contrat de travail* rather than the *contrat d'emploi;* the former carried in particular penal sanctions for absenteeism or other defective behavior judged to be in violation of the labor contract. The organization of trade unions was largely left in the hands of the Congolese extensions of the major Belgian unions, the *Fédération Générale du Travail de Belgique* (FGTB-Socialist), and the *Confédération des Syndicats Chrétiens* (CSC-Catholic); in the words of the Congo's trade union historian. "They assumed this role vis-à-vis the native workers by processes inspired by paternalism."[15]

[15] R. Poupart, *Première esquisse de l'évolution du syndicalisme au Congo* (Brussels: Editions de l'Institut de Sociologie Solvay, 1960), p. 112.

A number of other harassing provisions springing from the loins of paternalism affected the urban African. The sale of liquor to Africans was prohibited until 1955. This restriction dated back to the Brussels Anti-Slavery Conference of 1889-1890; initially, it was no doubt a humanitarian measure to halt the ravages of alcoholism and prevent unscrupulous exploitation. By 1945, however, this seemed to the new elite only an intensely irritating piece of discrimination. The same objections held for the nightly curfew imposed on Africans. Reference has already been made to the fact that Congolese were not in fact able to own land;[16] the justification for this was the desire to prevent speculators from obtaining valuable urban land. Africans were judged either by the summary police courts, presided over by the territorial administrator who sat as judge and prosecutor, or in "native courts," in accordance with traditional law which the urban elite strongly felt should not be applicable to them without their consent.

In the countryside, the paternal approach was even more thoroughgoing. The most striking application was in the practice of obligatory cultivation. This began on a limited scale in 1917; it was generalized and written into the legislation by the decree of December 5, 1933 on *circonscriptions indigènes*. The principal architect of the Congo's agricultural policy, Edmond Leplae, argued that constraint was a necessary part of the "educational" process; however, three decades after the "education" had begun in many cotton-growing areas it was still going forward.[17] The fact that, with the exception of former French Equatorial Africa, cotton has been introduced successfully as an African crop without maintaining compulsion for any prolonged period,

[16] Supra, pp. 44-45.

[17] Edmond Leplae, "Notes au sujet du développement de l'agriculture du Congo belge," *Bulletin Agricole du Congo Belge*, VIII (March-June, 1917), 3-39; (September-October, 1917), 172-217; Guy Malengreau, *Vers un paysannat indigène* (Brussels: ARSOM, Sci. Mor. et Pol., T. XIX, fasc. 2, 1949) p. 7.

if at all, suggests that the policy is at least open to question as an educational device. The constraint used was considerable; the 1947 Senate commission reported that about 10 percent of the adult male population spent some time in prison, in good part because of violation of the agricultural requirements. The condemnation could be made by the territorial administrator, as a violation of Article 45h of the December 5, 1933, decree, or could be treated as a "traditional" offense, with the chief imposing a "traditional" penalty, often a whipping, for the disrespect shown in failing to execute the planting orders he transmitted from the administration.[18] A study group of CEPSI in Elisabethville, investigating the problems of rural development, put its finger on the defects of education by constraint:

"When, some day, the history of social transformation in the Congo is written . . . the historian will without any doubt underline the disadvantages which our Colony has experienced and the dangers it has run, if in the meanwhile these have not engulfed it, from the fact that one had recourse for too long to imposed cultivation. Not only that, in so doing, we have seriously infringed upon the liberty of the Congolese—although this aspect is important in its own right—but our legislation of constraint, foundation of a policy of facility both in terms of agricultural technique and of the concomitant political and social action, has reduced to mediocrity the power of imagination and persuasion of the agricultural personnel, excluded all effective participation of native authorities, and sterilized the spirit of initiative in traditional societies."[19]

[18] Sénat de Belgique, *Rapport*, pp. 32, 68.

[19] "A propos des problèmes du milieu rural congolais," *Bulletin du CEPSI* (March 1957), p. 156. This study was inspired by and bears the mark of one of Belgium's finest colonial servants, F. Grévisse, who wound up his career as district commissioner at Elisabethville. In 1959-60, Grévisse was frequently consulted on Katanga affairs, both by Belgian authorities and *Union Minière*. However, he was strongly opposed to the secession and anti-Baluba policies which emerged in

The generalization of the *paysannat indigène* formula in the last decade of Belgian rule was, in the manner of its execution, another manifestation of the paternal approach. One of the main objects was to give improved supervision to the enforcement of INEAC crop rotation plans. In a distinguished study of the problems involved in entending this pattern on a large scale, Malengreau warned of establishing the settlements without a careful survey of existing land rights, and remarked on the dangers in the use of force.[20] The CEPSI study indicated that many *paysannats* had nothing voluntary about them but the name; some had been deserted by over 50 percent of their members.[21] Although the Ten-Year-Plan goal of 385,000 plots was not met, 200,000 had been established by the beginning of 1959.[22] The extent of surveillance is indicated by the extremely high deployment of staff; there was one agent per 320 farmers, as compared with one per 1,000 in Western Nigeria, and one per 20,000 in Northern Nigeria.[23] Some of the showpiece settlements, such as those at Gandajika (Kasai) and Buta (Orientale) were spectacular successes; many of the others, however, never got beyond the stage of administrative impositions, and disappeared with independence.

The Belgian system of administration, ultimately, failed to move beyond the paternal phase. Theoretically, Belgium, beginning with Liberal Minister Franck, adopted the Lugardian principles of indirect rule. However, the prac-

---

Elisabethville under the Tshombe regime, and withdrew from an active role.

[20] Malengreau, *Vers un paysannat indigène.*

[21] "A propos des problèmes du milieu rural congolais," *loc. cit.*

[22] *Rapport sur l'Administration . . . 1958*, p. 244.

[23] Hunter, *The New Societies of Tropical Africa*, pp. 116-17. Numerous interviews with former agricultural officers confirm the view that constraint was frequently used to establish and maintain the *paysannat*, although in many cases it was maintained that once operational, the peasant came to see the undoubted advantages of the scheme. The term *paysannat* in fact covered a wide variety of agricultural settlements.

tice in most areas tended to be much closer to the description advanced by the authoritative juridical commentary of Magotte on the 1933 decree embedding "indirect rule" in colonial legislation: "[The administration] . . . has maintained traditional organization to implant its own organization, but it has not left to the former its independence. On the contrary, the administration intervenes to a large degree in order to make the population evolve, instead of letting them crystallize in the conceptions and customs of the past."[24]

The tendency of the territorial administrators to do everything themselves, to place immediate efficiency above political education, persisted until nearly the end. In 1956, Malengreau noted that there was a deterioration of the functioning of rural institutions: "Traditional chiefs are less clever than previously in the exercise of their traditional functions. And this political incapacity seems to have as a principal reason the excess of solicitude of our administrative paternalism, which, through its continued interventions, has killed all spirit of initiative and encouraged the inertia of traditional authorities."[25]

Petillon summarized the process in 1952: "Our former conception of indirect administration, timid and mitigated as it might have been from the beginning, has not ceased being attenuated. Under the pressure of economic circumstance and war situations, with the praiseworthy desire to act better and more rapidly, we have taken everything into our own hands and directed the Congolese mass, for better

[24] J. Magotte, *Les Circonscriptions Indigènes* (La Louvière, Belgium: Imprimèrie Louvièroise, n.d. [1952]), pp. 50-51.

[25] *L'Afrique belge devant son avenir* (Louvain: Société d'Etudes Politiques et Sociales, 1957), p. 12. With the implementation of the decree of May 10, 1957, however, a genuine start was made toward depaternalizing local government. The ability of the *circonscriptions indigènes* to survive the shock of independence in most areas suggests in retrospect that Malengreau was too pessimistic, but also that paternal intervention had been for some time unnecessary and harmful.

or for worse, toward a well-being in conformity with our own concepts."[26]

Urban administration experienced the same shortcomings as that of the rural areas. One of the innovations of Belgian colonial organization which intrigued some observers was the *centre extra-coutumier* (CEC) which represented an extension of the Belgian version of indirect rule to the cities.[27] The decree of November 23, 1931, provided for the creation of a CEC council composed of members representing different ethnic groups and the designation of a "chief," on whom considerable administrative tasks could theoretically be devolved. There was, however, an escape clause which permitted these institutions to be "suspended" by the Provincial Governor. The key centers of Elisabethville and Jadotville immediately made use of this; Leopoldville refused flatly to create a CEC. Elisabethville had a "chief" from 1937-1943, but he found the ambiguity of his situation intolerable; unable to escape the stigma of deriving his authority solely from the Europeans, who were ever more conpicuous in the background, he simply could not stand the strain.[28] He was never replaced; even the "adjoint" was dismissed in 1946, and no new one designated until November 1955.[29] By the eve of World War II, only 24 *centres extra-coutumiers* had been created, involving 100,000 persons; this mechanism was really only used for the smaller towns.[30] After the war, creation of CEC's virtually came to

[26] Congo Belge, Conseil du Gouvernement, *Discours du Gouverneur Général*, 1952, p. 37.

[27] Hailey, for example, terms it "one of the most original initiatives of the Belgian administration." *Op. cit.*, p. 222.

[28] F. Grévisse, *Le Centre Extra-Coutumier d'Elisabethville* (Brussels: ARSOM, Sci., Mor. et Pol., T. XXI, 1951), pp 39-41. A former district commissioner at Elisabethville, Grévisse felt that the CEC experiment had been almost a complete failure as a method of effectively involving the African population in its own administration.

[29] P. Caprasse, *Leaders africains en milieu urbain* (Elisabethville: C.E.P.S.I., 1959), p. 95.

[30] Guy Baumer, *Les centres indigènes extra-coutumiers au Congo*

an end.[31] Paternalism again produced its inevitable vicious circle; capable chiefs could not be found to fill even the limited functions provided under this legislation, yet paternalism itself stood squarely in the way of the acquisition of the necessary political experience to become capable.

Refurbished and institutionalized paternalism then, despite its economic and social achievements, merely made more difficult and painful the changes which eventually were required. The habits of unilateral action became embedded all the deeper in the political style of the colonial structure. Malengreau's prophetic warning in 1947 laid bare the defects of the paternal response upon which Belgium was embarking:

"The object of paternalist policy is to make the African a being assisted, insured and pensioned, instead of making him a free man. . . . Each native is provided with his standardized house, mass-produced furniture, pre-determined scale of food, his free time regulated to the last detail and without a trace of imagination. . . . Man is turned into a sort of vegetable, in an anticipation of the mechanical earthly paradise of Bernanos. But at all times, men have found freedom in misery preferable to a comfortable slavery. . . . We must remember that liberty which has once been taken away is difficult to give back."[32]

That the warnings went largely unheard can be seen from the CEPSI study a decade later which noted with great concern a dangerous growth in passive African acceptance of whatever was given. "In a country where certain elements are demanding the right to self-determination, nothing is conceived nor directed in its execution except by a

---

Belge (Paris: Editions Domat-Monchrestien, 1939), p. 65.

[31] Guy Malengreau's contribution on the participation of Africans in political life, in *Compte Rendu des Journées Interuniversitaires d'Etudes Coloniales,* p. 28.

[32] Malengreau, "Le Congo à la croisée des chemins," *loc. cit.*

European to whom the natives bring the assistance which one might expect from a new worker."[33]

Paternalism as a frame of mind was debilitating to both partners in the metaphor. Spiraling postwar paternalism sapped African initiative, created a vast superstructure, such as the parastatal network or the *paysannats*, which were erected on the hypothesis of prolonged "arrested adolescence" and which tended by their mode of operation to verify the hypothesis. The fashioning of a system after the paternal image was so thoroughly done that intractable dilemmas were created for the moment when the father had to depart.

[33] "A propos des problèmes du milieu rural congolais," *loc. cit.*, pp. 170-71.

CHAPTER V

Desegregating Colonial Society

The Threat of Elite Disaffection

UPON return from his highly successful 1955 Congo tour, King Baudouin told the nation:

"I want to insist on the fact that the basic problem which now confronts the Congo is that of human relationships between black and white. It is not enough to equip the country materially, to endow it with wise social legislation, and to improve the standard of living of its inhabitants; it is imperative that the whites and the natives should show the widest mutual understanding in their daily contacts. . . . Before we realize this high ideal, gentlemen, much remains to be done."[1]

A fundamental preoccupation of colonial policy throughout the postwar period was summarized by the young King's statement. Now making its appearance was an educated African elite, which somehow had to be provided satisfactory status within colonial society. Until the early fifties, adaptation of the system was conceived of primarily in terms of elite satisfaction. In the later period, the problem of laying the structural foundations for a democratic, Eurafrican polity in the Congo and a broader Belgo-Congolese community came increasingly to the fore. But till the very end of Belgian rule "race relations" tended to be seen as the elemental cause of elite disaffection; desegregating colonial society was a *sine qua non* for achieving the vague vision of the Belgo-Congolese community. Accordingly it is appropriate to examine the steps taken to cope with the challenge of the emergent African elite.

---

[1] Speech to the Royal African Circle, Brussels, July 1, 1955, quoted in Ruth Slade, *The Belgian Congo* (New York: Oxford University Press, 1960), pp. 19-20.

There were two distinct stages to policy development on this issue. In a first phase, from 1945-1952, an effort was made to define in legal terms a special elite status, privileged in relationship to the African mass. These culminated in the 1952 decree offering immatriculation to "civilized" Congolese. However, the immense difficulties in defining the nature and scope of this reform foreshadowed its failure. In the succeeding years, primary effort was concentrated in achieving piecemeal desegregation in various specific areas of discrimination. Both of these phases will be explored in some detail, for the illumination they provide on the total decolonization process.

That elite satisfaction was the central issue in colonial policy was accepted in the early postwar years by all sectors in colonial society. African perspectives as well as European were shaped by the assumption that any early change in the Congo's colonial status, however desirable, was impossible. The question was posed in the second issue of the first publication edited by the Congolese (under the careful tutelage of the administration), when Paul Tshibamba-Lomami asked, "What will be our place in the world of tomorrow?"[2] The issue of évolué rights almost completely absorbed the attention of the emerging elite during the first postwar decade. And on the Belgian side, the significance attached to the problem was clearly stated by A. Sohier, the father of the decree on immatriculation:

"The objective to attain, is that the Belgians of Africa[3] feel truly Belgian, united with the Belgians of Europe in a single national community, the essential condition so that one day, free to decide on their future, they will choose the main-

[2] La Voix du Congolais, No. 2, 1945.

[3] In this context, Sohier is including Congolese, who had Belgian nationality, but were not Belgian citizens. The colonial literature contains a long and tedious debate as to what exactly the juridical content of the terms "Belgian" and "Congolese" was. To sample this discussion, see André Durieux, Nationalité et citoyenneté (Brussels: ARSOM, Sci. Mor. et. Pol., N. S., T. XXIII, fasc. 2, 1959).

tenance of the present association. Ineluctably, in a number of years which it is impossible for us to determine, so many factors being able to influence the course of events, the colonial form of our political organization must give way to another regime. We would hope that, this moment having arrived, the African society would be so indivisibly integrated to our own that it would not desire to separate, and that for the tutelary domination of one people by another will be substituted a comprehensive formula for national collaboration."[4]

The Immatriculation Decree

Immatriculation in fact has a hoary history. It was first instituted by a decree of May 4, 1895, in the Congo Free State days; it was then apparently designed to bring under European civil law those Congolese who had entered European service and wished to renounce their traditional status. It was next extended to cover automatically certain categories of Africans, such as soldiers, workers, or those attached to the mission settlements. This was inscribed in the *Charte Coloniale* at the time of *reprise*. However, the procedure fell into almost complete disuse; the colonial milieux regarded as excessive the indiscriminate grant of full civil rights to every soldier or domestic servant. Legislation was subsequently passed which imposed certain special regulations on the entire African population, whether or not immatriculated. Africans ceased demanding the status or trying to invoke what few rights might remain under it.

In the 1930's the issue reappeared, urged on by the assimilationist, direct administration wing of colonial opinion. The growing number of Congolese living permanently outside the traditional areas were considered a threat to colonial stability; these clustered in "Christian villages" around the mission stations, and *"fin de terme"* settlements of dis-

[4] Sohier, "La politique d'intégration," *Zaïre*, V, No. 9 (November 1951), 909.

charged soldiers and workers refusing to return to their villages of origin. Boma, Matadi, Leopoldville, Stanleyville, Jadotville, and Elisabethville were becoming urban centers with significant African populations, with new social policies seeking to stabilize a Congolese working force in towns. The first African priest in modern times[5] was consecrated at the Baudouinville seminary in 1917; this was the beginning of a slowly growing modern elite. A handful of Belgians advocated the revival of the immatriculation procedure of the 1920's, "to assure the close and permanent cooperation of the African to European activity."[6]

In 1931, the Commission for the Protection of Natives proposed a *"petite immatriculation"* for clerks, with the idea of establishing an intermediate category of persons, distinguished from the African population as a whole, yet also kept at a safe distance from European society. In 1935, a draft decree was prepared in the Colonial Ministry; after studying it, Monsignor de Hemptinne's Elisabethville subcommission of the Commission for the Protection of Natives produced a counterproposal in 1937 which called for the complete assimilation of the "rare individuals" who had thoroughly adopted "European civilization." The Katanga subcommission argued that only a few priests "as of today . . . are assimilated to our civilization." On the one hand, the subcommission continued, it was necessary to make clear that the door of European society was open to those who attained its standards, and, on the other, to avoid any

[5] During the period of substantial missionary activity in the old Bakongo kingdom, especially in the 16th century, a number of African priests had been consecrated, and in 1517 an African bishop. However, Portuguese interest and energy shifted increasingly from importing salvation to exporting slaves, and by the 19th century virtually nothing remained of the early Christian communities.

[6] L. Lotar, "L'immatriculation et l'ordre économique," *Congo,* 7th yr., T.I, No. 1, (January 1926), p. 34. See also the same author's "L'immatriculation des indigènes de l'état civil," *Bull. Séances,* ARSOM, (1937), pp. 54-58; "Le statut des immatriculés," *Congo,* 4th yr., T.I., No. 4, (April 1923), pp. 451-56.

premature expectations on the part of the mass by the establishment of precise and rigorous conditions. Nothing, however, materialized before World War II.

After the war, the question returned to the colonial agenda in the new postwar atmosphere. There was a vague feeling that the Belgians had acquired a war debt to the Congo and that a series of measures in favor of diverse elements of the Congolese population was necessary. There was growing African pressure for some step in this direction; symptoms of the times were the various articles in *La Voix du Congolais* on the subject. After the *Force Publique* mutiny in Luluabourg in 1944, a group of Luluabourg *évolués* had prepared a memorandum demanding "if not a special statute, at least a special protection of the government, shielding them from the application of certain treatments and measures which could be applied to a retarded and ignorant mass."[7] Certain significant steps were taken immediately. *La Voix du Congolais* was established. The administration created *Cercles d'Évolués* in many centers and often provided good facilities. Many Congolese leaders recall the 1945-1947 period as one in which the administration seemed genuinely concerned with their grievances.

In 1947 the Commission for the Protection of Natives "regretted" that its prewar proposals were not put into effect, as this would have forestalled the growing "color bar" allegations.[8] The Senate commission the same year noted that status of the African elite was "the great question of the moment." Although some provincial councils and the *Conseil de Gouvernement* had expressed their hostility to the idea of some sort of special card, the senators felt that something should be done to provide an intermediate class of

[7] *Dettes de guerre*, pp. 128-129. This important statement was the first public group petition for better treatment; the case for reform rested in part upon the claims that the *évolués* had played a key intermediary role in limiting the impact of the mutiny.

[8] Guebels, *Relation Complète . . . Commission Permanente pour la Protection des Indigènes*, p. 652.

transport on the boats and railroads, special rooms in hospitals, and to halt whipping in prisons for *évolués*.[9] The National Colonial Congress in Belgium also called for action in 1947. Governor-General Jungers, in his 1948 address to the *Conseil du Gouvernement,* indicated that some temporary solution would be found while the issue was being studied in some detail.[10] The normal laborious legislative process required for the issue of a decree was avoided by the device of an *ordonnance législative* of the Governor-General on July 12, 1948, establishing a *"Carte du Mérite Civique."*[11]

The *Carte* was to be available on application to those who had a record free of "uncivilized" practices, such as polygamy and sorcery, and crimes, such as theft or fraud, indicating a lack of integrity. Literacy was required, except for individuals with twenty-five years of "good and faithful service" in the administration or twenty years as a chief. There was a brief flurry of interest in the *Carte,* but the ordinance establishing it provided no concrete benefits for the cardholders, either legally or in terms of their daily treatment by the Europeans. Thus enthusiasm quickly gave way to bitter disappointment. By the end of 1952, only 452 *Cartes* had been issued;[12] the latest published totals at the end of 1958 indicated that a mere 1,557 had been distributed.[13] This stop-gap measure was thus almost completely ineffective. The verdict pronounced upon it by the liberal Catholic lawyer from Elisabethville, Antoine Rubbens, seems just: "Those who possess it," he argued, "are dis-

[9] Sénat de Belgique, *Rapport,* pp. 18-19.

[10] Congo Belge, Conseil du Gouvernement, *Discours du Gouverneur Général,* 1948, p. 34.

[11] The Governor-General had the legal authority to issue in an "emergency" ordinances which in Belgian constitutional law are regarded as "legislative," but these must theoretically be confirmed by a decree within six months. This does not seem to have been the case with the *Carte de Mérite Civique.* Piron & Devos, *Codes et Lois,* I, 152-53.

[12] Hailey, *op. cit.,* p. 226.

[13] Chambre des Représentants, *Rapport sur l'Administration . . . 1958,* p. 104.

appointed, having no uses for it; those who had it refused to them are embittered."[14]

In 1948, a special committee was appointed in Brussels, headed by Sohier, to seek a more permanent solution. The Sohier Commission was clearly aware of the implications of its task and recognized that "in a number of years . . . the colonial form of our political organization must cede the place to another regime."[15] A number of perplexing issues were posed: For whom should the new status be designed? Should it cover only a very few or be designed to cover a broad portion of the literate population? Should it be as-similative in character and formally establish as a goal the Europeanization of the African population? Should it give full or partial access to rights enjoyed by the European pop-ulation? Should immatriculated Congolese be encouraged to move into European quarters and identify themselves completely with the European population? Should chiefs have access to the status? What objective standard could be found for "civilization"? If assimilation were rejected as a principle, how was differentiation to be reconciled with the desire to reduce discrimination in legislation? Finally, what social group was to be the chosen ally of the colonial system in its efforts to effect the necessary transformations in such a way as to achieve goals which it defined for itself?

The Sohier Commission set to work with dispatch, and by the end of the year had prepared a draft decree. The central theme of the proposals was the provision for two levels of differentiated status. For a small number of com-pletely Europeanized Congolese, full equality with Euro-peans in all matters was to be assured. For a larger category of persons, the *Carte du Mérite Civique* would be retained; these people would come within the provisions of European civil, but not criminal, jurisdiction. Finally, the archaic im-

[14] Fedacol, *L'opinion publique coloniale* . . . , pp.10-12, reprinted from *Essor du Congo*, September 2, 1950.
[15] Sohier, *loc. cit.*, p. 909.

matriculation provisions of the Free State would be repealed.

Sohier published his proposals in the semi-official colonial journal *Zaïre* in 1949,[16] and at first only African opinion responded. However, the situation changed rapidly when the draft decree was debated by the *Conseil du Gouvernement* in 1950. "Perhaps never, since the existence of the Congo, has a question aroused such burning controversy," wrote the president of Fedacol, the settler association, in 1951.[17] Planter O. Defawe spoke for a broad segment of European opinion in the Congo when he warned:

"To accord assimilation now, even with severe conditions, is to throw sand in the works; . . . we will have created an active minority which will be the basis for shaking native society to its foundations. . . . It suffices to be acquainted with on the one hand our brave populations of the interior, and on the other the anomalous collection of so-called *évolués* to understand the disastrous effects which would result from granting the one the aura of authority, which would have as its first result the unleashing of violent movements of premature emancipation, followed by an odious tyranny of a tiny minority."[18]

Using the specious argument that the draft decree had been available to them only a few days before the meeting, some of the European members of the *Conseil* proposed that such an important matter be studied at leisure by the provincial councils then returned for debate at the *Conseil* the following year. However, those representing the Africans[19] reacted strongly, maintaining that such a delay would

[16] A. Sohier, "Le problème des indigènes évolués et la Commission du Statut des Congolais civilisés," *Zaïre*, III, No. 8, (October 1949).

[17] A. Maus in the introduction to Fedacol, *op. cit.*, p. 2. This interesting document reproduces a large number of articles and speeches on the immatriculation issue, which have in common their opposition to the proposed decree.

[18] O. Defawe, speech to *Conseil du Gouvernement*, July 20, 1950, in *ibid.*, pp. 7-9.

[19] It will be recalled that only two Africans were actually members

create bitterness and disillusionment amongst the Congolese elite.[20] The *Conseil* finally accepted the extraordinary procedure of convening special provincial commissions to study it, then to resubmit the decree to its *Députation Permanente* (a continuing standing committee).

The provincial commissions delivered "contradictory and often passionate" opinions concerning the draft decree.[21] The *Députation Permanente* gave it unenthusiastic endorsement in December 1950, but only after emasculating the proposal by suggesting that solely the principle of immatriculation be stipulated in the decree itself, and that the rights to which it would give access be gradually spelled out over the succeeding years through a series of supplementary decrees. Colonial opinion was nonetheless shocked when Governor-General Jungers, in his farewell address in 1951, rallied to the revised decree and warned that "the hand offered too late runs the risk of being refused."

The draft decree was then returned to Belgium, where Colonial Minister Wigny accepted the dilutions of content imposed by the colonial milieux; after a lengthy debate in the *Conseil Colonial,* the decree finally was promulgated on May 17, 1952. A frustrated Sohier warned of the danger which a certain racist section of colonial opinion represented,[22] and Malengreau commented that the reform had been voided of nearly all its content by the assault of colonial groups, with the residue only a very small advance over existing legislation.[23]

The final crystallization of forces had found the administration (after initial reluctance), some missions, and

---

of the *Conseil du Gouvernement* from 1947-1951, when six more were added. These latter replaced Europeans who had been designated to represent African interests.

[20] *Ibid.,* p. 4.

[21] *Courrier d'Afrique,* November 28, 1950, cited in *ibid,* pp. 76-79.

[22] Sohier, "La politique d'intégration," *loc. cit.,* pp. 913-16.

[23] Malengreau, "Chronique de politique indigène," *Zaïre,* VI, No. 9, (November 1952), 957-60.

nearly all African opinion in support of immatriculation, with part of the missions and nearly all European colonial opinion hostile. In the forefront of the opposition was the Katanga lobby, led by its most violent spokesmen, the influential editor of the *Essor du Congo*, Jean Sépulchre, and Monsignor de Hemptinne. "Opponents of the decree," wrote *Pourquoi Pas Congo* "were astonished to find themselves led by *Jean-Félix à la barbe fleurie* (de Hemptinne)."[24] The decree did in fact bear a strong resemblance to the legislation proposed by Monsignor de Hemptinne through his Katanga subcommission of the Commission for the Protection of Natives before the war. The problem had since changed, the Monsignor maintained; only African priests could really be called "civilized," and for the government to assume the responsibility of defining a "threshold of civilization" would be to create endless jealousies and in fact set back the achievement of a real Latin, Christian civilization in Africa.[25] The Katanga Chamber of Commerce and Industry, in a memorandum submitted to the Colonial Minister in August 1951, declared, "Our members are all directly concerned with native policy, and we don't hesitate to tell you that we consider inapplicable in the immediate future that proposed by [Jungers]."[26]

The African elite became increasingly attached to the project as it watched from the sidelines the arguments being marshalled against it. Two Congolese who have both since become politically prominent, J. P. Dericoyard and Antoine Omari,[27] wrote in a special issue of *La Voix du Congolais* in October 1950 expressing their indignation at some of the pretexts invoked by colonial milieux to deny

[24] September 25, 1951; quoted in Fedacol, *op. cit.*, pp. 133-36.

[25] From a memorandum prepared by Monsignor de Hemptinne and unanimously adopted by the Katanga subcommission of the Commission for the Protection of Natives, quoted in *ibid.*, pp. 52-56.

[26] *Ibid.*, p. 125.

[27] Dericoyard has twice held ministerial posts; Omari was briefly district commissioner in Maniema and later a special commissioner in Equateur.

them new status. One of the colonial arguments was that companies would be reluctant to hire immatriculated Congolese if they were forced to pay them at European scales; were such reluctance to materialize, Omari maintained, "it could create automatically amongst all the Africans a generalized hatred against Europeans."[28]

The Failure of Immatriculation

Criticisms of the decree were by no means all governed by a hostility to the emerging African elite; some, especially those of Rubbens, were proven by subsequent events to be particularly acute.[29] There were in fact three crucial misunderstandings between colonizer and colonized as to the content of the new system; these made the immatriculation experiment an unqualified failure.

In the first place, there was a misunderstanding about whom the immatriculated status was in fact destined for. The original project of the Sohier Commission foresaw a two-tiered arrangement in which the top rung would be accessible only to a very small group: African priests, two or three paramount chiefs, such as the Bami of Rwanda and Burundi and Antoine Mwenda-Munongo of the Bayeke,[30] a couple of the successful traders, and eventually university graduates when they began to appear. In all a tiny handful might be included, Sohier suggested in a meeting with

[28] Quoted in *ibid.*, pp. 47-49.
[29] A. Rubbens, "La querelle de l'immatriculation des indigènes," *Essor du Congo*, September 2, 1950, reprinted in *ibid.*, pp. 10-12.
[30] One problem faced by writers on African problems is whether or not to retain the Bantu prefixes on names of ethnic groupings. "Ba" in most Bantu languages, which cover all of the Congo except the northern fringe and the northeastern frontier area, is a plural prefix, referring to the group as a whole. The singular prefix, generally "mu," refers to an individual. Although the International African Institute has recommended that the prefixes be dropped, in the case of the Congo, this prescription has only recently been adopted by anthropologists and very rarely in any other writing. To conform to the usage most familiar to most readers, this study will retain the prefixes where they are generally used.

CEPSI in 1950.[31] In a memorandum opposing the decree, CEPSI asked why special legislation was required if the number involved was so small.[32] Jungers in his 1951 address spoke of a "still very limited number." Fedacol president A. Maus was right to inquire whether the executive was not going to be faced with the dilemma of either changing the content of the decree by admitting a much larger number or risk serious disappointment on the part of African opinion. The *évolués*, he argued, would not have been so interested in the "reform" if they had realized that it would only apply to a few dozen persons.[33]

African priests, the first category deemed fit to acquire the civilization cards, refused *en masse* to apply. They felt that their educational attainments spoke for themselves without any other external badge than their soutanes, and also that acceptance of this status would create an artificial barrier between themselves and their communicants.[34] Those few paramount chiefs who had been highly educated likewise found an immatriculation card beneath their dignity. At the end of 1958, only 217 family heads had received the card.[35]

Secondly, there was a misunderstanding as to what advantages the card would bring. Here the disappointment was similar to that engendered by the *Carte du Mérite Civique;* the decree in the course of its preparation had been shorn of all its practical effects. Rubbens pertinently observed in 1950 that the problem was being approached in the wrong way; rather than lose time trying to sort out the innumerable conundrums involved in defining who was to receive the card and how, the problem should be at-

[31] *Ibid.*, p. 32.
[32] *Ibid.*, pp. 28-39.
[33] *Ibid.*, p. 4.
[34] Malengreau, *loc. cit.*, p. 964.
[35] Chambre des Représentants, *Rapport sur l'Administration* . . . *1958*, p. 104.

tacked directly by immediately starting the elimination of racial differentiation which had crept into legislation.[36] Not only was the necessary series of implementing decrees slow to be issued and even slower to be applied but the principle usually adopted from 1953 on was that they were to extend to all Congolese, not just to those who had undergone the immatriculation process. The first of the promised further reforms was the decree of February 10, 1953, concerning the accession of Congolese to individual private landed property rights. The declaration of purpose attached to the act was quite explicit in rejecting limitation of its benefits to the immatriculated: "A fundamental principle regulates the matter: the natives must be able to achieve full individual property rights, without any restriction founded uniquely on racial distinction. . . . As the new system of immatriculation could be interpreted as restricting this faculty, it is appropriate to formulate without equivocation the principle . . . that any Congolese, immatriculated or not, can acquire registered land title."[37]

Thirdly, there were insoluble difficulties in establishing procedures and criteria for granting immatriculated status. Although earlier proposed drafts of immatriculation decrees had proposed a plethora of conditions, the final legislation stipulated only that the candidate had to be of age and "to justify by his character and manner of living a state of civilization implying an aptitude to enjoy the rights and fulfill the duties specified in written law."[38] The declaration of purpose made clear that it was not sufficient merely to have had European schooling, but "it must be shown by his acts that he is penetrated with European civilization and conforms to it." Thus, even a university graduate would not necessarily be eligible.[39] Rubbens was again incisive in

[36] Fedacol, *op. cit.*, pp. 10-12.
[37] Piron & Devos, *Codes et Lois*, I, 208.
[38] *Ibid.*, p. 55.
[39] *Ibid.*, pp. 55-56.

questioning the wisdom of creating a definition of eligibility to European status which many Europeans themselves could not pass.[40]

If the criteria were brief and vague, the procedures elaborated for processing requests were long and complicated. The magistrature was charged with obtaining all appropriate information about the applicant, and bans were posted at the nearest territorial seat. A bevy of European administrators descended upon the residence of the candidate. In the words of one applicant who was initially refused immatriculation for "immaturity," Patrice Lumumba,[41] "All the rooms of the house, from the living room, bedroom, and kitchen to the bathroom, are explored from top to bottom, with the aim of uncovering everything which is incompatible with the exigencies of civilized life."[42] Thereafter, the potential *immatriculé* is summoned with his wife to a hearing conducted by the head judge of the provincial court, which Lumumba described as follows:

"The applicant and his wife submit to a very thorough interrogation, including some complicated questions, of which some are dangerous traps, among others the following: What do you understand by immatriculation? Why have you sought immatriculation? What are the juridical advantages of immatriculation? What do you do during your leisure hours? What sorts of friends do you frequent? What are the books that you read, and their authors? In case of a family quarrel, do you leave your husband to return to your relatives? Do you share meals with your husband? Does he beat you? Does he let you manage the household? etc."[43]

The humiliating character of this process is evident, and

[40] Fedacol, *op. cit.*, pp. 10-12.
[41] Lumumba eventually won a reversal of this ruling by a court appeal.
[42] Lumumba, *Congo, terre d'avenir,* p. 64.
[43] *Ibid.,* p. 65.

86

was yet another cause of the failure of the immatriculation experiment.

The designers of the decree had hoped that it would have psychological shock value, would serve as a striking example of Belgian good will, and would thus enlist the support of the emerging elite for the terminal objectives which the colonizer might eventually fix for the as yet undefined permanent association with Belgium. However, the psychological effect was precisely the opposite of that intended; the elite was intensely irritated by the whole affair. The colonial circles which had forecast this reaction were in a sense proven right, although they were themselves responsible for the fulfillment of their gloomy prophecy by stripping the reform of all its meaning. In 1953, the African representative on the *Députation Permanente* of the *Conseil du Gouvernement* proposed that a *voeu* be adopted calling for the complete assimilation of *immatriculés,* but this was rejected on the grounds that "European public opinion wasn't favorable."[44] In Leopoldville, an *Association des Immatriculés* was founded to press for the economic and social advantages promised. The Congolese became convinced that the measure was simply intended as Belgian propaganda at the UN; a Leopoldville newspaper wrote in 1956, under the headline "Crisis of Confidence": "We need no other example than the discreditable humbug of immatriculation, where, once again, the government has lost face in promising a great deal, but giving nothing except a smoke screen."[45]

Coping with Color Bar

Although immatriculation per se was a non-starter, the problem with which it was designed to cope—the status of educated Africans—remained in the forefront of colonial

[44] *Ibid.,* p. 73.
[45] *L'Avenir,* August 25, 1956, quoted in *ibid.,* p. 66.

policy issues. If a legally defined special status for the elite was unworkable, then the alternative was to come to grips with the hardening color bar by a methodical elimination of the welter of discriminatory legislation which had gradually grown up.

It was sometimes argued, even by liberal colonial writers, that the racial barriers in the Congo were a "culture bar" rather than a "color bar."[46] Whatever the merits of this argument, the fact remains that, as Rubbens pointed out, ". . . the most ferocious Anglo-Saxon color-bar had never produced so many discriminatory laws, had never enacted so many measures of so rigid a segregation as our Belgian tutelage."[47] No doubt it was correct to argue that much discriminatory legislation had sprung from the paternalist hypothesis. Before World War II, this had created little stir; insofar as it was perceived, discrimination was passively accepted as being in the natural order of things. But after the war, tensions over this issue rapidly grew under the convergent impact of two phenomena.

On the one hand, there was the increasing size of the modern elite, self-conscious of its education and keenly sensitive to differentiated treatment which seemed to call into question their value as modern men. On the other, the European population was rapidly expanding. From approximately 35,000 at the war's end, the population shot up to 114,341 at the beginning of 1959. Cities such as Leopoldville, Luluabourg, Stanleyville, Bukavu, Kolwezi, Jadotville, and Elisabethville became important centers of European population. With the continually arriving families

[46] Even Malengreau makes this argument, while being the first to concede that many areas of discrimination existed and should be eliminated, in his contribution aimed at the English-speaking audience in Grove Haines, *Africa Today* (Baltimore: Johns Hopkins Press, 1955), p. 349.
[47] A. Rubbens, "Le colour bar au Congo Belge," *Zaïre*, III, No. 5 (May 1949), 503.

came a sharp rise in the standard of living of the European community. The larger the European community in any given center, the more it withdrew into itself and sealed itself off from contact with the African population. Thus, as the colonial system sought to purge itself of legal discrimination, it had to contend with social forces tending toward reinforcement of the walls of segregation.

The effort to reform colonial society to make it acceptable to the African elite proceeded in five basic areas: property ownership and residential segregation; education; relations with employers and equal access to all jobs; judicial treatment; and the more intangible field of social relations.

AFRICAN LAND OWNERSHIP

African aspirations tended to have more support on the property question than in other areas of discrimination, thanks to the theory referred to before and frequently advanced in colonial milieux that making property available to Africans was a key step in the creation of an African bourgeoisie. It should be noted that the rural and urban aspects of this issue were entirely different. At the elite level, the problem was most acute in the cities.

In theory, the right to own land apparently existed for Africans since the 1895 Congo Free State legislation on immatriculation; but even the theory was disputed and certainly non-application was the reality. By the end of World War II, the only exceptions were a handful of rural plots which the *Comité Spécial du Katanga* had ceded to Africans.[48] After the future King Leopold III had called for the generalization of individual peasant farming to bolster the African participation in the economy in 1933, a draft decree was prepared in the Colonial Ministry clarifying the right of Congolese to hold rural land, but this met with a lukewarm response in Leopoldville and a frosty one from the

[48] Malengreau, "De l'accession des indigènes à la propriété foncière individuelles du Code Civil," *Zaïre*, I, No. 3 (March 1947), 235; No. 4 (April 1947), 404.

Katanga.[49] The matter was then dropped and returned to the agenda after the war.

On February 23, 1953, a decree was promulgated declaring, "Any Congolese may enjoy all property rights organized by written legislation."[50] The problem would seem to have been settled by this; again, however, the gap between law and practice was enormous. As far as the cities were concerned, another clause in the decree stated, "The provincial governor will determine the *centres extra-coutumiers*, the recognized agglomerations and *cités indigènes* or portions thereof to which the present decree applies."[51] Only three of the six provinces ever took any steps to put this into execution, and the first of these was not until more than three years had elapsed. Kivu provided for acquisition of lots in the African quarters of Bukavu on June 8, 1956; Leopoldville province provided for property sale in some communes in the city of Leopoldville on December 31, 1957; and Katanga followed on November 25, 1958, with an executive order applicable to the various Katanga urban centers.[52]

Lumumba's bitter complaints about the failure to apply this decree were no doubt widely shared by the elite. A Congolese trader seeking a loan would be told that as collateral he had to obtain title to his land plot. Lumumba described his fate if he went to do this:

"He was told patience was required because the provincial measures of application of the Decree of February 10, 1953 were not yet taken or 'are under study,' or 'the lack of personnel has not permitted the administration to activate the study of local measures of execution,' or even 'execution is deferred until after the reconstruction of the African quarter by the *Office des Cités Africaines* and the delimitation of lots by the urbanization services.' These are the typical

[49] *Ibid.,* (March 1947), pp. 248-52.
[50] Piron & Devos, *Codes et Lois,* I, 209.
[51] *Ibid.,* III, 789.
[52] *Ibid.*

answers given to Congolese for four years, and will still be given during the years to come."[53]

Linked to the urban property problem was the issue of residential segregation. Beginning in 1898, the law required the complete separation of European and African quarters; the only exceptions to this rule were the domestic servants in Katanga cities, who were permitted to occupy *"boyeries"* located in the European quarter.[54] One of the anomalies with which the immatriculation status confronted Congolese card-holders was that on the one hand they could not acquire land in the European quarter and, on the other, they were in some senses legal "Europeans," and like other Europeans forbidden from holding land in the African quarters. Two small steps were taken in the final colonial years. Legal residential segregation was repealed in February 1959, and an experiment was made in Leopoldville in the application of the 1957 municipal reform to create a "mixed" commune through including in one of the European quarters a largely rural area containing a few African farmers. But in reality virtually no headway in tackling this problem had been made by the time of independence.

Individual holding of agricultural lands posed complex problems of the relations of the landholders to traditional chiefs and communities. At the mass level, one of the proclaimed objectives of the *paysannat indigène* system was to move toward individual holdings of land plots. Prince Leopold, in his 1933 speech, had called for development of African agriculture to be guided by the principle that "the native would be working, no longer as a salaried worker, but as a free peasant, owner of his land." The goal, he added, should be the "establishment of a *paysannat* in its most integral form, in such a way as to permit the native to accede to ownership."[55] The stated objective of the *paysannat*

[53] Lumumba, *op. cit.*, pp. 112-113.
[54] A. Rubbens, "Le colour bar . . . ," *loc. cit.* p. 505; Brausch, *Belgian Administration in the Congo*, pp. 21-22.
[55] Quoted in Infor Congo, *Le Congo Belge*, I, 266.

scheme, when it was decided in 1950 to generalize the formula, was to give the peasant permanent title to the land if he remained fixed on it and followed the required crop rotation cycle. This, however, never reached the stage of application. The carelessness with which the *paysannats* were often established meant that the humble peasant never felt very secure in his claim to the plot he occupied because the land distribution did not always proceed with full regard for traditional requirements for land use rights. Accordingly, peasant cultivators included in the scheme "were convinced that, sooner or later, they would be chased from the land by the real (traditional) proprietors."[56]

A quite different problem grew out of the more recent desire of a small number of prosperous cultivators to acquire title to lands for establishing on a moderate scale plantations of palm, rubber, or cocoa trees. Many experts questioned whether formal registration of land title by the administration was necessary, as reasonably permanent land use rights could be negotiated with the local clan or chief in whom land rights were invested by custom. Malengreau, for example, argued that registry of individual rural land titles would create new problems without solving old ones.[57] In any event, virtually no Congolese benefited from provisions of the decree of February 10, 1953, making Congolese as well as Europeans eligible for free land grants to individuals from domain lands of up to 100 *hectares.*[58]

[56] Malengreau, *Vers un paysannat indigène.* This work remains the classic study of the problems and promise of the *paysannat* formula. It was an inquiry written at the behest of the government to explore the successes and failures of the various pilot projects. By and large, the lucid analysis of Malengreau of the pitfalls in establishing *paysannats* has been borne out by subsequent events.

[57] Malengreau, "De l'accession des indigènes à la propriété foncière individuelle du Code Civil," *loc cit.,* p. 411. Lucy Mair has also argued that private land-holding has little magical effect on production. *Vers la promotion de l'économie indigène* (Brussels: Institut de Sociologie Solvay, 1956), p. 368.

[58] Piron & Devos, *Codes et Lois,* III, 787-89.

In the second major area of discriminatory regulation, education, the two sources of tension were admission to the European school system and access to higher education. A genuine difficulty grew out of the fact that the European population was for the most part not permanent, and the Belgian administration felt obligated to maintain complete equivalence of program with metropolitan schools for European children, so that they might be qualified for employment in Belgium. However, access to these schools became of crucial importance to the African elite after the war, especially at the secondary level, as through these schools lay the path into the higher status positions.

This issue became significant only after the war, when rapid expansion of the European population brought a swift growth in the European school network. Further, beginning in 1946, a laic school system was founded to provide the "freedom of choice" for the parents between Catholic and state education, which is traditional in Belgium. This soon provided another source of irritation; why, asked the Congolese, should they be denied the same freedom of choice. In 1947, one of the members of the Senate mission wrote, "The desire for a color-bar which reigns among the Europeans, especially the women, is such that, if either mulattos or Indians were admitted into white schools, numerous parents would remove their children."[59]

However, this step was taken in 1948, and in 1950 for the first time Congolese children were permitted to enter in very small numbers, despite the protests of a number of European families. But the humiliating procedures remained; African children applying for European schools had to appear before special commissions which verified not only their educational qualifications but also the general living standard of their families and their personal hygiene. In reality the door opened only a very small dis-

[59] A. Buisseret in Sénat de Belgique, *Rapport*, p. 82.

93

tance; in 1953, 21 African students were admitted to European schools in the Congo, and even in 1959 the figure was only 1,493, or substantially less than 10 percent of the European enrollments.[60] Even this modest headway was not made without backsliding; in 1958, a large number of African children were removed from European primary schools in Elisabethville on the grounds of hygiene and personal health. They were told at the same time that their condition was not serious enough to warrant medical attention.[61]

In 1952, Thomas Kanza set off for the University of Louvain, the first Congolese student to register in a university.[62] The permission accorded him to proceed to Belgium required some high level intervention from influential colonial personalities. In 1954, the Catholic Church stole a march on the administration, establishing Lovanium University outside Leopoldville; here again there was important opposition. In 1956, the Liberal-Socialist government riposted with the State University of Elisabethville. At this point, higher education rationed itself through the secondary bottleneck; less than 200 Congolese a year were being produced from the *humanités* cycle in secondary school necessary to qualify for admission to the university. As of 1960, there was a total of 30 holders of university degrees,

[60] Brausch, *Belgian Administration in the Congo*, p. 27.

[61] Slade, *op. cit.*, p. 30.

[62] This does not include a number of African priests who had pursued their higher studies at seminaries in Belgium, or in some cases Rome. This includes a few who later abandoned their religious vocations. An example of this category is Antoine Mwenda-Munongo, Bayeke paramount chief and brother of Godefroid Munongo, former Katanga Minister of the Interior. Mwenda-Munongo studied in Europe for six years between 1929 and 1935, first in Rome, then at the Institut Orban de Trivry, at Grand Halleux. See his biography in Pierre Artigue, *Qui sont les leaders congolais* (2nd. ed.; Brussels: Editions Europe-Afrique, 1961), pp. 250-52. Pierre Mambaya, President of Uele Province, likewise is a former student of theology, and actually was a priest for several years.

plus 466 African students in the universities of Lovanium and Elisabethville, and 76 in Belgian universities.[63]

JOB DISCRIMINATION

Closely related to the problem of education was that of access to employment and the discriminatory regulations in Congo work legislation. Again there was a real difficulty, never given adequate solution before independence, and a major plague of the independent state. This grew from the high level of remuneration paid to Europeans in the Congo, which was defended as necessary to recruit adequate personnel in Belgium. Historically, the Belgians had gradually withdrawn upward and had replaced Europeans in subaltern positions with Africans as they became trained and available. When, in the 1950's, a growing number of Congolese began to acquire the competence necessary for entry at the higher levels, the question arose as to whether they should receive the same pay as Europeans. This could be seen most clearly in the civil service; a prolonged impasse paralyzed progress on Africanization of the administration until 1959.

The civil service statute in force until 1959 had four categories; the top three, as well as the upper half of the fourth required a university degree. The rank and file clerks, all Congolese, were under a separate statute as "auxiliaries." The legislation was unclear as to whether the requirement of "Belgian nationality" in the regular civil service consti-

[63] These are official Belgian figures, made available by the former Ministry of African Affairs, alias Colonial Ministry. The Belgians argue, correctly, that the figure of 30 or less usually cited in the press is not a fair picture of their educational achievements, as there were nearly 500 priests, and 400 in technical fields, such as medicine and agriculture, with several years of post-secondary schooling which in the United States would be counted statistically as college graduates. The catch in this argument, in the context of the race relations issue, is that access to high-status positions in the administration and other sectors was reserved to those with "university" degrees, in the European sense.

tuted a barrier to Congolese entry.[64] The question was moot as long as there were no university graduates, but with the first graduating class emerging from Lovanium in 1958, something had to be done. Not only was there a handful of university graduates on the horizon but a growing number of Congolese auxiliaries could claim the complete *humanités* or equivalent secondary training required for entry into the lower half of the fourth category; there were two or three of these individuals as early as 1953, 40 in 1956, and about 400 by 1958.[65] The continued delay in facing up to this problem created a growing suspicion in African circles that the exclusively European character of the civil service was not, as alleged, merely a matter of competence, but a policy of discrimination.

Although the number that would actually benefit from any changes was relatively small, the issue was of absorbing importance to a much larger group with enough education to feel some stake in whether the Congo was to continue to be a state with a solid phalanx of Europeans at the top.[66]

In early February 1958, Colonial Minister Buisseret decided to set up new wage scales, involving a considerable salary reduction for the potentially integrated grades. This created a violent reaction among European functionaries, who demonstrated against the Minister in Elisabethville during a visit in February 1958.[67] This caused the Minister to reverse his decision and retain an "expatriation bonus"; (extra pay for overseas service); the catch was that this was in fact available not only to those recruited in Belgium but also to the small number of Europeans permanently resident in the colony and hired in the Congo. These few changed the expatriation bonus to a racial bonus.

This time it was the Lovanium students who responded

[64] Heyse, *Congo Belge*, I, 222.
[65] Brausch, *Belgian Administration in the Congo*, p. 30.
[66] R. Poupart, *Première esquisse de l'évolution du syndicalisme au Congo*, p. 89.
[67] Brausch, *Belgian Administration in the Congo*, p. 30.

96

with fury. A delegation from the University had been assured that there would be no discrimination in the new statutes. The 50 percent expatriation bonus, plus larger family allowances, was seen by the students as one more indication that they would never, no matter what their qualifications, be treated as equals by the colonizer. In April 1958, the students took a daring step in issuing an open letter to the Minister, reminding him of his promises. The memorandum referred bitterly to those who were Congolese when it came to exploiting the land and its wealth, but metropolitan when it came to determining the salary scale. They concluded with the threat that if satisfaction were not given, they were prepared to turn the Congo into a second Algeria.[68]

The rest of 1958 was filled with the exchange of angry communiqués between the administration, the European civil service union—AFAC—and the union of Congolese auxiliaries—APIC. The tenacity with which the European union resisted a single status was another important thread in the fabric of distrust woven by constant European colonial obstruction of African advance. By the end of 1958, AFAC had rallied to the principle of the *statut unique;* a year earlier, however, it had written:

"We are opposed to this formula because we don't see how one can join the status of Europeans and those of the auxiliaries without giving great advantages to the latter to the detriment of the former, at least the humblest of them. We have demonstrated the danger there would be to infringe further upon the acquired rights of functionaries of the fourth category and we have especially drawn serious at-

[68] Open letter from the Students of Lovanium, April 1958. See also Slade, *op. cit.,* pp. 28-29. During a visit to Lovanium in July 1958, the writer found this question to be the leading issue amongst the student body; at this point, it seemed of far more immediate importance than that of the political structures of the Congolese state. The somewhat extravagant threat to create a second Algeria was withdrawn a week later.

tention to the ineluctable consequences of such a process which would only engender rivalry, resentment and hatred between the two social classes which would be ranged against each other in trying brutally to force them together."[69]

Access to the civil service as a focal point of conflict was particularly important, as the state was by far the largest single employer of the emerging elite; few of the present Congolese leadership have not spent at least part of their careers as a functionary in the administration or one of the parastatal organizations. Further, the pattern set by the state would clearly have to be followed sooner or later by the private sector.

It was not, significantly, until January 13, 1959, that the new, unified civil service law was promulgated. Although it would no doubt have been issued in the end in any case, few doubted that the trauma of the Leopoldville riots played some role in the sudden publication of the reform. It is to be noted that civil service statutes are an administrative matter, in Belgian constitutional practice, and need not pass through the ponderous legislative channels; procedure cannot be blamed in this instance for the fact that ten years passed between first discussion and final enactment.

The hesitation in adopting the simplistic solution of extending European salary levels to all Congolese was certainly understandable; the experience since independence shows that this scale of remuneration for the civil service is

---

[69] *Bula Matari,* quoted in Poupart, *op. cit.,* pp. 87-88. *Bula Matari* was the quarterly bulletin of the European civil servant organization, AFAC. The title is pungent; "Bula (or Boula) Matari" is, according to legend, the name given to Stanley by the Africans of the Lower Congo, and means "he who breaks rocks." This apparently grew from the impression made by the use of dynamite. The metaphor appealed to the colonizer, and became widely employed throughout the Congo to refer generally to the colonial administration. In a way, it is in epigram the whole psychology of the colonial situation.

entirely disproportionate to the resources of the country. But the ambiguities as to the future role of Europeans in the Congo obfuscated this simple issue; according to the Eurafrican premise, Europeans were to be a permanent and integral part of the Congo scene. And thus a structural salary differentiation was perceived by the African elite as an outright racist measure. Had it then been possible to define the position of the European cadres as temporary, overseas technicians, then a clear and nonracial basis for a reasonable and legitimate distinction could have been found between nationals of the country and foreign subjects engaged to fill jobs for which there were no qualified Congolese. But Europeans in the Congo were certainly not prepared to accept this view of their future, even in 1959. This issue, it should be added, has been a vexing problem in most terminal colonial systems.

At another level, the elimination of job discrimination required an end to the distinction in labor legislation between the *contrat de travail* for Congolese and the *contrat d'emploi* for Europeans. Since 1939, the Belgians had been under pressure from the International Labor Organization (ILO) on this point, and it was a major African grievance in the postwar years. However, a storm of protest arose from employers when proposals were made to eliminate it. When a decree was passed June 30, 1954, it was more declaratory of principle than real reform. Belgium promised the ILO that penal sanctions would be eliminated by 1958, but in fact, it was not until after independence that the provision was finally removed from the legislation. In 1958, there were still 8,693 condemnations for violations of the *contrat de travail*.[70]

"Only the complexity of the problems arising has delayed the elaboration of a decree creating a unified labor statute," was the reply given to several members of the *Conseil Co-*

[70] Chambre des Représentants, *Rapport sur l'administration . . . 1958*, p. 18.

lonial who in 1958 expressed doubts about approving any further labor legislation which did not eliminate discrimination.[71] Shortly after the Leopoldville riots, the Governor-General finally used his authority to end the use of prison sentences, but not fines, for "the worker, who, out of bad faith in the execution of the *contrat de travail,* contravenes the obligations imposed by the decree, the convention, or usage."[72]

The *contrat d'emploi,* on the other hand, had no provision for sanctions of any sort. It is defined as applying to "any contract whose principal place of execution is in the Belgian Congo or Ruanda-Urundi and concerns an employee who is not a native of these territories or any other territory in Africa."[73] This law was said "in no way to establish a racial segregation by a disguised path; it proclaims the principle of non-discrimination to the degree compatible with the present state of evolution of the natives."[74] The Governor-General was given the authority to extend the application of the decree to any African, individually or collectively; however, this was not done even for the *immatriculés,* a fact on which Lumumba reflected with some asperity in his 1957 book.

EQUALITY IN THE JUDICIARY

On the judicial front, grievances of the Congolese centered upon their liability to judgment both before summary "police courts," where the territorial administrator served as both prosecutor and judge, and before "native courts," at times used by the administration to enforce application of its desires. Europeans, on the other hand, were only tried on criminal charges before duly constituted courts separated from the administration.

In the hands of the administrator-judges was a formida-

[71] Piron & Devos, *Codes et Lois,* III, 28.
[72] Article 84 of the unified code on the *contrat de travail, ibid.,* pp. 40-41.
[73] Article 2 of the legislation of the *contrat d' emploi, ibid.,* p. 12.
[74] From the report of the *Conseil Colonial, ibid.*

ble array of legislation which lent itself to arbitrary interpretation. The most widely used was the decree of July 24,
1918, which permitted seven days and/or 200 francs for
"anyone who commits in public any act, gesture, or declaration tending to mark or provoke mistrust or insurrection
against the established authorities."[75] In addition, the administration had plenary powers to rusticate an African;
this was deemed an administrative measure, and required
no judicial process. The procedure was most frequently invoked in the repression of messianic sects but was also popular as a means of ridding the region of an unruly chief or
any other thorn in the side of the administration. At the
beginning of 1959, 4,815 persons were on the relegated list.[76]

On June 24, 1955, a special commission was established
to undertake a study of judicial reform. This resulted in a
complete overhauling of the judicial system through the
important decree of May 8, 1958. Henceforward, all persons, European or African, were to be judged by the same
court; original jurisdiction would depend in all cases on the
seriousness of the infraction. Further, career magistrates
were to be placed as heads of the district courts, which left
only the territories with administration and justice linked.
Even here, the principle of separation was proclaimed as a
goal.[77] It is only fair to add parenthetically that even before
this reform the Congo had a greater separation of administration and justice than did most other African colonies. In
the early years, an effort was made to have a complete separation, and administrators frequently complained that the
magistrature was meddling and spoiling discipline by their
concern for legal proprieties.[78]

It was not, however, until April 15, 1960, that the new re-

[75] Piron & Devos, *Codes et Lois*, I, 344.
[76] Chambre des Représentants, *Rapport sur l'Administration* . . .
1958, p. 82.
[77] Piron & Devos, *Codes et Lois*, II, 5-22.
[78] Hailey, *op. cit.*, p. 619; A. Bertrand, "La fin de la puissance
Azande," *Bull. Séances*, ARSOM, 1943, pp. 270-71.

form went into effect. Once again, the administration had given the impression of retarding reforms, of preventing application of measures taken in the interest of the African elite. There was, indeed, a real difficulty in expanding the ranks of the magistracy to staff the new district court positions. It is hard to believe, however, that an administration which could achieve remarkable results in the economic and social sphere could not have found ways of implementing this measure at a time when it might have contributed to improving confidence between the Congolese elite and the colonial structure.

The native courts were felt by the elite in the urban centers to be composed of elders less educated than they, applying, often as de facto adjuncts of the police courts, a bastard *mélange* of pseudo-traditional legal principles.[79] Further, in the countryside, besides the bona fide application of customary law, traditional courts tended to be used to enforce agricultural regulations; the chief would instruct his subjects to plant cotton and, if they declined, could punish them for disrespect of his authority. There were moves to reform the traditional courts, especially those in the cities, to bring them in line with the 1957 municipal reform. These plans, like so many others, were overtaken by political events; a sweeping judicial reorganization is still one of the major institutional problems on the agenda of the independent Congo.

SOCIAL RELATIONS

The final sphere of racial friction was the pervasive area of social contact between the European and African communities. The number of Europeans in the urban centers who sought out social relations with Africans was small indeed; even in the countryside, the close if paternal relationship which had once existed between the administrators and their charges had considerably diminished despite the

[79] F. Grévisse, *La grande pitié des juridictions indigènes* (Brussels: ARSOM, Sci. Mor. et Pol., T. XIX, fasc. 3, 1949), pp. 47-55.

increase of Belgian personnel after the war. Belgian writers usually argue that Belgium was not a spawning ground for racist theories; as Buisseret's former assistant put it: "Most Belgians have never held any rigid color prejudices, and if they do appear they cannot be said to result from any officially expressed opinions on the innate inferiority of colored peoples.[80]

Some qualifications, however, are necessary. There can be no gainsaying the sincerity of official Belgium's desire after World War II to remove discrimination from official texts and to expunge it from human spirits. However, especially in the de Hemptinnian assimilationist theme in Belgian colonial thought, there is a strong presumption of the inferiority of the African. For example, the Katanga subcommission of the Commission for the Protection of Natives, expressing itself on immatriculation, declared:

> "Conscious of the present inferiority of the native of the Congo compared to the European;
>
> "Without trying to resolve the insoluble question of knowing whether the progressive evolution of this race will one day make it the equal of our own;
>
> "Recognizes that exceptional individuals can achieve this equality . . .
>
> "[Hopes] that this assimilation of the race placed under our tutelage take place with an extreme prudence, without losing sight of the inferiority in which almost the entirety of the native population finds itself."[81]

On a more vulgar level, the remarkably forthright autobiographical portrait of the Congo by the British wife of a Kivu settler reveals a set of attitudes shared by many Europeans in the Congo:

"Alphonse [a dismissed servant] . . . to me represented everything that Africa must modify and change, before it

---

[80] Brausch, *Belgian Administration in the Congo*, p. 19.
[81] Guebels, *op. cit.*, pp. 442-43.

and its people can be taken seriously and respected as responsible individuals. A complete lack of personal responsibility, deceit, laziness and pretension without foundation. . . .

"Perjury has no moral significance to a Congolese. He lies naturally to get himself out of trouble. . . . There is one way of persuading him to confess, and that is by force. Where days of persuasion and argument will not penetrate—a solid kick in the seat of his trousers may convince him that it is better to save everyone's time by telling the truth."[82]

It is somewhat disingenuous, therefore, to say that there was not an important racist element in colonial society. In the daily routine of life, there were for the African elite (as for Negroes in the United States) a thousand petty vexations, wounds to the *amour-propre*. Even the most casual visitor to the colonial Congo could not fail to observe this. Africans, whatever their status, were almost invariably addressed in the familiar *"tu"* form which French reserves for close friends, children, and as a patronizing expression of vague contempt. This practice was most pronounced in Katanga and Kivu, but to a lesser degree was found throughout the country (and, for that matter, in all of French-speaking Africa). The prohibition on sale of alcohol to Africans until 1955 has been mentioned; even thereafter, many European establishments refused to serve African clients, despite the fact that no law existed to prevent this discrimination. Many European shops had separate counters for Congolese clients, although not legally required to do so. An ordinance required that films to be shown to African audiences be reviewed by a special board of censors;

[82] D. P. Dugauguier, *Congo Cauldron* (London: Jarrold's, 1961), pp. 37-38, 48. Mrs. Dugauquier's blunt expressions are perhaps more characteristic of her Anglo-Saxon antecedents than the Belgian society which she adopted; however, there can be no doubt that her feelings were shared by a large part of the European community in the Congo.

as the film distributors never sought this authorization, Africans were excluded from the movie houses.[83] But much of what was most harmful lay not in formal barriers, but the banal, routine incident—such as the experience of a Belgian writer in mid-1959. When he took an African journalist into a bar on Leopoldville's swank Boulevard Albert, there were snide remarks on all sides, and sarcastic applause when they departed.[84]

There can be no question that this phenomenon caused anguish, even despair, at the more responsible levels of the administration and in Belgium itself. There is hardly a major policy pronouncement of the 1950's which does not appeal for an improvement in human relations as an essential part of any reform program. A decree was even enacted December 2, 1957, which inflicted up to one year imprisonment and/or 3,000 francs fine for "manifesting aversion or racial or ethnic hatred, or committing an act of a nature to provoke this aversion."[85] This law was designed to give a legal remedy to an African called a *macaque* (monkey) by a European; however, in practice, it was more frequently used by the administration in 1959-1960 against nationalist organizers.

The efforts of the colonizer, then, to gain the confidence and support of the emerging elite group through dealing with its specific grievances and defining for it an attractive status in the colonial society was a failure. Even had this been well-implemented, the Congo would undoubtedly have opted for independence; however, it is at least arguable that negotiations could have taken place in a more propitious environment had a gulf of mistrust about Belgian intentions not been built up by the persistent disappointment of the expectations of the elite group during this period.

[83] Brausch, *Belgian Administration in the Congo*, pp. 23-26.
[84] Francis Monheim, "Léopoldville en juin 1959," *Revue Générale Belge*, July 1959, p. 36.
[85] Piron & Devos, *Codes et Lois*, I, 321, article 75bis of the penal code.

✖✖

CHAPTER VI

From the Ground Up: The Communes

✖✖

Toward Urban Reform: A Decade of Gestation

THE first important reforms which looked toward the establishment of an organic structure to a Congolese state were the decrees of March 26 and May 10, 1957, establishing both urban and rural institutions based upon genuine consultations of the population. These are significant from several points of view. They were in the first instance reflective of the honored place which local institutions occupy in Belgian political values. From the time of Petillon's 1952 speech, the promise of constructing a Congolese state was to be fulfilled through a careful political architecture that began at the base. The first exercise of authority which derived from the population, rather than simple designation as an adjunct of European rule, was to be prudently confined to the local level. The theory went that political education of African officeholders required face-to-face contact with the populations for which they were to exercise authority, where responsibility could be enforced by the constituents upon their representatives. Immersion in the practical, humdrum issues of local administration would produce the pragmatic bent, the concern with immediate material problems, the aversion for "grand designs," which are valued political virtues in Belgium.

In addition to being the first cautious unfolding of the Belgian design for the future, the two decrees were the last to be fashioned according to the slow, traditional colonial decision-making processes: a decade passed in their preparation. They were also the last to be implemented in an environment where the administration was still clearly master of the situation, and African opinion played a small role in influencing their provisions. For these reasons, the twin decrees merit careful analysis here.

The earlier efforts to find an adequate form of urban government which was something other than pure direct administration had been notably unsuccessful. On the European side, beginning about 1920, there was pressure for the establishment of communal institutions for the Belgian quarters of the new agglomerations. A January 12, 1923, decree gave partial satisfaction in authorizing the creation of "urban districts." This was done in Leopoldville in 1923, Elisabethville in 1942, and Jadotville in 1943. The *Comité Urbain* permitted under this legislation was entirely European and was appointed by the provincial governor. The de facto practice developed, however, of accepting a list of candidates put forward by the European Chambers of Commerce.[1] Although their authority was theoretically restricted to the segregated European quarters, the urban committees could hardly fail to try to influence the administration of the surrounding African quarters.

On the African side, the failure of the *centre extra-coutumier* (CEC) experiment has been described earlier.[2] Cities burgeoned forth without organic structure. Not included in the CEC structure were the "workers' camps" and military garrisons, which often included large numbers of persons, especially in the Katanga centers. In Leopoldville, where the European *Comité Urbain* had opposed the creation of CEC's, a 1945 ordinance established a *cité indigène* for the African quarters.

While awaiting the completion of the over-all municipal

[1] Auguste (Mabika) Kalanda, *Organisation des villes au Congo Belge,* Mémoire de Licence en Sciences Politiques et Administratives, Université Lovanium, 1958, pp. 7-12. Kalanda, one of the most brilliant of the Congo's university graduates, later became Commissioner of the Civil Service in the *Collège des Commissaires,* and from April-December, 1963, Foreign Minister.

[2] Supra, pp. 70-71.

reform, the Leopoldville administration undertook an experimental innovation whose favorable results had some impact on the final shape of the legislation. The *cité* was divided into a series of zones beginning in 1953. Each block was asked to choose one or two representatives, in any way seen fit, in the absence of the European administrator. In some cases, a vote was taken; in others, where two ethnic groups were involved, there was frequently an agreement that each would designate one member. Zone councils were set up, with advisory functions, on the basis of these "consultations." Although "elders" tended to emerge from this system, and it was not accompanied by wide publicity, the administration did carry it through with some genuine interest; both the administration and African opinion felt that it had worked well.[3] At the level of the *cité*, however, the two *chefs de cité* in function since 1945 were from the so-called "Bangala,"[4] although the Bakongo were the largest element in the population. The legislation stipulated that the *chef de cité* was to be chosen by the administration, "taking into account the preferences of the inhabitants," but no way in which this was to be done was suggested, and it was certainly not applied in any meaningful sense.

The legislative history of the decree is summarized in Table 2. The decade of gestation meant that it was promulgated in a very different environment from that of the initial proposal. The objectives set for it changed considerably in the course of its preparation. There can be little question but that the final result was a considerable improvement over the first versions; at the same time, the years lost in slowly resolving a number of complex issues were precious,

[3] *Ibid.*, p. 31. Ville de Léopoldville, *Consultation du 8 décembre 1957* (1958) mimeographed, pp. 5-6.

[4] A generic label applied indiscriminately in Leopoldville to all persons who were "gens du Haut," who had arrived in the city from the upper Congo by boat. These nominations were a major grievance of the Bakongo, who felt that as the largest ethnic group in Leopoldville they were entitled to fill this post.

TABLE 2

Legislative History of the Decree of March 26, 1957 (*Statut des villes*)

	CONGO			BELGIUM	
Prov. Council	Prov. Govt.	Govt. Council	Govt. Gen.	Min. Col.	Cons. Col.
1948			Schoeller Comm. draft		
		Approved			
1949				Important changes	
			Restudied		
1950				. . . .	
1951			Petillon remolds in framework Belgo-Cong.		
1952			Community goal		
		Approved Nov. 1952	. . . .		
1953		to May, 1953			
				Reviewed	
1954					Special Commission
	Consulted on proposed changes			. . . .	
1955					Debated and modified
1956					
1957				March 26, 1957	
1958			Implemented: Jan. 1, 1958 Leo'ville E'ville Jadotville		
		Jan. 1, 1959 Coquilhatville Stanleyville Bukavu Luluabourg			

Vertical annotations in table: WIGNY; JUNGERS; DEQUAE; PETILLON; BUISSERET

and responsible colonial officials would agree with African opinion that what emerged was several years too late.

The issues at stake in defining this decree were indeed of great importance. Those involved in its preparation certainly felt that the formulas found for constructing the urban institutions would set a pattern for higher-level structures. Thus, further insight into the evolving perspectives of decolonization may be gained from examining further each of the three major issues which dominated the debate over this reform: structure and paritarism; elections; and the office of the burgomaster.

THE PARITARY PRINCIPLE

A recurrent conflict between Leopoldville and Katanga existed throughout the years of preparation of the urban reform decree on the structural issue; Leopoldville wanted a single, integrated municipality, while Katanga advocated a dual city, with European and African components. Closely linked to the issue was the strong European desire at the very least to entrench paritary representation into the new structures. In 1952, although disapproving the Katanga separate-development thesis, the administration promised that paritary representation would be a permanent principle:

"The paritary composition of the *Comité Urbain* is not based upon an effort to find a just balancing of interests and men. . . . The object pursued is essentially functional: to achieve the political collaboration of the two communities without the predominance of one over the other. This paritary composition is therefore independent of the relative importance of the two communities in any domain. Neither the economic development of the African population, nor the increase in the European population can be permitted to reopen it to question."[5]

[5] *Note documentaire* submitted to the XVIIth session of the *Députation Permanente*, cited in André Tshibangu, *La technique de nomination dans le Statut des Villes*, Mémoire de Licence en Sciences Politiques et Administratives, Université Lovanium, 1958, p. 52.

The administration's concept at this point was to have a unitary structure at the city level, with paritary participation in the urban council but with the European and African portions of the town each possessing its own autonomous structure and carrying out the most important part of routine government. This version passed the *Députation Permanente* in May 1953 and was returned to Brussels for transmission to the *Conseil Colonial.*

In the initial debates in the *Conseil Colonial*, however, serious reservations were expressed about the entrenchment of the paritary principle in the legislation; this was, after all, a racial principle hard to reconcile with the object of constructing a national community in the Congo based upon equality. Further, it was objected that the European city was in fact being accorded more autonomy than the Congolese agglomeration, since close administrative tutelage was to be maintained over the latter.[6] After the exchange of some heated memoranda, a counterproposal was made which called for a *cité urbaine* (European) and a *cité suburbaine* (African), with functionaries at the head of each.[7]

The *Conseil du Gouvernement* replied in 1956 with another counterproposal, instituting a three-tiered system of urban government. At the base would be a number of *quartiers*, grouped in a *cité européene* and *cité indigène*, with the whole unified under an urban council. The *Conseil Colonial* finally emerged with the solution, in eliminating the middle tier proposed by the *Conseil du Gouvernement*. To augment the psychological impact, the *quartiers* were to be called "communes." The paritary principle was discreetly concealed. The principle of one man–one vote was apparently embraced through granting city council representation on an equal basis to the various communes. That meant an African majority in this category of representa-

6 *Conseil Colonial, Compte Rendu Analytique*, 1954, pp. 1294-1310.
7 Kalanda, *op. cit.*, p. 68.

tion. There was a rough equality in the size of the communes (although the European ones were much less populous than African boroughs); therefore, in the large urban centers there were more African communes than European. But de facto parity was restored by sufficient dosage of interest-group representation, so defined as to be mainly European. For example, Leopoldville had eight African communes, two European and one "mixed," but wound up with a paritary *conseil de ville*; Elisabethville had four African and one European communes and had a small European majority on the first city council. The "mixed" commune in Leopoldville was to be another showpiece, but it was in fact a European suburban zone which merely included a handful of African peasants.[8]

DEFINING THE ELECTORAL PROCESS

On the representation issue, dilemmas existed in the early formulations, with the administration caught between European demands for election of their members, the fear of introducing elections in the African quarters, and a desire not to have conspicuous racial differentiation in the reform. Further, the murky reaches of Belgian constitutional tradition revealed one major juridical barrier to "elections." Article 22 of the Colonial Charter stipulated that "the executive power cannot delegate the exercise of its rights except to persons or bodies which are hierarchically subordinated. . . . The delegation of legislative power is forbidden." Thus if the new communal councils were to have any responsibility, they could not derive their authority from any source other than the Governor-General and ultimately the King. Therefore, they could not be "elected." When the spirit was willing, this obstacle could be and was in fact overcome by labeling the elections "consultations" and promising to respect their results in the nominations made.

In 1952, the administration view was that the "consultations" should be different for the European and African

[8] *Courrier d'Afrique,* Oct. 16, 1957.

quarters; in the case of the Europeans, they should be based on "consultations" of the populations, with candidates nominated by interest groups. For the Africans, there would be a mingling of a system akin to that employed for the *conseils de zone* in Leopoldville, with representation of ethnic and interest associations.[9] These schemes were finally abandoned as unrealistic. It was instead agreed that the decree itself would not specify what "consultation" meant, but by 1956 it was clearly intended that these would be genuine elections.[10] In the ordinance of execution of September 29, 1957, the franchise was defined as extending to males 25 years old and over.

SELECTING THE BURGOMASTER

The final issue was whether the communal burgomasters would be appointed functionaries or elected officials. In Belgian practice, the burgomaster is appointed by the Minister of the Interior, after consulting the communal council; this derives from an administrative tradition which requires that the chief magistrate of the local government unit be hierarchically subordinated to central authority. In Belgium, the proposals of the communal council are nearly always respected, but there are exceptions.

At the early stages of discussion, no serious consideration was given to the possibility of elected burgomasters in the Congo. However, once the decision was made to adopt the vocabulary of Belgian local governmental institutions, it was difficult to avoid including most of the content. The compromise was to permit the elected communal councils to propose to the provincial governor a candidate for the mayoral post, and let it be understood that the administration would try to accept the nominations, without committing itself in advance to do so in all circumstances. On the other hand, the city was headed by a functionary who was given very extended powers of *tutelle administrative*.

9 Tshibangu, *op. cit.*, pp. 45-46.
10 Kalanda, *op. cit.*, p. 75.

Tutelle administrative is a hallowed Belgian principle by which acts of local governments are subject to review and veto by higher authority if they are not deemed to conform with existing legislation or the general interest. However, in the 1957 statute this *tutelle* deriving from Belgian tradition was mingled with the paternal tutelage notions growing out of colonial administrative tradition. The European who was designated as first burgomaster was given the power not only to veto all acts of the communal burgomasters but to act in their place when he felt appropriate, which is contrary to Belgian practice.[11] Further, the entire two-tiered concept of urban government was at variance with the Belgian model. Belgian cities have no single municipal government; they are a conglomeration of autonomous communes. This somewhat chaotic method of governing large urban centers has thus far resisted all efforts of reformers to secure effective city-wide institutions. Thus the first burgomaster post under the Congo municipality reform had no Belgian equivalent.

The decree of March 26, 1957, then, had explicitly or implicitly resolved its dilemmas in a liberal direction. No structural distinctions between European and African communes were to be made, nor was the city to be governed on the basis of a simple diversion into a white and a black half. A uniform system of "consultations" was to be elaborated in such a way as to constitute genuine elections. A long step

[11] On the issue of *tutelle administrative* in the 1957 decree, see Albert Parisis, *Les finances communales et urbaines au Congo belge* (Brussels: ARSOM, Sci. Mor. et Pol., N.S.,T. XXV, fasc. 1, 1960), pp. 47-49. To be complete, we should add that in Belgium the central government has in some areas the power to act in the place of communal authorities if they fail to carry out statutory obligations. However, in fact such action is extremely rare. For example, in the major wave of strikes in March 1961, mainly in Wallony, the government did not dare take strong action against a number of burgomasters in Socialist constituencies who visibly sided with the strikers and failed to execute some Brussels directives. Soon thereafter, a large number of Flemish burgomasters flatly refused to administer a census including linguistic questions. No sanctions were taken in this case either.

away from the rigid paritary notions of 1952 had been made. The plurality of communes at the base of the urban structure reflected the much greater African population; with the *conseil de ville* having equal representation from the communes, de facto parity was retained through the interest-group representatives but without explicitly racial criteria. The burgomasters were to be nominated by the communal councils. As a Congolese student of urban reform suggests, the changes over the nine-year preparatory period made the end product a "profound and progressive" step.[12]

Thus what emerged was a rather complex, decentralized urban organization. The city was divided into communes, roughly equal in population (except that the European communes were much smaller than the African ones); the African communes averaged 20,000-30,000 inhabitants. Each commune had an elected council and a burgomaster nominated by the council, presumably from among its members. Most routine tasks of urban administration were performed at the commune level. At the city echelon, there was a council whose membership included representatives of the communal councils, with about one quarter of the seats reserved for interest group representation. At the apex was a first burgomaster, directly appointed by the provincial governor, and responsible only to him. The first burgomaster was ranking civil servant, and therefore by definition a European.

African Apathy

It is at first view surprising that the reform aroused very little interest among the African population until shortly before the first consultations were held. Lumumba, writing on the very eve of enactment, barely mentions the project, simply stating in the cryptic style which characterizes his book, "Reforms are being studied and will be promulgated

[12] Kalanda, *op. cit.*, p. 60.

at any moment. However, we don't yet know what their exact scope will be."[13] The administration itself remarked on this apathy and apparent indifference: "A few limited intellectual milieux and the press have contented themselves with observing that the decree offered only a framework and that only the ordinances of execution would make it possible to evaluate the 'democratization' promised since 1948. This attitude is characteristic. In effect, the state of mind is such that one takes note of nothing which is not direct, concrete—and sensational."[14]

The skepticism and limited interest with which the publication of the reform was greeted had two main roots. In the first place, the African community had played almost no role in the preparation of the decree. As Kalanda remarked: "One must carefully note that (Congolese opinion) is not a determinant in political decisions. It came, in this case, after the draft statute was ready for signature. The most relevant opinion remains that of the Europeans, for they alone have had weight, and influence the legislator in his final decisions."[15] At the end of 1956, the views of the *conseil de cité* in Leopoldville were solicited, and half a dozen meetings were held, two with delegations from the European *comité urbain*. Further discussions were held in June 1957 concerning the details of application; among the African councilors playing a prominent role were Joseph Ngalula and Cyrille Adoula.[16] However, as Kalanda remarked, these consultations came only at the very last minute.

The second factor tending toward African disinterest was the accumulated suspicion which was the residue of the series of unrealized promises and empty reforms described in the previous chapter. The juridical subtleties which led to calling elections "consultations" and for burgomasters to

[13] Lumumba, *Le Congo, terre d'avenir*, p. 39.
[14] Ville de Léopoldville, *op. cit.*, p. 14.
[15] Kalanda, *op. cit.*, p. 76.
[16] Ville de Léopoldville, *op. cit.*, pp. 9-12, 36.

be named by the administration after receiving the "advice" of the communal councils led to fears that this would prove to be yet another fraud. The Abako, by far the most dynamic political group at this time, demanded: "The people must choose their own representatives. They must not have imposed upon them the personal friends of functionaries or other *frotteurs de manche.* . . . If the government chooses councilors that the people do not accept, there will be discontent, even unrest and incidents."[17]

A Leopoldville daily on April 18, 1957, reflected a widespread belief when it stated, "One thing is already certain: the burgomasters will be imposed by the administration."[18] Even after the ordinance of execution was issued on September 29, 1957, announcing "consultations" for December, the suspicions were far from dissipated. The *Courrier d'Afrique* on October 3 conceded that the clause concerning "consultations" could be the "object of the most diverse interpretations." The Leopoldville Catholic daily added that it was wrong to imagine that this would be invoked in such a way as to falsify the election results, that the administration was aware what a disastrous error it would be to hold elections, and then ignore the results. However, two days later, the same newspaper remarked that many in the African quarter still had the "false idea that the burgomasters would be imposed."

Implementation of Urban Reform

The administration was determined to follow the rules. This reform was, after all, conceived by Belgium and embodied all the cherished Belgian norms of successful decolonization: it had been slowly and prudently elaborated with "patient empiricism," and was building cautiously from the ground up. Responsible officials were well aware of the failure of other reform measures; the system

---

[17] "Faut-il que le Gouvernement désigne ou que le peuple vote?", *Congo*, May 4, 1957, quoted in Kalanda, *op. cit.*, p. 75.
[18] Ville de Léopoldville, *op. cit.*, p. 40.

badly needed a success. In 1957, the measure was to be applied on a pilot basis in Leopoldville, Elisabethville, and Jadotville. Especially in Leopoldville, where the incipient nationalist movement was making itself felt, an enormous effort was deployed to obtain a real psychological impact through the consultations. Some 230,000 tracts explaining the electoral procedures were issued, with a final distribution of 85,000 on the eve of the polling to assure a maximum turnout.[19]

Two particular factors, not clearly foreseen, played an important role in the nature of the results. In the first place, the formula of single-member constituencies had been chosen, which meant that in both Leopoldville and the Katanga centers, a disciplined group could parlay a relatively small numerical majority into a sweeping electoral triumph. In Leopoldville, the Abako, representing primarily the Bakongo population, won 133 of 170 seats in the African communes with only 46 percent of the total vote. Secondly, the ideology of the administration, hostile to the formation of African political parties to contest the elections, was that the new statute was to provide schooling in the practical problems of local administration. Parties, in this theory, were superfluous, if not harmful, as they would introduce extraneous and demagogic considerations into the political campaign. The result was that the competition was structured by the existing associations, essentially ethnic. The metropolitan Belgian parties did make some effort to play a role, especially in Katanga, but the operation of the consultations served to make the ethnic factor paramount. The idea that men anywhere in the impersonal urban environment would not seek to make their voices effective by relying on some organized effort to profit from the competition was strangely naïve; the pattern of political behavior unintentionally set in these consultations was a fateful one for the country.

[19] *Ibid.*, p. 24.

TABLE 3

LEOPOLDVILLE ELECTION RESULTS ACCORDING TO REGION OF ORIGIN

Commune	Bas Congo				Lac Leo, Equateur				Kasai				Kwango-Kwilu				East			
	A	B	C	D	A	B	C	D	A	B	C	D	A	B	C	D	A	B	C	D
Kintambo	1827	12	7	28	578	3	3	27	105	–	1	5	1576	2	2	5	150	–	4	10
St. Jean	2951	18	10	61	922	4	8	28	270	–	1	5	1425	1	2	5	139	–	1	5
Kinshasa	2738	12	6	37	2107	9	11	45	739	4	6	20	2308	1	3	12	418	1	1	6
Barumbu	2108	16	8	42	1463	5	14	42	264	1	–	12	1167	–	–	1	197	1	1	7
Dendale	5206	24	17	67	1067	1	6	30	267	–	–	11	2266	–	2	5	116	–	–	6
Kalamu	2679	19	6	47	1644	2	7	21	437	–	5	21	689	–	1	6	125	–	1	4
Ngiri-Ngiri	3545	22	16	58	724	–	5	15	210	–	2	11	2577	1	1	5	76	–	–	4
Banda-lungwa	699	10	7	25	511	–	2	10	252	1	2	9	201	–	–	6	65	–	–	1
Total	21753	133	77	365	9016	24	56	218	2544	6	17	94	12209	5	10	45	1286	2	8	43

KEY: Columns A, B, C, and D in each case refer respectively to: A) number of votes received; B) number of elected councilors; C) number of alternates (runners-up); D) total number of candidates.

Bas Congo includes the two districts of Bas Congo and Cataractes, and for all practical purposes may be assumed to be exclusively inhabited by Bakongo. The Lac Leopold II District and Equateur Province region included two major groups, the "Bangala," and the Mongo. Kasai Province was represented in Leopoldville primarily by Baluba, Lulua, Batetela, and Basongye. The Kwango and Kwilu Districts had as their largest contingent the Bayaka, and also included members of many of the large number of tribes in the Kwilu, such as the Bayanzi, Bambala, Bangongo, Bapende, and Bambunda.

SOURCE: Ville de Leopoldville, *Consultation du 8 décembre 1957*, pp. 67–70.

119

In Leopoldville, as Table 3 shows, the great victors were the Bakongo; no one had been certain how strong the ethnic factor would be, and many Congolese intellectuals were shocked to find how extensive a role it had played. This was not the only factor, by any means. The vanguard role of the Abako had earned it considerable prestige. As Kalanda, himself a Muluba from Kasai, wrote in 1958, "They are the only ones who dare today express with firmness the as yet confused aspirations of the Congolese people."[20] None of the other ethnic associations came close to the coherence of doctrine or action of the Abako.[21] Further, there had been negotiations between the Abako and Bayaka groups earlier in 1957;[22] the great disparity revealed in Table 3 between the number of voters from this district and the number of its own candidates elected suggests that a large number of these ballots went to Abako candidates. Jean Bolikango and Paul Bolya, respectively the leading "Bangala" and Mongo personalities, were both defeated by Abako candidates.

The administration accepted with good grace the verdict of the polls, and invested with the burgomaster functions the six Abako candidates put forward by the communal councils which had a Bakongo majority. A temporary flurry of resentment was caused when European burgomasters were named for Barumbu and Kinshasa communes; this, however, was done only because the non-Abako majority in each case was deadlocked on a candidate to propose.

[20] Kalanda, op. cit., p. 73.

[21] Tshibangu, basing his conclusions on extensive interviewing during the election campaign, identifies four other major ethnic associations which were factors. These were Fedekaleo (Fédération Kasaienne de Léopoldville), Liboke lya Bangala, Fedequalac (Fédération de l'Equateur et Lac Leopold II—Mongo), and the Fédération Kwango-Kwiloise. All of these except Bolikango's Liboke lya Bangala and to a lesser extent the Mongo association were paralyzed by internal division. Both Fedekaleo and the Fédération Kwango-Kwiloise were undergoing leadership crises, with their presidents accused of embezzlement. Op. cit., pp. 119-23.

[22] ABAKO 1950-1960, pp. 67-68 (Brussels: CRISP, 1963).

When agreement was reached within these two councils, the European mayors were replaced by the Congolese nominees put forward by the councilors.

In the Katanga elections, canvassing by the three metropolitan parties was more active, and the vocabulary of politics was more ideological. The results, however, were virtually identical. The Kasai Baluba, the largest single group in the population of Elisabethville and even more so in Jadotville, enjoyed a clear social ascendancy, of which both they and other ethnic groups were keenly aware. They had no ethnic association as strong as the Abako; rather the strong sense of common purpose of the Kasai Baluba provided a basis for informal cooperation more advanced than that achieved by the numerous Katanga ethnic groups represented in the urban centers. No figures have been published as to the precise ethnic breakdown of membership on the four African communal councils of Elisabethville or the one in Jadotville. However, the nature of the majorities was clear from the fact that all five of those nominated as burgomaster were from outside the province of Katanga.[23]

Serious problems arose concerning the designation of the burgomasters in both Katanga cities. The conservative Catholic daily in Brussels, La Libre Belgique, denounced the "deplorable maneuvers [in Elisabethville] by the administration which evaded the problem for a long time and sought to influence certain councilors to modify their voters in Katuba, Kenya, and Albert communes."[24] The administration had sought to find a place as burgomaster for the former chef de centre of the Elisabethville CEC, a Muena Kanyoka,[25] and to avoid the designation of a solid phalanx of "strangers" from outside the province. However,

[23] For a brief but interesting account of the 1957 urban elections in Katanga, see Antoine Rubbens, "La consultation populaire du 22 décembre 1957 à Elisabethville," Problèmes Sociaux Congolais (September 1958), pp. 77-81.

[24] Quoted in Ville de Léopoldville, op. cit., p. 147.

[25] A tribe in southeastern Kasai, related to the Katanga Baluba. The name is often transliterated as Kanyok.

in the end, the nominations of the communal councils were respected, with two Kasai Baluba named for the communes of Kenya and Katuba, a Musongye from Kasai for Ruashi, and a Mukusu from Maniema district in Kivu in Albert. This last nomination was interesting in that the Bakusu were an ethnic group with very small representation in Elisabethville. The individual in question, Pascal Luanghy, enjoyed considerable prestige among the intellectuals, and had ably defended the interests of the elite in a syndical organization.[26] He won the nomination, therefore, solely on the grounds of his personal merits.

The one serious deviation from the principle of accepting the nominations made by the communal councils was in the African commune of Kikula in Jadotville. Here the administration, under pressure from some European milieux and the missions, prevented the nomination of Victor Lundula, later to be named by Lumumba as the first Congolese commander-in-chief of the *Armée Nationale Congolaise*. Lundula had earned the reputation of being too forthright in his advocacy of political change, and was alleged to be "anti-white" and "anti-mission."[27] When it became clear that he was likely to be a candidate as elections approached, he was hastily transferred from his job as a medical orderly in Jadotville to Kamina. However, 13 of the 17 Kikula counci-

[26] The Bakusu are closely related to Lumumba's tribe, the Batetela, and are the easternmost extension of the large Mongo culture cluster, which covers most of the central basin of the Congo, stretching from Lac Leopold II to Maniema, south of the Congo River. Luanghy in 1960 was elected president of the Ankutshu-Anamongo association, formed at a congress in Lodja (Kasai), and offering important support to MNC/L. Since 1960, he has served as permanent secretary in the Civil Service Ministry in Leopoldville.

[27] The latter allegation seems particularly ironic in view of Lundula's subsequent display of personal courage and *sang-froid* in preventing a massacre of the European population in Jadotville during the *Force Publique* mutiny July 10-11, 1960, and again when some extremists wanted to retaliate through a generalized massacre of the European population when the death of Lumumba became known at Stanleyville February 13, 1961.

lors nominated him despite his transfer. Katanga Governor Schoeller simply refused to accept his candidacy and named another person in his place. Lundula is an Otetela, and as in the case of Albert commune, personal competence was clearly the only important factor in his support.

The urban reform was extended to four more cities at the end of 1958—Coquilhatville, Stanleyville, Bukavu, and Luluabourg—plus two more suburban areas of Leopold-ville—Matete, and Ndjili. In the case of Stanleyville, the consultations had neither a political nor an ethnic character, and excited relatively little interest. In Bukavu, the Bashi constituted an unchallenged majority in the two African communes, but there was very little ethnic tension at this point. In Coquilhatville and Luluabourg, however, the competition was sharply ethnic, and provoked tensions which in the former case tore the province into several pieces after independence, and in the latter led to a large-scale massacre and the Calvary of the Baluba.[28]

In Equateur, the ethnic composition was essentially bipolar; the oldest residents, who generally occupied the higher status positions in urban society, came from the Mongo grouping. There had been in recent years a consid-erable influx of Ngombe from north of the Congo River and east of Coquilhatville. Of a 1954 population of 23,668, approximately 16,000 came from the Mongo group and 5,200 from the Ngombe ethnic cluster.[29] In the first elections, although the results in the African commune of Bandaka reflected the Mongo majority, there was a split in the ranks when it came to electing a burgomaster. Feelings ran so

[28] The Coquilhatville tensions in 1958 were still at a relatively low pitch, and in no way comparable to the Luluabourg situation. It was striking, in interviews in Coquilhatville, Stanleyville, and Bukavu in 1962, to find that even persons who had played political roles in the 1958 communal elections could barely recall them. Obviously, in the face of the momentous events in the Congo since that time, 1958 seems to belong almost to a prehistoric era.

[29] Frans M. de Thier, *Le centre extra-coutumier de Coquilhatville* (Brussels: Institut de Sociologie Solvay, 1956), pp. 111-13.

high during the prolonged deadlock among the Mongo that one Mongo group defected to the candidate of the Ngombe minority. This was a great shock to the Mongo community at Coquilhatville, which was accustomed to thinking of the city as "theirs," and it was one of the important factors leading eventually to the establishment of a Mongo political movement, Unimo.

At Luluabourg, the introduction of urban elections took place in a similar strikingly polarized ethnic composition. The Kasai Baluba accounted for 56 percent of the population, with another 25 percent Lulua.[30] The Baluba had first access to the new opportunities created by the modern sector, and were quick to capitalize upon them; at the time of the first elections, they formed indisputably the highest social caste in African society. At this stage, Baluba intellectuals were also making more radical demands upon the colonial system, and at least part of the administration became involved in aiding the Lulua candidates by counseling on electoral procedures and tactics and helping on the selection of contestants.[31] The Lulua were well equipped to make use of this help, as they developed a remarkably disciplined ethnic association, *Lulua Frères*. They succeeded in winning a majority of seats on the communal council and in installing both African burgomasters.[32] The Baluba then spurned an offer to share in the communal responsibilities.

Functioning of the Urban Communes

In the functioning of the urban communal institutions, a number of difficulties were encountered. The first and most dramatic was the foreseeable ambiguity in the role of the

[30] André Lux, "Luluabourg: Migrations, accroissement et urbanisation de la population congolaise," *Zaïre*, XII, No. 7 (1958), 8-9.

[31] A. Kalanda, *Baluba et Lulua: une ethnie à la recherche d'un nouvel équilibre* (Brussels: Editions de Remarques Congolaises, 1959) p. 99.

[32] Kalanda, *op. cit.*, p. 14.

burgomaster; this caused grave problems in Leopoldville and Elisabethville. Kalanda rendered the perceptive verdict that the *Statut des Villes* was in the final analysis an administrative decentralization rather than a democratization.[33] The dilemma grew in part from a similar ambiguity in the role of a burgomaster in Belgium itself, and partly from the colonial situation. The burgomaster was in the impossible position of at once representing both colonial authority and the spearhead of emerging resistance to it. The issue was immediately joined when Kasavubu, the most prestigious Congolese figure at the time, chose the occasion of his inaugural address as burgomaster of Dendale commune on April 20, 1958, to make a political speech articulating in moderate terms a certain number of grievances, such as the inadequacy of higher educational opportunity, restriction of freedom of the press and of association, the obstacles to entry of Congolese into the officer ranks of the army and police, and concluded: "Democracy will not be established until we obtain autonomy, be it only internal. Democracy is not established there where one continues to name functionaries instead of elected officials of the people . . . . There is no democracy until the vote is generalized. The first step is therefore not yet taken. We demand general elections and internal autonomy."[34]

The administration was indignant and maintained that Kasavubu's political speech was imcompatible with the exercise of his burgomaster functions. A week later, he was officially reprimanded by the Governor-General.[35] Having made his point, the Abako leader did not again use his mayoral chair as a political tribune. The Abako burgomasters were outspoken and effective in defending the rights of the African communes at the *conseil de ville,* and in seeking an adequate allocation of the total resources available

[33] Kalanda, *Organisation des Villes,* p. 100.
[34] *ABAKO 1950-1960,* pp. 132-136.
[35] *Ibid.,* p. 130.

to the city and communal control over the highly important *Fonds d'Avance* resources.[36] The Abako had a developed sense of its responsibilities to the population as a whole, and Bakongo and non-Bakongo alike felt that there was relatively little ethnic favoritism in the exercise of their burgomaster functions.

In Katanga, the experiment was off to a bad start because of the hesitation of the administration in accepting the nominations of the communal councils. Very rapidly a conflict of crisis proportions arose between the Baluba burgomasters and the European district commissioner, Leopold Henroteaux. A number of points of conflict were built into the statute by the excessive *tutelle* powers given the first burgomaster. Henroteaux followed the very popular Grévisse as district commissioner, and he was generally believed to lack the qualities of tact and diplomacy with which his predecessor had been well endowed. The affair eventually reached a point where the African burgomasters presented a petition to Katanga Governor Schoeller demanding the removal of Henroteaux. The administration became alarmed by the general deterioration in the political climate in South Katanga, especially in Elisabethville, where a malaise entirely new to the area was remarked.[37] African demands were quietly met; Henroteaux was transferred to Kasai.

Also, it is conceded on all sides that there was in Elisabethville thorough-going ethnic favoritism by the Kasai burgomasters in the allocation of favors, some important, which did lie within their authority. The greatest point of

[36] *Courrier d'Afrique,* Jan. 11, 28; Feb. 27; Mar. 25; April 29; June 24; July 29; Aug. 26; Sep. 9; Sep. 23; Nov. 25, 1958. Beside Kasavubu, Abako burgomasters Arthur Pinzi and Gaston Diomi were particularly outspoken in the debates. The *Fonds d'Avance* made possible easy financing terms for acquiring low-cost, decent housing; its loans were eagerly sought.

[37] See, for example, A. Rubbens, "La confusion politique au Katanga," *Revue Nouvelle,* T. XXVIII, No. 18 (October 1958) pp. 308-13.

friction came in the area of housing; the burgomasters in Elisabethville acquired an important voice in administering the *Fonds d'Avance* and in the award of urban lots. One student group found that 280 of 300 plots allocated in one of the communes went to Kasai Baluba.[38]

According to a Belgian expert on communal institutions who was investigating the operation of the new law at the end of 1958, "Certain functionaries treated the burgomasters like children, even using the word. Others required that any meeting with a burgomaster be preceded by an interview with an assistant. The third group contented itself with being present in an office of the former CEC transformed into a *maison communale*, saying: 'Do not bother to come looking for me; *débrouillez-vous.*' "[39]

The experiment had operated for only a year when the report of the *Groupe de Travail* and the obvious necessity to accelerate the creation of political structures for the Congo entirely transformed the situation. The decree of October 13, 1959, which was a part of the first step of implementation of the Working Group recommendations, introduced important changes in the structure of the urban institutions. *Tutelle administrative* over the communes was attenuated by being removed from the hands of the (European) first burgomaster and lodged with the more distant provincial government. The power of the communes was greatly increased at the expense of the city; real police powers and extended taxation authority were put in the hands of the communes. The single-member constituencies were replaced by multi-member voting districts and proportional representation.[40] By this time, however, the attention of both colonizer and colonized had become entirely absorbed by the debate over a timetable for independence and structures for the independent state.

[38] According to Venant Ngoie, formerly of Lovanium University, himself a Muluba from Katanga.

[39] Parisis, *op. cit.*, p. 49.

[40] *Ibid.*

Rural Local Government

Shortly after the promulgation of the first urban reform law followed the decree of May 10, 1957, which made potentially far-reaching changes in rural local government and was intended as a step toward rural communes. This decree, because its implementation did not take place at the vortex of political activity and did not involve the most active elements in the Congo's modern elite, is much less known than its sister urban reform. Although the changes made in the countryside also suffered from the tempestuous pace of decolonization and post-independence difficulties the system of rural government remains one of the most impressive and least heralded monuments to Belgian administration in the Congo.

It is unnecessary to offer in detail the historical evolution of Belgian policy toward African administration. From the very early days there have been two distinct schools of thought, one advocating with enthusiasm the Lugardian theses of indirect administration, the other, preoccupied with assimilation and/or efficiency, preferring direct rule. This debate has flowed along several lines of cleavage; perhaps the most important separated the more theoretical colonial specialists in Belgium itself and the more practical administrators in Africa.

Other bases for the division of opinion can be found. It is interesting to note that the greatest apostles of indirect rule have been Flemish and Liberal. This is true of both the major architects of the policy—Louis Franck, who was Colonial Minister from 1918-1924, and Georges Vanderkerken, who served as Governor in Equateur province under the Franck ministry, and thereafter, in numerous books and articles, was a wholehearted spokesman for indirect rule.[41]

[41] Inter alia, *Les sociétés bantoues du Congo Belge* (Brussels: Etablissements, Emile Bruylant, 1920); *La politique coloniale belge* (Antwerp: Editions *Zaïre*, 1943); *L'ethnie Mongo*, 2 vols., (Brussels: ARSOM, Sci. Mor. et Pol., T. XIII, fasc. 1 & 2, 1944); plus several articles in the semi-official review *Congo* in the interwar period.

Franck was the author of one of the classic pleas for Flemish nationalism, *Taal en Nationaliteit*. The philosophic postulates of indirect rule are remarkably concordant with the *weltanshauung* of a Flemish nationalist—a reaction against the cultural chauvinism of the French-speaking, Walloon element and its dominance in Belgian society. The same could be said for the Liberals; a reverence for a laissez-faire approach to traditional authority systems, encouraging them to evolve at their own pace to the new challenges of modernization, is consistent with many of the postulates of nineteenth-century liberalism.[42]

Important elements of the Catholic missions, incarnated in the person of Monsignor de Hemptinne, imbued with a sense of the superiority of the Latin, Christian civilization, were the motor elements in the assimilationist strand in colonial thought. Brausch and Vermuelen no doubt considerably overstate their case in charging Catholic missions with sabotage of indirect rule. However, it is undeniable that many missionaries viewed most traditional structures as being so linked by their ritual sanctions with practices incompatible with Christianity that their disappearance was a necessary prerequisite for fulfillment of the evangelical task.

Also, one may discern a divergence of view between

[42] For interesting examples of this philosophy, expounded from a (Belgian) Liberal viewpoint, see, in addition to the afore-cited works of Vanderkerken and those of Franck himself, Brausch, *Belgian Administration in the Congo;* V. Vermuelen, *Déficiences et dangers de notre politique indigène* (Brussels: Imprimerie I.M.A., 1952). Liberalism, of course, is a rather diffuse corpus of political philosophy, containing within itself contradictory strands. Lugardism and its Belgian variants are not consistent with the earlier utilitarian school of rationalizers and reformers, who followed in Jeremy Bentham's footsteps. For this group, India in the mid-19th century was a great laboratory for social engineering. However, half a century later when the naïveté of rationalizing India was apparent, and Liberalism had felt the impact of social Darwinism, indirect rule did fit remarkably well into a Liberal world view. It is interesting that most of the dedicated apostles of this administrative ideology in Britain and Belgium were Liberals.

those linked with areas where European settlement was important, in particular Katanga, and those whose experience was in the central basin, where there was no prospect of extensive European implantation. There is a total dissimilarity of view between, for example, Monsignor de Hemptinne of Elisabethville and Father Boelaert, whose missionary experience was among the Mongo near Coquilhatville.[43] Orientale province, especially from 1920-1933 under its greatest governors, de Meulemeester and Moeller de Laddersous, took considerable initiative in the pioneering of indirect rule policies, such as the "native tribunals," formalized by legislation in 1926, and the establishment of "sectors," or artifical groupings maintaining as much traditional content as possible in areas where traditional structures were segmentary or disintegrated.[44] Katanga, on the other hand, was reluctant to implement these provisions.

Historians of indirect rule cite as its starting point an 1891 decree permitting the recognition of chiefs by the state. Subsequent measures were adopted in 1906 and 1910, somewhat extending the earlier one. Then finally on December 5, 1933, was passed the basic legislation, which some could maintain was the culmination of a single policy consistently developed[45] and others could label a heretical innovation.[46] This confirmed the policy of establishing, as the administrative echelon below the purely European *territoire*, a *circonscription indigène* which could be either a *chefferie* or a *secteur*. "While respecting traditional organ-

[43] See, for example, R. P. E. Boelaert's article "Assimilation," *Aequatoria*, No. 1, 1951, reprinted in Fedacol, *L'opinion publique coloniale . . .* , pp. 70-75, or his communication to the Académie Royale des Sciences d'Outre Mer, "Vers un état Mongo?", *Bull. Séances,* ARSOM, 1961, pp. 382-91.

[44] A special issue of the *Congo* was devoted to these topics in July 1929, 10th year, T. II, No. 2.

[45] Among many examples that might be given, see the extract from the report of the *Conseil Colonial,* Piron & Devos, *Codes et Lois,* II, 211.

[46] J. de Hemptinne, *Un tournant de notre politique indigène* (Elisabethville: Edition de la Revue Juridique du Congo Belge, 1935).

ization, the legislator wanted to establish a single administrative system: he made of the chieftaincy the lowest echelon of the administrative organization, and the chief a functionary integrated into the system without prejudice to his traditional role."[47]

There is a strikingly continental, Cartesian quality to the concept of this diluted form of indirect rule. On the one hand, it eschews the ambiguities of a thoroughly indirect system, such as Northern Nigeria, with dual authority structures. More significantly, it sets a certain optimal size for a *circonscription*; if the traditional structure was too large, as in the case of the Lunda, it was simply broken up. If the traditional units were too small, a number were amalgamated into the "sector"—one of the innovations of the 1933 decree. In fact, the practice of recognizing segments and fragments of clans had gotten out of hand in the first decade after the *reprise*; the number of *chefferies* shot up from 450 in 1908 to 6,095 in 1919. The Stanleyville district reached a point where the average population of a chieftaincy was 150 adult males, with one clan which had a chief and no population.[48] The sector was an inevitable administrative corrective to this problem.

With an important modern administrative role placed upon him, the chief was inevitably subject to judgment from an efficiency standpoint by the administration. Although in general an effort was made in the case of the *chefferies* to respect the customary rules regarding succession, these were often complex and at times misunderstood by the administration, or sometimes not applied when understood. The dual nature of the chief, representing colonial authority to his subjects and representing his subjects to colonial authority, was an uncomfortable one, and in most of the major chieftaincies there has been at least one

[47] Piron & Devos, *Codes et Lois,* II, 211.
[48] Guy Malengreau, Course on *Politique indigène,* Louvain University. The author is indebted to Professor Malengreau for permission to use his excellent course notes.

instance of replacement of a chief, or of tampering with the succession.[49]

In the case of the sectors, an effort was made to find a notable with the leadership qualities and administrative ability necessary to carry out the tasks assigned to him. An interesting set of instructions from Orientale province in 1923 suggested how this might be done:

"The tradition must be studied, with the history of the tribe, its migrations, its rules of succession, etc., and the real present and past relationships among the various chiefs of groupings. Seek to discover among them one whom our occupation, our decisions, or our mistakes might have dispossessed, or whose authority has been diminished by an overly swift recognition of independence of his sly, cunning vassals. Do not forget that in certain districts groups were split to facilitate the rubber collection. . . . If there is no descendent of the former chiefs, one must seek out the most intelligent group chief who is capable of exercising an influence on the others; listen to him with greater attention, ask his advice frequently, try to get his colleagues to support him, point out publicly how he analyzes and solves problems with clarity, precision and equity; bring about by opportune questions numerous general expressions of adhesion . . . give to the chosen chief a more and more preponderant voice; excite his ambition by brief private interviews."[50]

[49] Tshombe gives an interesting list in *Discours prononcé par le Président du Katanga à l'occasion de la fête du 11 juillet 1962* (Elisabethville: 1962), pp. 5-9. To give only a small sampling, the Kasongo Nyembo of the Baluba Shankadi was relegated by a district commissioner in 1917. The administration interfered in the designation of the Lunda Mwata Yamvo in 1920. Beginning in 1892, M. Plancquaert chronicles a series of interventions and imbroglios with several Kiamfus of the Bayaka, in the Kwango, *Les Jaga et les Bayaka du Kwango* (Brussels: ARSOM, Sci. Mor. et Pol., T. III, fasc. 1, 1932), pp. 142-55. The Mwami of the largest Bashi grouping, Alexandre Kabare, was replaced in 1936 following his apparently voluntary departure as a result of a series of disputes with the administration.
[50] Province Orientale, *Politique indigène: instructions,* 1923.

The *circonscription indigène* was by the 1933 law given a "civil personality," which meant that it could have a treasury and collect some taxes. There was a council with a consultative role, with the members partly *ex officio*, in the case of chiefs of groupings which were component parts of the sector, or recognized elders in the case of a *chefferie*. Although the sector was not a traditional unit, it was kept ethnically homogeneous as far as possible; there were many areas where the tribes were so intersticed as to make this impracticable. With some rare exceptions, the chief would always be drawn from the local population.[51]

It is difficult to pass a single verdict on the success of the 1933 reform. The assimilationist currents, the paternal habits, and the premium upon immediate efficiency certainly caused the administration to intervene continuously in the operation of the *circonscriptions* in many, if not most, cases.[52] It would be wrong, on the other hand, to underestimate the important range of tasks performed through these instruments; order was maintained, justice provided, taxes collected, local roads built. Brausch argues with some jus-

[51] Biebuyck mentions two derogations to this principle in his study of the Bakumu. "La société kumu face à Kitawala," *Zaïre*, XI, No. 1, (January 1957), 9. There was no parallel for example, to the frequent use of Baganda as "chiefs" in non-Baganda areas of Uganda.

[52] However, even in territories under British administration, there was a good deal of intervention. Southall, in an interesting comparative study of British and Belgian methods of administration of the Alur tribe, which straddles the Congo-Uganda frontier, found some contrasts, but they did not add up to a dramatic differentiation in the degree to which rule had been "indirect." He found that the Belgians had in fact respected the traditional lineages in designating chiefs more closely than had the British, although removal was more frequent. He concludes that in sum indirect rule was more closely followed in the Congo, but less scope for training for self-rule had been given. A. W. Southall, "Belgian and British Administration in Alurland," *Zaïre*, VIII (May 1964), 467-86. See also Audrey I. Richards (ed.), *East African Chiefs* (London: Faber and Faber Ltd., 1960), for a series of case studies illustrating the degree to which the theory of indirect rule had been mingled with the practice of considerable intervention in the interests of effective administration and preparation for self-rule.

tice, "This system of local government, together with the economic infrastructure and the social achievements, was for years the chief strength of Belgian colonial rule."[53] The only extant African appreciation of the system, an interesting analysis of its impact on the segmentary Batetela structure, advances an original and basically favorable judgment:

"[The *circonscriptions*] gave the Batetela an interest in reasoning thenceforward, not within the framework of the family or the clan, which had lost its audience with the European authority, but rather in the framework of the chieftaincy and the sector. This state of mind put a brake on the secessionist tendency of certain overly ambitious family members (the family having become an entity without great importance), and facilitated a rapprochement between the clans, in previous times adversaries of any form of superposition; and the more the position of the *circonscriptions indigènes* became stabilized, by the reinforcement of its powers, the more the former elders were overshadowed by the new institutions. Thus the application of the decree . . . has been, for Otetela society, a very efficacious remedy to its internal plague, segmentation."[54]

1957 Rural Reforms

The 1957 decree introduced several important innovations in rural administration. The most fundamental of these involved the establishment of councils with deliberative powers and a dosage of members who were selected, "taking into account the preferences of the inhabitants." The ordinance on implementation on May 29, 1958, made it clear that these preferences were to be indicated by either direct or indirect elections, depending on local circum-

[53] Brausch, *Belgian Administration in the Congo*, p. 44.
[54] Antoine Wembi, *Influence de l'organisation administrative coloniale sur l'organisation administrative coutumière chez les Atetela*, Mémoire de Licence en Sciences Politiques et Administratives, Université Lovanium, 1961, p. 53.

stances. In the case of the sectors, the chiefs were to be elected for ten-year terms by the sector council, rather than being installed for life by the administration. This was of great importance, as 523 of the 867 *circonscriptions indigènes* by the end of 1958 were sectors.[55] The chiefs of the *groupements* which were the components of the sector were *ex officio* members, as were the elders in the case of a chieftaincy. The *centres extra-coutumiers* that were too small to be made eventually into cities were to be covered by this same act. Provision was made for "interest representation" on the councils; this was applied essentially to cooperatives.[56] No specific proportion of *ex officio* and elected members were stipulated. From interviews in a number of territories, it would seem that the percentage of indirectly elected members ranged from one third to somewhat over one half the total. It should be added that many of those designated in this way were, like the *ex officio* members, of high traditional status in their communities. The "elected" members were in fact chosen by an indirect process. Each village held a general meeting to designate a *mandataire;* the *mandataires* then served as an electoral college for the *circonscription.*

For inexplicable reasons, implementation of this important reform was delayed for over a year, until July 1, 1958. It was then up to the provinces to take their individual measures of application. Performance here was very uneven. In Equateur, the law was in good measure applied by the end of 1958. In Katanga, implementation came in early 1959. In Leopoldville, it was not until mid-1959 that the new sector councils were established. An interesting report by the former territorial administrator at Mweka, in Kasai, dated February 27, 1960, argued at great length the pros and cons of applying the decree to the complex Bakuba

[55] *Rapport sur l'Administration . . . 1958*, p. 75.

[56] See, for example, the list of associations to consult fixed by Orientale province, *Bulletin Administratif,* 1959, pp. 355-61.

traditional structure, analyzing the possible consequences of an electoral system of any sort. The Bakuba were admittedly a particularly difficult case, possessing one of the Congo's oldest and most sophisticated traditional authority systems; yet the fact that this debate seemed far from resolved early in 1960 suggests at least that application in Kasai had not been complete.[57]

Implementation of the measure in both Leopoldville and Equateur was accompanied by a very substantial reduction in the number of *circonscriptions*. In the latter province, the number was brought down from 220 to 92;[58] in Leopoldville the proportion was similar. The reduction was not required by the law but was argued as necessary to provide an adequate local tax base to support the expanded governmental infrastructure which was implied.

It had been foreseen when the decree was formulated that the intervention of the territorial service in implementation would be substantial; the Declaration of Purpose accompanying the decree stated: "The action of the territorial service will remain preponderant in the evolution of the *circonscriptions*. The territorial service retains its role of direction and control, in a word, *tutelle*."[59] A number of interviews with Congolese civil servants who had been involved as clerks in the application of the decree indicates that in many cases the intervention of the territorial service in the designation of the chief was decisive. On the other hand, beginning in 1959, the administration progressively lost its grip on the countryside, especially in Leopoldville province, and with it both the will and the capacity to manipulate the sectors in the traditional cavalier fashion.

The sector chief, because of his lack of traditional legitimacy, was a particularly vulnerable creature of the admin-

[57] *Renseignements sur la population du territoire du Mweka située sur la rive droite de la Rivière Lubudi (Région de Misumba) avec projet de réorganisation politique*, A. Lambert, 1960, mimeographed.
[58] *Rapport sur l'Administration . . . 1958*, p. 80.
[59] Piron & Devos, *Codes et Lois*, II, 211.

istration. The onerous nature of many of the administrative impositions on the countryside has been described earlier; the chief was given the unpleasant obligation of transmitting these orders to the villages. Subsequent events were to prove that, if they found national politics bewildering, the chiefs were certainly aware of the currents of history in their local areas. When it became clear that the colonial administration was a waning force, they and the emerging local political leaders generally found it mutually convenient to arrive at an understanding.

In addition to the chief and notables, the *circonscription* had a small bureaucracy of its own, composed of a *secrétaire* and a *receveur,* sometimes combined in one person. This embryonic bureaucracy was responsible for keeping the accounts, the civil registers, and other written aspects of administration. A primary education was required and the pay was relatively high by rural standards.

Also on a permanent basis, in addition to the chief and the clerks, was a *collège permanent* established by the 1957 decree. This is another feature of government drawn from Belgian practice; the communal council designated a small standing committee from its membership to participate actively in the administrative affairs of the commune. The size of the *collège* depended upon the number of inhabitants, and ranged from three to seven. Each member would occupy himself with one particular sphere of activity.

In his daily life the villager came into contact with the state through the institutions of the *circonscription*. It was here he paid his tax. If his goat were stolen, he sought redress through the tribunal attached to the *circonscriptions*. It was the sector which organized the market where he sold his surplus agricultural production or cash crops. It was the *circonscription* which built and maintained the local road which linked him with the outside world.

Political recruitment did not in general take place from

the *circonscription* institutions; neither the chiefs nor the clerks departed in vast numbers for the new opportunities in the political sector. In sharp contrast was the situation of the urban communes, where the May 1960 national and provincial elections stripped the councils elected in December 1959 of many of their ablest members.

Some confusion was introduced into the status of the May 10, 1957, decree by the report of the *Groupe de Travail,* made a mere six months after the reform had gone into legal effect and before any province but Equateur had advanced very far in the actual implementation. The Working Group proposed sweeping alterations, including universal suffrage for the election of the majority of members of the councils, participation of Europeans, and restriction of *tutelle* to that characteristic of metropolitan Belgian practice. On the one hand, the Working Group suggested that there was considerable urgency in the application of its proposed reforms: "These objectives will be pursued without hesitation. . . . To wish the evolution slowed might correspond to a logical conception, but would take little account of certain psychological necessities, the existence of external events."[60] At the same time, "We must see that the new norms[of the 1957 decree] enter progressively into the mores, in order to be able to pass, without danger, after several years of functioning, to the following phase of evolution."[61] The impression that the laboriously constructed institutions required by the May 10, 1957, decree would likely be scrapped in a very short period of time was a pretext for hesitation.

Be that as it may, even discounting the partial and occasionally authoritarian application in the countryside, the twin decrees reforming local institutions in 1957 are of considerable interest, as they were the first and last meaningful steps toward the creation of a Congolese state according to

[60] Groupe de Travail, *Rapport,* p. 28.
[61] *Ibid.,* pp. 47-49.

a purely Belgian blueprint. As a general proposition, one may state that those policies which were given real priority by the colonial system were competently executed. Local government, with economic and social development, was fully consistent with the permanent values of the system, and it is logical that these should constitute its most noteworthy achievements. But building from the ground up, although a principle with which few could quarrel as an abstraction, was, in fact, unrealistic as an eleventh-hour strategy for decolonization.

Certain aspects of the urban structure, originating in the Eurafrican perspective, complicated this operation. But in bequeathing to the Congo an impressive local rural infrastructure, Belgium provided a partial antidote for the inadequacies of the hastily erected superstructure which subsequent events have proved invaluable.

🌣🌣🌣🌣🌣🌣🌣🌣🌣🌣🌣🌣🌣🌣🌣🌣🌣🌣🌣🌣🌣🌣🌣🌣🌣🌣🌣🌣🌣🌣🌣🌣🌣🌣🌣🌣🌣

Disintegration of the System

🌣🌣🌣🌣🌣🌣🌣🌣🌣🌣🌣🌣🌣🌣🌣🌣🌣🌣🌣🌣🌣🌣🌣🌣🌣🌣🌣🌣🌣🌣🌣🌣🌣🌣🌣🌣🌣

The Economic Miracle Tarnished

THE startling change in Belgian policy since the "patient empiricism" of the early postwar years is comprehensible only against the background of the accelerating disintegration of the once monolithic colonial power structure. In 1957, after a decade of preparation, the first steps were taken for establishing local institutions on the Congo infused with a significant democratic element. In 1960, Belgium agreed to construct from scratch in less than five months provincial and national political institutions. *Le pari congolais* was totally alien to the political style and traditions of the colonial system; clearly it could not have been undertaken by a nation in which hard-headed practicality and realism are writ large in the political culture unless the range of policy alternatives was exceedingly narrow. As a preface to an analysis of the final stage of decolonization, therefore, a brief inquest concerning the demise of a once invulnerable organism is in order.

An awareness of the economic environment of the final colonial years is important to understand how sudden independence could in 1960 be accepted with very little resistance by Belgian opinion. Some observers assign to this factor a decisive role.[1] While this assessment seems exaggerated, there can be no question that rapid decolonization was more tolerable in face of some disturbing economic trends than it would have been in the boom period. By 1956, the fat years for the Congo were over. Social overhead and public debt were mounting at an alarming pace, and a relative decline in public revenue set in. A fifteen-billion-franc

[1] Robert West, for example, in a paper delivered to the Fourth Annual Meeting of the African Studies Association, New York, October 20, 1961.

1956 budget reserve had evaporated by 1960. Investment slowed in 1956-1957, and capital flight began in 1958. A small Belgian contribution to the budget was necessary for the first time since World War II in 1959 and would inevitably have grown in the following years (although by no more than what has been given as aid to the independent Congo). Unemployment was a serious problem in the large towns for the first time. The lean years were at hand, and the image of miraculous economic success became tarnished.

The phenomenon of disintegration can be seen in three dimensions: first, there was progressive intrusion of metropolitan Belgian political disputes into the Congo; second, there was a rupture of the traditional state-church-capital alliance; and third, there was a loss of control over the tempo of political evolution in the face of a burgeoning nationalist movement.

The Impact of Metropolitan Divisions

BELGIAN PARTIES AND THE CONGO

Belgian society has three great cleavages. It is a culturally plural nation, with its Flemish and Wallon components uneasily coexisting in a unitary state. Overlapping this cleavage is the religious one; although Belgium is almost entirely Catholic in the sense that it is not Protestant, only about half of its people are practicing Catholics, and many are strongly anti-clerical. The Masonic movement has had, in Liberal and some Socialist milieux, an important audience. The final cleavage is in social thought, between advocates of a free enterprise, capitalist economy and partisans of varying degrees of socialization. The *Parti Socialiste Belge* is predominantly Walloon, anti-clerical, and moderately socialist. The *Parti Social Chrétien* (before World War II, the Catholic party) is strongest in Flanders, is Catholic, and contains economic philosophies ranging from mildly socialist to very conservative. The Liberals are strongest in the

Brussels area, among French-speaking business and professional classes; they are anti-clerical, and economically conservative.

TABLE 4

POSTWAR ELECTION RESULTS IN BELGIUM

	NUMBER OF SEATS				
Year	PSC	Lib	PSB	Communist	"Volksunie" (Flemish nationalist)
1946	92	17	69	23	
1949	105	29	66	12	
1950	108	20	77	7	
1954	95	25	86	4	1
1958	104	20	83	2	1
1961	96	20	84	5	5

A glance at the arithmetic of Belgian parliamentary politics reveals that in the postwar period only the PSC has had an absolute majority from 1950-1954. Otherwise, the normal situation is a coalition government; from 1946-1950, there was a PSC-Liberal government, from 1954-1958 a PSB-Liberal government, 1958-1961 a return to the PSC-Liberal formula, and in 1961 what conservative Catholics termed an *alliance contre nature* with a PSC-PSB government. The critical period in Congo policy was 1954-1960; there followed two coalition governments which were bitterly opposed by the party out of power. Partisan diversions were unusually intense.

In 1954-1958, on one of the rare occasions in the twentieth century, the PSC found itself in the opposition. The PSB and Liberals had established an uneasy coalition. The two parties had totally divergent views on social policy; the one important area in which ideologies overlapped was anticlericalism. Sharp tensions were immediately generated on this issue. The Catholic Church feared a major assault on what it felt were its prerogatives both in Belgium and the

142

Congo and was in a suspicious, defensive mood. Militant advocates of a laic society saw a unique opportunity to reduce what appeared to them as unwarranted privileges which the Church had acquired during long years of Catholic-dominated coalition governments.

It was in this charged atmosphere that Auguste Buisseret, a Liberal from Liége, came to office as Colonial Minister in 1954. He found himself confronted with a permanent staff in Brussels which had little sympathy with his views, a colonial administration in Leopoldville headed by a nonpolitical Catholic, and a colonial structure in which the missions enjoyed considerable strength. Here was a situation he deemed intolerable and set about to alter. The first battleground was the very heart of the mission program in the Congo: schools. Buisseret had prepared a long chapter in the 1947 senatorial report on the educational system, where he had extensively criticized the mission efforts in this regard. His first step in 1954 was to appoint a special group to investigate the educational system; the result, foreshadowed by the membership of the group, was a scathing indictment of the mission performance.[2] Based on the findings of the investigation, Buisseret proposed the establishment of a laic educational network for African children and sharp cuts in subsidies to the Catholic schools. The Catholic missions threatened to shut down the entire school system if their subsidies were cut, and the Minister had to back down on this part of his program. However, he did introduce some state schools for Africans, almost entirely in urban centers.

[2] *La réforme de l'enseignement: Mission pédagogique Coulon-Deheyn-Renson* (Brussels, 1954). For indignant Catholic response, see *Objectivité 'sur mesure'* (Brussels, E. Vandenbussche, 1955). A more balanced critique from a Catholic viewpoint is offered in a review by Guy Malengreau, *Zaïre*, X, no. 4 (April 1956), 405-13. Many of the criticisms leveled at the educational system in the Congo were pertinent; on the other hand, the Catholic objection that anti-clerical animus pervaded the report is also undeniable.

Any increase in educational opportunity available to the Congolese was in itself praiseworthy. Also, the creation of an alternative to missionary education was favorably received by a substantial part of the Congolese elite. However, the effort to prune the Catholic educational system was a more dubious move, and the classic European struggle between laicism and clericalism seems to have unduly influenced the debate over educational policy during this episode. But most significant within the context of decolonization was that both parties to the quarrel took the fateful step of appealing for support outside of the colonial structure itself, to the as yet inarticulate African population. Buisseret justified his policies in part on the basis that they were in response to a widespread African demand. The missions in turn elicited Congolese testimonials for their position.

In 1956, all three major Belgian parties held congresses devoted to the Congo question. The conclusions were unexciting, and none mentioned independence. The PSB concluded, "The first task is to raise the standard of living of the inhabitants. The second is to help them in their apprenticeship of democracy in all domains of collective life." The PSC spoke of the right to autonomy and of increasing Congolese participation in decisions concerning their country. The Liberals concluded, "Our role is to construct the future of the Congo, for the welfare of Belgians and Congolese, in seeing that the promotion of the Africans is realized in conjunction with economic expansion."[3] *La solicitude toute nouvelle* of *la Belgique politicienne* was seen as an ominous cloud on the horizon by colonial milieux.[4] All parties, es-

[3] A useful summary of the three programs is given by Doucy in *L'avenir politique du Congo Belge,* pp. 26-31.

[4] Jean Sépulchre, *Propos sur le Congo politique de domain: autonomie et fédéralism* (Elisabethville: Editions de l'Essor du Congo, 1958), p. 7. See also the long citation from Sépulchre in Jacques Marres and Pierre de Vos, *L'équinoxe de janvier* (Brussels: Editions Euraforient, 1959), p. 12.

pecially the PSB and Liberals, pushed the creation of satellite political clubs and trade unions in the Congo.

Although parties were not allowed to participate as such in the 1957 communal elections, the Socialists and Catholics sought through the trade unions and political clubs to endorse candidates they regarded as sympathetic. The naïve illusions of this political paternalism were quickly deflated, however; the left Socialist weekly *La Gauche* sadly noted on December 21, 1957, "The news is now well confirmed to us, cruel and unmitigated; we were beaten in the Leopoldville consultations." In Katanga, Rubbens remarked on the numerous comments by Africans that they might have supported one of the informal lists put together by the European unions or parties if a member of their tribe had been included.[5] The effort of Belgian parties to create Congolese prolongations had in fact the opposite effect of that intended; instead of Europeans using Congolese, the Congolese played upon the newly revealed European divisions to weaken the hitherto invincible juggernaut. This result was predictable, but political partisanship in Belgium is strong. Once it became clear that the Congo was edging toward a new status, party leaders in all three camps inevitably felt a sense of paternal obligation to save the Congolese from the perdition which lurked in the platforms of the other parties.

FLEMISH NATIONALISM AND THE CONGO

The intrusion of the Flemish language issue provoked a different reaction from the Congolese; in this argument, he had a clear stake in preserving French as the dominant European language in the Congo. The issue posed the question as to whom the Congo was for; if it was essentially a Belgian entity, then there could be no argument against application of the Belgian bilingual requirements. But if the Congo was being administered in the interests of the Con-

[5] Rubbens, "La consultation populaire . . . à Elisabethville," *Problèmes Sociaux Congolais,* No. 42, pp. 78-79.

golese, then there could be no argument for the requirement of a European language without international currency.

This issue simmered from World War II on. The impo-
sition of the Flemish language never represented anything
close to a majority desire within the colonial establishment,
but the linguistic question is a politically dangerous one in
Belgium, and officialdom had to tread softly to avoid openly
antagonizing Flemish opinion in Belgium. Some measures
for improving the status of Flemish in the Congo were
taken by the Flemish André Dequae, who served as Colonial Minister from 1950 to 1954. When the State University of Elisabethville was founded in 1956, a costly special
Flemish section was set up for two, then one student. In
1957, heated debates took place in the *Conseil du Gouvernement* and provincial councils over the language policy in
secondary schools. Congolese delegates expressed themselves with great feeling on the question, as reflected in the
following intervention by future Leopoldville provincial
President Gaston Diomi:

"We see no valid reason for the study of a second language;
to impose a knowledge of Flemish, while it is not in the interest of the Congolese, would be pure colonialism. . . . I
feel, in a word, that imposing knowledge of Flemish on the
natives is equivalent to seeking one day to exclude from the
administration those Congolese who do not speak Flemish.
If by any chance we are obligated to study Flemish . . . we
will demand that all the functionaries speak our four native
languages, that all administrative documents be translated
in the four languages, and that we are addressed in our own
language in offices."[6]

Brussels–Leopoldville Tensions

Relations between Brussels and Leopoldville (and Boma

[6] From the *Conseil du Gouvernement* session of December 21,
1957, quoted in *La Voix du Congolais*, No. 143, (February 1958),
p. 103.

before it) had been a source of continued tension since the days of the Free State. When forceful ministers served at Place Royale (Colonial Ministry), the center of decision-making gravity clearly lay in Belgium, as under Jules Renkin (1908-1918) and Louis Franck (1918-1924). During periods of repeated political crisis in Belgium, the role of the Governor-General tended inevitably to grow; between 1924 and 1932, for example, ten Ministers passed through Place Royale, and during World War II the Congo was obviously under very little real control from the London exile government. Never, however, did the problem acquire the dimensions of the 1954-1960 period. There was constant hostility between Buisseret and Petillon. Buisseret sought to create a network of persons loyal to him, beginning with a powerful ministerial cabinet and extending through the colonial administration.[7]

There was a brief lull in the conflict from July to November in 1958, when the minority PSC government experimented with a "technican" Minister in the person of former Governor-General Petillon. This formula, however, proved not to be viable. Petillon failed to seize two major occasions to announce a new policy which might have captured the imagination, and his aloof behavior as "King's Minister" offended his political colleagues in the Council of Ministers.[8]

[7] There is an inexhaustible reservoir of *petites histoires* which reflect the serious tensions between Buisseret and Petillon. For some examples, see Marres and De Vos, *op. cit.*, pp. 10-16, 203-04; Van Bilsen, *Vers l'indépendance*, pp. 117-26. Brausch cites one typical example: in 1955, Leopoldville refused permission for future foreign Minister Justin Bomboko to go to Belgium for university study, because he proposed to enroll in the anti-clerical stronghold *Université Libre de Bruxelles;* Buisseret, eager to see Congolese students at ULB as well as Louvain, gave a categorical order requiring exit permission for Bomboko. *Belgian Administration in the Congo*, p. 54.

[8] Petillon might have used either the moment of the governmental declaration at the time of the investiture in July 1958 or more likely the ceremonies marking the 50th anniversary of Belgian rule in the Congo on October 18. This apparently had been his first intention; however, a visit to the Congo in August 1958 was a severe shock, as the deterioration in the political atmosphere during the short time

When the PSC found it necessary to enlarge the government by inviting the Liberals into coalition, Petillon was replaced by a PSC political figure, Maurice Van Hemelrijck, fresh from having settled the "schools war."[9]

The year 1959 was marked by several further incidents; an example was the colonial administration's reluctance to liberate three Abako leaders—Kasavubu, Daniel Kanza, and Simon Nzeza—imprisoned after the Leopoldville riots. The Minister came to the Congo himself and secretly arranged for their release and transport to Belgium.[10] As the year wore on, the Congolese leadership progressively lost interest in discussion with the administration and sought to negotiate directly with metropolitan officials. Similarly, the deepening crisis led Belgian authorities to short-circuit the traditional decision-making processes, and the administration was to a growing extent a passive spectator in a dialogue between Brussels and the emerging nationalist leadership.[11]

Dissolution of the Colonial Trinity

Not only was the colonial power structure threatened by the transplanting of Belgian party activity and metropolitan cleavages but its monolithic structure in the Congo itself began to break apart. The triple entente of state-

---

since his departure was striking. The *Groupe de Travail*, which originally would have been simply a drafting group, was then ordered to visit the Congo and hear testimony, which delayed its final report until December 24, 1958.

[9] The "schools war" was the metropolitan dimension of the bitter dispute over state v. church schools, whose Congolese repercussions were discussed earlier. Baldly stated, the conflict centered on the extent of use of public funds to assist Catholic schools. The solution found by Van Hemelrijck was through assuring adequate state support for both church and state school systems.

[10] *Congo 1959*, pp. 100-01.

[11] This point is well made by Prof. Jean Stengers of ULB, "Notre nouvelle politique congolaise," *Le Flambeau*, 42d yr., No. 7-8 (September-October 1959), pp. 453-76; No. 9-10, (November-December 1959), pp. 637-61.

TABLE 5

BRUSSELS AND LEOPOLDVILLE SINCE WORLD WAR II

	Colonial Minister	Party	Governor General	Party[a]
'45	Baron Albert de Vleeschauwer	PSC	Pierre Ryckmans	Catholic
	Edgard de Bruyne	PSC		
	Robert Godding	Liberal		
'46	Lode Graeybeck	PSB	Eugène Jungers	non-party
	Robert Godding	Liberal		
'47	Pierre Wigny	PSC		
'48				
'49				
'50	André Dequae	PSC		
'51				
'52			Léon Petillon	Catholic
'53				
'54	Auguste Buisseret	Liberal		
'55				
'56				
'57				
'58	Léon Petillon	Catholic	Henri Cornélis	Socialist
	Maurice Van Hemelrijck	PSC		
'59	Auguste De Schrijver	PSC		
'60	(Raymond Scheyven—Economic Affairs, Congo; PSC W. J. Ganshof van der Meersch—Resident Minister; Liberal)			

[a] Governor-Generals are not named on a party label, but all have been clearly identified with Catholic milieux, although not in a narrowly partisan sense (except Cornélis).

Church-capital was first deserted by its moral dimension, the missions. The Vatican was well aware of the dangers for the permanence of Christian communities in Africa if they remained identified with a moribund colonial system. The Church was rethinking its future, not only adapting its alliance with the colonial regime but accelerating the Africanization of its personnel and liturgy. And those in touch with the seminaries in the Congo knew that national sentiment was strong among the African clergy.

In June 1956, the Bishops of the Congo drew up an important declaration which placed the Church on the side of emancipation:

"All the inhabitants of a country have the duty to collaborate actively for the common good. They have therefore the right to take part in the conduct of public affairs.

"The trustee nation is obliged to respect this right, and to favor its exercise by progressive political education.

" . . . It is not for the Church to pronounce on the precise form in which a people's emancipation may come. She considers this legitimate so long as it is accomplished in charity and the respect of mutual rights."[12]

A number of distinguished Church leaders such as Van Wing of the Jesuits and Mosmans of the Pères Blancs were more outspoken. The latter wrote in early 1956 that the movement of ideas should be clear to all; independence was coming, and the time was past when political evolution could be harmoniously guided by Belgium. He added, in a particularly cogent analysis:

"The aspirations of the African will provoke, sooner or later, frictions with the established authorities, for despite all the loyalty and good will on both sides, the interests are too divergent to be harmonized without friction. The Church must remain above these oppositions. Accordingly, the formula of collaboration, which has been faithfully followed until now, runs the risk of making the Church appear entirely linked with the government. If it were thus, the Church would be held co-responsible for the inevitable errors of tactics, the delays, the blunders, in short for all the elements, often imponderable, which wound the Congolese in the most intimate way. . . . The independence of the Church must therefore be clearly affirmed."[13]

The precise role of the economic partner in the colonial alliance, the large companies, is obviously far more difficult to be certain about. What is perhaps most striking is the failure of the colonial corporations to oppose more actively

[12] Quoted in Slade, The Belgian Congo, p. 33.
[13] Reprinted in Guy Mosmans, L'Eglise à l'heure de l'Afrique (Tournai, Belgium: Castleman, 1961), p. 24.

the sudden acceleration of the decolonization process implied in the twin declarations of January 13, 1959. Hitherto, the companies had been well represented in the colonial councils through the application of the interest principle of representation. While never in the forefront of reform pressures, the large companies had on the other hand never been involved in the more extreme demands of the settler milieux. Their stake in the Congo was much too large for their behavior to be governed by short-term perspectives.

Stengers advances two interesting and persuasive hypotheses concerning the role of the colonial companies. In the first place, they had no alternative policy to purpose. It was clear to all that the status quo was untenable and that uncertainty could be removed only by some solution which could have the support of African leadership and opinion. Secondly, a sudden change in the traditional decision-making procedures caught the companies unawares. Until 1958 the fashioning of colonial policy was a slow procedure. The companies were well represented on various consultative organs and benefitted from a network of influence both in Leopoldville and Brussels established through the judicious distribution of places on boards of directors and the whole gamut of complex economic and social interactions which constitute influence. The fateful decisions involved in the promise of independence after the Leopoldville riots, however, were made by a very small group. Petillon, Van Hemelrijck, De Schrijver, and a handful of others took the step; Baudouin covered it with his prestige, and the companies were virtually silent.[14]

[14] Stengers, "Notre nouvelle politique congolaise," *loc. cit.* See the noncommittal attitude of Paul Gillet, governor of the *Société Générale*, before the general assembly of stockholders, February 24, 1959, reprinted in *Congo 1959*, pp. 54-55. In the same collection, there is a forthright statement in support of the policy from the head of *Cominière*, another large holding company with Congo interests, who warns employees that henceforward their efficiency ratings will give greater weight to their relationships with African employees. *Ibid.*, pp. 55-56.

Thereafter, the companies tried to adapt themselves to the tempestuous pace of events by a number of protective devices: economic guarantees, Belgian or Congolese, were sought; contributions were made to nearly all Congolese political parties, and Congolese politicians were courted assiduously; the organization of an "Economic Round-Table" in April-May 1960 was supported. The Eyskens government created a new post of Minister of Congo Economic Affairs in November 1959 to help soothe corporate uneasiness; Raymond Scheyven, respected by the business community despite his occasionally unorthodox views,[15] was named to fill the post. But these were helpless reactions to a situation which the corporations could no longer play a major role in controlling.

Deterioration of Administration Control

In the face of this deterioration of colonial solidarity, the sudden explosion of leaderless violence in Leopoldville on January 4 through 6, 1959, came as a virtual death knell for the system. The hour of demoralization had sounded for the Belgian governing elite in the Congo, which was fast losing confidence in its mission and right to rule. The indecision with which the administration reacted to the riots, first in hesitating to take firm action to restore order and second in failing to apply resolutely the decolonization policy set forth by the January 13 declarations, was symptomatic of the decay of the system. Although the January 13 declaration itself had been long promised, it is virtually certain that the explicit promise of independence would not have been included had it not been for the riots.[16] The adminis-

---

[15] For example, Raymond Scheyven, whose brother Louis Scheyven serves as Belgian Ambassador in Washington, returned from a long tour of Latin America in September 1961 with a highly favorable assessment of the Cuban Revolution.

[16] *Congo 1959*, pp. 35-36; Stengers, "Notre nouvelle politique congolais," *loc. cit.*, p. 457.

tration's reaction was to try to make the Abako leaders the scapegoats. Thousands of unemployed persons were expelled from Leopoldville, which had the ironic effect of politicizing the back country without reducing nationalist sentiment in the capital.

Beginning in mid-1959, a new dimension to the situation emerged; the administration progressively lost control of the critical area between Leopoldville and Matadi. A confidential report of acting Governor-General Schoeller, after a trip through the area, warned of the dramatic deterioration of the situation: "All the persons encountered agreed unanimously that, on a political level, contact with the population had become impossible. Directives, advice, efforts at persuasion, attempts at a dialogue, everything which comes from the administration, from Europeans in general or Congolese considered to be collaborators of the whites, is rejected without discussion."[17]

The administration was shocked to find how helpless it was before a mass movement of this nature. As Scholler's report pointed out, the passive resistance was so widespread that a major military operation would be necessary to deal with it by force. Few of the Europeans living in the interior were partisans of such a solution. In the months that followed, although nowhere was the deterioration of authority so complete as in the Bas-Congo, similar phenomena were noted in Kwilu, large parts of Orientale, and Maniema. At the same time, the Lulua-Baluba dispute in the Kasai had reached proportions where an administration-backed mediation effort resulted in the radical proposal (although modest in the light of what subsequently happened) to repatriate 80,000 Baluba from Lulua lands within a month.[18] Governor Bomans of Leopoldville province spoke for a

[17] *Congo 1959*, pp. 128-35.
[18] Convention of Lake Mukamba, negotiated by the Rae arbitration mission, December-January, 1959-1960, *Congo 1960*, I, 188-92.

153

large part of the administration when, in a letter to the Governor-General coincident with the beginning of the Round Table Conference, he urged:

"Disavowed several times, the territorial personnel has lost confidence and will not act unless it has the certainty that its action will be supported by the Belgian government.

"It is not too late to reestablish this confidence, but for that, the Belgian government must define clearly its position and the policy it desires to see applied.

"We cannot continue to live in this indecision which is at the base of the deterioration of the situation throughout the country."[19]

The Alternative of Force

Thus, as 1960 approached Belgian strategy was becoming oriented toward salvaging whatever agreement could be made with the Congolese leaders. The administration could not simply ignore the anarchic conditions developing in key regions. A policy of "firmness" implied the willingness to embark upon an adventure which might be prolonged and which might have created a unified nationalist front—something which did not yet exist. Further, to be seriously carried out, the policy implied not only the will to tolerate the torrent of international abuse which would have rained down but the readiness, in the last resort, to use Belgian troops.

Article 1 of the Belgian constitution includes a clause stipulating that "Belgian troops destined for the defense (of colonies) could only be volunteers." In 1953, Belgian military bases were established at Kamina in Katanga, and Kitona and Banana in the Bas-Congo; provision was made by a law of July 29, 1953, for the Governor-General to requisition the Belgian troops from these bases in case of serious disorders. On August 12, 1958, the Defense Ministry submitted to the *Conseil d'Etat* (*in tempore non suspecto*)

[19] *Ibid.*, pp. 136-37.

a proposed executive order establishing that any member of the armed forces could be assigned to the metropolitan bases, whether or not a volunteer. The following January, the *Conseil d'Etat* rendered its opinion that this would be compatible with the constitution and specified that these troops would be liable to requisition.[20] As 1959 wore on, a campaign of major proportions against any scheme to send European conscripts to the Congo developed in Belgium. The *FGTB* in November announced that it would "oppose by all means in its power" the dispatch of any soldiers to the Congo. The same day, Collard, a PSB leader in the Lower House, interpellated Defense Minister A. Gilson on his ministry's proposal, declaring: "Belgium could not support the weight of such a policy, engaging . . . at once its money and its sons . . . and even if it could, no matter what the class of the population, no matter what their political opinions, you may be certain that they want no part of a policy of that nature, that the Congo would not tolerate it either, and that it would be the final end of any hope of a peaceful solution."[21] According to Congo Economic Minister Scheyven, the government knew that it would receive no support from the United States or other NATO allies, that it would be condemned by the UN; Belgium was too small a country, too lacking in an imperial will to withstand this kind of pressure.[22]

In Search of Negotiations

The final step in the erosion of the system came with the formula accepted for the decisive negotiations on independence at Brussels in January 1960. The January 13 declarations had been based upon the assumption that Belgium would create the necessary structures of a Congolese state to which it could grant independence. Minister Van Hemelrijck then toured the Congo, contacting "all who could be

[20] *Congo 1959*, p. 273.
[21] *Ibid.*, pp. 274-75.
[22] Interview, Brussels, October 4, 1961.

considered as public opinion in the Congo of today." He added: "I have seen all the burgomasters and their councilors, I have seen the chiefs and the elders, I have seen delegations from the interior and the leaders of all the political movements, recognized, non-recognized, in formation or in process of dissolution. I have seen the most valid spokesmen of the ethnic groups, the leaders of cultural associations, associations of African employees, large family associations, mulatto associations, *immatriculé* organizations, veterans. . . ."[23]

There was, indeed, a very real problem of whom to consult at this stage. Even the Abako was not well organized outside Leopoldville until after the January riots, and other political movements were still clusters of intellectuals. For a legally inclined nation such as Belgium, it thus seemed entirely reasonable to require elections first, from whence Congolese spokesmen with a juridical mandate could emerge. However, this was suspected by the Congolese as being a scheme to arrange for the election of "stooge" leaders. Doucy's analysis of this phenomenon at the end of 1958 is pertinent; he observes:

"These political coteries include only a very small number of real participants. It is impossible to reply affirmatively or negatively to the question as to whether these political leaders represent effectively Congolese public opinion. One must avoid the mistake of facilitating the dialogue by considering as representative only six or seven particularly active groups. But one must also avoid considering that these men represent only themselves. The ideas they defend have a sociological significance; they are perhaps those of which the African mass dream, without having either the occasion or the means to externalize them."[24]

[23] Georges H. Dumont, *La Table Ronde Belgo-Congolaise* (Paris: Editions Universitaires, 1961), p. 9. Dumont was in Van Hemelrijck's cabinet.
[24] Doucy, *L'avenir politique du Congo Belge,* p. 60.

As seen by the Belgian administration, the dilemma in seeking a dialogue lay precisely in the situation analyzed by Doucy. Until nearly the end of 1959, there was still room for wishful thinking on the nature of emerging Congolese leadership; indeed, it was not until the May 1960 elections that militance was conclusively proven to embody the mood of the bulk of the population. The administration pursued the contradictory goals of seeking to strengthen persons it deemed moderate by investing them with the presumed prestige of recognition as an *interlocateur valable*. The nationalist audience was in most areas still potential rather than actual; the administration feared that granting too prominent a place in the dialogue to leaders most hostile to the colonial structure would simply facilitate nationalist expansion. Yet this approach backfired in three ways. First, nationalist leaders were probably helped more than harmed in the eyes of their followers by administration suspicion of them; colonial reticence to hear their grievances provided a useful mobilizational argument. Second, the recurrent administration tactic of bringing into the dialogue, as Congolese "spokesmen," persons felt by many Africans to be "soft on colonialism" redoubled suspicion of Belgian motives at a moment when a climate of confidence was a vital necessity. In the third place, the complicated maneuvers involved in this negotiating strategy meant that precious time was lost, that nationalist positions steadily hardened while the colonial structure slowly fell to pieces.

Another fateful episode was the resignation of Congo Minister Van Hemelrijck on September 2, 1959, in circumstances which led many Congolese to believe that his decolonization policies were being repudiated. The Minister by mid-1959 was in an extraordinarily difficult situation. On the one hand, he felt caught in the middle of the African nationalist debate over federal versus unitary structures, and was unable to meet the demands of all militant nationalist groups for a precise timetable for independence. On

157

the other side, he encountered growing hostility in various European quarters. He was splattered with tomatoes by Kivu settlers during a Bukavu visit in June 1959; an abortive plot for secession and proclamation of a settler dominated state in the eastern Congo was hatching in Kivu circles at this time.[25] Much of the colonial administration was in sullen disaccord with his policies.[26] The Socialist opposition gave him little respite. The final blow came when in late August it became clear that the Council of Ministers itself was unwilling to support his efforts to come to terms with Congolese nationalism. De Schrijver, his successor, in fact carried on virtually the same policies; however, his task was complicated by the initial suspicions he faced in negotiating with Congolese leadership. The MNC/L spoke for a wide spectrum of Congolese nationalist opinion in concluding that the Van Hemelrijck resignation "proved that the vague promise of independence contained in the January 13 government declaration is nothing other than an instrument of propaganda."[27]

At this point, the Belgian formula was for elections in December to choose territorial and urban communal councils, and to constitute thereby electoral colleges for the pro-

[25] See the illuminating account of this plot by one of its organizers in Dugauquier, Congo Cauldron, pp. 127-35. Contacts were established with settler milieux in Katanga and Orientale provinces; the plan was to arrest the colonial governors, win the support of the traditional chiefs, and proclaim independence. Arms were secretly collected in Bukavu, but the movement collapsed ignominiously when it became clear that only a fraction of the European community was prepared to join.

[26] The letters of André Ryckmans give valuable insight into the psychology of this period within the ranks of the administration. J. K., André Ryckmans, pp. 225-37.

[27] The incident of the dispatch of d'Aspremont Lynden to the Congo behind Van Hemelrijck's back was described in Chapter III, and Congo 1959, pp. 188-190. Symptomatic of the chasm of mistrust separating the colonizer and nationalist leadership in the latter part of 1959 were the careful plans made by the Abako-PSA-MNC/K Cartel to lay the groundwork for a government-in-exile. Herbert Weiss and Benoit Verhaegen, Parti Solidaire Africain (P.S.A.) (Brussels: CRISP, 1963), pp. 157-58.

vincial councils, which would select in their turn the national assembly. However, the militant nationalist wing, led by the Abako, the PSA, MNC/L and MNC/K, announced its refusal to participate in unilaterally organized elections. Beginning in May 1959, Congolese proposals emerged for direct negotiations by de facto leadership, in the form of a round table. The Kalonji wing of the MNC, in an Elisabethville congress on November 1, elaborated on the round table idea, suggesting that it be held in Brussels and have as participants the three Belgian parliamentary parties and the leading Congolese parties.[28] De Schrijver announced on November 3 a *colloque général* for Leopold-ville the last ten days of November, including Congolese and Belgian parties. The PSB riposted two days later proposing that the Belgian Parliament itself organize a round table in Brussels.[29]

On November 26, De Schrijver edged closer to the Brussels Round Table notion in suggesting *une grande conférence* in either Brussels or Leopoldville or both. The "Cartel" Abako-PSA-MNC/K[30] demanded that the Round Table be convened before the elections; Belgium felt it could not back down on the election schedule. Although MNC/K did not dare leave the field clear to the Lulua at Luluabourg and defected from the boycott, the Abako and PSA abstention orders were strictly followed in the Bas-Congo and Kwilu. The government was at this point caught between the PSB domestically and the Cartel in the Congo, which had demonstrated its capacity to block the implementation of any policy of which it disapproved. De Schrijver finally capitulated and on December 15 told Parliament:

"A conference, called a Round Table—I accept this expres-

[28] *Congo 1959*, pp. 239-40.
[29] Dumont, *op. cit.*, p. 15.
[30] The Cartel of federalist parties originated in an agreement between the Abako and PSA at the end of June 1959 to form a united front against the colonial administration. In November, the Cartel was enlarged by the adhesion of MNC/K and the smaller *Parti du Peuple*.

sion, no matter how romantic it may be and even if it evokes King Arthur—will have to take place in mid-January to hasten the installation of political structures in the Congo....

"M. Collard has posed questions to me on the subject of the Round Table. On the Belgian side, I have already explained that the deputies will attend this conference as the representatives of the Belgian people....

"I have never said that [the Congolese participants] had to be communal or territorial councilors. When I spoke of valid representatives, that meant that they had to be spokesmen of parties recognized as important. At the same time, the Minister stated that independence would be achieved in 1960."[31]

However, "independence" as envisaged by De Schrijver at this juncture still presumed continued Belgian sovereignty in several key policy fields (defense, foreign affairs, currency, and telecommunications).[32]

On January 19, 1960, the eve of the Round Table Conference, to the astonishment of the Belgian delegation the Congolese representatives announced the establishment of a *front commun*. These extraordinary negotiations thus opened with the Congo's yet fragmentary political movements having joined themselves into a single negotiation unit, across the table from a very divided Belgian Parliament. Not only had the colonial administration been completely excluded but the Belgian government had been placed in the humiliating position of having the negotiations in good part carried on by the Parliament. History offers no parallel for this formula of negotiating a decolonization agreement.

Was there any alternative to immediate Congo independ-

[31] *Congo 1959,* pp. 256-58.

[32] This problem of divergent Belgian and Congolese perception of the meaning of "independence" is dealt with in more detail in the following chapter. See the important decisions of the Council of Ministers meeting October 7, 1959, reproduced in *Congo 1959,* pp. 190-91; see also Dumont, *op. cit.,* p. 57.

ence at the end of 1959? This question will long be debated by historians. The object of this analysis has been to show that the policy choices open to Belgium by the time of the Round Table were very narrow. Had there been a single nationalist movement in the Congo which could have spoken authoritatively for the entire population, then there might have been some way to achieve agreement with appropriate guarantees to both sides on a phased power transfer over four or five years. But with militant nationalism fragmented, no single movement could bear the stigma of accepting a compromise which would leave it exposed to attack from its rivals. Short-lived accords among Congolese political movements, such as the *front commun* at the Brussels Round Table, were possible for militant goals, but not for moderate ones. A negotiated delay, then, was virtually out of the question. Could Belgium have imposed a longer transition period, perhaps by setting a terminal date with a solemn proclamation by Parliament? Given the profound distrust of Belgian intentions by militant nationalist parties, it is hardly conceivable that cooperation would have been available. Without nationalist cooperation, the dreary cycle of repression and mutual bitterness would have inevitably followed; delay would have lost its purpose. If this reasoning is correct, the Belgian decision on January 27, 1960, to accept June 30 as the date of independence was not cowardice or stupidity, as has often been suggested; if errors there were, these were made long before the Brussels Round Table. They were to be found in the smug complacence of the early postwar years in the invulnerability of the colonial mechanism. But self-confidence had been sapped by a crescendo of internal conflicts and the end of the era of record-breaking economic advance. And when the belated challenge from the long-docile subject finally came, the ruler was too demoralized to offer real resistance. The colonial power structure was in fact too far decomposed to organize gracefully its own demise.

CHAPTER VIII

░░░

A Structure for Independence

░░░

The Belgian Plan

THE final phase of decolonization began with Petillon's announcement before the Senate on July 10, 1958, that he intended to make as soon as possible, "a declaration on the problems of the administrative and political evolution of the Congo." To prepare the ground for this, a *Groupe de Travail* (Working Group) was designated, nominally headed by Pierre Ryckmans, who was replaced after he fell fatally ill by Petillon himself (after his removal as Colonial Minister). This preparatory commission included seven other members: three (De Schrijver, PSC; Buisseret, Liberal; Housiaux, PSB) represented the major parties in Parliament; one (Macquet) the *Conseil Colonial;* one (Van den Abeele) the Colonial Ministry; and two (Forgeur and Stenmans) the colonial administration. Petillon clearly had a blueprint in mind; the function of the Working Group was to win endorsement and sponsorship for the Petillon decolonization scheme. After spending three weeks in the Congo, hearing 212 African and 250 European witnesses, a report was drafted which contained the Belgian master-plan for structuring the Congo state. Ten days after the report was submitted, the Leopoldville riots transformed the situation, and the resulting government declaration of January 13 announced the proposals in an atmosphere of crisis.

During the eighteen-month surge to independence which followed, one may observe a dialectic interaction between radically opposed European and African conceptions of the guiding postulates of decolonization. However, under the twin impact of the progressive decomposition of the colonial mechanism and the profound suspicion of Belgian promises which a decade of disappointment and frustration had instilled in the Congolese leadership, the Belgian position was steadily eroded, and the outcome gave nearly complete satisfaction to African demands.

To recapitulate Belgian premises at the beginning of 1959, one may first recall that autonomy was to be granted to institutions created by Belgium in the final stage of the legitimate exercise of its sovereign colonial mandate. The Congo had been created by Belgium as an administrative entity; the task was now to be completed by giving it an organic political structure. In the words of the Working Group, "Belgium proposes to establish in the Belgian Congo an autonomous state, benefitting from a democratic regime, with respect for the rights of men and African values."[1] This did not mean that the views of the inhabitants would not be taken into account; "No measure engaging the future will be taken without consultation," the Working Group pledged.[2] But after consultation, Belgium intended to take the decision itself; "negotiations" were not proposed.

Although universal suffrage was accepted by the Working Group as a necessary legitimating principle for local institutions, the provincial and national institutions were to emerge from the local bodies via indirect elections. The inchoate nature of Congolese opinion created very real problems, as illustrated by the disparate list of persons Van Hemelrijck found it necessary to consult in early 1959 in his effort to win over "all who could be considered as public opinion leaders in the Congo of today";[3] it goes without saying, however, that the colonial administration had itself created this problem by refusing to extend basic political liberties to the African population until 1959.

It was assumed that these institutions would have some time to function under Belgian tutelage before the final decisions were made as to the future relations of Belgium and

[1] *Rapport du Groupe de Travail*, p. 27.
[2] *Ibid.*, p. 28.
[3] Supra, p. 156.

the Congo. Although paritarism as a formal principle was gone, it was presumed that there would be significant European participation in the political institutions, both through the retention of interest representation in the legislative assemblies and also directly through the electoral machinery.[4]

Finally, evolution had to proceed at the pace of some hypothetical common denominator for the country as a whole. The politically volatile areas, by this Cartesian formula, would have to wait for the more tranquil areas to catch up with them. Reforms had to be applied at the same pace to the docile reaches of Equateur as to the boiling Bas-Congo region.[5]

The African Reaction

The intrusion of nationalist claims into the dialectic was entirely new. As has been emphasized, policy-making had consisted of a series of compromises within the colonial establishment between statesmanlike spokesmen for paternal progress and intransigent defenders of colonial privilege. But now an African dimension entered, with an almost diametrically opposed vision of decolonization. Through this thought ran a constant motif of suspicion, a fear of being tricked just once again by an "indépendance-fiction". André Ryckmans summarised this psychology in writing of the re-

[4] *Rapport du Groupe de Travail*, pp. 17, 22-23, 27, 50-52, 61-62, 65. The paritary demands from European circles were far from silenced at the beginning of 1959. Fedacol, in its commentary on the government declaration on January 17 stressed its demand that "the principles of paritory representation, solemnly affirmed by Minister Petillon while he was Governor General, not be abandoned." *Congo 1959*, pp. 59-60.

[5] Any large African territory is likely to have different levels of politicization, with nationalist demands more intensely advanced in some regions than in others. In Nigeria, for example, the southern regions were responsible for most of the nationalist pressure; the politically less volatile North played a somewhat similar role in braking political evolution while it "caught up." However, the less systematic British tradition made possible the grant of self-government to the eastern and western regions while awaiting northern readiness for power transfer.

action to the governmental declaration: "For the Africans, the text is so confused that no one has understood it—or rather, all have thought they understood one thing for certain: that this obscurity concealed numerous snares, numerous escape clauses, a new policy of deception."[6]

African opinion required that the terms of decolonization be negotiated between the Congolese leadership and Belgium. The authors of the *Conscience Africaine* manifesto had declared in 1956, "We demand in the most explicit terms to be directly involved in the elaboration of the 30-year plan now under discussion. Without this participation, such a plan could not have our consent."[7] The embryonic group of intellectuals which became the *MNC* denounced the absence of African members on the Working Group, and averred that its conclusions were in advance suspect in their eyes.[8] This view was advanced with growing firmness in 1959, culminating in the refusal of the Abako Cartel to take part in the December 1959 elections.

Finally, this idea led to the demand for a provisional Congolese government which would itself organize Congolese institutions. The germ of this viewpoint can be first seen in the 1956 Abako response to the *Conscience Africaine* manifesto, where the notion of a 30-year plan is rejected in favor of immediate "emancipation."[9] The demand for "immediate independence" under the aegis of a "provisional government" became one of Kasavubu's principal themes; it was spelled out at a press conference in December 1959:

"This system [the blueprint of the Belgians] tends to give to the Congolese a Belgian independence and not an African independence. This *jeu de dupes* puts the Congo leadership in difficulty. Remember, when colonialism is in

[6] J. K., *André Ryckmans*, p. 226.
[7] *Congo 1959*, p. 14.
[8] *Ibid.*, p. 27
[9] *ABAKO 1950-1960*, pp. 37-44.

power . . . it can't permit parties to develop freely; and these parties can only develop the day when we have independence in our own hands. What will happen tomorrow, after these elections [of December 1959] which are not ours? The country will not accept institutions imposed upon it from outside. . . .

"We need independence immediately with a provisional government in each province and a federal government on the Swiss model. Then, under the protection of governments which will really emanate from the people, free elections can be held to set up a Congolese constituent assembly, and not an assembly *à la sauce belge*."[10]

Implementing the Groupe de Travail Blueprint

In summary, the decolonization plan proposed by the January 13 governmental declaration foresaw two initial steps. Firstly, it was promised that in March 1959, the *Conseil Colonial* would be enlarged by twelve members coming from the Congo, with one European and one African to be nominated by each of the provincial councils. The group was to be renamed the *Conseil de Législation* and would be considered an embryonic upper chamber. Secondly, the *Conseil du Gouvernement* and provincial councils would at the same time elect "consultative councils" from their membership to advise the governors on the exercise of their executive functions. By the end of 1959, the primary level institutions would be created by general elections for urban communal councils and territorial councils. These would constitute an electoral college for the establishment of provincial councils, promised for March 1960.

In fact, this scheme, illustrated in Table 6, was full of curious silences and contradictions. In the first place, no mention was made of a Congolese government; the proposed institutions merely offered greater checks upon the administration. Secondly, the attributes of the embryonic legisla-

10 *Ibid.*, pp. 272-75.

tive bodies were extremely vague. The *Conseil de Légis-lation* was presumably to have the same functions as the *Conseil Colonial,* but the very limited authority of this body has been described earlier.[11] Further, although there was to be at least an indirectly elected majority on the provincial councils and General (ex-Government) Council, the declaration made no allusion to the *Conseil de Législation;* apparently, the option of a nominated administration majority was being kept open. The two chambers were eventually to have jointly "the legislative competence . . . that the law would progressively recognize in them,"[12] but no timetable for any enlargement over the restricted existing powers was mentioned, nor was any date fixed for the constitution of the General Council as an indirectly elected body.[13]

The first concrete step was the election of the Consultative Council to monitor the executive actions of the Governor-General; this was done by the *Conseil du Gouvernement* on March 1, 1959. Four of the six elected were Congolese: André-Marie Edindali, born 1908, Orientale, later PNP[14] National Vice-President; S. Mudingayi, born 1912, Kasai, later a PNP Vice-President; Chief Omari Pene Misenga, Kivu, later associated with *Alliance Rurale Progressiste* (moderate, chief-led party); and A. Lopes, born 1921, Orientale, later a PNP National Vice-President.

The psychological impact of these designations was what might be expected. The Congo's worst fears seemed to be realized; no representation from the Lower Congo was included, and all four representatives were clearly marked, rightly or wrongly, as men from an older generation and sympathetic to the administration. They were, in fact, rep-

[11] Supra, pp. 24-26.
[12] *Congo 1959,* p. 47.
[13] See the interesting analysis of the Government Declaration made by Van Bilsen in *L'indépendance du Congo* (Tournai, Belgium: Casterman, 1961), pp. 59-64.
[14] *Parti National du Progrès,* a loosely-structured, moderate party which enjoyed the sympathy of the colonial administration.

TABLE 6

PLAN FOR NEW INSTITUTIONS, GOVERNMENTAL DECLARATION,
JANUARY 13, 1959

Chief of State		King			
					12 by Prov. Council
	majority either by Prov. Councils or Terr./Comm. Councils plus minority by interests	Govt. Council (Chamber of reps.)	elects 2	Legis. Council (Senate)	2 by Govt. Council
Central					6 by Belg. Parl.
					8 by King (from Belg. Colonial personalities)
Province		Prov. Council		majority by indirect elections; minority by interest rep.	
(rural)		(*District: Administrative echelon only*)			(urban)
	Territorial Council	directly elected majority; minority by interest rep.		City Council	Indirectly elected majority; minority by interest rep.
	Circonscription Council	Directly elected majority; trad. elders ex officio		Communal Council	All directly elected
		VOTER			

resentative of Congolese membership on the *Conseil du Gouvernement,* and merely reinforced the impression that the new policy was an extension of the familiar technique of choosing only those acceptable to the colonial administration to "represent" Congolese viewpoints. Governor-General Cornélis undid some of the damage by adding E. Kini, a sector chief from near Tshela, Mayombe, and connected with the Abako.

The six Congolese representatives on the *Conseil de Législation,* selected shortly thereafter, included only Albert Kalonji of what were then the more militant nationalists.[15] Although the reformed Legislative Council opened a

[15] Four of the other five, Maximilien Liongo, Hubert Sangara, Mathieu Kalenda, and Jean-Baptiste Alves, had excellent credentials in

series of meetings on May 11, 1959, and did serve as a useful platform for Kalonji, its role was insignificant. The days of leisurely reforms put together over a ten-year-period were over; the functioning of both the Legislative Council and the Consultative Council became overshadowed by more momentous events, and both faded into the background.

The next step was to be the elections for urban communal and territorial councils. These were really the key to launching the new structures, since the principle of legitimation from the ground up had been made their cornerstone. A decree of October 13, 1959, reformed the 1957 *Statut des Villes*.[16] The elected territorial councils were to be an innovation.

An *Arrêté Royal* of January 22, 1957, had first established territorial councils as an experiment. In his 1956 address, Petillon had announced that these would constitute the basic rural echelon where European and African representation would interpenetrate.[17] The executive order left the specific composition up to local determination, requiring only that it should represent as adequately as possible local interests and populations. It was to be a consultative body, "an organ of collaboration and information between the administrators and administered."[18] By the end of 1957, these councils had been constituted, in general with European majorities. Information gathered from interviews indicates

---

terms of competence, and in fact have all occupied important positions since independence and rendered distinguished service to the country. The point here is that in terms of the psychology of early 1959, these nominations seemed to imply an intent by the administration to assure that no militant nationalists were to occupy positions in the new institutions.

[16] Supra, pp. 127.

[17] Conseil de Gouvernement, *Discours du Gouverneur General,* 1956, p. 17

[18] André Durieux, *Institutions politiques, administratives et judiciaires du Congo Belge et du Ruandi-Urundi,* (4th ed.; Brussels: Editions Bieleveld, 1957) p. 53.

169

that, with some exceptions, those powerless bodies were not taken very seriously, although they did meet occasionally. The experiment had been undertaken because of a feeling that there should be some echelon of representation between the local *circonscription* and the vast province. Further, the territory was the most active administrative level in the Congo: "it exercises a profound influence on the administered, white and black, and they both refer to it spontaneously for the solution to their problems."[19]

The reformed territorial councils, established by the decree of October 2, 1959, were to have two-thirds of their members elected by universal male suffrage and one-third named by the district commissioner from traditional elders and local interest groups. There was, however, a profound contradiction between the purely administrative character of the territory and the existence of an elected council attached to it. The territorial administrator was exclusively responsible to the bureaucratic hierarchy; he was therefore in no position really to "consult" a representative territorial council. The territory did not have a "civil personality"; it had no budget of its own, and levied no taxes. Just what these councils could have done, had there been time for them to function, is not clear. If they had taken their representative functions seriously, there could have been grave conflicts with the administration; and if they did not, they served little use. In any case, no sooner had they been established than the Brussels Round Table accepted the principle of universal suffrage for the provincial and central representative organs. Thus the one real function that the territorial councils might have had, that of an electoral college, was removed. In most of Leopoldville province, the December elections were effectively boycotted, and the territorial councils were never constituted.[20]

[19] *Rapport du Groupe de Travail,* pp. 54-55.
[20] An ordinance of December 26, 1959, provided that in areas where the elections had been blocked, the territorial councils as

The Brussels Round Table: A New Start

The Round Table Conference in January-February, 1960, produced a radically different decolonization plan; the December 1959 elections marked the end of the Belgian effort to proceed with their own formula. In accepting negotiations with the Congolese political parties, there could be no other outcome than a scrapping of the scheme outlined by the *Working Group* and the government declaration in favor of a project closely in line with the demands being made by nationalist movements. Even on the eve of the Round Table, Belgian and Congolese positions remained a substantial distance apart; but the extraordinary structure of the meeting, which gave to the parliamentary opposition party the role of arbiter between the Congolese and the Belgian government, meant a triumph across the board for the Congolese platform.

The first skirmish of the meeting took place on the opening day, as the Congolese *front commun* insisted on a clarification of the nature of the meeting. A campaign had been conducted for the two weeks preceding the meeting in the conservative French-language press—*Le Soir* (a Liberal paper reflecting business viewpoints) and *La Libre Belgique* (Catholic)—urging that the sessions be considered a simple exchange of views and arguing that, from a constitutional viewpoint, Parliament could not delegate its powers to a negotiating committee.[21] Two days before the conference De Schrijver specified that the Round Table would make recommendations upon which the government would draw in preparing new legislation, provided that they were compatible with the international obligations of Belgium and its moral duties to the Congolese. The Congolese felt

constituted under the 1957 regulations remained in function. Piron and Devos, *Codes et Lois,* II, 190.

[21] *Congo 1960,* I, 23. From a juridical point of view, the argument is correct; however, with the three major parties engaging themselves to defend in Parliament the solutions found, the distinction became unimportant.

that this promise was too vague; under the impetus of the Abako Cartel, the *front commun* established as a prerequisite for proceeding with the meeting guarantees that its decisions would be binding upon the participants. Kasavubu declared in the second session, "It is after we have determined the object of the meeting that we will know whether or not the conference can take place or not. . . . We are here *pour trancher toute la palabre*. . . . Belgium must no longer decide anything without our agreement."[22] The following day, Moise Tshombe demanded elucidation by De Schrijver on what international obligations or moral commitments Belgium might have which would affect the issues they were to negotiate.[23] Satisfaction was given by the Minister's promise that he would pose the question of confidence in defending whatever agreements were made and the parliamentary groups' agreement that their parties would guarantee to support the solutions.[24]

The next divergence arose over the procedure of the meeting. As outlined in the draft agenda submitted by De Schrijver, the first problem was to define the political structures to be established, then to find a way to put them in place, and finally to decide on the time-table. For the Congolese, however, the first necessity was to establish the date of independence, which had to be virtually immediate and total. After a weekend interlude and a flurry of excitement

[22] *Comptes rendus,* Conférence de la Table Ronde Politique, Brussels, session of January 21, 1960.

[23] *Congo 1960,* I, 25.

[24] Three days later, however, the issue was posed again by Kasavubu, who seemed to require that the Round Table be considered a Constituent Assembly and that powers be transferred immediately. His argument was that all that was immediately necessary was that the Colonial Charter be abrogated forthwith, and agreement be reached on the composition of a provisional government, which would then itself take charge of organizing elections in the Congo. Kasavubu's extreme position was not endorsed by the *front commun;* his walkout when he did not obtain satisfaction was joined by only part of his own Abako delegation. Daniel Kanza, then Abako Vice-President, remained at the sessions.

over the release of Lumumba,[25] the *front commun* demanded that the date of independence be fixed forthwith and proposed June 1. After some hesitation over the technical possibilities of creating a state by that date, Senator Rolin, PSB spokesman, suggested that the date should be set between June 1 and June 30. The *front commun* re-examined the question, and Jean Bolikango declared to the assembly on January 27: "I have the honor of announcing to you the conclusion reached by the *front commun*. . . . The date of independence will be June 30, 1960."[26]

The issue of immediate independence was thus settled; the precise content of "independence," however, was not. On the same day, De Schrijver gave a long introductory intervention, exposing the various problems of political construction. He proposed a bicameral legislature, which would sit as a constituent assembly; in the passages in which he described the functions of the legislature, it became clear there was still a considerable gap between the Belgian and Congolese understandings of independence:

"The first parliament will have as a first task, the exercise of normal legislative power, for beginning July 1, Belgian Parliament and executive will only intervene in exceptional circumstances. Its second task will be to draw up the Constitution. For this, it seems to me reasonable to foresee a maximum delay of two years. . . .

[25] Lumumba had been charged with inciting to rebellion in connection with the serious riots in Stanleyville, October 30-31, 1959; his trial was concluding as the Round Table began, and on January 22, he was sentenced to six months' imprisonment. At this point, after the verdict, the MNC/L delegation, with support from a number of others, made his release in order to attend the Round Table a condition of their continued participation. On January 25, De Schrijver announced he had been given temporary release, which became permanent.

[26] G. Dumont, *La Table Ronde*, p. 50. It will be recalled that De Schrijver had told Parliament on December 15, 1959, that Belgium was prepared to grant independence in 1960, although with some powers still reserved.

"In the meantime, the power of the two Chambers will be extremely broad, but will not yet cover all spheres. The Belgian government considers that the greatest number possible of its powers would be transferred to the Chambers and to the Congolese government."[27]

The next day the Cartel responded with a communiqué requiring that "the independence of the Congo, of which the date is irrevocably fixed, be complete, with no reservation of competences in favor of the former colonial authority."[28] Adoula cited the minutes of a Belgian cabinet meeting on October 7, 1959, which had been leaked; at this time, De Schrijver had told the Council of Ministers that the proposed Congolese chambers would have real power, but certain matters would be reserved to Belgium. Among these were foreign affairs, defense, telecommunication, finance, and transport.[29] In response to Adoula's remarks, De Schrijver observed, correctly, that the government position had considerably evolved since October; his position now seemed to be that foreign affairs, defense, and finance would have to remain in part Belgian responsibilities.[30]

Again, Senator Rolin made a decisive intervention; he indicated that Parliament had not been aware that the government intended to reserve to itself certain powers, and added: "Yesterday I compared independence to the handing over of the keys to the trousseau of the new Congolese house. In my opinion, Belgium must, on June 30, hand over all the keys and the Congolese will decide what use they will make of them. In foreign affairs, in finance, everywhere they will find Belgians to assume responsibility. It will be for the Congolese to decide if they wish to replace them, or if, for a certain time, they will retain them. A state does not lose its independence because it is willing to

[27] *Ibid.*, p. 57.
[28] *Ibid.*, p. 58.
[29] This remarkable document is reprinted in *Congo 1959*, pp. 190-91.
[30] *Congo 1960*, I, 31.

have certain services performed on its behalf by another state."[31]

At the next plenary session, after a fortnight interlude of commission work, De Schrijver resolved the question by announcing on behalf of the government that "the independence of the Congo means that the Congolese government and parliament will be in possession of all the powers."[32]

With the questions of independence decided, the Congolese *front commun* ceased operating as an effective caucus. On the specific questions of structure and implementation, there were in most cases divisions of opinion amongst the Congolese delegations. The other major issues dealt with by the Round Table were the nature of the vote, the broad outlines of the state, and an interim participation by Congolese representatives in the establishment of the new Congo institutions. Another key issue was that of the areal division of power or "federalist" versus "unitary" structure, and will be considered in a later chapter.

The Belgian government had abandoned the notion of using the December 1959 winners as an electoral college at the central level for the lower house. However, the parties which had done well in these elections[33] wanted indirect elections maintained for the provincial assemblies. This question was not resolved by the Round Table. The decision was left up to a drafting committee which came to be dominated by the more militant parties which had boycotted the elections or only campaigned in a few urban centers; thus the *Loi Fondamentale* provided for universal suffrage at this level as well. It was further decided that Europeans would not be extended voting rights; the majority Congolese argument was that Belgians could not be given suffrage in the Congo until they had become Congolese citizens.

[31] G. Dumont, *op. cit.*, p. 63.
[32] *Ibid.*, p. 93.
[33] PNP, Conakat, ARP, chiefs.

This marked the final disappearance of the Eurafrican concept of the Congolese state.

Nature of the Loi Fondamentale

The constitutional system adopted by the Round Table and consecrated by the *Loi Fondamentale* was a parliamentary regime, copied with very few alterations from the Belgian blueprint. Here one finds dramatically expressed Mackenzie's observation that when the time comes to transfer power, the colonizer inevitably satisfies his conscience as to the integrity of his act by implanting a system modeled upon the democratic values and their structural embodiment which are cherished at home. The colonized likewise demands that, as surety for the sincerity of the power transfer act, he is bequeathed a constitution which is a replica of the metropolitan format.[34] In remarking on the regime chosen for the Congo, the *Loi Fondamentale*'s first commentator, Professor François Perin, observed:

"The big argument which tipped the scales in favor of the European tradition is the confidence which the functioning of the Belgian regime inspires in the Congolese. The political regime of Belgium has shown itself to be endowed with a rather surprising prestige, even amongst certain Congolese leaders least suspect of indulgence toward the colonizing nation. It is curious to note that the temptation to adopt the form of the metropolitan state is a constant phenomenon among young decolonized nations. The experiment is often disappointing, as the historical, economic, and sociological conditions of the new nations are profoundly different from those of the former rulers."[35]

Minister Scheyven stated this anomaly more bluntly in a speech June 8:

"I do not think that underdeveloped countries are ready for democratic formulas exactly the same as we know

[34] Mackenzie and Robinson, *Five Elections in Africa*, p. 465.
[35] *Congo 1960*, I, 106.

them. . . If the Round Table was in some senses a disappointment, it was on this point. I was there myself, and therefore I am one of the first responsible. But, to tell the truth, I didn't know, and I don't yet know today, what form of democracy is most suitable for the needs of the Congolese populations. But I hoped that at this political Round Table, there would be a Congolese who would stand up and say, 'Here, from a political point of view, is what is necessary for us, a democratic system, but more adapted to our needs.' We have presented to the Congo a political system like our own. . . There are communes, provincial assemblies, a bicameral system, a political system where the Chief of State is not responsible before Parliament, whereas most young countries need a single executive. We have set up a government which can be reversed in the course of the legislature, whereas the continuity of executive action is essential in a country in construction. We have installed an electoral system which fragmented representation."[36]

A major anomaly which crept into the constitutional framework with inadequate consideration of its consequences was the duality between a Chief of State and a Prime Minister. At the time of the Round Table, the problem was posed in a somewhat false light; the issue debated was not the merits of the dual executive, but whether the Belgian monarch should continue to serve as Chief of State for the independent Congo. The deep sense of its historic mission in the Congo led the dynasty to hope that this role would continue beyond independence; many Belgian political figures shared this desire. On the Congolese side, 29 of the 44 Round Table delegates wanted to see Baudouin remain head of state. Only a handful privately supported not only the rejection of the Belgian monarchy but the elimination of the ceremonial office of Chief of State.[37] But the possibil-

[36] *Ibid.,* pp. 106-107.
[37] François Perin, "La crise congolaise et les institutions africaines," *Civilisations,* XI, No. 3 (1961), 284-95.

ity of a presidential regime was not even formally discussed. A majority of both Belgians and Congolese wanted to leave open the possibility that King Baudouin might be chosen Chief of State; further, this was the standard model of constitutional democracy as practiced in Western Europe at this time. Thus, the dual executive was written into the provisional constitution. By the time the first Congolese government was invested in June 1960, there was no longer any support for retaining the services of the Belgian monarchy. But the Chief of State office was still there, to be filled by a Congolese political leader. The Chief of State-Prime Minister dichotomy was an invitation to conflict and instability.

Interim Government

Kasavubu's provisional-government demand returned to the forefront as agreement neared on the constitutional principles. On February 4, Lumumba submitted a proposal elaborated with Joseph Ileo and D. Kanza, which was in fact designed to "visualize" a transfer of power from the hands of the Governor-General to a special twenty-one member commission to be named by the Congolese delegates to the Round Table. De Schrijver at first wanted a series of consultative bodies at Brussels, Leopoldville, and in the provinces, whose mission would be to "cooperate" with the Belgian authorities in the preparation of texts and execution of decisions. At the same time, growing demands were being expressed by financial milieux, the European civil service union (AFAC), and other pressure groups for specific guarantees from the Congolese delegations.

Albert Kalonji on February 16 proposed solving both problems at once: "During the last few days, our exchanges of views have resulted in two sorts of demands:

"1) On the Belgian government side, the demand to have our assembly formulate a specific guarantee regarding the respect for property and persons, on the future of relations of friendship and technical and economic cooperation between Belgium and an independent Congo;

"2) On the Congolese side, the demand to assure a new form for the exercise of power during the period following the Round Table until the moment of complete independence of the Congo.

"We believe that there would be a considerable practical interest in linking these two demands and in giving them a practically simultaneous answer."[38]

The result was agreement on a series of executive commissions, to be designated at every level. In Brussels, a six-member group was to work with the ministry in preparing the text of the *Loi Fondamentale*, which was to be based upon the principles agreed upon by the Round Table. In Leopoldville, a six-member executive commission was to be named, with each province having one representative. These were to share decision-making power with the Governor-General. In March, it was decided to undertake a quasi-ministerial allocation of functions among the members of the Congo commission. Three-man executive colleges were to be adjoined to the provincial governors. The Brussels, Leopoldville, and provincial colleges were to be named by the Congolese delegates to the Round Table. The provincial colleges were in turn to designate three-man colleges to be attached to the district commissioners and territorial administrators.

This significant and wise move was a tardy and incomplete corrective to one of the fundamental defects of the decolonization process. The real Congolese leadership until this point had had no stake whatsoever in the preservation of order; it was not associated in the exercise of responsibility at any level. Meanwhile, Congolese political parties were rapidly extending their authority and in wide areas

[38] *Congo 1960,* Vol. I, pp. 44-45.

wielded considerable power. This dangerous gap between power and responsibility had already produced a pre-anarchical situation, not really desired by either Belgian or Congolese leadership. But it could only be solved by placing the new leaders in positions of responsibility and by giving the completely demoralized and discredited organs of the administration a new legitimacy.

At this date, their effectiveness was limited by the fantastic demands placed upon the leading figures; in addition to the executive college duties, parties had to be organized and an electoral campaign waged. In fact, by the time of the May elections, the executive colleges, especially at the central and provincial levels, had ceased operating.

Although the provincial councils had a less important role, the territorial college, had it been established earlier, might have been a valuable transitional institution. The selections were made by the Congolese members of the provincial colleges and took into account the locally dominant political movements. In other circumstances, a genuine contribution might have been made toward avoiding the loss of administrative control and development of habits of disobedience which applied not only to the Belgian administration but to its Congolese successor in the months following independence.

The establishment of territorial colleges did not occur until April, at which point electoral fever was reaching its apogee. Political observers who were present at the time report that the functioning of these bodies depended a great deal upon the personality of both the territorial administrator involved and the African members. Even where the former was disposed to make the measure operate, often the African members were afraid to accept the responsibility given, and indeed at this stage it was difficult to be identified with the administration. The period of the civil disobedience appeal had been followed by the extravagant demagoguery of the electoral campaign, and the mass was in no mood for discipline.

One spectacular effort was made by Territorial Administrators Antoine Saintraint and André Ryckmans at Madimba, in Bakongo country, to force authority upon the Congolese. Saintraint declared on April 21, on the occasion of the installation of the territorial college:

"Understand, gentlemen, that we cannot continue to accept responsibility without power or means. . .

"To illustrate our position, as of now we renounce treating new disputes which arise in the territory. The liquidation of pending affairs and the organization of the files will occupy us until the end of the month. The transfer of responsibility will be prepared. . . .

"Parallel to this symbolic closing of the territory, we must envisage the withdrawal of the European regional agents very shortly.

"We will remain at the disposition of the executive college for information and assistance that may be asked of us. . .

"I have nothing left to say but to appeal to all, young and old, men and women, to reestablish yourselves an authority and save your country from anarchy.

"To all of you, Bakongo of Madimba Territory, I confide as of today the patrimony, the buildings, the archives, the finances, the material of *your* territory. . . . Safeguard it as the clan chief safeguards his clan, as the village chief safeguards his village."[39]

With the general elections of May 1960 and the subsequent establishment of the provincial and national governments, the task of setting up an organic structure for the Congo state was completed. Beginning with the representative assemblies that emerged from these elections, the

[39] *Ibid.*, p. 145. This was an altogether exceptional gesture, however, and Saintraint and Ryckmans narrowly escaped severe disciplinary action for their daring initiative.

Congo was no longer Belgian. In a frantically compressed period, the Congo was launched into the world of independent nations with a regime closely resembling in its formal exterior the metropolitan model. It bore little resemblance to the Eurafrican Congo, eager to bind itself in a permanent association with Belgium, that had been the fond dream of earlier years.

The generosity of the final accommodation is striking; once Congolese opinion found organic expression for itself, Belgium bowed to its will. Some illusions had lingered: the triumph of the moderate parties and especially the local lists in the December 1959 elections had given rise to some hope that universal suffrage, while conceding the urban centers and the Bas-Congo to the militant groupings, would produce a "moderate" majority with the incontestable sanction of the election behind it. Further, the *Force Publique* remained entirely under European officers; the myth of its unimpeachable discipline had survived the four major mutinies since its establishment in 1888. Finally, the administration, despite the *statut unique* of January 1959, was almost entirely European. One may discern an unarticulated hope that through doubling the traditional bureaucracy with a political sector, the Congolese leadership would be content with the mere possession of formal authority, without seeking to use it in a way which would conflict with vital European interests.

There was certainly a widespread conviction that the Congolese leadership would be helpless without Belgian management of the massive bureaucratic machinery. Thus, by this reasoning, extensive Belgian involvement in the independent Congo would be in the joint interest of Belgium and the Congo leadership.

The results of the elections were respected. The man who had come to incarnate radical Congolese nationalism, Patrice Lumumba, was duly invested as Prime Minister; the man who founded Congolese nationalism, Joseph Kasavubu, was substituted for King Baudouin as Chief of State. It is hard to challenge the conclusion of the authors of the definitive chronicle of the last phase of decolonization: "The chance of succeeding was slight, but still one must prove it was not the only one. The *décolonisation ratée* of the Belgian Congo was perhaps inevitable."[40]

[40] *Ibid.*, p. 8.

CHAPTER IX

Elites: Chiefs, Clerks and Traders

Traditional Sources of Modern Prestige

IN THIS and the next three chapters, as a preface to analysis of the emerging political system in the Congo, a brief attempt will be made to portray Congolese nationalism and the society from which it sprang. A sense of tentativeness must necessarily attend such a venture, especially in seeking the sociological coordinates of nationalism. Congolese society in recent decades has been in a state of extraordinary flux. Although there is abundant raw data on Congolese peoples, relatively little is directed to the critical question of social change. In this opinion, there is no adequate theory of social change which can serve as a reliable framework for analysis. Thus the commentary on the Congolese society created by the colonial association will contain a considerable impressionistic element, with all the limitations of this approach. Impressionism, however, provided it is not dogmatically asserted and is offered as a first formulation rather than an established doctrine, represents a slight advance over silence, and in this spirit the following chapters are put forward.

A colonial society offers a classic example of the Weberian duality between traditional and rational elements in status. Superimposed upon the plethora of pre-colonial African societies was the bureaucratic colonial state, which added to the ascriptive traditional elite systems entirely new avenues of social mobility leading to achieved status.[1]

---

[1] Like most abstractions, the ascriptive-achievement dichotomy is rarely found in pure form. Most traditional systems include recruitment by achievement, especially if this is understood with reference to the needs of the particular community, rather than judged in terms of the material, technological culture superimposed by colonial rule. Thus, in a social system whose survival depended on war-making,

Access to the subaltern clerical functions in the colonial bureaucracy or its economic prolongations, the availability of Western education, the introduction of a monetary economy led to the emergence of a new elite, whose prestige reposed upon its success in assimilating the opportunities offered by the superimposed colonial society.

Traditional society did not disappear, even under the pressure of the three-pronged colonial penetration by state, Church, and companies. In areas where the colonial system encountered long-disintegrated political systems, as among the Bakongo,[2] segmentary systems, as in nearly all the forest zone of the central basin, and recently disrupted systems, as in Maniema and eastern Kasai, traditional leadership could easily be supplanted by a modern elite. However, in large parts of Katanga, the lake region of Kivu, northern Orientale, and some of Kasai, colonial occupation encountered well-organized political systems with an established elite group. These elites remain significant factors in large areas of the Congo. Thus a portrait of the elite must include both those whose avenue to leadership has been through high traditional status and those whose success has been through achievement in the modern sector.

Traditional society has always been far more fluid than the terminology usually used to describe it implies. Long before colonial occupation, contacts with the outside world were introducing changes in Congolese social systems. Jan Vansina has shown persuasively how, beginning in the fifteenth century, trade networks gradually extended inward

---

choosing leadership on the basis of warrior skill is recruiting by achievement. In this chapter, however, "achievement" and "ascription" are used in relation to the modern state. Thus a traditional ruler who obtains an important place in the modern state primarily because of his high traditional status is chosen for ascriptive reasons.

[2] This refers to the institutions of the old Bakongo kingdom, which flourished in the 14th-17th centuries, but had already reached a stage of advanced decomposition when the new wave of colonial penetration began to make its impact felt in the late 19th century.

from both coasts.[3] By the mid-eighteenth century, these circuits extended as far as the Luapula valley, the Congo's southeastern frontier. Through this trade nexus, manioc as a staple crop was transmitted to many parts of the country long before the founding of the Free State. Trading relationships stimulated structural transformations in a number of traditional communities, in function of the requirements of new economic patterns. New military technologies, especially firearms, also slowly spread and produced in their wake numerous changes. Nineteenth-century examples of the successful warrior chief are Ngongo Lutete, a Mukusu chief in Maniema who apparently rose from slave origins,[4] and Msiri, grandfather of Godefroid Munongo, former Katanga Minister of the Interior, who came from the Banyamwezi group in Tanganyika to establish a vast and well-structured political system covering a good part of Katanga province in the latter half of the nineteenth century.[5] Msiri, the Mwata Yamvo of the Lunda, and the Bateke "chiefs" found occupying the banks of the Stanley Pool near what became Leopoldville derived significant power from their trading activities.[6] Another example of traditional mobility

[3] Jan Vansina, "Long-Distance Trade Routes in Central Africa," *Journal of African History*, III, No. 3 (1962), 375-90.

[4] Ngongo Lutete, also claimed as an ancestral hero by the Basongye, emerged in a situation where enormous disruption had been caused by large-scale Arab slave and ivory raids; he was first an ally of the Arabs, then, shrewd judge of realities that he was, switched sides and played a major role in helping the Belgians defeat the Arab bands.

[5] On Msiri and the Bayeke empire, see F. Grévisse, "Les Bayeke," *Bulletin des Jurisdictions Indigénes et du Droit Coutumier Congolais*, V, Nos. 1-8. (January-February, 1937 to March-April, 1938); Auguste Verbeken, *Msiri* (Brussels: Editions L. Cuypers, 1956); René J. Cornet, *Katanga* (Brussels; Editions L. Cuypers, 1946).

[6] For the Bayeke exploitation of the copper mines, see J. de Hemptinne, "Les 'mangeurs du cuivre' du Katanga," *Congo*, VII, (March 1926), 371-403. On the Lunda, for recent studies see D. Biebuyck, "Fondements de l'organisation politique des Lunda du Mwaanlayaav en territoire de Kapanga," *Zaïre*, XI, (October 1957), 787-817, and a dissenting view from Leon Duysters, "Histoire des Aluunda," *Prob-*

through an alliance with progress is to be found in the cunning Kalamba, grandfather of the present Sylvestre Mangole Kalamba, who parlayed the prestige of association with the first European explorer, Van Wissman, into the position of paramount chieftaincy among the Lulua.[7]

Belgian policy did not emphasize the buttressment of traditional authority with either educational weapons or economic privilege. There were two experiments with the establishment of special schools for sons of chiefs. The first was at Buta, Orientale, under Franck's ministry. This was abandoned in 1929, largely under mission pressure. The official reasons were that it was unwise to remove prospective chiefs from their traditional environment and that it was often difficult to know in advance which of the often numerous chiefly descendants would succeed to office. Another explanation for the termination of the school experiment, which had been under the direction of a missionary order, is advanced by a Liberal advocate of indirect rule: "It must be remembered that most of the candidate-chiefs were sons of polygamists and likely to follow the example of their fathers on their return to the village. This was so true that the Fathers were reluctant to baptise the sons of chiefs. This can be easily understood. A school managed by Fathers,

---

lèmes d'Afrique Centrale, No. 40, (2d trim., 1958) pp. 75-98. For some biographical material on the commercial origins of the "chiefs" at Stanley Pool, such as Ngaliema, see Henry M. Stanley, The Congo and the Founding of its Free State, 2 vols. (London: Sampson, Low, Marston Searle & Rivington, 1885), I, 304-60.

[7] Kalamba the elder heard rumors of the explorer's presence, went to meet him and invite him to his "court." The prestige conferred by this alliance with the mysterious power which the first whites seemed to represent was obviously not enough; Kalamba also managed to be the first chief in the area to obtain firearms, and was quick to rally to the Free State agents and their successors. The administration in general continued to acknowledge his paramountcy, although it is far from being accepted by all Lulua today. For the fascinating account of Kalamba's rise, see A. Van Zandijcke, Pages de l'Histoire du Kasayi (Namur, Belgium: Collection Lavigerie, 1953), and Kalanda, Baluba et Lulua . . .

entrusted with the education of future polygamists, was hardly conceivable."[8]

In 1955 Buisseret tried to set up three state schools to train prospective chiefs and others for local government, but pressure from the Catholic hierarchy, which labeled the scheme a plot to remove the elite of the country from the mission schools and to create *Führerschulen* in the Nazi style, forced the closure of these in 1957.[9] Thus there was no equivalent for the emphasis on educating prospective chiefs which was a corollary of British indirect rule doctrine. There was no deliberate policy of excluding chiefs from education, but their location in rural areas has meant that their offspring have perhaps had a disadvantage in comparison with the sons of the modern, urban-dwelling elite.

Second, although the chiefs invested as heads of *circonscriptions* did receive a salary and a cut in the head tax and were authorized to continue collecting some of their traditional tribute, they were not in general economically prosperous, even by African standards. A number of voices were raised to warn against the loss of traditional prestige due to the mediocre economic standing of the chiefs in relation to the modern elite. The Commission for the Protection of Natives, reversing its earlier hostility toward traditional authorities, in 1951 solicited better treatment: "With a view toward rendering the material situation of the native authorities more healthy and more decent, and also to increasing as far as possible the prestige over the populations which they have the mission to lead, we request that for each category of chiefs a salary scale be established giving them a sufficient standard of living."[10]

Here the contrast with British policy was even sharper. There was nothing in the Congo remotely resembling the

[8] Vermeulen, *Déficiences et dangers de notre politique indigène*, p. 33.

[9] "Quand le maître d'école crée des maîtres," *La Libre Belgique*, June 1, 1955, quoted in Brausch, *op. cit.*, p. 53.

[10] Guebels, *Rélation complete*, p. 708.

material prosperity of Baganda chiefs, thanks to the allocation of large freehold estates to chiefs by the 1900 agreement, or of the Basoga chief in Uganda who in 1924 had parlayed indirect rule into an annual income of £ 3,500.[11] Nor did Congo chiefs in an important way capitalize on their traditional functions, as Balandier suggests has happened among the Bakongo in the other Congo republic.[12]

In the earlier period, there was considerable Belgian distrust of the really important paramount chiefs; Monsignor de Hemptinne voiced the views of many, especially in Katanga where traditional chiefs were most powerful, in writing in 1935, "among the petty chiefs we find a sincere loyalism, whereas the paramount chiefs have most often retained a hidden resentment toward us."[13] The catalogue of grievances of a paramount chief who has recently acquired the international reputation of excessive sympathy for colonial rule, the late Mwata Yamvo Ditende Yawa Nawezi III of the Lunda,[14] is instructive in this regard. Through the

[11] On the 1900 agreement between H.M. Government and Buganda, see D. A. Low and R. Cranford Pratt, *Buganda and British Overrule, 1900-1955* (London: Oxford University Press, 1960). Regarding Busoga, see Lloyd Fallers, *Bantu Bureaucracy*, (Cambridge: W. Heffer & Sons, n.d. [1956]) For extensive documentation on the material advantages of indirect rule for chiefs in former British West Africa, see Martin Kilson's forthcoming book, *Political Change in a West African State*.

[12] For example, the association in many ethnic groups of the chief with the grant of land-use rights gave real possibilities in this regard, once land began to have an economic rent. Balandier also shows in this interesting contribution how some rituals have become elaborated and serve as the nexus between the new wealth and social prestige; the more costly the ceremony, the more popular esteem of the chief is enhanced. Georges Balandier, "Structures sociales traditionelles et changements économiques," *Cahiers d'Etudes Africaines*, (January 1960), I, 1-14.

[13] de Hemptinne, *Un tournant de notre politique indigène*, p. 42.

[14] *Mwata Yamvo*, also transliterated *Mwaat Yaav* (and in other variants as well), is the title assumed by Lunda paramount chiefs since the early 18th century. Ditende Yawa Nawezi III died in June 1963 and was succeeded by Gaston Mushili, a grandson and also a close relative of former Katanga President Tshombe.

Cartesian working of Belgian "indirect rule," his traditional domain had been divided among different territories and even districts, which meant that the various segments of the Lunda empire had completely different channels of communication to the administration and little relationship with each other. Notables still maintain that the administration interfered in the choice of the Mwata Yamvo in 1920. Pockets of Tshokwe, a group whose ruling aristocracy is of Lunda origin but who had become their bitter enemies and virtually dismantled the Lunda empire from 1888-1898, had remained on Lunda territory; these had been recognized as independent chieftaincies by the Belgians. About 1955, the royal village, situated at a site of great ritual importance, had been required to move over 100 kilometers to a new location just outside the small town which was the territorial administrator's headquarters. In the postwar period, considerable administrative pressure had been exerted on the Mwata Yamvo to agree to the cession of 100,000 hectares to the *Compagnie Pastorale de Lomami,* a cattle-raising enterprize which belonged to the *Société Générale* group.

Similar evidence is presented by a former district commissioner who served in Azande country in the northern part of Orientale. From the eighteenth century, this martial group, with a formidable capacity for military organization, had been pushing southward into what is now the Congo, and had established control over and assimilated a large number of peoples from the Uele River north. The Azande had never solved the problem of peaceful succession, and politically the state remained entirely personalized in the chief. The death of a ruling chief brought about dissolution of his state and eventual reconstitution by whoever from the many eligibles in the ruling Avungara clan had the force and skill to carry out the rebuilding.[15] Azande chiefs were

[15] On the Azande, see P. T. W. Baxter and Audrey Butt, *The Azande and Related Peoples of the Anglo-Egyptian Sudan and Belgian Congo* (London: International African Institute, 1953); the innumerable articles of E. E. Evans-Prichard in *Zaïre, Africa,* and other journals.

seen as a definite threat in the early years. The administration was thus led to eliminate the major Azande rulers from 1910 to 1912. It should be added that once their power to resist had been definitively broken, the colonial administration became less hostile to Azande chiefs. In later years, the proximity of the indirect rule model in neighboring Uganda led to a warmer relationship between the Azande traditional elite and the administration.

In the very last years of colonial administration, when the paramount chiefs began to appear as bastions of moderation to be balanced against the burgeoning demands of the modern elite in the cities, attitudes underwent a sharp reversal in many colonial quarters. This was reflected in the aforementioned interest in improving the prestige of the chiefs and a special issue on the rehabilitation of chiefs in one of the major colonial reviews, *Problèmes d'Afrique Centrale,* prepared by five senior civil servants in 1959.[16]

Although the number of members of the traditional elite who occupy leading positions in contemporary Congolese society for purely ascriptive reasons is small, there is an interesting symbiosis whereby traditional elements, real or simulated, become an element in modern elite status. In discussions with members of the modern elite, one is struck by the frequency with which reference is made to a chiefly ancestry. Because the "chief" concept is so vague and covers a traditional leadership position ranging from the hamlet to the empire, the claim to it can be true in a number of different degrees; what is interesting is that it appears as one element legitimating a claim to modern prestige. Also, nearly all political leaders have manipulated traditional leadership symbols—the leopard skin, the fly whisk, the headdress. Tshombe made use of his son-in-law relationship to the late Mwata Yamvo in reinforcing his leadership claims. The most extravagant example of exploiting pseudo-traditional sanction for exercise of modern leadership was

[16] *Problèmes d'Afrique Centrale,* No. 43, last quarter, 1959.

Albert Kalonji's fabrication of the title of *mulopwe* of the Kasai Baluba for himself in a grotesque set of ceremonies in Bakwanga, Sud-Kasai, in February and March, 1961.

TABLE 7

SIX CHIEFS

CHIEF KIAMFU PANZU-FUMUBULU
Bayaka Tribe—b. ±1900—education: none
Background: Only rarely left his traditional domain of Kwango. He is by far the most "traditional" of the chiefs cited here. His traditional authority is particularly strong; there was little competition to it from any modern economic development, as Kwango is the poorest district of the Congo, with no large towns. Like his predecessors, he had occasional feuds with the colonial administration. In the early 1950's, he was able to force the transfer of a Belgian administrator he found *persona non grata*, an unheard of scandal in its day. He resisted the intrusion into his domains of the Abako and PSA in 1959, and supported the establishment of a local party based on the Bayaka, Luka. The Bayaka aristocracy is of Lunda origin, and symbolic relationships are still maintained with the Mwata Yamvo. In February, 1961, Kiamfu visited the court of Mwata Yamvo; the following month, separate provincial status was demanded for Kwango.
He has 25 wives and about 125 children.

CHIEF MWAMI ALEXANDRE KABARE
Bashi Tribe—b. 1913—education: primary
Background: Was selected as a child by administration to succeed his father, Rutaganda, who resisted colonial penetration from 1900 to 1916, and died in 1919. After growing conflicts with the administration and the missions, he left—voluntarily—for Elizabethville, in 1936 where he became a chauffeur. Several years later, he proceeded to Leopoldville, where he found clerical employment. In 1959, at the overwhelming demand of the population, he was brought back and restored to power. His adopted son, and heir apparent, Albert Kabare, received secondary training at a seminary and spent eight post-secondary years at Kisantu (Leopoldville), acquiring a diploma as medical assistant 1953. In 1960, although the Mwami was not a member of any political party, he was associated with the "moderate" groups, and his son Albert joined the PNP in May, 1960. However, he came into sharp conflict with the Kivu provincial government after independence, and allied himself with Stanleyville during the Kashamura and Omari regimes, in early 1961. In March 1962, a territorial council voted to remove him as Mwami. The crisis resulting forced central government intervention. In September 1963, he was voted First Vice-President of the Congo and honorary president of the Kivu branch of MNC/L. He has built up a large private militia since 1961.

ELITES: CHIEFS, CLERKS AND TRADERS

Chief Antoine Mwenda-Munongo
Bayeke Tribe—b. 1905—education: Seminary
Background: Grandson of the famous Bayeke chief Msiri, who was in
the process of consolidating an empire in the Katanga when the Belgians
arrived. The actual number of Bayeke who came from Tanganyika was
relatively small, augmented by the local women they took as wives;
thus Munongo's chieftaincy is not nearly so large as those of the others
mentioned in the table, but his prestige is considerable. Was brought
to Europe in 1929, spent four post-secondary years at a seminary in
Belgium when he seemed headed for the clergy. Instead, he served as
a teacher for two years, then spent 18 years as a clerk in the administration. In 1956, he was invested as Bayeke paramount chief; his predecessor, before his death, was nearly deposed by the administration. A man
of keen intellect, he is the author of a number of articles on Bayeke
traditions, law and history. His son, Bernard Munongo, is now completing his university education at Louvain. His brother, Godefroid,
was Katanga Minister of the Interior, and his cousin, Odilon Mwenda-
Mukanda-Bantou, was Conakat general secretary and later a Secretary
of State in the Katanga government. He was an outspoken critic of
what he felt to be the inadequate place reserved for traditional leaders
in the new institutions. Strongly supported the Conakat and the
Katanga secession.

Chief Kasongo Nyembo Emmanuel Ndaie
Baluba (Shankadi) Tribe—b. 1909—education: primary
Background: The paramount chief, by historic tradition although not
present reality, over all of the Katanga Baluba. A strong-willed personality, who, like the Kiamfu of the Bayaka, has had less direct
experience of urban life than some other chiefs, but has a shrewd
determination in the use of his considerable traditional authority.
One of the few chiefs to seek elected office, won a seat in the lower
house, on the Conakat ticket. The Kasongo Nyembo gave full support
to the Katanga secession; he was permitted to build up a well-armed
militia of his own. He has resisted attempts of the Balubakat leaders
Jason Sendwe and Prosper Mwamba-Ilunga to assert the authority of
Nord-Katanga province over his domains, since termination of the
secession. Deposed by Central government, January 1964, and rein-
stated in October 1964.

Chief Boniface Kabongo
Baluba (Shankadi) Tribe—b. 1900—education: post-primary
Background: Worked from 1924–1932 as a clerk in the private sector,
then for a decade in the recruiting services of *Union Minière*. He
succeeded his father in 1946, and from 1947 was a member of the
Conseil de Province, later the Government Council as well. He was one
of a group of notables who were brought to Belgium in 1953 for a long
tour. The Kabongo ruling when the Belgians arrived was a brother of
the sixteenth Kasongo Nyembo, and a part of the Luba empire. Under
Belgian administration, Kabongo became an independent paramount

193

chieftaincy. Assassinated by Balubakat youth group in October 1960, after he had rallied to the Tshombe regime.

CHIEF MWATA YAMVO DITENDE YAWA NAWEZI III
Lunda Tribe—b. 1890—education: post-primary
Background: Educated in Protestant mission schools. He is probably the most prestigious of the Congo chiefs; the Lunda political system was a remarkable construction which has resisted the corrosion of the colonial experience. His prestige had remained very high among Lunda, even in the urban centers. Sat in both the provincial and government council. In 1960, he made a two-month trip to the United States, under the sponsorship of the Protestant missions. He had established cattle farms in the Sandoa area and pushed hard for economic development of the region. In the 1950's, he made a spectacular progress amongst his subjects in Northern Rhodesia and Angola, to the consternation of the respective colonial authorities. He was a major supporter of the Conakat and the Katonga sessions. Tshombe was his son-in-law. Died in June 1963.

SOURCE: The biographical data is drawn in part from Pierre Artigue, *Qui sont les leaders congolais?* (2nd ed., Brussels: Editions Europe-Afrique, 1961). This is completed by interviews with Congolese sources, and Belgian missionaries and administrators who have served in the areas concerned.

In the Katanga urban centers, during the period of major recruitment in the 1920's, chiefs frequently sent delegates from noble lineages with the new recruits to the city to retain some leadership over them.[17] An extremely interesting sociological study of Elisabethville by Caprasse in 1957 shows that the role and prestige of elders remained considerable in African society. In a Gauss scale he constructed to essay a measurement of prestige, he found that among both educated and illiterate respondents the traditional element in prestige was highly significant, with educated notables preferred to illiterate ones. Although no comparable studies exist for other urban areas, it is reasonable to suggest that

[17] Grévisse, *Le centre-extra-coutumier d'Elisabethville*, p. 306. A similar phenomenon is found in the Northern Rhodesian copper belt towns. See A. L. Epstein, *Politics in an Urban African Community* (Manchester: Manchester University Press, 1958), pp. 28-38, *passim.* The British for a considerable period encouraged this, and based their urban administration on it, which was not the case in the Congo.

invocation of traditional prestige as a modern asset was most successful in cities such as Jadotville, Elisabethville, and Bukavu, where much of the population was drawn from areas where highly-structured traditional systems survived. In cities such as Stanleyville, Coquilhatville, or Leopoldville, whose populations were largely recruited from segmentary systems, traditional prestige was less important.

TABLE 8

PRESTIGE SCALE IN ELISABETHVILLE

Category	80 educated respondents	27 non-educated respondents
Traditional, aged, educated	7.75	7.70
Traditional, young, educated, wealthy	6.39	
Traditional, young, educated	5.33	5.24
Traditional, aged, illiterate, wealthy	5.08	4.98
Traditional, aged, illiterate	4.62	5.86
Non-traditional, aged, educated, wealthy	4.59	
Non-traditional, aged, educated	3.22	3.87
Non-traditional, young, educated, wealthy	3.06	2.30

SOURCE: P. Caprasse, *Leaders africains en milieu urbain*, pp. 147–55.

Bureaucratic Origins of the Modern Elite

To turn to the other pendant of the elite dualism, one finds an interesting recapitulation of its history in a manifesto published in 1961 by Lovanium University students:

"The Belgian divided the Congolese successively into two, then in three or even four new classes. In effect, at the beginning of the colonization, there were, on the one hand, the *basendji*[18] or natives, and on the other hand the soldiers of the *Force Publique* (first Hausa, then Congolese).

"The soldiers had as their noble mission the conquest of the regions inhabited by the *basendji* and their subjection to the

[18] A frequently-used slang term, meaning approximately "savage."

195

authority of the white man. . . . A new class then appeared, that of the 'boys' and native domestic servants of the colonizer. The Belgian used them to consolidate his authority over the country. At the beginning of the era baptized 'pax belgica,' the prestige of the domestics exceeded that of the soldiers. They became catechists and taught the Catholic religion, principal source of the general pacification of the Congo by the colonizers.

"As the children of the 'boys' and soldiers went to school, a new class grew up, that of the *évolués*."[19]

There is a great deal of accuracy to this summary. Access to primary education which went beyond the rudimentary catechism taught in the rural mission schools before World War II first went to the sons of those who in the early days attached themselves to the Europeans in one form or another. Workers at first were engaged for very short terms and then returned to the village; the soldiers and domestics were the first to settle with their families permanently outside the traditional milieu. The mission stations collected about them a miscellaneous group of uprooted persons, orphans, and victims of the enormous turmoil which accompanied the Belgo-Arab wars in the eastern Congo. The state set up schools at Boma and Nouvelle Anvers for *enfants recueillis*, operated by the missions. Missions themselves frequently bought slave children to educate as evangelizers. Both Protestant and Catholic missions made extensive use of "catechists," who, with a minimal acquaintance with Christianity, would be posted in one of the villages surrounding the mission station to serve as an intermediary.

The next generation, then, had sufficient education to find clerical places with the administration or the companies, and became permanently settled in the rapidly expanding urban areas. Their sons, or the third generation, form the bulk of the present university generation. University-pre-

[19] *Manifeste des universitaires congolais* (Leopoldville: n.d. [1961]).

paratory secondary schools are exclusively located in the medium and large towns. Until recently, most of the rural primary schools were not adequate to prepare for entry into the *humanités* cycle at the scondary level. It was possible to make the leap from the village to a higher education, but extremely difficult.

The notion of a modern elite is obviously an imprecise one. In the sense in which the term is being used here, it refers to those persons who have distinguished themselves from the mass by assimilating at least some of the tools of the civilization imported by the colonizer. The definition changes in the course of time; a "boy" was part of an embryonic modern elite half a century ago. After World War II, anyone with some post-primary education could probably be considered a reasonable candidate. Today, a secondary education or equivalent would be a fair criterion. Educational criteria are not the only ones; any form of successful entry into the new world created by the arrival of the colonizer, be it commercial or intellectual, would be relevant. And subjective self-identification would need to be included as well as objective attainment.

The most important aspect of the modern elite is that it is, to borrow Balandier's apt phrase, an "administrative bourgeoisie."[20] As a highly bureaucratized society, the potential employers for the new elite were invariably either a state or parastatal organization or a large enterprise. One way of illustrating this point is to examine the backgrounds of the 23 persons included in the first government of the Republic of the Congo; the constitutional requirements and exigencies of majority-hunting meant that this group was geographically and ethnically representative, and is a fair, if crude, random sampling of the modern elite.

One immediate qualification which should be made to Table 9 is that it omits the avant garde of the modern elite,

[20] Georges Balandier, *Sociologie des Brazzavilles noires* (Paris: Librairie Armand Colin, 1955), p. 123.

TABLE 9

The Modern Elite—Background of the First Congolese Government

	EMPLOYER		
NAME	State	Company	Other
Lumumba	clerk	salesman	
Gizenga			teacher
Bomboko[a]	clerk		research asst. Institut Solvay
Bisukiro	clerk		
Delvaux		clerk	
Th. Kanza[a]			teacher; internship, Common Market
Mwamba	clerk		
Gbenye	clerk		
Nkayi	clerk		
Yav	clerk		
Ilunga		clerk	
Songolo	clerk		
Lutula	clerk		
Masena	med. asst.		
Mbuyi	clerk		
Kamanga	med. asst.		
Rudahindwa	clerk		teacher
Mahamba	judge/clerk		planter
Ngwenze		clerk	
Mulele	clerk		
Kashamura		clerk	journalist
Mpolo	clerk		
Kabangi	clerk		

[a] University graduates

SOURCE: Data is primarily drawn from Artigue, *op. cit.*

NOTE: Only the major occupation has been listed in most cases, although several individuals have moved back and forth between the private and public sectors. It should be noted that the term "clerk" is used in a rather extended sense; duties of "clerks," like "secretaries" in the United States, range from routine functions to exercise of considerable responsibility in some cases. But in colonial society, all shared the status and formal hierarchial position of "clerks."

the priests. Former Belgian Africa is unique in the size of its African clergy; in large part this was because, until World War II, the sole avenue to secondary or higher education (not counting post-primary vocational schools) was through the seminaries. There is also no parallel for the priesthood's having served for so long as literally the sole channel into full acceptance as "civilized."[21] The first African priest was ordained in 1917 at Baudoinville at the seminary of the White Fathers; there followed first a tiny trickle, then after the war a steady stream. At the time of independence, there were nearly 500 African priests and four bishops; by the end of 1962, the number of African bishops had increased to 10. The Congo had more than a third of the total number of African priests for the continent.[22] The standing of the priests is perhaps no longer so high in relative terms, now that many other avenues of advance are open, but the success of the Church in adapting to independence and the demoralization of much of the political sector has left Catholicism in a stronger position than would have been thought likely in 1959.

The first means of education extending beyond the Bible-reading-elementary-arithmetic level came with the establishment of schools for clerks at Boma in 1906 and Leopoldville in 1907. In 1908, an agricultural school was established at Stanleyville. By 1948, in addition to the several grand seminaries, there was only a school for medical assistants and agricultural assistants at Kisantu which went beyond the secondary level. At the end of 1954, however, one student of Congolese elites maintained that there were 11,572 Africans of "relatively advanced education."[23] As of 1960 there were some 3,000 former students of the Catholic seminaries, beginning with the Congo's first President, Kasavubu. (During the days when the seminaries were the only secondary institutions, many Congolese feigned a desire to

[21] It will be recalled that as late as 1950-1951, during the debate over the immatriculation decree, many argued that only the priests could be considered as qualified for this civilization merit badge.

[22] Lecture by Monsignor J. Jadot, former chaplain to the *Force Publique*, Brussels, September 29, 1961.

[23] "L'évolution politique du Congo Belge et les autorités indigènes," *Problèmes d'Afrique Centrale*, No. 43 (1959), p. 54.

enter the priesthood until they could get the education, then discovered that they "had no vocation." When in 1959 the *statut unique* for the civil service went into effect, some 800 persons qualified for the fourth category, which required a complete *humanités* (university-preparatory) education.

TABLE 10

AFRICAN SCHOOL ATTENDANCE IN 1959

School level	No. of pupils	No. of African teachers
Primary	1,502,588	43,251
Secondary and higher	13,583	84
Technical & agricultural	17,142	734

SOURCE: Albert Pevée, *Place aux Noirs* (Brussels: Editions Europe-Afrique, 1960), p. 39.

Table 10 depicts the educational situation on the eve of independence. It should be noted in passing that the 44,000 African teachers, although many had barely a primary education themselves, constituted a significant elite element, especially in rural centers, where they rank high in relative intellectual attainment. There were 350 students enrolled in the two Congo universities, and 30 had received university degrees. However, in fairness, one should add to these a number of persons with post-secondary technical training, which in the case of the medical assistants amounted to six years; in American statistics, they would be counted as college graduates. They included:

130 medical assistants
250 agricultural technicians
30 administrative specialists
20 social workers
15 veterinary assistants

The secondary system had the defect of having a very small output of Congolese *humanités* diplomas; only 136 were graduated in 1960.[24]

[24] République du Congo, Ministère de l'Information et des Affaires

Congolese traders

The final avenue of entry into the modern sector is through the acquisition of economic prosperity. Here the Congo ranks far below most of West Africa or Uganda. The Belgians were never very active in the field of petty commerce in the Congo, but two major groups of "pariah entrepreneurs"—the Portugese in Leopoldville, Equateur, and western Kasai, and the Greeks in the areas lying to the east —have formed a major competitive barrier with their own tight nets of communications and peculiar aptitude for this brand of economic activity. Further, despite the belated interest of many in the rapid creation of a black bourgeoisie that would make common cause with colonial society, there were major institutional obstacles in the path of African entrepreneurs. Individual landed property was not made available to Africans until the last minute, and the absence of property, among other factors, made credit very difficult to obtain.

However, especially in recent years, an African trading class was rapidly emerging. A 1956 survey in Leopoldville showed that there were 7,000 self-employed persons; to the astonishment of the Belgian administration, and the tax-collectors, who had heretofore ignored this group, several had incomes of over $20,000 per annum.[25] Elisabethville in 1955 had 1,309 African traders who earned a total of 50,000,000 francs, although only two had an income over 100,000 francs per year. In 1953, 436 vehicles were owned by African traders in Leopoldville, while in Elisabethville in 1956 Africans possessed 82 trucks and 112 cars.[26] A handful of Africans accumulated substantial wealth; these have, for the most part, fared well after independence. The best-known example is the Tshombe family (it was the father who was

---

Culturelles, *Nouvelles congolaises*, Nov. 26, 1962, speech of Henri Takizala at UNESCO Conference, Paris, November 1962.

[25] Brausch, *Belgian Administration in the Congo,* pp. 4-5.
[26] Denis, *Le phénomène urbain en Afrique Centrale,* p. 339.

a successful entrepreneur, and not the Katanga President). Isaac Kalonji, also of Elisabethville, had a string of enterprises; he headed Fedeka[27] before independence and during 1961-1963 served as Vice-President of the Senate. Victor Nendaka, past president of the *Association des Classes Moyennes Africaines* (ACMAF), formed under the impetus of Buisseret in 1954, and since September 1960 head of the all-important *Sûreté*, had owned in Leopoldville a bar, travel agency, and insurance company. Table 11 gives a breakdown of the African entrepreneurial group; in evaluating the figures included, it should be emphasized that the great majority were very modest, one-man operations.

TABLE 11

Self-Employed Africans, 1959

Province	Planters	Artisans	Traders	Small Business	Liberal Professions
Leopoldville	1104	2582	4559	605	28
Equateur	51	19	161	25	
Orientale	252	90	1774	188	
Kivu	301	543	2446	193	
Katanga	53	112	2067	101	1
Kasai	720	221	106	464	

Source: Julien Kasongo's paper on the Congo in INCIDI, *Staff Problems in Tropical and Subtropical Countries* (Brussels: 1961).

Thus, one may conclude that the African elite which developed during the three-quarters of a century of symbiosis with the modern material civilization introduced by the colonizer was strongly shaped by the nature of colonial society itself. Access to the modern system was essentially through the subaltern roles in the bureaucracy of the colonial triad. High status had first been possible through the priesthood; this had enabled the Church to equip itself with an African clergy of superior attainments. For the rest, the dominant trait it summarized in Balandier's "administrative

[27] Ethnic association of Kasaiens, mainly Baluba, in southern Katanga cities.

bourgeoisie" term. Traditional elites, although not given special encouragement, have, in areas where differentiated, structured politico-social systems existed, held their own, and traditional prestige symbols remain of great importance.

The nature of elite recruitment has crucial significance in determining the political perspectives of the Congo's leadership. The "political resources"[28] available to the elite did not include economic power. The prospect of a transfer of political authority to this elite implied, at least for a long transitional period, a policy where the economic and political structures would be almost completely divorced. The new Congolese elite had virtually no vested interest in the economic and social status quo. At the same time, they were keenly aware that they, for the time being, lacked the technical capability of replacing or operating the vast economic infrastructure constructed by the colonial corporations. The resolution of the dilemma came through adoption of a hortatory socialism by much of the nationalist leadership. This combined the advantages of a doctrine which enjoyed great intellectual prestige as coherent ideology of protest in much of the world and an effective rationalization for the leading role of the state in post-colonial society. At the same time, the socialist vector of nationalist thought stopped well short of any immediate threat to the expatriate-controlled economic machinery: the engine of modernity must be kept running. From its bureaucratic genesis, the elite had derived one real vested interest: the state.

[28] To borrow Robert A. Dahl's useful concept. *Who Governs?* (New Haven: Yale University Press, 1961).

CHAPTER X

The Mass: Workers and Peasants

Urban Labor: A Proletariat?

IN AN analysis of nationalism, we cannot escape frequent reference to the led as well as the leaders. The components of the African mass—worker and peasant—if undefined, carry, from common usage with reference to industrialized societies, a host of connotations which may be irrelevant or worse. It is not our purpose here to suggest a general theory of social class in Africa. We propose only to make explicit our own reflections and assumptions concerning the sociological referents of the "mass," in both its urban and rural dimensions.

The importance of clarification is greatest with regard to the urban areas. The difference between the farmer of West Europe and the Congolese rural villager is so obvious that there is little temptation to infer that their political behavior may have identical determinants. But the difference between nineteenth-century Manchester and twentieth-century Elisabethville is at first glance less clear. May one foresee patterns of political behavior unfolding among Congolese workers parallel to those of working class groups in other polities at comparable stages of industrialization? Obviously, these important questions can only be answered by the future; however, it is relevant to explore urbanization patterns for insight into similarities and differences with those in other times and places, and the nature of the Congolese worker group as a social category.

Growth of Cities

The first and foremost element in the nature of the urban mass is its size, by African standards, and the rapidity of its growth. Only settler Africa can compare in the percentage of African wage-earners to population, and the number living outside traditional milieux. On the eve of independence 37 percent of adult males in the Congo were wage-earners, and 24 percent of the total population lived outside the village. This rapid transformation is summarized in statistics in Tables 12 to 16.

Belgian policy toward urbanization differed in important ways from those of other colonial occupants in Africa. Confronted with a massive labor shortage which threatened to bring economic expansion to a halt by 1926, the colonizer and the colonial corporations abandoned the policy of using only short-term, migrant labor. They began a program of stabilization of the working force in the towns, and planned cities on the assumption that they would be permanent abodes for African families rather than temporary dormitories for contract labor. Thus in Elisabethville by 1955, 43.4 percent of the population had lived there for more than ten years.[1]

Employment and Wage Patterns

The employment market for unskilled workers was dominated by a handful of giant firms; ten mammoth enterprises (including the copper mines of *Union Minière,* the diamond mines of *Forminière,* the tin mines of *Symétain,* and the gold mines of *Kilo-Moto*) absorbed one fifth of the labor force. Seventy of the 3600 enterprises in the Congo accounted for over half the working force.[2] Until the 1950's, policy was oriented toward the maintenance of a low-wage economy. This was made partially tolerable by administrative intervention to ensure that living costs of the African worker were kept low. Compulsory cultivation of staple food crops in the city hinterlands and enforcement of low prices for this produce by the administration transferred part of the social cost of low industrial wages to the rural population. Also, in many cases, large employers provided

[1] Denis, *La phénomène urbain en Afrique centrale,* p. 190.
[2] Merlier, *Le Congo de la colonisation belge à l'indépendance,* p. 168.

housing at nominal cost for their laborers. Even after the administration embarked upon a policy of forcing more efficient use of labor upon the companies by slowly raising the legal minimum wage in the last decade of colonial rule, the "minimum" for half the labor force was at the same time a maximum.[3] In 1946, a survey in Leopoldville revealed that

TABLE 12

GROWTH OF WAGE-EARNING POPULATION

Year	Wage-earners	Year	Wage-earners
1915	37,368	1935	377,531
1920	125,120	1937	491,634
1925	274,538	1940	536,055
1926	421,953	1945	701,101
1930	399,144	1950	962,009
1932	291,961	1952	1,070,346

SOURCE: Chambre des Représentants, *Rapports sur l'Administration...*

TABLE 13

PERCENTAGE LIVING OUTSIDE TRADITIONAL MILIEUX, BY PROVINCE

Province	% 1957	Province	% 1957
Leopoldville	27.65	Kivu	19.03
Equateur	21.62	Katanga	36.17
Orientale	23.02	Kasai	12.05

SOURCE: Inforcongo, *Le Congo Belge*, II, 20.

TABLE 14

GROWTH IN PROPORTION OF POPULATION LIVING IN TOWNS

Year	Total in towns	% of total population
1935	603,413	7
1940	1,017,899	10
1945	1,565,401	15
1950	2,162,397	19
1955	2,850,084	22
1957	3,047,734	23

SOURCE: Inforcongo, *Le Congo Belge*, II, 20.

[3] For various viewpoints on the general subject of wage policies,

TABLE 15

GROWTH OF MAJOR CONGOLESE CITIES

City	1935	1940	1945	1950	1955	1957[a]
Leopoldville	26,622	46,884	96,000	191,000	340,000	370,000
Elisabethville	23,000	27,000	65,000[b]	99,000	131,000	185,000
Stanleyville		15,000	20,000	35,000	55,000	78,000
Matadi		9,000	18,000	37,000	61,000	56,000
Coquilhatville	10,000	10,000	12,000	17,000	27,000	33,000
Bukavu		1,900	4,500	18,000	26,000	34,000

[a] The 1957 figures include Europeans, whereas the earlier ones do not. The European populations were respectively 21,000, 14,000, 5,000, 2,000, 1,000, and 4,000.

[b] 1946 figures.

SOURCES: Inforcongo, *Le Congo Belge*, II, 21; Thomas Hodgkin, *Nationalism in Colonial Africa*, p. 67; A. Romanuik, "Evolution et perspectives démographiques de la population au Congo," *Zaïre*, XIII, No. 6 (1959), 571.

TABLE 16

ORIGINS OF POPULATION OF NINE LARGEST CITIES

City	Territory	District	Province	Other Provinces	Other Countries
Leopoldville	20.3%	13.6%	33.3%	15.7%	17.1%[a]
Matadi	15.0	53.3	4.5	1.4	25.8[a]
Coquilhatville	5.5	41.2	32.9	17.1	3.3
Stanleyville	18.3	55.7	16.3	9.3	0.4
Bukavu	13.6	53.3	18.6	14.4[b]	0.1
Elisabethville	3.3	12.6	31.9	33.1	19.1[c]
Jadotville	10.7	11.8	28.2	39.9	9.4
Kolwezi	17.8	13.8	29.6	30.2	8.6
Luluabourg	38.3	33.3	24.8	1.4	0.2

[a] Mainly Angola.

[b] Including Ruanda-Urundi.

[c] Mainly Northern Rhodesia.

SOURCE: Jacques Denis, *Le phénomène urbain en Afrique Centrale,* p. 141.

see Fernand Bézy, *Problèmes structurels de l'économie congolaise* (Louvain: Editions E. Nauwelaerts, 1957); Arthur Doucy and Pierre Feldheim, *Problèmes du travail et politique sociale au Congo Belge* (Brussels: Les Editions de la Librairie Encyclopédique, 1952); R. Poupart, *Facteurs de productivité de la main-d'oeuvre autochtone à Elisabethville* (Brussels: Editions de l'Institut de Sociologie. Solvay, 1960); Joye and Lewin, *Les trusts au Congo.*

55 percent of the wage-earners were receiving the minimum legal wage of $.22 per day.[4] And in 1960, the ILO concluded that about half the workers in the Congo received no more than 110 percent of the minimum.[5] Salaries had, however, substantially increased during the interim. By 1959, the daily minimum salary ranged from $1 in Leopoldville to $.40 in the Kwango. As late as 1950, many rural wage-earners in Kivu had earned less than two cents a day.[6]

Rising wages were part of the general pattern of the "welfare colonialism" of the postwar years described in Chapter IV. The Congolese worker could hardly draw much sustenance from the knowledge that the Congo had tropical Africa's most elaborate welfare state; a comparison with Chad or Sierra Leone had little relevance. However, he could be aware that there was a visible rise in real wages and welfare services during the boom years. An ascendant curve of prosperity may not be an infallible cure for discontent, but its sedative effect was, in this case, undeniable.

The nature of each city's economic base resulted from important differentiations between them. In southern Katanga, one finds the most extreme example of an economy dominated by a giant mining firm, with its host of satellite activities. An important percentage of the African population lives in the relatively comfortable camps provided by *Union Minière* and the BCK railroad, the latter also a major employer. Industrial paternalism was most elaborate in Katanga; the UMHK worker was well cared for.

In Leopoldville, there are several important sectors of activity. As the capital, it is a center of administrative services. It is a key transport hub, as terminus for the Matadi-Leopoldville railroad and the river shipping system. There is a significant concentration of light industry, such as textile factories and beer distilleries. The construction industry em-

---

[4] Emmanuel Capelle, *La cité indigène de Léopoldville* (Leopold-ville: Centre d'Etudes Sociales Africaines, 1947), p. 54.

[5] Cited in Merlier, *op. cit.*, pp. 172-73.

[6] Bézy, *op. cit.*, p. 168.

ployed a large number in the postwar years, as Leopoldville's skyscrapers rose along Boulevard du 30 Juin (ex-Al-
bert). With several thousand European families, and nearly
every one employing at least one "boy," domestic servants
constituted an important class. Stanleyville's growth was
based upon administrative services, its usefulness as a
transport center and as regional agricultural market, and its
growing light industry. In Bukavu, on the other hand, over
one-third of the African wage-earners were "boys," or twice
the proportion of other cities, as low wages encouraged the
European families to engage two or three per household.[7]

Rural Exodus: Migration Routes

Since the postwar boom ran out of steam in 1956, an important new factor is that immigration to the cities has out-
run employment opportunities. During the great depression
of the 1930's, the population of the large centers dropped
substantially as people returned to their villages. They were,
it is true, legally bound to do so if they were without work,
but the experience of the 1957-1959 period showed that
such a regulation is extremely difficult to enforce if there is
an inclination to resist it. Rural exodus is a recent phenomenon and is no longer responsive to business cycle fluctua-
tions. Proof of this is the sharp rise in population in all
major urban centers since independence, despite an equally
sharp drop in employment opportunity. Since 1960, the
population of Leopoldville, by conservative estimates, has
reached 700,000; some estimates run as high as 1,300,000.

Migration to the urban centers shows a clear tendency to
follow the main axes of communication. For many years the
Congo River provided the main route into Leopoldville
from the east, while the Bakongo followed the rail line in
from the west. More recently, especially since 1952, a new
line of major migration has been established from the Bayaka country in the Kwango. The market for their one agri-

[7] Denis, *op. cit.,* p. 345.

cultural product, a kind of fiber, utterly collapsed, and desperate poverty drove large numbers of Bayaka by foot across 600-700 kilometers of sandy plateau.[8] Immigration into the South Katanga centers of Kolwezi, Jadotville, and Elisabethville has tended to follow the BCK railway coming from Port Francqui, Kasai. The other centers, such as Matadi, Stanleyville, Coquilhatville, Bukavu, and Luluabourg, have drawn their populations almost entirely from the immediately surrounding regions. Table 16 gives a summary picture of the human hinterland of the major centers.

Another significant aspect of migration, proved by a number of studies, is that migration from the village to the city generally passes through the smaller, regional centers. The villager experiments with town existence in a small community, where he remains rather close to clan and family, before plunging into the relative anonymity and traumatic experience of Leopoldville or Elisabethville. In Stanleyville, Pons found that although 66.5 percent of the population had been born in a village, only 28.8 percent had come directly from a village to Stanleyville.[9] Trade union leader André Bo-Boliko found that, of the 53 natives of Kutu territory in Leopoldville whom he sampled, 37 had migrated via a smaller center.[10]

Smaller Towns

An important distinction must be made between the large cities and small, regional centers. Romanuik suggests in a valuable demographical study that, as of 1956, of the 22 percent of the population classified by census-takers as town-dwelling, only 9.88 percent lived in major urban cen-

[8] For an excellent account of the plight of the Bayaka, see N. Bailleul, "Les Bayaka," *Zaïre*, XIII, No. 8 (1959), 823-41.

[9] International African Institute, *Social Implications of Industrialization and Urbanization South of the Sahara* (UNESCO: 1956) p. 254.

[10] Bo-Boliko, *Le comportement des travailleurs manuels congolais devant leurs rémunérations* (Mémoire, Ecole Sociale de Louvain, 1958, mimeographed), p. 67.

ters.[11] In the smaller, essentially rural centers, there is a far greater homogeneity in the population, and the continuing links with the surrounding countryside are much more intense.

A fascinating picture of the worker in a typical small center is painted by Bo-Boliko. The town of Nioki, situated in his home province, Lac Leopold II, may be taken as a representative small town. It has about 10,000 inhabitants and a single major employer, *Forescom*, a subsidiary of *Forminière*, in turn a subsidiary of the *Société Générale*. The low salaries in the minor centers are not enough for subsistence; most families cultivate land in the surrounding countryside. In 1956, most workers received $.30 a day with lodging provided by *Forescom*. Nearly 80 percent of the married workers had cassava fields, tilled by their wives; 67 percent supplemented their incomes by fishing nearly every weekend, especially in the two-month dry season when fishing is best. Somewhat surprisingly, most of the unskilled workers were dependent to an important degree on their families in the village. Seventy percent received packages from home two or three times a month, containing *chikwangue*[12] and smoked fish. In many families, the husband returned to the village as often as once a month; on important occasions, such as harvests or major fishing efforts, the chiefs summoned all back to the villages. The inquiry found no cases of workers sending money back to the villages. Bo-Boliko's estimate was that the supplements to income in the form of food from the village, and that raised or caught by the worker himself, amounted to one-third of his total income. On the other hand, the standard of living seems higher than might have been expected; the average worker possessed four shirts, three pairs of trousers, and one pair of

[11] A. Romanuik, "Evolution et perspectives démographiques de le population du Congo," *Zaïre*, XIII, No. 6 (1959), 571.

[12] A manioc bread which is a major dietary item in most of the Congo, where manioc is the staple food.

shoes. As many as 87 percent owned bicycles, and 26 percent had sewing machines.[13]

The Large Cities: Urban Sociology

The Congo had nine cities whose population exceeded 30,000 during the latest complete colonial census (1957): the six provincial capitals plus Matadi, Jadotville, and Albertville. It was in these cities that urbanization as an engine of social change had its fullest impact. They were too big for the inhabitants to supplement their income by tilling plots on the edges of the city. More tribes were represented; the community was less likely to be a mere urban prolongation of a single cultural group. There was greater occupational differentiation; these were not, like Nioki, the workers' compound of a single large enterprise. Immigration was from farther afield, and visits to the village were much more infrequent. Bo-Boliko found that Kutu men in Leopoldville returned home on an average of only once every four years; in Nioki, many visited the village once a month, and nearly all paid several visits a year.[14]

A vital aspect of all the urban centers, small and large, was their newness. There was no Congolese equivalent of the old Yoruba towns. In terms of Southall's useful dichotomy of African cities (old, slowly growing towns versus new, mushroom centers),[15] all Congo urban clusters were new, and almost none were more than large villages before World War II. Nearly all persons over 30 had been reared in a village or small community; only the current young generation contains any significant number of city-born. The sociological consequences of urbanization are thus only beginning to be felt.

Was the urban mass a nascent working class? Most students of Africa, including those who acknowledge an intel-

[13] Bo-Boliko, op. cit., pp. 40-57.
[14] Ibid., pp. 50-52, 129.
[15] Aiden Southall (ed), Social Change in Modern Africa (New York: Oxford University Press, 1961), p. 6.

lectual debt to the Marxian world view, have been cautious in using this term and have tended toward such formulations as "social category" in place of undiluted European social class concepts. Writers of the Marxist-Leninist school, such as Merlier and Woddis,[16] have assumed that the classic social-class frame of analysis is applicable, with few qualifications. Many African leaders, such as Sékou Touré, have argued that the entire African population had the role of a proletariat with the colonialist-imperialist system filling the role of the exploiting class.

Certainly in the case of the Congo, even more than in most West African social systems, there is pertinence to the view that there was little divergence in the economic interests of the African population in the terminal colonial period. The real economic cleavage, like the political cleavage, was between African and European. The employer, like the administrator, was European. In these circumstances, economic and political deprivation are intimately intertwined as a stimulant to nationalism.

Within the African community, differentiation was primarily in terms of social status rather than economic standing. Before independence, there was very little economic stratification. Bo-Boliko's 1957 sampling in Leopoldville found that the vast majority of monthly wages ranged from the 900 franc ($18) legal minimum to 2,000 francs ($40). Records of the Congo pension fund show that, of the over 1,000,000 employees of the private sector, only 25,000 earned more than $80 a month.[17] However, there was marked status disparity; this is defined in terms of distribution of prestige or social honors. Education, a white collar job, the ability to deal on equal terms with the Europeans

[16] Jack Woddis, Africa: The Roots of Revolt (New York: The Citadel Press, 1962); Merlier, op. cit. Although many will reject Merlier's premises, and regret his tendentious approach, his effort to systematically apply a social class analysis is original and rich in stimulating hypotheses.

[17] Bo-Boliko, op. cit., p. 75. Merlier, op. cit., p. 191.

were key criteria. The urban elite was distinguished from the workers almost solely in status terms before 1960; only after independence, when the elite gained access to well-remunerated political positions and upper echelons of the administration did economic stratification begin to appear.

Other important characteristics of the urban worker can be noted. For the migrant to the city, social atomization is an intolerable situation; towns have spawned a multitude of associations, providing the individual a structural basis for integration into city life. Especially at the level of the little-educated, unskilled worker, the most important of these were based on ethnic affinities as well as performance of necessary economic or social functions. (The nature of ethnic cleavage in urban society will be further explored in the following chapter.) The poignant summary by a Nigerian observer of the difficulties in building trade union loyalties could be equally valid, *mutatis mutandis,* to the Congo:

"The worker's own tribal organization, or 'improvement' union in the town provides benefits in desperate cases, financially assists those who want to get married, pays the burial expenses of a deceased parent, makes a present on the occasion of the birth of a new babe, honours the worker elevated to chieftaincy, and repatriates the destitute . . . It is this that explains the seeming paradox that whereas the worker will not regularly subscribe to the funds of a trade union (apparently because he is too poor) he does pay regular subscriptions to the funds of his tribal 'union'; and the contributions here are usually higher than those required by the trade union.

"Thus the trade union is caught in a vicious circle: it is deprived of funds because the services it ought to render are provided by non-industrial organizations supported by the workers, and it cannot provide rival services because it has not funds. The sociological factors are equally impressive. In the tribal 'union' for example, the worker can speak and be spoken to in a language he understands well, against a background of customs and traditions he comprehends. . . ."[18]

The nature of traditional kinship structure meant that the African worker was part of an extended family which was likely to have members at various levels of the status strata. This gave to the emerging urban structure a set of vertical linkages which militated against any sharp horizontal cleavage in the African community, even when, after independence, greater economic differentiation became visible. This is in contrast to Western kinship systems, based primarily on the nuclear family, with meaningful expectations of mutual obligation extending only to the immediate members.[19]

Another qualification derives from the newness of Congolese cities; the urban worker has not yet irrevocably broken with the countryside. In nearly all cases, at least a theoretical option of return to the rural homeland is open. There is a village where he could be received as a returning member and reintegrated. Many, especially of the older generation, intend to retire to the village in their old age. It may be that another generation or two will produce an unskilled labor group, born and bred in the city, whose rupture with the rural village is complete; this would be a rather different social group from the present urban immigrant.

The unskilled worker group was placed in a situation of exceptional economic vulnerability by the accelerating rural exodus. Since unemployment became a permanent phenomenon about 1957, there has been in every town a veritable reserve army of unemployed. The colonial economic and political structure inhibited the organization of workers by

[18] T. M. Yesufu, quoted in Richard Sklar, *Nigerian Political Parties* (Princeton: Princeton University Press, 1963), p. 496.

[19] Martin Kilson makes this point rather differently, in noting the "asymetrical" structure of what he calls the middle class—"the fragmented or uneven manner in which persons enter the middle class, without carrying their own immediate social unit along." "Political Change and Modernization," *Journal of Modern African Studies*, I, No. 4 (December 1963), 437-38.

various restrictions. But even had freedom of association existed, the bargaining power of the worker would have been small indeed. It is significant that the only effective union in defending African material grievances was APIC, which represented the modern elite in the civil service. A professionally qualified employee was difficult to replace; a replacement for the unskilled worker loitered just outside the compound gates.

As a group, then, the urban workers as yet lacked clearly expressed goals or the collective self-awareness which would have marked them as a social class. The status differentiation within the African community had not led to any generalized antagonism between worker and clerk, except when status strata became identified with particular ethnic groups. Indeed, the striking fact is that the worker was able to identify so completely with the objectives articulated by the clerks. A special emissary of Buisseret in 1956 was astounded to note at the APIC Congress in 1956 an audience of 1,500 "gave deafening applause to the extremist position of leaders in support of demands affecting no more than 20 of them."[20] South of the border in Northern Rhodesia, the prolonged copperbelt strikes of 1955 were directed at equal access to all jobs in the mines, a grievance which concerned in the short run only the skilled workers and clerks who were competing with Europeans. The urban mass was easily mobilizable for political objectives once these were formulated by the elite, whether, as in Stanleyville, in support of a comprehensive nationalist movement, or, as in other cities, filtered through an ethnic or regional screen.

Genesis of Rural Frustration

The Congolese peasant was more affected by the colonial

[20] G. Smet, "Rapport sur le mission effectuée au Congo Belge du 31 mars au 24 aout 1956, concernént la politique salariale," quoted in R. Poupart, *Première esquisse de l'evolution du syndicalisme au Congo* (Brussels: Editions de l'Institut de Sociologie Solvay, 1960), p. 89.

system than has been the case in most of tropical Africa. This phenomenon is a consequence of the thoroughness of the workings of the colonial mechanism; the administrator came to count the villager, collect his head tax, perhaps innoculate him, and certainly to put him to work building roads and tilling the fields. The missionary, Catholic or Protestant, came to evangelize him; no village was likely to be very far from a mission station, which would very likely have established a catechist in the village. And company agents would come to the village to recruit him.

IMPACT OF THE FREE STATE

From a distance, the impression might be gained that the period between "pacification" and elimination of Free State abuses, and the emergence of a modern nationalist movement was one of quiet administration and gradual economic and social development. However, this image would need to be completed by consideration of the series of major crises which punctuated the *pax belgica*. The Free State period was particularly harsh in its impact in three major areas (see Map 1): 1) In the area from Matadi to Leopoldville, where between 1890 and 1898 the first railroad was constructed. It was not so much the railroad construction itself in this instance, for which a majority of the labor force was recruited elsewhere in Africa,[21] but the cruel burden of portage. All imports and exports, from stationery to steamboats, had to be carried on Bakongo backs over 200 miles of rugged terrain; it is estimated that some 50,000 men were occupied in this calvary.[22] 2) In large parts of what is now Equateur province, the Lac Leopold II area, and parts of Kasai, where the concessionary companies

[21] René J. Cornet, *La bataille du rail* (Brussels: Editions L. Cuypers, 1947), pp. 174-76, 248, 330.

[22] A. J. Wauters, *L'Etat Indépendant du Congo* (Brussels: Librairie Falk Fils, 1899), p. 348. The Free State was obviously aware of the urgency of ending dependence on portage for access to the interior; Stanley had remarked that "without a railroad, the Congo is not worth a penny." Great priority was given to the railroad, which was expensive and difficult to construct.

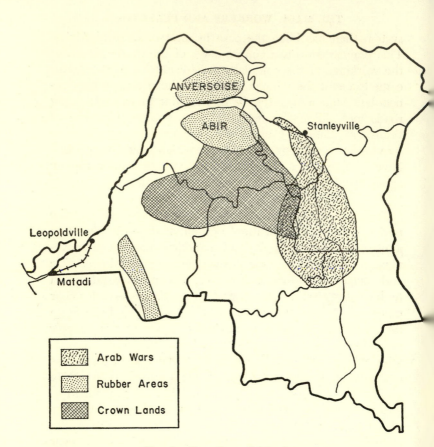

ANVERSOISE

ABIR

Stanleyville

Leopoldville

Matadi

Arab Wars

Rubber Areas

Crown Lands

MAP 1. Free State Crisis Areas

collected "red rubber." This area was confined essentially to those parts of the forest zone then under effective occupation and was especially severe in the concessions of the ABIR and Anversoise Companies. 3) The areas in eastern Kasai and western Kivu (Maniema) where the populations were caught between the marauding Arab slave and ivory traders and expanding Free State occupation. The dislocation of societies in these areas was enormous; the period between

218

1890 and 1895 was one of massive devastation. Although both Arab and European were present in only small numbers, both mobilized an awesome number of Congolese auxiliaries; between the initial Arab-organized slave raids and the military operations of the Free State to eliminate the Arab factor, the toll was heavy indeed.

THE WAR EFFORT: I

World War I had significant repercussions in the Congo. With a large part of metropolitan Belgium occupied by Germans, the Congo was called upon to make a war contribution, in particular to support costly military campaigns to help seize German Africa. Although the army itself was not large, 260,000 porters were required for its logistical support.[23] This was not comparable in scale to the World War II "war effort," but any crisis so serious for the colonizer could not fail to be felt by the colonized. One may note that it was during World War I that the 60-day forced labor provision was instituted by an ordinance-law of the Governor-General, on February 20, 1917, and the much-used law of July 24, 1918, was enacted.[24] The tone of the 1919 report of the Commission for the Protection of Natives reflects the mood of the times, with its sense of genuine alarm at a number of abuses, and especially the apparent depopulation through the rapid spread of sleeping sickness and other diseases.[25] "The Congolese population spared neither its blood nor its efforts," wrote the Commission;[26] the war had prevented the administration from coming to grips with the problem of epidemic disease and subordinated long-run policy considerations to the immediate objective of contributing toward winning the war.

[23] E. Leplae, "Histoire et développement des cultures obligatoires de coton et de riz au Congo Belge de 1917 à 1933," *Congo,* 14th yr., T.I., No. 5 (May 1933), p. 655.

[24] This law, described earlier, gave plenary power to the administration to impose a 200 franc fine or a week in prison for any "disrespectful" word, act, or gesture.

[25] Guebels, *Rélation complète,* pp. 159-225.

[26] *Ibid.,* p. 161.

LABOR CRISIS

The next crisis came in the labor shortage encountered by the mid-1920's. Minister Franck had embarked upon an ambitious development program, with some financial aid from Belgium. During this period, two major railroad projects were carried out, the reconstruction of the Matadi-Leopoldville line and the Port-Francqui-Katanga connection. The Kasai diamond mines, Orientale gold mines, and Katanga copper mines each employed over 20,000 workers. The Lever plantations were just getting underway with their palm oil development and were engaged in large-scale recruitment. The number of wage-earners more than doubled from 1920 to 1925, growing from 125,120 to 274,548. Then at the peak of the crisis, with a booming Congo economy, the number of earners shot up in one year to 421,953.[27] By 1926, the problem of labor recruitment had become extremely serious; such desperate measures as the importation of Chinese coolies and generalized conscription were seriously proposed, and the latter measure was vetoed only at the level of the Council of Ministers after passing the *Conseil Colonial*.[28] The administration was increasingly drawn into the recruiting process; the use of force was widespread, and villagers fled into the forest at the approach of the administrator. The colonizer did face up to the situation and, despite the protests of part of the private sector, placed serious controls upon forced recruitment, even at the price of slowed economic growth.[29]

DEPRESSION REPERCUSSIONS

This emergency was barely beginning to ease when the Congo was hit by the reverse phenomenon; from a crisis of excessive expansion, the colony suddenly collided head on with the world depression, beginning in 1929. Because the Congo had moved closer to a modern, export-oriented economy, it was more vulnerable than most of tropical Africa to

[27] See Table 12, p. 206.
[28] Buell, *The Native Problem in Africa*, II, 506.
[29] *Ibid.*, pp. 544-50.

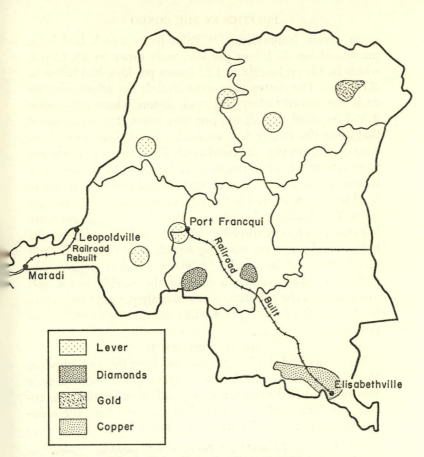

MAP 2. Labor Intensive Centers, 1920's

a world crash. *Union Minière* fired 15,000 workers, and the European population of the Congo dropped by one-third.[30] Palm oil processing plants stayed in operation only "thanks to an increasingly regular and active administrative pressure, the prices offered to the African producer having be-

[30] Pierre Ryckmans, *La politique coloniale* (Brussels: Les Editions Rex, 1934), p. 63.

come almost insignificant."[31] Palm fruits which had been purchased for .25 francs per kilo, were down to .05. Copal, which had been bought at 1.25 francs per kilo, had fallen to .25 francs. The cotton gins were closed; the administration itself was forced to buy and stock cotton, whose cultivation it had required, at half the previous price. It was estimated that an entire family had to work two to three months to earn enough to pay the head tax.[32] Chambers of commerce were clamoring for instructions to be given to the administrators to force deliveries of agricultural produce at prices fixed near zero, to enable the European firms to weather the crisis. The discharged workers sent back to the villages were becoming factors of disorder. "Revolts and threats of revolts have already sent up warning signals that there is a limit which must not be passed."[33] The Congolese peasant obviously had little understanding of the world market and saw only that the colonizer was suddenly paying him a mere fraction of the former price while continuing to make him produce.

THE WAR EFFORT: II

No sooner had the Congo emerged from this period when World War II occurred. The Belgian government-in-exile was under Allied pressure to expand greatly gold, tin, cobalt, tungsten, and rubber production. To satisfy these demands, a "war effort" was undertaken which made a sub-

[31] O. Louwers, *Le problème financier et le problème économique au Congo Belge en 1932.* (Brussels: ARSOM, Sci. Mor. et Pol., T. III, fasc. 2, 1933), pp. 30-31.

[32] *Ibid.,* pp. 31-32. In evaluating figures given in Belgian francs, one must remember that on several occasions since the colonial venture was launched there have been major devaluations of the franc; the postwar franc is only 3% of the value of the 1914 gold franc. For future reference, the following table is inserted:

1914	1.00	1926	.16
1919-1923	.25	1927	.13
1924-1925	.20	1945 to present	.03

Stengers, *Combien le Congo a-t-il couté à la Belgique?,* p. 318.

[33] Louwers, *op. cit.,* pp. 42-45.

stantial contribution (and not only in uranium) to the Allied victory.[34] However, the price paid by the colonial system, and especially the peasant, was very high. In 1942, compulsory cultivation was extended to 120 days, and the collection of wild rubber in the forest, abandoned after the Free State days, was resumed. Monsignor de Hemptinne, who felt that neither Latin Europe nor especially the Congo had any further interest in a war involving Germans, Bolsheviks, Anglo-Saxons, and Asians, warned in a famous letter to the Minister of Colonies, de Vleeschauwer, in December 1943: "In one place, the food situation is becoming aggravated to the point of threatening famine; in another, the villages are disintegrating; elsewhere, there is depopulation. The native populations have been deeply troubled by an ill-considered war effort, and this has been singularly aggravated by the agitation amongst the whites."[35] As in the case of the depression, the peasant could have had little appreciation of and certainly bore no responsibility for the outbreak of a European war.

THE COTTON QUESTION

At the end of World War II, a rural exodus began to be observed. Rubbens wrote in 1945 that the flight of cotton planters was unmistakable; in Lodja, where there had been 20,737 farmers in 1940 there were only 16,000 in 1943. Cotonco had indicated that the number of cotton planters in Lomami was down from 58,000 in 1940 to 45,700 in 1943.[36] The beginning of the rural exodus was a major reason for the establishment of the *paysannats indigènes* in an effort to fix the peasant on the soil. The cotton export companies in particular had a large stake in African production, relying exclusively on deliveries by Congolese peasants; they exerted strong pressure for, and helped finance, the agricultural reorganization, through assigning their own agents to the *paysannats*.

[34] Ryckmans, *Etapes et jalons*, pp. 166-86.
[35] Quoted in Gilbert, *L'empire du silence*, pp. 23-29.
[36] *Dettes de guerre*, p. 45.

The cotton question is of great importance, and is a key to understanding the system of compulsion to which the peasant was subjected. It had been introduced as a crop in 1917, and with it an ordinance establishing compulsory cultivation. Production increased relatively slowly at first, then in the 1930's extended very rapidly, rising from 23,000 tons in 1932 to 127,200 tons in 1939. By 1933, there were 700,000 cotton planters.[37] Grévisse, speaking of Katanga, notes: "It is not true that the territorial personnel had been diverted from its principal mission only since the war. The alteration of the territorial ideal began about 1935 with the introduction or extension of obligatory crops. On this occasion, the representatives of the Agricultural Service have assumed a great ascendancy over other authorities, to a point where many territorial administrators have felt obliged to abandon their own missions."[38]

After the war, however, a ceiling seemed to have been reached, and even this was threatened by the looming menace of a flight from the countryside and the alarming contraction of the forest zone before an enveloping savanna in the north of the country. Malengreau summed up the problem in his study on the *paysannat*: "Unfortunately, even in exceeding the maximum of 60 days of obligatory cultivation authorized by the Decree of 1933, which by the way is becoming a growing practice, and even in requiring the native to work just about continously throughout the year, it is not possible . . . to go beyond a certain ceiling . . . considered to be much too low."[39]

The organization of the cotton export trade had one peculiarity which led to an extension of the crop which some agricultural experts felt to be excessive.[40] The objective was

[37] Brixhe, *op. cit.*, p. 19; Leplae, "Histoire . . . des cultures obligatoires," *loc. cit.*, p. 650.

[38] Grévisse, *La grande pitié des juridictions indigènes*, p. 42.

[39] Malengreau, *Vers un paysannat indigène*, p. 8.

[40] B. Van de Walle, *Essai d'une planification de l'économie agricole congolaise* (Brussels: INEAC, 1960), pp. 41-44.

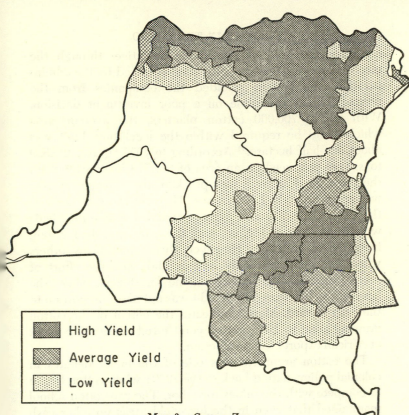

	High Yield
	Average Yield
	Low Yield

MAP 3. Cotton Zones

"High yield" indicates an annual production of over 2000 metric tons per territory. "Average yield" means a production per territory of between 1000 and 2000 tons, and "low yield" indicates less than 1000 tons.

SOURCE: B. Van de Walle, Essai d'une Planification de l'économie agricole congolaise (I.N.E.A.C., 1960)

to assure a stable price to the producer, a widespread practice in Africa through marketing board arrangements. However, the method of price determination was such that the companies could first deduct their operating expenses, profits, and *oeuvres sociales*. The system was harmful in that it permitted the companies to overexpand their network of processing plants in areas where the price to producers did

225

not offer any kind of reasonable incentive; through the mechanism of obligatory cultivation enforced by the administration, the system shielded the companies from the normal market discipline on a poor investment decision. With nearly 700,000 cotton planters, the average area which could be required within the legal time limit was about one-half hectare.[41] According to 1957 figures, 129,829 tons were produced on an area of 331,774 hectares.[42] With the price fixed at six francs per kilo, the average revenue was approximately 1,100 francs. There were areas, such as the Uele, Gandajika and parts of Sankuru, where the yields were substantially higher, and the cultivator had strong incentive to cultivate. However, there were many others where the yield was only half as high, and the effort of several months (particularly in the forest zone where the land had to be cleared by hand) was out of all proportion to the cash reward. Map 3 indicates the entent of the cotton growing area; in 1957, cotton constituted nearly 80 percent of African export crop production.

The cotton argument was one of the major debates in colonial policy, dating back to the 1930's when cotton began to compete with the mines for labor. The pro-cotton school maintained that even in the low-yield areas no other cash crop would grow, so that the meager cotton revenues were better than letting the region stagnate in a subsistence economy. Whatever the merits of this argument, to the rural population, cotton was an extremely unpopular crop; many peasants considered it simply a tribute levied by the European ruler. It is interesting to note that many of the low-cotton yield areas, such as North Katanga, Maniema, much of Sankuru, and parts of Orientale, coincide with zones of radical nationalist response.

Crops were not the only brand of forced labor which irritated the villager. Bo-Boliko perceptively summarizes the

[41] One hectare = 2.471 acres.
[42] Inforcongo, *Le Congo Belge*, II, 96.

several negative causes of the rural exodus from Kutu territory, which does not lie in the cotton zone: "What annoys
the villager of the region the most are the *corvées* to which
they are subjected. The most striking of these are the obligation to assure the transport (by hammock) of any person
black or white traveling in the name of the state and his
baggage, or else to execute tasks such as the repair of roads,
construction and maintenance of houses for colonial agents.
It is superfluous to add that the work of the state has priority over all other activity of traditional subsistence and for
those who complain, it's the prison which makes the wheels
go round."[43]

Another problem relating the rural subject to the system
in a nexus of conflict was the land question. Significantly,
Kasavubu first came to public notice in 1946 with a speech
on "the right of the first occupant," an indication of the growing seriousness of this problem. The amount of land conceded to Europeans under the Free State was fantastic, and
has been estimated to total as much as 27 million hectares, of
a total land area of 234 million.[44] After the *reprise*, the original concessions were renegotiated and reduced, but major
new grants were made to the Lever group. Figures from
1944 indicate that a total of 12 million hectares had been
alienated to Europeans.[45] In 1929, a new dimension was
added with the establishment of a national park system. As
in every country, these public reserves are no doubt appreciated by the community as a whole, but are highly
unpopular with those who are displaced by the parks. The
parks cover a vast area, some 4,000,000 hectares.[46] In particular, the beautiful Albert Park in the Kivu mountains and
Upemba Park in North Katanga were subjects of prolonged and bitter dispute between the administration and
the peoples affected.

[43] Bo-Boliko, *op. cit.*, p. 25.
[44] Merlier, *op. cit.*, p. 58.
[45] *Ibid.*, p. 70.
[46] *Ibid.*, p. 61.

The land issue simmered just below the surface in the postwar years. On the one hand, the administration was under pressure both from individual settlers and large companies to make available substantial new land concessions for coffee in the northeast, oil palm and rubber in the forest zones, and extensive cattle ranching in the southern savannah.[47] On the other, the traditional communities became somewhat more conscious of their own rights, not only in terms of customary concepts of land tenure but also in terms of the land concession procedures of the colonial administration. The formal requirements of establishing that land for concession was legally vacant (i.e., not under effective cultivation or other use by the local Congolese population) were now taken more seriously by many in the administration. Concessions of more than 500 hectares had to be submitted to the *Conseil Colonial*;[48] several of its members, led by Father Van Wing, were openly critical of what they felt to be excessive land grants. Two special commissions were named to study this issue in the 1950's. The reports were never made public, but are known to have made some controversial recommendations for declaring certain zones "saturated" and closing them to any further concessions. With the exception of the Bakongo, the rural communities most affected lacked the spokesmen to articulate their grievances on this issue; only muffled overtones of the dispute broke into print.[49] Until urban nationalism came into its own, especially after the Leopoldville riots, many responsible colonial officials felt the land problem was the most serious crisis faced by Belgium in the Congo. At the same time, it was somewhat localized, and had reached critical

[47] For an extreme statement of these demands on behalf of individual settlers, see Emile Dehoux, *L'effort de paix du Congo Belge* (Brussels: Robert Stoops, 1946).

[48] Article 15, *Charte Coloniale*.

[49] For example, the illuminating article by E. Boelaert, "Les trois fictions du droit foncier congolais," *Zaïre*, XI, No. 4 (April 1957), **399-427.**

dimensions only in the Lower Congo, Kwilu, Kivu, and some parts of northern and western Katanga.

A new element after the war, especially beginning with the implementation of the Ten Year Plan in 1950, was the generalization of primary education in the countryside. There were not only quantitative but qualitative changes; during this period, rural schools became something more than the rudimentary institutions of the earlier years. As this movement gained momentum, it came in the late 1950's to coincide with another, the halt in the spectacular growth rate of the early postwar years. In both rural and urban areas there began to appear a social group which proved highly volatile—a disoriented youth. The primary education often made traditional village life intolerable, yet the economic slowdown and secondary bottleneck meant that access to satisfactory advance in the modern sector was blocked. These were the groups who became the "muscle" of the nationalist movement, who filled the ranks of the numerous militia that parties established in early 1960. They also constituted an element which parties themselves soon became afraid of, and have been the authors of considerable violence in the post-independence period. Their frustration made them susceptible to the appeal of militant nationalism, but the nationalist leadership came to realize that it could not offer them full satisfaction after independence. The Executive College, including Kasavubu, Lumumba, Anicet Kashamura, and Remy Mwamba, voted unanimously on March 25, 1960, to dissolve all private militias.[50]

The Congo under Belgian administration was committed to a forced pace of economic development. In rural areas, this meant that the village populations had to be coerced into the cash economy. The alliance between capital and administration assured that investment was well-remunerated, and the social cost inevitable in rapid economic transformation fell largely on the peasantry. To situate this in

[50] *Congo 1960*, I, 75-76.

historical perspective, we need add that in every case of rapid development, those directing the process placed the burden upon peasant and worker. In this sense, the experience of the Congolese villager is comparable to the role of the immigrant in American industrialization, working classes in Western Europe, and of workers and peasants in the Soviet Union in the 1930's and more recently China.

The totality of policies pursued in rural areas—land alienation, national parks, creation of *paysannats*, obligatory cultivation, other forced labor, relocation of villages along roadways—imposed modernity on the countryside. If we follow Martin Kilson in suggesting that integration into a cash nexus is the key factor in distinguishing the political transition from traditional to modern, then we may conclude that there is no parallel in tropical Africa for the degree of penetration of a modern economic-social system throughout the entire territory.[51] If we add to this the impact, first of evangelization, then education, we find the simultaneous infusion of new norms, of new cosmologies. Finally, the rapid extension of a feeder road system, the airplane, and the radio after World War II joined with the other rail and river routes to provide channels of social communication which eroded the isolation of the rural village. The colonial system had in good part succeeded in eliminating the subsistence economy, in methodically reconstructing an entire society by its own blueprint. In the words of Governor-General Ryckmans, "It is not only a matter of furnishing seeds or providing new techniques; it means redoing the education of an entire people, of modifying profoundly its mentality—of giving it a new soul."[52]

But at the same time, the colonial system had engendered a profound frustration at the level of the mass. This is

[51] Kilson, *loc. cit.* In our view, Kilson's approach is a more useful way of conceptualizing the penetration under colonial auspices of a modern economy than the misleading "rural proletariat" analysis put forward by Merlier, *op cit.*

[52] Ryckmans, *Etapes et jalons,* pp. 137-38.

perhaps the key to understanding the astounding politiza-
tion of a large part of the countryside in so brief a period of
time. Symptoms of the frustration broke through in the
widespread outcropping of syncretic religious movements.
These, however, in their millennial, apocalyptic vision of
change reflect the conviction that the colonial system was
impregnable, a permanent source of humiliation. When the
perspectives suddenly changed, when "Boula Matari" was
clearly on the run, there followed in many sections the explosive outburst of a radical form of rural nationalism.[53] It
was not a programmatic radicalism; its objectives were
limited to the destruction of the system and the end of the
humiliation.

Worker and peasant, then, had a very different reaction
to the colonial system from that of the elite. The latter was
frustrated by its lack of status in the system and the multiple psychological wounds of pervasive racial discrimination.
The former sought an end to the process of being dragged,
wrenched, and tugged into a modern society. This was not a
Luddite revolt against modernity; indeed, the village core
of the traditional world was fast emptying. But the oppres-
sive, omnipresent system had to go. No more taxes, no more
cotton, no more census-takers, no more vaccinaters, no more
identity cards, no more army recruiters. Whether such a
happy world could exist was, of course, beside the point.

[53] The rural radicalism thesis was originated by Herbert Weiss, in
a paper delivered before the African Studies Association, Oct. 20,
1961, summarized in *African Studies Bulletin*, IV, No. 4 (December
1961), 8-9.

CHAPTER XI

xxxxxxxxxxxxxxxxxxxxxxxxxxxxxxxxxxxxxxxxxxxxxxxxxxxxxxx

The Politics of Ethnicity

xxxxxxxxxxxxxxxxxxxxxxxxxxxxxxxxxxxxxxxxxxxxxxxxxxxxxxx

The Challenge of Cultural Pluralism

No ANALYSIS of the emerging political system in the Congo can escape grappling with the elusive problem of "tribalism," or ethnicity. This is a transcendent issue for the Congolese polity, and indeed poses the very question of the polity's continued existence. For seventy-five years, the numerous African societies preexisting the scramble for Africa had superimposed upon them the "steel grid of colonialism," to use Coleman's evocative metaphor.[1] Despite the intensity of this historic experience, the time span involved is less than the lifetime of some Congolese. It was foreseeable that the conflict of loyalty between the new nation, *née* colonial state, and the diverse ethnic entities which were incorporated within its artificial boundaries would be a challenge to the new leadership.[2]

Although all new African states are confronted with this problem in varying degrees, most have managed to contain it within tolerable limits; Zanzibar and Rwanda are the major exceptions. In many cases, independence was achieved under the tutelage of a single party. In others, such as Nigeria and Uganda, ingenious constitutional arrangements have been devised to insure a balance between the major component parts of the state. In most, a liberal dosage of authoritarianism has been necessary.

It is tempting to approach this problem by establishing an analytic dichotomy between traditional and modern,

[1] James S. Coleman, "The Character and Viability of African Political Systems," in *The United States and Africa* (New York: American Assembly, 1958), p. 27.

[2] See for example, the excellent analysis in Rupert Emerson, *From Empire to Nation* (Cambridge, Mass.: Harvard University Press, 1960), pp. 89-131.

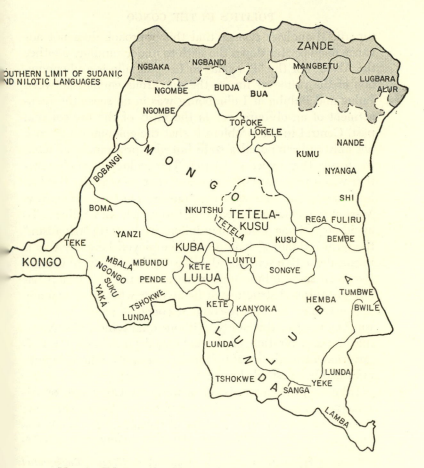

MAP 4. Ethnographic Map of the Republic of the Congo

anachronism and progress. The very term "tribalism" is tainted and carries the unspoken implication of antithesis to progress. Indeed, the word "tribe" came into the vocabulary of discourse on Africa only in the nineteenth century, as a pejorative expression for "state" or "kingdom."[3] But even

[3] Philip D. Curtin, *African History* (New York: Macmillan Company, 1964), p. 38.

233

superficial analysis reveals that this approach does not advance one very far down the path to understanding. Neither the Abako nor the "Bangala" in Leopoldville is a phenomenon of the primeval forest; the disastrous conflict between Lulua and Baluba at Luluabourg was in no sense the reenactment of an obscure war in the mists of the pre-colonial past. Central to the problem is that the colonial experience not only superimposed a state but also profoundly affected the preexisting African societies. The ecology of modernization was a process which operated not only at the level of individuals but also with the "culture clusters," to borrow Merriam's useful analytical unit,[4] to which they adhere. To avoid any stigma which may inhere in the term "tribalism," the term "ethnicity" is in general employed here. By this is meant the active sense of identification by nearly all Congolese with some ethnic unit, whether or not this group has any institutional structure of its own, or whether it had any real existence in the pre-colonial epoch. And by "nationalism," as used in this study, without qualifying adjective, is meant the aspiration of the colonized population for self-government of the new political community whose boundaries had been established by the colonizer.[5]

Ethnicity, of course, is not a uniquely Congolese or African phenomenon. Careful scrutiny of the ethnic arithmetic

[4] Alan P. Merriam, "The Concept of Culture Clusters Applied to the Belgian Congo," *Southwestern Journal of Anthropology*, XV, No. 4 (Winter, 1959), 373-95.

[5] This is essentially Coleman's definition, in *Nigeria, Background to Nationalism*, pp. 1-7, and in his article, "Nationalism in Tropical Africa," *American Political Science Review*, XLVIII (June 1954), 404-26. This narrower sense is chosen over the broader and equally tenable definition used by Hodgkin (*Nationalism in Colonial Africa*, pp. 9-25) merely for analytical convenience, to distinguish a loyalty matrix based upon the nation-state in gestation with that which has an African culture cluster referent smaller than the nation-state, or astride the modern boundaries. For a recent and stimulating discussion of the metaphysical problems involved in defining the concept of African nationalism, see Ali A. Masrui, "On the Concept 'We are All Africans,'" *American Political Science Review*, LVII (March 1963), 88-97.

in a political ticket in any New England state will illustrate its universal aspects. Handlin's chronicle of the immigrant communities in America reveals some interesting parallels with the social and political behavior of the new immigrants to Congolese towns.[6] Recent grave difficulties in Canada and Belgium show that problems of political instability persist in culturally plural nations at all levels of economic development.

Students of African politics have not, until recently, been especially preoccupied with this issue. One obvious reason was that ethnicity as a norm of political behavior was largely obscured in the colonial period. Reaction to the colonizer was a transcendant obligation, and until the metropolitan power had irrevocably committed itself to departure it could not be clear just how significant an element ethnicity would be. Further, the stereotype of the "detribalized" urban, educated African had been established by earlier generations of administrators and anthropologists beginning with Lugard. This new breed of African was purported to be totally "Europeanized," and "cut off from his people." A useful concomitant of the "detribalization" premise was that the educated African could be considered as *ipso facto* unrepresentative; he could not pretend to challenge the "natural rulers" who held sway in the Native Authorities.[7] In a more recent period, the detribalization myth was quietly absorbed into other streams of thought. The term was often used by scholars as simply synonymous with urbanization.[8] The study of African politics began to attract

[6] Oscar Handlin, *The Uprooted* (New York: Little, Brown and Company, 1951). On the universality of this phenomenon, see also John S. and Leatrice Macdonald, "Urbanization, Ethnic Groups and Social Segmentation," *Social Research*, XXIX, No. 4 (Winter, 1962), 433-48.

[7] This idea is suggested by Paul Mercier, in an excellent and important article, "Rémarques sur la signification du 'tribalisme' actuel en Afrique noire," *Cahiers Internationaux de Sociologie*, XXXI (1961), 61-80.

[8] Godfrey Wilson, for example, entitled his study of Broken Hill,

many who were sympathetic to the aims of African nationalism, who were not anxious to serve colonial propaganda by
emphasis upon themes which might be exploited to dis-
credit nationalist movements. On its side, the nationalist
leadership was bent on proving that it was shorn of ethnic
reflexes.

Several interesting hypotheses concerning the political
role of ethnicity have been advanced in other African con-
texts. Immanuel Wallerstein[9] has noted the tendency toward the formation in urban centers of new solidarity
groups with an ethnic label and some rough relationship
with a traditional grouping. He argues that the transfer of
identity from the rural, customary social group to a hybrid
urban one is a crucial step toward national integration, as
the artificial character and lack of genuine historic roots or
organic structure of the town ethnic reference groups will
insure their transitional character and will be less of an
obstacle to a national loyalty than a continuing sense of full
membership in a bona fide traditional society.

A rather different thesis is advanced by Aristide Zolberg,
in a study of the *Parti Démocratique de la Côte d'Ivoire*
(PDCI).[10] He argues that the Houphouet-Boigny party op-

An Essay on the Economics of Detribalization (Livingstone, Northern
Rhodesia: Rhodes Livingstone Institute, 1941-42). The word "detribalization" is not, however, used in the text. E. Hellman, in *Rooiyard:
A Sociological Study of an Urban Native Slum Yard* (Capetown: Oxford University Press, 1948), makes explicit use of the notion of
"detribalization," defined as permanent residence outside the tribal
area, severance of relationships with the chief, and lack of dependence
on rural relatives for support or performance of ceremonies. This
does not necessarily imply a complete rupture with rural areas, and
even less a total loss of ethnic identity. See also J. C. Mitchell, "Urbanization, Detribalization and Stabilization in Southern Africa: A
Problem of Definition and Measurement," in UNESCO, *Social Implications of Industrialization and Urbanization in Africa South of
the Sahara*, pp. 693-711.

[9] Immanuel Wallerstein, "Ethnicity and National Integration," *Cahiers d'Etudes Africaines*," I (July 1960), pp. 129-39.

[10] A. R. Zolberg, "Effets de la structure d'un parti politique sur
l'intégration nationale," *Cahiers d'Etudes Africaines*, I (October
1960), 140-49.

erated at two levels; at that of the leadership, it was successful in establishing new relationships, in "transferring the
political power previously held by traditional authorities
to the central organs of a modern government." However,
at the level of the mass, "the cells of the party have maintained, and even reinforced, the solidarity of ethnic and
family links." The PDCI found that the only way it could
communicate was through ethnic sections; efforts to make
these sections geographic failed. Yet the process is circular;
in making the ethnic cells the foundation for its political
communication and action, the PDCI is infusing urban ethnic solidarity groups with a modern function they did not
previously possess, and thus it strengthens them. There was
even talk of reorganizing the Triechville quarter of Abidjan
on an ethnic residential pattern and ending the present
scrambling.

The most systematic study of the problem has been conducted by several scholars associated with the Rhodes-Livingstone Institute in Northern Rhodesia, especially J. Clyde
Mitchell, A. L. Epstein, and Max Gluckman.[11] Perhaps because the Copperbelt towns have so much in common with
most Congo urban agglomerations, especially the nearby
South Katanga centers, the hypotheses which they have
developed seem particularly useful. Vincent Harlow, although one of the first to face the problem, misses the point
in only treating the rural aspect of tribalism.[12] Tribalism,

[11] See especially J. Clyde Mitchell's *The Kalela Dance* (Manchester:
Manchester University Press, 1956); A. L. Epstein's *Politics in an
Urban African Community* (Manchester: Manchester University
Press, 1958); Max Gluckman's "Tribalism in Modern British Central
Africa," *Cahiers d'Etudes Africaines*, I (January 1960), 55-70. For an
important work situating the problem in the rather different setting of
South Africa, see Philip Mayer, *Townsmen or Tribesmen* (Cape-
town: Oxford University Press, 1961).

[12] Vincent Harlow, "Tribalism in Africa," *Journal of African Administration*, XII (January 1955), 17-20. Harlow was one of the
first to argue that it was inadequate to assume simply that tribalism
was rapidly dissolving; he cites the example of the Chagga in
Tanganyika having recently chosen a paramount chief, a position

these scholars argue, must be seen in two dimensions. In the countryside, tribalism "involves participation in a working political system, and sharing domestic life with kinsfolk; . . . this continued participation is based on present economic and social needs, and not merely on conservatism."[13] In the towns, a new form of ethnicity grows up; it is not a group bound in a patterned structure, but a solidarity network with ethnic boundaries. The town-dwellers display their ethnic origin in the language they use, their way of life, which enables others "immediately to fit their neighbors and acquaintances into categories which determine the mode of behavior towards them." Mitchell continues: "For Africans in the Copperbelt 'tribe' is the primary category of social interaction, i.e., the first significant characteristic to which any African reacts in another. Frequently relationships never penetrate beyond this and tribes appear to one another to be undifferentiated wholes."[14]

Mitchell argues further that there should be no surprise in finding that ethnic identity serves as the most significant category of day-to-day social interaction, despite the emergence in the urban environment of new, non-ethnic prestige and status strata: "There is a constant flow of newcomers into the towns from the various rural districts from which the Copperbelt draws its labor supplies. They are not immediately absorbed into the prestige system which could possibly supply an alternative principle of social interaction. Instead their own ethnic distinctiveness which they took for granted in the rural areas is immediately thrown into relief by the multiplicity of tribes with whom they are cast into association. Its importance to them is thus exaggerated and

---

which had no sanction in history. But the "tribalism" he talks about is not exactly the same phenomenon as the urban-centered ethnicity which has constituted such a problem for the Congo.

[13] Gluckman, *loc. cit.*, p. 55.

[14] Mitchell, *op. cit.*, p. 32.

it becomes the basis on which they interact with all strangers."[15]

From these studies emerges the fruitful hypothesis that political behavior can be analyzed in terms of a multiplicity of roles, the relative importance of each at any given time dependent upon the situation. An urban African is, in economic terms, a worker *vis-à-vis* his employer, the mining companies. With reference to the dominant European society, the African is simply an African. And within the compound or African quarter of the town, he is related to an ethnic reference group. In a situation where the transcendent conflict is with his European employer, as during the Copperbelt strikes of 1935 or 1940, the ethnic role is of very little importance; the same can be said of crisis situations where the central issue is that of the continued hegemony of the settler-colonial complex. The 1959 Leopoldville riots, a brief but nearly total mobilization of the African *qua* African in an anomic response to the colonial situation, is a case in point. But in the internal politics of an African trade union, where the issue may be the leadership of ethnic group A or B embodied in the persons of rival candidates, the situational context is entirely different, and the African relates himself to the conflict through his ethnic role.

Mercier adds the further suggestion that this situational analysis needs to be extended to reactions in terms of ethnic role itself. Ethnic identity is highly ambiguous and fluid. Within every large group, there are recognizable subdivisions. In a situation where perceived conflict is with an external group, social action relates to the larger ethnic referent. But when threats from outside the group diminish in intensity, then the locus of conflict and cleavage may transfer to the subdivisions of the larger group.[16] For example, when the Bakongo were confronted with the "Bangala" in

[15] *Ibid.*, p. 29.
[16] Mercier, *loc. cit.*

Leopoldville, a high degree of solidarity was attainable. When the issue was election of members to the executive committee of the Bakongo movement, Abako, friction between Bakongo subgroups (Bantandu, Bandibu, Manianga, Mayombe, and others) came to the surface.

With this general introduction, a return to the specifics of the Congo environment is now in order. It is undeniable that the events of the past few years have brought to the surface, and, by all indications, increased, ethnic consciousness. The first problem is to seek out the roots of ethnicity as a contemporary phenomenon and then to examine successively some of the particular elements of the Congo situation which have made its political impact especially intense, in comparison with other African experience.

The Phenomenon of "Super-Tribalism"

The focal point of the modern political process is urban, and it is to the city one must initially turn. The first point to note is that urban ethnic reference groups involve a major simplification of the innumerable groupings of the countryside. Jean Rouch first called attention to this phenomenon, calling it "super-tribalism."[17] Wallerstein has described this in West Africa; Mitchell ably summarizes it for the Copperbelt, on the basis of an ingenious survey he undertook to establish a scale of "social distance":

"The main point that emerges from the experiment is that the more distant a group of peoples is from another, both socially and geographically, the greater the tendency to regard them as an undifferentiated category and to place them under a general rubric such as 'Bemba,' 'Ngonï,' 'Lozi,' etc. In this way, from the point of view of the African on the Copperbelt, all tribes other than those from his particular home area tend to be reduced into three or four categories bearing the label of those tribes who, at the coming of the

[17] Jean Rouch, "Migrations au Ghana," *Journal de la Société des Africanistes,* XXVI, No. 19 (1956).

Europeans, were the more powerful and dominant in the region."[18]

This reductive process is completed when the individual himself accepts, at least in terms of his relations with other groups, the new label which others have put upon him. Caprasse found this to be the case in Elisabethville:

"It seems that it would be the phenomenon of ethnic regroupment which could explain, in part, a federation of all the Kasai Baluba; one forgets, little by little, the multiple subdivisions to retain only the similarities and to regroup on their basis. It is according to the same principle of reduction to the essential lines, it seems, that two groups as antagonistic, in the *cité*, as the Kasai Baluba and the Baluba Shankadi [of Katanga] have tried, at various times to federate in a single association, because, according to informants involved in these efforts, there was a common ancestor for the two groups."[19]

"Super-tribalism" began to appear simultaneously with the first clusterings of heterogeneous Congolese populations around Free State outposts. For example, in eastern Kasai, much of the population was dislocated and disorganized as a result of the Arab incursions and the subsequent campaign against them. At a very early date, an uprooted class, no doubt including many Baluba but also many others, took refuge around the European posts. Visiting Lusambo, Kasai, in 1908, Hilton-Simpson, a member of the famous Torday-Joyce anthropological expedition, reported an "enormous" African population. A number of separate ethnic villages were grouped about the post; however, "in addition to these, there is a very large mixed population of natives belonging to no particular village, who are generally termed Baluba by the white men of the Kasai, but who in reality belong to that tribe no more than to any other."[20] These included the

[18] Mitchell, *op. cit.*, p. 28.
[19] Caprasse, *Leaders africains en milieu urbain*, pp. 36-37.
[20] M. W. Hilton-Simpson, *Land and Peoples of the Kasai* (London: Constable & Co., 1911), p. 72.

former Arab slaves, the uprooted, the outcasts, many of whom had no idea from what village they came. This group no doubt successfully became "Baluba."

Artificial Ethnicity: The "Bangala"

The most striking example of an urban ethnic group which is a pure specimen of "super-tribalism" is the Leopoldville "Bangala." The most recent ethnological study of the region in Equateur which was believed to have been their home states: "We believed for a long time in the existence of a people called the Bangala, speaking Lingala and possessing very definite ethnic and cultural characteristics. . . . We know today with certainty that, in all the Belgian Congo, there exists no ethnic group bearing this name."[21]

The origins of the myth are not entirely clear. Stanley, the first foreign visitor to the region, first used the name. He drew attention to the Bangala, whom he termed the "Ashanti of the Congo," "unquestionably a very superior tribe"; in the same breath, he remarked that they only amounted to a string of villages extending ten miles along the Congo River banks, near what is now Nouvelle Anvers.[22] His attraction to this small cluster led him to deposit Coquilhat amongst them with the task of establishing a station in 1883. Coquilhat gave great impetus to the myth, in lending credence to the tales spun by Mata Buike, a village chief at his station; "if these reports are correct," he wrote, "Mata Buike governs one of the most vast states in equatorial Congo."[23] That he did take them seriously is indicated by his estimate that there were 110,000 Bangala.[24] He was more than a little disconcerted when one day Mata Buike told him that he

[21] H. Burssens, *Les peuplades de l'entre Congo-Ubangi* (Tervuren Belgium: Musée Royal du Congo Belge, 1958), pp. 14, 37.

[22] Henry M. Stanley, *Through the Dark Continent* (New York Harper & Bros., 1878), II, 301-02.

[23] Camille Coquilhat, *Sur le Haut-Congo* (Paris: J. Lebegue et Cie. 1888), p. 202.

[24] Cyr. Van Overbergh, *Les Bangala* (Brussels: Institut International de Bibliographie, 1907), p. 65.

was not a Bangala after all, but that this name referred to the peoples downstream.[25]

This would never have been more than a historical anecdote were it not for Coquilhat's success in persuading a large number from the area surrounding his Equateur station to enter the service of the state. They formed an important part of the *Force Publique* rank and file in the early years, and also the bulk of the crews for the river steamers. And they began settling around the European post at Stanley Pool.

The recruitment extended rapidly along the river banks, and with it the boundaries of the "Bangala" tribe began to grow. An early state officer, Lothaire, observed: "Take a contingent of workers engaged aboard the steamers, or workers in the state posts along the Congo River, choose them from all the tribes of the area; they all become Bangala. They will tell you . . . 'We are Bangala.' Even if they belong to hostile groups, while out of their areas they will unite."[26]

The myth of the Bangala was given anthropological sanction when a volume which was dedicated to the Bangala was included in the important ethnological survey of the Congo, directed by E. de Jonghe. An ethnic map was published which indicated that the "tribe" covered an enormous area, extending from Coquilhatville 400 miles upstream, and running inland some 100 miles on each side of the river. An immediate *caveat* was entered by the first Protestant missionary to establish a post in the area where Stanley and Coquilhat had discovered the tribe: "In a work published in Brussels the term 'Bangala' is made to cover a vast area. . . . This includes a dozen or more different tribes, talking as many distinct languages, having various tribal marks, possessing in many instances very different customs . . . among whom there is nothing in common except their

[25] Coquilhat, *op. cit.*, p. 244.
[26] Quoted in Van Overbergh, *op. cit.*, p. 55.

black skin and backwardness in civilization." Speaking of the cluster of villages which had formed the "Bangala" heartland, he added, "The natives themselves never used the name Bangala."[27]

The legend was consolidated by the adoption of "Lingala" as a language for the army and communicating with the population. This river trading language was especially influenced by Lobobangi, but also included infusions from Swahili, Kikongo, and other more local river dialects; the simplified version used by Europeans refined out most of the inflectional elements difficult for non-Africans to learn.[28] It was widely believed that this synthetic *lingua franca* was the Bangala language, as the name given it implies; here again Weeks is enlightening:

"This heterogeneous mass of humanity [the Africans stationed at Nouvelle Anvers], often numbering over two thousand soldiers, workmen and women, held communication with each other by means of the 'trade language.' The smartest of the natives in the towns adjacent to Diboko [Nouvelle Anvers] quickly learned this jargon, and used it more or less fluently when communicating to State soldiers and workmen, and the white men hearing the natives of the neighborhood talking this lingo jumped to the conclusion that it was their own tongue in which they were conversing and thus called it the Bangala language, and by that name it was generally known on the Upper Congo."[29]

In later years, in Leopoldville, all *gens du Haut,* or immigrants, arriving from up the river were referred to as Bangala. The Bakongo in particular referred to all non-Bakongo as Bangala, and the term came to be accepted by all but the Kasaiens, Mongo, and Kwango-Kwiluites. An

[27] John H. Weeks, *Among Congo Cannibals* (London: Seeley, Service & Co., 1913), pp. 161, 165.
[28] Burssens, *op. cit.,* p. 16; G. Hulstaert, *Carte linguistique du Congo Belge* (Brussels: ARSOM, T. XIX, fasc. 5, 1950), p. 24.
[29] Weeks, *op. cit.,* pp. 48-49.

ethnic federation, Liboke-lya-Bangala, was organized which, according to one African source, in 1957 had forty-eight affiliated tribal associations, and 50,000 members.[30] Both Europeans and Africans tended to analyze Leopoldville society in terms of a Bakongo-Bangala duality, and the 1957 urban elections were generally described in these terms.[31] One major Congolese political leader, Jean Bolikango, linked his political fortunes with the reconstitution of a *grande ethnie bangala;* significantly Bolikango is one of the rare personalities who was actually born in Leopoldville, of parents who came from Lisala, a Ngombe region. It is instructive to observe that the Bangala movement was at its height when the entire nascent political process was centered upon Leopoldville. More recently, Bolikango has sought to assert Bangalahood as a legitimating principle for the new province of Moyen-Congo. He faces great obstacles, for the dominant group in the province considers itself Ngombe. The major dissident group in the province, the Budja of Bumba territory, equally rejects the super-tribal label exported from Leopoldville.

An interesting variant of super-tribalism was the use of regional administrative units as well as tribal entities as bases for self-identification. Biebuyck and Douglas have pointed out that although "administrative units often cut across tribal and linguistic boundaries, . . . to some extent their very existence has created solidarities of another kind."[32] In Leopoldville, in the years preceding the urban elections, of the five major ethnic associations, three bore the name of administrative divisions rather than tribes, even in the case

[30] Tshibangu, *La technique de nomination,* p. 121.

[31] See, for example, Mobutu's report of the elections, *Avenir,* Dec. 9, 1957; M. C. C. De Backer's section on the "Bangala," *Notes pour servir à l'étude des groupements politiques à Léopoldville* (Brussels: Inforcongo, 1959, mimeo), I, 11-12; and Merriam's analysis of "Bangala parties," *Congo: Background of Conflict* (Evanston, Ill.: Northwestern University Press, 1961), pp. 157-67.

[32] Daniel Biebuyck and Mary Douglas, *Congo Tribes and Parties* (London: Royal Anthropological Institute, 1961), pp. 19-20.

of Fedequalac (Federation of Equateur and Lac Leopold II), which was a purely Mongo movement. In Elisabethville, Grévisse notes that in the early postwar years the Bakasai was an effective ethnic federation which in fact grouped several tribes, Baluba, Lulua, Basongye, Batetela, and Kanyoka; they were indeed all lumped into a single undesirable category of "strangers" by those from southern Katanga.[33] These regional loyalties tended to give way to more specifically ethnic ones in the last years before independence. The Bakasai group, for example, could not survive the emergence of the aggressive and dynamic Lulua Frères organization, about 1953, fueled by a reaction to Baluba hegemony in Luluabourg and environs. The one major example of a solidarity appeal based upon an administrative subdivision was the PSA, based upon Kwilu district.

Emergent Ethnic Awareness

But the ethnic awareness produced by urban environment has not been exclusively super-tribal. In cases of large, cultural communities lacking centralized structures, such as the Mongo, or retaining only an historical recollection of them, as the Bakongo, urban experience produced a sharpened sense of unity within the group which was entirely new in its intensity. Co-existence with other ethnic groups engendered a heightened sense of the cultural identity which set the Bakongo, for example, apart from the Bangala. Differential opportunities, social standing, or treatment by the administration reinforced this self-awareness and provided a bill of grievances which spawned active ethnic organization and aggressive assertion of ethnic claims.

THE BAKONGO

In Leopoldville the Bakongo felt threatened by the growing use of Lingala not only as a language of administration but as a language of education to the detriment of Kikongo.

[33] Grévisse, *Le centre extra-coutumier d'Elisabethville*, p. 308.

Further, the administrator appeared to the Bakongo to take a clear stand against them by choosing both postwar *chefs de cité* from the Bangala (the post was created in 1945). In the manifesto which was the call for the foundation of the Bakongo movement, Abako, the appeal for unification of language and people is clear: "All Bakongo are brothers from the same stock: Kongo Dia Ntotila. However, since the collapse of our beloved Kingdom provoked by the incessant wars with our neighbors, the Bayaka, and the slave traffic of the last three centuries, we are no longer united. . . . Let us concentrate our efforts and intellectual capacities so that we will . . . never fail in this grand national task we would like to undertake."[34]

Thus, although the problems of Leopoldville did not directly concern the Bakongo hinterland, and the Abako was not at first a movement with strong roots in the countryside, the sense of external threat from both colonizer and his alleged ally, the Bangala, was gradually transmitted. The latent capacity for unified action was strengthened by a remarkably potent historic myth. Balandier remarks that in the remotest village there is not a Mukongo who cannot recite the tale of San Salvador, "where all were born, where each clan still has its street, and where each one has relatives to receive him."[35] The sense of ethnic unity had in an earlier period found religious expression in the countryside, as the rural areas were swept in 1921 by Kimbanguism, and subsequently by related prophetic movements. Sharpening pressure on land, especially in Mayombe, where extensive concessions had been made to European forestry, oil palm, and cattle ranching enterprises, provided a rural grievance which readily fused with the protest message of the urban elite.

THE MONGO

Another example is the gradual rise of an ethnic self-con-

[34] *ABAKO 1950-1960*, pp. 10-12.
[35] Georges Balandier, *Sociologie actuelle de l'Afrique noire* (Paris: Presses Universitaires de France, 1955), p. 39.

sciousness among the Mongo. This far-flung culture cluster stretches from the Nkundo-Mongo of Lac Leopold II to the Batetela-Bakusu of Sankuru and Maniema. There was never any central political structure in this segmentary society, nor is there any evidence of an active sense of ethnic identity predating colonial penetration. Various Mongo subgroups identified themselves to early travelers by one of the subgroup or clan designations. The basis for positing Mongo unity—the legend of common descent from the single ancestor Mongo, similarities in language, and related social organization and ritual—became slowly apparent to European analysts, but the Nkundo-Mongo of the Coquilhatville region had no notion that hundreds of miles to the southeast, in Maniema, the Bakusu also spoke of Mongo as the founder of their people. The initial wave of anthropological writing makes no mention of the Mongo as a discrete cultural grouping.

It was the task of four major writers, three missionaries and an administrator, to accredit the thesis of a single Mongo people. These four, E. Boelaert, G. Hulstaert, E. P. A. de Rop, and Georges Vanderkerken, became dedicated advocates of Mongohood; Vanderkerken urged the unification of the Mongo in a single province, Boelaert after independence called for the creation of a Mongo state, and all urged the fusion of Mongo dialects into a single Lomongo, to be used both in education and administration.[36] It is no mere coincidence that all four were Flemish; the parallels are striking between what was advocated for the Mongo and demands then formulated by the growing Flemish

[36] To cite only a sampling of the many writings on the Mongo by these four we may mention Georges Vanderkerken, *L'ethnie Mongo;* E. Boelaert, "De Nkundó-Mongó, een volk, een taal," *Aequatoria,* I, No. 8 (1938), 3-25; Boelaert, "Vers un état mongo," *Bull. Séances* (ARSOM, 1961), pp. 382-91; G. Hulstaert, *Les Mongo: Aperçu général* (Tervuren, Belgium; Musée Royal de l'Afrique Centrale, 1961); E. P. A. de Rop, *Bibliografie over de Mongo* (Brussels: ARSOM, Sci. Mor. et Pol., N.S., T. VIII, fasc. 2, 1956).

nationalist movement for the unification and development of their language and people.

The first public defense of the Mongo unity hypothesis appeared only in 1938, or more than half a century after the establishment of permanent European posts in the Mongo zone. Boelaert was the innovator, with an article "De Nkundó-Mongó, een volk, een taal" (The Nkundo-Mongo: One People, One Language), and consolidation of the Mongo case came in 1944 with the publication of former Equateur Governor Vanderkerken's massive, two-volume study, *L'ethnie Mongo*. Writings on the Mongo developed rapidly; de Rop, in his 1956 *Bibliografie over de Mongo*, was able to assemble nearly 100 pages of assorted studies on the Mongo and their sub-groups. These four played a role in catalyzing the awareness of Mongo unity comparable to that of Van Wing among the Bakongo.

The idea of Mongohood then became rapidly transmitted to the emerging Mongo elite in the cities, especially Coquilhatville and Leopoldville. Although Boelaert records a "very beautiful and very nationalist poetry"[37] arising in the countryside in response to the grave demographic crisis which seemed to traverse many Mongo areas from the Free State rubber collection days until World War II, the Africanization of Mongohood was first publicly undertaken in Leopoldville in the early 1950's. Joseph Ileo, Antoine-Roger Bolamba, Paul Bolya, and Eugene Ndjoku were among the best-known Mongo intellectuals; they were frequent contributors to *La Voix du Congolais* in this period and a number of articles appeared, especially from Bolamba's pen, on the richness of the Mongo cultural heritage. They began to dissociate themselves progressively from the "Bangala" category to which they had been assigned in earlier years. Although in 1951, they had joined in founding the Liboke-lya-Bangala, soon afterwards they split off to found their own group, Fedequalac. Bolamba argued, "More

[37] R. P. E. Boelaert, "Vers un état mongo," *loc. cit.*, p. 383.

than persons of other races [tribes], the Mongo are proud of their land, their past, and their language." He quotes extensively from a 1956 article by a Mongo compatriot entitled, "Nous ne sommes pas des Bangalas":

"If we defend our name, it is not by egoism or mistrust, but because it suits us. . . . The Mongo or Nkundo group occupies a vast stretch in the central basin of the Congo. We find ourselves at Lake Tumba, or the Ruki, to the Lukenie and Lomami. . . . We are astonished to bear a name which is not ours and which has no significance. . . . In the history of our ancestors, we are told that no neighboring group was our master, nearly all were inferior to the Mongo. Therefore we are discontent when people try to degrade us."[38]

The importance of the cluster of Leopoldville intellectuals in the establishment of a modern movement for the unification of the Mongo was emphasized in an interview with the author by the president of Unimo, the Mongo party. The movement extended to Coquilhatville, where the Mongo hegemony did not seem threatened until the successive upsets by Ngombe candidates for the burgomaster position in 1958 and 1959, which were made possible by the disunity of the Mongo councilors.[39] Boelaert observed: "Objectively speaking, the Mongo present all the characteristics of a people. . . . It seems to me evident that, in an ethnic community which does not form an administrative entity or a state, national consciousness is natural, but remains latent as long as it is not obliged to externalize itself before internal or external dangers."[40]

THE BASONGYE

Exploration of the antecedents of the new Basongye province of Lomami is also enlightening. The idea originated

[38] "Vie, coutumes et moeurs des Mongo de l'Equateur," *La Voix du Congolais* (April 1958), p. 373. Bolamba later became an MNC/L militant, and was a member of Lumumba's government.

[39] Interview, Eugene Ndjoku, Coquilhatville, July 21, 1962.

[40] Boelaert, *op. cit.*, p. 383.

with a group of Basongye intellectuals in Luluabourg, led by Alois Kabangia and Dominique Manono.[41] When the first elections in Luluabourg took place in 1958, the contest was entirely dominated by Baluba-Lulua hostilities. The Basongye elite perceived that there would be little place for them on the Luluabourg political stage if competition were to follow ethnic lines, as the Basongye were only a small minority of the urban population. The natural line of retreat was to Basongye homeland, where they first organized as a political party, the *Mouvement de l'Unité Basong(y)e* (MUB). In 1962, with the creation of new provinces, Basongyeland achieved separate administrative status. The sequence of events is particularly interesting. The first active impetus came from the urban elite; a ready-made audience was found for the appeal to ethnic unity. Modern amenities, such as schools, were believed to have been withheld from the Basongye; there was growing fear of their aggressive neighbors to the south, the Kasai Baluba. Sanction for the idea of Basongye unity could be found in the proud history of this people, the exploits of the great nineteenth-century warrior chiefs, Pania Mutombo and Ngongo Lutete, the martyrdom of the paramount chief Lumpungu II (hanged by the colonial administration in 1936 on the allegation of "barbarous practices"), and cultural achievements in metal and wood-working.[42]

The examples could be continued, but the point is clear. The need for a unified ethnic self-assertion was first felt in the city. However, there was fertile terrain in a latent and inarticulate receptivity to such an appeal from the city to the country. The precipitation of political events created a

[41] Central Minister of Economic Coordination and Planning, then Civil Service, February 1961–June 1964.

[42] Interview with Dominique Manono, President, Lomami province, Kabinda, June 29, 1963. See also the fascinating account of 1959-60 political evolution as seen from a Basongye village in Merriam, *Congo: Background of Conflict*, pp. 173-94. Ngongo Lutete is also claimed as a native son by the Batetela-Bakusu.

sense of urgency felt first by the urban elite, but quickly communicated to the rural constituencies.

Messianic Sects and Ethnicity

The role of messianic sects and secret societies in the rise of ethnic self-consciousness in rural areas deserves passing mention. Fundamentally, the motor force in these movements was an apocalyptic reaction to a colonial situation which seemed beyond any secular remedy. The millennial vision provided the means for transcending a temporal situation which was intolerable yet beyond the power of the African to alter. What is relevant for present purposes is that these movements had an important part in externalizing the latent sense of unity among an ethnic group through the avenue of a common ritual. This is most conspicuous in the Kimbanguist movement among the Bakongo. In Balandier's words, "Its extension was less influenced by national frontiers than ethnic boundaries; it expressed the profound reactions of a group which had preserved the sense of its unity."[43]

Kitawala, the other major millenarian sect in the Congo, is rather different. Kitawala is an Africanized offshoot of the American Jehovah's Witnesses. In Northern Rhodesia, where it was tolerated, the movement verged on being an Africanized Protestant movement, or an "Ethiopian" church, to use Sundkler's dichotomy.[44] In the Congo, where it was rigorously suppressed, it became far more radical and "Zionist" in nature. It had great appeal, especially to segmentary,

[43] Balandier, "Messianismes et nationalismes en Afrique noire," *Cahiers Internationaux de Sociologie,* XIV (1953), 49.

[44] B. C. M. Sundkler, *Bantu Prophets in South Africa* (2d ed., New York: Oxford University Press, 1961). Sundkler, in his classic and pioneering study of this phenomenon, divides the movements into "Ethiopian" and "Zionist" categories. The former merely Africanize an existing church and maintain the doctrine, ritual, and structure; the latter, often led by prophets, are African movements, drawing on Christian symbols and doctrine, but infusing many traditional ritual elements, and constituting a more radical form of reaction.

disintegrating societies. In the most detailed study of the phenomenon yet to appear, Biebuyck shows that Kitawala took on the contours of the ethnic group which absorbed it. Although the movement penetrated a large number of tribes, once adopted it became domesticated. Among the Bakumu in Kivu and Orientale, for example, where Kitawala was at the root of a major revolt in 1944, the movement tended to acquire a segmentary structure similar to that of the Bakumu. The message of Kitawala provided for the Bakumu a means of expressing in a radical and "modern" manner the pent-up frustrations of the colonial experience. It gave the society a substitute for its crucial ritual figures, the circumcizers, who had been suppressed by the colonial administration as "barbarian." And it strengthened its sense of its own identity and unity confronted with the colonizer; the unity, however, was in the first instance Kumuhood, not yet a broader commitment to a Congolese nationalism. The degree of self-consciousness of the Kumu identity was probably entirely new and in this sense modern.[45] It could thus be argued that the messianic sects had a dual role: on the one hand, by providing a channel for the externalization of radical hostility to the colonial regime, they created a pre-disposition toward subsequent diffusion of explicitly nationalist ideas; on the other hand, they served to catalyze a sense of ethnic unity and identity.

Roots of Ethnic Tension

In noting the emergence of new forms of ethnic identity, it is well to recall that recent research has repeatedly shown how fluid traditional systems were. Boundaries lacked definition, and identification was highly relative. Individuals, groups, and communities were constantly on the move;

---

[45] Daniel Biebuyck, "La société kumu face au kitawala," *Zaïre,* XI, No. 1 (January 1957), 7-40. In subsequent discussions, Biebuyck was of great assistance in elucidating the exact relationship of Kitawala and a sense of ethnic identity.

communities were dissolving and reforming; some tribes disintegrated, new ones were formed. The Azande are an excellent example of this; they have occupied their present location for less than two centuries, and initially constituted only a band of invading warriors. Language and culture were successfully imposed on the earlier strata of population in a matter of one or two generations.

The rise of ethnic consciousness as a response to the humiliations and frustrations of colonial subjugation is a natural phenomenon; it is often argued that the elimination of the deep inferiority complex imposed by the colonial situation requires an aggressive reassertion of one's own past, language, myth, and culture. In the countryside, where most areas were relatively homogeneous, filtering nationalism through the ethnic prism does not usually create overwhelming problems. However, in the city this often is a two-edged sword; unity is argued not only in the positive terms of the values of the group but also with regard to the threat to it posed by others. As Caprasse put it, in the case of Elisabethville:

"If the tribal association exalts the prestige of its own group, it also maintains that which opposes it to other groups. So well does a tribal association do this that . . . it prevents a complete restructuration of social groups . . . in setting one against another. . . . The origins, the objectives . . . of the Bena Lulua association are typical of this frame of mind: the Bena Lulua have united to achieve a hegemony for their group in opposing others. It is equally typical that the counter to this . . . has been the organization of other vast ethnic regroupings whose leaders concede that they organized to 'do in' the too-powerful Bena Lulua association."[46]

The impulse toward hegemony on the one hand and the fear of it on the other are the common threads in the aggregation of hostility aspect of ethnicity. In many cases the

[46] Caprasse, *op. cit.*, p. 37.

location of a city in an area considered to be within the tribal lands of a given group is a cause for conflict; this group asserts a claim to hegemony based on its traditional association with the land. In Leopoldville, the Abako wrote in 1957: "Each immigrant from the upper Congo is considered as an inhabitant of the country. . . . But they are obliged to respect the rights of the inhabitants in whose milieu they live. . . . Leopoldville, Brazzaville, the Kwango, Angola and Pointe-Noire formed in days of yore and for centuries . . . the ancient Kingdom of Congo, a state divided in 1885 between France, Belgium and Portugal. Leopoldville is therefore, like the rest of the Bas-Congo, Bakongo territory."[47]

A similar phenomenon can be observed in most cities; the Lulua consider Luluabourg to be on their land; the Bashi believe that Bukavu is situated upon their property; Coquilhatville is felt to be a Mongo possession. Where, as in Bukavu, no single, large, aggressive group challenged the claim (except the European settlers), tensions among Africans did not arise. Where, as in Luluabourg, another group achieved social predominance, the conflict was acute. Where, as in Stanleyville, the city happens to be situated in a transitional zone, not really considered by the nearest major groupings, Lokele to the west or Bakumu to the east, to be part of their lands, an important potential cause for friction is eliminated.

A numerical majority is another basis for a hegemony claim. In Leopoldville this was invoked by both Bakongo and Bangala; the former in 1954 justified their nomination of candidates for the vacant *chef de cité* post by the argument, "Given that 82 percent of the Leopoldville population is Bakongo, the Abako which represents this proportion feels itself obliged to give its views on this question."[48] The Bangala, retorted one of their journalists, Mwissa Camus,

[47] *ABAKO 1950-1960*, p. 104.
[48] *Ibid.*, p. 30.

"have for a long time constituted the majority in Leopold-ville."[49] In Luluabourg and the South Katanga centers, the Kasai Baluba felt that their absolute majority in the former and their relative preponderance in the latter gave sanction to aspirations for a leading role.

A crucial factor in urban ethnic tension is the tendency in some cities for social status stratification to overlap ethnic divisions. It is a general phenomenon in Africa that there are important differences both in access to the moderniza-tion process and in receptivity to it. On the opportunity side, there are such variables as location near a major zone of urbanization, early extension of missions and therefore schools, situation on a major communications axis, and a dense population which attracted recruiters. On the pro-pensity to modernity side, one may mention the nature of the traditional social systems and adaptability of their value system, the degree of success in resisting colonial occupation and penetration of the area by the accoutrements of mod-ernization, the degree of cohesion or dislocation at the mo-ment of colonial conquest, and the nature of the customary economy.[50]

Successful Response to Modernity

In the Congo, the three most successful groups have clearly been the Bakongo; the Congo River trading peoples, Bobangi, Lokele, and others; and the Kasai Baluba. Al-though no precise figures are available, these three together probably constitute a majority of the present generation of university students[51] and a very substantial proportion of the

[49] Quoted in De Backer, op. cit., I, 11.

[50] Coleman has a most interesting chapter on this theme in Nigeria: Background to Nationalism, pp. 332-52. See also Apter, on the Ba-ganda and Ashanti, in The Political Kingdom in Uganda; Balandier on the Bakongo and Fang, in Sociologie actuelle de l'Afrique Noire.

[51] A breakdown of Lovanium students by (old) province can be found in "Données complémentaires sur l'enseignement supérieur dans la République du Congo," Etudes Congolaises, V, No. 10 (De-cember 1963), 8. This shows that Leopoldville and Kasai accounted

elite. In the case of the Bakongo, Balandier remarked that it was one of the best prepared societies in Central Africa for European contact. Their prolonged contact with the coast had instilled in this people a keen commercial sense and a habit of serving as intermediaries. Skilled agricultural techniques produced cash crops to market in the several major urban centers which developed in Bakongo country or its fringes: Leopoldville, Matadi, Boma, Thysville, and Brazzaville. "It must be noted," Balandier added, "how much this ethnic group sought at an early date to multiply its contacts with colonial society." Two railroads, a dense road network, large-scale missionary penetration, both Protestant and Catholic, beginning with Grenfell's Baptist Missionary Society in 1878, all combined to make the group's adaptation with the modern process a striking success.[52]

The river traders enjoyed a somewhat similar advantage. For the most part, their villages lined the Congo but did not extend inland. Their structure was shaped by the central place which the river trade played in their pre-colonial life.[53] The first explorers established the belief that many of these peoples were potentially useful for the purposes of the colonizer and "open to civilization"; they were generally

---

for 64.7 percent of the enrollment. Of these, beyond any doubt the majority are Bakongo and Baluba, respectively.

[52] Balandier, *Sociologie actuelle de l'Afrique Noire*, pp. 293-353. It is interesting to note that the Abako quotes this evaluation with evident pride in a memorandum rebutting an anti-Abako article in a Catholic missionary news service release. *ABAKO 1950-1960*, pp. 103-11.

[53] See, for example, Stanley's descriptions of the clusters at Stanley Pool and Bolobo in *The Congo and the Founding of its Free State*, I, 295-369, 517-24; II, 1-2. The "chief" of the site of Leopoldville, Ngaliema, was in fact an ivory trader of slave origins. In Bolobo, which Stanley describes as a settlement of 10,000, the leading figures were also traders, some of whom Stanley estimated to be worth as much as £6,000. On the Lokele, see H. Sutton Smith, *Yakusu* (London: Marshall Brothers, n.d. [1912?]). For an excellent study of the pre-colonial extent of trading circuits, see Vansina, "Long-Distance Trade Routes in Central Africa," *Journal of African History*, loc. cit.

described as "well-built, strong, and intelligent."[54] State and mission posts were established along the river, and nearly a generation had passed before really effective occupation of the hinterland had been achieved. A generation advance in access to education made a crucial difference. There was also substantial recruitment for the *Force Publique* and the European posts in these areas; many moved to towns in the early phases of colonial rule.

The Kasai Baluba present the most striking case of all. A major, if not *the* major factor in their situation was the state of dislocation in which this society found itself at the moment of European penetration. Large numbers fled to the safety of the European posts at Luluabourg and Lusambo; to these were apparently accreted miscellaneous other uprooted populations, who became lumped by the Europeans as "Baluba."[55] As Kalanda put it, comparing the situation of the Baluba and the Lulua (who themselves historically are an earlier wave of Baluba migrants from Katanga) at the time of colonial occupation:

"Therefore, at the outset, there was a difference in the situation of the individual; on one side, the Muluba, disorganized and left on his own in brutal fashion by the slave wars, on the other, the Lulua integrated into a stable social organization. This difference created amongst the former a personal insecurity which he did not hesitate to cure through individual adaptation to the change and by the feeling of self-assurance which his personal experience acquired in travelling gave him. The Muluba thus became a man who counts above all on himself, on the established [colonial] authority. And, through his travels, he learned of price differences between regions, and the trading possibilities these provided."[56]

[54] Stanley, *Through the Dark Continent*, II, 301-02. A. J. Wauters, *L'Etat Indépendant du Congo* (Brussels: Librairie Falk Fils, 1899), p. 270.
[55] Supra, pp. 241-42.
[56] Kalanda, *Baluba et Lulua*, pp. 95-96.

Another theory was that the social mobility possible within traditional Baluba structures, as with the Ibo in Nigeria, had instilled in them a sense of drive for promotion even within customary society. The chieftaincy, before traditional practices were altered by the procedures of the colonial administration, was not linked to any family or lineage; any notable could aspire to the office, and win it with the assent of the incumbent chief and notables through a judicious blend of prestige and purchase. Most other high ranks in the traditional community were also acquired through wealth and achievement, rather than through genealogical prescription.[57]

On the European side, as with the Bangala, a stereotype was established that the Baluba were a particularly dynamic group, superior to other tribes. The explorers Livingstone, Cameron, and Von Wissman were all greatly impressed by the Baluba; Von Wissman declared that they, "more than any other people in Africa," were a fertile field for missionary action.[58] At this stage, mission strategy, with still limited resources, required a choice of "key tribes" as spearheads for penetration. Factors in the choice were the

[57] A. Verbeken, administrator-cum-historian, in "Accession au pouvoir chez certaines tribus du Congo par système élective," *Congo,* 14th yr., T. II, No. 5 (December 1933), pp. 653-57, suggests that the colonizer implanted a hereditary method of succession unwittingly, assuming that all traditional systems must be established on this principle. See also, Jean Weydert, *Les Balubas chez eux* (mimeographed, 1938), p. 1; Edmond Verhulpen, *Baluba et Balubaïsés du Katanga* (Antwerp: Editions de l'Avenir Belge, 1936), p. 186.

[58] A. Van Zandijcke, *Pages de l'histoire du Kasayi* (Namur, Belgium: Collection Lavigerie, 1953), p. 85. Jan Vansina has conclusively established, through close textual analysis of different editions of Von Wissman's work, that the "Baluba" he describes in glowing terms were in fact Lulua, later to acquire the reputation of mediocre adapters relative to the "Baluba." However, Von Wissman did describe his Lulua as Baluba, and those reading his books assumed that he was talking about those who became known as Kasai Baluba. Incidentally, this further reinforces the thesis that there was very little awareness of separate identity on the part of the Baluba and Lulua at the time of colonial penetration.

259

apparent receptivity to new ideas, and a language which gave access to a large area. The translation of the Bible, for the Protestants, and training missionaries in the use of the language involved a major commitment of resources, and the decision had to be carefully weighed. The Baluba qualified on both counts, and both Catholics and Protestants from the outset made them a target group.[59]

From the early days, one can find signs of a growing Baluba stature. The missions used them as catechists; the state employed them as soldiers and messengers; the companies engaged them as buyers of palm fruits and wild rubber. The Nyim, Bakuba paramount chief, sent a memorial complaining in 1910 of the growing Baluba populations in Bakuba areas; he protested "the development of Baluba centers of Luebo, Gallikoko and Ibanche born around the Protestant missions, which thus escaped from his authority, and whose inhabitants often molested his subjects, treating them with scorn as uncivilized people."[60]

The construction of the BCK railroad in the 1920's gave the Baluba a new and decisive advantage. They were easily recruited for the construction work, and then tended to settle as farmers along the rail line, which provided a profitable means of transporting their crops to market. The Baluba came to be a large majority in all the towns which grew up along the rail line; at Port Francqui, for example,

[59] Slade, *English-Speaking Missions in the Congo Independent State (1878-1908)* (Brussels: ARSOM, Sci. Mor. et Pol., N.S., T. XVI, fasc. 2, 1959), pp. 103-05. The belief in "superior" and "inferior" tribes was widely established in the European view of Africa in the latter 19th century. For interesting evidence, see Philip D. Curtin, *The Image of Africa* (Madison: University of Wisconsin Press, 1964) pp. 226, 414-31.

[60] J. Nicolai and J. Jacques, *La tranformation des paysages congolais par le chemin de fer. L'exemple du B.C.K.* (Brussels: ARSOM, Sci. Nat. et Med., T. XXIV, fasc. 1, 1954), p. 81. Vansina reports discovering in the Luebo archives evidence of Bakuba discontent with the Baluba influx as early as 1905; a local administrator had had the imprudence to install a Muluba as chief in a Bakuba zone, which provoked a sharp protest from the Nyim.

80 percent of the population was Baluba. In the other direction, the rail opened a path to the Katanga mining centers, followed by a growing number of persons.[61]

By the 1950's, over 100,000 Baluba were to be found in the Congo's ten largest cities.[62] No ethnic group compared in its dispersion throughout the urbanized Congo. They were frequently referred to by themselves and others as the "Jews of the Congo." Their role and situation in many towns was similar to that of "strangers" in West African communities. Their high status was conspicuous; their migration appeared to be under European protection. As with "stranger" communities in West Africa, they had a reputation for superior industriousness and were often preferred by employers. The colonial situation exempted them from any obligation to come to terms with the ethnic group(s) dominant in the surrounding area. And, it might be added, the sudden withdrawal of European patronage left them exposed to the reprisals of the local communities.[63]

Poor Adaptation: The Bakuba

As an example of unsuccessful response to modernization, the Bakuba are a classic case. They had developed one of Africa's most remarkable traditional structures. It was, in fact, a state which included a number of ethnic groups, each retaining a sense of its cultural identity as well as political membership in the Bakuba state. The institutions reflected an interesting balance between autonomy and central control.[64]

[61] For a fascinating account of the effects of the construction of the rail link from Elisabethville to Port Francqui, see Nicolai and Jacques, op. cit.

[62] Denis, Le phénomène urbain, p. 142.

[63] See Elliott P. Skinner's valuable article, "Strangers in West African Societies," Africa, XXXIII, No. 4 (October 1963), 307-20.

[64] The Bakuba, and among them the Bushong, have attracted some of the ablest anthropologists. The first and still classic study is that of E. Torday and T. A. Joyce, Notes ethnographiques sur les peuples communément appelés Bakuba, ainsi que sur les peuplades

As early as 1909, however, the Torday-Joyce anthropological expedition found them in critical condition:

"One must not forget that when they first received the visit of a white man, about 25 years ago, they formed an all-powerful nation, possessing all the traditions associated with a conquering race and endowed with the inflexible pride which is found in a history and tradition such as theirs. This national pride has naturally engendered a highly developed conservative spirit which can be considered the dominant trait of the Bushongo spirit. Conservatism appears in all the aspects of the primitive life. If one bears in mind the conservative spirit of the Bushongo and the great pride which is its cause, one may easily understand the enormous moral shock experienced by the Bushongo nation, and, by extension, each of the individuals composing it, when the great empire which had existed from time immemorial trembled before men whose name had been completely unknown forty years earlier."[65]

Although the Bakuba's artisan skills had been highly developed and they had carried on an extensive trade, the system tended rather to withdraw within itself. When the BCK railroad was built through Bakuba land, the Bakuba refused to supply labor for it and were greatly provoked at the growing Baluba settlements on their land. The existence of this new communications axis did nothing to stimulate their links with the modern economy. Although Luluabourg was less than 200 miles away, and linked by rail and road, the Bakuba constituted less than 1.5 percent of its popula-

apparentées (Brussels: Ministère des Colonies, 1911); their most recent student is Jan Vansina. Among his numerous writings on the Bakuba, particular mention may be made of "L'état kuba dans le cadre des institutions politiques africaines," _Zaïre,_ XI (May 1957), 485-92; _De geschiedenis van de Kuba_ (Tervuren, Belgium: Musée Royal de l'Afrique Centrale, 1963); _Le Royaume Kuba_ (Tervuren, Belgium: Musée Royal de l'Afrique Centrale, 1964).

[65] Torday and Joyce, _op. cit.,_ p. 13.

tion.[66] The 1947 census showed their total population to be 73,000 which had declined by 5,000 since 1938, symptomatic of a demoralized society. None have occupied a post of any prominence in national politics, and only a couple have been active in provincial affairs in independent Congo. In 1959-1960, they reinstituted a poison ordeal, long in disuse, in the hope that it would resolve their growing problems of insecurity. Beginning in late 1960, they began attacking and dislodging Baluba and Lulua settled on land believed to be theirs; since then, they have virtually cut themselves off both from neighboring peoples and the modern administrative system. For the Bakuba, independence was an opportunity for withdrawal.

Competitive Modernization

It is in the urban environment that the process of response to the modernization ferment introduced by the colonial system becomes a competitive one, and groups become aware of differentials in access to modernity.

There was a curiously circular character to the process; once the perception of relative advance by one group began, it rapidly strengthened ethnic self-consciousness on the part of the group which felt deprived. From that point forward, the conviction of discriminatory behavior by the favored group found daily corroboration in a thousand petty events: the expulsion of one child from school, the promotion of one clerk. Even in the colonial period, the leading Africans in a community were in a position to make decisions important to other Congolese. For example, many large firms had Africans in their personnel departments, who did at least the initial screening for job applicants; as in any country, a certain number were guilty of ethnic favoritism, and in each incident was seen a systematic pattern by the excluded group. Likewise, in the schools, by the postwar years, the bulk of primary and some secondary school

[66] Lux, "Luluabourg," Zaïre, loc. cit.

teachers were African. In Luluabourg, Lulua frequently charged that the Baluba teachers were blocking the advances of Lulua children in the schools. Again, parents everywhere are quick to conclude their child is the victim of partiality. Sometimes it is true, but whether true or not, it gains ready credence and fuels the tensions.

There can be no doubt that in Luluabourg and the Katanga cities the Baluba had a marked advantage, although the distinction was nowhere near as complete as the frequently-heard allegation that "all the top jobs are held by Baluba." One recent study of Elisabethville showed that, although the Baluba (of Katanga and Kasai), plus other natives of Kasai whose numbers were relatively small, constituted 55 percent of the population, they occupied 71 percent of the trading and artisan class.[67] This shows that there was a clear lead but that it was far from a total commercial hegemony. Even more illuminating are statistics on the level of education in Luluabourg drawn up by Lux (Table 17).

TABLE 17

LEVEL OF EDUCATION BY ETHNIC GROUP: LULUABOURG[a]

Level	Baluba[b]	Lulua[b]	Average of all groups
None	6.6%	11.2%	8.5%
Incomplete primary	23.5	30.3	25.5
1st primary cycle	37.2	35.1	36.1
Complete primary	18.6	16.1	17.7
1–2 years secondary	7.5	4.7	6.3
3 or more years secondary	6.6	2.6	5.9

[a] SOURCE: A. Lux, "Luluabourg," *Zaïre*, XII, Nos. 7, 8 (1958).
[b] Baluba were 56% of the Luluabourg population, Lulua 25%.

The table shows that the real Baluba educational lead over the Lulua was much less than the perceived advance.

[67] J. Benoit, "Contribution à l'étude de la population active d'Elisabethville," *Problèmes Sociaux Congolais*, No. 54 (September 1961), p. 17.

Lead there was, but the Lulua were catching up. Yet the unshakable belief that the Baluba were systematically excluding the Lulua from rightful status in their own city led to the foundation of *Lulua Frères* in 1952, and a militant expression of grievances since about 1950.[68]

The competitive response to modernization opportunities was capable of engendering very serious tensions in the urban centers. In instances such as Luluabourg, Kolwezi, Jadotville, Elisabethville, and Coquilhatville, where one well-represented group was able to acquire a perceptible status lead, both ethnic consciousness and ethnic tensions were heightened. It should be noted that these tensions were between two relatively favored groups. The Lulua were well-established in the modern sector relative to groups such as the Bakuba, or Bakete, for whom opportunity was completely lacking or receptivity was small, and at a disadvantage only when compared to the most effectively modernized group.

Colonial Policy and Ethnicity

In a variety of ways, the modern administrative system

[68] The Musée Royal d'Afrique Centrale anthropologist, Dr. F. Maesen, tells of finding, during a field trip in 1954, in every Lulua village furious meetings every Sunday morning, the subject of which was the Baluba menace and how to deal with it. It should be added that in the Baluba-Lulua case, there were other grievances aside from those arising from Luluabourg. Many Baluba cultivators had settled on Lulua lands; this migration had begun before European occupation. However, the railroad had greatly accelerated it. Moreover, about 1925, the administration had organized the Baluba on Lulua lands into independent chieftaincies, a source of great irritation to the Lulua chiefs. Also, other peoples than the Lulua were involved, in particular the Bakuba. Vansina found the Bakuba paramount chief ready to fight over the issue of Baluba (and Lulua) squatting as early as 1953; see "Le régime foncier dans la société Kuba," *Zaïre*, X, No. 9 (November 1956), pp. 899-926. Ironically, the Nyim was invited to serve as chief arbitrator in the Lake Mukamba talks in January 1960 designed to find a solution to the "Baluba problem"; his son represented him on the commission, which proposed to eliminate the friction by the removal of 100,000 rural Baluba to their own areas.

introduced by the colonizer tended unconsciously to breed ethnic awareness. Every time a form was filled out, there was a blank for "tribe." In this, the individual was generally encouraged to list his identity with a large group, rather than to cite his clan or subgroup; for example, administrative convenience favored the classification of "Baluba" rather than "Bakwa Kalonji," although in the first instance the clan identity was often more meaningful. The simplification of several major languages and their reduction to writing by missionary and administrator has also strengthened a potent vehicle for cultural identity. There has been a curious feedback of ethnographic research, mainly by missionaries, into the emergence of ethnic self-consciousness. Van Wing, among the Bakongo, Boelaert, Hulstaert, and de Rop, among the Mongo, lived for many years with the peoples they studied, and they developed a very genuine attachment to their respective cultures. Their works were avidly read by the new elite; many were taught in schools and seminaries by the missionary-anthropologists. For example, Edmond Nzeza-Nlandu, founder of the Abako, attributes to his studies under Van Wing a decisive impact in appreciating the richness of the Bakongo cultural heritage.[69]

Several other aspects of Belgian colonial policy, and in particular the sequence of decolonization, have served to embed ethnicity at the heart of the political process. The authoritarian character of the colonial regime until it began to collapse after the January 1959 Leopoldville riots obstructed the formation of organizations on a non-tribal basis capable of aggregating grievances; this in turn gave an ex-

---

[69] René Lemarchand, "The Bases of Nationalism among the Bakongo," *Africa*, XXXI, No. 4 (October 1961), 346. One may also note that all these missionaries were of Flemish origin. It seems plausible that the constant struggle in Belgium to assert the equal place of Flemish language and culture may have predisposed many Flemings to sympathy for indigenous cultures in the Congo, threatened by the assimilative implications of acculturation.

ceptional preeminence to the tribal associations, which were tolerated. Although there were some other types of prepolitical groups, such as alumni associations and the African civil service union, APIC, it was only through the tribal association that there was a mass-elite nexus. As latent frustration coalesced into articulated grievance, no adequate structural channel aside from the ethnic association emerged through which these could flow. It is indisputable that the introduction of elections at the very vortex of ethnic tension and competition in the cities in 1957 and 1958, without permitting the free organization of political movements to structure the competition, built up a linkage between ethnicity and politics in five crucial urban centers (Leopoldville, Coquilhatville, Luluabourg, Elisabethville, and Jadotville) which could not be eradicated by subsequent events.

There is probably some significance in the fact that Belgium differs from other major colonial occupants of Africa in being culturally plural herself. In an encounter with Britain, France, or Portugal, African peoples were confronted with a colonizer possessing a highly integrated nationalism with centuries of history and common experience. Belgium as a country was born in 1830, only half a century before the Congo Free State. The Belgian national image, on the other hand, was schizophrenic; tension between Walloon and Fleming is highly visible and was recognized in the Congo once an elite began to emerge equipped to remark that Europeans were not simply an undifferentiated and distant ruling class.

An interesting illustration of this point is found in one of the Abako's arguments for a federal state which would permit considerable cultural autonomy; in an article entitled, "What is a People and a Nation," they argue: "It suffices to observe the perpetual mistrust and misunderstandings between Flemings and Walloons to convince oneself of the danger there is to unite men of different origins. We do not

267

want to meddle in the internal affairs of our Belgian friends, but we cannot help saying that if the union between Flemings and Walloons were conceived on a federal basis, the almost interminable quarrels which have often broken forth between these two tribes would have been avoided. Belgium herself offers us proof of the danger there is in united men of different origin."[70]

The importance of this point should not be exaggerated; obviously the model for Congolese nationalist expression was not consciously Belgian; it was influenced by the unitary models of the mass single-party sort. Nonetheless, it remains true that assertions of ethnic nationalism find a sanction in Belgian history and a "demonstration effect" in the Belgian example absent in other colonial situations.[71]

In addition to the passive, demonstration effect role of the colonizer in legitimating ethnic consciousness, it was frequently alleged, especially in the months before independence, that there was an active, diabolical "divide and rule" plan. This argument can indeed be substantiated in part; Boelaert, for example, cites the case of the district commissioner who, in preparing a study on the feasibility of unifying Mongo dialects, concluded that it was fully possible but "inopportune" as it might become a vehicle for unity and nationalist expression.[72] It is perhaps not entirely coincidental that, after a major revolt in 1931, in the provincial reorganization of 1933 the Bapende were divided between Leopoldville and Kasai provinces, with communication between the two made difficult.[73] In

[70] *Notre Kongo,* November 19, 1959.

[71] There are minor cultural subnationalisms in Scotland and Wales, but these in no way are comparable in intensity or impact to the Flemish-Walloon split. Irish nationalism might well have had significant repercussions in British African territories had it not reached its decisive point at a stage before nationalist ideas were in the ascendant in Africa.

[72] Boelaert, "Vers un état mongo," ARSOM, *Bull. Séances,* loc. cit., p. 385.

[73] This insurrection was provoked by the first serious effort to

268

Katanga, the two largest traditional systems, the Lunda of Mwata Yamvo and Baluba of Kasongo Nyembo, were administratively dismantled through division into different territories and districts; this meant that the different segments of these kingdoms passed through entirely different administrative channels.

However, the connection of the colonizer to this phenomenon was less in terms of a cleverly-framed grand design of division, but the cumulative effect of many individual, ad hoc actions. For example, the next-to-last colonial governor of Katanga, J. Paelinck, had spent most of his career in Kasai and had developed many friendships in Baluba circles; a great scandal resulted from his delivery of a farewell address in Elisabethville in 1958 in Tshiluba, the Kasai dialect of the Luba language. This was interpreted by the South Katanga peoples as "proof" of the systematic hostility of the administration. In Leopoldville, there was a widespread conviction in Bakongo circles that the important Scheutist missionary order was partial to Bangala; some concrete evidence of this seemed to be found in the distribution of a violent attack on the Abako and, by extension, on the Bakongo by the Catholic news agency Dia.[74] The colonial administration reacted instinctively against whatever seemed to be the most militant expression of nationalism. Thus, in Leopoldville, the pioneering role of the Abako had as its natural result a search for "moderates" by the colonizer among the Bangala. In Kasai, radical articulation of the nationalist views seemed at first to be emanating from Baluba circles, especially in the persons of Albert Kalonji and

---

fully occupy and administer Bapende country, which lies south of Kikwit, in Kwilu district, running over to Tshikapa, in Kasai. The repression was on a large scale and is very much a vivid memory in the area today. This was the last of the traditional-led, primary resistance movements to colonial rule. It is now a heroic epic in the local legends, and was used by the modern Bapende leaders, of whom Antoine Gizenga is the best-known.

[74] *ABAKO 1950-1960,* pp. 103-12.

Joseph Ngalula; the latter was the first to mention the word "independence" in Luluabourg in April 1959. The reaction of part of the administration was to find renewed sympathy for the grievances of the Lulua, "oppressed" by the haughty Baluba.[75]

A last fillip was given to ethnic self-consciousness by the crisis atmosphere in which the surge to independence took place. The role of crisis in producing ethnic catalyzation has been frequently observed; Southall noted: "Times of crisis and violence tend to throw people back on racial and ethnic lines; . . . traditional solidarity of ethnic and kinship groups goes deeper than newer special interests."[76] Balandier observed that in Brazzaville "it is a question especially of quasi-groupings [Bakongo and Mbochi] which become real particularly under exceptional circumstances [such as elections]. . . . It is furthermore these circumstances which efface temporarily the internal divisions which enfeeble each of the two groups."[77]

The final months of Belgian rule were times of acute insecurity and uncertainty about the future. The violence of the political campaign in areas where there was real inter-party competition, the visible fears of the European community, the outbreak of ethnic disorders, all contributed to an atmosphere of anxiety.[78]

The circumstances of independence posed acutely for the

[75] This culminated in the famous Dequenne report, proposing for the first time a massive removal of Balubas from Lulua lands. *Congo 1959*, pp. 210-13. This point is documented in detail by Kalanda, *Baluba et Lulua.*

[76] Southall (ed.), *Social Change in Modern Africa*, p. 40.

[77] Balandier, *Sociologie des Brazzavilles noires*, p. 119.

[78] Merriam records an interesting example of this point, in documenting the perceptions of the pre-independence months in a small Basongye village. At a secret meeting in May 1960, the villagers reached the decision that no further "strangers" were to be admitted. Further, the villages relocated and consolidated in order to protect themselves against the "treacherous Baluba," believed to be armed and plotting. *Congo: Background of Conflict*, pp. 173-94.

individual Congolese the question of his ethnic identity. The May 1960 elections particularly became largely an ethnic census; the voter was called upon to relate himself to the political process through his ethnic self-identification.

The Congolese response to colonial subjugation, then, was in part an intensified ethnic awareness. The stigma which attaches to "tribalism" as "backwardness" is unfair to the Congolese; there is nothing inherently more "backward" about Bakongo cultural self-assertion than there is in Flemish or Quebec nationalism. The corollary assumption that "detribalization" is an automatic consequence of material progress seems, on the basis of Congolese evidence, wholly unrealistic. Modernization has accelerated the transformation, but not the disappearance, of ethnic identity patterns. Some have been greatly strengthened, others have been absorbed. It is at least plausible to argue that the long-run impact of modernity is toward consolidation of ethnic self-consciousness on the part of larger groups.

The crux of the matter is that the many obstacles which cultural pluralism creates for nation-building will be present for a long time. The chronic discords which arise out of the conflict of loyalty between the ethnic community and the modern state have in all times and places been difficult to accommodate. The particular colonial experience has worked to make ethnic loyalties in the Congo stronger and supra-tribal identification probably weaker than in most other African states.

Ethnic loyalty in itself is a natural and indeed a necessary phenomenon; psychological liberation requires pride in ones antecedents, and the Congolese has an ethnic identity as well as a Congolese and African self. However, on the negative side of ethnicity, a solidarity which feeds on hostility to others in the national community creates grave difficulties for the stable and efficient functioning of the political system. The development of appropriate political methods of harnessing the positive and shackling the negative is a vital post-independence challenge to the wisdom of the Congolese elite.[79]

[79] President Azikwe of Nigeria has recently made an important contribution to this debate, in his address entitled "Tribalism—a Pragmatic Instrument for National Unity," delivered to the Political Science Association of the University of Nsukka in early 1964. Here he poses the central question of how the notion of tribe with its negative connotations can be transformed into "community" and constructively incorporated into a strategy of nation-building.

For an interesting analysis, with similar findings, based on Indonesian evidence, see G. William Skinner, *Social, Ethnic and National Loyalties in Village Indonesia* (Yale University Cultural Report Series, 1959).

CHAPTER XII

XXXXXXXXXXXXXXXXXXXXXXXXXXXXXXXXXXXXXXXXXXXXXXXXXXXXX

The Rise of Nationalism:
From Primary Resistance to Political Parties

XXXXXXXXXXXXXXXXXXXXXXXXXXXXXXXXXXXXXXXXXXXXXXXXXXXXX

THE rise of nationalism and the related emergence of political parties have in the recent past served as a basis for the study of African political systems. One important justification advanced is that nationalist parties "give better guidelines to African politics than those formal institutions of government which were set up by French and British colonizers at least in part as a condition for their recent political withdrawal, and are being changed by Africans after independence."[1] This argument is almost indisputable during the pre-independence phase of nationalist development, when parties were the only significant part of the modern political process which were entirely Africanized. During the terminal colonial period, when the legitimacy of the colonial state was challenged by nearly the entire population, the "people" were in a sense outside of the state, and the nationalist party, especially when united, incarnated the nation. In a symbolic sense, this withdrawal from the colonial state was consummated in the Congo when, during the last months before independence, the population in many areas ceased paying the head tax due the state and instead bought, for a roughly equivalent price, party membership cards.[2]

[1] Ruth Schachter, "Single Party Systems in West Africa," *American Political Science Review*, LV (June 1961), p. 294.
[2] For an excellent, thorough study on the origins and development of Congolese parties see René Lemarchand, Political Awakening in the Congo: The Politics of Fragmentation (Berkeley, Calif.: University of California Press, 1964), scheduled for publication by the University of California Press in 1965. There is now a remarkably good documentation on Congolese parties. See especially the two CRISP volumes, *ABAKO 1950-1960* and *Parti Solidaire Africain (P.S.A.)*; M. C. C. De Backer, *Notes pour servir à l'étude des "Groupements Politiques"*

This chapter will inquire into the pattern of development of Congolese nationalism. This evolution can be seen as a series of responses to the colonial situation, beginning with the flat rejection which motivated primary resistance movements, and culminating in the demand for Africanization of the state created by the colonizer. We will first consider the development of nationalism as a political doctrine which asserts the explicit claim to African self-government of the territory established by colonial partition. We will then examine the stages of development of African movements directed against the colonial pattern, leading up to the mature form of nationalist organization, the political party, which arises to assert and enforce nationalist doctrinal objectives.

Nationalism as a Political Doctrine

Nationalism as a political idea in the Congo is almost a contemporary phenomenon. There was no explicit, public demand for independence from a Congolese figure until 1956. The first public assertion of African grievance dates only from 1944;[3] on the heels of the Luluabourg mutiny,

---

à *Leopoldville*, 3 vols. (Brussels: Inforcongo, 1959); M. Crawford Young, "Congo Political Parties Revisited," *Africa Report*, VIII, No. 1 (January 1963), 14-20; J. C. Willame, "L'évolution des partis politiques au Congo," *Etudes Congolaises*, V, No. 10 (December 1963), 37-43. *Etudes Congolaises* contains current, documentary material on party evolution.

[3] This omits the picturesque episode of Panda Farnana and his *Association des Noirs* in Belgium. Farnana, a Mukongo from Boma, was a permanent resident of Belgium. He attended the Brussels Pan-African Congress in 1921, speaking on behalf of the Congo, and subsequently attended some of the National Colonial Congresses. His message was equality of treatment for Africans and opportunity for advance, in line with the position of most African intellectuals of the day. Andersson reports that he had some followers in the Bas Congo, including two brothers. The movement subsequently was placed under the patronage of the Royal Family, which took some interest in Farnana; it had, however, very limited influence and no direct relationship with the later emergence of Bakongo nationalism via the Abako. On Farnana, see Efraim Andersson, *Messianic Popular*

an anonymous "group of *évolués*" issued a tract which asked for some recognition for the embryonic elite as a reward for their educational attainments and loyalty during the uprising.[4] Kasavubu caused a brief sensation in Leopoldville in 1946 with a speech on the theme of the "rights of the first occupant" in land tenure, which in its context was an audacious criticism of the extent of land alienation to companies and missions in the Lower Congo. By and large, however, the preoccupations of the elite in this period were epitomized by Paul Lomami-Tshibamba's famous question in the second issue of *La Voix du Congolais*, "What will be our place in the world of tomorrow?" Equal treatment for Europeans and educated Congolese in the colonial framework would have satisfied (temporarily) nearly all until the early fifties. An account of Mrs. Paul Robeson's 1947 session with Leopoldville *évolués* is enlightening in this regard:

"She asked them how they envisaged the future of their country, if they wanted independence, what their political aspirations were. . . . [To] her disappointment, the *évolués* did not seem visibly interested in independence, nor emancipation. They were unaware of what was going on in the world. They had a certain number of grievances, which were centered about what one called, ten years later, human relations."[5]

The first overt demand which went beyond elite status to open the question of Congolese self-government came in August 1954 from the Abako. In a lettter to the administration, the Bakongo movement announced its list of candidates for the vacant post of *chef de cité*. "Given that the African population of Leopoldville is 82 percent Bakongo, the Abako which represents this percentage is obliged to

---

Movements in the Lower Congo (Upsala, Sweden: Studia Ethnographica Upsaliensia XIV, 1958), pp. 256-57; and Pierre Daye, *Problèmes congolais* (Brussels: Les Écrits, 1943), pp. 170-71.

[4] The memorandum is reprinted in *Dettes de guerre*, pp. 128-29.
[5] Van Bilsen, *L'indépendance du Congo*, p. 47.

give its views on this matter," the letter explained.[6] The administration was not in the habit of eliciting African views about such nominations, and even less of being confronted with unsolicited nominations from an organization which implicitly claimed to be the political spokesman for the majority.

Two years later the first open demand for independence was heard. Van Bilsen had in the interim published his 30-year plan, the three Belgian political parties had all held special congresses on the future of the Congo, and the Catholic bishops in the Congo had issued a statement engaging the Church to support "emancipation."

At this critical stage, the Governor-General in his 1956 annual address gave the impression that the administration was retrenching even on the timid pace of reform then envisaged.[7] A small group of African Catholic intellectuals began meeting regularly; the most prominent members were Abbey (now Bishop) Joseph Malula, Joseph Ileo, and Joseph Ngalula. With some encouragement from a handful of sympathetic professors at Lovanium, in particular Jean Buchmann, a manifesto was prepared which echoed the Van Bilsen plea for total emancipation over a thirty-year period. The Abako riposted with a counter statement, which for the first time advanced the slogan of "immediate independence."[8] Both statements repudiated the Belgo-Congo-

---

[6] *ABAKO 1950-1960*, pp. 29-30.

[7] This little-noted factor is stressed by F. Grévisse, at that time district commissioner in Elisabethville and one of the rare administrators who enjoyed real relations of confidence with the emergent elite. He argues that the colonial administration still had some psychological momentum in its favor, especially at the moment of King Baudouin's triumphant tour in 1955. However, the failure to capitalize upon this success by swift reforms was followed in 1956 by the indication that all progress was to be halted pending a rapprochement in the hearts and souls of European and African, and development of local structures. "Evolués et formation des elites," *Livre Blanc: Apport Scientifique de la Belgigue au développement de l'Arique centrale* (Brussels: ARSOM, 1962), I, 404.

[8] The two manifestoes are reprinted in *Congo 1959*, rev. ed., pp.

lese community goal which remained Belgian official policy.

Although a goal of self-government was coming into evidence, the nature of the independent state and means of achieving it remained shrouded in obscurity. Further, the articulation of the independence objective was only encountered in Leopoldville. Lumumba, writing in Stanleyville at the end of 1956, still expounded themes which bore little relationship to the radical Pan-African nationalism which he came to espouse in 1959; Eurafrica, racial equality, status for the elite, and the Belgo-Congolese community summed up his program.[9] Not until April 1959 was the word "independence" pronounced in Luluabourg.[10]

It was in 1958, or only two years before independence, that nationalist thought began to take form. Two events transformed nationalist debate from the vague assertion of terminal goals to serious consideration of ways and means. Several hundred Congolese, including a number of the most prominent members of the elite, were brought to Brussels for the world's fair. This offered the first real occasion for those from the different urban centers to meet each other. A Brussels branch of *Présence Africaine* was established which also brought the Congolese into contact with the currents of nationalist thought from the rest of French-speaking Africa and with anti-colonial left groups in Belgium. A series of discussion sessions were organized, where uncompromising militance rather than timid nuance was encouraged.

The other precipitant was the establishment of the *Groupe de Travail* in August 1958 to formulate a decolonization plan. The mere fact of soliciting views on the future

9-24. In the printed version of its countermanifesto, the Abako used the more ambiguous term "immediate emancipation." However, in his oral delivery, Kasavubu had stated "immediate independence." Charles-André Gilis, *Kasa-Vubu au coeur du drame congolais* (Brussels: Editions Europe-Afrique, 1964), pp. 78-79.

[9] Lumumba, *Le Congo, terre d'avenir*, pp. 191-209.

[10] By Joseph Ngalula; Kalanda, *Baluba et Lulua*, p. 22.

forces an effort to make explicit vague aspirations. The Working Group was a catalyst for the formation of both the *Mouvement National Congolais* and the Conakat in Katanga. The former sought to present a united Congolese viewpoint in support of rapid independence, and the latter to defend Katanga regional interests.

After the Leopoldville riots and the twin messages of January 13 had promised independence, the focus of debate shifted to two specific issues: the timing of power transfer and the distribution of power between the center and the provinces.[11] With the goal of independence conceded by the colonizer, nationalist parties competed in large part through the brevity of the timetable they were prepared to concede for decolonization. The Abako slogan of "immediate independence" had already established the framework for this competition; the deadline was to be very short. The absence of a single, comprehensive nationalist movement rendered inevitable the triumph of the most radical demand. In the highly competitive political atmosphere of 1959, no movement could long bear the animus of "moderation." In April, the Luluabourg congress of political parties, dominated by the MNC, set January 1961 as the deadline for the establishment of a provisional Congolese government which would decide on the independence date. The Abako called for a Congolese central government in March 1960; in May, Lumumba demanded a Congolese government by the end of 1959. None of the militant movements were publicly willing to accept de Schrijver's October proposal of a four-year plan for phased power transfer. In January 1960 the Congolese delegates at the Brussels Round Table unanimously required full independence for June 1960.

Thus nationalist thought emerged in unusual circumstances in the Congo. Through 1958 it was with rare exceptions only timidly expressed, primarily in Leopoldville.

[11] The "federalist" v. "unitary" debate will be dealt with in Chapter XVII.

Suddenly, the entire colonial atmosphere was transformed, and with it the nature of nationalist demands rapidly became radicalized. Competitive denunciaton and rivalry in radicalism became the motifs of nationalist expression.

Why Was Nationalism Retarded?

The question then arises as to why conscious nationalist thought should be so late in developing. One obvious cause is the absence until World War II of an elite with even secondary education, excepting the African clergy; this has been explored in Chapter IX. Another major explanation lies in the fact that the colonial administration did not permit parties to exist, nor did it permit the type of political activity usually associated with parties. Legal parties are almost everywhere closely related to an electoral process of some sort, which provides some means of constitutional pursuit of power or at least influence. Although political liberty was certainly not unrestricted in British and French colonies, from the end of World War II it was recognized as legitimate in a broadening sphere of activity. In British Africa, there were elected local councils and growing elected membership in central legislative councils; in French Africa, there were elected delegates to the National Assembly and elected territorial councils. A vigorous and colorful African press dates back to 1858 in Ghana, with Charles Bannerman's *West African Herald;* in French Africa, *L'éclaireur de la Côte d'Ivoire* was launched in 1935; in the Congo, the first independent African newspapers, *Quinze* and *Congo,* began only in 1957 and were quickly suppressed. It was not until August 1959 that freedom of association and press were legally granted in the Congo, although de facto toleration dated from the Leopoldville riots.

The almost total isolation of the Congolese population was another important factor. Before 1958, literally only a handful of educated Congolese had been abroad. A $1,000 deposit was necessary to obtain a passport; evidently, this put overseas travel out of reach for all who were not under the sponsorship of some organization which could put up the money. Even if the deposit could have been found, the administration was not obliged to deliver a passport.

The list of those who had traveled is not long. Beginning after World War I, a number of priests received advanced theological schooling in Rome or Belgium. In both World Wars, *Force Publique* units served in other parts of Africa, and a few in Palestine and Burma; the garrisons, however, were kept away from large cities, and the impact appears to have been slight.[12] Some Congolese sailors worked the Matadi-Antwerp run, but there is no evidence of any significant political communication through this channel. Thomas Kanza left for Louvain University in 1952, the first Congolese university student (excepting theology); however, in 1959 there were only fifteen Congolese students in Belgium. In 1953 and again in 1956 hand-picked delegations of Congolese notables toured Belgium.[13] Antoine-Roger Bolamba, later Minister in several governments, represented the Congo at the Rome Conference of Negro Artists and Writers in 1956. Isaac Kalonji, Senate President from 1961 to 1963, spent several months in the United States in 1956 and 1957. Brazzaville was easily accessible to Leopoldville residents; this was the one small leak in the dike of isolation built around the Congo.[14] Large-scale contact with

[12] Some of the veterans of these expeditionary forces have become prominent. Victor Koumorico, oldest member of the Congolese Senate and President of Lac Leopold II province, fought in Tanganyika in World War I. Victor Lundula, first Commander-in-Chief of the *Armée Nationale Congolaise*, and Gaston Diomi, an Abako leader, served in Burma in World War II. In discussions with veterans of these campaigns, the author could find no evidence that this experience had had any noteworthy influence on their political perspectives.

[13] Lumumba was a member of the 1956 group.

[14] Lumumba confided to a European friend that a visit to Brazzaville in 1947, where he was served a glass of mineral water in a European cafe, was one of the traumatic experiences of his youth.

the outside world dates only from the Brussels Exposition in 1958, where several hundred Congolese were brought to Belgium as showpieces for the Congolese pavilion. There can be no more eloquent demonstration of the degree of isolation of Congolese until 1958 than the fact that one brief paragraph can provide a nearly complete catalogue of external contacts.

Stages in Development of Nationalist Movements

To complete the analysis of the development of Congolese nationalism, it is appropriate to review the stages in the evolution of political structures founded on the ideological goal of Congolese self-rule.

Five partially overlapping stages in the evolution of the nationalist movement may be distinguished:

1) Primary resistance movements
2) Messianic and syncretic sects
3) Urban riot and violence
4) Pre-political modern associations
5) Political parties

We propose to examine briefly each of these stages and to discuss at somewhat greater length the particular characteristics of the political party system which was the culmination of Congolese nationalism.

PRIMARY RESISTANCE

Primary resistance movements, defined as armed opposition to the establishment of colonial occupation and usually led by traditional rulers, were widespread, as illustrated by Map 5. These were most frequent when the Free State agents encountered well-structured traditional states in areas remote from the colonizer's initial operating bases.[15]

Pierre Clement, "Patrice Lumumba (1952-1953)," *Présence Africaine*, No. XX (1st quarter, 1962), p. 67.

[15] The most thorough single source for these is Deuxième Section de l'Etat-Major le la Force Publique: *La Force Publique de sa Nais-*

Such chiefs had the military capacity to offer in some cases prolonged resistance to colonizers, which the unorganized, segmentary systems of much of the central basin were helpless even to attempt. These revolts were not situated in areas where rubber collection had been imposed; it was the traditional structure which saw itself threatened by colonial penetration. Examples of this type of primary resistance are the Azande, Bayaka, Baluba Shankadi of Kasongo Nyembo, and Bashi.

A somewhat different type of insurrection was exemplified by uprisings of the Babua (1903-1904, 1910) and the Budja (1903-1905). Neither of these were centralized systems; both felt the impact of harshly enforced rubber and ivory deliveries of the "red rubber" era. These were peasant uprisings of a sort, a reaction of the entire society to the severities of the Free State. There were many other more localized insurrections of this nature, or even individual acts of resistance. For example, the Abir rubber company reported that no less than 142 of its Congolese "sentries" were assassinated in the first seven months of 1905.[16] But the dispersed, small communities of most of the forest zone had no real chance of armed resistance; their best defense was retreat further into the forest, away from European posts and transport routes.

A third and particularly interesting variant of the primary resistance theme was the mutiny of two sizable armed bands from the *Force Publique*. In 1895, the Luluabourg garrison killed its commander and dispersed in eastern Kasai, where various units held out against punitive expeditions for several months. An even larger mutiny occurred

sance à 1914 (Brussels: ARSOM, Sci. Mor. et Pol., T. XXVII, 1952). Hereafter cited as *La Force Publique . . . à 1914*.

[16] *The Congo. A report of the Commission of Enquiry appointed by the Congo Free State Government* (New York: G. P. Putnam's Sons, 1906), p. 72. A sentry was a Congolese auxiliary, posted in a village outside his area, to ensure by whatever means were necessary that rubber deliveries were met.

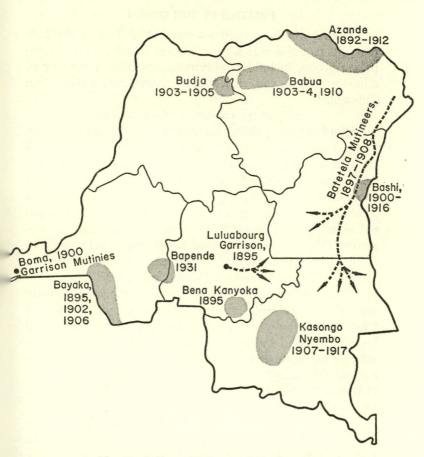

MAP 5. Primary Resistance Movements

in 1897, when most of the Dhanis column destined to win
Leopold a bridgehead on the Nile rose against the European
officers in Ituri, then fanned out southwards. In 1903,
elements of the mutineers attempted to link forces with an
insurrection against British rule in western Uganda. They
retreated into Maniema, and finally North Katanga; the
last pockets of resistance were not eliminated until 1908.

283

Although both these mutinies were attributed to the Batetela, in fact this was a generic term which covered a disparate group, including representatives from a number of ethnic groups in eastern Kasai, Maniema, and northeastern Katanga.[17]

SYNCRETIC RELIGIOUS MOVEMENTS

In the long run, primary resistance was doomed to failure. By its nature, it was localized. There was no turning back the clock on colonial penetration. By the time of the *reprise* in 1908, this phase was virtually over. It was soon succeeded by a second stage, where a synthesis of ideas and symbols assimilated from the colonizer and traditional ritual elements was found in messianic and syncretic movements. This represents a period when no secular remedy to the frustrations engendered by the colonial situation seemed available. The disequilibria introduced in traditional communities by colonial contact found temporary remedy through the millenial dream, or through adaptation of Christian symbols to supplant ritual functions which had been suppressed by the colonial administration, or to cope with an outbreak of witchcraft symptomatic of social dislocation.[18] These appeared nearly simultaneously at both ends of the country: Kimbanguism in 1921 in the Lower Congo, and the Mwana Lesa movement entering Katanga in 1925.

In the Kimbanguist example, the Bakongo character was explicit, and the movement reappeared periodically in various forms. The long contact with Christian doctrine

[17] The exact antecedents of this intriguing episode remain obscure. In addition to *La Force Publique . . . à 1914,* see "Mutineries au Congo Belge," *Bulletin Militaire,* No. 21 (March 1947), pp. 20-84; F. A. Vandewalle, "Mutineries au Congo Belge," *Zaïre,* XI, No. 5 (May 1957), 487-514; Auguste Verbeken, *La Revolte des Batetela en 1895* (Brussels: ARSOM, Sci. Mor. of Pol., N.S., T. VII, fasc. 4, 1958); Van Zanijcke, *Pages de l'histoire du Kasayi.*

[18] For two interesting inquiries into the history and sociology of messianic movements in Europe, see Norman Cohn, *The Pursuit of the Millenium* (New York: Harper Torchbooks, 1961), and E. J. Hobsbawm, *Primitive Rebels* 2nd ed. (New York: Praeger, 1963). See also *Supra,* pp. 253-54.

and especially Christian symbols in the Lower Congo seems to have predisposed the Bakongo to expressing frustration through this channel; messianism can be traced back to 1704, when a female prophet, Beatrice, galvanized Bakongo country with a message from God to return to the deserted capitol of San Salvador and reunite the kingdom.[19] In 1872, the Kyoka movement swept Bakongo areas in Northern Angola, with an appeal for destruction of all fetishes. Thus Bakongo country was fertile terrain for both the prophetic message and mass response.

To this predisposition to the messianic appeal must be added the intense dislocations of the early colonial period in the Lower Congo. Although there was little wild rubber collection in this zone, the demands imposed upon the Bakongo for porters were extremely heavy. All goods destined for the Upper Congo and the rubber and ivory to be exported had to be carried on Bakongo backs for 300 miles of hilly, difficult terrain between Matadi and Stanley Pool, until the railroad was completed in 1898. Not long after, sleeping sickness decimated the Lower Congo; this was attributed to the European, and engendered a deep bitterness. Van Wing estimated in 1920 that the Bakongo population had declined by two-thirds during this period.[20] In 1914, the Bakongo revolted at the capital of the ancient

[19] On this remarkable incident, see Louis Jadin, "Le Congo et la Secte des Antoniens. Restauration du royaume sous Pedro IV, et la 'sainte Antoine' congolaise (1694-1718)," *Bulletin de l'Institut Historique Belge de Rome*, fasc. XXXIII (1961), pp. 411-601. The literature on Kimbanguism is extensive and excellent; for the best accounts, see Georges Balandier, "Messianismes et nationalismes en Afrique Noire," *Cahiers Internationaux de Sociologie*, XIV (1953), 41-55; Efraim Andersson, *Messianic Popular Movements in the Lower Congo*; Paul Raymackers, "L'Eglise de Jesus-Christ sur la terre par la prophête Simon Kibangu," *Zaïre*, XIII, No. 7 (1959). See also Charles-André Gilis, *Kimbangu: fondateur d'eglise* (Brussels: Librairie Encyclopédique, 1960); Jules Chomé, *La passion de Simon Kimbangu* (Brussels: Les Amis de Présence Africaine, 1959).

[20] R. P. Van Wing, *Etudes Bakongo* (Brussels: Bibliothèque Congo, 1921), p. 290. This affirmation was dropped from the revised edition, published in 1959.

kingdom, San Salvador, in Angola; although many across the border in the Congo watched with approval, they dared not risk open insurrection against the Belgians. This was the atmosphere in which Kimbanguism emerged. The social costs of modernization were heavily felt; the prosperity which was later built upon it was not yet in evidence.

In March 1921, Simon Kimbangu, a former Protestant catechist, began to reveal divine messages which he had been receiving for some time, suggesting that he had been given a special mission to assure the salvation of his people. The news of Kimbangu spread rapidly, and soon the roads were filled with long processions of pilgrims to the prophet's village, not far from Thysville. In June, with workers deserting their jobs in droves and the first signs of overt civil disobedience, a warrant was issued for his arrest. He lay concealed virtually under the nose of the administration for three months, though thousands of Africans knew where he was hidden, and in September gave himself up. During his imprisonment and court martial, he was cast by the Africans in the role of Christ before Pontius Pilate. In November 1921, his death sentence was commuted by King Albert to life imprisonment in Elisabethville, where he died in 1952.

However, the removal of the prophet did not suppress his message. In January 1924, several thousand Congolese demonstrated in Thysville against the imprisonment of several Kimbanguist followers. In 1935, Salvation Army missionaries were widely greeted as Kimbanguists reincarnated in European form; the red letter "S" on the collar lapel was believed to stand for "Simon." In 1939, Simon Mpadi, a Salvation Army village sergeant, broke away and announced himself as Kimbangu's successor; his "Khakist" movement made several appearances during the war years. By the 1950's, the religious channel for the venting of frustration tended to be supplanted by the modern, secular nationalism of the Abako.

In the eastern Congo, the emergence of the messianic popular movement was foreshadowed by the appearance of secret societies whose ritual was almost entirely traditional. This was logical enough, given that Christian symbols had not become familiar through centuries of sporadic missionary activity, as in the Lower Congo. In Sankuru, a bloody revolt was led by a movement known as Epikilipikili in 1905; the followers believed they were given supernatural protection by a potion called Tonga-Tonga. This movement spread to a number of groups in Kasai, extending as far as the Bashilele in the southwestern part of the province. The Punga movement arose in Katanga shortly thereafter and developed a complicated secret hierarchy and ceremonial rites.[21]

The first sect to exhibit explicitly Christian elements was that of Mwana Lesa (son of God), which penetrated southern Katanga from Northern Rhodesia in 1925. After an incident in which a number of persons were drowned in a total immersion baptismal ceremony, the leader, Tomo Nyirenda, was deported to Northern Rhodesia, where he was hung in 1926. However, beginning in 1930, Kitawala appeared in Katanga urban centers and slowly spread northwards, then down the Congo River valley. Its extension was no doubt facilitated by the administrative practice of rusticating leaders of the movement in distant areas. The alarm of the administration at the remarkable flowering of Kitawala and related rural social protest movements in religious form was reflected in enactment of a decree on August 25, 1937, authorizing the dissolution of rural associations.[22] In 1944, Kitawala was involved in a major insurrection among the Bakumu in Orientale and Kivu. Its slow

[21] Ed. de Jonghe, "Formations récentes de sociétés secrètes au Congo Belge," *Africa*, IX, No. 1 (January 1936), 56-65.

[22] At first the greatest fear was that sects would sweep the towns, especially Leodpoldville; see "A propos du Kimbanguisme," *Congo*, 5th yr., T. II, No. 3 (October 1924), pp. 380-88. This forecast proved wrong: millennial activity was primarily a rural phenomenon.

spread can be measured by the successive dates at which it was dissolved by provincial edicts:[23]

Katanga	1937	Kivu	1944
Orientale	1943	Equateur	1946
	Leopoldville	1948	

Kitawala, unlike Kimbanguism, was not in the first instance linked to a specific ethnic group and met with a receptive audience among many; however, once adopted, as argued earlier, it tended to become assimilated into the society. Its structures, function, and doctrine varied somewhat in the different communities which were affected by it.[24] It should not be concluded that these were the only such movements; the list of dissolved associations of this nature totals about fifty.[25] These movements had in common their radical rejection of European domination, but their response was through the escape to the apocalyptic dream rather than a nationalist program.

URBAN RIOT

A third phase in the evolution of a nationalist response was the emergence of a series of large-scale urban disorders, attributable to frustration and hostility toward the colonial

[23] Frans Gevaerts, *Vadé Mecum à l'usage du Service Territorial* (Brussels: Ministère des Colonies, 1953), pp. 30-33.

[24] The most authoritative study of Kitawala structures, as they appeared in the Kazembe (Lunda) chieftaincy in the Luapule valley, just across the frontier in Northern Rhodesia, is provided by Ian Cunnison, "A Watchtower Assembly in Central Africa," *International Review of Missions*, XL (October 1951). The movement was tolerated in Northern Rhodesia, and thus was more accessible to foreign researchers. In the Congo, where it was vigorously suppressed, it became far more secretive and xenophobic in character, very little of real value became known in detail concerning its internal structures. See, in addition to Biebuyck, "La société kumu face au Kitawala," *Zaïre*, XI, 7-40, Jean Comhaire, "Sociétés secrètes et mouvements prophetiques au Congo Belge," *Africa*, XXV (January 1955), 54-59. For the role of the related Watchtower movement in Nyasaland, see George Shepperson and Thomas Price, *Independent African* (Edinburgh: University Press, 1958).

[25] Gevaerts, *op. cit.*, pp. 30-33.

situation of the town wage-earners. These differ from primary resistance movements in that they were not headed by traditional rulers, nor did they reject the modernization which accompanies colonial rule. They were leaderless, mass movements, whose participants had partially entered the modern sector. They were anomic; there were no explicit objectives. They were ephemeral outbursts rather than sustained revolts. The culmination of this form of response, the Leopoldville riots of 1959, profoundly marked both the nationalist movement and the decolonization process.

Although some manifestations of urban unrest were recorded prior to World War II, the major examples occurred after 1940. It was not until this period that towns of any size developed. The first sizable urban riot grew out of a wildcat strike of African employees of *Union Minière* in December 1941. Troops were called in; they opened fire, and at least sixty casualties resulted among the workers.[26] At Matadi, in November 1945, dock worker demonstrations led to armed intervention and an official toll of seven dead and nineteen wounded.

A somewhat different manifestation of this phenomenon was the Luluabourg mutiny in February 1944. Unlike the "Batetela" mutinies in 1895 and 1897, these mutineers were not irregular auxiliaries, but trained soldiers. Their experience and frustrations were not unlike those of the newly urbanized unskilled worker. The mutiny produced in its train a night of rioting and looting in the city, in which a part of the population participated. The mutineers then sought to disperse and disappear into the countryside.[27]

[26] The strike was probably touched off by the example of a walkout by subaltern European employees a short time before. The shooting apparently began while a Belgian administrator was negotiating with the striker-demonstrators; he barely escaped being killed by the first salvo.

[27] The igniting spark was the announcement that the troops were to be vaccinated. The rumor spread that the vaccination was really to be a mass poisoning of the soldiers. See "Mutineries au Congo Belge," *Bulletin Militaire*, No. 21 (March 1947), pp. 20-84; F. A.

These are all overshadowed by the massive Leopoldville riots of January 4-6, 1959. This sudden eruption broke out on a Sunday afternoon, when a scheduled Abako meeting had to be postponed because administrative authorization was refused. For a brief period, the explosion mobilized virtually the entire African population of the city. Police and troops could only seal off the European residential quarters; for one night all control over the African quarters was relinquished to a leaderless mob, which vented its fury on Portugese shops within its zone, and such visible symbols of the colonial system as the social centers and Catholic missions. Official figures give the death toll as forty-nine Africans; nearly all concede this falls short of reality, and many Africans were convinced that there had been several thousand casualties.[28] It is appropriate that January 4 has been designated as a national holiday since independence, in memory of the "martyrs of independence." It was at once the most decisive single event in the surge to independence and singularly prophetic of the revolution without revolutionaries which followed in 1960.[29]

We may note that these first three stages had in common an essentially mass character and a diffuseness of goals. All were clearly movements in reaction to the colonial situation;

Vandewalle, "Mutineries au Congo Belge," *Zaïre*, XI, No. 5 (May 1957), 487-514; *Dettes de guerre*, pp. 36-37.

[28] On the Leopoldville riots, see "Sociologie d'une emeute," *Courrier Africain*, Jan. 16, 1959; Commission parlementaire chargée de faire une enquête sur les événements qui se sont produits à Léopoldville en janvier 1959, *Rapport* (Chambre des Représentants, session 1958-1959. Document Parlementaire 100/3, March 27, 1959); Marres and de Vos, *L'équinoxe de janvier*.

[29] To be complete, mention should also be made of the Stanleyville riots, October 30-31, 1959. These broke out in disputed circumstances, after a congress of nationalist parties; tension on both European and African sides was very high; this was Stanleyville's first open exposure to militant nationalist expression. Thirty Congolese were killed in the two-day disorders. For different versions, see *Congo 1959*, pp. 219-38; Jean Van Lierde (ed.), *La pensée politique de Patrice Lumumba* (Brussels: Editions Amis de Présence Africaine, 1963), pp. 75-124.

the first two were essentially rural in base, while the third was an urban phenomenon. The first was a hopeless rejection of an irreversible fact. The second transcended colonial reality through the apocalyptic vision.[30] The third lashed out blindly, but without clearly formulated purposes. Leadership by the modern elite and explicit goals are found in the last two stages of the growth of nationalism—the pre-political associations and political parties.

PRE-POLITICAL ASSOCIATIONS

African group activity prior to the emergence of parties can be divided into four categories: unions, alumni associations, *cercles des évolués*, and tribal associations. Of the first, the only real example is APIC.[31] This was founded in 1946, prior to which in fact no African labor organization had been tolerated. However, the legislation in effect from 1946 to 1957 placed so many obstacles in the path of union organization that APIC was not very effective outside Leopoldville. It did, however, play a significant role in exerting pressures for a unification of the civil service statutes and access for Congolese to the upper ranks of the colonial administration.[32] Although this issue was of political importance, this in itself was not a nationalist demand.

The *cercles des évolués* and the alumni associations had certain common features. The former were organized under the patronage of the administration immediately after the war. They were set up not only in the major urban centers

[30] This is not to suggest that messianic movements did not have religious goals; it would be wrong to imply that their religious content is entirely irrelevant. But in this discussion, we are only concerned with their political function and their place in the evolution of a nationalist movement.

[31] The two major Belgian unions, *Fédération Générale des Travailleurs Belges* (FGTB-Socialist) and *Confédération des Syndicats Chrètiens* (CSC) tried to organize Congolese branches. Their paternalist operation and European direction, as well as restrictive legislation, kept their membership and impact small until political parties began to emerge.

[32] Poupart, *Première esquisse . . . du syndicalisme au Congo*, pp. 88-90.

but in many smaller towns; attractive clubhouses were built. They did serve as a social center and forum for discussion of the problems, even the frustrations, of the elite. However, they were usually closely monitored by the administration, which was normally represented by a European functionary at the meetings; they clearly fell within the paternal elite-satisfaction epoch.

The alumni associations were under mission sponsorship; the major ones were *Association des Anciens Elèves des Pères de Scheut* (ADAPES), *Union des Anciens Elèves des Frères Maristes* (UNELMA), *Association des Anciens Elèves des Frères Chrètiens* (ASSANEF), and the *Anciens Elèves des Pères Jésuites,* and, in Elisabethville, the *Cercle St. Benoit.* ADAPES dates from 1925, but had little real activity before the war. However, after the war it had 15,000 members, and many future leaders emerged from its ranks; Bolikango was the president for a number of years. The closest approximation to a comprehensive movement was UNISCO, a federation of alumni associations. Fundamentally, however, compared with similar groups elsewhere in colonial Africa, these associations were restricted in the scope of their demands and weakened by the close surveillance of a still highly authoritarian colonial system. Their contribution was in providing some organizational experience to the new leadership.

The most important pre-political groups were the tribal associations. These were the only organizations which by their nature included both elite and mass. They were the only effective, wholly African organizations, formed to help adjust to the colonial situation, both in the humble functions of mutual benefit and in assertion of comprehensive political programs. The oldest known tribal association in Leopoldville is the *Fédération Kasaienne,* founded in 1916; the *Fédération Kwangolaise* dates from about 1925.[33] The first

[33] This information is from Lemarchand's forthcoming book.

292

Bakongo association was established in 1940.[34] In Katanga, note was first taken of the existence of ethnic associations in 1926; in the late 1920's, such bodies as the *Société des amis de Kasongo Nyembo et Kabongo, Compagnie des Batetela,* and the *Société des Basong[y]e de Tshofe* were given official recognition. In 1932, when the *centre extra-coutumier* was established, the tribal associations sought to obtain the de facto right of nominating representatives; this was at first accorded, but later ignored.[35] The associations which were recognized, and large ones could not afford not to be, were required to have European counselors who attended the important meetings.

There was an important change in the character of these groups after the war. Caprasse, who has made the most thorough study of Elisabethville tribal associations, found that the pre-1945 groups were limited in membership, and served as a bridge between the administration and the group. They were much more traditional in leadership; in the cases of ethnic groups with centralized traditional structures, the tribal association was an urban extension of the traditional system. Problems were referred to the chief in the final instance.[36] In the postwar years, however, the modern elite moved into leadership positions. Here an important difference is found between Leopoldville and Elisabethville. In the capital, where traditional structures had disappeared among most of the peoples which constituted the population, groups such as the Abako did not have to dose their executive committees with uneducated elders. In Katanga, on the other hand, a careful balance was necessary. Elders, often with a kinship link to the chief, were needed for their traditional prestige, still influential among the less educated rank and file. On the other hand, the young educated element was essential, both to provide the technical capacity

[34] *ABAKO 1950-1960,* p. 10.

[35] Grévisse, *Le centre extra-coutumier d'Elisabethville,* pp. 46-47, 312-13.

[36] Caprasse, *Leaders africains en milieu urbain,* p. 68.

to operate the organization effectively and to retain the interest of the elite in the association.[37]

Two ethnic associations stand far above all others in dynamism and effectiveness, the Abako and *Lulua Frères*. To the former must go the laurels as the real founders of militant Congolese nationalism; until early 1960, the Abako was the spearhead of the independence movement. Kasavubu's election to the presidency of Abako in 1954 was a milestone in the evolution toward a nationalist movement that went beyond the problems of racial discrimination and immatriculation cards. Their successful organization to win the 1957 Leopoldville elections made them in fact the first real Congolese political party.

The *Lulua Frères* are a different phenomenon; this was essentially a reaction to the relative frustration of the Lulua in the modernization process. Its remarkable discipline and organizational success were directed against the Kasai Baluba in particular, rather than against the colonial system. Chief Kalamba apparently also desired to use the body as a vehicle to insure recognition by all Lulua of himself as paramount chief. There is no parallel for the scope of its organization; after recognition by the administration in 1952, sections were rapidly installed throughout the Congo and in the neighboring territories of Angola, Northern Rhodesia, Burundi, and Congo (Brazzaville). By 1954, it had forty sections; its bank deposit increased from 16,071 francs in January 1953 to 350,000 francs in March 1954.[38] Caprasse notes that it was the most cohesive and effective tribal association in Elisabethville; it set up its own tribunal, to handle all cases involving Lulua. In 1956, it had 1,580 members and had adjudicated 33 cases; its monthly general

---

[37] *Ibid.*, pp. 48-49.

[38] On the *Lulua Frères* movement, see Kalanda, *Baluba et Lulua*. He maintains that a high European functionary and an influential missionary were involved in its establishment. The other information is drawn in part from the Kasai Sûreté *Bulletin d'Information* notice on "Activité Kalamba et association Lulua-Frères."

assemblies had an average attendance of nearly 500.[39] Like the Abako, the introduction of urban elections in 1958 served as the occasion to become overtly political. In 1960, under the sobriquet *Union Nationale Congolaise*, the movement ran in alliance with MNC/L, which then seemed the most effective way of accomplishing its ethnic objectives.

The emergence of militant ethnic associations may no doubt be seen as a symptom of the imminent appearance of nationalist political parties. Certainly the fact that militance first emerged through the medium of the tribal association set up a dialectic peculiar to the Congo; where subsequent ethno-political movements emerged, they reacted as much to the original groups as to the colonial system. When colonial resistance evaporated shortly after the appearance of a modern nationalist movement, the compulsion for unity was removed.

The pre-political association has traditionally served as the organizational apprenticeship for the modern elite which subsequently assumes the lead in nationalist political parties. This was equally true in the Congo; nearly all the leadership which emerged in 1959-1960 had occupied posts of responsibility in one or more of the organizations which proliferated in the major towns. The often humdrum techniques of managing a modern organization—record-keeping, maintaining accounts, running meetings, electing officers— were slowly acquired. Lumumba, for example, was either president or secretary of no less than seven associations in Stanleyville in 1953—testimony to his boundless energy and skill in organizational situations.[40] These associations rapidly multiplied in the postwar years and to a certain extent

[39] Caprasse, *op. cit.*, pp. 25-26, 35.

[40] He was president of the Stanleyville branch of ADAPES, and *Mutuelle des Batetela;* and Secretary of *Amicale des Postiers Indigènes de la Province Orientale, Association des Evolués de Stanleyville,* and *Groupement Culturel Belgo-Congolais.* Pierre Clement, "Patrice Lumumba (Stanleyville 1952-1953)," *Présence Africaine,* No. XL (1962), p. 73.

served as channels for ventilating grievances. However, the potential role of the association both as a training ground and organ of expression was limited in comparison with those in former French and British territories by the more authoritarian character of the colonial regime. Many were under paternal supervision of the colonial system; all were subject to the sharp restrictions on associational rights which continued until 1959.

POLITICAL PARTIES

The final stage, the emergence of Congolese political parties per se, can be dated from the first elections in December 1957. The first political group to obtain recognition as a party was *Action Socialiste*, authorized in December 1957. At the same time in Elisabethville, Gabriel Kitenge and Antoine Rubbens, a European lawyer, formed the *Union Congolaise* to present a slate of candidates for the municipal elections; in the words of its confounder, this was intended to be anti-ideological (i.e., hostile to the metropolitan party efforts to set up Congo branches), opposed to tribal divisions, and nationalist. In the absence of a Catholic party, it rallied a number of Catholics who were offended at the anticlericalism of other candidates.[41]

The only really effective political organization in the 1957 elections, however, was the Abako, not yet officially a political party. *Action Socialiste,* and to a lesser extent *Union Congolaise,* suffered from their European roots. The efforts of Belgian parties, especially the Liberals and Socialists, to set up a network of Congo branches has been described in Chapter VII; although many African leaders at one time took part in these political groups as a place for exchange of ideas with Europeans, the paternal assumptions of political activity funneled through Belgian political parties were out of date. What the Congolese elite desired was to organize their own political movements, not to have politics organ-

[41] Rubbens, "La consultation populaire . . . ," *Bulletin de CEPSI,* No. 42, p. 78.

ized for them under European tutelage. It is true that *Action Socialiste,* which later became the *Parti du Peuple,* involved several leaders of ability, including, in the early stages, Adoula, and its socialist philosophy had a considerable audience among the intellectual group. However, the PSB and FGTB parentage proved an obstacle to effective mass action.

Union Congolaise, on the other hand, like the *Conscience Africaine* group, had links with progressive Catholic intellectuals. The PSC attitude was rather different from the Liberals and PSB; the party by and large felt that European parties should be kept out of the Congo. The 1956 PSC Congress, devoted to the colonial problem, recognized that it was legitimate to create political groups in the Congo but regretted that those existing were branches of Belgian parties; it was desirable that parties be the expression of the aspirations of the Congolese populations.[42] This view found an echo in the *Conscience Africaine* manifesto of 1956, which argued:

"National union is necessary because all the population of the Congo must become aware above all of its national character and its unity. . . . This leads us to take a position on the introduction into the Congo of political parties from Belgium. Our position is clear; these parties are an ill, and they are useless. . . .

Political parties respond to no need in the present political and administrative structure of the Congo; we have neither a Parliament, nor elections. Further, the Belgian political divisions have no relevance to the Congo; they were born from historic circumstances particular to Belgium."[43]

Political party activity gradually accelerated in 1958; the MNC was founded in October in Leopoldville, Cerea in

---

[42] Doucy's summary in *L'avenir politique du Congo Belge,* p. 29.
[43] *Congo 1959,* p. 15.

Bukavu in August, the *Confédération des Associations Tri-bales du Katanga* (Conakat) in October (although the latter did not become avowedly a political party until July 1959). The Government Declaration induced a trickle then, by mid-1959, a torrent of political parties. Over 100 led at least an ephemeral existence during the last 18 months of colonial rule. By the end of 1959 the only parties which had real organizations in the countryside, however, were the Abako and PSA, and both of these had sunk real rural roots only in the last half of the year. Elections were held in December 1959, but at a stage in the debate over the timing and terms of independence which had led most political parties to either boycott them, or to delay the decision to participate until it was too late to mount a real campaign, except in urban areas. The only serious rural electioneering was done by the Abako and PSA to enforce their boycott order.

It was on the heels of the Brussels Round Table that political organization got underway throughout the country on a grand scale. The parties were thus working under enormous time pressure, and every available shortcut was taken. In some areas, this was intimidation and violence; in most it was unbridled demagoguery, extravagant promises, and appeals for ethnic solidarity. Each provincial capital produced its own flowering of parties, which then extended into the rural hinterland, seeking as a natural electoral clientele the groups ethnically related to the party leadership.

Consequences of Short Party Life Span

Important consequences flowed from the very short life span of the parties, and the fact that they had no responsibility in the exercise of power until, in a limited way, the creation of the executive colleges beginning in March 1960 and, in an extended sense, until the provincial and national governments were established in June 1960. In their brief existence, they undertook two major functions, the sale of party cards and the selection of electoral lists. The former took place on an astonishing scale in some areas; Abako, PSA, and MNC/L achieved nearly complete sales in their respective areas. The latter was by far the most difficult, and was a substantial educational experience. With a proportional representation electoral system, the party had the responsibility of drawing up electoral lists for each voting district; these were the administrative district for the national Chamber of Deputies and the territory for the provincial assemblies. The task of drawing up a list which at once gave satisfaction to the various aspirants to leadership and to the electorate through a judicious balance of groups and regions was an extremely delicate one, and a maturing experience for all involved.

However, despite the educational experience of this period of intense organizational effort, there was no time to consolidate gains. With independence looming on the horizon, and elections even closer, there was a strong temptation to postpone resolution of any problem which did not demand immediate action. Many of the promises made were not only extravagant but contradictory; the same post-independence jobs were pledged several times over. The lack of responsibility for the conduct of government made possible a thorough-going attack on the administration; the leadership intended only the administration as organized by the colonial powers, but too often the mass believed that all administration was to be done away with, except for the maintenance of welfare services. And the earlier lack of access to responsible posts for the elite made easily credible the thesis that all difficulties resulted from the machinations of the colonizer.

Another important dimension to the problem of brief time span was the fragmentation growing out of the lack of contact among the various regional elites. The problem is rendered acute by the accidents of geography, which placed

299

Leopoldville and Elisabethville, the two poles of growth of the country, at opposite extremities, with entirely different populations and subject to different external contacts—Leopoldville with Brazzaville and former French Africa, Elisabethville with Northern Rhodesia and settler-dominated southern Africa. The four other provincial capitals were major regional centers, and, as far as the African population was concerned, each lived almost entirely separate from the others.

Here again the introduction of politics at the local level through municipal elections tended to establish a pattern of politics whereby the approach to national issues was to a large extent determined by the imperatives of the local competition. This can be seen as the thread linking many of the confusing alliances and shifts through 1959 and 1960; in Katanga, the Balubakat had at first been allied with the Conakat but rallied to a unitary platform in reaction to the ethnic exclusiveness and European associations of the latter. In the Kasai, the Lulua party, *Union Nationale Congolaise,* saw the alliance with MNC/L as a protection against the militant Baluba aims of MNC/K. In Leopoldville, the rivalry of the PSA and Abako was a major determinant of the attitudes of both parties, and the rallying to the unitarian platform by the former in early 1960 was dictated in part by the suspicions of separatist intentions on the part of the Abako.

Only two parties made a serious effort to organize nationally, MNC/L and the *Parti National du Progrès* (PNP). The former did achieve a remarkable degree of expansion in the three short months between the Round Table and the May elections. Lumumba, the crucial figure, had been in jail from early November 1959 until the Round Table on charges of having caused the Stanleyville riots at the end of October. In his absence, the party had been in disarray. But in spite of Lumumba's organizational *tour de force,* between the conference and the election, the party won only thirty-three of one hundred and thirty-seven seats in the Chamber of Deputies, with eight more taken by allied parties in Kasai. The failure of MNC/L to win a real base of support in either of the key economic poles of the country, Leopoldville or South Katanga, was of critical importance in subsequent developments. Lumumba was confronted with insuperable obstacles outside of Stanleyville and its regional hinterland of Orientale province, and areas of Kivu, Kasai, and Equateur where an ethnic appeal was possible. In each provincial situation, he was confronted with an already polarized situation; he had to make a choice of alliance with one or another existing group, earning thereby the bitter hostility of the other.

The PNP was a rather different sort of enterprise. The party was formed in November 1959 as a loose coalition of numerous local movements, mainly rural in base. At the time of its establishment, only Abako and PSA had a rural structure. There seemed some reason to believe that a combination of "moderation," support from traditional leaders, and the sympathy of much of the colonial administration might well produce a parliamentary majority, even on the assumption that the militant parties would sweep the cities.

Finally, parties were confronted with agonizing difficulties in sorting out leadership. Most major parties experienced serious tensions in this respect. Daniel Kanza created a dissident wing of the Abako; relations between the Leopoldville and Kikwit leadership in the PSA, in the persons of Gizenga and Kamitatu, were very tense at several points; the MNC split into Lumumba, Kalonji, and Nendaka wings with the second becoming progressively an exclusively Baluba movement and the third having little audience; Cerea developed Kashamura, Weregemere, and Bisukiro wings. It is difficult to discern any real ideological divergences beneath these fractures; they seem much more explicable in relation to the telescoping timetable, the lack of satisfactory means for selection of leadership. Like most leaders in all parts of the world, Congolese leaders are ambitious and obey an inner compulsion for the exercise of power. This is a property of all political systems; the successful ones develop adequate mechanisms for selecting those who can best serve the polity in fulfilling their own ambitions. This is extraordinarily difficult to achieve when neither time nor procedures are available.

The May elections formally registered the fragmentation of Congolese political movements. The radical nationalist parties in general, and MNC/L in particular, were the psychological victors, as their vote exceeded expectations. The leading three parties had between them only a bare majority of 69 of the 137 seats in the Chamber of Deputies; nine parties had seven or more seats. The fragmentation was equally visible at the provincial level. Only in Orientale did

TABLE 18

SEATS WON, MAY 1960 ELECTION

PARTY	NATIONAL		PROVINCIAL ASSEMBLIES					
	Chamber of Deputies	Senate[a]	Leo-poldville	Equateur	Orientale	Kivu	Katanga	Ka
MNC/L	41[b]	19	2	10	58	17	1	
PSA	13	4	35					
Cerea	10	6				30[c]		
Cartel Katangais	7	3					23[d]	
Abako	12	4	33					
Puna	7	7		11[e]				
Unimo	1	2		8				
MNC/K	8	3					1	
PNP	15	3		5	6	5		
Conakat	8	6					25	
Other	15	27	20	26	6	18	10	
TOTAL	137	84	90	60	70	70	60	

[a] Indirectly elected by provincial assemblies.
[b] Including direct alliances.
[c] Including all three wings.
[d] 18 Balubakat, two ATCAR, two Cartel Katangais, one MNC/L.
[e] Including two from alliance.

MAP 6. May 1960 Elections*

* In this map, the PNP is not separately indicated, but included in the category of local and individual lists.

SOURCE: Adapted from *Carte électorale du Congo,* prepared by J.-H. Pirenne. (Brussels: ARSOM, 1961)

any single party have a majority of provincial assembly seats. Nigeria and Uganda are the only other African states where no one party has a majority in the national legislature. In Nigeria, there are clear majorities at the regional level, and in Uganda the UPC appears on its way to becoming a majority party. But the Congo was exposed to all the weaknesses of coalition government at both provincial and na-

303

TABLE 19

SUMMARY OF TEN MAJOR PARTIES

Party	Founding date	Major Congresses	Leaders	Areas of strength
MNC/L	October 1958	Stanleyville, Nov. 1959, Mar. 1961—series of regional congresses, March, April, May, 1960, Luluabourg, Coquilhatville, Inongo, Stanleyville	Lumumba Gbenye	Orientale (all), Maniema, Sankuru, Tshuapa, and Lac L pold II districts plus by alliances parts of Kasai, Lulua, Kabinc districts.
PSA	April 1959		Kamitatu Gizenga	Kwilu, parts of Kwango districts
Cerea	August 1958		Kashamura Bisukiro Weregemere	North Kivu, South Kivu districts
Balubakat	November 1959		Sendwe Ilunga	Katanga urban cen Tanganika, Haut Lomami districts
Abako	1950		Kasavubu Kanza Diomi	Leopoldville city, I Congo, Cataractes districts
Puna	March 1960	Lisala, Mar. 1960; Gemena, Jan. 1961	Bolikango	Mongala
Unimo	January 1960	Boende, Jan. 1961	Bomboko Ndjoku	Coquilhatville, Equ teur, Tshuapa districts
MNC/K	July 1959	Elisabethville Oct.–Nov. 1959	Kalonji	Luluabourg, Kabin West Kasai distric
PNP	November 1959	Coquilhatville Nov. 1959	Bolya	Scattered pockets; northern Equateur Orientale, south central Kivu, parts Kasai provinces
Conakat	October 1958		Tshombe Munongo	Katanga urban ce Haut Katanga, Lu districts, scattered pockets, North Ka

tional levels, aggravated by the fact that many of the parties themselves were internally fragmented.

Weakness of Congolese Parties

Thus, an evaluation of the place of Congolese political parties in the political system and process must take into account a number of important variants from the normal African pattern. They were born in an environment where the nationalist awakening was very belated and had tended to be preceded and accompanied by a reinforcement of ethnic self-consciousness. The authoritarian character of the colonial system had given less leeway for the acquisition of experience in African associational activity than had been the case in former British or French territories. The vanguard in militant, radical nationalist expression was assumed by an ethnic movement. The vast size of the country, with its two major poles of modernization at opposite ends and several major regional centers in between, each developing its own distinct African elite until 1958, created a built-in fragmentation problem which was given little time to be overcome. And when the elite did begin to communicate nationally, the dissolution of colonial resistance provided little of the compulsion to unity which has been a vital argument elsewhere for advocates of a single independence movement. The unfolding political process happened to situate the first power contests at the various regional levels, and thus unwittingly catalyzed a local polarization to a degree impossible to overcome in the time available. Symptomatic of this is the striking fact that Congolese parties are the only significant ones in Africa to adopt specifically ethnic names; there are no important parallels for the Abako, Unimo, and Balubakat.

The compressed pre-independence life span of parties meant that many costly shortcuts were taken. The key single event in the existence of nearly all major parties was the electoral campaign of 1960. An organization and relationship with the population tailored to the short-term requirements of electoral success was hastily woven together. Further, as the parties at the time of the campaign all lay nearly completely outside the colonial system, they could afford a sort of politics-on-credit with unlimited promises individually and collectively, to be delivered after independence. The foreclosure date would have created grave difficulties for parties in the best of circumstances. Time and circumstance again conspired to block the consolidation of the spectacular triumph of electoral organization by such parties as MNC/L, PSA, and Abako into the sort of continuing solidarity nexus mobilizing governors and governed to a common pursuit of the goals of social transformation and economic advance, which such parties as PDG, TANU, and the CPP have at least partially succeeded in becoming.

Congolese political parties in 1960 were not comparable to those in other independent states; their *sui generis* traits seem more important than their similarities. From this it would be logical to expect that their function in the post-independence state would diverge sharply from the African model.

CHAPTER XIII

A Profile of Independence: 1960-1963

LESS than a fortnight after independence, the Congo's army had mutinied against its entire officer corps, its richest province had seceded, and its European functionaries were in flight. The effort to transform overnight the colonial juggernaut into a functioning independent African state had failed. The Congo had become a world crisis of the first magnitude, which for a time threatened to produce a dangerous, great power confrontation. Not until 1963 did the Congo become again effectively one country, with a single government which for a time enjoyed indisputable legitimacy.

We do not propose to give a detailed account of the Congo crisis; this would be a book in itself, and a large number have already been written.[1] Rather, as a prelude to analysis of the emerging post-independence political sys-

---

[1] By far the most objective and complete picture of the crisis is the series of volumes published by CRISP. Running documentary accounts are provided in the *Institut National d'Etudes Politiques (ex-Institut Politique Congolais)* excellent monthly, *Etudes Congolaises*. In a documentary line, see also the two special issues of *Chronique de Politique Etrangère*, *La crise congolaise*, XIII, Nos. 4-6 (July-November, 1960); and *Evolution de la crise congolaise*, XIV, Nos. 5-6 (September-November, 1961); and A. Stenmans, *Les premiers mois de la République du Congo* (Brussels: ARSOM, N.S., T. XXV, fasc. 3, 1961). Most of the many journalistic accounts were heavily weighted by the emotional intensity of the crisis and the particular political options of the writers. An incomplete list of the more useful testimonials and descriptions would include Van Bilsen, *L'indépendance du Congo;* Colin Legum, *Congo Disaster* (Baltimore: Penguin Books, 1961); Devos, *Vie et mort du Lumumba;* Marcel Niedergang, *Tempête sur le Congo* (Paris: Librairie Plon, 1960); Serge Michel, *Uhuru Lumumba* (Paris: René Julliard, 1962); Pierre Davister, *Katanga: enjeu du monde* (Brussels: Editions Europe-Afrique, 1960); Francis Monheim, *Mobutu: l'homme seul* (Brussels: Editions Actuelles, 1962); Gilis, *Kasa-Vubu;* Conor Cruise O'Brien, *To Katanga and Back* (New York: Simon & Schuster, 1962); Jules Chomé, *La crise congolaise* (Brussels: Editions de Remarques Congolaises, 1960).

307

tem, this chapter will recapitulate briefly the major political developments of 1960 through 1963 to enable the reader to situate the analysis of the emerging political system in the following chapters. The drama which was enacted in these four years was of extraordinary complexity; interwoven were developments in the four poles of de facto political autonomy which emerged, actions of the United Nations and a number of world powers who were drawn into the situation, relationships with the former colonizer, and evolution in the provinces. To offer a compressed and comprehensible overview we are forced to simplify and select certain aspects which are most relevant to the remainder of the volume. We will summarize the psychology of the situation on the threshold of independence; the diverse dimensions of breakdown, military and administrative; the fragmentation of the polity; the slow reconstruction of a single state; the Adoula government and its opposition; and some social and economic consequences of breakdown.

Psychological Climate of Independence

The emotional dimension of the final stage of decolonization is a key to understanding the explosion which followed independence. The whole atmosphere at this time was charged with uncertainty and insecurity. Beneath the external surface of delirious joy lay fears and suspicions of diverse sorts. The most absurd rumor would find a ready audience; from top to bottom, there was a predisposition to give immediate credence to tales of foul conspiracy. For example, on July 7, the arrival of a Soviet plane at the Leopoldville airport sent a report surging through the city that Russian invasion was imminent; 2,000 Congolese soldiers were dispatched in haste to the aerodrome. On the European side, the process was similar; there was a widespread belief that a Communist takeover was planned, embellished by reports that small groups of soldiers in the months prior to independence had been evacuated via Uganda and

Ethiopia to Soviet bloc training areas for rapid indoctrination. There were recurrent reports of a Polish freighter standing offshore, laden with armaments for insurgents.[2]

Plots indeed there were; Belgian *Force Publique* Commander Janssens admits in his memoir that he planned after his dismissal to fly to Luluabourg or Elisabethville to organize resistance to the Lumumba government.[3] Ganshof van der Meersch, Resident Minister to the Congo the last six weeks, makes it abundantly clear in his report on the accomplishment of his mission that he did everything legally possible to avoid a Lumumba government, and was subjected to pressure by many who argued that "at any cost" a different leader must be found.[4] The Katanga secession plot had been going through long incubation; the first overt attempt to secede was in December 1959, and a second was made three days before independence. There can be little doubt that the Soviet Union did see real opportunities in the Congo situation to weaken "imperialist" positions in Africa and, partly through the Belgian Communist party, made vigorous efforts to develop a clientele and alliances amongst the Congolese leadership, with showers of invitations to Prague, East Berlin, and elsewhere. Western powers were disturbed by the fluidity of the situation and devoted considerable resources to blocking any extension of Soviet influence. It would be surprising if Touré and Nkrumah had not hoped that the Congo would join the Ghana-Guinea union to give decisive psychological impetus to the embryonic pan-African state.

Nothing could be more natural than uncertainty in this situation. No one could be sure exactly what the next day

[2] *Congo 1960*, I, 6. See also for this thesis, Pierre Houart, *La pénétration communiste au Congo* (Brussels: Centre de Documentation International, 1960); Edouard Mendiaux, *Moscou, Accra et le Congo* (Brussels: Charles Dessart, 1960).

[3] Janssens, *J'étais le général Janssens*, pp. 219-30.

[4] W. J. Ganshof van der Meersch, *Fin de la souveraineté belge au Congo* (Brussels: Institut Royal des Rélations Internationales, 1963), pp. 176-298.

would bring; independence was really inconceivable for both Europeans and Africans. For the former, a tiny minority in an African state of which it controlled nearly all the wealth, it was impossible to foresee the reaction of leaders or mass to the new situation when the European community was no longer protected by the formidable instruments of colonial order. For the latter, it could hardly seem true that the Europeans were suddenly and peacefully surrendering; surely, many reasoned, there must be some devious scheme.

EUROPEAN FEARS

European insecurity took a number of forms. In the private sector, business was alarmed, and the stock quotations of the colonial companies fell sharply. A spokesman for colonial capital, Liberal Senator Hougardy, declared after the Brussels Round Table: "The Belgian delegates, seeking to reassure the Africans, have terrified the Europeans. In abandoning reserved powers, the government has provoked in Belgium a veritable panic. . . . For let us not forget that in many countries, independence is accompanied by horrible tumults."[5] But no guarantees were obtained; business sought to win the good will of political leaders by financing their election campaigns, by trying to put on a public face of good will while privately taking what measures they could to protect their investments.

More important was the insecurity of the administration personnel. Their future was particularly unpromising. Their experience seemed to have little relevance in finding new positions, and many had reached an age at which beginning a new career would not be easy. Unlike their British or French counterparts, their pensions and status were entirely linked with the colonial state; they had no claims on the metropolitan power. Although a law was passed (over the opposition of Belgian civil service unions) on March 21, guaranteeing integration into the metropolitan ranks of

[5] G. Dumont, *La Table Ronde Belgo-Congolaise,* p. 167.

310

those functionaries who were officially declared unable to continue their careers in Africa, the measures of application necessary to put the law into legal effect were not taken until June 28. There were known to be "black lists" circulating of "anti-African" functionaries to be sacked at the first opportunity. The general climate of insecurity among the 10,000 European civil servants is reflected in a letter sent to the King on May 8 by the European unions:

"On the eve of Congolese independence, the European population of the Congo asks itself anxiously about the nature of the protection that Belgium is prepared to give to its nationals.

"The fear expressed by our compatriots is far from being vain and unjustified.

"Many Congolese publications contain virulent appeals to racial hatred, and even encouragements to massacre of the Belgians, and rape of our wives and daughters.

"Large sections of the native population identify independence with our expulsion, even by bloody means. . . ."[6]

Many sent wives and children home in anticipation and shipped out much of their movable belongings.

AFRICAN UNCERTAINTIES

On the African side, at the mass level, conceptualization of independence was difficult. It was to be something good; electoral promises indeed had given the people reason to believe that spectacular gains were in sight. It was evident that independence was to mean that no one was going to be peremptorily ordered about by Europeans; one could even dare openly express one's defiance of Europeans by throwing stones at cars or shaking a fist as the administrator strolled by. There was never the kind of mass political education campaign which parties like TANU and the PDG carried on to explain the opportunities and responsibilities of independence. The payment of an "independence bonus"

[6] *Congo 1960*, II, 523-24.

was general for all firms, to try to meet the vague expectation of some concrete benefit. The transport workers at Leopoldville were on strike as independence came; the first serious post-independence incidents, which left ten dead at Coquilhatville on July 4, were caused by unfulfilled expectations.[7] Cessation of cultivation was widespread; in many cases, full mechanization of agriculture had been promised during the election campaign, and the peasants very sensibly were waiting for the tractors to arrive.

For the leadership, several incidents looked ominous. The physical gold stock representing part of the foreign exchange reserves was removed from Leopoldville to Brussels. There were complicated technical explanations for this, relating to the liquidation of the colonial Central Bank, which had been headquartered in Brussels, but the move was quickly understood by the Congolese as a sort of theft; Kasavubu issued a communiqué on April 14 demanding the immediate return of the gold "arbitrarily transferred to Belgium."[8] In April and May, reinforcements were sent from Belgium to the metropolitan bases at Kamina and Kitona. In May, Ganshof van der Meersch was named as Resident Minister; these measures, taken to reassure European opinion, alarmed the Congolese. Lumumba reacted by demanding on May 18 the immediate withdrawal of the Belgian troops; he expressed the misgivings of many in adding, "The principal objective of the Belgian government is to establish a stooge government which it will control. . . ."[9]

DISCONTENT OF CLERKS AND SOLDIERS

In the early months of 1960 two important groups developed the conviction that they were being left out in distribution of the fruits of independence—the clerks and the soldiers. Most of the political leaders had been recruited from the former category, and the future looked bright in-

[7] Stenmans, *Les premiers mois,* p. 4.
[8] *Congo 1960,* I, 87.
[9] *Ibid.,* I, 81-82.

deed for them; the political sector was to be entirely African. But prospects were very different for those remaining behind in the bureaucracy. The administration was to remain mostly European in the upper reaches, with promotion to the highest ranks blocked by the university degree requirement, which the growing numbers of students would have but the present generation of functionaries could never obtain. Belgium offered in March training programs in various Brussels ministries; the Congolese Executive College insisted that the choice of candidates be made by the political parties. On May 22, there was a stormy session of the *stagiaires* in Brussels, during the course of which their spokesman complained bitterly of the declarations which future Foreign Minister Bomboko had made concerning their extremely modest perspectives. Bomboko, then a member of the political commission in Brussels, declared bluntly, "It is not in three months that someone can make a first secretary out of you."[10]

The depth of feeling of the civil servants is reflected in a communiqué of APIC on March 15, which stated:

"Having learned of the guilty and demagogic attitude of certain Congolese political leaders, during and after the Round Table, especially concerning the career guarantees accorded by them to metropolitan functionaries, APIC protests energetically once again against these guarantees and demands the immediate departure of all the non-technical civil servants and even the reduction of the present level of European technicians in the administration. It recalls to public opinion that the career guarantees accorded by the aforementioned leaders constitute gratuitous promises binding only on themselves. . . . Conscious of its responsibilities, APIC feels that the guarantees accorded will maintain the mass of workers in the blackest misery. . . . APIC will mobilize all the national working forces to support, with

[10] Albert Pevée, *Place aux noirs* (Brussels: Editions Europe-Afrique, 1960), pp. 74-76.

all the means at its possession, its just demands. It reaffirms its ardent desire to see Congolese occupy forthwith and before June 30, 1960, the posts of command in the administration. It desires a Congolese administration with a Congolese government."[11]

A similar trend was noticeable in the army. Here a dual process was in operation; on the one hand, the nationalist movements, especially in the period before the Round Table, were deeply distrustful of the *Force Publique,* particularly its commanding officer. The right-wing political opinions of General Janssens were well-known, and there was legitimate reason to fear that at some point the *Force Publique* would be called in to wipe out the fragmented nationalist groups by force. Verhaegen and Gérard-Libois conclude:

"The Congolese leaders . . . sought to limit the risks . . . in destroying or paralyzing the essential means for a colonial war, the *Force Publique.* They did this aided by Congolese opinion and by their political organizations, in establishing, each with his own ethnic group, contacts and close relations with the Congolese non-coms and certain leaders amongst the soldiers. Thus, it was a secret for nobody that Kasavubu, as of 1959, could count on the support and fidelity of the adjutant Nkokolo, of Mukongo origin, future colonel and commandant of camp Leopold II [Leopoldville]."[12]

To this was added, beginning in 1960, a growing malaise among the troops about the obstinate refusal of Janssens to permit any acceleration of the plodding Africanization program, which would have produced the first Congolese officers in 1963. There was here, as with the clerks, a feeling that the political leadership was failing to assure an equitable distribution of the opportunities for advance established by the achievement of independence. Lumumba him-

[11] *Congo 1960,* II, 522.
[12] *Ibid.,* II, 1072.

self, who had the responsibility for defense within the Executive College, as well as in the first government, was the target for considerable resentment. Although as independence neared, the nationalist parties associated themselves with the demands for Africanization in the army, the first Prime Minister had declared in a Brussels speech shortly after the conclusion of the Round Table, "It is not because the Congo is independent that we can turn a private into a general."[13] A campaign of anonymous letters from the troops began; during information hours, officers were bombarded with questions as to "why independence was not for the soldier."[14] Several of the Congolese political journals printed similar communications; their tenor is typified by the following passages:

"It is with great shock that the Congolese soldiers have learned via the press of the various declarations made by Congolese leaders on their return from the Round Table. . . . It astonishes us to see our African brothers forget us. . . . There will be two branches of Congolese independence. First there will be . . . the class of the great Congolese leaders and their white counselors. These will benefit from all the advantages of the new independent state. . . .

"A second dishonored wing, which will include the inferiors, the criers of 'Vive Independence' on June 30, 1960, will be and remain the servants of the first branch.

"M. Lumumba judges us incapable of taking the place of the officers. . . .

"Dear Lumumba, friend of the Europeans . . . we guarantee you the infernal ruin of your powers as long as you insult us as ignorant and incapable of taking the places of your white brothers. . . ."[15]

Mutiny of the Force Publique

Thus, stability hung on the razor's edge as independence

[13] *Courrier d'Afrique*, March 4, 1960, quoted in *ibid.*, I, 350.
[14] Ganshof van der Meersch, *Fin de la soveraineté*, p. 313.
[15] *Congo 1960*, I, 350.

was proclaimed on June 30. Breakdown could have come at any number of points. As it turned out, the first place to give way was in the army. This engendered in almost instant succession the Katanga secession and the flight of Belgian civil servants. With the government deprived of its instrument of coercion, it was at the same time rendered powerless to deal with the crisis touched off by the mutiny. The climate of fear and suspicion on all sides led each group to place the worst construction upon the actions of others. Events surged hopelessly out of control, with all parties helplessly reacting to what appeared to be the fulfillment of their gloomiest forebodings.

On July 5, General Janssens had summoned the African non-commissioned officers of the army detachment garrisoned in Leopoldville for a meeting following the first overt act of indiscipline the previous afternoon. He wrote on the blackboard the phrase "After Independence—Before Independence" and bluntly announced, "The *Force Publique* continues as before."[16] That same evening, troops in Thysville, ordered to march on Leopoldville to cope with incipient indiscipline, refused to obey their European officers. The first mutiny in modern times of an army against its entire officer corps began.

The next day, Lumumba tried to temporize by promoting all soldiers one grade and announcing the dismissal of General Janssens. The mutiny spread to other parts of the Lower Congo, but not as yet elsewhere. On July 8, the decision was taken to Africanize the entire officer corps, retaining a small cadre of politically acceptable Belgian officers as councilors. But panic had swept the European community in Leopoldville on the nights of July 7 and 8, as the first reports of incidents of violence began arriving from the Bas-Congo. On July 9, for the first time the mutiny spread to other parts of the Congo. The Belgian government decided to use metropolitan troops to protect Belgian lives and

16 *Ibid.*, I, 372.

property, if possible with the accord of the Congolese government. In Elisabethville, the mutiny began to take on more murderous overtones; five European civilians including the Italian vice-consul were shot down at an ambush established by mutineers. In Luluabourg, nearly the entire European population barricaded itself in a large office building, which was surrounded by mutineers.

Belgian Intervention

The following day, the first Belgian troops arrived in Luluabourg, Kamina, Jadotville, and Elisabethville. Lumumba and Kasavubu, who were touring the country to appeal for calm and to designate the new Congolese army commanders, agreed in Luluabourg on July 11 to accept the presence of the Belgian troops, provided their mission was restricted to the protection of persons and property. The situation was somewhat improved in Leopoldville and the Bas-Congo, and for a brief period there seemed some possibility of limiting the damage.

However, two decisive events took place on July 11 which led to a total rupture between Belgium and the Congo. In Matadi, Belgian naval forces unleashed an entirely unnecessary bombardment of the city, which had already been completely evacuated by Europeans. Although Congolese fatalities were reported to be nineteen, the news transmitted immediately over the excellent *Force Publique* communications net to garrisons throughout the country was that a generalized massacre had taken place, with hundreds of deaths.[17] Almost immediately in areas as widely separated as Thysville (Lower Congo), Tshuapa (Equateur), and Goma (Kivu), mutineers set off after Europeans to avenge Matadi.

Meanwhile, at the other end of the Congo, an even more important event transpired; Katanga declared its "independence," and Belgian troops were used to disarm and

[17] Ganshof van der Meersch, *Fin de la souveraineté*, pp. 418-19.

317

expel all troops who were not from pro-Conakat zones in the province. A military and technical assistance mission was rapidly mounted, including regular Belgian officers as well as former *Force Publique* personnel. It was obvious that here the Belgian intervention went far beyond the officially announced goal of protecting European lives; the Katanga secession was being supported by Belgian military force. On July 12, Lumumba and Kasavubu were refused authorization to land at Elisabethville airport.

In all, between July 10 and 18, Belgian troops intervened in 28 localities, 16 of them in the provinces of Leopoldville and Katanga. In the prevailing atmosphere of panic and incomprehension, this added to the Matadi bombardment and protection afforded the Katanga secessionist regime seemed in the eyes of many Congolese to accredit the thesis that Belgium was "reconquering" its lost colony. With the exception of the short-lived Luluabourg agreement, the interventions took place without authorization by the Congolese government, in formal violation of the Friendship Treaty signed the day before independence (but never ratified by either parliament).

Until July 12, much of the Congolese leadership was inclined to agree that the Belgians were the aggrieved party. The parliamentary debates are instructive on this point; on July 12, Arthur Pinzi (Abako) introduced a motion in the lower house calling for an expression of apology to King Baudouin and to other foreign nations for the atrocities committed by the mutineers. The deputies observed a minute of silence for the victims, and the feeling of shame was expressed by numerous members. The following day, however, the news of Matadi, the refusal to allow the plane bearing the President and Prime Minister to land at Elisabethville, the realization of the import of the Katanga secession, and the humiliating treatment to which Lumumba and Kasavubu were subjected by Belgian refugees on their arrival at Leopoldville totally altered the mood; shame became wrath.[18] On July 11, Lumumba had been willing to authorize the continuing presence of Belgian troops at Luluabourg for a provisional period. Three days later, he and Kasavubu sent a telegram to Premier Khrushchev urging the Soviet Union to keep close watch on the Congo situation for any Western plot against its sovereignty, and they announced a rupture of relations with Belgium.[19]

Anatomy of Violence

With some widely scattered exceptions, particularly in the Bas-Congo and Tshuapa district in Equateur, the population did not join in the attacks against Europeans. The nature of the violence was significant. Although there were moments when large-scale killings might have occurred, the final toll of European lives in the initial weeks was relatively small, certainly less than two dozen. There were spectacular exceptions, such as the assassination of André Ryckmans and his companion on a rescue mission at the Inkisi bridge in the Lower Congo, and the machine gun ambush in Elisabethville. However, the clear emphasis was less a desire to liquidate then utterly to humiliate. The rapings are significant in that light; the European woman was the ultimate taboo of colonial society, as in the southern United States. Men were forced to walk barefoot, and were spat upon; women were violated in the presence of their husbands and children. Priests and nuns were paraded nude before the public. These acts were infused with the sadism

[18] République du Congo, Chambre de Représentants, *Annales Parlementaires*, 1960.

[19] On July 12, the Council of Ministers, presided over by Vice-Premier Gizenga in the absence of Lumumba, appealed for U.S. troops to intervene in the Lower Congo. A subsequent "clarification" indicated the American troops were to be under UN auspices. The same night, in the midst of their journey through the eastern Congo, Lumumba and Kasavubu cabled the UN asking for military intervention. It is almost certain that there had been no communication between the Council of Ministers and Lumumba-Kasavubu concerning these separate initiatives. However, it is significant that the telegram to the Soviet Union followed these other communications.

and wanton cruelty of mob behavior, but the symbolic humiliation of the European-run colonial society stands out.[20]

The psychology of the mutiny is ably summed up by the authors of *Congo 1960,* who note that in case after case the same pattern of mutual fear and misunderstanding appeared:

"1) reciprocal panic fed by false news, by the declarations carried by the radio, and by rumors spread, systematically or otherwise, among the two populations;

2) amongst the white population: preventative constitution of self-defense groups, action of armed Volunteer Corps; parallel to this action: efforts made to remove or neutralize the arms of the soldiers of the *Force Publique,* with or without the complicity of the officers;

3) On the part of the soldiers, the fear of being killed by the whites, civilian or military, led to the desire to

[20] Characteristic of many of the testimonials is the following account of events in the Djolu region, in Tshuapa district of Equateur:
"Troubles in the Djolu region began on July 11, 1960. Father . . . of a mission in this region took in some refugees, including a man seriously wounded by a shot from a native soldier. The next day, Father . . . was arrested by two soldiers and beaten across the back and knees. He was obliged to lie flat on the ground and then to run about several times. . . . On this same day, July 12, the nuns were put into a punishment cell with two women and a baby, according to a statement made by two of the nuns. The native soldiers attacked the first nun and, after a painful struggle, managed to rape her. Then they attacked another, and with the help of yet another soldier, tried to rape the Sister. Two of the soldiers stamped on her. The nun fainted, and one of the other sisters asserted that the victim had just expired. The soldiers were frightened and ran away. . . . At 0530 hours the party of white prisoners, both men and women, were taken to another prison. They were all naked, including the priests and nuns, and their hands were tied behind their backs. They were incarcerated in a cell block where some twenty women and children were already imprisoned. The soldiers wanted to know why the nuns were not affiliated to Lumumba's political party, and whether they had sexual relations with the priests; each was promised a soldier for the night. Subsequently, the captives were taken by a truck to Mompono accompanied by the insults of the native population."
Congo 1960, II, 477.

seize, by attack if necessary, the arsenals and arm depots, and then, the hunt for Europeans to disarm them, with search of house and vehicle. Sometimes the soldiers oppose the departure of the civilians and imprison their officers to hold some whites as hostages and thus avoid being attacked by airplanes or parachutists;

4) once the metropolitan forces have intervened, virtually all the white population leaves when the Belgian troops can no longer guarantee their security. The white officers of the *Force Publique* must abandon their men. The population pillages, if the soldiers do not stop them."[21]

By the middle of the month, the entire European officers corps of the army and police had been replaced. The civil servants had been guaranteed by Belgium on July 8 that in Leopoldville and the Lower Congo they were considered unable to continue their functions, and assured of the application of the provisions for integration into the metropolitan civil service. On July 12, the Belgian ambassador in Leopoldville announced that the measure would be applicable throughout the Congo (except Katanga); this led to a massive flight by most of the 10,000 functionaries. The European population, which had reached a high of 110,000 at the beginning of 1959 and dropped to a little over 80,000 at the time of independence, now fell to an estimated 20,-000, of whom a large number were in Katanga.[22] This unsought revolution, on top of Africa's most remarkably telescoped decolonization, produced the continent's most Africanized political system.

Toward the Overthrow of Lumumba

With this fundamental watershed of Congolese history passed, one may divide the post-independence developments into two phases: 1) a slow downward spiral of dis-

[21] *Ibid.*, I, 425.
[22] *Ibid.*, II, 1080-82.

integration, which reached its nadir with the announcement of the assassination of former Prime Minister Lumumba in February 1961 and which saw the Congo split into four principal fragments: Katanga, South Kasai, Congo (Leopoldville), and Congo (Stanleyville); and 2) a gradual improvement and trend toward reunification with, as the major steps, the unanimous investiture of the Adoula government in August 1961 at the Lovanium Parliament and the liquidation of the Katanga secession at the beginning of 1963.

During the two months between the outbreak of the mutiny and the overthrow of the Lumumba government, the determinate goals in the action of the Prime Minister were the elimination of the Katanga secession and the consolidation of the authority of his government. However, Lumumba faced imposing obstacles on both counts. His own army was leaderless, and could only be brought under control over a long period. Beginning July 15, with the arrival of the first UN detachments, the effective military forces were those of the UN and, until their final withdrawal from the Congo (minus Katanga, August 7) and Katanga (September 4), Belgian metropolitan forces. Accordingly, Lumumba was powerless to act except through diplomacy. He tried various means to force the UN to eliminate the secession, seeking support at different stages from the West, the Afro-Asian group, and the Soviet bloc. Meanwhile, his council of ministers was large, heterogeneous, and unwieldy. Under the enormous strains of the crisis atmosphere, cleavages quickly became evident. Different ministers perceived the events in somewhat different ways and were susceptible to varying influences, domestic and external. The cabinet as such never was able to function harmoniously. At the same time, Lumumba's relations with Kasavubu had never been intimate, before or after independence. The compromise by which Kasavubu became Chief of State and Lumumba Prime Minister had been achieved with great difficulty in June; the constitutional duality between the two offices was fraught with potential conflict.

The UN objectives were not the same as those of Lumumba.[23] UN policy was necessarily a function not only of the Congolese situation per se but also of the alignments within the Security Council and General Assembly and other UN responsibilities, present and future. Preventing a great power confrontation and preserving the UN structure for future peace-keeping missions takes priority over any missions set by the Congolese government. Further, a number of senior UN officials came to share with many Western and some Afro-Asian chancelories the growing lack of confidence in Lumumba's judgment; his behavior viewed from abroad frequently seemed erratic and irrational. Thus there was from the outset a fundamental misunderstanding between Lumumba and the UN on the objects of the international intervention. To the Prime Minister, the central purpose was to preserve order and restore the integrity of the national territory, including Katanga; the UN was a surrogate for the duly constituted Congo government, acting at its behest. For the UN, the object was in the first instance to prevent the Congo crisis from becoming the occasion for a larger world conflict; the Secretariat had to retain its freedom of action, and was responsible to a majority in the Security Council and General Assembly, not the Congolese government.

It rapidly became clear to the Prime Minister that the UN did not intend to take decisive action to reduce by force the

[23] For an analysis of UN action, see especially O'Brien, *op. cit.*; Joseph P. Lash, *Dag Hammarskjöld* (London: Cassell, 1962); Arthur Gavshon, *The Mysterious Death of Dag Hammarskjöld* (New York: Walker and Co., 1962); Stanley Hoffman, "In Search of a Thread: The UN in the Congo Labyrinth," *International Organization,* XVI, No. 2 (Spring, 1962), 331-61; Robert C. Good, "The Congo Crisis: A Study of Postcolonial Politics," in Lawrence W. Martin, *Neutralism and Nonalignment* (New York: Frederick A. Praeger, 1962), pp. 34-63; Arthur Lee Burns and Nina Heathcote, *Peacekeeping by U.N. Forces* (New York: Praeger, 1963).

Katanga secession. The crucial moments came on August 5 when UN special representative Ralph Bunche concluded in Elisabethville that UN troops scheduled to arrive in Katanga would be met by force. He therefore recommended postponing their dispatch. A week later, Hammarskjold himself negotiated with Tshombe the conditions under which UN troops would relieve Belgian detachments, on the basis of an August 9 Security Council mandate "not to intervene in any internal conflict." On August 8, the Baluba state of South Kasai had followed the Katanga into secession.

Soon thereafter, Lumumba determined to seek whatever external support he could find outside the framework of the UN. He summoned an African summit conference for Leopoldville August 25-31; this proved to be a failure as no chiefs of state attended, and the conference was unwilling to endorse direct military assistance to the Lumumba government. By this time, Lumumba had decided to undertake himself a military offensive against South Kasai and Katanga. On August 26, Bakwanga, the South Kasai capital, was occupied by ANC units without resistance. However, this expedition took a catastrophic turn, and by August 29 the reconquest of South Kasai was turning into a massacre of Baluba civil population. These acts, which Hammarskjold asserted "had the characteristics of the crime of genocide,"[24] discredited the Lumumba government at a critical moment. When ten Soviet aircraft and sixty trucks appeared in response to Lumumba's appeal for direct assistance at the beginning of September, the Prime Minister appeared to have opted for a Soviet alliance.[25]

[24] In a statement to the Security Council, September 9, reprinted in *Congo 1960*, II, 805-06.

[25] From Lumumba's point of view, by the end of August only the Soviet Union seemed prepared to give him full and unconditional support in his drive to restore national unity and consolidate his rule. The miscalculation lay in failing to appreciate fully the repercussions of this act both in consolidating the hostility of the West and in

In the capital, opposition rapidly mounted. Lumumba had the fatal disadvantage of lacking any large body of supporters among the Leopoldville population. Had the capital been Stanleyville, or even Luluabourg,[26] the course of history might have been different. But in Leopoldville, leaders of five significant groups in the population, Bakongo, Bangala, Baluba, Bayaka, and Mongo, were openly hostile to Lumumba by early August. These constituted the overwhelming majority of the population and readily participated when frequent anti-government demonstrations took place. The Catholic Church feared his laicist convictions in general and the threats to remove from Church control the University of Lovanium in particular. Three trade unions, the *Union des Travailleurs Congolais* (UTC), *Fédération Générale des Travailleurs Kongolais* (FGTK), and APIC, issued statements critical of the government in early August.[27] The only daily newspaper, *Courrier d'Afrique*, and an important weekly, *Présence Congolaise*, were both anti-Lumumba.

Constitutional Impasse: The Lumumba Revocation

This set the stage for another vital dimension to the

---

temporarily alienating even those who supported his nationalist objectives. Soviet bloc personnel began arriving in large numbers at the end of August, which reinforced the psychological impression that a Soviet "takeover" was in the offing. Another factor contributing to this impression was that Lumumba ceased to be accessible to those bearing counsels of prudence by mid-August; there appeared in his entourage persons with an extremist reputation, such as Serge Michel, a Russian émigré who had become a self-proclaimed Algerian citizen, and Felix Moumié, leader of the *Union des Populations Camerounaises* (UPC). The real influence of these persons was perhaps limited, but the psychological impact, especially on Western embassies and news media, was substantial.

[26] The Brussels Round Table had called for Luluabourg as a provisional site for Parliament and presumably the government, but this proposal was abandoned when Lulua-Baluba rioting grew more violent in the following weeks.

[27] UTC is of Catholic inspiration, while FGTK is a descendant of the Congo branches established by the Belgian Socialist FGTB.

breakdown: the collapse of the constitutional parliamentary regime set up by the *Loi Fondamentale*. On September 5, President Kasavubu read over the national radio network an ordinance revoking Prime Minister Lumumba from his functions. The constitution required that all presidential acts bear the counter-signature of two ministers; this stipulation was met by Foreign Minister Bomboko and Minister Resident in Belgium A. Delvaux. The act created a complete impasse, which was overcome only a year later by the unanimous parliamentary agreement on the Adoula government.

Legally, Kasavubu's act was based upon Article 22 of the constitution, which states with pristine simplicity, "The President names and revokes the Prime Minister." At the same time, Kasavubu named Ileo as *formateur* to set up a new government. Article 22 is a textual replica of Article 65 of the Belgian constitution; the problem with its insertion in the Congo document was that it was not accompanied by the accumulated political traditions relevant in Belgium. In fact, in the more authoritarian days of King Leopold II, this clause had been used by the King to inform a Prime Minister that, as he no longer enjoyed royal confidence, he should resign. At the present time, however, it is contrary to Belgian constitutional usage, if not letter, for the King to use this clause.[28]

There was nothing in the *Loi Fondamentale* that made Belgian usage binding on the Congo, even if it were unam-

[28] In August 1960, Baudouin is reported to have summoned Prime Minister Eyskens to inform him that he no longer had confidence in his government. Eyskens, however, indignantly refused to resign and defied the King to invoke Article 65 and revoke him. Quite obviously, for Baudouin to have done this would have reopened the *question royale*, so the matter was dropped. Interview with Professor F. Perin, Brussels, February 9, 1962.

It should be added that in these precedents the article was not formally involved as in the Congo case. Rather the King informed the Prime Minister that he had lost confidence in him, which in a different era was sufficient in some instances to produce a resignation.

biguous. Indeed, it was by no means clear what the role of the President was to be. Obviously, a Chief of State elected by Parliament cannot be compared to a hereditary monarch; Kasavubu, as the father of Congolese nationalism, was a political figure, not just a symbol. Lumumba himself initially desired the presidential office, rather than the Prime Minister's post.[29] He obviously saw it as being far more than the ceremonial post of the King of the Belgians.

The *Loi Fondamentale* had the fatal flaw of providing no method to secure a definitive interpretation of constitutional ambiguities. Articles 226 to 236 provided for a Constitutional court, but its functions were restricted to the delivery of opinions on the compatibility of legislative measures with the *Loi Fondamentale*, conflicts in the division of powers between central and provincial authorities, and the legality of administrative acts where no other recourse existed. In any case, this court has never been established, and the interim substitute, the Belgian *Conseil d'Etat*, could hardly have been used, given the lack of diplomatic relations. Article 51 states:

> The authoritative interpretation of laws belongs only to the Chambers.
>
> For the interpretation of the present law, the Chambers may ask the Belgian Parliament the interpretation which it gives.

This is the only explicit provision for problems of interpretation of the *Loi Fondamentale* itself, and it goes without saying that in the best of circumstances it is unimaginable that, on an important constitutional question, the Belgian Parliament could have been accepted as an arbiter. And yet, in a narrow juridical sense, the Belgian Parliament had enacted the law, and was thus alone competent to rule on legislative intent.[30]

[29] *Congo 1960*, I, 285.
[30] Documents prepared in Stanleyville to establish the "legality" of

At any rate, at this critical juncture, the UN accepted the legality of the revocation and closed the radio and airports; Hammarskjold told the Security Council on September 9 that the act was constitutional in his judgment. Lumumba was thus unable to organize an immediate counter-coup.

The impasse became complete when, on September 7, the Congo Chamber of Representatives, by a vote of 60-19 of a total of 137 members, resolved that the revocation was annulled, as well as Lumumba's clearly illegal gesture of revoking Kasavubu. The Senate followed suit the next day by a 41-2 vote, with 6 abstentions, of 84 members. At this point, only Lumumba and 4 of the 27 ministers[31] had been revoked; Kasavubu's thesis was that Ileo as *formateur* was in function until he could present himself before the Chambers, as were those ministers who had not been included in the revocation ordinance. Ileo, his backers argued, had not been able to appear before the Chambers, and the Lumumbists only legal recourse was to introduce censure motions against the ministers who countersigned the ordinance. Once the act of revocation had been signed, it was argued that the Lumumba government could not be considered even to have "caretaker" functions.

On September 12, Ileo announced the composition of his government. It was quite clear, however, that there was no

---

the Gizenga regime are an interesting reflection of the difficulty in finding any clear judicial answer to the question of the legality of Lumumba's revocation. The clauses of these edicts which seek to prove that Kasavubu violated his constitutional oath in acting illegally repose on very vulnerable arguments. The very fact that two drafts were considered, based on quite different lines of reasoning, is evidence in itself of the impossibility of constructing a clear legal case. *Congo 1961*, pp. 161-64.

[31] Remy Mwamba (Balubakat), Minister of Justice; Christophe Gbenye (MNC/L), Minister of the Interior; Anicet Kashamura (Cerea), Minister of Information; Antoine Bolamba (MNC/L), Secretary of State for Information and Cultural Affairs; Antoine Gizenga (PSA), Vice-Premier; and Jacques Lumbala (PNP), Secretary of State to the Presidency. The Secretaries of State were not considered members of the Council of Ministers.

possibility of obtaining a parliamentary majority for it. Two days later, Mobutu held the famous press conference announcing that the army was "neutralizing" both the President and Prime Minister and designating a *Collège des Commissaires* composed of university students to serve as a caretaker government until the end of the year. The joint session of the two Chambers September 13, where with several members short of a quorum and with armed troops in the hall a vote was taken according extraordinary powers to Lumumba, proved to be the last meeting of Parliament until the reconciliation at Lovanium nearly a year later.

Thus, in another ten-day period, exactly two months after the first breakdown, the constitutional framework of government collapsed. It could hardly have lasted much longer in any case; there is strong evidence that Lumumba himself had lost patience with the niceties of parliamentary democracy and felt that effective realization of nationalist goals could only be achieved through a centralized, presidential regime, headed by himself. Belief in the imminence of a Lumumbist coup was one precipitating factor in Kasavubu's decision. In the same way, suspicion by the Prime Minister that opposition groups were gathering strength for a move against his government led him to formulate plans for a coup of his own.

The principle of constitutionalism is necessarily weak in most newly independent states. Radical African nationalism has not in general offered it a large place in its pantheon of political values; the state structure at the moment of independence suffered the dual defect of its colonial antecedents and the features which the colonizer would frequently require as a price for his departure. The mass single-party, not the state, incarnated the sovereign "general will" of the people, and, until profound reforms of the state could be carried out to excise colonial anachronisms, the revolutionary promise of African nationalism was not to be shackled by legalism. Constitutional arguments, in general, were the refuge of opposition groups, which in the premises of the single-party state were anti-national and threatened the yet-fragile independent regimes with paralysis. It is thus hardly surprising that the *Loi Fondamentale* framework did not long survive.

Emergence of Stanleyville Government

Beginning September 15, Lumumba was confined to the Prime Minister's residence, encircled by a UN guard to protect him against arrest and a second cordon of Congolese troops to prevent his escape. The UN, which had initially given de facto support to Kasavubu, quickly retreated to a position of "neutrality" and refusal to take a position for either party; with large blocs of states rapidly forming in support of the two contenders, this attitude of the Secretariat was dictated by its constituency. Slowly, the new Kasavubu-Mobutu-College of Commissioners tandem consolidated an uneasy control over Leopoldville and the formal institutions of government. By October, it became clear that the Lumumbist groups could do nothing from Leopoldville, and the possibility of a negotiated reconciliation with Kasavubu seemed remote; accordingly, the strategy emerged of establishing a rival government in Stanleyville and carrying on the struggle from there.

In November, Vice-Premier Gizenga arrived in Stanleyville, the support of the provincial government was assured, and pro-Mobutu officers were removed from the army detachments. By the end of the month, Lumumbist control over Orientale had been consolidated. At the same time, Lumumba on November 27 began his spectacular escape attempt. He got as far as Port Francqui by December 2, when he was recaptured in a zone inhabited by Kasai Baluba; a few more miles, and he would have had nothing but friendly territory between his convoy of eight automobiles and Stanleyville. He was then imprisoned at the military camp in Thysville, and on January 17 transferred with

Senate Vice-President Joseph Okito and Youth Minister Maurice Mpolo to Elisabethville, where almost certainly all three were assassinated shortly after the plane landed.[32]

However, the Stanleyville regime gathered momentum in December-January. A handful of gendarmes overturned the pro-Leopoldville Kivu government of Jean Miruho on Christmas, and Anicet Kashamura took over under Stanleyville authority on January 2. Stanleyville troops penetrated as far as Manono in North Katanga by January 10, without meeting resistance; a North Katanga province (Lualaba) had been proclaimed on October 20, in Stanleyville. The Sankuru district of Kasai was also under Stanleyville control, and on February 24, some Stanleyville units briefly won over the Luluabourg garrison. This, however, was the high water mark of Stanleyville.

The Struggle for Reunification

Thus by the end of 1960, the Congo was splintered into four autonomous fragments, Leopoldville and Stanleyville (each claiming to be the legitimate capitals for the entire country) and Bakwanga and Elisabethville (claiming to have seceded); each possessed its own armed forces. The first half of 1961 was marked by a complex pattern of military maneuvers, negotiations through various intermediaries, round tables, and ephemeral alliances. The three major poles, Leopoldville, Stanleyville, and Elisabethville, each had a clientele of international supporters, which lent global ramifications to their contest.

The presence of the UN forces ruled out a solution by force; what resulted was a war of attrition while intermit-

[32] A wave of political assassinations followed. In February, 7 Lumumbists, headed by Joseph Finant, first President of Orientale province, were executed in an atrocious ceremony near Bakwanga, after being "tried" for "crimes against the Baluba nation" by a "traditional court" of Baluba chiefs. Shortly thereafter, 15 political prisoners were shot at Stanleyville as reprisals; these included the Minister of Communications of the Lumumba government, Alphonse Songolo. This was without doubt the nadir of the Congo crisis.

tent negotiation proceeded. There were remarkably few genuine confrontations between the various armies. The real victims were the civil populations in the areas through which the armies moved; most of the fatalities which occurred during this period were the result of encounters between one of the armies and the local population, as in North Katanga or the fringes of South Kasai.

In the play of alliances, Leopoldville occupied the central position. At various times, there were alternative options of allying with Stanleyville against Elisabethville, or vice versa. Thus, when Stanleyville's military expansion was at its peak, in February 1961, with a wave of antagonism to both Leopoldville and Elisabethville authorities following the Lumumba assassination and a new UN mandate February 21 seeming to hint the disarming of Mobutu's troops, a military alliance was quickly signed between Leopoldville, Bakwanga, and Elisabethville on February 28. However, the conjuncture rapidly changed, and by early April Leopoldville was embarked on serious negotiations with Stanleyville, which eventually led to the reconvening of Parliament in July.

In the dialogue with Stanleyville, in addition to the alternative option of a Katanga alliance, Leopoldville enjoyed a number of important advantages. The assassination of Lumumba removed Stanleyville's only outstanding leader. Leopoldville possessed the central administrative infrastructure of the country. Embassies and the UN headquarters were situated in Leopoldville, providing superior access to the external world. The College of Commissioners and subsequently the Ileo government were able to construct, from very tenuous beginnings in September 1960, a power base with Mobutu at the head of the army and Nendaka reorganizing the security police (Sûreté). Stanleyville proved highly vulnerable to a supply blockade established on the Congo River from December 1960 to April 1961; Sudan forbade the use of its territory for the transit of military sup-

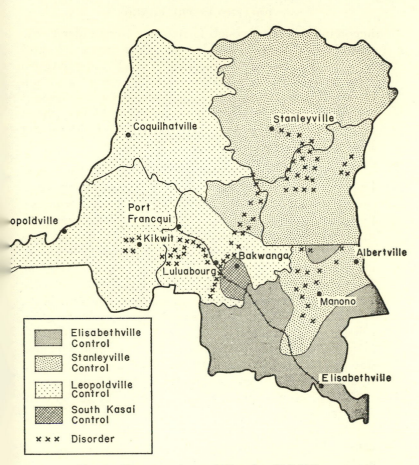

MAP 7. Fragmentation and Disorder, 1960-1962

plies, and there was no real way for the external support from the Soviet bloc and those Afro-Asian states backing Gizenga to be more than verbal.

The impasse at the level of constitutional legitimacy and international recognition did not of course prevent the four governments from operating, with varying degrees of success. In Leopoldville, the College of Commissioners did an important and effective job in restoring some order to the central administrations and beginning the immense task of adjusting the country to the fundamental changes which had occurred. The entire existence of the Lumumba government had been dominated by the crisis, and almost none of the ministries had really begun to function. Most qualified observers would agree with the evaluation of the present head of the Congo Bank, Albert Ndele:

"From July 1 to September 29, 1960, the country was no longer really governed. No law, no ordinance, no important decision was made. It suffices to leaf through the *Moniteur Congolais* [official gazette] for this period to appreciate this. One finds that two executive orders had been promulgated, one on September 5 restricting civil liberties, the other on August 16, 1960, installing a special military regime. To be complete, one should add three orders of the Finance Ministry on questions of administrative routine. . . .

"Within the administration, the functionaries, lacking top-echelon personnel and governmental directives, found it impossible to make the administrative machine function. The public services were paralyzed by absenteeism and riddled with the gangrene of political favoritism. . . .

"Finally, no measure was taken directly by the government to assure the continuity of fiscal receipts and supplies. No disposition was taken to halt the financial hemorrhage caused by the massive transfer of capital and reserves abroad."[33]

With the help of the UN and the International Monetary Fund, a Monetary Council, to be the embyro of a National Bank, was established; exchange controls were effectively imposed, and an import licensing system established. The primary schools were reopened on schedule in September, and with some delays the secondary schools as well. There

[33] Albert Ndele, speech, Nov. 9, 1960, quoted in *Congo 1960*, II, 883-87.

was some established authority with whom the UN could work in technical assistance projects.

From the standpoint of administrative effectiveness, Katanga was governed reasonably well in the areas not hit by the Balubakat uprising. Although the posts of command were in a formal sense Africanized in July 1960, the level of European technical assistance and de facto control remained high. Katanga also had the advantage of very high tax and export duty earnings from the rich mining complex, which made it better able to afford the extravagant levels of ministerial salaries and army wages which have kept the Leopoldville public finances under continuing pressure. In Katanga, unlike the rest of the Congo, Belgian functionaries in the crucial July days were given a strict order by Belgian officials to remain; departure was declared to be a "grave dereliction" of duty.[34] A high social cost was paid for the apparent tranquility in South Katanga, however. There was a systematic persecution of political opponents to the Tshombe regime, under the direction of Interior Minister Munongo's ruthless security police. When the UN opened a camp for political refugees in September 1961, it quickly filled with 70,000 persons, mainly Baluba. The fact that so large a number chose the appalling misery of the refugee camp to their city homes is eloquent testimony to the harshness of the Conakat government toward those who were lukewarm in their enthusiasm. The "pacification" efforts periodically conducted by the mercenary-led Katanga gendarmes in Balubakat areas of North Katanga were often little more than terrorization carried out by indiscriminate reprisals against whole regions.[35]

Stanleyville had great difficulties. The coexistence of the provincial government and the "central government" of Gizenga was an uneasy one. The effective administrative functions were carried out by the former; indeed, this very

[34] *Ibid.*, II, 871.
[35] For a graphic description, see O'Brien, *op. cit.*, pp. 140-66.

fact led the provincial authorities to place greater priority on the health of the economy and, in consequence, on the maintenance of European enterprise. The Gizenga cabinet was in reality a government in exile, and its real activity was limited to the diplomatic field and the effort to extend its authority by military force on the Leopoldville government. It had no administrative activity as such. But, considering the difficulties and lack of external assistance, in many ways the Orientale provincial government functioned reasonably well.

The South Kasai government also had some noteworthy achievements to its credit. In September 1960, with the actual operation of the government primarily in the hands of Ngalula and a group of Baluba intellectuals, a state was created from scratch. The ghetto of South Kasai made real strides in coping with the agonizing refugee problem, with substantial assistance from the UN and the diamond-mining firm, *Minière du Bakwanga* (*ex-Forminière*). But the administration itself was established with very little outside assistance; a solidarity born of an abiding sense of persecution and the relatively large modern elite of the Kasai Baluba enabled a functioning system to emerge, until Kalonji's extravagances and enthronement as "Mulopwe" produced a split with the intellectuals and the departure of Ngalula. An *Essor du Katanga* correspondent, returning from South Kasai in March 1961 after having seen the utter disorganization on the heels of the military massacre in September 1960, reported a *saissisant* progress. A census had been taken, agriculture and justice reorganized, a system of rural communes established, selling and purchasing cooperatives created. "All along the roads of South Kasai, a very homogeneous people regroups itself, cooperates to overcome the obstacles. . . . There are certainly striking parallels with the history of Israel, which indeed are frequently cited."[36]

Three round table conferences were held in the first part

[36] *Essor du Katanga*, March 3, 1961.

of 1961, in Leopoldville, Tananarive, and Coquilhatville. Their object was to negotiate a settlement of the constitutional impasse. Throughout this phase, Katanga insisted that the *Loi Fondamentale* could not be the basis for reunification, and only a far looser, confederal form of association would be acceptable. Stanleyville, on the other hand, argued that a rigid application of the *Loi Fondamentale* could be the only basis for solution and that Parliament, not a round table, was the appropriate body to conduct the discussions. The Leopoldville round table (January-February) included neither Elisabethville nor Stanleyville,[37] and little of lasting significance emerged. The Tananarive conference was organized and dominated by Tshombe in March, and the Katanga theses of confederal association were momentarily endorsed by the Leopoldville representatives. At Coquilhatville in April and May, Leopoldville again had the upper hand, and Tshombe was arrested and held for two months in the capital when he walked out in protest over the abandonment of the Tananarive confederal principles. Stanleyville was absent from all three. The permanent significance of these meetings lay in acceptance of the principle of new provinces, a federal structure, and the convening of Parliament to bring an end to the governmental crisis.

Reconciliation at Lovanium: Adoula Government

Under UN encouragement, agreement was finally reached to convene Parliament in isolation at Lovanium University in July. All groups were represented, except Tshombe's eight Conakat deputies; the Katanga authorities had finally reneged on an agreement to attend, despite Western pressures. The Leopoldville coalition and Western milieux feared that Conakat votes would mean the difference between investiture of a Gizenga government and

[37] There were several participants from the Lumumbist bloc, but these held no mandate from Stanleyville.

one headed by a Leopoldville political figure. South Kasai, however, was in attendance.

As the session began, the votes were divided almost equally between two coalitions, the "Nationalist Bloc" (essentially the Stanleyville group) and a "National Democratic Bloc" (essentially Leopoldville). The Nationalist Bloc candidate was elected president of the Chamber of Deputies, 61-57, reflecting the narrowness of the division. However, a unanimous compromise was found on the issue of a new government; Parliament agreed that neither the Ileo nor the Gizenga governments could be considered the legal successor to the Lumumba government, and it found in Cyrille Adoula a leader who could be accepted by both groups. Adoula had served as Minister of Interior in the Ileo government, and was therefore a Leopoldville man. On the other hand, he had consistently defended the unity of the Congo and opposed the Katanga confederal theses; further, while Interior Minister, he had put an end to persecution of pro-Lumumba elements in Leopoldville. He had not been implicated in the Lumumba assassination.

On August 2, Adoula received a unanimous vote of confidence. His government represented a careful balancing of the political groups present at Lovanium; of the 27 ministers, 16 had been associated in 1960 with the Lumumbist bloc, and Gizenga retained his position of Vice-Premier. This broad representation was in part facilitated by the enormous size of the cabinet. In addition to the 27 ministers, there were 15 secretaries of state. The Congo thus entered a new phase; the constitutional crisis, which began on September 5, 1960, was now over. There remained the tasks of eliminating the last bastion of secessionism—South Katanga—reducing remnants of dissidence in Stanleyville, beginning to define permanent institutional structures to replace the provisional *Loi Fondamentale,* and restoring the economic and social circuits which had been damaged by the long crisis.

338

Despite the unanimous vote in Parliament, elements in the Lumumbist bloc were uneasy about the Adoula government. Their suspicions related to the degree of vigor with which Katanga would be crushed, the susceptibility of the government to Western influences, compromises which might be made in the unitarian structure of the country, and continued control of the primary instruments of force by Mobutu and Nendaka. In October Gizenga returned to Stanleyville "to pack his suitcases," and began trying to reconstitute the old power base. A fortnight after his arrival in Stanleyville, a new provincial government in Orientale was invested, which supported the Gizenga dissidence. Pro-Gizenga administrators were installed in Maniema and Sankuru districts; the Orientale and Kivu units of the ANC appeared to be under Gizenga control. In early November, the Stanleyville threat seemed very real indeed.

However, there was a fundamental difference between the post-Lovanium Parliament situation and the period in early 1961. Gizenga was now in overt rebellion against a government of indisputable pedigree; he was no longer head of a regime which could make a debatable but plausible claim to be the legitimate successor to the Lumumba government. The arguments of "legality" which had been so fervently advanced by Stanleyville in the earlier period now rebounded against Gizenga. The situation rapidly turned against him. General Lundula, in Stanleyville eyes the legitimate commander-in-chief of the ANC, rallied to Leopoldville on November 11. The same day, Stanleyville troops were responsible for the atrocious massacre of 13 Italian aviators in UN service at Kindu, which further discredited the Gizenga enterprise in the UN and internationally. By January 15, the Chamber of Deputies voted a motion of censure against Gizenga by the overwhelming vote of 67-1 with 4 abstentions. On January 20, he was arrested and transferred to Leopoldville and subsequently sent to the island of Bula-Bemba in the mouth of the Congo River, where he remained under confinement until early July 1964. Stanleyville as a potential base for dissidence was further weakened by the division of Orientale into three provinces in August 1962 and the placing of the city itself under direct central administration in September of the same year.

Elimination of Katanga Secession

The Katanga secession was a far more difficult obstacle to overcome.[38] However, the existence of a legitimate government in Leopoldville made possible a concerted effort to deal with the problem. The UN Security Council resolution of February 21 had authorized the use of force in the last resort to bring about the immediate removal from Katanga of all foreign military personnel and political advisers who were not under UN orders. On August 28, the UN undertook a massive round-up of unauthorized expatriate personnel; the surprise sweep was initially highly successful, and some 338 mercenaries and 443 political advisors were caught and expelled. The UN was induced to halt its operation on the basis of a promise of voluntary cooperation; this permitted a regrouping by mercenaries and Katanga forces. On September 13, UN forces attempted to resume the operation, this time with the more extended objective of bringing the secession to a close.[39] However, the surprise advantage was lacking, and the UN suffered a humiliating reverse.

In December, a second round took place between the Katanga gendarmes and the UN. This time, the UN was better prepared, and a number of the key installations in

[38] On Katanga developments, see O'Brien, *op. cit.*; Gérard-Libois, *Sécession au Katanga;* Davister, *Katanga: enjeu du monde;* P. Davister and Ph. Toussaint, *Croisettes et casques bleus* (Brussels: Editions Actuelles, 1962); République du Congo, *Les entretiens Adoula-Tshombe* (1962).

[39] O'Brien, *op. cit.*, pp. 219-88. This interpretation of the mission was apparently not shared in New York.

Elisabethville were seized. On December 15, Tshombe cabled President Kennedy indicating his willingness to meet with Adoula, provided that guarantees for his security were offered. The meeting took place at Kitona, in the Lower Congo; UN representative Ralph Bunche and American Ambassador Edmund Gullion took part at a critical stage in the negotiations. The result was an eight-point accord which basically accepted the Leopoldville terms. However, no sooner had Tshombe returned to Elisabethville than the agreements were called into question; by various dilatory tactics, without actually denouncing the accords, Katanga authorities never applied more than a small part of them.

March to June, 1962, was consumed by intermittent negotiations between Adoula and Tshombe on the whole range of problems posed by reintegration of Katanga—military, financial, administrative, and constitutional. These discussions took place in Leopoldville under UN auspices, with considerable UN and other diplomatic pressure to obtain a compromise settlement. Although measurable headway was achieved on some issues, on the basic question of the nature of central-provincial relationships, Tshombe did not move far from his Tananarive confederal positions. The Katanga leader was offered the post of Vice-Premier, and several times during the course of the negotiations rumors swept Leopoldville that Tshombe was about to become central Prime Minister. But on June 26, the talks were broken off, and the negotiators could not even agree on a final communiqué.

The failure of the Adoula-Tshombe talks convinced most observers that there was no possibility of an agreed reintegration of Katanga; Tshombe would not concede more than a loose and unworkable confederal link. The UN, however, had suffered humiliating reverses in Katanga. To withdraw from the Congo without having assured the reunification of the country would have been to concede complete failure, especially given that many UN members believed that UN policies in July-August, 1960, had made possible initial consolidation of the secession. The United States, and to a lesser extent Britain, was convinced that stability elsewhere in the Congo was unlikely if the Katanga secession were permitted to stand. Belgium, which had initially given vital technical and military support, if not diplomatic recognition, to the secession, had gradually altered its Congo policy since the PSC-PSB government of Théo Lefèvre, with Paul-Henri Spaak as Foreign Minister, replaced the more conservative PSC-Liberal coalition of Gaston Eyskens in April 1961. By mid-1962, Belgium as well was prepared to go a long way toward coercing Tshombe to accept genuine reunification, despite the potent Katanga lobby at Brussels.

The next step, then, was the U Thant Plan, announced August 10, 1962. The scheme was a package plan, proposed as the arbitrator's solution; its specific proposals were not negotiable. The main points were provision for preparation by UN experts of a federal constitution, proposals for equitable distribution between center and provinces of tax revenues and foreign exchange earnings, integration of the armed forces, general amnesty, and Conakat participation in the central government. The sting in the tail was a timetable for the application of economic sanctions to Katanga if the plan was not accepted. Tshombe was too shrewd to be snared so simply; on September 3, he "accepted" the Thant Plan. As with the Kitona "accords" previously, however, the application of its provisions proceeded at a snail's pace.

In North Katanga, there had been intermittent fighting with various ANC units since January 1961. During the course of 1962, the ANC made some headway, and central authority over a substantial part of the north had been assured, albeit loosely. By December 1962, tension was growing in the South Katanga cities, and the expectation grew that a final trial of force with the UN was close at hand. On December 28, the third round began; this time, the UN was prepared with sufficient air and ground strength to push the operation to a conclusion. On January 3, UN forces occupied Jadotville. Several tense days followed while the participants watched to see if the oft-brandished Katanga threats of a "scorched earth policy" and the demolition of the *Delcommune* and *Le Marinel* dams would be implemented.[40] However, on January 14, Tshombe announced to the world that the Katanga secession was terminated.

In Search of a Constitution

Thus the Congo had become a single country again, and attention could be turned to other problems. The nature of the political system had been profoundly altered by the decision in March and April, 1962, to break down the six old provinces; by mid-1963, twenty-one new provinces had emerged. In the shadow of the Leopoldville-Elisabethville conflict, important powers had quietly slipped from central into provincial hands. Adoula had proved adept at balancing the disparate political forces in Leopoldville and maintaining himself in power at the head of shifting coalitions (cabinet shuffles took place in February and July 1962, and April 1963). However, the administration never succeeded in developing a genuine popular base.

The constitutional debate had begun in earnest at the Brussels Round Table prior to independence; based on its general instructions, a working group elaborated a provisional basic law, the *Loi Fondamentale,* which was adopted for the Congo by Belgian Parliament. This was intended as a transitional document only; Congolese leaders agreed that a definitive constitution could be elaborated only by the Congolese themselves, after the country enjoyed full sovereignty. The Leopoldville, Tananarive, and Coquilhatville round tables in 1961 all gave their attention to the future

[40] The dams had been mined, although it remains a moot point whether this was done sufficiently to accomplish more than partial destruction. Had the dams been destroyed, however, not only would the financial loss been staggering but the resulting flood would have taken many thousands of lives along the Lufira and Lualaba valleys.

constitution, with contradictory results. At Coquilhatville, the Ileo government was requested to establish a special constitutional study commission; this was set up shortly after, under the chairmanship of the first Congolese law graduate, Marcel Lihau. At the same time, a group of three UN-designated specialists, headed by Justice Minister T. O. Elias of Nigeria, prepared a draft constitution. During the course of the Adoula-Tshombe negotiations, the central government position was developed from these various documents.

When the Adoula-Tshombe talks broke down, a new group of four UN experts, again headed by Elias, prepared another draft constitution, which formed a part of the arsenal of the U Thant Plan. In March 1963, a parliamentary commission began to examine the by now extensive working documents, operating primarily on the basis of the UN draft. This proved tedious and slow; by July, less than one-fourth of the work had been completed. Parliament was summoned on August 31, 1963, to sit as a constituent assembly and to devote itself exclusively to the task of completing the constitutional draft. However, the deputies refused to confine their attention to constitutional labors, and, on September 29, the Chambers were indefinitely adjourned by President Kasavubu. A special constitutional commission was established by presidential ordinance, composed of representatives of the central government, provincial governments and assemblies, trade unions, employers, youth and student organizations, and churches; this commission began its work in Luluabourg on January 13, 1964, and completed a draft constitution in April.[41]

[41] Specifically, the Luluabourg commission included: 4 delegates of the central government; 2 of each provincial government; 2 of each provincial assembly; 2 of each recognized trade union; 2 of each recognized employer association; 2 of cooperatives per province; 2 of the Conseil National de la Jeunesse; 2 of the press; 2 of student organizations; 2 of the Catholic Church; 2 of Protestant churches; and 2 of the Kimbanguist church.

It will be noted that political parties were not accorded representation. Only the national student union, *Union Générale des Étudiants*

Opposition Groups

Although Adoula had been unanimously voted into office as Prime Minister, throughout nearly all of his tenure there has been a shifting bloc of opposition which claimed fidelity to the Lumumbist heritage of radical nationalism. Membership in this opposition cluster varied; the most consistent participants were a fraction of MNC/L, led by Christophe Gbenye, of Orientale, and the Gizenga wing of the PSA, which had openly split in 1962. The Gizenga dissidence in Stanleyville represented the first phase. From early 1962 until the adjournment of Parliament in September 1963, the opposition operated mainly within the Chambers, constantly trying to gather the votes needed for a censure motion and at times obstructing government business.

An entirely new phase of action opened in October 1963 with the establishment in Brazzaville of the *Comité National de Libération* (CNL), committed to the forcible overthrow of the Adoula government. In November, a plot to seize and assassinate Mobutu and Nendaka very nearly succeeded. By December, a sizable insurrection had broken out in the Bapende-Bambundu areas of Kwilu province, which was where PSA-Gizenga had drawn its support.[42] There appeared to be emerging the tactic of seeking "liberated areas" in different parts of the Congo, in zones where the various leaders involved in the CNL had a local following. Appeals had been made for Soviet bloc and Afro-Asian assistance; the CNL was seated at the Afro-Asian Peoples' Solidarity Conference in Algiers in March 1964. The major participants in the CNL were a segment of MNC/L, led by Babua leaders Gbenye and Egide Bocheley Davidson; PSA-Gizenga; a dissident Lulua movement,

---

Congolaises, refused to participate. "La commission constitutionelle à Luluabourg," *Etudes Congolaises,* VI, No. 1 (January 1964), 22-30.

[42] It is not entirely clear whether the CNL approved of the Kwilu uprising, led by Pierre Mulele, or whether this was in part an independent initiative of Mulele.

TABLE 20
MINISTRIES OF CENTRAL GOVERNMENT SINCE INDEPENDENCE

Ministry	Lumumba[a] government June–Sept. 1960	Collège des[b] Commissaires Sept. 1960–Feb. 1961	Second Ileo[c] government Feb.–Aug. 1961	Adoula[d] government Aug. 1961–July 1962	Revamped[e] Adoula government July 1962–April 1963	Revamped[f] Adoula government April 1963–June 1964
1. National Defense	Lumumba (MNC/L)	Kazadi (MNC/K)	—	Adoula	Anany	Anany (PDC)
2. Foreign Affairs	Bomboko (Unimo)	Bomboko (Unimo) (Bomboko)	Bomboko (Unimo) (Bomboko)	Bomboko (Unimo)	Bomboko (Unimo)	Mabika-Kalanda (PDC)
3. Foreign Trade	Bisukiro (CEREA)			Bisukiro (CEREA)	Anekonzapa (PNP)	Yava (Conakat)
4. Justice	Mwamba (Balubakat)	Lihau	(Lihau)	Mwamba (Balubakat)	Weregemere (CEREA)	Bomboko (Unimo)
5. Interior	Gbenye (MNC/L)	Nussbaumer	Adoula (MNC/K)	Gbenye (MNC/L)	Kamitatu (PSA)	Maboti (Abako)
6. Finance	Nkayi (Abako)	Ndele	Nkayi (Abako)	Pinzi (Abako)	Bamba (Abako)	Bamba (Abako)
7. Economic Affairs	Yav (Conakat)	Mbeka	Dericoyard (PNP)	Eleo (MNC/L)	Dericoyard (PNP)	Nyembo (Conakat)
8. Public Works	Ilunga (UNC)	Mukendi	Ilunga (UNC)	Ilunga (UNC)	Delvaux (Luka)	Delvaux (Luka)
9. Communications and Transport	Songolo (MNC/L)	Kashemwa	Mukwidi (PSA)	Kama (PSA)	Ilunga (UNC)	Ilunga (UNC)
10. Agriculture	Lutula (MNC/L)	Lebughe	Mopipi	Weregemere (CEREA)	Tshala-Mnana (MNC/K)	Tshala-Mwana (PDC)
11. Labor and Social Security	Masena (PSA)	Bokonga	Kimvay (PSA)	Kisolokele (Abako)	Diamusumbu (MNC/L)	Nguvulu (PP)

						Lutula (MNC/L)
	(MNC/L)			(MNC/L)		
13. Public Health	Kamanga (COAKA)	Tshibamba	—	Kamanga (COAKA)	—	Bolya (Unimo)
14. Mines and Energy	Rudahindwa (REKO)	—	Mahamba (MNC/L)	Rudahindwa (REKO)	Bolya (Unimo)	Mahamba (MNC/L)
15. Land	Mahamba (MNC/L)	—	—	Mahamba (MNC/L)	Mahamba (MNC/L) (Mahamba)	———
16. Social Affairs	Ngwenza (Puna)	—	—	Asumani (MNC/L)	Uketuenge (MNC/L)	Massa (RADECO)
17. Education	Mulele (PSA)	Cardoso (MNC/L)	Bizala (MNC/K)	Ngalula (MNC/K)	Ngalula (MNC/K)	Colin (Abako)
18. Information	Kashamura (CEREA)	Bolela	Bolikango (Puna)	Ileo (Unimo)	Colin (Abako)	Bolamba (MNC/L)
19. Youth and Sports	Mpolo (MNC/L)	—	—	Mongali	(Uketuenge)	Agoyo (MNC/L)
20. Economic Coordination and Plan	Kabangi (MUB)	(Mbeka)	Kabangi (MUB)	Kabangi (MUB)	Massa (RDLK)	Kamitatu (PSA/K)

a There were six others of ministerial rank: Gizenga, (PSA) Vice-Premier; Delvaux, (Luka) Minister Resident in Belgium; Kanza, UN Delegate; and Bolya (Unimo), Grenfell (MNC/L), Kisolokele (Abako), and Genge (Puna) without portfolio.

b Bomboko, President of the College, headed both Foreign Affairs and Foreign Trade; Mbeka combined Economic Affairs and Economic Coordination and Plan. Few of the students had any marked party identification.

c Bomboko again headed both Foreign Affairs and Foreign Trade; Dericoyard combined Economic Affairs and Middle Classes; Lihau and Mukwidi headed their departments without ministerial rank.

d In February, Gbenye became Vice-Premier and was replaced at Interior by Kamitatu; Bolikango became Vice-Premier as well.

e Land, Mines and Energy were united under Mahamba; Social Affairs, Youth and Sports were unified under Uketuenge.

f There are three others of the ministerial rank: Kasongo (MNC/L), Vice-Premier for Economic Coordination; Masanga (Conakat), Vice-Premier for Social Affairs; and Ileo (Unimo), Minister without portfolio for Katanga Affairs.

(continued next page)

TABLE 20 (concluded)

MINISTRIES OF CENTRAL GOVERNMENT SINCE INDEPENDENCE

Ministry	Lumumba[a] government June–Sept. 1960	Collège des[b] Commissaires Sept. 1960–Feb. 1961	Second Ileo[c] government Feb.–Aug. 1961	Adoula[d] government Aug. 1961–July 1962	Revamped[e] Adoula government July 1962–April 1963	Revamped[f] Adoula government April 1963–
21. Civil Service	—	Bindo	Bolya (Unimo)	Masikita (Luke)	Kabangi (MUB)	Kabangi (MUB)
22. Parastatals	—	—	Kisolokele (Abako)	—	—	—
23. PTT	—	—	—	Mungamba (MNC/L)	Mungamba (MNC/L)	Mungamba (MNC/L)
24. Portfolio	—	—	—	Badibanga (MNC/K)	—	—
25. Traditional Affairs	—	—	—	Lumanza (PNP)	—	—

[a] There were six others of ministerial rank: Gizenga, (PSA) Vice-Premier; Delvaux, (Luka) Minister Resident in Belgium; Kanza, UN Delegate; and Bolya (Unimo), Grenfell (MNC/L), Kisolokele (Abako), and Genge (Puna) without portfolio.

[b] Bomboko, President of the College, headed both Foreign Affairs and Foreign Trade; Mbeka combined Economic Affairs and Economic Coordination and Plan. Few of the students had any marked party identification.

[c] Bomboko again headed both Foreign Affairs and Foreign Trade; Dericoyard combined Economic Affairs and Middle Classes; Lihau and Mukwidi headed their departments without ministerial rank.

[d] In February, Gbenye became Vice-Premier and was replaced at Interior by Kamitatu; Bolikango became Vice-Premier as well.

[e] Land, Mines and Energy were united under Mahamba; Social Affairs, Youth and Sports were unified under Uketuenge.

[f] There are three others of the ministerial rank: Kasongo (MNC/L), Vice-Premier for Economic Coordination; ... (Gizenga) and Ileo (Unimo), Minister without portfolio for Katanga Affairs.

348

Union Démocratique Africaine, headed by André Lubaya; and the small personal following of Kashamura, in Kivu.

Another and very different type of opposition to Adoula came from the trade unions. The unions began to be a genuine social force only after independence, when the paternal shadow of European sponsors was totally removed. There are three major national unions: FGTK (heir of the socialist union before independence); UTC (successor to the Catholic union); and the *Confédération des Syndicats Libres du Congo* (CSLC—an unsuccessful effort to unite all unions, but including important membership of civil service and teachers' associations). The total union membership is impossible to know; only the UTC gives figures on dues-paying members (65,000). The others make no distinction between dues-payers and "sympathizers"; the FGTK and CSLC thus claim 70,000 and 200,000 supporters, respectively, but these figures are certainly too large. Congolese trade unionism has some distinctive features: it is in good part a white collar movement. The most throughly organized groups are civil servants and teachers, who occupy a relatively privileged employment situation. It is also worth noting that, by definition, membership is among the employed workers; the lowest social strata, the massive ranks of the unemployed, are not directly represented.

The opposition of the unions has been not to specific governments, but to "politicians" in general. They have not supported the Lumumbist rump nor the CNL. Their consistent demand has been for the application of a meaningful austerity plan, with the reduction of the extravagant emoluments received by ministers and parliamentarians, government and opposition alike. The union position was epitomized in the extraordinary spectacle of a general strike called for March 31 and April 1, 1962, in which the sole demand was reduction of politician salaries; no wage demands for the unionists were advanced. Although the government effectively prevented the strike from succeeding,

TABLE 21. CHRONOLOGY OF MAJOR EVENTS, 1960-1963

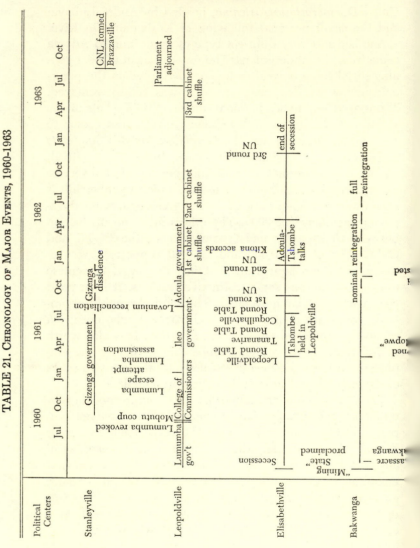

the gesture was highly significant. The divergence between the unions and the Lumumbist rump was made dramatically clear in their differing reactions to the adjournment of Parliament. Whereas the Lumumbist group set up an insurrectional liberation committee in exile, the unions approved the decision, demanding only that it be followed up by a purge of the government itself and the constitution of a reduced cabinet of *salut publique*, composed only of persons exempt from suspicions of profiteering. The unions accepted participation in the Luluabourg constitutional commission, and have played an active role in the initial phases of its work.[43]

Social and Economic Repercussions

The cumulative impact of newspaper headlines concerning the Congo in this period produces an image of utter chaos and disorder, especially in 1960 through 1961. Although the country could hardly be said to have had an efficiently functioning system during that time the term "chaos" considerably distorts the real situation. The period of total hiatus was relatively brief; the infrastructure of a country does not disappear in three months. Provincial and local governments continued to operate in Leopoldville, Equateur, Orientale, and, with reservations, in Kasai. The school system was maintained; few of the Catholic missionaries ever left, except in the most troubled areas, and Protestant families evacuated in July began returning in September. River and rail transport was maintained in most areas. Road maintenance, which lapsed in 1960, had resumed in 1961, although the secondary roads, which depended on local government finance, were less well maintained than the main routes. In areas such as

[43] On the political role of Congolese unions, see "Les syndicats et la politique congolaise," *Etudes Congolaises,* VI, No. 2 (February 1964), 19-26; "Notes et documents sur le syndicalisme congolais," *Travaux Africains,* No. 2-5 (May-September 1963), CRISP; *Congo 1962,* pp. 168-90.

Kwilu, where extensive plantations existed, thousands of kilometers were maintained by the companies. In the medical field, although the WHO recruitment of 200 doctors was not a fully adequate replacement for the 700 Belgian doctors who had departed, hospitals and dispensaries were kept open. Medical supplies, however, often were very scarce. Ironically, in this field, finding a permanent solution involved aggravating the immediate problem; most of the 130 Congolese medical assistants who at first replaced the departed European doctors received scholarships to undertake the two or three years supplementary university training which would qualify them as doctors. Although there have been some smallpox outbreaks, no major epidemics have occurred, and the smallpox threat was met by an efficiently organized mass innoculation campaign.

Severe and prolonged disruption was a local rather than a general phenomenon. Three different types of serious disorders may be distinguished:

1) Areas affected by constant troop movements. The hardest hit was North Katanga, ravaged by the punitive actions of the Katanga gendarmery, the countermovements of ANC forces, and irregular "youth" bands, some operating in "police" uniforms but not under effective control of any civil authority. Another badly disrupted area was the region surrounding the South Kasai state; during the Kalonji regime, frequent efforts were made to enlarge the frontiers of the diamond kingdom, an enterprise whose primary victims were the local civil populations. No one will ever know the casualty figures resulting from these operations; most observers believed that 20,000 deaths in North Katanga alone was a minimum figure.

2) Areas where the strains of independence produced serious ethnic disorders. These were mainly confined to former Kasai province, where the widely dispersed Baluba were forced back into the ethnic homeland of South Kasai. The important role which Baluba had played as traders,

cash crop producers, and clerks in areas where they had settled added to the economic and social cost of their expulsion from non-Luba zones. The relative absence of large-scale expatriate enterprise in Kasai further aggravated the impact; one of the few major concerns, the diamond-mining company *Forminière*, was forced to terminate its operations in the Tshikapa zone by the end of 1961 because of continuing ethnic tensions and the impossibility of policing the dispersed diamond fields. The fall in marketed agricultural production was 75 percent from 1958-1962, a far more disastrous drop than experienced in other provinces.[44]

3) Areas where vexatious measures were taken against expatriate persons and property. In practice, this meant only Kivu during the Kashamura-Omari regime from January to August, 1961. Kashamura in particular had revolutionary intent without revolutionary plan; in a capricious and arbitrary manner, he provoked the flight of nearly all Europeans and totally disorganized the economy of the region. In the rest of the zone, under Stanleyville authority prior to the Lovanium reconciliation, however, no significant measures were taken against expatriates except during the period of peak tension over the assassination of Lumumba. A substantial European population remained in Stanleyville itself throughout the period. Elsewhere, except for regions disrupted for the first two reasons above, Europeans encountered after the first wave of panic no hostility either from the population or officials. Indeed, the massive departures in July and total Africanization of the public sector had the ironic effect of exonerating the Belgians from blame for the sharp drop in rural income and rise of urban unemployment. By 1963, the European population was back up to an estimated 60,000.

[44] Pierre Dupriez, "Transformations dans la structure des exportations de la République du Congo depuis l'indépendance," *Cahiers Economiques et Sociales*, No. 3 (March 1963), pp. 15-16. The actual production fall may not have been quite so sharp, as local consumption of formerly marketed food crops, such as manioc, probably increased.

Thus, words such as "chaos" and "anarchy" are far too sweeping to summarize adequately the consequences of breakdown. On the other hand, there were major changes in the social and economic landscape. With the repeal of the administrative controls which ineffectively restricted emigration to the cities, there has been a large-scale rural exodus. Some estimates of the present Leopoldville population run as high as 1,000,000, as compared with less than 400,000 in 1959. The growth of the city is clearly demonstrated by the construction of ramshackle houses covering a very large area on the hills surrounding Leopoldville which were vacant in 1960. Unemployment figures are difficult to estimate but are generally conceded to cover at least 50 percent of the working population, and to total well over 100,000 in the city of Leopoldville. In the countryside, there has been a marked shriveling of the rural trading network; traders operating out of the smaller centers abandoned many of their village posts, which had served both to buy produce and sell the supplies in demand by the rural African. Thus it has become more difficult to market crops other than those purchased by the large companies and to find goods to buy with the cash that can be earned. The Congo has been forced to import crops such as cotton and rice which it formerly exported.

Mining production has by and large been maintained, especially in Katanga. However, industrial diamonds, the second largest mineral export in the colonial period, were until the end of 1962 largely exported by fraud; this is reflected in the astonishing fact that Belgium in 1961-1962 became the largest client of the Congo (Brazzaville) which in 1961 set up a diamond-purchasing office fed by the smuggling racket. Political unrest has at times interrupted, but not halted, gold production in Orientale and tin mining in Maniema and North Katanga. As an enclave type of operation, most mines really depend very little on the local government authorities for services, aside from the maintenance of a minimum of order.

The completely unreal valuation of the Congo franc created an uncontrollable and almost institutionalized smuggling business in many products, especially in the eastern parts of the country, until a major devaluation in November 1963. The franc, which before independence was on a par with the Belgian franc at 50 = $1, fell to a black market rate which seemed to stabilize at around 250 = $1 about mid-1962, while officially there was only a minor devaluation to 65 = $1 in November 1960. The 1963 devaluation set the exchange rate at 150 = $1. The government was caught in an uncomfortable pinch; for products such as coffee, where producers were required to export through regular channels and to convert their export earnings into francs at the official rate, they would be forced out of production. Thus the anti-smuggling measures were often half-hearted. The problem was magnified by the disruption growing out of the period of fragmentation, and the Congo River blockade; at this time the whole zone under the control of the Stanleyville regime developed new trading patterns.

There has been, at the same time, a remarkable upsurge in production for the domestic market. These local industries, predominantly in the Leopoldville area, have had their growth limited mainly by difficulties in obtaining necessary imported materials. Cement production grew from 95,169 tons in 1961 to 145,000 tons in 1962, excluding that of Katanga; sugar was up from 28,520 tons to 41,000 in the same period, and beer increased from 1,235,000 hectoliters to 1,702,000. Electricity consumption in Leopoldville rose from 119,601,076 kilowatt hours in 1960 to 148,863,700 in 1962. In other parts of the country, it has remained stationary.[45] This change in consumption patterns reflects an inter-

[45] These figures are found in Fernand Herman's excellent survey, "La situation économique et financière du Congo en 1962," *Etudes Congolaises,* IV, No. 3 (March 1963), 6-8.

esting development: the tendency of economic growth to be concentrated at the Leopoldville and Katanga poles. For any enterprise which depends to an important extent on decisions taken by the central authorities, for example in the field of import licenses, situation near Leopoldville is of inestimable advantage.

Thus, what is perhaps most surprising is that the damage was not much greater; the economic and social infra-

TABLE 22

AGRICULTURAL PRODUCTION, 1959–1962[46]

Products	1959 exports	1960 exports	1961 exports	1962 exports
		METRIC	TONS	
Palm oil	183,610	168,891	153,055	151,721
Cotton	39,836	42,367	15,282	12,900
Coffee	56,541	58,582	33,937	21,154
Rubber	40,173	35,557	37,551	35,679
Palm kernals	39,836	20,439	12,702	18,473
Cocoa	3,852	5,229	4,966	5,687
Bananas	31,099	33,383	28,336	25,187
		CUBIC	METERS	
Timber	173,898	151,966	116,473	104,260

SOURCE: Société Commerciale Anversoise and Société Belge d'Extrême Orient Réunies, *Main Congo Agricultural Products, 1962.*

[46] It should be noted that the drop in coffee production is by no means entirely connected with the crisis. The price of robusta, the strain which is most widely produced in the Congo, fell from 40.5 francs per kilo in 1957 to 17.5 francs per kilo in 1961. (One Orientale coffee grower told the writer that in 1957 his cost of production was 12 francs per kilo.) The very high coffee prices resulted in a great over-extension of coffee by both European and African producers. The sharp fall in cotton, on the other hand, is definitely attributable to the unpopularity of this crop and the constraint used to force its cultivation. Smuggling also accounts for some of the reported drop in coffee, cotton, tea, quinine, and pyrethrum exports. It is worth adding that in Rwanda and Burundi, which had no post-independence breakdown, production of the major export crop, coffee, fell by over half in the first independence harvests. This suggests that the problem for crops like cotton, raised by African producers, was in large part the inadaptability of the authoritarian methods of constraint which were an important dimension of colonial agricultural policy.

structure is remarkably intact. The toll taken by the break-down has been heavy in human life and suffering; however, in its violent aspects, it has only involved a fraction of the country. In those regions which escaped serving as a battleground in the power struggle, a new equilibrium was achieved fairly quickly.

TABLE 23

MINERAL PRODUCTION, 1959–1962[47]

Product	1959	1960	1961	1962
		T O N S		
Tin	13,187	11,100	4,295	6,903
Copper	290,403	300,675	293,500	296,996
Cobalt	8,431	8,222	8,400	9,683
Zinc				
concentrates	118,000	193,004	182,000	166,990
Cadmium	99	209	190	307
		K I L O S		
Germanium	13,643	25,100	14,000	8,006
Silver	148,307	123,300	108,000	49,626
Gold	11,985	11,055	1,508	7,325

SOURCE: *Ibid.*

[47] The figures for diamonds, number two in export value among minerals in 1957, are not available; although organized exploitation of the Tshikapa fields has stopped, the more valuable Bakwanga deposits are being mined at a vigorous rate. Nearly all the diamond production, however, was illegally exported during 1961-1962.

CHAPTER XIV

The Political Sector:
Parliament, Parties and Politicians

A MAJOR casualty of the Congo crisis has been the political sector, hastily grafted onto the ponderous colonial bureaucratic state in the weeks before independence.[1] "Politicians" are often an unpopular breed with the rank and file; the very word carries vague overtones of the cynical exploitation of public office for private ends. In the Congo, however, the extraordinary circumstances of independence have served to enlarge the gap between rulers and ruled and to produce a particularly sharp sense of alienation on the part of the mass. Dumont argues that this has become the standard pattern for independent Africa;[2] even if his severe judgments were to be entirely accepted, it would remain true that the Congolese path from the euphoria of revolutionary expectation to the demoralization of unfulfilled promise was extremely short. This chapter will examine in this context the functioning and fate of representative assemblies, provincial and national, and the political parties; also, we propose to analyze the phenomenon of political leadership from the perspective of three post-independence years.

[1] "Political sector" is used to describe the congeries of institutions and men related to the electoral process. It means, therefore, the Parliament and provincial assemblies, the leaders selected by these bodies to occupy ministerial functions, and the political parties organized to compete for these offices. The term is in distinction to administration or bureaucracy; the dichotomy, as always, is clearer analytically than on the terrian, as many administrative nominations were based upon political criteria, a phenomenon obviously not unique to the Congo. However, the term and the distinction are widely used in the Congo and, despite the blurred edges, are valid and useful.

[2] René Dumont, *L'Afrique noire est mal partie* (Paris: Editions du Seuil, 1962).

Inadaptation of Parliamentary System

The Congo began its independent existence as a parliamentary democracy on the classic Western European model. Few observers, European or African, felt that this system would be adequate for the needs of the Congo; the *Loi Fondamentale* was merely to serve as an interim arrangement until a permanent constitution could be prepared by the Congolese themselves. As a transitional regime, the replica of the Belgian system had the advantage of the respectability which the parliamentary system has in classic democratic theory, despite its recent retreats before presidentialists and technocrats. Although most observers agreed that a strong government was required, each tacitly assumed that it would be a strong government to his own respective tastes; clearly, a weak government was better than a strong hostile one. At the time that the constitutional principles were agreed upon, no one could be sure what the results of the May elections would be; a "strong" government could have meant either a PNP government, relying heavily on its European functionaries and officers, or a radical nationalist MNC/L regime. A parliamentary system as a start could seem like handy insurance to all parties in the dialogue.

Other African experience suggests that parliamentary regimes there have little future; as Buchmann shows in his useful study, the trend toward presidential regimes set in quickly, and has been general.[3] The only major exception, Nigeria, has retained a parliamentary system as a reflection of the problems of scale and the present impossibility of obtaining consensus on a single leadership. Presidentialism is a means of remolding the institutions of the state to fit the single party; democracy, argue the theoreticians of the mass single party, is achieved through free discussion within the party, rather than within a parliament. The role of a for-

[3] Jean Buchmann, *L'Afrique noire indépendente* (Paris: Librarie Gale de Droit et de Jurisprudence, 1962).

359

mally organized opposition was negative; "A responsible opposition with a definite alternative policy in which its members sincerely believes . . . is rare indeed in a newly independent state," wrote Julius Nyerere.[4]

Initial Difficulties

The first symptoms of the difficulties of parliamentarianism were not long in coming. The election results themselves were a warning; although the MNC/L's triumph was striking in comparison to what had been forecast, Lumumba's party still had only 33 seats, or 41 counting the direct alliances with two ethnic parties in Kasai, out of a total of 137. In all, 15 parties won seats, and no other party had more than 15 seats in the directly elected lower chamber. There is no historic example of a parliament which has functioned well in modern times with this degree of dispersion of party strength. The number of parties itself understated the degree of latent fragmentation; the parties were in most cases far from being coherent, disciplined groups. This became starkly clear when Lumumba presented for a vote of confidence a government in which 94 percent of the party voting strength in Parliament was represented; he barely obtained the necessary vote of confidence, with a mere 54 percent of the votes.

Secondly, the Parliament deeply wounded itself in maladroitly making its first legislative act the raising of its annual salary from the 100,000 francs provided by the *Loi Fondamentale* to 500,000 francs, despite the opposition of Lumumba. In the lower house, the vote was overwhelming; the Senate vote was less so.[5] The resentment of the population was reflected in the plaintive intervention of PSA deputy Vital Bula on July 19, 1960: "Our parliamentary salary has not yet been paid, despite the fact that ru-

[4] From "One-Party Rule," reprinted in Paul Sigmund (ed.), *The Ideologies of the Developing Areas* (New York. Frederick A. Praeger, 1963), pp. 197-202.
[5] *Congo 1960*, II, 647.

mors already fly that it is exhorbitant. . . . Where is this salary, for which we are threatened by the population?"[6]

The example set by Parliament was immediately followed by the provincial assemblies; the Leopoldville Assembly on July 12 voted 72-5, with 3 abstentions, to triple its wages to 300,000 francs.[7] This proved to be one aspect of Leopoldville policy that Katanga was eager to follow; it is noteworthy that the longest article in the Katanga constitution promulgated August 8, 1960, had to do with salaries of deputies and the various fringe benefits of the office. Article 30 of the Katanga constitution must surely be unique in entrenching welfare legislation for the deputies into the basic law of the land.[8]

During 1960, Parliament was in fact only very briefly in session. It did succeed in organizing itself; in the first elections, for the officers of the lower chamber, there was a temporary crystallization into two blocs, the "nationalist" bloc and the "bloc démocratique national"; the former was composed of MNC/L, Cerea, Balubakat, and PSA, while the latter rallied Abako, Puna, PNP, MNC/K, and, temporarily, the Conakat. The discipline shown on this occasion, with spokesmen for each "bloc" rising to remind members who the caucus candidates were gave some brief hope that an effective parliamentary coalition might emerge. Lumumba, in particular, counted on being able to fashion a reliable majority, especially in the Chamber of Representatives, through a rally of the parties which more or less shared MNC/L's program of militant nationalism and a unitary state. But with internal tensions in nearly every party, Par-

[6] République du Congo, Chambre des Représentants, *Annales Parlementaires,* July 19, 1960, p. 10.

[7] République du Congo, Etat de Léopoldville, *Compte Rendu Analytique 1960,* (mimeographed).

[8] The complete text of the Katanga constitution may be found in *Congo 1960,* II, 755-61. One may add that the parliamentary workload prescribed in the Katanga constitution had been substantially reduced from that set forth in the *Loi Fondamentale.*

liament rapidly became unpredictable. When Lumumba departed for the UN on July 22, Parliament went on vacation; on his return, the Prime Minister suggested that the return of Parliament be delayed for three months so that study tours might be organized for the members.[9] There were several confused sessions at the beginning of September, but Mobutu sent the members packing on September 14.

Lovanium Parliament

Parliament's finest hour was at the Lovanium conclave in July and August, 1961. Here the legislature played its potential role, arriving at a unanimous vote for the Adoula government, restoring unquestionable legal authority to Leopoldville, and paving the way for the eventual reduction of the Katanga secession. From this point forward, it was in session except for brief intervals until adjourned sine die in September 1963. The only major achievements have been the legislation breaking the six former provinces into 21 and the adoption of a controversial law organizing the city of Leopoldville as a federal district, not to be part of any province.[10] In July 1962, the remnants of the Lumumbist parliamentary coalition announced they were going into "opposition." This was first demonstrated when Adoula presented a shaken-up cabinet for an expression of confi-

[9] *Ibid.*, II, 654.
[10] When this was adopted in June 1962 feeling ran high between the Bakongo, who claimed that Leopoldville was part of the old Bakongo kingdom, and as such should be part of their province, and the Bangala, who argued that the Bateke and Bahumbu are the original proprietors, and support the "neutralization." There has been continued conflict over such matters as the police jurisdiction in suburban zones, and the right of the Bakongo to place their capital in a Leopoldville suburb. At one point, early in 1963, police of the Kongo Central (Bakongo) province halted all deliveries of food provisions, much of which come from the Bas Congo. An agreement with the Abako was finally reached on March 12, 1963, by which some suburban zones were conceded to the Bakongo province in return for relinquishment of Bakongo claims on the capital itself.

dence by the Chambers. Although the opposition mustered 44 votes, against 60 for the Prime Minister,[11] a closer scrutiny of the vote reveals the incoherence of the parliamentary divisions. Most of the MNC/L deputies did oppose, but the rest of the opposition was an odd lot of bedfellows: Tshombe's Conakat delegation, which ironically had been sitting with the Parliament in Leopoldville and whose obvious objective was simply to weaken the central government; half the Abako delegation, incensed at the government's proposal for "neutralizing" Leopoldville; most of the Puna delegates, out of solidarity with their leader Bolikango, who was left in the cold by the cabinet shuffle; and the Gizenga wing of the PSA.

Close observers of parliamentary labors discerned a slow improvement in technical competence in 1962; part of the initial ineffectiveness could certainly be attributed to the total inexperience of nearly all members in the conduct of a deliberative assembly. The quality and organization of debates were far better in 1962 and 1963 than the often disorderly, incoherent sessions of 1960. A certain number of deputies, such as Felicien Kimvay (PSA/K) and Emile Zola (Abako), developed into skilled debaters. But Parliament from the outset tended to be a tribune for the opposition to whatever government held power. Ministers, who were almost all members of Parliament, rarely attended sessions; because of the inflated size of all councils of ministers since independence, this removed a significant number of votes. The government case was seriously put only when a censure motion was before the house; in its final months, the work of Parliament came to be dominated by a series of such motions aimed at various ministers. Disappointed of-

[11] For a brief period, the opposition maintained that the Adoula government had become illegal, as his 60 votes were 9 short of the absolute majority required for a vote of confidence. The dispute centered on whether the vote had been one of confidence in the constitutional sense or was a simple expression of continued support for a continuing government which had been revamped, not replaced.

fice-seekers were an important element in the opposition at any given moment. These circumstances combined to give a negative motif to much of the debates.

Parliament as a Guild

One consistent pattern to be seen in parliamentary behavior is a strong sense of corporate solidarity. It is revealed in the very strong reactions in all sections of Parliament, including the government benches, to the persistent rumors in November 1962 that a dissolution or permanent vacation was being plotted. The government decreed a state of military rule under the direction of security police chief Nendaka and arrested four prominent opposition deputies[12] on charges of a plot to join with Tshombe in a regrouping of the eastern half of the Congo. In a stormy session on November 23, 1962, the Chamber of Representatives demanded the cancellation of the two measures; both were seen as part of a move against Parliament. The incident blew over when Adoula backed down on both counts, although Justice Minister Weregemere did lose his post as a consequence through a vote of censure.[13]

Even more revealing was the incident which cost Vice-President Jason Sendwe his post in December 1962. At the very moment when the Katanga crisis was attaining its final paroxysm, the prestigious Balubakat leader Sendwe happened to become involved in a street brawl with Senator Pierre Medie (MNC/L-Kasai). The origins of the dispute were entirely non-political; it all began with a fight between street gangs of youths in which Sendwe's and Medie's sons were on opposite sides. The two fathers appeared on the scene; Sendwe brought some soldiers, who administered a sound thrashing to the Senator. The following week, in a

[12] Gbenye (MNC/L), Edmond Rudahindwa (Reco), Simon Malago (Reco), and Marcel Bisukiro (Cerea). Reco is a local party led by the Bashi chiefs, allied with the Lumumbist bloc because of a complicated dispute over the Mwami position in the Kabarè chieftaincy.

[13] *Courrier d'Afrique,* November 25-26, 1962.

charged atmosphere, Sendwe was faced with a censure motion; in the colorful terms of the newspaper account, his effort to defend himself "was punctuated throughout by hostile cries of the majority of the senators, like Christ before the Jews."[14] Sendwe was deposed by an overwhelming vote of 45-4, with 3 abstentions; the case for censure rested entirely on his alleged misconduct toward a senator, despite the timid suggestion of one or two orators that the moment was ill-chosen to disgrace the titular head of the Katanga opposition to the Conakat.

Parliament was a permanent obstacle to any serious austerity program; one should quickly add that it was far from the only one. Effectively attacking this problem meant eliminating many *situations acquises;* this is extremely difficult in any democratic system. In an extraordinary tract, the largest Congolese trade union, the *Union des Travailleurs Congolais* (UTC) in March 1962 bitterly attacked parliamentarians and other political figures, maintaining that austerity projects had twice been rejected by Parliament on the grounds that "the Congo is a rich country." According to the UTC's calculations, with family allocations and fringe benefits included, deputies earned a salary of over 600,000 francs per year.[15] As an agency to enforce government responsibility in the field of public finance, it was clear that the Parliament was a complete failure. Several austerity projects have since been submitted to Parliament by the government, none of which were passed.

Low Parliamentary Prestige

The damage done to parliamentary prestige by refusal to reduce its exorbitant remuneration was reflected in a mor-

[14] *Ibid.,* December 30-31, 1962.

[15] Reprinted in *Etudes Congolaises,* II, No. 5 (May-June, 1962), 96-97. Only the Governor-General and Vice-Governor General drew higher salaries in the pre-independence period, although some allowance must be made for the depreciation of the currency.

dant April Fool's Day "news report" appearing in Leopold-ville's leading daily in 1963:

"Those who daily pour abuse on our politicians for their dishonesty and thirst for money must now make honorable amends when they learn that a national austerity program has been unanimously adopted by the representatives of the nation. . . .

"From now on deputies and senators will receive no more than the 100,000 francs specified by the *Loi Fondamentale*. This salary will obviously be subject to taxation like the income of every other Congolese citizen. . . . Furthermore, as parliamentary service is a civic mission, a disinterested service rather than a lucrative trade, the parliamentarians have decided to pledge 33 percent of their salary to a charitable fund for the unemployed and the aged. . . .

"Having noted that numerous parliamentarians remained unemployed outside of the few days of sessions, they have decided that in the interim they will resume productive work. . . .

It was also decided to reimburse the 'bonuses' and other 'presents' offered by embassies and foreign governments to parliamentarians and other politicians. These sums will be reimbursed, not to the embassies but to the Congo Treasury. Optimists hope to recuperate 3.25 billion francs in this way."[16]

Another paper added, " . . . the title 'deputy' has become the object of public derision. It is by the term 'deputy' that one designates a scoundrel or a ne'er-do-well."[17]

Another index of the failure of Parliament to establish its credit was the lack of public reaction to the adjournment sine die by President Kasavubu on September 29, 1963.

[16] *Courrier d'Afrique,* April 1, 1963, reprinted in *Etudes Congolaises,* IV, No. 5, (May 1963) 109-11.
[17] "L'opinion publique et le Parlement national," *Présence Congolaise,* November 3, 1962.

Aside from the rump of opposition parliamentarians who then moved across the river to form the National Liberation Committee (CNL) there was almost no hostile reaction to this decision. The three Leopoldville dailies all approved the move, as did the trade unions. This was less an indication of support for the government than a display of aliena-nation from Parliament as a forum for opposition.

Provincial Assemblies

At the provincial level, the assemblies started with a less complicated problem, as the number of groups represented in each was much smaller. What is striking is the fact that all six of the provincial assemblies reached a total impasse by 1962. In the cases of Katanga and Leopoldville, the pro-vincial governments could only be formed when the Bel-gian Parliament hurriedly voted an amendment to the *Loi Fondamentale* on June 15, 1960, making it possible for a provincial government to be established with a simple ma-jority present as a quorum, rather than the two-thirds ini-tially required. In every province but Orientale, with its overwhelming MNC/L majority, important regions felt in-adequately represented; as a result demands for separate provinces came from the Abako in Leopoldville, Unimo in Equateur, the Maniema deputies in Kivu, the Balubakat in Katanga, and MNC/K in Kasai. The provincial govern-ment, in the spirit of the *Loi Fondamentale,* was supposed to reflect the general composition of the provincial assembly and include a proportional representation of all tenden-cies.[18] Although all but Katanga did give reasonable ap-proximation in 1960 to a proportional representation for re-gions and political parties, important groups in all assem-blies (except Orientale) were strongly dissatisfied with the results.

In Leopoldville, Equateur, Katanga and Kasai, the ten-

[18] Ganshof van der Meersch, *Fin de la souveraineté belge au Congo,* p. 189.

367

sions reached a point where opposing groups frequently refused to sit together. Equateur is a somewhat colorful example of the problems of the provincial assemblies. The
Unimo group had been deeply distressed from the outset
at what it considered an inequitable distribution of ministries. Beginning in April 1961, the Mongo deputies met separately. In an effort to achieve a reconciliation, the provincial assembly was called back into session in September.
Tension was so high in Coquilhatville that the whole assembly boarded a river steamer and anchored for a week
down the Congo River from Coquilhatville to be able to
meet in isolation.[19]

Even the one politically homogeneous assembly which
seemed to have every prospect of functioning harmoniously,
Orientale, did not. In November 1960, when the Lumumbist regime was established at Stanleyville, the handful of
PNP delegates, led by Chief Kupa, took refuge in Leopoldville with a certain number of "moderate" MNC/L deputies. During the early months of 1961, as negotiations went
forward for some formula of accord between Leopoldville
and Stanleyville, there was considerable tension within the
provincial government and assembly and between them
and the Gizenga central government, apparently reflecting
divergences in the sense of urgency in reaching agreement.[20] Other signs of the internal assembly dissensions
were the sharp struggles over the post of assembly President; Dominique Kehleko, who emerged as provincial
"boss" after his election as provincial assembly president in
April 1961, won reelection in April 1962 by a narrow 31-27

---

[19] *Courrier d'Afrique,* October 23, 1961.

[20] *Congo 1961,* pp. 202-06. In a session of the provincial assembly
on April 10, 1961, reported in *Uhuru,* the Lumumbist daily in
Stanleyville, April 11, 1961, Assembly President Babadet denounced
the existence of "traitors" within the assembly, alleged to have attempted to form a delegation to attend the Tananarive Conference in
March and subsequently to have endeavored to organize a "reconciliation" delegation to negotiate with the Ileo government.

vote, after an earlier session whose legality had been challenged by the loser.[21]

A curious distinction in the *Loi Fondamentale* between provincial and central representative assemblies made resignation from the provincial assembly by those elected as ministers mandatory, whereas at the central level ministers continued to hold their parliamentary seats.[22] Further, the continuation of any other salaried governmental position rendered the individual disqualified for further parliamentary service. These provisions were the source of endless disputes in provincial assemblies, especially in Kasai and Orientale. Beginning in 1962, the tactic of appealing for central reversal of provincial assembly votes on the grounds that disqualified deputies had taken part in the vote became widespread. It was on these grounds that Jean Foster Manzikala protested the October 1961 vote turning him out of office as Orientale president. Similarly, Barthélémy Mukenge appealed for reversal of a Kasai assembly vote in December 1961 which replaced him with André Lubaya as provincial head. After the creation of new provinces, the tables were turned, with Lubaya demanding central intervention against President Francois Luakabwanga of Luluabourg province on grounds that five disqualified deputies had taken part in the vote of investiture.

Thus the representative institutions at the provincial level fell victim to the same difficulties as those on the national plane. The parties did not function effectively in maintaining a coherent approach to problems. Fragmentation and bickering were the salient features of their activity; few of the assemblies ever even performed the fundamental task of voting a budget in the 1960-1962 period. Performance was somewhat better in the new provinces. By and large, the most able elements had been attracted to the national Parliament in 1960; the Congo's narrow elite could

[21] *Uhuru*, April 20-21, 1962.
[22] Articles 198-203.

hardly furnish overnight the personnel to fill the 641 elective posts in the provincial and national assemblies. It is hardly surprising that the average level of the provincial deputies would suffer under these circumstances.

A frequent phenomenon in all parts of the Congo has been conflict between deputies, provincial and national, and the administration. Administrators have felt that the deputies have needlessly stirred up the population against them, incited to civil disobedience, and generally misunderstood the distinction between legislative and executive functions. It has been a widespread practice to ban deputies from travel in the interior, especially in moments of tension; political meetings are, to say the least, discouraged. Typical of this problem was an incident observed personally while visiting the Mongala district capital of Lisala. A provincial deputy had just succeeded in suborning a detachment of local police, and sought to turn the territorial administrator at Bumba out by force, primarily on ethnic grounds.[23] Large army reinforcements had to be rushed to the scene and the administration was for some time thereafter paralyzed by the death threats which had been showered upon its members during the height of the storm.

Political Parties

Central to the failure of representative institutions has been the shriveling of their vital communications nexus with the mass via political parties. This is a major element of differentiation of the Congo with other African states, especially those such as Ghana, Guinea, Ivory Coast, and Tanganyika founded upon the mass single party. Even the three major parties which had developed a cohesive organization and leadership with a program of militant nationalism—Abako, PSA, and MNC/L—rapidly experienced a

[23] Bumba, a small river town in one of the Congo's best ricegrowing areas, is dominated by the Budja group. The territorial administrator was Ngombe, the largest ethnic group in Mongala district (now Moyen-Congo), but not in the territory of Bumba.

370

dislocation of their grass roots structure after independence. From 1960 through 1963, parties had become nothing more than caucus groups at the various assemblies, with a nominal extra-parliamentary organization consisting of a central committee whose functions were limited to the issue of an occasional communiqué.

THE PRICE OF INEXPERIENCE

A number of factors in the pre-independence history of Congolese parties, set forth in Chapter XII, presaged difficulties in their becoming a permanent and vital part of the political process. The extremely brief time available to construct political parties, the lack of time or procedures for selection of leadership, the subordination of permanent organization requirements for the short-term exigencies of winning the fateful May 1960 elections, the fragmentation and ethnic roots of many parties, the heavy mortgage to extravagant and unrealizable campaign promises, all these and other factors suggested that at best parties would have been in for a difficult period of readjustment and reorganization.

Independence and the ensuing breakdown, however, overtook parties before this problem could begin to be faced. The creation of a political sector with a large number of positions to be filled had drained off the better part of the leadership at the moment of independence; in addition to the 641 elective openings in Parliament and the provincial assemblies, each province had ten ministers plus a president, and the central government had a cabinet which reached a height of 42 persons during Adoula's initial government. Those who were left quickly found governmental functions of responsibility when the Belgian exodus suddenly opened up 10,000 top civil service positions, plus several thousand more in the network of parastatal organizations.

In different ways, the parties in many areas did serve as the nominating machinery for the designation of leadership. Through the obligation to present for the elections a list of candidates in order of preference, the party played a decisive role in selecting the persons who were to sit in the assemblies. And in areas where party life had been real the party was a key element in selecting the personnel to replace the departed Europeans, especially in the extremely important territorial service. Who directed a bureau of a ministry was often important only to the persons involved in competing for the position; who occupied the post of territorial administrator was of vital significance for a region averaging four-fifths the size of Belgium and containing perhaps 100,000 people.

Thus, by August 1960 the political parties had largely been absorbed into the various mechanisms of the state. In the mass single-party states, the party has succeeded in maintaining its identity and structure separate from the state, despite the frictions this entails.[24] In the Congo, in most cases, the party made administrative nominations from within the ranks of the administration itself; only the MNC/L widely departed from this practice and placed explicitly political criteria above technical administrative experience. This was a logical consequence of the fact that MNC/L alone of the Congo parties was really influenced in its organization and operating principles by the mass single-party models, which at that time were especially the PDG and CPP.

EFFORTS FOR A NATIONALIST FRONT

The failure of a single party to emerge was of fundamental significance for both the role of the party and the structures of the state itself. The mission set for the mass

[24] See L. Gray Cowan's discussion of this point in the instance of Guinea in Gwendolyn N. Carter (ed), *African One-Party States* (Ithaca, N. Y.: Cornell University Press, 1962), pp. 177-215. See also the most interesting article on Tanganyika by John R. George, "How Stable is Tanganyika?" *Africa Report,* VIII, No. 3 (March 1963), pp. 3-8, 12. Clement Moore found a similar pattern in Tunisia, described in his forthcoming book on single-party rule in that country.

party by its theoreticians as sole interpreter of the general will is only valid when it is genuinely single. Touré argues that national unity was achieved through the independence struggle; "We do not intend to lose our unity just to adapt ourselves to a [Western] political system which would deteriorate and reduce our political strength."[25] The Lumumbist dream was that the MNC/L would be invested with a similar mission by the Congo's electors, as the incarnation of the indivisible sovereign will of the people. According to Lumumba's intimates, he was particularly impressed with the Ghanaian model, and "had an almost supernatural conviction that the destiny of the Congo was bound to the existence of a single party [MNC] led by an undisputed chief."[26] However, the failure to achieve this goal meant that the polity could have only the state itself as the reflection of its fragile unity; political parties, being many, became factors of disunity rather than integration. And when it could no longer claim to incarnate the community, the political party could not claim to be a higher law than the state. This view was set forth in an interview by an outstanding MNC/L leader in Stanleyville: "The experience of Ghana and Guinea in this field is not relevant for the Congo. They have a single party; we have a number of parties. The function of a party in our circumstances is to govern through the state, not to exist outside of it."[27]

To date, only the struggle against the colonizer has been of sufficient force to galvanize the populace in tropical Africa into unified action. The evidence substantially indicates that a mass single-party cannot at this stage be formed once

[25] Carter, *op. cit.*, p. 192, cited from *Texte des interviews accordés aux representants de la presse par le Président Sekou Touré* (Conakry, 1959).

[26] *Congo 1960*, II, 566-67.

[27] Interviews with Dominique Kehleko, provincial president of MNC/L for Orientale, and president of the provincial assembly, Stanleyville, Aug. 8, 1962. Although Kehleko is quoted, a similar argument was made to the writer by several other leading MNC/L officials.

power has been transferred. Parties which are able to dominate a new state can use its instrumentalities to absorb the opposition, but the prospects for this occurring without firm control of the state seem dim at this historic stage. The fates of the Sawaba party in Niger and the UPC in Cameroon are instructive; to many observers at the time of independence both seemed as parties more in the African mainstream, with more dynamic leadership and program than those to whom power was transferred. But both have been progressively weakened, to virtual impotence in the UPC case, by the many weapons, both of inducement and deterrence, which control of the mechanism of the state (and French armed support) has given the ruling parties.

This was not so clear in 1960 as it seems today. A major theme in Congo party history from 1960 to 1963 was the continuing effort of the Lumumbist bloc to achieve a unification of "nationalist" parties.[28] There are indications that Lumumba before his death had hoped to achieve this through the rapid establishment of a presidential regime and a unicameral parliament, with a referendum or general elections providing the occasion to obtain a new and overwhelming mandate from the people. In June 1960, he was hoping that this might be realized before the end of the year.[29] The first step was taken through the organization of a Lumumbist bloc in Parliament.

This movement was interrupted by the breakdown of the central institutions, but resumed at the beginning of 1961.

[28] There is an invidious implication in the use of this term that these groups which did not share the world view of Lumumbism were not nationalists; this is certainly not true. Nearly all Congolese were "nationalist" in the sense of rejecting a status of subjugation to the European colonizer. There were, however, differences in the militance of expression of hostility to the colonial regime and the emphasis on local or national loyalties. In this section, the term "Lumumbist bloc" is used, rather than "nationalist," by which they described themselves. By "Lumumbist" is meant a vision of nationalism which is radical in its opposition to the colonial regime and unitarian in its design for the independent state.

[29] *Congo 1960,* II, 566-67.

At the Leopoldville Round Table of January-February 1961, a *Front Nationaliste Congolais* (Fronaco) was formed by representatives of the MNC/L, PSA, Cerea, Balubakat, Coaka, *Union Nationale Congolaise, Mouvement de l'Unité Basong(y)e,* Unibat, and Alco.[30] Fronaco functioned only for the duration of the meeting.

In Stanleyville there were new efforts in this direction beginning in March 1961. *Le Monde* correspondent Rouleau reported that at the extraordinary MNC/L congress called in March 1961 to elect a new president to succeed the deceased Lumumba there was a general desire to create a "patriotic front" regrouping all Lumumbists; Gizenga at this point seemed the logical head.[31] Over the next six months, the Lumumbist front gradually frittered away its energies over who would lead and who would absorb whom. Gizenga was refused permission to organize a PSA chapter in Stanleyville; his position was that the other parties could not be expected simply to join the MNC/L. The MNC/L leaders, on the other hand, felt that there should be some recognition for the MNC/L's vanguard role in propagating Lumumbism.

At the end of August 1961, negotiations were reported to be taking place in Leopoldville between Kamitatu and Gbenye with a view toward forming a Lumumbist cartel including MNC/L, PSA, Puna, and Balubakat.[32] Gizenga, just elected to a post as Vice-Premier in the Adoula government, but not yet in Leopoldville, sought to beat his rivals to the draw. At the beginning of September, he announced in Stanleyville that the PSA and MNC/L had been fused as the *Parti National Lumumbiste* (Panalu), with himself as

[30] Coaka, *Union Nationale Congolaise,* and *Mouvement de l'Unité Basong(y)e,* were ethnic-regional parties in Kasai, allies of MNC/L. Unibat was the Bateke party, representing a small tribe situated near the city of Leopoldville, and Alco was the small Kanza dissident wing of the Abako.

[31] Eric Rouleau in *Le Monde,* March 31, 1961.

[32] *Le Soir,* September 2, 1961.

the leader. He claimed to be the unique successor to the mantle of Lumumbism because, on the one hand he incarnated the MNC by succeeding Lumumba to the prime ministership (according to Stanleyville), and on the other was national president of the PSA.[33] MNC/L President Gbenye, Vice-President Joseph Kasongo, and Orientale province President Manzikala immediately returned to Stanleyville to announce that no decision could be taken until an MNC/L congress was held.[34] A congress was in fact held in October 1961, which rejected the idea of any unification until a "Congress of Nationalists" could be organized.[35] An MNC/L Youth statement in January 1962 noted that Gbenye, in a recent visit to Stanleyville, "confirmed before the provincial committee of MNC/L and the handful of PSA leaders present the rejection of unification until the Congress could be organized." "The idea in itself," the memorandum continued, "is not bad, and we must necessarily arrive at this unification without too much delay, but without inconsiderate precipitation either."[36]

During the last part of 1961 and early 1962, the chances for a regrouping were definitely compromised by absorption of much of the Lumumbist bloc into the Adoula government and by Gizenga's adventure in Stanleyville. In July 1962, the remnants of the Lumumbist groups announced that they were refusing further support to the Adoula government; included in this were the Gizenga wing of PSA, a fraction of MNC/L, and part of Cerea. However, the Kamitatu wing of PSA remained firmly in support of the government. Following the July 1962 shake-up, there were also two Cerea ministers and seven from MNC/L in the Adoula

[33] *Ibid.* Kamitatu was the provincial president of the PSA, a hierarchy of titles which had little relevance as the PSA was only organized in Leopoldville province, with the insignificant exception of some votes obtained in Kasai from ethnic groups centered in the PSA's home district of Kwilu, but spilling over into Kasai.

[34] *Le Monde*, September 3, 1961.

[35] *Uhuru*, January 28, 1962.

[36] *Ibid.*

cabinet. A new phase of activity by groups invoking the Lumumbist heritage began in October 1963 with the formation of the CNL in Brazzaville. By the end of 1963, this movement seemed no closer than its predecessors to achieving either genuine national support or even internal cohesion. The leadership was disputed by Gbenye and Lubaya. Pierre Mulule's Bapende-Bambundu insurrection in south Kwilu, beginning in September 1963, appeared to be yet another variation on the theme of nationalist opposition. The real backing of the CNL remains limited to the regional following of the principal figures involved;[37] the radical mass single party is as far from realization as in 1960.

PARTIES AS CAUCUS GROUPS

Thus, by 1962, party activity outside the assemblies had all but ceased. In mid-1962 the writer visited all of the areas of Abako and PSA strength; there was no sign of political activity on the part of either. No party cards had been sold since 1960; the former party cadres, for the most part, now represented the state and were more anxious to have local taxes paid than party fees. The PSA office in Kikwit, cradle of the party, was locked by the Army in November 1960 and not reopened for more than two years. At Stanleyville, party activity lasted longest; in early 1962, there were still occasional MNC/L manifestations, both in the provincial capital and some of the regional centers. However, a Lovanium University fact-finding team studying the new provinces in January-February, 1963, found that all party activity had ceased.[38]

[37] Documents purportedly seized from Soviet diplomats in November 1963 shed interesting light on the complex internal divisions of the CNL, if these papers may be assumed to be authentic; they were reprinted in Le Progrès, November 26, 1963. For another fascinating and plausible analysis of the CNL, see the lengthy interview with former Stanleyville ambassador to China, Bernardin Diaka, in Courrier d'Afrique, January 6, 1964.

[38] The delegation included Benoit Verhaegen, S. J. Lacroix, B. Ryelandt, and J. C. Willame of the Institut de Recherches Economiques et Sociales, Lovanium University.

From independence until 1963 parties had no mission in the political system outside of Parliament. The administration had assimilated much of the anti-political bias of the pre-independence bureaucracy; there was little disposition to see a role for parties as an agency for social mobilization or political education. And the parties, stripped of their cadres, demoralized, and fragmented, were in no position to play this role. Parties bore the "politician" stigma in the interior, which means broken promises and profiteering; the rank and file were discontent with the disappointments of independence, but not inclined to articulate their grievances through parties.

During this period, then, political party activity was largely confined to Parliament and to a lesser extent the provincial assemblies. This was partly because the active party cadres were largely absorbed into the assemblies or received political appointments.[39] Equally important was the absence of any obvious reason for preserving a local network of party sections. These had been created for anticolonial action and electoral campaigning, both of which had been accomplished. Local activists would have been placed under intolerable pressure to explain the non-fulfillment of campaign promises. The general disillusionment which quickly spread to many rural areas would have made unthinkable local party activity aimed at winning enthusiasm for the government.

As parliamentary caucus groups, parties had mixed success. The most effective discipline was maintained by the Abako, perhaps explicable in terms of the high ethnic solidarity of the Bakongo. Abako delegates almost always voted as a bloc, and only rarely was an Abako speech made at variance with the group viewpoint. This cohesion is all the more remarkable in that the group lacked any recog-

[39] Each minister had a "political cabinet" of up to 12 persons; this alone created a potential of 7,500 patronage appointments to jobs for which no minimum qualifications were stipulated.

nized leader. President Kasavubu did not take part in day-to-day caucusing, and no Abako member in the parliamentary delegation was publicly acknowledged as its chief. This discipline helped give the Abako a bargaining power out of proportion to its numbers in Parliament. With only 12 of 137 seats, the Abako was represented in 1963 not only by the Chief of State but also in the key Ministries of Finance and Interior, as well as Information.

The other consistently disciplined voting groups were the two wings of PSA, Kamitatu and Gizenga. The party had formally split in 1962, as the outgrowth of tensions dating back to its founding in 1959.[40] However, each of the two wings remained united in parliamentary action, with the Kamitatu group supporting the Adoula government, and the Gizenga followers opposing.

MNC/L, on the other hand, became totally fragmented. Even before the fall of the Lumumba government, a few MNC/L deputies had defected. After the Lovanium reconciliation, a significant group of MNC/L members always served as ministers even after Gbenye announced in July 1962 that the party was going into opposition. MNC/L was never able to replace its first leader; although an extraordinary congress was held in Stanleyville in March 1961 to elect a new president (Gbenye), the question was never held to have been fully resolved. At different times, Joseph Kasongo, Charles Badjoko, Gabriel Lassiry, and Antoine Kiwewa all advanced claims to the succession. The splintering of Orientale into three provinces further weakened the party. Although MNC/L was substantially the largest parliamentary party, its fragmentation and leadership competition made it ineffective as a party after 1961.

By late 1961, the most important group in the capital was not a political party at all, but an informal caucus known as the "Binza Group." Its principal members were army com-

---

[40] For detailed evidence of early symptoms of the subsequent split, see *Parti Solidaire Africaine (P.S.A.), passim.*

mander Mobutu, security police chief Nendaka, perennial Foreign Minister Justin Bomboko, national bank president Albert Ndele, and Interior Ministry permanent secretary Damien Kandolo. This group owed its effectiveness to a political situation where effective power derived from control of key organs of power in the central governmental structure, rather than a countrywide organization. It was an anonymous coalition; its existence did not become widely known until mid-1962, and even into 1963 references to the Binza Group in the press were infrequent. Adoula was consistently supported by the group, in close communication with it, but not a participant. It is also worth noting that the group was not marked ethnically or regionally; the individuals listed are from four of the six old provinces, and no two of them are from the same ethnic group.

PARTY REBIRTH: A NATIONAL GOVERNMENTAL PARTY?

In early 1963, the long shadow of anticipated elections began to transform the perspectives of party leaders. By the letter of the law, urban council elections should have taken place no later than December 1963; only in Bukavu, of the major centers, was this requirement met. More important, the *Loi Fondamentale* unambiguously provided for national and provincial elections by June 1964. Although the prerequisites of a new constitution, a new electoral law, and a new census made this timetable unlikely even at its origin, the growing expectation that elections might be within sight stimulated efforts at both national and provincial levels to found or reestablish political parties. Elections would recreate a real function for a grass roots structure for parties.

The Binza Group and other leading figures in the central government began to seek ways to establish a national, pro-governmental party to assure a continuation in power by the present Leopoldville leadership in the event of elections. Despite the advantage of control of the instruments of the state, these efforts were, at least in their initial phases, not marked with great success. Two parallel enterprises in party construction have gone forward since mid-1963, the *Parti Démocratique Congolais* (PDC), led by Defense Minister Jerome Anany, and the *Rassemblement des Démocrates du Congo* (Radeco), headed by Minister of Social Affairs Jacques Massa. Although considerable energy has been displayed by the promoters of these projects, and sections have been founded by both groups in a number of provinces, neither seems to have won either complete support from key provincial leaders or a real mass audience. A congress organized by Radeco in Luluabourg in August 1963 foundered precisely on the issue of whether the party was to be a real national movement or a loose coalition of regional parties. Massa's own regional movement in Lac Leopold II, *Rassemblement Démocratique Africaine* (RDA— ex-RDLK), refused to fuse with Radeco.[41]

Provincial Party Activity

Also of significance was a rebirth of political party activity at the provincial level in the latter part of 1963. The first major party congress was convened by PSA (Kwilu) in June 1963; by the end of the year, the dominant movements in eight other new provinces had followed suit.[42] The capacity to organize a political congress was one fair indicator of the coherence and effectiveness of the provincial government. On the other hand, a congress of itself does not establish permanent roots at the local level for a party.

In most cases, the party congress resulted in a vote of confidence for the existing provincial leadership. In several

[41] For a report of the Luluabourg Congress, see *Présence Congolaise,* September 7, 14, 28, 1963; see also "L'evolution des partis politiques au Congo," *Etudes Congolaise,* V, No. 10 (December 1963).

[42] Kongo Central—Abako; Kwango—Luka; Cuvette Centrale— Unimo; Moyen Congo—Puna; Ubangi—*Mouvement de l'Evolution Démocratique Africaine* (MEDA); Nord-Katanga—*Parti Progressist Congolais-Balubakat;* Lomami——MUB; Sud-Kasai—*Rassemblement du Peuple Luba* (RPL); Unité Kasaienne—*Parti Démocratique National* (Padena—ex-Coaka).

cases, there was grumbling in the ranks to be overcome; the Abako leadership, for example, confronted murmured complaints of loose administration of party funds, regional favoritism for Mayombe, and excessive ethnic chauvinism. Several small, dissident parties, centered on Bakongo subgroups, had bitterly criticized the leadership of Kongo Central President Moanda (Alco—Manianga; PNCP—Batandu; UDEA—Bandibu). Although the dissidents were not all reabsorbed, the congress itself was generally rated a psychological success for the leadership.[43] In Sud-Kasai, twenty-nine movements and associations of varying significance were absorbed into the RPL behind President Ngalula; the RPL was proclaimed the "single party" in Kasai Lubaland.[44] On the other hand, at the PPC-Balubakat congress at Albertville in January 1964, North Katanga provincial President Jason Sendwe was defeated by 28-3 in a contest for the party presidency; he wound up winning no major party office.[45]

Not all party congresses were successful. The PSA meeting in Kikwit did not manage the reintegration of the Gizenga wing of the party, and only three months later the disaffected Bapende-Bambundu regions of Kwilu began to be infiltrated by Pierre Mulele's irregular bands. The aborted Puna congress in Lisala in January 1964 led to serious disorders in which 12 persons, including the local mayor, lost their lives.[46]

Some indication of what elections might produce was provided by a series of local ballots during 1963. Municipal voting took place in Kikwit (Kwilu), Bumba (Moyen-Congo), Bukavu (Kivu Central), and Kabinda (Lomami); Cuvette Centrale held rural elections. In Kikwit, there was a straight contest between the Kamitatu and Gizenga wings

[43] "Le Congrès de l'Abako," *Etudes Congolaises,* V, No. 8 (October 1963), 34-41.
[44] *Courrier d'Afrique,* November 1-2, 3, 1963.
[45] *Le Progrès,* January 31, 1964.
[46] *Courrier d'Afrique,* February 21, 22-23, 1964.

of the PSA. The Kamitatu forces won all three burgomaster posts, with a two-thirds majority in two of the three communes and a slight majority in the third. This result seemed to derive both from relatively weak representation of the city population of the Bapende-Bambundu ethnic groups which form the support for PSA-Gizenga and, no doubt, from PSA/K's advantage in controlling the Kwilu provincial institutions.

In Bukavu, the political situation was much more complex. Of the 45 seats on the three communes, MNC/L was the largest single winner, with 18 seats and 2 of the burgomaster posts. In interpreting this result, it is important to note that MNC/L in Bukavu has as its honorary president Mwami Alexandre Kabare of the Bashi, a highly structured traditional system whose seat is close to Bukavu and which is strongly represented in the Bukavu electorate. Various primarily Warega parties (PDC, Unerga, PSC, ABL) won 13 seats, as did the party dominant in 1960, CEREA. At the end of 1963 Bukavu remained the only major center where elections had been organized in an entirely competitive situation, where the results were unpredictable to the provincial authorities, and where the winners represented groups at odds with provincial leadership.[47]

The Bumba results were an interesting indicator of emerging political patterns. This Congo River station had in 1960 been divided between MNC/L and Puna. However, the post-independence period saw a rapid awakening of Budja ethnic consciousness in reaction to what was considered Ngombe domination. The establishment of an Ngombe-dominated province, Moyen-Congo, with Bumba as a minority appendage was the breaking point. The central government was forced to declare a state of exception in

[47] Kivu Central President Simon Malago ran afoul the truculent Mwami Kabare shortly after his election in August 1963 as had his predecessors; see *Courrier d'Afrique*, August 30, 1963; *La Presse Africaine*, Bukavu, October 26-November 1, 1963. For the complete results of the communal elections, see *La Presse Africaine*, January 25-31, 1964.

Bumba in November 1963 and to assume direct administrative responsibility. Under central government supervision, municipal elections were held in January 1964. These resulted in an overwhelming triumph for a newly formed Budja party, Unida, led by André Genge; the latter had been a co-founder of Puna in 1960, at a time when the ethnic polarization in the region had not yet emerged. A congress of the Budja people was held in October 1963. Here, speaker after speaker "stepped to the tribune to denounce publicly the attitude of Moyen-Congo authorities toward the Budja people." The orators decried "the 'Ngombeization' of the territorial police and the provincial administration and, in conclusion, expressed the desire to see the Budja regions separated from the present province of Moyen-Congo.[48] In this instance, the electoral process consolidated and ratified an ethnic dissidence which was largely a product of post-independence politics. The main competition was provided by Anany's PDC, which won only one of 21 seats as opposed to 19 won by Unida.

In Cuvette Centrale, a rather different electoral operation was carried off in June 1963. The rural government structures were reorganized to delegate greater power to the local institutions, the former *circonscriptions indigènes,* and new councils were elected. This was implemented with considerable energy by the provincial government; the elections were spaced over several weeks, so that provincial leaders could explain personally their aims. The exercise was part of a general effort to adopt mass mobilization techniques familiar from African single-party models—with the difference that Mongohood, rather than Congolese nationalism, was the ideological basis.

The conclusion which may be drawn from a survey of provincial party activity in 1962-1963 is that the expectation of elections will force provincial leadership to organize political organizations capable of contesting them. Where rea-

[48] *Présence Congolaise,* October 19, 1963.

sonable homogeneity has been attained at the provincial level, the leadership should be capable of achieving a plebiscitory endorsement of its position. Where provinces are badly divided, an unpredictable electoral contest will ensue, whose terms will be defined by the nature of the local fragmentation. In neither situation will a national movement find its task easy.

PARTIES: AN EVALUATION

Thus the prospect of elections serves to regenerate parties, both at a provincial and national level. But neither as an electoral committee nor as a parliamentary caucus does the party fulfill the role of continuing political education and legitimation of the polity which the model comprehensive African nationalist party is expected to play. Party labels do remain in general use as part of the political vocabulary; their multiplicity, recurrent internal crises, and high mortality do not presage their disappearance. But parties are still far from having a clearly defined role in the political system.

Illustrative of this fact was the conspicuous absence of political parties at the Luluabourg constitutional commission, which began meeting in January 1964. In 1960, when Belgium sought to designate to the Brussels Round Table delegates who could be considered de facto representatives of the Congolese population, it was to political parties that the colonizer had to turn. In 1963, when the Congolese government sought to constitute a similar group, the appeal was made to central and provincial governments and assemblies and to various syndical organizations—but not to parties. The coherent parties, such as Abako, would be represented through the provincial delegations they controlled. In the case of fragmented parties, such as Cerea or MNC/L, it would have been virtually impossible to name a single delegation which could be considered as legitimately representing all of the party.

385

Anatomy of Leadership

Another prism for examining the political sector is its leadership. The political style and roles played by the leaders provide insight into the nature of the political process and the place of the "political sector" within it. If one examines the leaders who have emerged and succeeded in the independent Congo, in the central government, the first observation to be made is that nearly all of the key persons are from the Leopoldville milieu. Kasavubu, Adoula, Mobutu, Nendaka, Bomboko, Ndele, all have been closely associated with the capital for some time. The only "outsider" to carve a key niche for himself is Kamitatu, whose career prior to independence had been almost entirely in Kikwit. Nendaka, although a Mubua (an Orientale tribe little represented in Leopoldville), had been a successful trader for a number of years prior to independence. One of Lumumba's fatal weaknesses was the lack of support in the city of Leopoldville itself.

Leaders from the eastern half of the country face a very difficult choice in opting for the national or provincial arena. Whereas a leader from Kwilu or Bas-Congo can involve himself at the national level while retaining his local base of support, this is extremely difficult for the men from Stanleyville, Bukavu, or Elisabethville. Prolonged absence from home means that others arise as replacements; the lack of a network of old colleagues and ethnically related persons in Leopoldville makes the exercise of effective power at the national stage very difficult. The experience of Gbenye is an interesting example of this phenomenon. Prior to 1960, he had occupied a leading position in Stanleyville; in 1959, he had become assistant burgomaster for the city. During the Gizenga period in Stanleyville, his power was at a zenith. He was elected to replace Lumumba at the extraordinary MNC/L congress in March 1961. One of the conditions of support for Adoula by the Lumumbist bloc was the inclusion of Gbenye as Minister of the Interior in the government of reconciliation. However, transplanted to Leopoldville, Gbenye rapidly found that he was unable to avail himself of the theoretical powers of his ministry. He could not dislodge Nendaka from the security police, despite his publication of an ordinance relieving Nendaka of his duties in December 1961. Nendaka's response was to place the Minister under virtual arrest. At the same time, Kehleko emerged as the dominant figure in Stanleyville; Gbenye had lost on both counts.

Style and Situtation: Before Independence

Successful Congo leaders can for the most part be distinguished from the best-known leaders of other tropical African states by the different political style employed. On the national level, only Lumumba can be said to be in the charismatic tradition of Nkrumah, Modibo Keita, Houphouet-Boigny, Azikiwe, or Nyerere, although others, such as Kasavubu, Kamitatu, or Kalonji, had a similar role regionally.[49] One may well wonder whether this form of leadership is not part of the phenomenon of revolt against colonial rule, rather than a permanent element on the political scene. Effectiveness in the colonial era derived in large measure from the leader's capacity to articulate with courage and if possible with rhetorical flourish the profound desires of the population to throw off the colonial yoke. A recurrent theme in interviews dealing with the question of leadership was the enormous prestige which went to those who would stand up and tell the Europeans *les quatre verités*. Caprasse notes in his Elisabethville study:

"An attitude of opposition or more dissatisfaction removes all the barriers, whether they be tribal or socio-economic. From whatever side it comes, it is applauded. When one

[49] David Apter first applied in a systematic way the Weberian notion of charisma as a central element in African leadership. *The Gold Coast in Transition* (Princeton: Princeton University Press, 1955).

seeks the success of certain leaders, it seems to us significant to discover that they owe it to the audacity with which they underline their role of intermediary between the population and the European. Our informants emphasize that these leaders were not afraid to seek out the competent authorities . . . to transmit a complaint or protest against measures taken."[50]

It is clear that Kasavubu first made his reputation in this manner; despite the fact that he is not a captivating public speaker, he spoke out at a time when it took real courage to make even an oblique criticism of the colonial system. In the pre-independence period, Kasavubu was an electrifying name in the Bas-Congo area. Albert Kalonji won his political spurs in the same way; in the provincial council of Kasai, he made points which were daring in their day. Lumumba, however, brought to this task not only audacity but an exceptional oratorical ability and the capability of expressing himself well not only in French but in three of the four major vehicular languages of the Congo: Swahili, Lingala, and Tshiluba.[51]

Post-Independence Leadership

After independence, this style of leadership became less relevant. The men that have emerged from the period of breakdown present a rather different kind of public image. An Adoula has little of the magic capacity for communicating with a crowd of a Touré or a Nyerere. Rather, he embodies the ideal public servant; he is intelligent, hard-working, untouched by any of the scandal which has discredited many Congo figures, not suspect of ethnic chauvinism.[52] He

[50] Caprasse, *Leaders africains en milieu urbain*, p. 91.

[51] For a nearly complete collection of Lumumba's political statements, 1958-1960, see Van Lierde (ed.), *La pensée politique de Patrice Lumumba*.

[52] See Lloyd Garrison's interesting and sympathetic biographical article, "Adoula Tries to Bind up the Wounds," *New York Times Magazine*, May 12, 1963, pp. 25, 89-93.

has no real electoral base; he was born in Leopoldville, and has never sought, as did Bolikango with the Ngombe, to reestablish links with the Budja country, in Bumba territory, from whence his parents came to the capital.[53] His reputation was consolidated by his conduct as Minister of the Interior in the second Ileo government, from February to July, 1961, when he brought an end to the wave of arbitrary arrests and to the atmosphere of intimidation which reigned in the dark days of early 1961. He is skilled in the juggling of political combinations in Leopoldville. He keeps himself somewhat apart from any single group, to retain his freedom of maneuver as the political arbitrator. Accordingly, he has never been a part of the Binza Group, despite his reliance on their continued support. Also, through 1963 he refused to identify himself personally with either of the two attempts to form a national, pro-governmental party (PDC and Radeco), although he clearly remains in close communication with both sets of organizers. One measure of his success is that he is one of the rare Congolese leaders who has seldom been accused of corruption or nepotism; his opponents have been restricted to attacking his policies and not his person.

Lumumba's "spiritual heir," Gizenga, might have succeeded in replacing Lumumba at the Lovanium Parliament had he been endowed with a more dynamic political personality. During his reign at Stanleyville, however, he rarely left his official residence and public appearances were very few. For one three-month period, in early 1961, he is reported to have remained enclosed in his riverside mansion. The numerous anecdotes to be heard in Stanleyville concerning his obsession with assassination plots are no doubt considerably exaggerated, but the credence they seemed

[53] He has been under considerable pressure in 1963 to espouse the claims of the Budja for a separate province; although he appeared briefly at a Budja congress in October 1963, he refused office in the Budja movement and declined to support its regional claims.

to be given is indicative of Gizenga's drab public image.[54] Gizenga had his historic role thrust upon him largely by circumstance. Although he had been out of the country for several months in 1959-1960 and had been less conspicuous on the pre-independence scene than a number of other nationalist figures, his designation by Lumumba as Vice-Premier made him the successor to Lumumba's functions (on the Stanleyville assumption that Kasavubu's revocation of both him and Lumumba was illegal) when the first Prime Minister was first imprisoned, then assassinated. Subsequently, when Gizenga himself was imprisoned in January 1962 on charges of having organized a rebellion, he gradually became a symbol for opposition to the Adoula government. Repeated censure motions were brought against the government and individual ministers for the failure to bring Gizenga to trial or release him.

Kasavubu represents another generation and another leadership style. Although he seldom toured the Bakongo countryside and never gave flamboyant speeches in each village square in the Lumumba or Nyerere manner, he had attained during the pre-independence period, a position of almost supernatural respect through his leaderhip of the Abako, the 1956 Abako manifesto, and especially his inaugural speech as burgomaster of Dendale commune on April 20, 1958. In August 1959 the acting Governor-General Schoeller wrote in reporting on a visit to the Lower Congo: "One single thing counted: immediate independence; one single person was competent to decide everything: M. Kasavubu. Although the latter was practically unknown in

[54] Merlier's critique from the left of Gizenga's leadership is an interesting reflection of this point: "The legalism of Gizenga completed the political confusion on the ideological plane. . . . Concerning the political situation of the moment, the ideas of Gizenga incarnated the illusions of radical Congolese clerks: the power of Gizenga represented the "legal" authority, on the basis of the *Loi Fondamentale* and parliamentary prerogative. In reality this rudimentary viewpoint led straight to the triumph of a capitalist military dictatorship in the Congo." *Op. cit.*, p. 337.

the District [of Cataractes] last January 4 [date of the Leopoldville riots], his personality is now veritably deified, is the object of a blind and fanatic mass submission."[55]

Born in 1913, Kasavuvu is in fact older than most Congolese leaders. He is not a traditional chief; these have disappeared in much of the Bakongo area. He has, however, employed traditional symbols, such as the leopard skin and the "Roi Kasa" title by which he became known in 1959.[56] There was also a religious dimension to his charismatic political personality, a logical outgrowth of the importance in Bakongo country of religious protest movements, especially Kimbanguism and related prophetic sects. In 1959 pictures were circulated in the Lower Congo which showed Peter giving the keys of the kingdom to Kasavubu, on the instructions of Kimbangu.[57]

[55] *Congo 1959,* p. 129.

[56] Jean-Pierre Paulus in "Pour un fédéralisme congolais," *Terre d'Europe,* No. 9 (March 1959), has a picture of Kasavubu seated on a throne placed on a leopardskin-carpeted dais, receiving oral petitioners on their knees. One hears rumors in Leopoldville that he is related to a clan from whence chiefs were drawn; this tale is interesting for its existence, not for its veracity. Leadership thus tends to create the myth that it is traditional. Another persistent rumor about Kasavubu is that his grandfather was one of the several hundred Chinese coolies brought in by Leopold II in 1891 to help build the Matadi-Leopoldville railway. This is denied by his biographer Gilis, *Kasavubu . . .* pp. 341-42. It seems on the face of it unlikely, as the part of Mayombe where Kasavubu was born was virtually unpenetrated at the time of railroad construction. No recruitment was done in this area until several years afterward; pacification was not completed until 1894, after the disappearance of the Chinese, and the first posts and plantations were set up in the following years. Cyr. Van Overbergh *es Mayombe* (Brussels: Institut International de Bibliographie, 1907), pp. 434-35.

[57] Raymaekers, "L'Eglise de. . . . Simon Kimbangu," *Zaïre,* XIII (1959) 682. Kasavubu himself never belonged to the Kimbanguist Church. He was raised as a Catholic and nearly completed training as a priest. Gilis indicates that one of the most bitter experiences of his life was his sudden expulsion from the seminary, for no apparent reason; *op. cit.,* pp. 31-35. Parenthetically, it is worth noting that two prominent Kimbanguists have occupied significant political posts since independence; Emmanuel Bamba, Minister of Finance from May

Since independence, however, Kasavubu has played the role of elder statesman, rather than of active leadership. He remains somewhat above the political fray, enveloped in a shroud of mystery. Few understood his behavior in the agitated summer of 1960; he accompanied Lumumba on the tour of the Congo immediately after the mutiny, and co-signed the July 14 telegram to the Soviet Union calling for a close watch on the situation. In late August, as opposition groups were coalescing and a move against the Lumumba government was clearly in the offing, Kasavubu's cooperation with the government was essential. No one could be sure what he would do, and his speech on the radio announcing Lumumba's revocation was apparently a surprise to virtually everyone.[58] But after the speech, he retired to his official residence and left the execution of his decision to others. The yearning for reunification is a constant feature in Bakongo ethnic nationalism, and as a popular hero Kasavubu automatically came to embody this. However, he has taken the oath of office to the entire Congo seriously and has become somewhat disassociated from the particular goals of the Abako. For example, he did sign the ordinance neutralizing the city of Leopoldville, bitterly opposed in Bakongo circles.

Perhaps the best summary of Kasavubu's leadership style is offered by one of his closest friends and admirers, Professor Van Bilsen: "M. Kasavubu is the most African of the statesmen I have been able to meet. He is profoundly conscious of his mission to preserve the unity of the Congo, and to equip his country with the structures relevant to its present stage of development. Although he was the first and most intransigent nationalist, he is not by nature revolutionary. Neither does he have a dynamic temperament.

1962 until June 1964 and Charles Kisolokele, eldest son of Kimbangu, who served as Labor Minister in 1961-62.

[58] *Congo 1960*, II, 688-90. For another account from Kasavubu's authorized biography see Gilis, *op. cit.*, pp. 265-86

He lets time act for him, and tries always to proceed by persuasion and not by violence."[59]

The leader closest to the Pan-African model in 1960-63 was probably Kamitatu, Minister of the Interior in 1962-63, and previously Leopoldville provincial president. In his pre-independence days, Kamitatu gave the PSA its dynamic impulses. He was of all the leaders perhaps closest to the rural mass. He only took up residence in the capital after independence. In 1960, he was one of the most radical nationalists; those who observed his campaign were deeply impressed by both the content of his message and his ability to communicate it. He successfully bridged the gap between pre-and post-independence politics by an exceptional intelligence and a keen sense of political power and organization. Although he was ideologically inclined to the Lumumbist bloc, he did not leave his post as provincial president in Leopoldville to join the Stanleyville group. He understood the importance of control of the local administration; from his provincial post he was able to exercise a decisive influence in the nominations of the Kwilu district commissioner and the territorial administrators in the PSA district. A discerning appreciation of the sources of power in Leopoldville combined with a will to act have made him a key factor in the political equation. But his mode of operation is now radically different from that of 1959 and 1960; the problem then was to mobilize the mass against the colonial regime. Today's problem is to govern, to maneuver through the labyrinth of forces, internal and external, which operate in Leopoldville.

The case of Albert Kalonji also merits brief mention in a survey of leadership. It is ironic that a leader of the ethnic group which probably has had the greatest access to education and modernization should deliberately adopt a style of action which was a caricature of traditionalism. Kalonji was well-educated and in 1958 opened his own office as an

[59] Van Bilsen, L'indépendance du Congo, pp. 217-18.

accountant. In 1957, he was named to the Kasai provincial council, and immediately became known for his radical statements of opposition to the colonial regime. His prestige grew during his period as a guide to the Congolese pavilion at the Brussels Exposition and subsequently as the most outspoken Congolese member of the *Conseil de Legislation* (alias *Conseil Colonial*) during 1959. When Ileo, Adoula, Ngalula, and several other intellectuals of the MNC sought to find an alternative leader to Lumumba in July 1959, Kalonji seemed a logical choice because of his flamboyant personality and capacity for mass communication. The Kalonji wing of the MNC soon became in his hands a Baluba ethnic party.

Although most Congolese leaders made use of traditional symbols to communicate with the mass, Kalonji soon carried this to the point of obscurantism. A leading Muluba intellectual and Foreign Minister from April to December, 1963, Mabika-Kalanda, described in these terms Kalonji's manipulation of the admixture of superstition in political perceptions of the mass: "Kalonji declared that he had returned from the *Conseil de Legislation* session in Belgium with independence in his pocket [physically]. The Belgians, he said, had done everything to prevent his return; he had been thrown out of the plane into the Atlantic Ocean with a stone tied around his neck. But his magic power had been too strong for the Belgians, and he had been able to safely return to his people."[60]

After an unsuccessful effort to lead a parliamentary opposition to the Lumumba regime, Kalonji returned to take command of the South Kasai government, which seceded first from Kasai province then from the Congo. In February 1961, the seven Lumumbist prisoners were executed in a macabre ceremony, at which Kalonji was present. The fol-

[60] Mabika-Kalanda described this incident in personal discussion and also cited it in an interesting lecture, "Croyance et politique," given at the Institut Politique Congolais, Leopoldville, June 8, 1962.

lowing month, he took the final step of trying to concoct a traditional sanction for his authority; the description of this process that Kalonji gave to a reporter not long afterward is most interesting:

"On the morrow of the Tananarive conference, I convinced Parliament.[61] I had a draft constitution. . . . My term would have been seven years. But the members did not like my solution; they wanted me to be president for life. The traditional chiefs then convened, pointed out that if, upon my death, another president had to be named, there would be competition amongst the diverse clans, each feeling that it would be its turn to provide the Head of State. To avoid these dissensions, they preferred to revert to the custom of the ancient Baluba empire, and to name me Mulopwe [paramount chief], which would assure my succession to my descendents. . . . The ceremonies followed our most ancient traditions. My father is the son of a dispossessed chief. Following upon his removal from the chieftaincy, my grandfather embraced the Catholic religion: that's how I am a third generation Christian. My father could accordingly be invested as Mulopwe. . . . In the course of the same ceremony, he was crowned, then abdicated in my favor. This was the desire of the chiefs, who wanted me to be Mulopwe not only for my courage, but also by descent. At the moment each of them is presenting me to the populations over whom he exercises power, and ordering them to recognize me as the sole chief. . . . Simultaneously, secret ceremonies are going forward which will result in my becoming divine. These are very difficult tests. . . . I was kept for two nights awake all night in the cemetery, to have me enter into contact with the spirits. . . . The final ceremony . . . is beyond imagination. The chiefs will dress me as a native, and for

[61] The *Etat Minier* constitution had created a bi-cameral legislature, with a lower chamber composed of the deputies, senators, and provincial assembly members elected from South Kasai constituencies. An upper house composed of chiefs was added.

certain circumstances, I will not be able to dress otherwise. I will have an entire leopard skin. All the chiefs will be there. It is really the return of our most ancient traditions."[62]

Whatever the chiefs may have thought of this procedure, the intellectuals had no taste for it. Ngalula, the real organizer of the state, was driven out of South Kasai by Kalonji in July 1961, and Kalonji's kingdom foundered. He himself was condemned by a Leopoldville tribunal in December 1961 to a two-year prison term for crimes committed while in office. He subsequently escaped into exile to return as Minister of Agriculture in Tshombe's cabinet in July 1964. However, as Kalanda observed, this style of leadership can at least be successful temporarily in a demagogic sense, since the belief pattern at the mass level remains an amalgam of modern materialism and magic. It can hardly serve as an organizing principle for a modern state.

Leaders and Led: A Nexus Defective

What emerges from a survey of the "political sector" in the Congo is its failure to perform its function as a buckle binding the populace to the polity. The roots briefly sunk in 1959-1960 quickly shriveled. Representative institutions became corporate guilds of parliamentarians. Parties lost touch with both rural and urban masses and now face an uncertain future. Leaders no longer had need of the led; the system was turned within itself. The sources of power were in the capital, not the countryside. Like Spanish moss, the political sector had its roots in the air, not in the ground.

There can be no doubt that there is a profound sense of alienation on the part of the population. The UTC's "general strike" appeal against the system, the ministerial salaries,

---

[62] José Peraya in *Dernière Heure*, April 2, 1961. Other Kasai leaders interviewed denied the authenticity of Kalonji's claim. The old Luba empire had been centered in Katanga, not Kasai. There had never been a "Mulopwe" for Kasai Baluba.

and the parliamentary abuses, failed as it was bound to do with unemployment rates over 50 percent. But the demand that "politicians" cease living off the back of the nation represented a nearly unanimous view, among the elite as well as the mass.

The problem is widely recognized in the Congo by all sectors of opinion, but it is simpler to analyze than to solve. Initially, mass alienation took the form of apathy, of withdrawal, of social demobilization. However, beginning in September 1963, some opposition leaders began forging a revolutionary strategy in the crucible of peasant discontent. Revolts, primarily rural-based, began to break out, at first widely scattered and closely linked to local grievances. In April 1964, largely under the impetus of Gaston Soumialot, a web of rebellion was spun over the entire northeast quadrant of the Congo. Alienation was ignited, and engulfed for a time all which lay in its path; its choice targets were those who stood as the local representatives of the "system," the provincial politicians and territorial civil servants. The somber spectacle of massacre and assassination was a grim warning to all African elites that peasant inertia might not always afford immunity from social accountability.

CHAPTER XV

The Administration and Judiciary: Resurgent Bureaucracy

Bureaucracy and the Post-Colonial State

ONE year before independence, André Ryckmans wrote to a friend:

"I think it is an intellectual fraud to wish to name an African . . . Minister of Interior before there is a single territorial administrator. It is a fraud which will satisfy no one; it is also a grave danger, because if all goes well, the Minister will say, 'It's because of me,' and if it goes badly, he will say, 'The European executants sabotage the work'. . . . But [administration] REFUSES to do this. The Minister [Van Hemelrijck] has *formally* declared during his visit to Thysville: 'Yes, yes, we are thinking of it, but supervised, led, supported by Europeans . . . the responsibilities remaining in the hands of the latter'. . . . You can imagine the fury of the territorials here, who are prepared to help and train these persons, but are reproached with being retrograde, faced with the attitude of people like the Minister and the bureaucrats in Leopoldville who refuse what we ask with all our heart, on the pretext that the Congolese aren't yet ready."[1]

The heart of the colonial system had been its bureaucracy. With system and purpose, it had penetrated and organized the Congolese society; it created an elite in its own image, whose access to the modern world was through the subaltern ranks of the administration. As Ryckmans suggests, the formula for decolonization was the creation of a political sector outside the bureaucracy, rather than introduction of a real program of Africanization within it.

[1] J. K., *André Ryckmans*, pp. 232-34.

And a salient feature of independence has been the relative failure of the political sector and the resurgence of an Africanized bureaucracy.

In all African states, the accelerated Africanization of the key jobs in public service has been a crucial problem of the power transfer period.[2] If we view the political system as concerned with the authoritative allocation of resources, the immense conflict potential in this process becomes clearer. No colonial power in Africa had really established a training and Africanization program which envisaged power transfer as soon as it in fact took place. Accordingly, independence meant the sudden redistribution of a very large number of high-level positions. In the African context, these posts simultaneously rewarded the holder with the exercise of meaningful power, high status, and a level of remuneration which made him, relative to the mass of citizens, a wealthy man. As most of the contestants were far from retirement age, the distribution appeared to have a permanent, irrevocable stamp. It is hardly surprising that this process is capable of generating great tensions, even when relatively controlled and orderly. In the Congo, where Africanization was abrupt and total, the impact was intensified. Parenthetically, we may suggest that in most African states the Africanization process has been a prime source of ethnic tensions.

The bureaucracy is of crucial significance not only as a fulcrum of conflict but also as the primary armature of the modern state. The role of public administration in a developing country goes far beyond its tasks in industrialized societies. Not only does it provide essential public services but it serves as the major element of cohesion in the face of the risk of disintegration. If, as in the Congo, political parties are unable to carry forward the task of national integra-

[2] Reflective of this is the fact that a recent book entitled *Public Service in the New States* (Kenneth Younger) is in reality entirely devoted to the problem of Africanization (and Malayization) (New York: Oxford University Press, 1960).

tion, the administration must carry much of the burden.[3] In this chapter, we will examine the Africanization issue, the functioning of central and local administration, and the judiciary.

Africanization Before Independence

The steps leading to the adoption of the *statut unique* have been reviewed earlier.[4] The situation at the moment of independence can be briefly summarized. Only a tiny handful of Congolese had acceded to posts of responsibility within the administration. Joseph Yumbu[5] was assistant director of N'Dolo prison in Leopoldville. Bolamba[6] edited the administration-sponsored (and supervised) review *La Voix du Congolais* and was made an attaché to the Ministry in Brussels by Buisseret. Bolikango, for a long time a teacher in the Catholic mission schools, was in 1959 named Assistant Commissioner of the Information Department of the central administration in Leopoldville, the highest pre-independence position occupied by a Congolese. Alphonse Sita[7] became youth commissioner for the Governor-General in early 1960. Julian Kasongo[8] was made an attaché by Van Hemelrijck and retained in this post by

[3] For some interesting reflections on the role of the bureaucracy, see F. Gazier, "Les problèmes spécifiques de l'administration publique en pays sous-développés," *Civilisations*, XI, No. 2 (1961), 143-55; E. de Bethune and A. Wembi, "Le problème de la sous-administration dans les pays d'Afrique noire indépendante," *Civilisations*, XII, No. 4 (1962), 446-56. See also the uneven survey, Joseph LaPalombara, *Bureaucracy and Political Development* (Princeton, Princeton University Press, 1963).

[4] Supra, pp. 95-99.

[5] An influential Abako leader who became interim president during Kasavubu's period of confinement in 1959 and participation at the Round Table in 1960.

[6] Secretary of State for Information and Cultural Affairs in the Lumumba government and Minister of Information since April 1963.

[7] A Mukongo, he never entered politics; he remains first secretary of the Ministry of Social Affairs in Leopoldville.

[8] From 1961-1962 private secretary to the Prime Minister.

De Schrijver. Théo Idzumbuir[9] occupied a similar position with Governor-General Cornélis. Hubert Sangara[10] was appointed to the Board of Directors of the Belgian state airline Sabena.[11]

The *statut unique* of January 13, 1959, set up seven ranks; this law, whose provisions are summarized in Table 24, in essence simply fused the earlier dual schema, which had four ranks limited in fact to Europeans, and an auxiliary service whose top grade was tangential with the lowest rank of the European service. Only one Congolese was recruited for the top grades of the unified system via the normal path of Belgian entry—a university degree and a competitive examination.[12] Some 742 Congolese were integrated into the new fourth category, previously all-European, by August 1959. However, the greater part of these were in Leopoldville; in Katanga, for example, by January 1960 only 35 Africans had been promoted to formerly European grades: 17 agricultural officers, 7 health officers, 5 clerks, and 4 territorial officers.[13]

To complete the picture, two other tardy steps toward Africanization of the territorial service deserve mention. On a political level, the provincial executive colleges named three-man African executive colleges for each district and territory; these took office in April 1960. Secondly, at the

[9] Finished his university training in Geneva and since 1962 has headed the Congolese delegation to the UN.

[10] He has since become president of Air Congo. When Sabena was founded in 1923, 25% of the capital was provided by the Congo, on the grounds that the colony would benefit from the development of the airline. This was a somewhat embarrassing situation for Sabena as Congolese independence neared; the price for the repurchase of these shares made the establishment of Air Congo with a reasonable fleet of DC-3's, DC-4's, and DC-6's.

[11] This list of Congolese holding posts of responsibility before independence was prepared by Francis Monheim, "Le problème des cadres au Congo," n.d.

[12] This was Mabika-Kalanda. One other candidate from the first Lovanium graduating class of 1958, Tshibangu, also made the trip to Brussels for the examinations in 1959 but did not pass.

[13] Brausch, *Belgian Administration in the Congo*, p. 30.

TABLE 24

Statut Unique

Rank	Annual pay range	Minimum education required	Type of position
1	Over 440,000	University	Provincial commission
2	325,000–440,000	University	District commissioner Territorial administra Chief police commissioner Bureau chief
3	225,000–325,000	University	Assistant territorial administrator Police commissioner Assistant bureau chie
4	90,000–225,000	Upper half: two years university Lower half: complete secondary	Territorial officer Police sub-commissio Office supervisor
5	73,250–90,000	Secondary	Chief clerk
6	45,000–73,250	Secondary	Clerk
7	Less than 45,000	Four years primary	Office boy

Source: Piron and Devos, *Codes et Lois*, II, 430–65.

TABLE 25

Composition of Civil Service, 1960

Rank	European	African
1	106	0
2	1,004	1
3	3,532	2
4	5,159	800
5-7	0	11,000

Source: INCIDI, *Staff Problems in Tropical and Subtropical Countries*, p. 174.

end of 1959, each territorial administrator was asked to select the ablest clerk in his territory as an auxiliary for a one-year training period; the plan was to conclude this apprenticeship with a practical examination, and, if success-

fully completed, name the candidates as territorial officers.[14] Both measures came too late to have much practical
effect, although the latter step did create in many places a
clear heir-apparent for the territorial administrator at the
moment of departure half a year later.

Africanizing the Territorial Service

Politically, the crucial element in the situation created
by the European exodus was the transfer of power within
the territorial service. Although little noted at the time,
the way in which this transfer took place was a crucial
shift in power toward the provinces. Belgian tradition
prescribed that a functionary in one of the top three
categories, named by the King, would be placed at the
disposition of the Governor-General for assignment. Those
in the territorial service would be posted to a province;
the provincial governor in turn would assign him to a
district, and the district commissioner had the authority
to determine his utilization within the district.

Thus the provinces took on the function of naming
Africans to replace the departing Belgians. In fact, in most
cases the leader of the dominant political group in the
region supervised the nominations, usually on the basis of
administrative criteria and regional-ethnic compatibility.
In Leopoldville province, for example, Provincial Vice-
President Diomi superintended the replacement process
in the two Bakongo-dominated districts of Bas-Congo and
Cataractes, while Provincial President Kamitatu made appointments in the rest of the province. In Equateur, Unimo
leader Njoku toured the Mongo areas to designate administrators, while Provincial President Eketebi did the same
in the north of the province.

The importance of this process was by no means lost on
Lumumba, but too much else was happening to allow the
central government to make a real effort to direct the

[14] *Ibid.*, pp. 30-31.

Africanization process. In Orientale, the provincial government could itself be entrusted with this responsibility, but nowhere else was there a fully "Lumumbist" provincial government. In Kivu, the MNC/L had been largely excluded from the Miruho government; in Kasai, Provincial President Mukenge was from the Lulua party, *Union Nationale Congolaise.* Although the party was allied with the MNC/L on a national level, Mukenge, closely related to Lulua chief Kalamba, represented the moderate wing of UNC; further, the entire alliance reposed essentially on ethnic factors, and was more an anti-Baluba front in Lulua eyes than an ideological community of views. In Equateur, although the MNC/L was represented in the government, it played little role in the nominations in the territorial administration.

The issue came to a head in the case of Maniema, where the MNC/L had won 9 of 14 seats in the provincial assembly. Miruho named Antoine Omari[15] as district commissioner for Maniema. As a Mukusu, Omari was ethnically linked with the dominant ethnic group; however, he had failed to follow the consigns of the March 1960 Lodja Congress, which called upon the Bakusu and all related groups of the Akutshu-Anamongo culture cluster to support MNC/L.[16] The central government tried to name its own candidate, MNC/L militant Gaston Soumialot.[17] For

[15] Antoine Omari is not to be confused with Adrien Omari, who replaced Kashamura as provincial president of Kivu at the end of February 1961.

[16] The Lodja Congress, which took place March 9-12, 1960, saw a regrouping of the Batetela-Bakusu tribes and their decision as an ethnic group to support the political movement of their favorite son, Lumumba. The congress voted unanimously "that all Bahamba, Batetela, Bakutshu, Bakela, Basongomeno, Bangengele, Benamashila, Bahina, Benamatepa, Bakongola, Bena Lubunda, Bena Samba, and Bena Malela should thenceforward bear only the name Akutshu Anamongo." Anamongo means "descendents of the single ancestor Mongo." See for the resoultions of the Lodja Congress *Congo 1960*, III, 7-18.

[17] Soumialot was not a Mukusu, but a Musongye, a group mostly situated in Kasai. He was a key leader in the 1964 revolt.

a time, both candidates fought for effective control of Kindu. In October 1960, Omari won a brief victory when Soumialot was arrested and imprisoned in Bukavu. However, with the Kashamura period Soumialot was returned to power in Maniema—although this time by the authority of the new provincial regime, not the central government.

Colonial law, which remained in force until abrogated, in this instance supported provincial prerogative. The relevant provision of the civil service statute reads:

"The Governor-General determines the province or the branch of the central government in which officers of the first four ranks will exercise their function.

"The general secretary and department heads allocate within their branches and the provincial governors within their respective territorial subdivisions, the officers placed at their disposition by the Governor-General. . . .

"The officers of the territorial service posted to a district and those of other services put at the disposition of the district commissioner by the provincial governor are assigned within each territory by the district commissioner. However, the assignment of officers who by their grades are entitled to administer a territory is subject to the prior approval of the provincial governor."[18]

Thus, legally, the nomination of Soumialot by the central government was irregular; all that could be done was to place him with the rank of district commissioner at the disposition of the Kivu provincial authorities. The central government could only have made its powers felt in this field had it been politically feasible to "scramble" the appointments and to assign persons to the territorial service outside their region of origin; for example, the law theoretically empowered Leopoldville to assign all Bakongo functionaries to Kivu. However, in most areas, especially

[18] Article 35 of the *Arrêté Royal* of January 13, 1959, Piron and Devos, *Codes et Lois*, II, 436.

during the desperate crisis of 1960, this would have been (and still is) absolutely out of the question.

By July 12, when Belgium officially announced that the option of integration into the metropolitan administration would be applicable to all colonial functionaries (except those in Katanga) and the exodus of European civil servants became virtually complete, the process of Africanizing the territorial service was underway throughout the Congo. Even in Katanga, where the Europeans were ordered to remain at their posts, they were forced to relinquish many of the nominal posts of command to Africans and to retire to the ambiguous role of councilor-technician. Tshombe declared on the Katanga radio on July 13:

"Certain malicious persons have spread the rumor that we wish to cede the power to the Europeans. The facts themselves refute these lies.

"The first task of the ministers has been to organize as rapidly as possible the Africanization of personnel. This has already been done for the districts and the territories. Here is the list of appointments for district commissioners and territorial administrators. These appointments take effect immediately."[19]

For the most part, the nominations were made from within the ranks of the administration. The senior clerk, who in many instances had already been named "auxiliary" at the beginning of 1960, was in general the first logical choice if he was not for some reason ethnically or politically incompatible. There had been no deliberate policy of transfer of African personnel from one region to another by the colonial regime; the bulk of the clerks would be from the region in question. However, those ethnic groups which had had early access to the facilities of modernization, particularly education, tended to be heavily represented in the ranks of the clerks; further, they had them-

[19] *Congo 1960,* II, 723.

selves dispersed widely from their own homeland. This was most striking in the case of the Kasai Baluba; however, it was also true of the Bakongo and the riverain peoples of Equateur labeled "Bangala" in Leopoldville.

Initially, such "scrambling" as took place in the July 1960 appointments was internal to a sphere of influence of a political movement. For example, within the PSA-dominated district of Kwilu, territorial administrators in a number of cases were posted to a territory not dominated by their own ethnic group. It would have been out of the question, however, for a Mukongo or a Muluba to be selected.[20] The same policy was followed by MNC/L, on a broader scale as the area dominated was much larger. Here the rationale was that the administration which would implement the nationalist program of the party had to be operated by those who had proved their party fidelity. A number of persons from outside Orientale province received posts of command in the territorial service as well as in the ministries of the province; in nearly all cases, these came from the MNC/L heartland of Maniema-Sankuru.[21] But the requisite of party loyalty produced in the end a similar result; although genuinely national in aspiration, the MNC/L was regional in fact.

During the first year of independence, *"chacun chez soi"* became a powerful slogan. The Baluba of South Kasai were both physically removed from administrative posts in areas like Luluabourg and attracted by the challenge of establishing their own Baluba state. In November 1960,

[20] By 1962, during the writer's visit to Kwilu, this had been made a systematic principle of administration. All territorial administrators were in charge of territories other than their own; on the other hand, all came from the Kwilu district.

[21] An interesting reflection of the tendency of administrative divisions to create their own loyalties was the complaint voiced by a number of persons to the writer in Stanleyville in mid-1962 about the excessive number of "strangers" in both the territorial service and provincial administration; these were for the most part MNC/L militants from Maniema and Sankuru, outside of Orientale province.

serious incidents in Kikwit resulted in the departure of most of the Bakongo remaining in the ranks of the Kwilu administration. In March and April, 1961, the movement for Kwango autonomy, stimulated by the recognition of a Kwango state at the Tananarive Conference, resulted in the expulsion of most of the Kwiluites remaining in civil service positions in that district. In Bukavu, the return of the Miruho government in August 1961, after the inflammation of ethnic tensions during the Kashamura-Omari regimes, was the signal for the departure of many Bakusu.

Provincial and Central Administration

In the provincial and central ministries, the abuses in the replacement of the departed Europeans were much more serious than in the territorial service. In the first place, the consequences of an inadequate appointment were not immediately felt, as in the case of a territorial administrator, who exercised a real post of command. Secondly, and most important, one cannot underestimate the enormous pressures placed upon the newly installed ministers. Each of them was confronted with a virtual army of political and ethnic clientele, camped on his doorstep, who expected a reward for their support. The complete disorganization at the central level engendered by the crisis left the ministers unprotected by any established neutral criteria by which they could escape these claims. It is, after all, less than a century since an American president was assassinated by a disappointed officeseeker; for the Congolese leader, neither law nor party could provide a discipline permitting a rational solution of this problem. The positions were obviously open, or could be created. Only a superhuman act of will could have enabled a minister to escape substantial concessions.

One escape valve was through the mechanism of the "political cabinet" which each minister could create. Belgium itself, and continental administrative tradition in general, provided the model for this. A minister was entitled to a private secretariat to advise him on the "political" aspects of his function, as opposed to the purely "administrative" recommendations which emerge from the civil service. This procedure leads to serious conflicts in Europe; one need go no further than the Colonial Ministry in Belgium to observe its effects.[22] In helping to solve the immediate problems of rewarding the clientele, the establishment of these ministerial cabinets built a duality of authority which became a permanent source of friction and paralysis, as well as of cost. The size of these cabinets was considerable, as shown by Table 26. Prior to creation of new provinces, there were approximately 100 ministerial rank political figures; the new provinces added 150 more.

TABLE 26

TABLE OF ORGANIZATION, MINISTERIAL CABINETS
(PROVINCIAL AND CENTRAL)

Title	Number	Salary (annual)
Chef de cabinet	1	343,200 B. frs.
Chef de cabinet adjoint	1	312,000
Secrétaire de cabinet	1	280,000
Secrétaire particulier	1	240,000
Attaché de cabinet	4	234,000
Attaché de presse	1	220,000
Commis	2	156,000
Huissier	2	31,200

SOURCE: "Traitements, grèves, et politique d'austérité," *Etudes Congolaises*, II, No. 5 (1962), 12.

Another major problem was the need for extensive administrative reorganization in order to create departments for the numerous ministers. The colonial administration, at the central and provincial level, had been broken down into the following departments:

General Secretariat

[22] Buisseret made extensive use of his political cabinet to bypass the Colonial Ministry functionaries, whom he believed to be dominated by conservative, Catholic influences.

409

Security police

Ten-year plan

1st *Direction:* Political, administrative, judicial, and religious affairs

2nd *Direction:* Native and social affairs

3rd *Direction:* Finance

4th *Direction:* Economic affairs

5th *Direction:* Agriculture, European settlement, and veterinary services

6th *Direction:* Public works and communications

7th *Direction:* Medical services

8th *Direction:* Education

The exigencies of cabinet formation for the central government led to the creation of twenty recognizable ministries under the Lumumba government; this was reduced to fifteen under the *Collège des Commissaires,* but shot back up to twenty-four under the Adoula government. It was inevitable under these circumstances that there would be overlapping ministries and serious jurisdictional conflicts.

The extravagant degree of administrative fragmentation not only drains away public funds from potential investment uses but establishes numerous duplications of functions which absorb the energies of public servants in jurisdictional contests. Economic policy is split between the Ministries of Foreign Trade, Finance, Economic Affairs, and Economic Coordination and Plan, without mention of the very important Monetary Council, which reports to the Prime Minister's office. The Ministry of Middle Classes competes with the parastatal *Société de Crédit aux Classes Moyennes.* Social issues are the domain of the Labor, Social Affairs, and Youth and Sports Ministries. Interior and Civil Service Ministries have a running conflict over authority to make civil service appointments.

Although the problem was less severe at the provincial

410

level, with the governments limited to ten ministers by the *Loi Fondamentale,* it was not entirely absent. In Orientale, for example, two separate ministers had authority in the allocation of import licenses and quotas; the running battle between them was a serious problem for the province in 1961-1962.

Toward a Civil Service Statute

The promotions that were made during the Africanization of 1960 inevitably placed many in positions far above those to which their civil service rating entitled them. This was initially done by "encommissionment," rather than "nomination." The former is a temporary designation which does not entitle the bearer to a salary commensurate with his post, but rather with his previous civil service rank. The functionaries thus did not immediately benefit materially from the promotions they had received in 1960.

The *statut unique* was clearly inapplicable in the new situation. Pending preparation of a new law completely revamping the civil service structure, on April 21, 1961, Ordinance 33 was issued which sought to regularize the situation.[23] According to one commentator, "in granting new advantages to the civil servants under the statute, already in a privileged situation in relation to the workers under contract and the private sector, the Ordinance increased to an insupportable point the tension between the categories of privileged citizens and the immense majority of the population."[24] Its central principle was to resolve the distortion between the top and bottom of the civil service scale by raising the top slightly and the bottom several-fold. It was to have been retroactive to January 1, 1961.

The UTC responded by threatening a general strike, and the monetary authorities warned of the disastrous

[23] *Moniteur Congolais,* 2d yr., No. 14, March 18, 1961.
[24] Benoit Verhaegen, "Les syndicats et le nouveau contrat de louage de services," *Etudes Congolaises,* I, No. 3, (July-August, 1961), 27.

inflationary effects; the government was thus led to postpone application of the Ordinance. In 1962, the new salary
scale of Ordinance 33 was finally applied, with "forced
savings" of the retroactive portion. However, the government was very sparing in the number of permanent "nominations" actually made to the top two ranks of the civil
service; many of the positions on the administrative organization chart were filled with only temporary designees,
who were maintained on their old pay base. The revised
civil service law was finally promulgated on July 13, 1963.

Generational Conflict: The University Graduates

One measure of great importance was the policy adopted
toward the university graduates, a trickle which would
shortly be a flood. An administrative regulation issued in
July 1961 (Ordinance 51) provided that access to the
top category and the upper half of the second rank would
be open only to those who had received an efficiency rating of "very good" for three successive years prior to 1960;
this was unmistakably a move directed against the university graduates, who were disqualified entirely under this
stipulation.

This generational conflict between an older group for
whom no higher educational facilities had existed in its
youth and which cites long experience, albeit in subaltern
posts, and the wisdom of mature age, and a young generation emerging from the universities of Europe and
Africa is a tension found in most new African states. The
Congo's problem differs only in degree; yet the workings
of history and Belgian policy have been such to make the
contrast between generations particularly sharp. There is
no parallel in tropical Africa for the achievement of independence before literally any of the university-trained
generation were ready to enter public life; only Bomboko
among the top Leopoldville leadership has a university
degree. The simple device adopted would not have been

412

so dramatically discriminatory against the university-trained generation in any other country.

The hostility toward the university generation is illustrated by a letter to Kasavubu from Bakongo clerks in the administration which was printed in the Abako weekly in April 1960, protesting the requirement of examinations for promotions:

"This measure has been designed to favor the university students and other diploma holders; . . . as a reward for the services they have rendered to the colonialists. . . . Even in our Abako, we have no knowledge of a single university student who has agreed to serve even as secretary for the movement. They belittle our work and consider us as primitive. . . . We have done everything ourselves, and therefore, we must not be forgotten. . . . We have won our independence with our little bit of French, we will govern the country with this same little bit of French [for ten or fifteen years, until they are really trained]. . . . We have learned by experience, which the university students are incapable of doing. Consequently, we intend to occupy all the positions and we will make good use of our experience."[25]

The resentment of the university students is reflected in a manifesto they published in 1961:

"It has often been said that the Congo lacks trained persons. Yet we see nonetheless that the Congolese university graduates are kept away from political responsibilities. If one or the other has been given some responsibility, it was in most cases by a politician from his tribe, in function of a short-sighted policy.

"It has often been said that university graduates are theoreticians, and have no experience. One thing, however, is clear; in the matter of experience, at least concerning the problems of the modern world, no Congolese has very

[25] *Notre Kongo*, April 17, 1960.

TABLE 27

Civil Service Reform

Rank	Job Title	Number (1962)	Annual salary[a] before independence	Proposal, Nov. 1960	Ordinance 33, April 1961	Civil service law, July 1963	Education required for future recruitment
1	General secretary	1	380,000 C frs.	300,000	405,600	429,000	Reserved for those in civil service before 1960
	Provincial secretary	10	325,000	280,000	374,400	379,500	
	Director	70	280,000	.....	343,200		
	Provincial director	41	225,000	240,000	312,000	313,500	
	Assistant director, central government	239	.....	.....	280,800		
2	Principal bureau chief	10	185,000	200,000	234,000	264,000	5 years univ.
	Bureau chief	501	135,000	180,000	218,400	247,500	4 years univ.
	Assistant bureau chief	825	90,000	160,000	202,800	231,000	
3	Principal office supervisor (Rédacteur)	980	73,250	130,000	171,600	181,500	.....
	Office supervisor	1,230	55,500	110,000	156,000	165,000	2 years univ.
	Assistant office supervisor	1,590	45,000	90,000	140,400	148,500	6 years secondary
4	Chief clerk	1,321	40,000	75,000	109,200	115,500	
	Principal clerk	3,618	35,000	60,000	93,600	99,000	4 years secondary
	Clerk	1,406	30,000	50,000	78,000	82,500	2 years secondary
	Total	11,842					

Source: "Traitements, grèves, et politique d'austérité," *Etudes Congolaises*, II, No. 5, pp. 5–7; *ibid*, V, No. 9. (Nov. 1963), p. 97.

a include fringe benefits which add approximately 25% to the salary total.

much in the political, administrative, or military field. The experience of the majority of the present leaders is limited to having been clerks, soldiers, or teachers. We don't know any Congolese who has had a long experience in the art of commanding, of conceiving or of supervising a task of great scope.

"International opinion is sometimes stupefied to see that in our country more than one simple soul tries to play the part of leader, and refuses the collaboration of the intellectual elite of the nation."[26]

There are of course two sides to this story; Coleman enters a perceptive caveat on this point:

"Apart from the fact that Western education is a requisite for running a modern state, most Africans have regarded it as a grace-giving process. Did not European colonial bureaucrats and settlers rationalize their dominant position in terms of education, with which 'civilization' was synonymous? . . . This uncritical equating of education with special rights and legitimacy has endowed the educated African with an exaggerated sense of superiority and special legitimacy. Politics have been permeated with the presumably uncontestable assumption that the educated have a divine right to rule."[27]

The fact remains that the present university generation is highly dissatisfied with a situation where access to their normal career outlet, the civil service, is at the relatively modest level of assistant bureau chief. A provisional solution in a number of cases has simply been to assign university graduates to ambassadorial posts abroad; Cardoso in Washington, Itzimbuir at the United Nations, Thomas Kanza in London, André Mandi in Rome, Paul Mushiete at Paris, Joseph Mbeka at the Common Market, are all from

[26] *Manifeste des universitaires congolaises,* pp. 8-9.
[27] Almond and Coleman, *Politics of the Developing Areas,* pp. 282-83.

the first group of university degree-holders. But this kind of answer will obviously not last long; in 1962, the Lovanium enrollment was up to 700, and nearly 900 in 1963. The state university of Elisabethville had 200 students, and a new Protestant university in Stanleyville was being established in 1963. There were over 1,000 Congolese in secondary and higher educational institutions in Belgium in 1961-1962. By 1967, it is estimated that the secondary academic cycle will be producing annually 7,000 potential university students instead of the 150 at the time of independence and 550 in 1962.

The salary problems for the top servants of the state are likewise creating a string of conundrums. When one adds to the civil service salaries those of the political sector, the army and police, and the very well-remunerated teachers, the total cost in 1962 came to over 15 billion francs, or nearly 90 percent of all public expenditure. The revenues of the state, excluding external aid, came to only 4 to 5 billion francs.[28] The state is thus crippled by its own overwhelming payroll; there is absolutely no money left to undertake the kind of vigorous public investment program which might help create new opportunities for those now sitting in the university lecture halls, as well as those lounging unemployed in the streets.[29]

It should be added that the 100,000 persons occupying menial positions in the employ of the state are not included under the civil service statute; these are hired

[28] This whole problem is given remarkable summary in "Traitements, grèves, et politique d'austérité," *loc. cit.*, pp. 1-32.

[29] The situation of the public finances has been considerably improved by the reintegration of Katanga and devaluation with a dual exchange rate (150 francs per dollar to obtain Congo francs; 180 francs per dollar to obtain foreign exchange). The system is in part a 20% surtax on imports, but is expected to yield 10 billion francs in revenue in 1964. Total government revenue for 1964 is estimated at 34 billion francs, which brings a balanced budget within sight. However, salaries still consume an exorbitant part of public revenue. *New York Times*, April 25, 1964.

"under contract." In April 1962, following a brief civil service strike, the upper level of this category was brought within the protection and privileges of the statute, which added approximately 10,000 persons to the 11,842 cited in Table 27. Theoretically, these are all eventually to come within the purview of the statute; the cost of this operation, however, would be prohibitive if the present salary scales are maintained.

Technical Assistance

Guinea is the only African parallel for the abrupt transfer of administrative responsibility from European to African. In the Guinean case, the exclusion of Africans at the top level during the colonial period had not been so complete, although the number of senior African civil servants was not large. Further, the tightly organized and disciplined PDG took over much of the responsibility of governing the polity. In the Congo, the clerks were suddenly confronted with the entire burden of managing the country, with virtually no direction at the top in the early days of independence. It is true that the UN technical assistance program provided some invaluable assistance in preventing irreparable damage in certain highly technical sectors and in the domain of public finance and management of customs collection and exchange controls. But the fact remains that the UN concept of technical assistance placed it parallel to and outside the Congolese administration; further, it functioned only at the provincial and central levels.[30] Fundamentally, the bureaucrat

[30] The evaluation of the UN technical assistance in *Congo 1960* is an excellent summary:

"With the exception of certain achievements, at times spectacular but in special fields, such as civil aviation, the relief of the South Kasai populations, the clearing of the Matadi port, the civilian assistance operation could be considered at the end of 1960 as a failure, despite the magnitude of the resources allocated and the quality of much of the personnel. . . .

"The UN felt that it could resolve entirely new problems, of a

417

sat alone behind his desk, surveying helplessly a world of disorder. What is remarkable under these circumstances is that so much of the routine administrative function was maintained in the central administrations, and in many of the territories the new administrator in a large number of cases maintained a reasonable degree of public order.

A handful of Belgian functionaries stayed on throughout the crisis period in 1960, and, beginning in the fall of 1960, a certain number responded to appeals to return by central and provincial authorities. It will be recalled that at the moment of independence, there were 10,000 Belgian functionaries, not counting those employed by the parastatal organizations, plus 8,000 lay teachers. In January 1961, the Congo government employed 2,268 Belgian civil servants, plus 308 lay teachers. Of this total, 1,168 served in Katanga. The number of technicians fell slowly during 1961; at the end of the year, there were only 1,500, plus 1,000 lay teachers.[31] By early 1963, the figure, including 589 teachers, stood at 2,179.[32]

It is noteworthy, however, that none of the Belgians occupied a position in the command hierarchy of the administration. They were attached as "technicians" or "advisers"; the exact nature of the role had a thousand

---

scale never before attained, by using its habitual procedures; pilot projects, juxtaposition of the UN and local services, councilors placed at the disposition of the Congolese administration, with a central brain-trust controlling the whole operation.

"These classical methods of technical assistance implied the existence of an administration and a local government, perhaps defective, but capable of being made effective by external assistance. This minimum condition was not fulfilled in the Congo." Vol. II, p. 1091.

[31] The figures are from J. Gérard-Libois, "L'assistance technique belge et la République du Congo," *Etudes Congolaises*, II, No. 3, 1-11.

[32] "Assistance technique belge à la République du Congo," *Travaux Africains*, CRISP, No. 20, March 4, 1963, pp. 11-12. Of these, 655 were in Katanga and 863 in Leopoldville, mainly with the central government. Figures for the other (old) provinces: Equateur, 124; Orientale, 127; Kivu, 113; Kasai, 132.

variations, depending upon the personalities of the Europeans and Congolese involved and the kind of working relationship which grew up. In a number of ministries, the Belgian technicians visibly performed a great deal of the important work; in others, they were assigned to tedious and menial tasks. There was a general conviction among the technicians, and among a growing number of Congolese, that they were not being used effectively, and could not be as long as they were excluded from positions of authority. It is likely that there will be some limited reincorporation of Belgian technicians into the bureaucratic hierarchy, but the formidable difficulties in de-Africanizing will operate to restrict the scope of this reintegration.

There was considerable variation in the amount of Belgian technical advice received at the local level. In the province of Equateur during 1962, there were sixty Belgian technicians attached to the local administration. At the district seat of Lisala, there were no less than five, and throughout the province there was at least one attached to every territory. However, in the two districts of the Lower Congo, there were only two Belgian technicians altogether. And in a tour of all the territories of Kwilu district in April 1962 there were only two technicians, one of whom performed virtually no work. The other, it should be added, had remained at his post throughout the difficult period and had been given important responsibilities in supervising the accounts and functioning of the local governments, the *circonscriptions indigènes*. His remarkable industry, constructive attitude, and real dedication to the well-being of local government rendered him very popular with the Congolese administrators. But the important fact is that he was the exception rather than the rule; only in Equateur and Katanga were there significant numbers of Belgians involved at the local administrative level after the 1960 crisis.

419

Adaptation of the Judiciary

One of the areas of Congolese government most disorganized by the European exodus was the judiciary; in the words of one jurist, "Impartial and competent observers have not hesitated to affirm that the worst catastrophe in

TABLE 28

JUDICIAL ORGANIZATION, JUNE 30, 1960

	Modern judicial hierarchy			Traditional courts		
	Jurisdiction		President of tribunal	Jurisdiction		President of tribunal
Echelon	Penal[a]	Civil[b]		Penal	Civil	
Circonscription (sector, chieftaincy)				1 month 1000 frs.	Unlimited	Chief
Territory	2 months 2,000 frs.	none	Territorial Administrator	Appellate only		Territorial Administrator
District	5 yrs.[c]	50,000 frs.	Magistrate			
Province (*Tribunal de Première Instance*)	Unlimited	Unlimited	Magistrate			

[a] This refers to the maximum sentences which could be imposed at each le it was the decision of the *parquet* (attorney-general) to select the echelon at wl to prosecute, depending upon the maximum penalties permitted by the law viola and upon whatever sentence appeared appropriate to the prosecution if convic were obtained.

[b] This refers to the maximum value which could be at stake in civil suits introdr at any given echelon. The traditional courts could obviously only entertain litiga between persons subject to traditional law.

[c] There was no limit to the amount of a fine which the district tribunal was powered to levy.

this series of disasters has been the disappearance of the judicial apparatus in the greater part of the Congo. . . ."[33]

Table 28 shows that the key element in the judicial structure as reformed on the eve of independence was the

[33] J. Sohier, "Problemes d'organisation judiciaire dans l'Etat du Katanga," Publications de *l'Université de l'Etat à Elisabethville,* I, (July 1961) 112.

district tribunal. In order to function legally, this court had to be presided over by a magistrate, with a doctor of law degree. The first Congolese doctor of law, however, was not graduated until 1962. When Lovanium was first established, the administration required that no law faculty be included; subsequently, the number eligible for admission to the study of law was for several years blocked by the requirement of a knowledge of Greek. Greek was only taught in the European secondary schools, which had but a handful of Congolese students; the majority of Congolese were trained in the mission-run schools which followed the *humanités congolaises* program, and did not include Greek.[34]

There were, at the beginning of 1959, 168 magistrates to operate the reformed judicial system;[35] the 1958 reform, applied in 1960, in fact required a substantial increase in this figure, as for the first time the district courts were to be removed from the administration and put under the charge of the magistrature. However, virtually the entire corps of magistrates departed in the 1960 exodus. This skill proved to be especially difficult to replace, as not only the French language capability was necessary but also a legal training based upon the continental traditions of Roman law and the Code Bonaparte. Further, unlike many of the administrators, the departed magistrates had no difficulty whatsoever in finding attractive new career opportunities in Belgium; a certain number also moved over to Katanga, which did maintain its European armature in the judicial field. When the first storm had passed, the College of Commissioners and various provincial authorities sought to persuade either the former colonial magistrates or other Belgians to restore the judicial apparatus. The success of these recruiting efforts was very

[34] Antoine Rubbens, "La décolonisation du droit et de l'organisation judiciaire dans la République du Congo," *Bull. Séances*, ARSOM, 1961, p. 798.
[35] *Rapport sur l'Administration . . . 1958*, p. 17.

limited, and, by the end of 1961, it was clear that some other interim solution was essential.[36] In September 1961, the Congolese Minister of Justice requested that the UN recruit fifty magistrates; by the end of 1962, this figure had not been reached, but enough jurists from Egypt, Greece, Haiti, Lebanon, and Syria had been found to restore to the former district courts at least a qualified president.[37]

In the interim, the former court clerks were temporarily commissioned to keep the judicial structure functioning as far as possible. Many had long experience in handling the routine work of the judiciary and had been disciplined in the proud traditions of independence and dedication to the supremacy of the law of the Belgian magistracy; Rubbens provides an interesting summary of the functioning of this improvised judicial system:

"We had stated that the Congolese magistrates named after the exodus of Belgian magistrates were generally the clerks of the courts and public prosecutors. All had therefore a practical acquaintance with judicial operations and if some of them applied the formulas which were familiar to them without always understanding the basis, there were others who in simplifying the formulas applied a sound justice. 'When they did not know the law or the custom, they judged by equity,' a functionary of the Ministry of Justice has observed. . . .

"The authority of these de facto magistrates was not really disputed by either the defendants or the local administrations; cases were heard, judged, and executed."[38]

The neutrality of the judiciary was relatively well maintained. An indication of this is that in 1962 this was the only sector of government where a virtually complete regionalization of personnel had not taken place. In Lisala, for

[36] Rubbens, "La décolonisation du droit," *loc. cit.*, pp. 802-03.
[37] *Progress Report No. 13 on United Nations Civilian Operations in the Congo during November-December, 1961*, p. 52.
[38] Rubbens, "La décolonisation du droit," *loc. cit.*, p. 800.

example, the acting public prosecutor was a Muluba from Kasai; at Kikwit, only one of the four acting Congolese magistrates came from the district of Kwilu. There was little pressure for Africanization of the judiciary; the acting Congolese magistrates are proud of the job they have done but are the first to request the designation of qualified magistrates to head the courts.

The problems of the judiciary will begin to find a solution in 1964, when the *Ecole Nationale de Droit et d'Administration* (ENDA) at Leopoldville will begin turning out sixty magistrates a year. Lovanium has also greatly accelerated its output of lawyers; sixty of the eighty students enrolled in the Law Faculty in 1961-1962 had started university study after independence. In the meanwhile, projects have been prepared, both in Leopoldville and Elisabethville, to complete the pre-independence judicial reform by removing from the territorial administrators their powers to judge petty criminal infractions and by unifying the customary and written law jurisdictions.[39]

Urban Government and Politics

A breakdown at the top echelons of a political system offers an unusual occasion to measure the viability of its local structures. In this context, Belgium's last carefully executed reform, the twin decrees on urban and rural councils of 1957, deserve reexamination in the light of post-1960 experience.[40]

[39] *Ibid.;* J. Sohier, *op. cit.* South Kasai during its period of autonomy actually implemented a reform of this nature.

[40] Supra, Chapter VI. The material on urban institutions was mainly obtained by interviews in Leopoldville, Coquilhatville, Stanleyville, Bukavu, and Elisabethville. I have insufficient data on Luluabourg as a municipality, although the presumption is that the massive population displacements have taken their toll. The study of local rural institutions is based especially on a visit to all parts of former Leopoldville province, except Lae Leopold II district and to Coquilhatville, Boende, and Lisala, or three of the four former district seats in Equateur. For Orientale, Kivu, and Katanga, the information was

The urban communal institutions clearly emerge second best in the context of independence. It will be recalled that many aspects of these institutions were postulated upon an incorrect assumption as to the future Congolese political system. As Chapter VI has shown, the principle of European-African parity was still in vogue when the 1957 decree was formulated, and little was done to expunge it in the 1959 reform. The two-tier structure of commune and city was erected to permit entire autonomy for the purely European residential quarters; at the *Conseil de Ville* level de facto parity was achieved by a heavy dosage of interest-group representation, balancing the African plurality which emerged from demographic arithmetic.

Further, because of the telescoped political evolution of 1959-1960, most of the ablest African communal councilors elected in December 1959 had resigned these seats to take up service at the provincial and national level in May 1960. From 1957-1959, when election to urban bodies was the highest level of politically achieved status, the communal institutions had attracted the able and the ambitious. In 1960, they lost their glamour and suffered a real decline in the average ability of the council members.

The communal institutions have had to contend with enormous strains. With the lifting of controls on population movement, ineffective though these may have been, the exodus to the cities has taken on fantastic proportions; many centers have apparently doubled in size. Unemployment is at an extremely high level. Especially difficult to deal with are the large numbers of young persons with some education but not enough really to lift them from the unskilled labor category; these formed the raw material for the youth gangs used by a number of political movements in 1960 as private militia, and more recently

collected only by interviews with provincial officials in the respective capitals, and is hence more derivative.

organized criminal groups. Many, especially the unemployed, have ceased paying rent on public housing they occupy; eviction would be an intolerable political risk. In Bukavu, there is a special problem of squatters who have illegally occupied the housing in the former European quarter. Faced with this challenge, burgomasters have tended to avoid attempts at enforcement of regulations which are beyond their effective power to apply.

The former European communes have been particularly disorganized. Burgomasters frequently departed in 1960 along with many of the communal councilors. These in any case no longer adequately represented the commune, as many Congolese moved into the houses which went with the new positions of responsibility to which they had been promoted. African burgomasters were appointed to replace the Europeans, and a minimum of administration is carried on through them. But in many cases they have become almost functionless.

At the level of the city, the European members have either voluntarily withdrawn or, in the case of Leopoldville, were discharged by the First Burgomaster Daniel Kanza in 1961. Although the *Conseil de Ville* meets with reasonable regularity in Leopoldville, one may doubt whether in fact a legal quorum (50 percent) is present. However, this is a matter of little concern to the population, which pays almost no attention to the workings of the *Conseil de Ville,* as long as the essential services which it has come to expect from the municipal administration are available.

One curious feature of the Leopoldville urban institutions is that the largest single element in the population, the Bakongo, is entirely unrepresented in them. The Abako, it will be recalled, boycotted the December 1959 elections which designated the incumbent communal councilors.[41] The participation in the elections ran from 17.26

[41] The PSA also boycotted, but this was less important in Leopold-

percent in Ngiri-Ngiri to 39.98 percent in Kinshasa, with the greatest single winner, the Bayaka party Luka, taking 63 of 225 seats. However, the Abako accepted the results, and the new communal councilors were set up on the basis of this minority vote. Perhaps it is a measure of the degree to which communal institutions have become politically invisible that this anomaly is seldom a matter for polemic or even for conversation.

Conflict between the burgomaster and communal council has been frequent. In Leopoldville, these have arisen over entirely local and indeed banal problems; they are not unlike executive-legislative skirmishes in all democratic systems. In an established system, formal procedure and informal usage prescribe limits for these disputes. The Belgian legacy has left the burgomasters with a heavily bureaucratic set of norms, which places little value in wheedling an unruly and, from their point of view, obstructive council. Thus, when conflict comes, the instinctive reaction of many burgomasters is to do without the services of the communal councils. Several in Leopoldville have either ceased functioning or experienced long interruptions. Those so inclined have been abetted by councilors who in some instances seem to view the councils as a trade union of members. The level of remuneration of councilors has been a constant issue; in one commune, the councilors voted themselves each a plot of land from the communal domain, a move which was vetoed by the city.

Some insight into the operation of Leopoldville communal councils may be obtained by examining the operation of Dendale since 1960. It was this commune where Kasavubu was burgomaster from 1958 to 1960. In the 1957 elections, the Bakongo predominance was reflected

___

ville, where natives of Kwilu composed only about 10% of the population.

in a sweep of 24 of 25 council seats by the Abako. This was further shown when only 24.63 percent of the voters turned out in the face of the Abako boycott of the December 1959 elections. At that time Luka, the Bayaka party, won 11 seats; Assoreco, an ethnic alliance of Bangala took 10, and the PNP won 2. By a vote of 12-10, a Muyaka burgomaster was installed. Thereafter, the "party" labels ceased to have any relevance in the operation of the communal councils. The council has continued to meet approximately monthly and has concerned itself with the street and sewer problems which are the warp and woof of local government. A Mongo councilor indicated in an interview in June 1962 that discussions were going forward as to how to avoid a return to power of the Bakongo in the assumption that more elections might be held.

In Coquilhatville, a rather different picture emerged. There had been two communes, one European and one African. The end of residential segregation with independence removed the entire *raison d'être* for the dual tier, and it has virtually disappeared. The communes still have a formal existence, but the real administration of the city was carried out at the level of the city, with the help of an able Belgian technician who had been a district commissioner before independence. The essential work of urban administration went forward, somewhat hampered and definitely rendered unnecessarily expensive by a municipal structure which was no longer relevant.

Until September 1962, the city of Stanleyville was the personal fief of Bernard Salumu; it was the only Congo town which had a real "boss." Salumu operated through a political organization personally loyal to him, although bearing the jeunesse MNC/L label. He had been first named district commissioner of Haut Congo, of which Stanleyville was a part, and subsequently first burgomaster of Stanleyville. He is one of the most colorful

Congolese political figures; his mother, Madame Bangala, must be one of the Congo's most eminent women.[42] She organized a flourishing commercial network, especially after 1960, and much of the manioc and fish for the Stanleyville markets passes through her hands. Some insight into the personality of her son is obtained in a revealing communiqué issued by Salumu in February 1961:

"I am obliged to speak frankly before public opinion to those who want to do me in, to those who plot against my life, to those who are jealous of my life, to those who are jealous of my political worth, both intrinsic and extrinsic. . .

"The late Prime Minister understood what I was. This is why he never traveled without taking me along, because he knew that, in addition to my political talents, I was a real body-guard. . .

"My dear brothers, before independence, nobody was unaware of the situation of my family from a financial point of view. No *Stanleyvillois* is unaware that I was one of the ablest clerks in town. . . . Who does not know that before independence, before politics became in vogue. . . I was one of the first to fight against social injustice? . . . Everyone knows that I am one of the great revolutionaries of all time."[43]

The opponents of Salumu accused him of installing a Lokele regime in Stanleyville. The central government

[42] This is a fascinating social phenomenon which hopefully some future Congolese sociologist will explore. The African food market is one area (before 1960 virtually the sole area) where expatriate traders did not monopolize the commerce. Marketing is traditionally carried on by women in much of Africa; the marketplace is a key nexus of social communication, as the truck driver delivering the goods picks up the latest news of all sorts, and transmits it to the villages along his route. The role of the Nigerian marketwomen in Herbert Macauley's Nigerian Democratic Party in the early years of Nigerian nationalism is cited by James Coleman in his classic *Nigeria: Background to Nationalism* (Los Angeles: University of California Press, 1958), p. 86.

[43] *Uhuru*, Feb. 25, 1961, cited in *Congo 1961*, pp. 207-09.

managed to arrest him in September 1962, which put an end to his role in Stanleyville.

The effectiveness of urban government in Bukavu had been almost completely undermined by the repeated turmoil and instability at the provincial level. Kashamura put in his own supporters, to replace those who had first held office in 1960. When Miruho returned to power in August 1961, he in turn dismissed those installed by the Kashamura-Omari regime. The new incumbents themselves came into sharp conflict with the trio of special commissioners named in May 1962 by the central government when Miruho became embroiled with the Bashi dynastic dispute. Kashamura's "revolution" had left many loose ends, such as the squatting problem referred to above, and the operation of local urban government would have to be considered minimal.

Elisabethville is obviously a special situation, situated at the vortex of a world crisis. Effective control of the capital city of Katanga was too important to too many people to be left to the burgomasters. The 1959 elections had been very close; of 86 seats in the four African communes, the Conakat had won 25, and the Balubakat, 21, with its Fedeka (Kasai Baluba) ally taking 10. In each commune, the independents and splinter groups held the balance, and the Balubakat came out somewhat better in the bargaining; three of the four burgomasters were from the Balubakat Cartel (two Katanga Baluba and one Tshokwe). The fourth was a Conakat Mubemba. By the end of July, the Conakat overtures to the Balubakat to win their support for secession had ended, and the three Cartel burgomasters were replaced; however, in each case, the Conakat-designated successor was from the same ethnic group as his predecessor. In July, Tshombe designated an African, Pius Sapwe, to replace the former European first burgomaster.

In a purely administrative sense, the Elisabethville

municipal institutions were maintained at a reasonable level of efficiency; as in all sectors of Katanga life, there was a large measure of European technical assistance. The suppression of the Balubakat on the one hand, the pervasive activities of Interior Minister Munongo's efficient police on the other placed the communal bodies within an environment where it behooved them to restrict their interests to the strict execution of administrative tasks. However, the Baluba burgomasters of Albert and Katuba communes were accused of failing to support the Tshombe regime during the second UN-Katanga skirmish in December 1961 and were suspended from their functions.[44]

For the towns no adequate answer can really be offered to the basic question: Who governs? As a tentative hypothesis, it is suggested that, leaving aside the special cases of Salumu and Munongo, the question itself is not yet relevant. Before 1960, urban administration was characterized by its colonial, bureaucratic tradition; at the same time, it provided the first level where African political leadership uncontestably legitimated by an electoral process could be asserted. In 1960, the municipalities were deserted both by the colonial bureaucrats and by the aspiring African leaders, who moved up the ladder to positions with broader horizons. The complicated structure of the cities makes it difficult to use these institutions themselves, through discriminating use of patronage and municipal powers, to construct a real political machine, such as that of Lamine Guèye in Dakar. The potentially important economic groups in a community are much more interested in the favors allocated at a provincial or national level, in particular import licenses and foreign exchange. The communes continue as best they can to fulfill those functions which are prescribed by colonial tradition, although they are limited by the lack of means to implement controversial or unpopular decisions. If the question

[44] Gérard-Libois, *Sécession au Katanga*, p. 248.

were really pursued as to who "runs" Coquilhatville or Bukavu, the most accurate response would be that no one does, yet. Real disorder is prevented by the local police, and the population obtains minimal administrative services, but there is not yet a discernible "power structure" to the urban community.

Rural Local Government

In the countryside, the picture is somewhat different; the stability of the *circonscription indigène* (CI) has been surprising. Caution is necessary in generalizing, as the situation varies from one region to another, depending on how effectively the May 10, 1957, decree had been applied by the Belgian administration and the amount of real disorder in the region in the wake of independence. On one extreme, in Equateur there was no discontinuity whatsoever; on the other, disruption was severe in the fought-over areas of North Katanga.

For the villager, the most significant echelon of government is the sector or, for some more specialized services, the territory. At the lowest level, each village has a recognized headman, and there is a *chef de groupement,* generally a clan or lineage chief, who enjoys administrative cognizance at the level of several villages. However, the effective capillaries of modern government are the CI's, which are equipped with the external symbols of an administration: a respectable officebuilding, at least one permanent functionary, typewriters, files, account books, and a treasury of its own. The CI has a squad of policemen, a tribunal, and it generally organizes a marketplace. It retains some auxiliary agricultural monitors who work under the supervision of the more highly trained agricultural officer who is posted at the territory. As any officer in the territorial service will tell the visitor, "if the territories and the CI's function, the country functions."

Prior to independence, there was a general tendency to

dismiss the sector chiefs as mere creatures of the colonial administration, as faithful domestic servants rewarded with a CI all their own by grateful European functionaries for years of devoted service. There was some truth to this notion in Free State days, but in recent years it has become a caricature. The sector is an artificial administrative creation, but it has been in existence sufficiently long to seem a normal part of the scene and provides a certain number of services to which the population has come imperceptibly to attach value. The indirect elections and reforms brought about by the May 10, 1957, decree permitted a new legitimation of the sector chiefs which seems to have preserved the institution of CI's as an effective and functioning instrument of government. Despite the resentment frequently expressed before independence by political leaders toward the sector chiefs, the striking fact is that, with the exception of the Bakongo areas where the chiefs were replaced to a man, the vast majority either remained in function after independence or returned to office after temporary dismissal.

The Bakongo represent a special case in this regard. The paradox of the vitality of the historic myth and high value attached to the cultural traditions of the group and the nearly complete atomization of the society is again perhaps relevant. In this case, the sector chief was trespassing on hallowed ground in decorating his functionary role with the appurtenances of authentic traditional authority.[45] Whereas the former clerk who equally served the colonial administration could now be a territorial

[45]In discussions with the writer Biebuyck has suggested as another cause the fact that the sector chiefs received personally part of the royalties from land concessions, which especially in Mayombe were an explosive issue. The quasi-religious linkage of land tenure with the mystic conception of the clan as a community of the ancestors, the living and the yet unborn made this usurpation particularly resented. Royalties should only have gone to clan chiefs, to receive them on behalf of the community; knowing who these were, however, required the wisdom of Solomon.

432

administrator without suffering any stigma, the sector chief in the Lower Congo was branded as an interloper. In February 1960, the sector chiefs of the Bas-Congo district issued a communiqué illustrating the uncomfortable situation in which they found themselves: "We ask . . . that the political leaders designate our replacements as of today, given the number of assaults upon us and damages caused to our property."[46] At the Brussels Round Table, the Abako was the most hostile of all the parties to reserving any status for chiefs in the new state.[47] Further, the 1957 reform was implemented in the Lower Congo in June 1959, at a time when it was too late to be well executed by the European administration, and too early to be taken in hand by the Abako itself.

In the Kwilu, there was a purge of sector chiefs, but not a complete replacement; in some territories, there was a 50 percent turnover. However, even where the chief was dismissed, the *secrétaire-receveur* remained, giving some continuity. According to a Belgian technician whose function it was to oversee the accounts of the sectors, there had been a lapse in their functioning in the months preceding and following independence, but by 1961 they were again close to normal. A fair index of their effectiveness is that by 1962, they collected the head tax, which in this prosperous region was about 250 francs, with approximately the same success as before independence.

In Lisala, both the new Congolese administrators and the Belgian technicians assisting them affirmed that the CI's were for the most part functioning as well as before independence. For example, in 1961 in the territory of Lisala, the head tax was collected from 18,881 of 22,836 taxpayers. The customary courts of the territory judged 3,535 cases, approximately the same as before 1960.

This suggests that much of the long-standing argument

---

[46] *La Libre Belgique,* February 23, 1960.
[47] G. Dumont, *La Table Ronde,* pp. 111-12.

as to whether Belgian rule was "direct" or "indirect" may have been irrelevant. It is at least clear that in many areas the CI's, as agencies of local government, have shown a remarkable resilience. Whether the pseudo-traditional decoration and terminology used to describe them has been important to their success is difficult to say; to this observer, it would seem rather that they are accepted because they have the comfortable familiarity of something which has long been a feature in rural life. They provide services which are significant to the population, and in regions where there was a temporary breakdown in their function the inconveniences of anarchy have probably enhanced their prestige. The 1957 reforms made an important contribution through the introduction of a flexible electoral principle in constituting the councils and, through them, designating the chief.

The importance of prescription as a legitimating principle in the countryside is impressive. The best illustration of this is the resumption of payment of the head tax. The rate fixed, although it varies according to the wealth of the region, is relatively high for a peasant; were there massive resistance to payment, it would be impossible to collect. Yet this has existed as a sort of tribute levied by the state as long as present generations can remember. In 1960, in the politicized areas, the villager bought a party card rather than pay the state tax. In 1961, however, the parties withdrew from the countryside, and payment to the state was resumed.

The relative solidity of the rural local institutions has been of inestimable service to the Congo in the difficult period while the search for effective government at a provincial and national level goes forward. The lurid newspaper descriptions of anarchy and terror in the countryside were entirely inaccurate, except for a very brief period in July 1960, and thereafter only in certain zones, such as North Katanga. Society has had a precious buffer against chaos in its local government. These embryonic rural communes seem likely to remain one of the most lasting and useful Belgian contributions to the government of an independent Congo.[48]

Bureaucracy Resurgent

In sum, the Congolese bureaucracy is a crucial element in the political system. The heavily bureaucratic tradition of the Belgian colonial system has left an indelible mark. It has bequeathed to the administrative elite which succeeded it the norms and attitudes of a bureaucracy little trammeled by political harassment. A visitor to the interior cannot fail to be impressed by the almost unchallenged position of the administrator at the territorial seat. Even those individuals who were party militants in 1960 tend to regard political activity as such and "politicians," especially deputies, as public nuisances to be excluded if possible. Political ideologies never took root, and there is accordingly no alternative offered for the administrative criteria of successful government: public order and increased production. No better illustration of this can be offered than the recent reintroduction of compulsory agriculture in Orientale and Kwilu in 1962. The recourse to constraint is interesting both in reflecting a characteristically "administrative" rather than "political" solution and in marking a return to the procedures of the colonial bureaucracy.[49] It is completely natural to the new Congolese administrator that he should conform to the standards which are familiar to him.

A close scrutiny of the structure and operation of the

[48] In many of the new provinces, plans for further reform of the rural local governments were being prepared, and during 1963 some were implemented. As these initiatives have been entirely provincial, there is no single pattern being followed. There is insufficient evidence on the real changes effected by the various reforms to be able to evaluate their significance.

[49] The texts of these edicts are printed in *Travaux Africains,* CRISP, No. 9 (November 16, 1962).

bureaucracy yields many insights into the nature of the Congolese polity. The most effective element in the administration is the territorial service; this in itself is a continuity with the past. Belgium always prided itself on the elite nature of its territorial service. Today the nature of the post thrusts responsibility upon the incumbent, and many have risen to the challenge. The swollen administrations of the provincial capitals and Leopoldville have been less successful. Ministries are grossly overstaffed in relation to their real product and hampered by paralyzing jurisdictional conflicts. Nonetheless, the tasks of the bureaucracy are more concrete than those of the "political sector," and many are acquitted surprisingly well. The relative weakness of political institutions in the Congo serves to magnify the importance of the bureaucracy.

The bureaucrats constitute a relatively satisfied element in Congolese society; *Etudes Congolaises* observes wryly that the once-militant civil service union, APIC, will no doubt undergo "profound modifications" in its functioning, as, "for the first time since its creation, its objectives seem to be fully realized."[50] The urgent need to reduce the administrative scale and retribution to a level commensurate with the real needs and financial possibilities of the independent state is a major challenge to its leadership. The other crucial, though less immediate, problem is the absorption of the emerging university-trained generation, so that their talents and training can be constructively harnessed by the community as a whole. The discriminatory provisions relegating the university elite to what is felt to be second-class status are not an adequate answer to this problem. If one is not found, the *colline inspirée* of rapidly expanding Lovanium University will shortly cast an ominous shadow over the city of Leopoldville.

But this should not obscure the merits of the bureaucracy. Not only did the bureaucracy serve as the recruiting

[50] "Traitements, grèves, et politique d'austérité," *loc. cit.* p. 29.

ground for the nationalist leadership in the pre-independence period but the fundamental power transfer came when the European exodus permitted a total Africanization of the administration. Perhaps the explanation for the lack of a revolutionary social credo to accompany the revolution can be found in this fact. The administrator is not by nature a revolutionary; his rationale is the governance, not the transformation, of society. The political program of the bureaucratic elite of the Congo was the Africanization of the administration, not a root-and-branch remaking of colonial society.

░░░

CHAPTER XVI

The Politics of Force: Army and Police

░░░

Role of the Military in Developing Areas

ON JULY 5, 1960, the colonial correspondent of *La Libre Belgique* wrote:

" . . . The *Force Publique* remains the miracle of the Congo which was Belgian. The F.P. is today the only solid institution of this country. Its soldiers have an *esprit de corps:* They are no longer Bangala, Bayaka, or Bakongo, they are from the *Force Publique*. They all have the same martial air, the same ear-to-ear smile, the same efficiency too. The *Force Publique* has made a prodigious demonstration: well led, well trained, the Congolese are capable of achieving great things."[1]

Events the day that the article appeared considerably embarrassed a capable journalist; yet with the immediate turmoil of the mutiny now fading into history, the statement regains its relevance. No summary of the Congolese political system can ignore the instruments of force within the society. In any political community lacking in consensus, a sense of its identity, and adequate legitimation for its political structures, the role of force must necessarily be large.

Indeed, the role of the military throughout the underdeveloped portions of the world had been until recently greatly underestimated; as Lucien Pye observes: "Only a few years ago it was generally assumed that the future of the newly emergent states would be determined largely by the activities of their Westernized intellectuals, their socialistically inclined bureaucrats, their nationalist ruling parties, and possibly their menacing Communist parties. It

[1] J. K. (Van der Dussen), quoted in *Congo 1960,* I, 363.

occurred to few students of the under-developed regions that the military might become the critical group in shaping the course of nation-building."[2]

The scholar, as several contributors to the RAND-sponsored study of *The Role of the Military in Underdeveloped Countries* remark, has tended to have a strong bias against the military and hence an aversion to serious examination of its sociology and place in the nation-building process. Yet in Asia the army has proved to be an important, if not preeminent, factor in Laos, South Korea, South Vietnam, Burma, Indonesia, and Pakistan. In the Middle East, the officer corps have come virtually to incarnate nationalism and the desire for modernization in countries where traditional monarchies have disappeared; only Lebanon is a real exception. In Africa, only three countries had significant armies at the time of independence. In Sudan, the army assumed power two years after independence, in 1958; in Algeria, the *Armée de Libération Nationale* played a pivotal role in the power struggle of July 1962 and remains a major factor in the political equation; and in the Congo, the army first overthrew the independence settlement by its mutiny, then in September 1960 imposed a caretaker government. Unemployed ex-soldiers murdered President Olympio of Togo in January 1963; in late 1963, army units were involved in uprisings in Dahomey and Gabon. In January 1964, consecutive mutinies in Tanganyika, Uganda, and Kenya nearly disrupted three relatively stable regimes.

The role of the military has by no means been entirely negative; few could dispute that the officers have brought reasonably successful government to the United Arab Republic or Pakistan. In the early stages of political development, there are indeed certain characteristics of the mili-

[2] "Armies in the Process of Political Modernization," in John J. Johnson (ed), *The Role of the Military in Underdeveloped Countries* (Princeton, N. J.: Princeton University Press, 1962), p. 69.

tary which are of very positive value to the polity. As Edward Shils has remarked, the army "is ubiquitous, it recruits from all parts of the country, and, most important of all, it is national in its symbolism."[3] Further, Pye adds, armies "as rationalized structures, are capable of relating means to ends."[4] The experience of military service provides a mechanism, an intensive acculturative experience for the recruit, and a shift from traditional to rational behavior; the good soldier becomes a modernized man. The structure of discipline in the army provides a relatively high degree of psychological security; acculturation proceeds in a very different environment then for the individual who migrates to an urban center with its anxieties and tensions.[5]

Nature of the Force Publique

In the Congo, as elsewhere, the army has received relatively little attention from researchers. What has been written is of a practical bent and deals with the effectiveness of the army as a military machine, or its history.[6] Yet the *Force Publique* was the first major avenue to modernity for the Congolese; in the early years, its acculturative impact was of great importance. As the Lovanium students observed, "on the morrow of colonization, the Congolese were divided into two classes, soldiers and natives."[7] Even before the missions, the army was able through its iron discipline and the complete removal of the recruit from

[3] Edward Shils, "The Military in the Political Development of the New States," in *ibid.*, p. 32.

[4] *Ibid.*, p. 74.

[5] *Ibid.*, pp. 80-81.

[6] The most thorough study of the *Force Publique* deals only with its early days; for this, see *La Force Publique de sa Naissance à 1914.* See also F. Ermans, "Organisation militaire de la Colonie," *Encyclopédie du Congo Belge*, pp. 815-26; "Mutineries au Congo Belge," *Bulletin Militaire*, No. 21 (March 1947), pp. 20-84. For more recent history of the *Force Publique* and ANC, see Janssens, *op. cit.*; Francis Monheim, *Mobutu, l'homme seul* (Brussels: Éditions Actuelles, 1962); *Congo 1960*, I, 333-70.

[7] *Manifeste des universitaires congolais*, p. 2.

his traditional moorings to create a group of persons sharply distinct from the rest of the population. In the early years of this century, many of the earliest non-traditional towns were composed of former soldiers who refused to return to their own clan. Special "villages *fin-de-terme*" were reserved for them; some of these still carry this name, and can be found scattered about, especially in Sankuru district. Both the administration and private sector were eager to hire former non-commissioned officers as headmen, or, in a number of cases, as "chiefs."

The nature of the *Force Publique* diverged sharply from that of other tropical African armies. Unlike Britain, France, and Portugal, Belgium would send no metropolitan troops for the colonial conquest. Nor could the Free State long bear the moderate cost of recruiting "auxiliaries" along the west coast of Africa, or in Zanzibar. The Congo had to be quickly organized so that it could conquer itself, so to speak. Although the *Force Publique* was formally founded only in 1888, by 1897 it numbered 14,000, of whom 12,000 were Congolese.[8] Throughout most of its existence, its strength was somewhat over 20,000. The European complement of officers and non-commissioned officers was small; during the most difficult part of the conquest, the Arab Wars of 1892-1894, there were only 120 Europeans with the army in all of the Congo. By 1905, there were 360 Europeans, and in 1953, only 788.[9]

The Belgians endured a searing experience in 1895 when the "Batetela" of the Luluabourg garrison mutinied and killed their commanding officer. This was followed by a revolt of the "Batetela" in the Dhanis column marching for the Nile in 1897, then a third mutiny near Boma in 1900, again attributed to Batetela. The lesson drawn from these experiences was that the army had to be very carefully ethnically integrated, in such a way as to prevent the domination of any

[8] Ermans, *loc. cit.*, p. 816.
[9] *Ibid.*, p. 824; Slade, *King Leopold's Congo*, p. 173.

single ethnic group at any unit level, even the squad. The army with its very small corps of expatriate officers would only be a secure instrument if it were so scrambled that no group resistance could emerge; discipline could then operate on the isolated individual, who by himself posed little threat. The Belgians could bank upon the postulate that being Congolese or even African would be an insufficient factor of solidarity for the black troop to unite against the white officer.

The impetus for ethnic integration was given renewed life when the Luluabourg garrison again mutinied in 1944. The findings of the inquests held on this disaster centered upon the revelation that there had been carelessness and dereliction in the application of the scrambling principle. Instructions were reiterated that at least four tribes had to be represented in each platoon. Further, care was urged in the categorization of recruits from the cities, where new forms of ethnic identification were emerging: "In the great African cities, those from the central basin call themselves Mongos. Those from Luebo, Kabinda, Kamina . . . label themselves Kasais. The black proletariat of the cities is progressively losing its consciousness of small tribal differences. . . . These are elements which one must take into account, to avoid endangering security. . . ."[10]

In the early days, the Free State tended to concentrate its recruiting of soldiers among the "martial races"; this reputation was acquired by the Bangala, Batetela-Bakusu, and Azande.[11] The great mutinies showed the dangers of this policy to the colonial system, and thereafter levies for the *Force Publique* were distributed throughout the Congo. Thus in 1960, the composition of the army, probably more than any other institution, including the civil service, reflected with reasonable accuracy the population as a whole.

A considerable effort was deployed to instill in the

[10] "Mutineries au Congo belge," *loc. cit.*, p. 36.
[11] *La Force Publique de sa Naissance à 1914*, pp. 39, 52-54.

Force Publique a loyalty to itself and to the great symbols of the colony, such as Leopold II and the Belgian crown. *"Congo uni, pays fort"* was the slogan of the army in 1959-1960. This was done through an active troop information program, troop newspapers, and the organization of veterans' association. Much of this was assimilated by the troops, and is very visible in the attitudes of the officer corps today. The army is not partial to pan-African nationalism, but its loyalty to the political community as a whole exceeds that of most other sectors of Congolese society.

The Congo army was more a national body than other tropical African military forces.[12] The careful ethnic integration and sense of a national mission enhanced its potential role in the nation-building process. The failure of political parties or representative institutions to make much contribution was a de facto abdication to the civil service and the army. In most of independent tropical Africa, the scales have thus far tipped in the other direction. The political sector has been substantially better organized, and the armies much less so. It is thus hardly surprising that the Congo should have been, after the Sudan, the second African state to experience a military *coup d'etat* (excluding the UAR).

Africanization: Background to the Mutiny

The events of independence, however, were a fearsome strain for the Congolese army. Overnight, the whole of its

[12] For data on other African armies, see James S. Coleman and Belmont Brice, Jr., "The Role of the Military in Sub-Saharan African," Johnson, *op. cit.*, pp. 376-79; William Gutteridge, *Armed Forces in New States* (London, Institute of Rare Relations, 1962); George Weeks, "The Armies of Africa," *Africa Report*, Vol. 9, No. 1 (January 1964), pp. 4-21. On the general topic of military role in developing nations, see Morris Janowitz, *The Military in the Political Development of New Nations* (Chicago: University of Chicago Press, 1964); Fred R. von der Mehden and Charles W. Anderson, "Political Action of the Military in the Developing Areas," *Social Research*, Vol. 28, No. 4 (Winter 1961).

officer corps disappeared. Soon thereafter, the political fragmentation of the country was reflected in the emergence of four separate armies. Leaderless bands of mutineers committed atrocities without number in 1960-1961; the new Congolese officers had a daily battle to regain control over the troops and to restore discipline to the army. The successful mutiny of an entire army against its entire officer corps is a phenomenon virtually unique in history.

The immediate cause for the breakdown in the army, which was described briefly in Chapter XIII, was the implausible obstinacy of its last European commander, General Janssens, in refusing to permit any real acceleration in the Africanization program he had devised, or to make any other psychologically reassuring gestures to the troops. Although the General argued that this was simply a desire to maintain standards, in his *apologia pro vita sua* he makes clear that there was also another dimension: " . . . the strict and absolute discipline . . . was based especially on the prestige of the leaders and . . . the prestige of the officer was reinforced by the prestige of the white. . . . One could not sap, later, the prestige of the European without sapping that of the officers. An Africanization which could only be achieved by a devaluation of the ranks, would necessarily compromise this indispensable discipline."[13]

The General indeed had a little plan for Africanization, but in its concept, scope, and pace, even without the illumination of subsequent events, it appears singularly inadequate. In 1953, when independence began to loom as a possibility in the Sudan, a British program of accelerated officer training produced nearly 400 new junior officers by the time of independence in 1956;[14] the Sudan was not conspicuous for its advanced educational system. At the end of 1958, when the Working Group was completing

[13] Janssens, *op. cit.*, p. 23.
[14] Johnson, *op. cit.*, p. 368.

work on a plan which foresaw Congo independence in perhaps five years, a scheme was announced with great fanfare which would have produced fourteen second lieutenants after ten years.

With all the cautious empiricism that could be mustered, an Africanization program was launched in 1945. The "build-from-the-ground-up" approach was carried to its logical extreme; five primary schools, and later a secondary school, were established by the *Force Publique* itself, to train from the cradle up, primarily from the offspring of soldiers, the future officer candidates. Even had this timetable been adhered to, theoretically the first applicants for the Belgian Royal Military Academy should have entered in 1957, after the twelve-year primary-secondary cycle had been completed. However, in December 1958, it was announced that the first group had nearly completed junior high school. The *Ecole des Pupilles,* the *Force Publique*-operated secondary school in Luluabourg, accepted its first students in 1953, with an entering class of 28; only 14 of this group remained at the end of 1958.[15] And these had yet to complete secondary school, then the Royal Military Academy in Belgium, and finally the Junior Officer Academy. It was proudly announced that for the 1958-1959 entering class at the *Ecole des Pupilles,* out of 1,950 applicants, only 23 were selected. Africanization by this program would have taken generations. Further, it entirely excluded the possibility of promotion for the Congolese non-commissioned officers; only their children could profit from the new opportunities. The requirement that the potential officer corps should be largely inbred and had to be trained in army-run schools throughout their educational career is hard to reconcile with any inherent complexities of the military vocation.

Some concessions were made in the last months before

[15]"L'avenir de la Force Publique Congolaise—formation de spe-cialistes et d'officiers congolais," quoted in *Congo 1960,* I, 342.

independence, but these could hardly be said to have responded to the threat posed by a growing *malaise* in the army ranks. The ten-year plan was telescoped to four, and the first group of fourteen Congolese cadets went to Belgium in May 1960 to prepare for entry to the Royal Military Academy. A warrant officer school was opened in Luluabourg in September 1959, and the first group of nine non-commissioned officers began the course. On March 25, 1960, it was announced that a competitive examination would be organized in all of the military camps of the Congo June 27-29 for entry to an officer training program; candidates had to be between sixteen and twenty-six, however. This still excluded most of the non-commissioned ranks in the army, as the grade of corporal or higher in the old *Force Publique* could usually only be earned after long service. Only on June 10 was it announced that competitive examinations to accede to the officer corps would be offered within the ranks; warrant officers even had the hope of promotion by seniority. None of these last-minute measures would have produced any Congolese officers before 1962 at the very earliest.[16]

On July 8, however, the Council of Ministers decided to Africanize the entire command structure of the army, and to invite merely as councilors a number of Belgian officers, such as Colonels Henniquiau, Marlière, Maertens, who had the reputation of being sympathetic to Congolese desires for a more rapid transformation of the ANC than Janssens had prescribed. Lundula was designated Commander-in-Chief, with the rank of General, and Mobutu was named a Colonel, Chief-of-Staff. The formula for the selection of the new officer corps reversed the Belgian plan; it was a massive promotion of the non-commissioned grades. The government communiqué announcing the measures gave no details as to how they were to be carried out; apparently the central authorities hoped only to exercise some control over

[16] *Ibid.*, pp. 343-46.

the nomination of field grade officers. The company grade officers were then designated by the newly appointed post and unit commanders; apparently, in some instances, the troops participated in this process, giving it the character of an election. However, in most instances, length of service and non-commissioned rank were key criteria in winning promotion.[17] On July 9, delegations were sent to different parts of the Congo to superintend the installation of the new Congolese officers. Lumumba and Kasavubu toured the garrisons of the Lower Congo; Kasongo, President of the Chamber of Representatives, and Colonel Henniquiau visited Stanleyville; Colonel Nkokolo, newly named as commander of the key Leopoldville military camp, was sent to Elisabethville; and Colonel Mobutu himself visited the outposts in his native Equateur.

Emergence of Mobutu

During the following months, the ANC was for the most part a "disorderly rabble," to borrow UN Congo Chief Dayal's description. The junior officers had little authority over their troops. The political crisis in Leopoldville saw many of the leading political figures seeking to make use of bands of soldiers from their region or ethnic group. The curious result of this was that Mobutu's *coup d'etat* of September was rendered possible, based on his firm control of a very small number of men. The bulk of the army was simply too disorganized to play a role; at this point, it was capable of unified action only in support of its corporate grievances. These were the regular payment of the sharply

---

[17] The extent to which lower-ranking commissioned grades were filled by election remains a matter of dispute. ANC officers interviewed by the writer denied that this had taken place. In the Army ranks there is a curious legend emerging about the mutiny, which reinterprets the event as an unprovoked flight by European officers, and fails to include any recollection of the misdeeds of the mutineers. Mobutu's biographer, Monheim, claims that elections were Lumumba's idea, vigorously opposed by Mobutu; *op. cit.*, p. 98.

increased salaries and resistance to UN moves to disarm them.

The UN initially assumed that the Congolese army should be entirely disarmed then reorganized and retrained under UN auspices. General Alexander, a British officer commanding the Ghanaian troops, began the process by disarming the Leopoldville garrison beginning on July 15. For a brief period, the Congolese government had agreed to the Alexander plan. However, the necessary conditions for the disarmament of the army to be acceptable were the rapid retreat of Belgian troops and vigorous UN action in the Katanga. With Belgian detachments remaining in Katanga while Tshombe was organizing his own gendarmery, and Hammarskjold's fateful retreat at Elisabethville on August 6 indicating that no immediate UN action was envisaged against the Katanga regime, the Lumumba government was no longer willing to tolerate the disarmament of its army. This in its turn permitted the ANC to be the arbiter of the crisis in September.

Chief-of-Staff Mobutu during the July-September period was able to win the support or at least the tolerance of the older elements in the army, as well as control of the elite *Prévôté Militaire* (Military Police), and a newly-created "commando" battalion based at Thysville. He had two vital advantages over his commanding officer, General Lundula: in his seven years' service, from 1950 through 1956, in the *Force Publique*, he had developed a wide set of acquaintances among the non-commissioned officers; General Lundula's thirty-month service had been during World War II. Secondly, Colonel Mobutu was a resident of Leopoldville, and had all the advantages of being on home ground; as a journalist and MNC/L militant, he was well-linked in the political circuits. General Lundula, on the other hand, had never lived in Leopoldville; he had spent most of his career in Jadotville, where he was well-known and deeply respected. When Kasavubu revoked him as

448

Commander-in-Chief on September 12, Lundula made no resistance, and the command of Leopoldville passed effectively into the hands of Mobutu.[18]

Another critical factor in Mobutu's success was his placement of officers upon whom he could rely in strategically located garrisons. The military camp in Leopoldville itself was placed under the command of a Mukongo known to be loyal to Kasavubu, Nkokolo. The only other military camp close enough to Leopoldville to be able to influence the situation was Thysville; this camp was commanded by Colonel Bobozo, who had been Mobutu's drill sergeant at Luluabourg in 1953 and 1954.[19] Also, Mobutu himself had supervised the designation of new officers in Equateur and at the key military complex of Luluabourg. The first crop of nine who had been trained at the Luluabourg Warrant Officer School, beginning during September 1959, were placed in command of the infantry regiments. With the help of Moroccan General Kettani, then heading the UN military group charged with helping to reorganize the Congolese army, Mobutu also constituted a battalion of parachutists to serve as a Pretorian Guard. This group, now 800 strong, was stationed around Mobutu's residence and until 1962 was under the command of Major Tshatshi, also of unquestioned fidelity to Mobutu. At Thysville, Mobutu also had at his disposition an armored squadron, only a few hours from Leopoldville.[20]

The installation of the *Collège des Commissaires* and his own designation as Commander-in-Chief gave Mobutu the opportunity he needed to consolidate control over the army.

[18] Monheim, *Mobutu*, p. 123.
[19] *Ibid.*, pp. 28-29.
[20] A distinction need be made in 1960 between the support of officers, and the effective support of the units they commanded. At the time of the coup, Mobutu could only count on a small number of disciplined troops; however, the placement of officers on whom he could rely in Kasai and Equateur at least assured that these units would not be likely to be used against him. Only as relative discipline was slowly restored were these units a real asset to Mobutu.

The student commissioners, who were only reluctantly accepted as a de facto authority by the UN, were completely dependent on the protection that those units controlled by Mobutu were able to afford them. Power at this point was a highly relative concept; a little could go a long way, given the nearly complete absence of any effective competitor. The ability to move a few armed men about Leopoldville was of decisive importance.

ANC Divided: Leopoldville and Stanleyville

Mobutu set to work providing himself with an officer corps on which he could depend and which had some rudimentary training. He had only a minimum of Belgian assistance; after the mutiny, only seven Belgian military personnel remained with the troops, including three chaplains.[21] In addition, Colonel Marlière remained during most of this period in Brazzaville, and was of some assistance. Finally, on December 15, 1960, Mobutu called back Colonel Marlière and nine other Belgian officers to rejoin the army as technicians. None of the Belgian officers wore uniforms or exercised any command position; their experience and counsel were certainly of real help to the ANC, but the salient fact is that direct Belgian involvement in the reorganization of the ANC was not large.[22]

In Stanleyville, the control of the third groupement[23] was central to the establishment of the Gizenga government. Although for a time Mobutu seemed to be gaining the upper hand, by November the Lumumbist groups had won out. On November 26, General Lundula arrived in Stanleyville and took command; in the following weeks, he succeeded in bringing under his control the troops of Orientale. In Bukavu, the garrison remained loosely under

---

[21] *Ibid.*, p. 189. These included two at Leopoldville, two at Thysville, one at Irebu (Equateur), and three at Luluabourg.

[22] *Ibid.*, p. 190.

[23] A *groupement* is roughly equivalent to a regiment.

Leopoldville control until December 1960, when Stanley-ville authority was established.

Thus, by the end of 1960 the ANC had broken into two groups, one at Stanleyville under Lundula, and one in Leopoldville under Mobutu. Meanwhile, South Kasai and Katanga had created new armies from scratch. So each of the four fragments of the Congo had an army of its own. General Lundula's Stanleyville forces, ironically, were paid for by Leopoldville; their salaries were met from Leopold-ville's resources, to which Orientale at that point was making virtually no contribution. However, Lundula's forces suffered a substantial handicap in being unable to receive any effective aid, either in material supplies or technical assistance. Although Lundula was able to bring the Orien-tale detachments under reasonable control, his authority over troops dispatched to North Katanga, Kasai, and Kivu was tenuous. UN Civil Operation Chief Dayal remarked in February 1961, "In the military field, the authority of General Lundula over the ANC troops stationed in Kivu has never been effective."[24] One of the curious aspects of this period of schizophrenia in the ANC was that the composition of the troops remained mixed; many soldiers from areas controlled by Leopoldville served under General Lundula, and vice versa. Both sides augmented their strength by recruitment, presumably among groups deemed to be friendly. On independence day, the army had 23,076 troops; a year later, the strength had shot up to 35,000, not including Katanga or South Kasai.[25]

A further complication in the Stanleyville picture was the private militia established by Gizenga, which some sources

[24] In a note on February 22, 1961, quoted in *Congo 1960*, II, 1017. Verhaegen gives as the strength of Lundula's forces in early 1961 a battalion at Stanleyville, two companies at Basoko (Orientale), a bat-talion at Watsa (Orientale), a battalion at Rumangabo and Goma (Kivu), two companies at Bukavu, and 200 men in North Katanga, *Congo 1961*, pp. 200-01.

[25] "Traitements, grèves, et politique d'austérite," *Etudes Con-golaises*, II, No. 5 (May 1961), p. 11.

claim amounted to a battalion recruited among the Stanley-ville youth. Kashamura tried to do the same at Bukavu. These groups were not under Lundula's orders.[26] Also, the Balubakat youth group had been armed in North Katanga, creating another uncontrollable and undisciplined body of troops.[27]

Other Armies: Katanga and South Kasai

In Katanga, the first acts of the Tshombe government were to call in Belgian troops to disarm and expel the ANC detachments in Katanga. Under Belgian Major Crèvecoeur, a Katanga gendarmery was created at top speed. At first, Tshombe and his Belgian advisers wanted order maintained and protection against an ANC invasion assured by Belgian troops for one year or eighteen months. Both Belgium and Katanga, however, had to give way before the Security Council resolution of August 8 and growing international pressures. The relief of Belgian troops by UN forces began on August 12, and on September 10 Belgium announced that the withdrawal of all "operational troops" in Katanga had been completed.

Substantial technical assistance was given by Belgium to the Katanga gendarmery.[28] All of the small aircraft of the *Force Publique* were flown to Katanga and put at Tshombe's disposition. Newspaper accounts in early September indicated that Katanga had received 25 airplanes, 100 tons of arms and munitions, 89 officers from the *Force Publique*, 326 Belgian junior officers and soldiers who had volunteered for detached service in Katanga, and 70 agents of the Belgian gendarmery.[29] By September, the Katanga gen-

26 Monheim, *Mobutu*, p. 240.
27 *Congo 1961*, p. 311.
28 Belgian assistance to the Katanga is detailed by Gérard-Libois, *Sécession au Katanga*, pp. 127-41.
29 The *London Daily Mail*, from its Brussels correspondent, September 10, 1960, quoted in *Congo 1960*, II, 771-72. See also Gérard-Libois, *op. cit.*, p. 177-91.

darmery was in a position to undertake its first military operations against the dissident populations in the Balubakat zones of North Katanga.

The Katanga gendarmery had several unusual features, in addition to the important degree of Belgian assistance in its early organizational phases. Beginning in late 1960, European mercenaries were recruited for a special "international company," composed largely of adventurers recruited in Southern Rhodesia, South Africa, and Europe. By February 1961, the *affreux* numbered 200.[30] At the time of the first UN moves to remove the mercenaries forcibly, their number had grown to 442. In most cases, these operated as separate units, although at times they worked in tandem with Katanga troops.

Secondly, the gendarmery was almost entirely constituted of newly recruited troops. Only 300 of the 2,800 Congolese *Force Publique* soldiers stationed in Katanga at the time of the mutiny were retained.[31] It is difficult to know exactly the number of troops in the gendarmery; UN reports set the figure at about 11,600 in mid-1961,[32] but the figure of 19,000 was generally cited to the writer during a visit to Elisabethville in August 1962. The recruitment was almost entirely restricted to areas which had been loyal to the Conakat in the May elections. Commanding the gendarmery for its first year was Major (later Colonel) Crèvecoeur. After he departed, under UN pressure, General Masuku Muké nominally took over command; after the first UN-Katanga hostilities in August and September, 1961, the Katanga information services for the first time began to project the image of an Africanized force with "*Muké le victorieux*" purportedly in charge.[33]

On the vulnerable frontiers of Katanga, some of the pro-Conakat traditional chiefs were permitted to maintain their

[30] *Congo 1961,* p. 233.
[31] Conor Cruise O'Brien, *To Katanga and Back,* p. 220.
[32] Gérard-Libois, *op. cit.,* p. 192.
[33] O'Brien, *op. cit.,* pp. 223-24.

own gendarmes. This was true in the case of Baluba paramount chief Kasongo Nyembo, who had supported the Conakat from the outset. He recruited a battalion of men who were given modern arms and Katanga gendarmery uniforms but were in fact under his command. His crucial location on the Kasai frontier, near the Kamina air base, made it seem necessary to establish the "Kasongo Nyembo's Own" infantry battalion; the virtual autonomy this gave the chief was a small price for Tshombe to pay. This obviously resulted in a substantial accretion to traditional power. Whether these troops have been completely disarmed and dissolved remains to be seen, although Kasongo Nyembo was arrested and jailed in Leopoldville in December 1963.[34] The Bayeke chief, Antoine Mwenda-Munongo, likewise had a detachment of his own warriors with modern equipment.

The little kingdom of South Kasai likewise organized its own gendarmery after the ANC invasion of August and September, 1960. This last army numbered some 3,000 men in 1961 and was assisted by nine European officers.[35] It was obviously not a match either in organization, armament, or training for any of the other three; its commanding "general" was 22-year-old Floribert Dinanga. This force was large enough to launch offensives to wrest control of Kabinda, Dimbelenge, and Lusambo to the detriment of Luluabourg (and the local populations). In its formative period, a certain amount of aid had come from Katanga; at two points, Kalonji signed military protocols with Elisabethville. The gendarmery had a certain elan in its early days, when the Baluba seemed everywhere to be victimized

[34] *Le Progrès*, December 30, 1963. The Kasongo Nyembo on January 4, 1963, agreed with UN authorities for a regrouping of troops under his authority and their cooperation with the UN. There is no indication, however, that they have been disbanded, or will be really reintegrated into the ANC. Louis Mandala, "Chronique des événements politiques congolais," *Etudes Congolaises*, IV, No. 3, (March 1963), 56.

[35] *Le Monde*, March 5-6, 1961.

by the circumstances of independence and the multiple external threats engendered a reaction of strong ethnic solidarity. However, by 1962, when the South Kasai state was rent by internal feuding and no longer seemed threatened from the outside, this impetus to effectiveness disappeared. When Kalonji made his spectacular escape from Leopoldville in September 1962 and briefly recaptured power at Bakwanga, the rapid dispatch of two ANC battalions was sufficient to provoke the flight of both Kalonji and "General" Dinanga, and the rallying of the South Kasai gendarmery to the central government.[36] The greater part of these troops were absorbed into the ANC in 1963.

Reunification of the Army

One of the most difficult problems in reunifying the Congo has been that of bringing these several military fragments together. In the case of the two wings of the ANC, a major obstacle was the question of who was the legal Commander-in-Chief. According to Stanleyville, the revocation of General Lundula in September 1960 by Kasavubu had been illegal. Leopoldville, however, maintained that Mobutu's elevation to the rank of Commander-in-Chief was irrevocable, and that Lundula had been legally removed from all command functions. The "government of reconciliation" unanimously invested by the Lovanium Parliament did not immediately solve the military problem. From August 16 to 18, Prime Minister Adoula made a formal visit to Stanleyville, to mark Stanleyville's recognition of the new coalition government. Subsequently, a Stanleyville emissary in Cairo on September 2 published what purported to be an accord reached between Adoula and Gizenga during the Prime Minister's visit; a key clause in this was an alleged pledge to "maintain General Lundula as Commander-in-Chief of the unified army."[37]

[36] *Congo 1960*, II, 801-07; *Congo 1961*, pp. 244-49; *Courrier d'Afrique*, October 4, 1962; *Présence Congolaise*, April 6, 1963.
[37] *Congo 1961*, p. 499.

Another element of discord was General Lundula's desire to throw the ANC into the campaign to eliminate the Katanga secession. Neither Leopoldville, the UN, nor Western powers were enthusiastic about this course of action. On September 14, Lundula cabled Adoula to announce, "My troops are ready to march on Katanga the moment that orders are received from Leopoldville." Mobutu's *"Bureau d' action psychologique"* riposted with a communiqué denouncing "certain politicians who try to use the troops under their control for political ends," and adding, "It is not for the ex-General Lundula, revoked by the Chief of State, but supported by certain politicians, to put his troops at the disposition of the government. . . . The whole *Armée Nationale Congolaise* is at the disposition of the government."[38]

At the end of October, a rapprochement was achieved with the arrival in Leopoldville of a military delegation from Stanleyville. A joint offensive was launched, with Lundula's troops invading Katanga from the north and Mobutu's from the west.[39] This provided a basis for unification of the army; on November 11, General Lundula arrived in Leopoldville for the first time since 1960. Lundula tacitly accepted the Leopoldville interpretation of his legal situation as having been revoked; he agreed to serve under Mobutu, retaining his rank as Major-General and commander of the third *groupement*.

Lundula's acceptance of these conditions marked the beginning of the end for Gizenga's attempt to reconstruct a power base in Stanleyville. Gizenga reacted to the news of Lundula-Mobutu reconcilation by trying to replace Lundula with Colonel Pakassa, who was ethnically related to Gizenga. Pakassa was immediately discredited when his men

[38] *Ibid.,* p. 508.
[39] Lundula's troops, moving through mostly friendly territory, penetrated to Albertville, while Mobutu ordered his troops to halt near the Kasai frontier, after a few light skirmishes with Katanga forces, and some serious acts of indiscipline in Luluabourg and Luputa.

massacred the thirteen Italian airmen at Kindu.[40] Lundula had resumed control of the third *groupement,* which still contained some officers and units loyal to Gizenga. The General continued to exert pressure for a more vigorous participation of the ANC in Katanga, and clearly had some reservations about Mobutu; he had told a correspondent of *Le Monde* in May 1961, "I am persuaded that General Mobutu has sold out to the Belgians—we have proof—but the Mobutists are our brothers."[41] However, Lundula was also motivated by a strong devotion to legality. Although he no doubt had some sympathy with the political position, if not the person, of Gizenga, his role in ending the Gizengist dissidence was decisive; it was Lundula who arrested Gizenga in January 1962. In Kivu, Lundula accompanied Prime Minister Adoula on December 17, 1961, to Bukavu, where a cluster of officers loyal to Gizenga and the Stanleyville "commandos" had kept the area in a state of permanent insecurity. Provincial President Miruho demanded that the army be brought under control, as his provincial government had to remain under the constant protection of the Malayan UN detachments. Lundula agreed to see to the transfer of the Gizengist officers and the removal of the "commandos"; this completely transformed the situation in Kivu.[42]

[40] Pakassa was present at Kindu, nominally in command of the troops, when these atrocities occured. However, the UN report on the events exonerated Pakassa of any responsibility for having personally ordered the assassinations; his fault was only incapacity to control those under his command, and his efforts to conceal the truth from the UN for four days. Pakassa was arrested by the central government in January 1962; in 1963, he escaped and joined the CNL in Brazzaville as "military councilor." He was arrested in Paris in December 1963 en route to Moscow and Peking for traveling on a false passport. Although extradition requests by Belgium, Italy, and Congo were refused, he was sentenced on this charge to one month in prison in February 1964.

[41] *Congo 1961,* p. 202.

[42] *Ibid.,* pp. 477-78. This interpretation was confirmed to the writer by a number of interviews in Bukavu.

The Katanga gendarmery represented a far more difficult problem. Katanga insisted that it not be simply disbanded and that its commander General Muké be permitted to retain his rank. But during the prolonged 1962 negotiations between Adoula and Tshombe, no firm agreement was reached on whether the gendarmery would remain a separate entity, merely pledging its allegiance to Leopoldville, or whether its troops would be totally integrated into the ANC through being incorporated into other units. Further, Katanga wanted a guarantee that the ANC itself would not be deployed except on a token basis in Katanga. Both during the Adoula-Tshombe talks and under the terms of the U Thant Plan in 1962, the assumption was that the entire Katanga gendarmery would be absorbed one way or another.[43] However, since the secession was eventually terminated by force and not negotiation, Leopoldville did not feel obliged to carry out this costly promise to inflate the military ranks by 25 percent. Only 2,000-3,000 were actually absorbed into the ANC.[44] Nearly 10,000 men simply disappeared, with their weapons; a number are reported to have regrouped in Angola.[45] Most were brought into the ANC when Tshombe came to power.

Character of the ANC

With ANC unity restored, Mobutu gradually strengthened his position during 1963 by a careful rotation of officers and the removal from command positions of those who appeared wanting in enthusiasm for the Leopoldville regime. By the end of 1962 General Lundula had been relieved of his command of the third *groupement* in Stanley-

[43] Gérard-Libois, *op. cit.*, p. 265, 274.

[44] J. Anthony Lukas, "The Congo Tries to Build an Army," *New York Times Magazine,* July 21, 1963. Similar figures were provided the writer in interviews with ANC officers, June-July, 1963.

[45] "Storm Signals in Katanga," *The Times* (London), March 2-3, 1964.

458

ville and brought back to Leopoldville as military councilor to Defense Minister Anany.[46] Lundula's old deputy in Stanleyville, Major Leonard Losso, was also brought to Leopoldville and given the honorific post of commander of the embryonic Congo air force. Former Katanga gendarmery commander Muké fills a headquarters position as well.

Meanwhile, the key command positions were given to officers unquestionably loyal to Mobutu. Colonel Leonard Mulamba replaced Lundula in the crucial Stanleyville post; he quickly established his own authority and transferred officers suspected of nostalgia for Gizenga days. Mulamba is an energetic and decisive officer; he frequently tours the dispersed outposts of his farflung command area (all of former Orientale and Kivu provinces), and has been prompt and firm in dealing with occasional disciplinary problems.[47] The military command of a newly formed fourth *groupement* for South Katanga was entrusted to Colonel (now General) Louis Bobozo. The campaign against the Mulele insurrection in South Kwilu, beginning in December 1963, was led by Major Tshatshi, who earlier had commanded Mobutu's elite paratroop battalion.

A constant stream of proposals to "retrain" the ANC had come forward ever since the mutiny. Initially, these assumed the disbanding and total reorganization of the army; however, it soon became clear that this approach was wholly impractical. In January 1963, Mobutu put forth his own retraining plan; this called for the assistance of Belgium, Israel, Italy, Norway, and Canada, under UN supervision. The UN found the NATO complexion of the training group unacceptable and declined to sponsor the scheme. The plan finally became simply a Belgian project, with a small assist from Israel. Beginning in mid-1963, 170 Belgian officers

[46] Lundula has accepted his removal with apparent good grace; he is near retirement age and seems devoid of personal ambition.

[47] The material on the ANC in 1963 is drawn in good part from interviews with a number of officers in June-July, 1963, including Mulamba.

were scheduled to be attached to the ANC to organize the retraining. However, by the end of 1963, only a part of the Belgian contingent had arrived, and no formal retraining program had been launched. On the other hand, the expanded Belgian assistance to the ANC officer corps could be expected to contribute toward its effectiveness.

Another important development is the growing number of young officers and sergeants who have received the six to eighteen-month training course in Belgium. By July 1963, 380 had returned from training in Belgium and another 300 were then receiving instruction in the former metropole.[48] The first small contingent of Congolese graduates from the Belgian Royal Military Academy returned in 1963. Those chosen for training in Belgium have for the most part been young and somewhat better educated than the older generation of *Force Publique* veterans.

Despite the improvements, the ANC is far from being a fully disciplined body. It was involved in several clashes with civil populations during 1963, with at least two leading to extensive casualties. There was in each case some provocation, but the army's reaction was in general out of proportion to the requirements of the situation.[49] Still, these excesses were a far cry from the anarchic indiscipline of

[48] Lukas, *loc. cit.*

[49] The most serious disorders were in former Kasai province, both in January 1963. At Katanga near Mweka on the BCK rail line, a band of Lulua irregulars trying to enlarge Luluabourg province ambushed an ANC patrol. The retribution was swift, and about 400 deaths resulted. Meanwhile, in South Kasai the ANC was called in to put down a revolt by Kalonjist bands; casualty estimates ran as high as several thousand, but these may have been exaggerated. In Boma, in Bakongo country, hostility of the local population to the "stranger" troops led to serious clashes between soldiers and civilians in March 1963, although no deaths resulted. Throughout 1963, sporadic incidents occurred between the ANC and both European and African civilians in South Katanga. Mutual suspicion remained high, and the risks of more serious incidents remained. At the time of writing, no reliable casualty figures were available to indicate the scope of ANC repressive action against Mulelist bands in Kwilu, beginning in December 1963.

1960; although brutal, the army is an instrument of established authority.

Within the officer ranks, new alignments were beginning to replace the old Leopoldville-Stanleyville divergence. Two basic groups could be seen emerging:

(1) The old non-coms, who had been promoted in 1960 to the top command posts. In some cases, typified by General Bobozo, these were little-educated men, who qualified mainly on the basis of their long service (in Bobozo's case, more than thirty years). Others, like Major Tshatshi, or Chief of Staff Major Jacques Puati, were young, although they had had several years of pre-1960 service. However, they could never be spared by Mobutu for overseas training.

(2) The young officers, markedly more educated and endowed with the prestige and self-confidence of overseas training. These were viewed with some reserve by the old non-coms, who expressed the characteristic veteran's distaste for the greenhorn and felt they needed a number of years experience as small unit leaders before they could be entrusted with important responsibilities. The young officers, on the contrary, were keenly aware of their higher educational attainments and superior training and were already impatient for promotion and command positions.

The military elite constitutes a distinct group in Congolese society, with a social experience very different from that of the political-administrative elite. Even when posted in camps near large cities, the officers do not belong to the same social circuits as other leaders. They are generally stationed outside their home region and frequently marry women of other ethnic groups. The careful ethnic integration of military units meant an ethnically diverse officers mess. Apoliticism is inculcated as a political ideal; army buildings are full of posters announcing that political discussions or activity are forbidden. The use of Lingala as the command language gives the army a linguistic unity.

In its deployment, the ANC follows the traditional pattern

set under the colonial administration. Under this scheme, the army was divided into two elements. On the one hand, there were the *troupes campées*, organized into three *groupements*[50] and stationed at half a dozen major military camps in various parts of the country. Their mission, a largely spurious one, was external security; the notion that a major military deployment was needed for these purposes grew out of the hardy legends from Free State days of a colony surrounded by *convoitises* and the minor military action in which *Force Publique* detachments had been involved in the two World Wars. On requisition by the civil authorities, these troops could be used for internal security purposes, with a hierarchy of procedures. At one end of the scale, there was the *promenade militaire*, which was a simple display of force; "despite their peaceful character, they are of a nature to greatly impress the native and give him a good idea of our power."[51] A police operation was similar, only under command of the local administrator; "it had no other object than to intimidate the inhabitants, to erect a barrier to movements of persons, and disperse mobs."[52] A military occupation came next; still under civilian command, this meant settling a sufficient armed force among a hostile population and requiring the population to feed and service them. Finally, there was a military operation; in this instance, the civilian authority simply gave the military free rein to take offensive action against dissident elements.[53]

The second major category of troops were those "in territorial service"; in 1959, these were rebaptized "gendarmes." They were deployed one company to a district, with an average of half a platoon per territory. They were directly under the command of the local administrator, and had a

[50] The 1st *groupement* covered the provinces of Katanga and Kasai, the 2nd Leopoldville and Equateur, and the 3rd Orientale and Kivu.
[51] *Receuil à l'usage des fonctionnaires,* p. 174.
[52] *Ibid.,* p. 141.
[53] Janssens, *op. cit.,* p. 61.

constabulary mission. These troops were under a less rigid disciplinary regime than those at the military camps, although both were equally part of the *Force Publique*. An ordinance of May 11, 1960, taken by the central Executive College, introduced an important innovation in giving the gendarmes the right of initiative under their military commander in the maintenance of order, without waiting for the formal request by the administrator.[54]

Provincial Police

Parallel to the gendarmery, a second internal security force operates at the local level, the territorial police. This body was organized separate from and in addition to the *Force Publique* in 1926, to carry out the more routine functions of maintenance of order. The police differ from the gendarmery in that they are locally recruited and thus, unlike the ANC, are ethnically related to the populations among whom they are stationed. Also, they are under provincial rather than national authority. They are less well armed than the gendarmes, but very much a factor at the local level. In every territory, there is a detachment of territorial police under the command of a police commissioner, responsible both to the territorial administrator and, since independence, to the provincial minister of the interior. Before independence, there was a definite overlapping in the functions of these two bodies.

There had been, beginning in 1954, a sharp, subterranean struggle between the *Force Publique* and the territorial police on their respective missions. Although Janssens oriented the army in its training and equipment toward the external defense role, he was also insistent on retaining the constabulary function. A Colonial Ministry study in 1954 recommended the establishment of a gendarmery based upon the territorial police. On December 30, 1955, Colonel Charlier of the Belgian national gendarmery was named to

[54] *Congo 1960*, I, 340-41.

head the reorganized force; he arrived in Leopoldville only in August 1956. Faced with the hostility of both the administration and the *Force Publique,* the reorganization never really was implemented. The official designation of the *Force Publique* detachments on territorial service as "gendarmes" ended the experiment.[55] Had this reform been implemented, and the army units assigned to territories been replaced entirely by "gendarmes" under provincial control and locally recruited, the post-independence implications for provincial-central relations would have been enormous.

After independence, the fact that these forces were under provincial authority took on entirely new significance, and the overlapping missions were a potential source of serious conflict. In Leopoldville, in late 1961 and early 1962, the remnants of the Lumumbist bloc made some use of the PSA control of the provincial Ministry of the Interior and hence the Leopoldville territorial police as a counterpoise to the ANC and the national security police. Skirmishes between provincial police forces over "disputed territories" after the creation of new provinces suggested another potential risk in the existence of small armies under provincial command; Lac Leopold II and Moyen-Congo clashed at Bolobo sporadically in 1963, and Lomami and Maniema forces narrowly averted a serious clash at Kasongo early the same year. The Leopoldville police mutinied in May 1963; only swift action by the ANC headed off a potentially serious threat to the central government.[56] The

---

[55] Ganshof van der Meersch, *Fin de la souveraineté belge au Congo,* pp. 385-86; see also Janssens' bitter complaints about this maneuver to reduce his jurisdiction, *op. cit.,* p. 27.

[56] The government siezed the occasion to make a display of forceful action by dismissing the entire police units involved in the short-lived mutiny, which was caused by material grievances. Subsequently, a number of those dismissed were recruited into other provincial police forces. In passing, it may be noted that this also permitted the Abako (which held the central Ministry of Interior) to rid Leopoldville of a police force it felt had been regionally recruited in Kwilu by the PSA provincial Minister of Interior.

ANC also disarmed and reorganized the Kwango police in August 1963.[57]

Although the police did not participate in the 1960 mutinies, the Europeans who had monopolized the commissioner ranks virtually all departed in the aftermath. It is generally believed that a large number of policemen shifted into the ANC, where pay became much better and more regular. At the same time, there was a massive recruitment of new elements into the police forces. Provincial leaders were quick to appreciate the political importance of having an armed force at their disposition; new police commissioners were named, with political reliability (as judged by provincial authorities) a major criterion. No one knows today for certain how large the police forces are for the entire Congo. Provinces tend not to report the full strength of their forces to the central government. One economist estimated the figure at the end of 1962 at 10,000 without counting Katanga, as against 7,000 for the entire country on the eve of independence.[58] A number of observers in the Congo felt this figure to be a minimum, perhaps underestimated by half.

Security Police

The final element in the military-police complex is the security police (*Sûreté*). In colonial days, this omnipresent, clandestine branch of the police had the missions of preserving internal security and the surveillance of immigration and movement of persons. It had eighty-one European agents and an enormous web of occasional "informers";[59] in early 1961, one Abako periodical published several pages of names and addresses of persons alleged to have been in-

[57] *Courrier d'Afrique,* August 30, 1962.

[58] Gérard Duprieé, "Les rémunérations dans l'ancienne province de Léopoldville," *Cahiers Economiques et Sociaux,* Université Lovanium, No. 2, (December 1962), p. 31; Ganshof van der Meersch, *Fin de la souveraineté belge,* p. 277.

[59] *Ibid.,* p. 379.

formers on Abako activities, according to documents left behind by the Belgians.[60] A security police report on the *Lulua Frères* movement which has become available since independence likewise reflects the extensiveness of the informer network, the penetration of organizations under their surveillance, and the *Sûreté's* access to bank records. The "gumshoes" were not particularly popular; the director of the security police wrote plaintively during the tenure of Resident Minister Ganshof van der Meersch the last six weeks of Belgian rule in the Congo, "At this time, for the first time in its existence, the services [of the Sûreté] . . . were used in an intensive manner."[61]

Reference should also be made to the existence of a separate security section attached to the *Force Publique*. In normal circumstances, the separate jurisdictions were relatively clear, but in times of crisis jurisdictional conflicts would come to the surface. Also, each province had, through the territorial police, its own security police group, in the pursuit of its legal mission of "collecting informaton."[62] This had particular relevance in Katanga, where the provincial administration and European opinion tended to be in chronic conflict with Leopoldville.

Lumumba regarded the control of the *Sûreté* as an important element in consolidation of MNC/L hegemony. It was to be under the Ministry of the Interior, whose first incumbent was MNC/L leader Gbenye. The first director was Christophe Muzungu, a Musongye who had been a faithful MNC lieutenant since 1958 and had remained loyal to Lumumba after the July 1959 split in the MNC. Lumumba's opponents claimed that during the brief period

[60] *Kongo dia Ngunga*, April 11, 1961. This journal was edited by the first president of Abako, Edmond Nzeza-Nlandu; the following issue appeared more than two months later with apologies for the delay resulting from a suspension because of publication of an "article threatening security."

[61] Ganshof van der Meersch, *Fin de la souveraineté belge*, p. 373.

[62] *Ibid.*, p. 377.

of Lumumba's effective rule the security police had been entirely politicized and heavily infused with Batetela-Bakusu elements. The failure of the *Sûreté* to play an effective role on Lumumba's behalf at the time of the revocation and the Mobutu takeover, however, suggests that this may have been more of a desire than a reality. Any leader seeking to reinforce his position obviously needs to be sure that the security police is not an instrument of the opposition, and preferably a positive weapon in his own hands.

When José Nussbaumer was appointed Commissioner of the Interior in the *Collège des Commissaires,* his first act was to purge the security police. Kasavubu revoked Muzungu,[63] and Victor Nendaka was named in his place. Nendaka proved to be an effective choice, from the Leopoldville point of view, and he quickly converted the *Sûreté* into a potent instrument.[64] He was considered an apostate by the Lumumbist groups, and in the last months of 1960 and early 1961 the security police struck hard at pro-Lumumba elements in Leopoldville. Many of the excesses of this period were no doubt the work of the numerous private bands organized by various political groups in the name of the *Sûreté.* However, when Adoula became Minister of the Interior in the Ileo government, which assumed the reins of government in Leopoldville in February 1961, he sought to regain control over the mechanism. A decree-law was promulgated on February 25, which formalized the right of the *Sûreté* "to conduct searches and

[63] Muzungu was subsequently among those executed in Bakwanga in February 1961.

[64] Nendaka has an interesting background. He is one of the rare Congolese leaders who had accumulated independent wealth and came from a commercial rather than a bureaucratic background. He had tried to found his own wing of the MNC in April 1960; he had previously been MNC/L vice-president, and served as an interim leader during the period November 1959-January 1960, when Lumumba was incarcerated on charges of having instigated the Stanleyville riots of October 1959.

seizure of goods, papers, and documents of all persons of whatever nationality suspected of threatening the security of the state at any time or place,"[65] but which required the express authorization of Adoula or his delegate. The executions in Elisabethville and Bakwanga of persons who had been transferred to those places from Leopoldville led Adoula to be more explicit; in denouncing these atrocities, he declared on February 20 "from this day forward, no arrest can be made except on instructions from the judiciary or my own order."[66]

When MNC/L President Gbenye became Minister of the Interior in the Adoula government, he also sought to assert his control over the security police. Matters came to a head when, on December 13, Gbenye's cabinet released the following communiqué: "The cabinet of the Minister of the Interior informs the public that effective December 12, M. Victor Nendaka has been placed at the disposition of the civil service [for reassignment], and no longer belongs to the staff of the *Sûreté Nationale*. He is therefore no longer authorized to identify himself as Director of the *Sûreté*."[67]

Nendaka immediately contacted General Mobutu, who sent a detachment of paracommandos to surround the Ministry of the Interior and offices of the *Sûreté;* an officer told Gbenye that if he dared set foot in the security police offices he would be arrested forthwith.[68] Five days later, the *Moniteur Congolais* carried the text of an ordinance signed on July 15 by the Ileo government, which announced the nomination of Nendaka as Director of the *Sûreté*, effective July 1, 1961.[69] This consecrated the autonomy of the *Sûreté*

[65] Decree-Law No. 1/61, published in *Moniteur Congolais,* No. 8, March 9, 1961.

[66] *Congo 1961,* p. 123.

[67] Quoted in *ibid.,* p. 504.

[68] According to a press conference by Gbenye on December 13, 1961, in *ibid.*

[69] *Moniteur Congolais,* No. 24, December 18, 1961. Earlier Nendaka held his post, in a legal sense, by commission, not formal nomination by the Chief of State, which is a permanent appointment. It is normal

from the Interior Minister; henceforward, in effect, Nendaka was responsible directly to the Prime Minister. This remained largely true when Gbenye was replaced by Kamitatu in February 1962.

This incident illustrates some of the sources of strength of the *Sûreté* in the political system. Nendaka is a key member of the Binza Group and has worked closely with the ANC and all governments since the downfall of Lumumba. At a crucial moment, Nendaka could count upon Mobutu's paracommandos to support him. An ambitious and shrewd man, Nendaka has been able to bring the security police under his full control. The broad mandate of the *Sûreté* as a sort of political police gives it extensive influence; the threat of imminent arrest is a powerful weapon. Further, its clandestine nature gives it the possibility of a broad range of *sub rosa* activities which escape public surveillance. By their nature, the security police are likely to be well-informed on matters such as Swiss bank accounts and the dubious financial transactions of certain political figures, which can constitute in the right circumstances important leverage. Although at first the *Sûreté* was effective mainly in Leopoldville, it had by 1962 restored its network in most of the country.[70]

---

that there is a lag of some weeks before laws are published in the official gazette, but the timing of this particular ordinance was clearly related to the Gbenye dispute. The same ordinance named Damien Kandolo permanent secretary in the Interior Ministry. Kandolo also played an important role in this affair. An Otetela, like Lumumba, he had been one of the highest ranking Congolese civil servants before independence, and a former leader of APIC. Lumumba named him *chef de cabinet* and his personal *attaché* in charge of the *Sûreté;* he rallied to the *Collège des Commissaires,* and became Nussbaumer's assistant. He later became Adoula's *chef de cabinet* during the latter's tenure as Minister of the Interior, and by the aforecited ordinance became entrenched as the top civil servant in the Ministry.

[70] From personal experience, the writer can attest to the existence of a *Sûreté* net extending down at least to the district level in 1962. When at Lisala, questions were raised about the validity of a visa, it turned out there were at least two *Sûreté* representatives; in

The *Sûreté*, like the ANC, is carefully scrambled. In 1963, in only one of the twenty-one provinces was the head of the national security police branch a native of that province. As most key political personnel travel by air, the maintenance of surveillance on movements of significant figures is not difficult. The *Sûreté* and the ANC cooperate closely in the provincial capitals; both have their own communication nets with Leopoldville. Although there was some Belgian technical assistance in restoring the *Sûreté* in Leopoldville and, more important, in providing training in Belgium for a number of *Sûreté* agents, European personnel have been few in number, confined to Leopoldville, and in no way comparable to the extensive expatriate role in the Katanga *Sûreté*.[71]

Role of Coercive Instruments in the Polity

In the matrix of force, accordingly, one finds on the central side the army and *Sûreté* and on the provincial side the police. By far the most important of these forces is the ANC, which draws support from its alliance at the summit with the security police. The provinces draw some bargaining power through their jurisdiction over the territorial police, but ironically General Janssens' 1959 triumph in preserving the gendarmery role for the *Force Publique* gives the central government one of its major trump cards, in the right to have its units deployed throughout the countryside.

There should be no illusions about the drawbacks of the army; its strength is really the weakness of other elements

---

Coquilhatville, where the writer was invited for an interview, about ten persons were observed to be lounging about the *Sûreté* officers.

[71] A cluster of security organizations grew up in Katanga. The *Sûreté* was under Interior Minister Munongo's control; there was also an external intelligence office and a military intelligence section. In October 1960, a coordinating security agency attached to the presidency was established, manned by eight Europeans. Gérard-Libois, *op. cit.*, p. 141.

in the polity. The army like Parliament, is a powerful pressure group which demands satisfaction of its own requirements. A pay cut for the army would be unthinkable. Because of its broad-based recruitment, the army units are likely to feel little identification with the region in which they are stationed; when on the move, they live off the land. Should some dissident villager shoot down a soldier, the troops may be counted on to exact savage reprisals. The troops are feared and disliked by the bulk of the population; the traditional hostility has now been exacerbated by the feeling that the soldiers have been given unreasonably high pay.

The high cost of the army is another very serious shortcoming. Part of the cost may be imputed to the Janssens heritage of an exaggerated external security mission, which was given a new lease on life by the Katanga crisis. For the most part, this is simply due to very substantial pay raises granted to the army since 1960, as well as the sharp increase in its size. The army salaries in 1962 amounted to 20 percent of the total Congo payroll, which was nearly 90 percent of public expenditure.[72] In 1964, the ANC budget was estimated at 10 billion francs of a total projected government expenditure of 34 billion. The ANC had a budget allocation of 1 billion in the pre-independence 1960 budget, or 3 billion, adjusting for subsequent devaluation. The enormous military expenditures of Katanga were not far behind those of Leopoldville, although the exact figure was a closely guarded secret in Elisabethville.[73] The soldiers have done better than the police in salary increases; according to calculations of the *Institut de Recherches Econo-*

[72] Traitements, grèves, et politique d'austérité," *loc. cit.*, p. 15.

[73] Not only did the Katanga gendarmery compete with Leopoldville in salary levels, but large expenditures were made for purchase of aircraft and other heavy military equipment, as well as the pay given the several hundred European mercenaries. In 1962, Gérard-Libois cites the figure of nearly 2.5 billion francs, or 47% of the budget. *Op. cit.*, p. 227.

miques et Sociales (IRES) at Lovanium, non-commissioned grades and privates are earning on an average 347 percent of their pre-independence salary, while police agents have advanced by 240 percent.[74] Although no figures are available for the 534 army officers or 166 police inspectors and commissioners,[75] it is reasonable to conclude from the solutions adopted in the civil service that their salaries are somewhat higher than the pre-independence scales for the Europeans occupying these grades. In the words of IRES: " . . . It is appropriate to recall that before independence the soldiers and police were very poorly paid, despite the fact that they received free food and lodging. . . . This fact justifies no doubt the desire they had to obtain a stronger purchasing power in monetary terms. It is not less true that in terms of the absolute level of remunerating the army . . . figures amongst the great beneficiaries of independence."[76] The rebellion of 1963-1964 has led to a further large-scale inflation of the army's size, which indeed military leaders had urged even before the insurrection began.[77] At least 10,000 former Katanga gendarmes were brought into the ANC as soon as Tshombe came to power, and recruitment has been going forward in areas believed to be of proven fidelity to Leopoldville, especially the Lower Congo and former Equateur province.

Probably the safest prediction that could be made concerning the future of the Congo in the coming decade is that the ANC will play a central role. Although shaken by the disgraceful performance of a number of units against rebel bands, the officer corps is likely to regain its self-confidence. The new officers have in many cases now had

[74] Dupriez, "Les rémunérations," *loc. cit.*, pp. 31-33.
[75] Figures from "Traitements, grèves, et politique d'austérité," *loc. cit.*, p. 12.
[76] Dupriez, "Les rémunérations," *loc. cit.*, p. 32.
[77] A law proposing the incorporation of 2,000 new recruits was before Parliament in April 1963; *Courrier d'Afrique,* April 11, 1963.

training periods abroad. Nearly four years of experience have been on intensive apprenticeship under fire; many who obviously did not measure up to their new responsibilities have been weeded out, and command positions put in the hands of those who have proven their worth in difficult circumstances. The task of resurrecting a disintegrated army was a challenge which can scarcely be underestimated. Those who have succeeded have developed a confidence in themselves which tends to be matched by a sense of impatience with the apparent ineptness of the "politician" element. The officer corps is genuinely national in outlook, although its attitude is not to be confused with the radical pan-African nationalism of the mass single-party form of national consciousness. Although Mobutu himself had at times appeared to be disposed toward compromise, during the 1962 Katanga negotiations the ANC was one of the main elements opposed to any settlement which did not guarantee the effective unity of the country. However, the approach is more technocratic than political, which seems to be a universal characteristic of military elites.[78]

The Congo is thus likely to provide tropical Africa its first experience of a political system in which a large role devolves upon a military elite. Far too little is yet known about the army to be certain what the consequences of this will be, although some relevant insights may be obtained from Asian experience. The army is unlikely to offer an adequate permanent alternative to forms of political organization which are more capable of generating real consent

[78] One may here cite the difference in approach to the nationalist goal of pan-Arab unity between the military elite ruling in Egypt and the Baath parties of the Middle East. The former seeks to mobilize behind it the support of the mass, but in a clearly authoritarian fashion, while the latter prefers achieving the same goal through the normal democratic processes, trusting implicitly in the transcendent qualities of their political message to secure massive backing. See Shils, "The Military in the Political Development of New States," Johnson, *op. cit.,* p. 40.

and legitimation. As an interim superintendent of modernization, however, its potential role merits careful evaluation.

Coleman and Brice have offered a first formulation of an inventory of problems likely to arise in this situation; among these, relevant to the Congo, is the fact that the officer ranks have now been effectively filled, and there will be relatively little opportunity in the next few years for the absorption of those undergoing training at the Belgian Royal Military Academy and elsewhere.[79] The general educational level of the former non-commissioned officers who now fill the officer ranks is not high; the *Force Publique* was not a high status career before independence, and non-commissioned officers had in general been promoted from the ranks. Their education had largely been within the army itself. The army will require the collaboration of the bureaucracy; it does not have the cadres to rule by itself. The army is not popular and is unlikely to become so; military rule in the Congo could never have the popular acceptance which it does in the UAR.

The fragility of the army, and the costs of the elite unit policy, became very clear during 1964, when a series of humiliating reverses were inflicted upon the ANC by rebel groups, often with only rudimentary armament. The army had to keep reliable units in the critical areas of Leopoldville and southern Katanga. When rebellion took place on only one front, in Kwilu, the ANC was able, after great difficulties, to disperse the rebels. But when revolt broke out in several areas at once, there were simply not enough dependable units available; the undisciplined battalions proved worse than useless. Further, purging unreliable troops carried its own risks; many of the "simbas", or rebel troops, were former ANC soldiers, eliminated because of suspected Stanleyville sympathies in an earlier period. And yet the ANC remains the frail prop upon which the continued unity of the Congo rests.

[79] *Ibid.*, pp. 394-405.

✄✄

CHAPTER XVII

Federalism: The Quest for a Constitution

✄✄

The Image of Federalism

"Federalism," declared an MNC/L provincial congress in April 1960, "results in practice in a dangerous ethnic separation and tribal wars." The analysis of federalism continued in the following terms:

"This federalism, were it to be realized, would plunge the smaller ethnic groups under the domination of other tribes;

"Proof has come to light concerning certain federalist leaders which demonstrates sufficiently that the federalism thus advocated camouflages clearly separatist and imperialist aims;

"Through this pseudo-federalism, certain persons wish to install neo-colonialism, the brother of that reactionary form which has just been interred."[1]

No, declared the Abako, unitarism is the real danger; "federal unity is better than any other." Through its organ *Notre Kongo,* a rather different interpretation of "federalism" was put forward:

"The Bakongo have more confidence in a man of their people, just like those of the Kasai. . . . This . . . obliges us to adopt a federal formula for the unity of the Congo, without which, the country will head toward great tribal struggles . . . We repeat, unity is dangerous, especially when colonialism still follows its trail; it is not colonialism which should unite us, but we ourselves must feel the need to unite. . . . We do not say that it is impossible to unite with a neighbor of different origin. . . . But this must be

[1] *Congo 1960,* I, 176.

freely consented, without any external interference or colonialism."[2]

Thus spoke the adversaries; the issue of federalism served as the great coalescing dispute, on either side of which the political battlelines formed in 1959 and 1960. The circumstances of independence provided a de facto resolution of this issue in rendering the unitary dreams of the Lumumbist coalition inapplicable; yet no easy answers emerged to the difficult dilemmas of a real dispersion of power. If the pre-independence polemic was unenlightening, the issues were very real. The quest for political institutions that are at once stable and effective is far from over and is fundamental for the successful organization of independence. For this reason, the problem of finding a viable relationship between the center and the parts bears careful analysis. In this chapter, we will explore the roots of federalist movements, the de facto metamorphosis of the polity from centralized colonial state to loosely structured federation, and the successive efforts to define the distribution of power within the Congolese state.

Federalism in New Nations

With relation to the new nations of Africa and Asia federalism has most frequently been seen, as the MNC/L resolution suggests, as a camouflage for conspiracies of diverse sorts. For Indonesia, federalism was a Dutch plot to detach the outer islands from the Java heartland. For Nkrumah, federalism was a maneuver of unscrupulous opponents to capitalize on traditionalist and tribalist elements in behalf of reaction.[3] In East and Central Africa, federation schemes were suspect as devices by which settler communities in Kenya and Southern Rhodesia could fasten their grip over much larger areas where Europeans were

---

[2] *Notre Kongo,* November 1, 1959; May 15, 1960.
[3] Kwame Nkrumah, *I Speak of Freedom* (New York: Praeger Paperbacks, 1961), pp. 71-84.

little represented in the population. Ivory Coast and Gabon viewed the old *Afrique Occidentale Française* and *Afrique Equatoriale Française* federations as budgetary maneuvers by Paris to offset the administrative deficits of the poor savannah territories of Chad, Ubangi-Chari, Niger, Soudan, and Upper Volta on the relatively prosperous coastal units.[4] And, in the case of the Congo, many African leaders (outside the Congo) were convinced that federalism was a constitutional formula hatched in the board room of *Union Minière.*

Until recently, the study of federalism had been centered upon the three continental nations constituted by former British colonies—the United States, Canada, and Australia—plus the unique, multicultural state of Switzerland.[5] In these cases, an original, fundamental compact had been agreed upon by preexisting sovereign entities to form a single state with a written constitution which could not be unilaterally changed. In the recent words of a student of the applicability of federalism to new nations: "Devised as a form of constitutional government to express imperfect unity of multi-nationalism, federalism is a particularly complicated form of Western democracy based on bargains and compromises. Originally, its main merit was thought to be the way in which it secured a dispersal of power in the interests of weak government."[6]

Renewed interest in the theory and practice of federalism grew out of the drafting of a new federal constitution for West Germany and subsequently the quest for a formula

---

[4] Elliot J. Berg, "The Economic Basis of Political Choice in French West Africa," *American Political Science Review,* LIV, No. 2 (June 1960), 391-405.

[5] The classic study of classic federalism remains K. C. Wheare, *Federal Government* (3rd ed.; New York: Oxford University Press, 1953).

[6] F. G. Carnell, in his chapter, "Political Implications of Federalism in New States," in Ursula Hicks (ed), *Federalism and Economic Growth in Underdeveloped Countries* (New York: Oxford University Press, 1961), p. 16.

for Western European political community.[7] The first real application[8] of the theory to the developing areas was in India, where the problem of accommodating within a single political community a diversity of linguistic and communal groups posed extraordinary difficulties.[9] Burma likewise adopted a nominally federal constitution, but the failure of constitutional government to operate and the multiple insurrections makes this a dubious example of functioning federalism. In Malaya and subsequently Malaysia, a federal constitution was also adopted. But the fundamental diversity in the Malayan polity between Malays, Chinese, and to a lesser extent Indians is not geographically distributed, and thus federalism does not really help on the basic problem. In Africa, federal theory was ransacked to find an adequate constitutional form for Nigeria. The vitality of Buganda as a modernized traditional system made necessary a highly complex and ingenious federal system in Uganda. Federalism has been adopted, perhaps only transitionally, by Cameroun to cope with the problem of fusing areas with dissimilar colonial experiences.

The problem in the Congo was not the classical federal challenge of providing a framework for union without unity to a series of operative political units; rather the crucial issue was to find a means to accommodate local

[7] Two important studies were commissioned as part of the European integration campaign: Robert Bowie and Carl J. Friedrich (eds), *Studies in Federalism* (Boston: Little, Brown & Co., 1954); and Arthur W. MacMahon (ed), *Federalism Mature and Emergent* (Garden City, N. Y.: Doubleday & Co., 1955).

[8] The Latin American "federations" are excluded from this discussion, as the four states which have nominally federal constitutions qualify in only a purely formal sense. These are Mexico, Venezuela, Argentina, and Brazil. In the latter case, one could come closest to rational argument that there is a real federalism, as regionalism is strong, and some of the twenty-one federal states, such as Sao Paulo and Rio Grande del Sul, have a very real sense of local self-consciousness.

[9] Naresh Chandra Roy, *Federalism and Linguistic States* (Calcutta: Firma K. L. Mukhopadhyay, 1962).

loyalties which only partially coincided with the administrative subdivisions of a tightly decentralized, bureaucratic, foreign-owned and operated enterprise. Here the Congo is at absolute variance with all other successful federations. There is no example of a viable federal structure which has grown from a comparable situation. If one restricts the scope of comparison to the significant Afro-Asian experiments in federation devolving from what had been a single colonial entity, it is immediately evident that India, Nigeria, and Uganda differ sharply from the Congo in this regard. The British Raj sat atop a complicated and highly differentiated administrative structure; much real authority was vested in the provinces, not to mention the princely states. Although the subdivisions were not entirely coincident with the ethnic components of the Indian population, they had a long history and had been important centers of political life and decision-making. Since 1953, important concessions have been made to linguistic boundaries in redrawing provincial frontiers, but the fact remains that the modified federalism adopted by India did not represent a sharp break with the structures of the colonial state.

In the case of Nigeria, the three regions have not only served as major administrative subdivisions but represent three clearly distinct components of the Nigerian nation. The Hausa-Fulani-dominated, Muslim North was not linked to the rest of the country until 1914; although the eastern and western regions only appeared in 1939 through a regrouping of the several southern provinces, each had a single dominant ethnic group, the Ibo and Yoruba, respectively. Political party organization reflected and reinforced the three regions. Thus federalism in Nigeria was a natural outgrowth of the style of colonial administration and of the structure of African response to colonialism.[10]

[10] For a useful discussion of the emergence of a federal solution for Nigeria, see Donald S. Rothchild, *Toward Unity in Africa* (Washington: Public Affairs Press, 1960), pp. 148-77.

In Uganda, the British pattern of indirect administration had been matched by several remarkably effective traditional systems, especially the Buganda, which had internalized modernization to a considerable degree. Here the constitutional problem was the disparity between the insistence upon very large autonomy by the Buganda and the preference for more centralized forms of government by those areas lacking a structured and functioning traditional system. The solution was found in a particularly interesting constitution, which permits some regions greater autonomy than others, thus incorporating a hierarchy of federal relationships within a single constitutional framework. Buganda will be most federal, the three kingdoms of Bunyoro, Toro, and Ankole will have lesser but substantial autonomy, while the other districts will have local government not really federal at all in its relationship to the center.

Tradition of Centralism

Centralization is a deep-rooted principle of colonial administration in the Congo. From the beginning of the Congo Free State, when the effective reins of command were held in Brussels by Leopold II and his general staff, there was little disposition to permit local autonomy. With the *reprise*, there was a period when power devolved both to the administrative capital of Boma and to the four provinces; Katanga from the outset has been a special case which will be discussed below. The provinces were briefly headed by Vice-Governors from the First World War until 1933,[11] but these were reduced to "Provincial Commissioners" by the highly centralizing Tilkens reform, with the four provinces reorganized into six. Since World War II, administrative decentralization has been a con-

[11] These were organized as follows: Vice-Governor General for Katanga, 1910; Province Orientale, 1913; Equateur, 1917; Congo-Kasai, 1919. A. Massart, *Notice de la carte des subdivisions administratives du Congo Belge et du Ruanda-Urundi* (Brussels: ARSOM, 1950).

stantly invoked slogan, with major reorganizations in 1947 and 1957. Although the latter did provide some budgetary autonomy for the provinces, few would argue that these "decentralizations" went very far toward altering an extremely centralized system.

The provinces were formally created only in 1914; at that time, there were only four. Prior to that time, the Congo had only been organized into districts. In 1933, Kivu was separated from Orientale, and the Congo-Kasai province was divided into Leopoldville and Kasai. The latter received a small portion of Katanga as well. Since that time, the provinces have remained stable, but only Katanga enjoyed real continuity and a personality of its own as an administrative entity. Orientale to a lesser extent possessed a colonial legendry deriving from its great proconsuls, Meulemeester and Moeller de Laddersous from 1920 to 1933 and its reputation as a laboratory for experimentation in new administrative methods.[12] However, this mythology operated at an entirely European level, and had little relevance for the new African state which was to be created.

Whatever the theoretical merits of federalism for the Congo in 1960, the fact is that strong federalist movements arose at the two poles of development, Elisabethville and Leopoldville. These unrelated but parallel demands gave decisive orientation to pre-independence political development and constitutional debate. The phenomenon of Katanga separatism has a longer history, and may accordingly be examined first.

Roots of Federalism: Katanga

EUROPEAN ANTECEDENTS

A sense of separate development by Katanga goes back

[12] It will be recalled that Orientale was the great incubator for the foundations of the Belgian indirect rule formula, the native courts, and the "sectors" as "traditional" reconstructions where no viable customary systems remained.

to the very beginnings of the Free State. In 1891, Leopold II turned over to a charter company, headed by Albert Thys of the CCCI,[13] the organization of the occupation and exploration of Katanga. One of the inducements offered to the chartered *Compagnie du Katanga*, full property rights over one-third of the total land area of the future province to be awarded on a checkerboard pattern, quickly proved to be totally impracticable. In 1900, the Free State and the *Compagnie du Katanga* agreed to pool their land domain in the hands of a new organism, the *Comité Special du Katanga* (CSK). Although the state held two-thirds of the seats on the board of directors, the CSK was in fact a private corporation, which was given plenary powers in the management of the public domain. From 1900 to 1910, the CSK organized the administration of Katanga and had only tenuous contacts with Boma; it organized its own military force. At the time of the *reprise*, the CSK had 77 European administrative agents and 1,000 African soldiers.[14]

The state formally took over the administration of Katanga in 1910 but established it as a Vice-Government General, largely autonomous of the capital at Boma. The first Vice-Governor was Major Wangermée, who coincidentally was the representative of the CSK in Africa.[15] In 1910, the railroad from the south reached Elisabethville, and thus Katanga became linked to the outside world through the Rhodesias and South Africa. It was faster to travel to Boma via South Africa than to make the painful overland and river boat voyage, which required several weeks. Europeans followed the rail lines north, and in its

---

[13] The *Compagnie du Congo pour le Commerce et l'Industrie*. The CCCI was a holding company which organized a number of enterprises in the Congo; after the death of Thys in 1915, these were absorbed into the *Société Générale* empire. Joye & Lewin, *op. cit.*, pp. 19-20.

[14] René Cornet, *Terre Katangaise* (Brussels: L. Cuypers, 1950), p. 153.

[15] *Ibid.*, p. 156.

early days Elisabethville was more of an Anglo-Saxon than Belgian city; its first newspaper was published largely in English. At this time, one must recall, South Africa was riding the crest of a wave of dynamic expansion. Rather than a pariah nation virtually excluded from the world community by its obnoxious racial policies, it represented for many a seductive example.

The Vice-Governor had separate legislative powers, and the communications problem made Boma directives difficult to enforce in Katanga. Nevertheless, there was from the beginning complaint about "centralization." A. de Bauw, director general of the CSK, wrote in 1920: "A country of industry and commerce, where private interests are preponderant and where the general conditions are entirely different from those of the rest of the colony, Katanga can hardly be adapted to the administrative methods inherent to a centralization of powers at Boma. The defects of this system have been innumerable times revealed, and one may hope that before long, this province will regain the autonomy necessary . . . to assure its economic development and a good administration."[16]

The same year, de Hemptinne, the future Apostolic Vicar of Elisabethville (who had arrived on the first train into Elisabethville), published under his name a "reorganization plan" signed by eleven persons who constituted a "who's who" of early Katanga. This called for the elimination of the administrative capital of Boma; the Governor-General should be resident in Brussels, and would, with the Colonial Minister, make some limited decisions on over-all orientation of colonial policy. The provinces would establish their own budgets and make some contribution to a central budget according to a quota which would be fixed once for all. The subsidization of the poorer provinces was a problem for Belgium, not Katanga.[17]

[16] A. Debauw, *Le Katanga* (Brussels: Veuve Ferd. Larcier, 1920), p. 78.

[17] J. de Hemptinne, *Le gouvernement du Congo Belge: Projet de*

The ambitious railway construction of the 1920's brought Katanga slowly into a closer transport web with the rest of the Congo. The advent of airplane transportation about the same time made the sulky province much too accessible for its liking. Under Governor-General Lippens, who was particularly favorable to colonial financial interests, instructions had been given in a circular of January 25, 1922, calling for "the broadest delegations of his powers to the provinces."[18] But in 1933, a sweeping centralization was imposed, with the defenestration of Katanga's vigorous Vice-Governor, Gaston Heenen, removal of all legislative discretion from the provinces, whose chiefs received the ignoble title of "provincial commissioner," and the removal of a slice of Katanga in favor of the newly created Kasai province. The howl of dismay from Katanga is summarized in the pungent prose of *Essor du Congo* editor, Jean Sépulchre: "Promoted to the highest post, in disregard of all common sense and contrary to the general desire, by pure capriciousness, tolerated by pusillanimous and *arriviste* politicans, devoid of any professional conscience and contemptuous of their responsibilities, favored by a general atmosphere of depression and despicableness, the dictator Tilkens has hatched a plan of radical overthrow of our whole colonial structure."[19]

---

réorganisation administrative (Brussels: Librairie Dewit, 1920). The signers were: de Meulemeester, president of the Katanga Appeals Court; Wangermée, *Union Minière du Haut Katanga* (UMHK) representative in the Congo; Grandry, chief of traffic service, Katanga railways; Cousin, director of Katanga Railways; Mathieu, director of the *Banque du Congo Belge;* Cambier, director of Intertropicale, Anglo-Belgian Trading Company; Valkenberg, Director of *Société Commerciale et Minière;* Lens, Legal Advisor of Katanga government and CSK; Massaut, head of legal staff, UMHK, and Katanga Railways; Habran, editor of *Etoile du Congo.*

[18] Cited in Jean Sépulchre, *Propos sur le Congo politique de demain: Autonomie et fédéralisme* (Elisabethville: Editions de l'Essor du Congo, 1958), p. 50.

[19] *Ibid.,* p. 62. This colorful passage was a reprint by Sépulchre of an editorial he wrote in the *Essor du Congo* on July 3, 1933.

Two years earlier, with threats of centralization in the air, the European milieux in Katanga had made their first public threat of separation; "independence" for Katanga was mentioned as a possibility, and a list of "ministers" for the first Katanga government was published.[20]

During this period, the European community's sense of a Katanga particularism remained strong. Civil servants, once posted to Katanga, generally remained there throughout their careers. The temperate climate created the image of a region particularly adapted to European settlement; the more tropical, humid, lower zones of the central basin and the Lower Congo were felt to be malaria-ridden and unsuited to prolonged European residence. The Rhodesian copperbelt with its large European population was in immediate proximity; the example of political development which seemed to be heading toward settler-dominated independent status on the South African model was close and convincing. Passengers for Katanga usually left the boat at Benguela, Angola, for the direct railway connection rather than entering through Matadi-Leopoldville-Port Francqui. And all watched with furious frustration as the skyscrapers rose in Leopoldville, while Elisabethville remained an unimpressive, provincial town. The mushroom city of Leopoldville was considered a parasitic plant, with its roots plunged deep into the mineral wealth of Katanga.

After World War II, European interests in Katanga became better organized; in 1944, the *Union pour la Colonisation* (Ucol) was founded in order to deploy "all efforts to obtain for the white population of the Congo the liberties granted by the Belgian constitution to its nationals, and to promote by all available means the growth of European settlement."[21] In 1950, provincial settler associations

---

[20] The writer is indebted to René Lemarchand for this prophetic episode. The list of "ministers" was published in the *Essor du Congo*, in June 1931. Needless to say, all were European.

[21] Ucol Statutes, Article 2, quoted in René Lemarchand, "The

throughout the Congo formed the *Fédération des Associations de Colons du Congo et du Ruanda-Urundi* (Fedacol). At first, the political goal of the Katanga settler groups was simply greater autonomy for Katanga within the colonial framework, as well as a grant of political rights to themselves.[22] However, as the pace of events elsewhere accelerated, the search began for a formula of adaptation acceptable to the Europeans; Sépulchre wrote in 1957:

"For the last several years, alerted by the irreversible transformation of Africa, [the Kantanga Europeans] have distinguished themselves by their ardor in seeking the right formula, which will avoid having the Congo overtaken by events. . . .

"Autonomy and federalism were obviously irrelevant ideas when Belgium took over the colony. . . . Only the slow unfolding of fifty years of Belgian rule in Africa has, through the accumulation of experience, observations and reflection, brought these new ideas little by little to our attention. The fact is that today, . . . especially in the Katanga, they are more and more necessary owing to the notorious incapacity of our governments to define and prepare the future . . . *La Belgique politicienne* has demonstrated its congenital ineptitude."[23]

It would be wrong to exaggerate the real importance of the settler element in the Congo or even in Katanga. Although the European population in Katanga, which stood at 33,918 in 1959, was comparable as a proportion of the total population (2.08 percent) to that of Kenya or the Federations of Rhodesia and Nyasaland, only 3,065 fell into the "settler" category.[24] Of this figure, only 31.8 per

---

Limits of Self-Determination: Katanga," *American Political Science Review*, LVI, No. 2 (June 1962), 407.

[22] Sénat de Belgique, *Rapport de la Mission Sénatoriale . . . 1947*, pp. 38-39.

[23] Sépulchre, *op. cit.*, pp. 7-8, 23.

[24] Defined as a person exercising an independent profession, whether

cent were actually members of Ucol-Katanga.[25] However, during the era when the African 98 percent remained entirely silent, this group partially compensated for its miniscule size by its strident voice. Despite the support of some Liberal members of parliament, the settler group was ineffective as a lobby in Brussels. However, as shown in Chapter II, the nature of the consultative machinery within the Congo itself and the access to the organs of opinion, particularly the press, permitted the settler group to exert pressures within the colonial framework out of all proportion to its real importance. Further, although there was a long-standing hostility between the settlers and the large colonial companies,[26] many of the Europeans in the administration and the private sector shared the views of the settlers. In any event, the significant point is that the growing "federalist" movement in Katanga was, until 1959, entirely European in origin.

Beginning in 1956, the notion of a vague sort of "federalism" for the Congo, largely undefined, was advocated by a variety of observers who were reflecting on the future. Van Bilsen seems to have been the first to propose openly a federal structure, in 1955-1956; the idea did not originate with him, but he was the first to discuss in concrete terms the terminal colonial goals.[27] From a more conservative

---

agricultural, commercial, or liberal, and thus established on his own behalf, rather than simply as a member of the private or public bureaucracies stationed in the Congo.

[25] *La Fédération Congolaise des Classes Moyennes* (FEDACOL), *Organisation et action des colons au Congo,* CRISP, *Courrier Hebdomedaire,* No. 25 (July 3, 1959).

[26] The settlers accused the companies of wishing to monopolize the service functions which they felt they could perform. There was also dispute over access to the limited labor supply and agricultural pricing policies which assured a low-cost food supply to the workers but made European farming unprofitable for many commodities.

[27] Van Bilsen, *Vers l'indépendance,* p. 6. It should be added that Van Bilsen quickly backed away from his first federal proposals, which were designed more to provide a formula for associating Ruanda-Urundi with the Congo than to cater to Katangan preferences. By

viewpoint, Professor Paul Coppens of Louvain University made similar proposals in 1956.[28] Support from an unexpected source came when Professor Arthur Doucy, a well-known Socialist figure and head of the *Institut de Sociologie Solvay*,[29] published a detailed set of proposals for reorganization of the Congo on federal lines in early 1957.[30] Sépulchre noted with evident relish that the "ideas of Doucy are especially close to our own."[31]

In 1957, Ucol published a brochure summarizing its ideas, in which for the first time its federalist scheme was put before the public.[32] The federal idea, as it then stood, called for a "federation of political entities, including Belgium and an unspecified number of major Congolese administrative divisions, with each enjoying very large internal autonomy. Sépulchre added that "independence, by common agreement, was excluded." Citing Doucy's proposals, he suggested tentatively that in addition to Katanga, a second

---

1958, when Ruanda-Urundi was clearly destined for separate evolution, and "federalism" had become a settler war cry, he ceased advocating it.

[28] Paul Coppens, *Anticipations congolaises* (Brussels: Editions Techniques et Scientifiques, 1956).

[29] Since 1961, the "Solvay" in the title has been removed. The Institute, attached to the Free University of Brussels, has been in the past seen as dominated by an anti-clerical approach; it includes both Liberals and Socialists. During 1960, a number of its representatives played an important political role, as advisers to various political parties. Doucy himself was closely linked to the Balubakat (as was Mme. François Perin), and later was certainly not preaching the virtues of federalism, Mme. P. Bouvier was counselor to Unimo, whose leading figure, Bomboko, had studied at the Institute. Guy Spitaels and his wife, Mme. Spitaels-Evrard, were associated with the PSA. The financial interests were intensely irritated with the Solvay role, especially in Katanga, and the Solvay group ended its financial support of the Institute as a result.

[30] A. Doucy, "Sociologie coloniale et réformes de structure au Congo Belge," *Revue de l'Université Libre de Bruxelles,* Nos. 2-3, (January-April, 1957), pp. 212-29.

[31] Sépulchre, *op. cit.,* p. 34.

[32] A summary was published in the *Essor du Congo,* April 2, 1957.

European-dominated state could be created by joining the Kibali-Ituri district of Orientale to Kivu. The rest of Orientale could then be joined with Equateur and Lac Leopold II, the Kwango-Kwilu incorporated with Kasai, and the Bas-Congo placed on its own to create five regions in function of their relative interest to Europeans.[33]

In Belgium and elsewhere in the Congo, there was considerable suspicion of the federalism advocated by Katanga Europeans; Sépulchre mourned that he and his colleagues were the object of constant calumnies of this subject. A single Katanga weekly had let slip the word "separatism" to describe their aims; "The use of this unlucky word, so contrary to the general sentiment, threatens to do great harm to the *belle cause* which we all have at heart." Separation, he claimed, would not receive a single vote on a referendum.[34] However, the occasional threat of secession as a means of pressure on Brussels and Leopoldville was deemed a useful weapon to achieve settler goals.[35]

Also, until 1959, the federal idea met with general hostility on the part of the African population. The Ucol manifesto which accompanied the federal proposals called for emphasis on vocational education for Africans, stationing of European troops in the cities to protect against external "or other" enemies, outlawing unions, intensification of European settlement, and an improvement of the roads to Northern Rhodesia to facilitate commercial and military traffic.[36] The federal state was to be based upon paritary European-African representation at all levels. Rubbens observed in 1958, "the whites of the Katanga having opted for a federalism to remove themselves from the preponderance of black influence at Leopoldville, the Congolese

[33] Sépulchre, *op. cit.*, pp. 9, 51-52.
[34] *Ibid.*, pp. 24-25.
[35] Gérard-Libois, *Sécession au Katanga*, p. 22.
[36] A. Rubbens, "La confusion politique au Katanga," *Revue Nouvelle*, October 1958, p. 311.

reacted immediately in requiring the maintenance of national unity."[37] Sépulchre admitted: "We must not conceal from ourselves the huge obstacle that we will encounter in the generalized complex of distrust of the African toward any proposal from the Congo white in the way of future policy. . . . On this subject, we have been very disappointed to read in the weekly *Katanga*[38] an article . . . whose author, M. Kishiba, launches into a veritable frenzy of suspicion . . . that autonomy is a trick to trade one colonizer for another and that the Congolese were not interested except on condition of having it all to themselves."[39]

Federalism Africanized

Thus, until the Leopoldville riot watershed in Congolese evolution, the Katanga thread of federal thought was characterized by its vagueness and its European roots. The central element in it was a desire for restoration of the administrative autonomy which the province had enjoyed during the early colonial years. The concept was posited on the assumption of European paramountcy, or at least parity, in the future state, which was in any case some time off. In this form, federalism had no chance of African support; it had rather the effect of covering over the latent cleavages in the African community, by casting the indigenous population in its African, rather than its ethnic role. No African leaders, whether they later participated politically through the Conakat or the Balubakat, found any attraction in the perpetuation of European domination.

In 1959, however, the content of Katanga federalism was entirely transformed; the European aspect became muted, and the ethnic tensions of the South Katanga urban

[37] *Ibid.*, p. 312. During a visit to the State University of Elisabethville in July 1958, the writer was struck by the strength of feeling of the African students on the federalism issue and settler intentions.

[38] Favorable to the Rubbens-Kitenge party, Union Congolaise, founded at the time of the December 1957 communal elections.

[39] Sépulchre, *op. cit.*, p. 33.

centers became grafted to the federal debate. This became possible when the January 13 Government Declaration scrapped the paritary principle and forecast a Congo founded upon universal suffrage. Chapters VI, XI, and XII have described the background to ethnic conflict in Elisabethville and Jadotville; it will be recalled that the December 1957 election had resulted in a clear triumph for the "strangers," with all four African communes in Elisabethville and that of Jadotville nominating burgomasters from outside the province.[40] The full effect of this was not, as in the case of Leopoldville, immediately perceived and felt; the electoral campaign itself was conducted in the lexicon of European political labels, with ethnic support not openly solicited in the hustings. It was really the sectarian behavior of the Kasai Baluba burgomasters which catalyzed the hostility of the "losers," the "authentic Katangans."[41]

Another dimension of the coalescent ethnic cleavages which predisposed the "authentic Katangans" to the settler alliance was the preemption of nationalist positions by Kasai Baluba. In November 1955, an ethnic association grouping the latter, the *Association de Baluba-Central Kasai au Katanga* (later renamed *Fédération Générale . . .*, abbreviated as Fegebaceka) was formed in the Katanga cities and rapidly became a focal point for opposition to settlers, Catholic missions, and the large corporations. Anti-settler demonstrations were organized on the occasion of visits to Elisabethville by Ministers Buisseret (February 1958) and Petillon (August 1958); the *Sûreté* accused the leaders of being in clandestine contact with Northern Rhodesian nationalists and the Abako. Fegebaceka was

[40] It will also be recalled that in the case of the Jadotville commune, the nominee, Lundula, was not accepted by the administration, although not because he was not "Katangan."

[41] During the first nine months of the tenure of the new burgomasters, until September 1958, they were assured of the sympathy of Katanga Governor J. Paelinck. Paelinck had served most of his career in Kasai, spoke fluent Tshiluba, and was widely believed to be partial to Kasai Baluba.

491

dissolved in November 1958, and its two leading figures expelled from South Katanga.[42]

Social tensions among the African population were sharpened by the unemployment which was associated with the Congo recession beginning in 1957, and in particular with the 50 percent drop in copper prices on the world market. The impact of unemployment was most strongly felt by the populations of Katanga origin, who tended to occupy the lower positions and were most subject to layoffs. In 1958, the administration began repatriating some of the unemployed to their regions of origin; very few Kasai Baluba were affected by these measures. Here control of the African communal administration by Kasai burgomasters facilitated the obtaining of permanent residence permits by "strangers," which obviously contributed to the bitter resentment of "authentic Katangans" at the performance of Kasai burgomasters and fears of what might happen if a similar hegemony were achieved at a provincial level. A letter written by future Katanga Interior Minister Godefroid Munongo to the provincial governor on February 13, 1959, is particularly interesting in this regard:

"The Katangese of birth wonder with reason if the authorities are not deliberately granting permanent residential permission to the people from Kasai in our towns so that the natives of this province can, thanks to their ever-growing number, crush those from Katanga. This fact could well cause in the near future violence between the inhabitants of the two provinces. We would respectfully point out to you that very numerous are the native sons of Katanga who would like to work in the great cities of their province; mercilessly, they are told that there is a decree forbidding access to the towns. And yet they are the ones who should have priority."[43]

[42] Gérard-Libois, *op. cit.*, pp. 14-15.
[43] Quoted in Lemarchand; "The Limits of Self-Determination: Katanga," *loc. cit.*, p. 411.

In October 1958, the resentment of the Kasaien domination of the municipal institutions led to the founding of the *Confédération des Associations Tribales du Katanga,* or Conakat;[44] following dissolution of the Fegebaceka, the Kasai Baluba had regrouped under Isaac Kalondji's *Fédération Kasaienne* (Fedeka). In February 1959, Jason Sendwe's *Association des Baluba*[45] joined the Conakat. Thus, at this stage, the tensions, while partly expressed in ethnic terms, also were in good part based upon acceptance of the administrative entity of Katanga as a valid coordinate of reference. The Kasai Baluba were "foreign" not only because they were Baluba but also because they came from

[44] Some of the leading groups joining the Conakat were the *Groupement des Associations Mutuelles de l'Empire Lunda, Fédération des Tribus du Haut Katanga, Association des Basonge, Association des Bena Marunga, Association des Ressortissants Bahemba, Association des Minungu.* Lemarchand, "The Limits of Self-Determination: Katanga," *loc. cit.,* p. 410. The imminent arrival of the *Groupe de Travail* to hear testimony on the future institutions of the Congo was an important factor which stimulated the formation of Conakat at that particular moment.

[45] The *Association des Baluba* was founded in 1957. It should be noted that the association was by no means the first based upon this clientele; a constant process of dissolution and reforming had taken place. There had been previous Kasai associations, as well as periodic efforts to establish federations regrouping all persons who bore the Baluba label. The word "Baluba" covers an enormous variety of people. Within the Luba group can be found three of the world's four major kinship systems—patrilineal, matrilineal, and double descent; a wide variety of political structures can also be found, ranging from the well-structured states of Kasongo Nyembo, Kabongo, Mutombo-Mukulu to the segmentary, stateless "river" Baluba. The Baluba Hemba, in northeast Katanga, are really a variety of peoples, having in common a petty-state system and a heavy Baluba cultural influence, especially in language. One can perhaps identify five major groups: 1) Baluba Shankadi, the survivors of the old Baluba empire, with Kasongo Nyembo the senior chiefly line; these are located in northwest Katanga. 2) "River" Baluba, of the Lualaba Valley, and Lake Kisale; these were the core areas of Balubakat strength. 3) Baluba Hemba, of northeast Katanga. 4) Baluba Bambo, or Kasai Baluba, who apparently emigrated from Kasongo Nyembo's domains about two centuries ago. 5) Lulua resultant from an earlier out-migration from the Katanga heartland.

Kasai. The Katanga Baluba at this point shared the resentments of their Conakat partners at partisan use of communal office. Two of three university students invited to draft the Conakat constitution were in fact Katanga Baluba.

In May 1959, the Conakat leaders for the first time publicly announced their desire for "an autonomous and federated state" with political and administrative control in the hands of "authentic Katangans."[46] At this point, European "federalists" perceived new opportunities and decided upon an entirely new policy direction. The European and African autonomy desires sprang from different sources, but they were now dedicated to a common goal. The *Union Katangaise* (political arm of Ucol) applied for membership in the *Rassemblement Katangais*, the political party founded by the Conakat in July 1959. The Conakat-settler cooperation rested on an uneasy basis; Tshombe did not support the Ucol program for large-scale European settlement nor any of its earlier paritary ideas. The analysis offered by Evariste Kimba, a leading Conakat personality and later Katanga Minister of Finance, as to the reasons for the establishment of the Conakat is instructive:

"To show the settlers that the Katanga was not a desert before the arrival of the Europeans and that this province could not serve as an outlet to certain settlers who have dreamed of making the region a zone of massive European settlement, for reasons which are sufficiently clear;[47]

"To affirm the presence of native Katangans to the administration, whose evil policy is to represent the Katanga,

[46] *Ibid.*

[47] A standard refrain of colonial propaganda is the argument, similar to that invoked in the case of South Africa, that the Haut-Katanga was a virtually uninhabited zone, barren, uncultivated, undeveloped. This thesis, expounded by Minister Buisseret in his inaugural address to the State University of Elisabethville in November 1956, maintained that the Europeans were really the first arrivers on the scene to take up permanent settlement and, accordingly, were no more "settlers" than the African populations.

in provincial and national assemblies, by Congolese delegates inhabiting the Katanga, but coming from other
provinces;

"To combat the policy of the large Katanga companies
who have recruited a large part of their labor force from
outside the province. This policy has handicapped the
Katanga tribes in their material and intellectual development, owing to the fact that most important schools are
found only in the industrial centers, and accessible only
to children whose parents have a legal domicile in these
localities;

"To avoid any repetition of the results of the communal
elections of 1957."[48]

In a Conakat meeting of March 1960, Tshombe angrily
declared: "[I] no longer intend to be depicted as a stooge
of the settlers; these gentlemen have collected a great
deal of money in the name of the Conakat, over which
they have retained control. . . . In short, the finances are
in the hands of the settlers; the rupture must be clear, if
need be brusque."[49]

It is interesting to note that the set of economic arguments, crucial to the Europeans, only became assimilated
to the African stream of federalism at a late date. None of
the leading African figures had spent time in Leopoldville; Katanga itself was completely in the center of their
preoccupations.[50] The capital only forced itself upon their
attention with the acceleration of political activity in mid-
1959 and the rise to prominence of the unitary nationalist
creeds preached by Lumumba.[51] While Kasavubu and the

[48] *Congo 1960*, I, 226.

[49] From the minutes of the Conakat Central Committee, March 3,
1960, quoted in *ibid.*, p. 233.

[50] Lumumba himself never visited the Katanga centers until January
1960, when he was briefly imprisoned in Jadotville after conviction in
Stanleyville on charges of inciting to riot. His first voluntary visit was
in March 1960.

[51] An interesting reflection of the parochial orientation of the

Abako monopolized the avant-garde positions in Leopold-ville, the twain would ne'er meet; the Abako was as un-interested in Katanga as was the Conakat in the Bas-Congo. But the first national congress of unitary parties took place in Luluabourg in April 1959, and a new threat loomed on the horizon. It became immediately linked with the old, as the Kasai Baluba, alarmed in their turn by the growing xenophobia of the Conakat, found the unitary theses of Lumumba particularly attractive as a guarantee of their security.[52] In the words of Davister, "In fact, for people considered as strangers in a region, the only chance to be able to remain where they were was to see the triumph of a unitary Congo."[53] It thus seems no accident that the first public commitment of the Conakat to federalism came in May 1959, on the heels of the Luluabourg congress, which forced upon Conakat leaders an expansion of their scope of concern from the immediate problem of distri-bution of power within Katanga to the broader issue of Katanga's relationships to the rest of the Congo. And at this point, the patient explanations of the Conakat's Euro-pean entourage concerning the high cost of Leopoldville began to find fertile ground.

At the same time, the notion of actual separation began to fuse imperceptibly with the federal claims. Although as a verbal threat this had been a topic of parlor debate and a settler lever against the administration for a long time, it never advanced beyond the stage of armchair bravado until 1959, when the precipitation of events suddenly made this idea of immediate relevance. In No-

---

Katanga leaders was the fact that all the top Conakat leadership opted from the provincial rather than national offices in May-June, 1960.

[52] This is not to suggest that the intellectual merits of the unitary nationalist program were not also a factor. Far more was at stake for the Kasaiens at that moment, however; the program of the Conakat, promising the Katangisation of the state, threatened their livelihood, and with it their very place in modern society.

[53] Davister, *Katanga enjeu du monde,* p. 78.

vember 1959, increasingly suspicious of separatist ideas rapidly germinating in Conakat circles as well as its European associations, Sendwe's *Association des Baluba* withdrew from the Conakat, thus rupturing the group's pan-Katangan unity.[54]

In December 1959, came the first open threats of independence for Katanga. *Union Katangaise* distributed a pamphlet to all post boxes in Katanga, calling for a postal referendum on the issue of whether Katanga should declare its independence if full satisfaction was not given on the federal program.[55] In an interview with Minister De Schrijver in Elisabethville on December 2, the *Union Katangaise* delegation warned the Minister that the Belgian government, "in wishing to defend a (unitary) structure . . . would rapidly provoke in Katanga the consolidation of the opinion, already so widespread both among Congolese and Europeans, that the moment has really come for Katanga to seek by all peaceful means its own independence." Later that same month, during Baudouin's Elisabethville stopover in the course of his rapid pulse-taking tour of the Congo, some persons schemed to use the occasion for a declaration of Katanga independence.[56]

Thus, the perspective of power transfer produced a curious alignment of forces, European and African, summarized by Gérard-Libois: "Thus emerged the image of cartels or at least solidarities and collusions between, on the one hand, European settlers, 'authentic Katangans,'

[54] During the period July-November, 1959, with the membership both of the Katanga Baluba and European settlers, Conakat could pretend to speak for the entirety of the Katanga population, European and African. Gérard-Libois, *op. cit.*, p. 27.

[55] *Le Katanga devra-t-il prendre sa propre indépendance?* (Elisabethville: Imprimerie A. Decoster, 1959).

[56] Gérard-Libois concludes persuasively that the December 1959 secession plot was less a serious scheme than a sham destined primarily to reinforce Katanga bargaining strength in negotiations on the future structure of the state. Those brandishing the threat at this stage entirely lacked the means to effectuate it. *Op. cit.*, pp. 33-36.

conservative and Catholic Europeans of the public and private sectors and missionary milieux, while on the other were found 'turbulent' African elements from Kasai, Europeans of a laic, anti-clerical background, and 'progressives' black and white."[57] The more radical views, first of the Fegebaceka and later of the Balubakat, and their apparent hostility to Catholic missions and large corporations tended to draw into this political spectrum Belgians who identified with the PSB (suspicion of the trusts) or the Liberal party (anti-clericalism). These included a number of persons inserted in responsible posts in the Katanga provincial administration by Buisseret during his 1954-1958 ministry, some of the academic staff of the State University of Elisabethville, and others connected with a social center maintained by the *Institut de Sociologie Solvay*. There was a cumulative effect of European polarization about the Conakat and Balubakat contenders; the conspicuous sympathy of the anti-clerical Left for Sendwe reinforced the support of the clerical Right for Tshombe, and vice versa. A. Decoster's anti-clerical daily, *Echo du Katanga*, was (before independence) pro-Balubakat, while Sépulchre's Catholic-oriented *Essor du Congo* backed the Conakat. Doucy, a well-known socialist figure and head of the Solvay Institute, served as adviser to the Balubakat at the Brussels Round Table, and Mme. Perin was sent to Katanga to give political counsel. On the other hand, the settler activists of *Union Katangaise* and conservative-Catholic milieux in the companies and the administration were visible in the Conakat entourage. As Vice-Governor Schoeller remarked in March 1960, "nowhere in the Congo are Europeans so intimately mixed in the activities of the Congolese political parties."[58] The grafting of irrelevant European antagonisms onto the political contest in Katanga helped to make it more bitter.[59]

[57] *Ibid.*, p. 23.
[58] *Congo 1960*, I, 236.
[59] See Lemarchand's interesting analysis, "The Limits of Self-

Thus it can be seen that although the roots of the autonomy movement as a European grievance extend almost back to the days of Msiri, federalism as an African idea is almost contemporary. Clearly, no self-respecting creed could admit to such compressed historical antecedents, and no African movement could publicly flaunt the European paternity of the federal idea. The artificiality of the Katanga movement in its African dimension was a serious constraint; the search for a Burkean prescriptive legitimation for the Katanga idea is thus interesting. Msiri's grandson has provided one interesting proposal as a sanctifying myth:

"The Katanga existed long before the arrival of the whites. Its copper has always been exploited by the natives. It had a money . . . and several armies. . . .

"We had an administrative and judicial organization which met the needs of the country. Between the different chiefs of Katanga, there existed defense pacts for protection against external enemies.

"The Congo, for its part, owes its existence only to King Leopold II and Belgium . . . who after the Berlin Conference . . . sent his emissaries to inform the traditional chiefs inhabitating that part of Africa later called the Belgian Congo that they depended on King Leopold II . . .

"But it was only in 1891 that the Belgians occupied the Katanga without the consent of the traditional authorities of the time or the inhabitants. Certain traditional chiefs were assassinated, among them the Emperor Msiri.

Determination: Katanga," *loc. cit.*, pp. 411-12. Some distinction may be made perhaps between the Conakat and Balubakat entourages. In the former case, European influences were more extensive and represented more firmly-rooted vested interests (missions, permanent settlers, companies). In the latter instance, the apparent community of ideological orientation between the Baluba movements and the Belgian Left was a central causal factor for the linkage. No doubt one may also discern a sort of paternalism of the Left, a vague desire to save the Congolese from the clutches of Church and capital.

"Despite the oppression of which the Katanga populations were the victims, the Katanga remained unsubmitted to Belgium from 1891-1910.

"Beginning in 1910, the Katanga had a special statute. A Vice-Government General was erected. . . . The Katanga was accordingly a protectorate like Uganda . . . or Ruanda and Urundi.

"But for unknown reasons, and despite our energetic protests, we were annexed to the colony in 1933. . . . As a sign of protest, the Vice-Governor, M. Gaston Heenen, resigned. This date marked the origin of Katangan nationalism.

"All the chiefs joined his protest. But the colonial power did not see this solidarity with equanimity. To stifle Katangan nationalism, the chiefs, judged dangerous because of this sentiment, were deported.

"The chief Katanga Kyanana, now President of the House of Chiefs, was deported in 1933, and permitted back in his own area only in 1950. There were several cases of rustications in the families of Kasongo Nyembo, of Mutombo Mukulu, of Mwata Yamvo, of Mwenda [Munongo], and many other chiefs.[60]

Tshombe garnished this analysis with some insights of his own in his address marking the second anniversary of secession:

"To serve certain political designs, people have pretended that the Katanga did not exist, that it was a construction of the colonizers. This is to deny that, when the first white explorers discovered the part of Africa called the Katanga, they found three monarchies which were not only bound by family, economic and social links, but, and this is by far the most important, their historic destiny had been linked for centuries. These links existed among themselves

---

[60] Godefroid Munongo, *Comment est né le nationalisme katangais* (Elisabethville, mimeographed, June 16, 1962).

and themselves only. They did not exist with other neighbors. These monarchies constituted in the heart of Africa an entity apart, matured slowly over a long historic period, with July 11, 1960, only the manifestation of an awakening self-consciousness. . . .

"When the Belgians and the English, the former coming from the north and the latter from the south, tried to lay their hands on the Katanga, the Baluba, Lunda, and Bayeke chiefs were united in the face of the new danger which threatened their sovereignty, and fought with all their feeble force.

"While in the Congo, Stanley and the other functionaries sent by Leopold II succeeded in having signed more than a thousand treaties by which chiefs renounced their sovereignty, here, the Baluba, Lunda, and Bayeke refused to sign or to recognize the flag of the so-called Congo Free State. This was, once again, the manifestation of this common historic destiny which I have just mentioned. It was for the first time the common resistance to a foreign effort to impose its will in Katanga."[61]

Needless to say, much of this history requires some strained reinterpretation of what is generally accepted to be the truth.[62] Katanga was not a natural entity; when its

[61] M. Tshombe, *Discours prononcé par le president du Katanga à l'occasion de la fête du 11 juillet, 1962* (Elisabethville: 1962), pp. 4-5.

[62] The hypothesis of a league of Katanga chieftaincies preceding the colonial era is an original one. It is true that there are mystical bonds between the Mwata Yamvo of the Lunda and the Kasongo Nyembo of the Baluba. The legendary Muluba hunter, Ilunga Tshibinda, married the Lunda queen Lueji, apparently about the end of the 16th century; he was the grandson of a brother of a Kasongo Nyembo, and their son, Mwato Lusenji Naweji, was the first to take the title of Mwata Yamvo. On this, see Edmond Verhulpen, *Baluba et Balubaisés du Katanga* (Antwerp: Editions de l'Avenir Belge, 1936), pp. 73, 134; Leon Duysters, "Histoire des Aluunda," *Problèmes d'Afrique Centrale*, No. 40, 2nd quarter (1958), pp. 75-98. The explorer Cameron, the first European to visit the Kasongo Nyembo, remarked: "Kasongo was inflated with pride, and asserted that he was the greatest chief in the whole world. The only one, in his opinion, who

borders were defined by King Leopold II and Albert Thys, it is doubtful whether either had heard of the three Katanga monarchies. The May 1960 national election results, in which the *Cartel Katangais* (Balubakat and ATCAR) had a narrow plurality over the Conakat, 110,000 to 104,000, suggest that Katanga nationalism was hardly monolithic and the three kingdoms were far from covering the entire population. But the Katanga myth was Africanized; the old tale about Europeans building a copperbelt in the wilderness has been transformed to resistance folklore, and an exaltation of those who fought the colonizer.

To outside observers the Katanga pole of federal sentiment suffered from its apparent associations; almost every caricature of evil in Africa seemed to be included in one unholy coalition. There were European settlers, large cor-

---

could compare with him was Mwata Yamvo . . . who was also a Muluba [sic], and belonged to the same family as Kasongo." Verney L. Cameron, *Across Africa* (New York: Harper & Bros., 1877), p. 326.

However, Msiri and the Bayeke only arrived in Katanga from Tanganyika in the mid-19th century. Msiri was in the process of constructing a state, which might well have lasted but for the untimely arrival of the Belgians in 1891. However, he was hardly greeted as a welcome addition to the royal table in Katanga; contemporary reports spoke rather of a hostility between Msiri and the established chiefs which facilitated the task of colonial conquest. On this, see Auguste Verbeken, *Msiri* (Brussels: Editions L. Cuypers, 1956), and Grévisse, "Les Bayeke," *Bulletin des juridictions indigènes et du droit coutumier congolais*, V, Nos. 1-8 (1937-1938). Although the domains of Msiri and Kasongo Nyembo were within Katanga, the Lunda empire spilled over into Angola and Northern Rhodesia. Neither the Baluba Hemba of Northeast Katanga nor the "River" Baluba of the Lulaba Valley and Lake Kisale area, the core of Balubakat strength, were organized as part of any of the three kingdoms. Munongo's interpretation of the dissidence of a number of paramount chiefs in the 1930's as having resulted from reading Sépulchre's articles in the *Essor du Congo* is the most ingenious historical reinterpretation of the collection. Dissidence there was, but other sources indicate that the causes were quite different, among them having been the application of the decree of December 5, 1933, reorganizing the *circonscriptions indigènes*. On the other hand, it is true that the Katanga chiefs had no interest in signing up with the Free State and that it was only, as Tshombe says, "brutal force" which subdued them.

porations,[63] and African leaders who were at best ethnic chauvinists, if not downright toadies for the European interests. Autonomy was thought to be demanded in order to selfishly conserve the full benefits of the Katanga mineral wealth to the detriment of the poorer regions.

In fact, as an African movement, federalism first emerged as a byproduct of the tensions engendered by modernization. As it became involved in the dialectic of power transfer, it progressively assimilated the older arguments of the earlier European autonomy movement. The complete absence of communication among the African elites of Elisabethville and Leopoldville until the virtual eve of independence is a factor which cannot be underestimated. A hardened framework of mutual distrust already existed by the time these were established.[64] Even the contacts of

[63] The role of the large corporations, especially *Union Minière* and the *Société Générale*, is much more complex than is generally believed by the world at large. One must carefully distinguish between the activity of the companies as such and that of their employees, and also between the Brussels and Elisabethville offices. There is every reason to believe the analysis of Glinne, from the Left group of the PSB, who argues that the companies were willing to use the secession threat as leverage, but did not want to have their bluff called. "Le pourquoi de l'affaire katangaise," *Présence Africaine*, XXXII-XXXIII (June-September, 1960), pp. 49-63. Both the Conakat and the Balubakat Cartel received large subsidies from the companies; many qualified observers, such as former Elisabethville district commissioner Grévisse, were convinced that, in terms of the ethnic arithmetic, the Balubakat Cartel was going to win, and there was too much at stake for the companies to risk betting on a losing horse. In my opinion, the most reasonable interpretation of the behavior of colonial corporations is that they were simply bewildered by the pace of events, had had little experience in other countries to provide perspective in survival techniques for periods of political effervescence, and pursued simultaneously several contradictory policies in order to hedge as many bets as possible. See Lemarchand's useful discussion on this subject, "The Limits of Self-Determination," *loc. cit.*, p. 41. See also Gérard-Libois, *op. cit.*, pp. 321-22 and *passim*. On the other hand, there can be no doubt, as Lemarchand argues, that UMHK fully supported the secession in July 1960, in its initial stages.

[64] Perhaps the only level at which communication was taking place was among the students at Lovanium University. It is interesting to note that the president of the Lovanium student council during 1958-

503

the Balubakat Cartel were dominated by the local situation in Katanga; outside alliances were sought primarily as a foil to the Conakat, not for their own sake. The Katanga leadership saw few perspectives for the kind of role in Leopoldville to which they came to feel their economic contribution to the country entitled them; this further reinforced the parochialism which had grown from the constraints of the colonial past. The federal doctrine proposed was extraordinarily vague and really boiled down to two elemental ideas: first, that access to responsibility should be limited to those from the province, and second, that the Katanga tribute to Leopoldville should be as small as possible. In these two notions, one can see the fusing of the two historic strands in Katanga federalist aspirations.

Roots of Federalism: Bakongo

The other federal pole, that of the ethnic self-awareness of the Bakongo, was of an entirely different character. The fascinating growth of a militant Bakongo self-consciousness has been described in Chapters XI and XII, and need not be repeated here. What is relevant at this juncture is an examination of the meaning attached to the federal idea and the process by which federalism came to be seen as the constitutional vehicle for the fulfillment of Bakongo aspirations. The Abako set the whole framework for the constitutional debate by its adoption of a federalist platform.

The assertion of federalism as a political aim was only made publicly late in April 1959, a little more than fourteen months before independence.[65] Until the Leopoldville riots and the Government Declaration, the issue of govern-

---

1959 was a Lunda student, Paul Malimba; political consciousness was already strong at Lovanium, and Malimba then fully shared the nationalist sentiments of his colleagues, although he later rallied to the Tshombe regime.

[65] *ABAKO 1950-1960*, pp. 205-08.

mental structures was so remote that there was little point in public discussion. In its early days, the Abako directed its energies to a cultural renaissance of all Bakongo, including those of Congo (Brazzaville) and Angola. In 1956-1958, Van Bilsen suggests that Kasavubu was inclined to a confederal structure, with much more diffuse links with the rest of the Congo than those urged in 1959.[66] The 1956 Abako Manifesto chided the authors of *Conscience Africaine* for their appeal for a single national union but no parties; political parties were essential to triumph over the colonial adversary, and as it is "pure utopia to seek to rally all Congolese to a single opinion," these had to be several.[67] Other than this indirect hint of an assumption of pluralism in the political community, there is no reference to federalism.

The experiences of 1957-1958, with parts of the colonial administration seeking to mobilize the Bangala as a counterpoise to Bakongo "extremism," were of great importance in solidifying Abako dispositions toward a federal formula. The administration and some Catholic mission milieux had considerable success in convincing a number of Bangala leaders that the Abako was a xenophobic movement which planned to establish a "Revolutionary Fanatic Party," claimed Leopoldville as Bakongo property, and nurtured separatist ambitions.[68] Most Bangala leaders felt that the "immediate independence" platform launched by the Abako in 1956 was unreasonable, and were prepared in 1959 to give full support to the Government Declaration. Bolikango, in 1957, told one writer: "The Abako leaders are petty and mean-spirited who are only concerned with tribal demands. A movement like this is condemned from the start because it is confined to a sterile regionalism."[69]

[66] Van Bilsen, *L'indépendance du Congo,* p. 219.
[67] *ABAKO 1950-1960,* p. 39.
[68] *Ibid.,* pp. 101-11; Gilis, *Kasa-vubu au coeur du drame congolais,* pp. 82-87.
[69] Labrique, *op. cit.,* p. 181. Dericoyard, an Azande long resident

The reaction to this in many Abako quarters was to conclude that only the Bakongo wanted independence; the others, in opposing the Abako, were opposing its independence demand. In the words of the Abako weekly:

"For a long time, the Abako had deployed all its efforts for unity. . . . Up to the moment when it demanded independence, the Abako did it on behalf of everybody.

"Protests then arose on all sides, claiming that the Abako had no right to speak in the name of all, and that it should concern itself uniquely with the problems of the Bas-Congo.

"The press published on this subject violent attacks on the Abako. The colonial administration stepped in, and one saw the birth of a host of associations, whose leaders, if one may believe the rumors, were in the hire of the colonial administration to oppose the action of the Abako. . . .

"The Abako had proposed unity, the others refused this proposal. It was their absolute right. But let them not come now and talk about unity today. The Abako was hounded both by the colonialists and all the ethnic groups for having wanted unity; it heard the voice of reason, and abandoned this idea."[70]

Mingled with the resentment at finding their earlier demands on the colonial administration unsupported or even opposed by other groups was the strong ethnic pride which was a central part of Bakongo solidarity. In this perspective, it was not surprising that peoples in their view less culturally advanced would not share the avant-garde aspirations of the Bakongo. "If our Bangala friends pass themselves off as the grand masters in the field of civilization, why haven't they civilized their own brothers in their respective regions?" asked *Notre Kongo*. "*Que d'êtres prim-*

in Leopoldville and subsequently a Minister in the second Ileo and revamped Adoula governments, added at the same time, "the Abako is at once a linguistic and a separatist movement whose aggressive designs are undeniable."

[70] *Notre Kongo*, November 1, 1959.

itives dans le Haut-Fleuve!"[71] The arguments advanced by a clandestine Bakongo group, the *Mouvement de Résistance Bakongo,*[72] in April 1959, to justify rejection of the decolonization program set forth in the Government Declaration, are illustrative of this point:

"[addressed to the Belgian Parliament] . . . Need we remind you that [the Bakongo] do not want to hear about the Government Declaration, and that they ask in consequence immediate independence?

"We know that we cannot oblige our African brothers who see the question from another angle to hitch themselves to our wagon. As we would like to have our opinion respected, so we respect that of others. We have, on the path of progress, three centuries of advance on the other ethnic groups of Central Africa.

"We demand . . . the partition of Belgian Africa."[73]

Bakongo ethnic self-awareness further implied irredentist dreams; the reassertion of the cultural unity of the Bakongo necessarily applied to those inhabiting Angola and Congo (Brazzaville). The crucial historic legitimization provided by the invocation of past glories of the ancient kingdom of the Bakongo made it inevitable that longing glances would be cast at the neighboring territories and consideration given to ways and means by which the post-colonial political community might in one way or another permit a reconstitution of the historic unity. One option would sim-

---

[71] *Ibid.,* February 17, 1960.

[72] The Abako had been dissolved after the January riots, for which it has been falsely blamed by the administration. In June 1959, it was reformed as the *Alliance des Bakongo* (Abako), this time overtly a political party. The *Mouvement de Resistance Bakongo* was a temporary replacement for the Abako during the period of dissolution.

[73] *ABAKO 1950-1960,* pp. 203-05. These statements need to be placed in perspective; the more extreme ethnic chauvinism was never expressed by the responsible, upper echelons of the Abako leadership, by such men as Kasavubu. But it did reflect views widely shared in the rank and file of the movement, especially in times of political tension.

ply be the secession of the three component parts of the old empire from their colonial affiliations to create a Bakongo state. This was hinted by *Notre Kongo,* in an article entitled "Kongo Uni, Pays Fort"[74] in late 1959:

"We will thus have the name Kongo in the three parts [Belgian, French, and Portuguese] of the empire which will permit us to regroup under a unitary or federal form. It is with this object that the *Mouvement de Regroupement des Populations Kongolaises,* in a declaration published in Leopoldville, has taken an inventory of the riches and future possibilities of a United Kongo. The *Union des Populations d'Angola* (UPA)[75] on its side wants nothing more than to see the colonial divisions of Kongo suppressed by decolonization itself. In a response given to an overly curious journalist, the Abbey Fulbert Youlou let it be understood on the subject of Kongo: *'Tout ce qui se ressemble, se rassemble.'* "[76]

A variant to this idea was the proposal that Bakongo reunification could be achieved in the framework of a larger political community. The various colonial entities of Central Africa could be fused into a vast *Union des Républiques d'Afrique Centrale* (URAC). URAC, said the Abako weekly, could be "the point of departure for pan-Africanism." The delegates at the Kisantu Congress in December 1959, it was maintained, were thinking not only of the Congo, but of AEF, Ruanda-Urundi, Tanganyika, Kenya, the Rhodesias, Nyasaland, and Angola. "URAC therefore responds to the desires of our populations seeking to recover the national unity of the Kongo in the

[74] Bakongo spelled with a "K" the "Kongo" which is held to be the domain of the Bakongo. The title is an adaptation of the slogan made famous by the psychological services of the *Force Publique,* "*Congo Uni, Pays Fort.*"

[75] Political movement headed by Holden Roberto, formed in 1954, in good part based on the Bakongo areas of northern Angola, which launched the armed insurrection against the Portuguese in March 1961.

[76] *Notre Kongo,* November 19, 1959.

boundaries of the Ancient Kingdom of Kongo. URAC also responds to the desires of other Africans who saw in their separation from the populations of the Kongo ominous signs of a dark and unhappy future should the gates to the sea be closed to them for some time."[77]

Fundamentally, however, these projects, however fondly cherished, came hard up against the realities of the decolonization process. In 1959, it was growing clearer every day that the independence demand was likely to be met much more rapidly than anyone had dared dream when the slogan was first launched. To the south, there was clearly no end in sight to Lusitanian intransigence; the UPA was not talking in terms of an ethnic regrouping, at least in public. To the north, Youlou was preoccupied with consolidating his position as head of state in the Brazzaville Republic, which he had precariously obtained in November 1958 by subverting one member of Jacques Opangault's party in the territorial legislature to alter the majority. The Abako leaders had to decide then and there what strategy to adopt in the face of Belgian intentions to proceed with the organization of a unitary, albeit decentralized state.

It was the end of April 1959 when the three Abako leaders, Kasavubu, Diomi, and Nzeza, made the first official statement on behalf of the Abako calling for a federal structure. They expressed their pleasure that nationalism had now spread to other parts of the Congo and denied "the gratuitous affirmation" that the Bakongo intended to impose their will on other peoples of the Congo. They continued:

"The unity of the Congo, which we admit in principle, would be desirable in the sense of a sort of federation of autonomous provincial entities.

"The difference of the degrees of evolution of Congolese populations should be seen as a stimulant for the ones and

[77] *Ibid.,* January 17, 1960.

an encouragement for the others. . . . Diversity does not necessarily exclude unity.

"The Congolese nation will be freely formed by a common agreement of all the peoples of the Congo. . . . Imposed, the unity of the Congo will always remain vulnerable."[78]

In June 1959, the federal views of the Abako were re-affirmed in more precise terms; the economic unity was accepted as indispensable to rapid development. Politically, it was argued, only "autonomous local power linked at the summit by commonly accepted institutions" could preserve the unity of the country. "Overly centralized and authoritarian power . . . would lead fatally to secession."[79] On June 21, the Abako submitted to Van Hemelrijck a plan for an "autonomous republic of Kongo Central," which was coterminous with Leopoldville province, less Lac Leopold II district. Federalism achieved nationalist respectability in the indignant reaction of Van Hemelrijck to this proposal: *"L'heure est à la fermeté,"* the Minister exclaimed, adding a warning that sanctions would be taken against the Abako leaders if they diffused and propagated this scheme.[80]

The choice of the Kongo Central boundaries is most interesting; in fact, only two of the four districts included, plus about half the city of Leopoldville, were inhabited by Bakongo. At this point, in mid-1959, the PSA was just beginning to be organized in Kwilu, while Kwango was as yet little touched by the nationalist awakening. Thus there was no immediate protest from the non-Bakongo regions at being included in what was clearly intended to be a Bakongo-dominated province. At the abrupt rejection of their plan the Abako went into a phase of total opposition, with civil disobedience rapidly spreading through the

[78] *ABAKO 1905-1960*, p. 207.
[79] Published June 3, 1959, quoted in *ibid.*, pp. 208-09.
[80] *Ibid.*, pp. 229-35.

Bas-Congo. In the context of the sudden explosion of the latent frustrations and hostility to the colonial system throughout the Congo, there was a tendency for political prestige to be proportionate to the purity of the intransigence. It was thus that the PSA, even as it gained in strength, was anxious to avoid a public dispute with the Abako.

In August, Acting Governor Schoeller and Secretary Stenmans sent alarming reports to Brussels, indicating that acceptance of the federal theses of the Abako was an absolute prerequisite to regaining communication with the activist wing of Congolese nationalism.[81] Stenmans noted that all the Bakongo feared being stifled in centralized institutions; he suggested that the difference was not very great between a decentralized unitary state and a federation. During the last half of 1959, despite Lumumba's success in Stanleyville, the political evolution was really dominated by the interaction between the Abako and the colonial administration. The Abako was an irresistible pole of attraction, with its success culminating in the Kisantu Congress, bringing together the PSA, MNC/K, and PP, among others.

The Bakongo federalism, then, was sharply distinct from that of Katanga. This was seen as a form of government which would guarantee cultural autonomy to the Bakongo; nothing was more unthinkable to a Mukongo than the prospect of being subjected to the orders of those from outside the region. (This form might also facilitate the realization of the Bakongo reunification dream, should circumstances ever prove propitious for this.) The separatist strand in Bakongo nationalism was in large part an outgrowth of the early articulation of the independence demands. Convinced that their region was more highly developed than those of the interior, they were unwilling to accept the proposition that their independence should

[81] *Congo 1959,* pp. 135-46.

await the further development of other provinces. There was no interest in the economics of federalism; the Abako manifestos on the subject never discussed this aspect, except to endorse the hypothesis that the preservation of the economic unity of the country was desirable.

The one element which Abako and Katanga federalism had in common was the extraordinary vagueness on the real details of the proposed federation. Prior to the Brussels Round Table the only tentative formulation of a distribution of functions between the center and the provinces was that proposed by the Kisantu Congress; this summary list shows every sign of haste and does not begin to attack such crucial conflicts of a federal system as the delineation of fiscal domains, or police jurisdictions, or recruitment and supervision of the administration.[82] The equally fundamental issue of the viability of the provincial components of the projected federation was not even debated; the "existing administrative subdivisions are retained, in principle."[83] The energies and attention of the Congolese leadership were at this point entirely absorbed in the exigencies of the dialogue with Belgium and the struggle for power within the fragmented nationalist movement.

Implicit Federalism: Loi Fondamentale

It belonged to the Round Table Conference to make a tentative determination on the issue of "federalism." The similarity of their slogans would have seemed to have been a logical basis for an alliance of its advocates. In the event, however, the disparate origins of the two federal theories, and lack of previous communication between them, had an opposite result. Although there had been at the Kisantu corridors observers from both the Conakat and the Balubakat,[84] the Conakat, in particular, had little feeling of

[82] *Ibid.*, pp. 299-300.
[83] *ABAKO 1950-1960*, p. 299. Resolution 2 of the Kisantu Congress.
[84] *Congo 1959*, p. 260.

community with the radical nationalism of the Abako Cartel, despite their mutual adherence to federalism. They resented the fact that the pace of political evolution was being dictated by the Abako in a dialogue from which they were excluded. The Conakat federalism suffered in Abako eyes from the stigma of its European antecedents and associations. The Abako Cartel wound up not pushing the scheme of its six federated republics adopted at the Kisantu Congress; instead, on January 29, the Cartel issued a communiqué which represented a considerable retreat from its Kisantu federalism: "The Cartel is preoccupied with the unity of the Congo, without which no economic expansion or social progress can be realized. This unity seems to it the only guarantee of an equitable division of the national wealth for the benefit of the entirety of the Congo populations."

The statement added that a unitary state would create strong regional reactions and that unity could best be preserved through a federal structure.[85] Three days later, an even stronger statement was made: "The frontiers of the regions must coincide with the present provincial boundaries. The Cartel opposes in addition any right of secession for regions or parts thereof. If one of them would provoke such a secession, or would try to seize power in the central state, the federal government would have the right to dissolve the regional authorities until legality has been reestablished."[86]

The federalism-unitary controversy, which indeed had been the primary issue at debate among the contending Congolese political groups, was regarded by the Belgians as the most dangerous question at the Round Table.[87]

[85] *Congo 1960*, I, 37.
[86] *Ibid.*
[87] It will be recalled that the Belgian policy, defined in the report of the Working Group, was to promote a unitary state, representing a continuity with the traditions of colonial administration, but with considerable decentralization, which in fact was also a continuity of

There was at this late date no desire on the part of the colonizer to profit from the dispute. On the contrary, the objective of the Belgian delegation was to "defuse the bomb."[88] It is beyond doubt that little purpose would have been served by provoking detailed discussions on the thorny problems of federal relationships, as such debate could only have proceeded in a factual vacuum. The Congolese delegates at that time lacked the experience, and the many able Belgians counseling them were hardly better equipped in the special field of federal government. Thus the dominant mood of the Round Table was to seek solutions on the issue of areal dispersal of power which could achieve consensus, and avoid semantic quarrels.

The Round Table made no decision on the terminological issue as to whether its proposals should be considered as constituting a unitary state, with considerable decentralization, or a federal structure. Even the Conakat rather quickly abandoned its demands that the provisional constitution be clearly labeled "federal."[89] The only disputes came in the preparation of a list of respective attributes of the provincial and central governments. It is noteworthy that in the debates the Abako made virtually no effort to augment the role of the provinces; the list which the Lumumbist unitary bloc was willing to concede to the provinces was for the moment acceptable to the Abako Cartel. The issues really in dispute dealt with matters which seemed relevant to the Conakat. The most heated exchanges took place over the regulation of mining rights and payment of royalties. The Conakat initially proposed a system by which the central government would be fi-

---

policy advocated since 1945 but never effectively implemented. Despite the Schoeller-Stenmans memoranda of August 1959, this remained official policy until the Round Table, although with diminishing conviction as Belgium came to accept the idea that independence would not be organized and granted unilaterally, but negotiated with the most representative groups.

[88] *Ibid.*, p. 36.

[89] G. Dumont, *La Table Ronde Belgo-Congolaise*, p. 88.

nanced by voluntary contributions from the provinces. In the end, the fiscal predominance of the central organs was affirmed, and some satisfaction was given the Conakat on the issue of mining concessions by an agreement that these would be made by the provinces, subject to certain general regulations, to be laid down centrally.

The crucial decision made at the Brussels Round Table, which paved the way for the transformation of the Congo from centralized state to federal system, was the recasting of the province from an administrative into a political structure. The provincial governments were to derive from assemblies elected by universal suffrage. The provincial president differed, then, in an essential way from his predecessor, the provincial governor; the president was elected by the assembly and was responsible to it. The provincial governor had been named by the Governor-General, and was hierarchically subordinate to him. Provincial institutions appeared to replicate the structures of a modern state, with ministers and deputies; lower echelons (district, territory, and *circonscription*) never lost their predominantly administrative character. The provinces shared with the new national government the glamour of being an object of electoral rivalry in May 1960. Provincial departments were to be transformed into ministries; department heads would no longer be senior Belgian functionaries, serving the last stretch of a colonial career, but young Congolese, recruited through political competition.

The provinces were not given extensive delegated powers by the *Loi Fondamentale*. However, the very creation of intermediate institutions, deriving their sanction directly from the provincial electorate, made it possible for the province to expand into the vacuum caused by central paralysis. Further, certain important central controls over the provinces never became operative. In particular, the central government was to be represented in each province by a state commissioner, to be named by the Chief of State and confirmed by the Senate (after consulting the respective provincial president); this provision in fact was never carried out. In addition a constitutional court was to be established to arbitrate conflicts of attribution between the central and provincial governments; this also was never done.

In sum, the *Loi Fondamentale* was a truce rather than a settlement. By definition, it was intended merely to permit the launching of the Congolese state. The militant wing of Congolese nationalism wanted to have the final constitution entirely created by the Congolese themselves, to insure against colonial jurisdiction. Belgium was no longer sure which formula it wanted, as the traditional predisposition toward unitary institutions was sapped by suspicion of the unitarists. Although neither the Lumumbist unitarians nor the Abako nor Conakat federalists were satisfied with the law as it stood, all accepted it.

Beginning with the Round Table areal distribution of power was discussed in practical detail. But the issue occupied the delegates for only one week, from February 5 through 12. The *Loi Fondamentale* was drafted in less than six weeks after the adjournment of the Round Table and was submitted to the Belgian Parliament on March 31. Although the working group which collaborated on its drafting had available some material on the Swiss and Nigerian constitutions, as well as the unitarian Ghana model, very little was drawn from these. According to one of the drafters, it was felt that there was no mandate for them to try to resolve any of the difficult questions, except insofar as a solution was indicated by the Round Table resolutions and proceedings. All involved, Congolese and European, had felt that this was an adequate working document which would do provisional service until a definitive constitution could be drawn up.[90]

[90] Interview with Jean-Marie Kititwa, Kivu representative on the

It is instructive to recall the prolonged and controlled experimentation which led to the preparation of a genuine and functioning federal constitution in African circumstances. In the case of Nigeria, beginning with the Richards constitution of 1945, major new constitutions or alterations were made in 1951, 1953, 1954, and 1957, before the adoption of the final constitution for independence. Almost continuous negotiations and constitutional conferences resulted in a system which represented a genuine consensus rather than a makeshift compromise.

Crisis and Power Dispersal

The post-independence crisis provided a virtually complete rupture in the constitutional system as foreseen before independence. The tightly structured administrative centralization had been effectively ended, and there could be no real prospect of reestablishing it on its former lines. The various specialized services at the central level were no longer capable of insuring that whatever directives they might prepare would be followed by the provinces. The control over the local administration was in fact lost in July 1960.[91]

Nowhere was centralization before independence more complete than in the field of public finance. Not only were all significant taxes paid to the central government but government disbursements were made entirely from Leopoldville. The treasury operations in the Congo had become a highly sophisticated affair, adapted to permit use of electronic computers. This whole system became entirely inapplicable after the breakdown, not only because of the loss of necessary technicians but also for the more elemental reason that the government simply lost all control over its expenditures. The budgetary mechanism

---

political commission appointed by the Round Table to participate in the drafting, Bukavu, August 11, 1962.

[91] Supra, pp. 403-08.

collapsed, especially at the provincial level; the previously extraordinary procedure of the *"débit d'office"* for an emergency expenditure not provided for in the budget became a generalized practice. The provinces made payments, using whatever stock of currency was available in the local branch of the *Conseil Monétaire,* successor to the *Banque Centrale.* As one of the Congo's key financial advisers has observed: "Although Leopoldville authorities paid without distinction all the provincial expenditures, they no longer exercised any control over the authorities who made them. No longer constrained to present a justification for their operations, no longer receiving any visit from itinerant inspectors of the central government, sheltered from any penalties which the weakness of the government rendered illusory, the local authorities spent without justification and without end."[92]

Until 1962, no province (except Katanga) had a budget. Although each province still had to show that the payments it was making were in fulfillment of some charge upon the province, there was simply no longer any need for a budgetary provision before a financial obligation could be contracted. This system was obviously completely intolerable, and in March 1962 an important reform was prepared by the Ministry of Finance. The central government simply made a global payment to the provinces and left it to them to be responsible for all their expenditures. These bills, such as salaries for functionaries and teachers, which were still actually paid from Leopoldville, were deducted from the provincial subsidy. In addition, the provinces were permitted to keep such taxes as they collected.

For present purposes, what is most interesting about this important reform is that it was entirely a de facto adjustment to the new circumstances of independence. This question was never discussed during the debates on "fed-

[92] H. Leclercq, "L'inflation congolaise," *Cahiers Economiques et Sociaux,* No. 1 (October 1962), pp. 9-10.

eralism," yet it marks one of the most significant steps to legally consecrated provincial autonomy. As Leclercq remarks, the central government in the final analysis was driven to use the weapon of autonomy to enforce discipline upon the provinces, which it no longer was able to impose from above.[93]

Simultaneous with the growth in provincial autonomy there has been a more subtle weakening of the grid of economic and social relationships which had begun to make the Congo more than simply an administrative entity. It was an article of faith on both Belgian and Congolese sides that the unity of the Congo was an economic necessity. A well-integrated transport net funneled the products of the country toward the single outlet to the sea at Matadi. Kasai corn and Maniema rice fed the great urban centers of South Katanga, whose copper exports kept the state coffers supplied both with tax revenue and foreign exchange. Katanga's mine products were in good part shipped as a matter of national policy via the *"voie nationale,"* even though it was longer and more costly than the direct rail link to the sea through Angola.[94] The BCK rail route through Katanga and Kasai, kept solvent by Katanga ore shipments, brought with it intensive agricultural development through the countryside it traversed.

Fragmentation in 1960-1961 had as a corollary the rupture of economic unity. Katanga products all were ex-

[93] *Ibid.,* p. 16. The fascinating tale of the impact of governmental breakdown on the operation of public finance and foreign exchange is well told in the several studies of Leclercq and also the lucid analyses of Fernand Herman, formerly an economics professor at Lovanium, more recently a technician with the *Conseil Monétaire.* See Leclercq, *Conjoncture Financière et Monétaire du Congo,* 1st and 2nd bulletins, *Notes et Documents,* Nos. 5, 21, IRES, Université Lovanium, 1960-1961. See also the various Herman articles in *Etudes Congolaises.*

[94] Due to chronic foreign exchange deficits since independence, the higher cost caused by necessity to transfer from rail to boat at Port Francqui, then back to rail from Leopoldville to Matadi, is partly compensated by the saving in hard currency which must be paid for shipment through Angola.

ported via Angola or the Rhodesias. South Kasai diamonds reached world markets through various circuitous channels. Coffee and tea in former Orientale and Kivu provinces were exported, mostly illegally, into Uganda. The sporadic hostilities in Katanga destroyed key bridges on the Katanga rail lines. Ethnic hostilities in Kasai forced trains to change crews three times in the 300 kilometers between Port Francqui and Luluabourg. Completion of reunification in January 1963 has brought some progress toward rebuilding the old economic circuits; the acute foreign exchange crisis is a compelling force operating in this direction. To date, however, the eastern part of the country remains significantly less integrated with the rest than during the colonial period.[95]

The rapid expansion of urban centers, especially after World War II, appeared to be producing a growing social integration of the diverse populations. The large cities were all polyglot, and urban experience was believed to be producing a modern man shorn of ethnic reflexes. But the disorders accompanying independence made *"chacun chez soi"* a potent slogan, and there was a widespread unscrambling of populations. The most spectacular example was that of the retreat of Kasai Baluba to the ethnic homeland of South Kasai; a minimum of 250,000 inhabitants were forced to flee other parts of former Kasai province. The UN refugee camp established at Elisabethville in September 1961 was flooded with 70,000 persons, largely but not exclusively Kasai Baluba; these were repatriated to their regions of origin in May and June, 1962. On a smaller scale throughout the country, similar population movements took place. Employment in the provincial civil services was almost entirely restricted to those indigenous to the province. The provincial fragmentation in 1962 produced in its

[95] For further analysis on this point, see Louis Baeck and Christian François, *Analyse économique de situation et étude du commerce exterieur du Congo; Evolution au cours de l'année 1960 et du Ier trimestre 1961* (Leopoldville: IRES, 1961, mimeographed).

train a new round of movements. Kwiluites and Bakongo were forced to leave Kwango. Many Bakusu left Bukavu for Maniema. Azande departed Stanleyville for Paulis. Ngombe in Coquilhatville retreated to Lisala. The Bakongo province, Kongo Central, intimated that its schools would be restricted to children from within the province.[96] Although precise figures are lacking, one may conclude that there has been, at least temporarily, a real diminution of the trans-ethnic linkages which had grown up around the modern economic and administrative circuits introduced by the penetration of the colonial state.

There can be little doubt that the de facto independence of two important regions of the Congo, South Kasai and Katanga, significantly contributed toward the official recognition that the Congo's structures were to be federal. As early as July 17, 1960, less than a week after secession, Tshombe began advocating the reconstitution of "a confederation" of the former Belgian Congo, starting from Elisabethville; this was apparently the position of Belgium at this time. On July 26, Foreign Minister Wigny cabled to Count d'Aspremont-Lynden, officially mandated counselor to the Katanga regime: "Belgium rejoices especially in the recent declarations of M. Tshombe, by which he affirms that he considers the Katanga as the hub of a future confederation of the states of the Congo. The rallying of other provinces of the Congo to the Katanga is therefore to be encouraged, although obviously with discretion."[97] The Katanga regime was at the same time pursuing means of consolidating its independence, but its utter lack of success in obtaining any recognition, and its ostracism by virtually the entire world led to simultaneous exploration of possibilities of resuming ties with the Congo on its own terms.

In the dark days of late 1960 and early 1961, there

[96] *Présence Congolaise*, April 13, 1963.
[97] *Congo 1960*, II, 745.

seemed little hope that the Katanga secession could be ended except through large concessions. The UN was not disposed to use force at this time, and the ANC was much too weak to be a match for the rapidly growing Katanga gendarmery. While Stanleyville proclaimed its fidelity to Lumumba's unitary doctrine, Leopoldville was, by the beginning of 1961, prepared to accept "federalism" as a basis for reunification.

The Round Tables: Leopoldville, Tananarive, and Coquilhatville

With the convening of a Round Table Conference in Leopoldville from January 25 to February 16, 1961, an experiment began in the negotiation of a political and institutional settlement among de facto authorities, by-passing the paralyzed legal institutions. The first Round Table, organized at the invitation of President Kasavubu, failed to bring together either Stanleyville or Katanga, although both were partially represented by sympathizers. The unitary state was rejected; the debate centered upon the issue of whether a "federal" or "confederal" formula should be found. The commission on structures finally opted in its majority for the federal solution.[98]

The next in the series was the Tananarive Conference, March 8 through 12, 1961. Tshombe now was at his apogee. A brief advance of Stanleyville troops as far as Luluabourg and Port Francqui produced an atmosphere of anxiety in Leopoldville immediately after the Round Table. On February 21, the UN Security Council adopted an important new resolution which for the first time explicitly authorized the use of force "in the last resort" to prevent civil war and provided for the immediate removal of all foreign military personnel and political counselors not belonging to the UN command. In Leopoldville, this resolution was at first misunderstood as a threat to disarm Mobutu's

[98] *Congo 1961*, p. 14.

troops and to force a UN solution to the governmental crisis; accordingly, an Elisabethville-Bakwanga-Leopoldville military axis was hastily negotiated on February 28. The Tananarive Conference was an outgrowth of the military accords.[99]

Tananarive came surprisingly close to bringing together all the major actors, de facto or de jure, although many came only reluctantly.[100] But the absence of Stanleyville was decisive in preventing the legitimation of this conference. Tshombe arrived at the conference armed with a project of a confederal constitution. His proposals served as the basis for discussion; he, unlike the other delegations, was accompanied by a juridical counselor. A foreign jurist invited by Kasavubu was expelled within two hours of arrival by Malagasy officials at the request of the Katanga leaders.[101] The atmosphere at Tananarive was one of astonishing entente. The Katanga resolutions were, with minor Leopoldville amendments, adopted, but the apparent accord fell apart as soon as the participants returned to their capitals.

The Tananarive formula of "confederalism" went far beyond the demands the Conakat had made before independence. The situation, they argued, had changed; now Katanga was no longer a petitioner humbly seeking some autonomy, but a sovereign state prepared to make some limited concessions in the confederal interest. In fact, the concessions were extremely limited. Virtually, the sole function of the confederation would be the conduct of

[99] *Ibid.*, pp. 19-27.

[100] *Ibid.*, pp. 27-30. There were apparently divergences of view at Stanleyville as to the wisdom of participation at Tananarive. A telegram arrived in Tananarive from Dayal, then UN chief in the Congo, indicating that Gizenga had agreed to come; there is no reason to suppose that this was sheer falsification by Dayal. The UN itself at this point, despairing of the situation, would have been happy to see any meeting which brought together all Congolese leaders. See also Pierre Davister and Philippe Toussaint, *Croisettes et casques bleus* (Brussels: Editions Actuelles, 1962), pp. 37-52.

[101] *Congo 1961*, p. 134.

international relations; this was merely an admission by Katanga of its own inability to secure the international recognition which would permit it to carry on foreign affairs. Kasavubu was recognized as president of the confederation, but the component states were all to be "sovereign." A Council of States was to meet occasionally, but only to decide by unanimity; such decisions as might be taken were to be implemented by an *"Organisme de Coordination,"* presumably to be financed by an annual fund drive. It is astounding that those articles of confederation could have been unanimously accepted by the participants. The Alice-in-Wonderland character of this meeting is above all a commentary on the utter demoralization of the participants at this nadir of Congolese history. The wave of political murders in Elisabethville, Bakwanga, and Stanleyville; the lack of any promising avenue of escape from the political impasse; the cumulative impact of months of disorder and insecurity alone make plausible this momentary surrender.

The third and final step in the series of Round Tables was the Coquilhatville Conference, from April 24 to May 28, 1961. Once again Stanleyville was not represented, and Tshombe walked out on the second day of the meeting.[102] However, Coquilhatville was by far the most serious of the three Round Tables. The Tananarive mood was entirely past; the confederalism which had been joyfully endorsed was now rejected by virtually all except Kalonji and Tshombe. The conference began as a continuation of Tananarive, but ended by completely rejecting the Madagascar conclusions. The resolutions of the conference were to serve as the basis for drafting of a federal constitution by a commission aided by UN experts.[103]

[102] To be arrested by the ANC when he tried to embark for Elisabethville and transferred to a gilded captivity in Leopoldville, where he remained until his release by Mobutu and the Leopoldville authorities on June 22.

[103] République du Congo, *Documentation technique du Governe-*

On May 13, as the Coquilhatville Round Table moved toward its final phases, Kasavubu announced his intent to summon Parliament back into session, a suggestion immediately endorsed by the delegates present. Although the Coquilhatville results were not as roundly denounced in Stanleyville as had been those of Tananarive, the Lumumbist bloc was by no means prepared to abandon the unitarian terminology which had been a central tenet of Lumumbism; Gizenga in his "governmental declaration" in Stanleyville on May 15 reiterated Lumumba's pledge regarding guarantee of "respect of cultural particularities" and "broad administrative powers" for the provinces within the unitarian framework.[104] Adoula himself, in his governmental declaration on August 2, used terms which differed very little in substance, despite nuances in tone:

"In elaborating a draft constitution, my government will be inspired by the idea of the national unity of the Congolese people, whose sovereignty must be represented by a central power which can defend the territorial integrity of the Congo Republic. Furthermore, my government will take into account the regional diversities which characterize our vast country, and the desire of the inhabitants of the diverse territories to obtain in fields which are of regional rather than of national concern, a local autonomy, which will permit an administration more closely linked to the population and more conscious of its interests."[105]

The word "federalism" was nowhere used, and no reference was made to the results of the Coquilhatville Conference.

Federalism and the Katanga Negotiations

Tshombe arrived in Leopoldville in March 1962, and from

---

ment concernant les résolutions du Coquilhatville (Leopoldville, 1961), p. 26. The resolutions are reproduced in Congo 1961, pp. 74-94.

[104] Congo 1961, pp. 166-81.
[105] Ibid., p. 423.

April until June negotiations in pursuance of the Kitona agreements (ending UN military action in December 1961) were conducted, in an effort to reconcile the still sharply divergent constitutional theses. The Katanga delegates had not taken part in the preparations of the Leopoldville draft constitution, as promised at Kitona. The drafting was done by a commission headed by Marcel Lihau[106] and aided by a team of three UN experts, led by the renowned Nigerian constitutional scholar-cum-politician, T. O. Elias. On its side, Katanga prepared another project of its own, with the help of a young Elisabethville lawyer. The content of the negotiations is given able summary by Gérard-Libois:

"These positions—fundamentally antagonistic—were very clearly expressed during the first meetings and by the first proposals made during the discussions. If some narrowing of the differences was achieved, this was very often the result of a UN mediation or 'advice' given the two sides by interested Western countries. It must be noted in addition that many of the agreements on specific points were only acquired—precisely as during the Belgian-Congolese Round Table of January-February, 1960—by a formulation which left to each side a broad scope of interpretation. Further, these compromises were not sufficient to unclog the negotiations: they are terminated at the end of June by a declaration of failure, with the two parties refusing even to sign a joint communiqué."[107]

The Adoula proposals in their first form did not use the word "federal"; they were in fact very close to the *Loi*

[106] Lihau, who had been Justice Commissioner in the College of Commissioners, completed his law degree at Lovanium in 1962, and thus became the first Congolese university-trained jurist.

[107] J. Gérard-Libois, "Les structures du Congo et le Plan Thant," *Etudes Congolaises*, III, No. 8 (October 1962), 5. For a complete record of the Adoula-Tshombe negotiations, see the excellent White Book prepared by the central government, *Les entretiens Adoula-Tshombe* (Leopoldville: 1962).

Fondamentale. The proposed distribution of powers was virtually identical; the only significant difference was that, rather than providing an exhaustive list of provincial attributions, the project allocated "residual powers" to the states. Given the extensive list of central powers, this concession was not important. The central government was to have a special representative in each provincial capital, similar to the stillborn *Commissaire d'Etat* provision of the 1960 basic law.

A modified version of the Adoula proposals, submitted April 30, used for the first time in an official document of the central government the term "federal." There was some reduction in the powers attributed to the central government, mainly by simplifying the list. The intervention rights of the ANC were defined, and procedures by which the central authorities could enforce the application of one of its edicts in a province were specified. The delegation to provincial administrative services of the execution of functions attributed to the center was made possible, and the right of provinces to recruit their own technicians was granted.

The Katanga negotiators objected that all forms of intervention by the ANC must be proscribed and the provinces equipped with their own armed forces; there could be no special representative of the central government in the provinces, and all administrative agencies in a province had to be under the direct authority of the provincial president.[108] The list of provincial functions proposed by Adoula was termed *absolument dérisoire* and the addition of the "federal" designation purely formal. On May

[108] It is interesting to recall in this connection that this was one of the crucial questions left obscure in the oldest federal constitution, that of the United States. A decisive step toward effective central power in the American federal system was the decision of the Washington administration to have a separate federal service, and in particular independent federal revenue collectors, rather than relying on the states to perform these functions on behalf of the federal government.

527

5, Tshombe presented a Katanga draft; while this represented some advance over Tananarive, the central institutions envisaged were emasculated. All federal military units stationed in a province would be under the sole command of the province, which would have in addition its own gendarmery. All federal functionaries in a province would be under the authority of the provincial president, who would be the representative of central authority in the province. All taxes were to be collected by the provinces, and some revenues turned over to the central government, according to a fixed ratio.

It may be seen from the content of the Adoula-Tshombe arguments that the nature of the debate had changed in an important way. In 1959 and 1960, while "federalists" and "unitarists" opposed each other with furious polemic, the issues were mainly symbolic. Illustrative of this is that the most heated disputes at the Brussels Round Table centered about the question of "mining rights." This was far from being the central question in the definition of the structures of the state. However, it admirably served as a catalyst for the animosities on each side; for the unitarian group, as well as the militant nationalist wing of the federalists, "mines" incarnated the copper empire of UMHK, the suspected neo-colonialist designs of Belgium and her trusts. For the Conakat, the issue of mining rights symbolized the pathological urge of those Congolese failing to qualify as authentic Katangans to seize their resources and, through them, to perpetuate the subordinate social position which native Katangans, less the apostates of the Balubakat alliance, felt they had suffered under the reign of the Kasai Baluba. After two years of intensive political education, it was a wiser set of negotiators who maneuvered cagily; what was at issue in the 1962 discussions went to the heart of political power and its distribution. Elisabethville and Leopoldville were talking about money, organization, and force; the financing of power (partition of the fiscal domain and foreign exchange), the organizational capacity to implement a decision (administration), and the capability to enforce it (army and gendarmery).

With the collapse of the hopes for a negotiated settlement through direct confrontation of Tshombe and Adoula, the UN was impelled to move more actively into the debate. Time was running out, as both UN officials and Tshombe were well aware. The U Thant Plan, unveiled in August 1962, was a general formula of compromise, including a guarantee of a federal constitution, backed by the threat of economic sanctions if Katanga failed to comply. Although Tshombe formally accepted the plan, it became clear by the end of the year that dilatory tactics were again being used, and in the final analysis it was only through a brief and nearly bloodless display of UN military force, December 28 through January 17, that the Katanga secession was terminated.

Toward Luluabourg

With the Congo at last reunified, the terms of the federalism debate changed; it was no longer a bargaining process to secure the voluntary return of the prodigal province, and it thus became removed from the arena of world politics. However, the nature of the polity had entirely changed since 1960. A consensus had emerged during the prolonged period of negotiations for reunification; concessions made by central authority could not simply be retracted. Provincial authorities had acquired autonomy in a number of once-centralized matters through the inability of the central government to enforce its theoretical prerogatives. The creation of new provinces in 1962 had on the whole strengthened the provinces by establishing more homogeneous units. There were no effective national political parties. A general loosening of social and economic linkages had taken place. The reintegration of Katanga had the ironic effect of removing the stigma from provincial autonomy demands; these could no longer be suspect of having been inspired by Tshombe. A trend toward corporate provincial solidarity against "Leopoldville" has become visible; a clear symptom has been the sharp hostility toward central government expressed at three interprovincial conferences held in 1962 and 1963.[109] The third of the series, held at Boma in September 1963, went farthest in this direction; as one observer summarized, "The debates of the Conference were dominated from beginning to end by unanimous complaints against the central government and national parliamentarians."[110]

Against this background work slowly went forward toward formalizing the new central-provincial relationships. A second team of UN experts, again led by T. O. Elias, prepared a draft constitution, whose terms were made known in December 1962.[111] The list of federal and provincial powers, although not differing markedly from the *Loi Fondamentale,* was more explicit and better defined. The system of posting a central commissioner in each province to represent federal authority—a source of constant dispute—was dropped, but the federal services remained under central control. Residual powers remained with the provinces, but this was of little import when such an exhaustive definition of jurisdiction was made. A constitutional court was provided, this time competent to interpret the constitution as well as to settle federal-provincial disputes.

[109] In Leopoldville (October 1962), Coquilhatville (February 1963), and Boma (September 1963). This antagonism toward the central government was a recurrent theme in interviews with authorities in 14 provinces conducted by the writer in 1963.

[110] "La Conférence Interassemblées de Boma," *Etudes Congolaises,* V, No. 9 (November 1963), 19.

[111] It is produced in extenso, along with the legal commentaries of the drafters, in *Travaux Africains,* CRISP, Nos. 12, 13, and 14 (December 15, 20, and 24, 1962). An abridged version appears in *Etudes Congolaises,* III, No. 10 (December 1962), 1-27.

In the fields of force and finance, the federal government was clearly paramount. Not only the mission of external defense but the key role of gendarmery was retained by Leopoldville. The *Sûreté* was a federal service, and the strength and equipment of the provincial police forces was fixed by a federal law. In the fiscal area, the major sources of tax revenue, customs, corporation taxes, personal income taxes, and royalties, were all centrally fixed and collected. The federal government could also levy excise and consumption taxes concurrently with the provinces. The constitution did stipulate that provinces were to receive 50 percent of the export duties collected from products originating in the province, as well as 50 percent of all royalties from mining or other concessions. If a province were to ask for a federal subsidy, which would seem in practice inevitable given the restricted fiscal domain of the provinces, the federal government could require that the provincial budget or that portion to be subsidized by the federal government be submitted for approval.

The UN draft served as the basic working document for the parliamentary commission which began meeting in April 1963, and subsequently for the Luluabourg constitutional commission convened by the Chief of State in January 1964. A noteworthy semantic modification was made to the UN draft in the elimination of the word "federal" throughout the projected constitution adopted in April 1964 by the Luluabourg working group; however, there were no major alterations in the substantive distribution of powers.[112]

Thus out of the pre-independence polemic has gradually emerged a broad consensus over a constitution which is federal in fact, if not name. At the same time, the breakdown in 1960 destroyed the centralized colonial state. For

[112] The text of the Luluabourg draft constitution is printed in *Courrier d'Afrique,* April 18/19, 1964, *et seq.*

better or for worse, unitarian formulas will not be viable for the foreseeable future. Federalism has many disadvantages for a young nation searching for its very preservation. It became, however, through force of circumstance a necessity. Intricate constitutional formulas cannot juggle away the problems of the Congo. However, a system which places real power at a level where it can be responsibly exercised, and where there is some meaningful awareness of linkage between the rulers and the ruled has much to commend it during the period of self-administered political apprenticeship through which the Congo is passing. The constitutional frame which is emerging will doubtless provide central authorities with more potential power than they can effectively exercise at this stage. There will be ample scope for the gradual reemergence of a strong, central government, as the human resources to utilize the central potential become available, and as political structures capable of generating consent for more centralized rule emerge.

CHAPTER XVIII

Fragmentation: The New Provinces

New Provinces as Political Innovation

To COMPLETE the analysis of the new contours of a Congolese state, we must survey briefly the process of decomposition of the original six provinces and the emergence of
twenty-one new units. The transformation of six into
twenty-one entirely changes the character of the Congolese
polity. Although it is too early for definitive judgments on
the new provinces, there is ample material for speculation
on their origins and nature.

The wholesale redrawing of its internal boundaries is
another remarkable Congolese political innovation. The
closest comparison is again with India and the partial re-
drafting of provincial lines which came in the years following 1953, when Nehru retreated from his hostility to linguistic states, he retreated to permit the formation of Andhra.[1]
The revisions, however, have been piecemeal, and the Indian
Government has so far succeeded holding part of the line of
resistance to parochial linguistic nationalism. Even for Afro-
Asia's most prominent example of an assault on poverty in a
constitutional democratic framework, the linguistic state
problem engenders explosive tensions, and has been contained with the greatest difficulty. In Africa, Nigeria has
talked intermittently about the creation of additional regions, and in 1963 it established a new Midwest Region. One
might speculate that what has been done in the Congo virtually requires the opportunity created by the over-all disorganization. In normal conditions, the strains imposed by this
process could not perhaps be risked; in the Congo, there
was less to lose, and the de facto developments made pos-

---

[1] Libya also redrew its provincial boundaries in 1963, but as part
of a shift from a federal to a unitary system.

MAP 8. The New Provinces of the Republic of the Congo
(*Shading indicates former provinces, labeled in parentheses*)

sible by the frailty of the central authority rendered the
wholesale surgery finally necessary.

The Entering Wedge: First Symptoms of Fragmentation

The possibility of altering the provincial frontiers was
hardly broached, even by the federalists, until 1960. The
fragmentation process got its real impetus from the high

534

tensions generated by the May 1960 elections and the ensuing formation of provincial governments. The initial presumption of retention of the six provinces, which had been
the operating hypothesis of all delegations at the Brussels
Round Table, was first breached in South Kasai and Bas-
Congo; the seeds of divorce were sown in June 1960 in
North Katanga, Maniema, and the Mongo south of Equateur, when these groups felt excluded from the formation of
provincial governments. But it was impossible to open the
door a crack to let only real hardship cases creep through.
The flood gates were thrown wide open, and an initial
equilibrium was found at the level of twenty-one individual
provinces.

KONGO CENTRAL

In the case of the Bas-Congo, the results of the general
elections came as a rude shock. Abako leaders had not
really believed that they would not be the largest party in
the Leopoldville provincial assembly. The census figures
clearly forecast the outcome in showing that there were approximately 1,200,000 inhabitants in the Kwilu and only
800,000 in the Bakongo areas; but somehow this evidence
was overlooked.[2] An uneasy accord was negotiated with the
PSA for the formation of a coalition provincial government,
by which the Abako was to have the presidency of the assembly and four ministries, while the PSA had the provincial
president plus four ministers. On the first vote, however, the
accord was violated, and a PSA candidate was elected to
head the assembly.[3] Three days later, the Abako pro-

[2] Guy Spitaels, of the *Institut de Sociologie* (Solvay), and some-
time adviser to the PSA, suggested that many Bakongo were convinced
that these figures had been fabricated by the colonial administration
as a subtle yet malignant way of belittling the unruly Bakongo.

[3] This was not simply an act of ill will, but a reflection of the
serious internal divisions of the PSA at this moment, and the well-
intended but bizarre and ineffective procedure designed by the *Loi
Fondamentale* to insure proportional representation of all parties in
the provincial governments. Under this curious system, all ten
ministers were elected on a single ballot, with each assembly member

vincial deputies issued a communiqué, declaring in part:

". . . Noting the strange attitude of certain political parties in coalition in the province, tending to minimize the importance of the Bakongo people that they subjectively and unjustly call a minority;

"After fruitless efforts with these parties to assure an equitable distribution of the portfolios;

"Given the lack of sincere and loyal collaboration which looms on the horizon in all fields . . . the unity of Leopoldville province is found greatly compromised. . . .

"We, representatives of the Bakongo people, . . . resolve to form ourselves our own provincial government in a Federal Congo."[4]

Belgian Provincial Governor Stenmans intervened to assure that this might be legally done, but not until after the constitution of a central government which could establish the procedures for formation of new provinces. The Belgian mandate, he argued, was to maintain the provinces in their existing form until independence. After arduous negotiations, a temporary solution was found, with a new post of vice-premier established for Diomi (Abako), while Kamitatu (PSA) was provincial president. However, in March 1961, the Abako deputies elected Vital Moanda as "president" of the province of Kongo Central, and offices were set up in Binza, a suburb of Leopoldville. At the end of 1961, the

---

to vote only once for one name. Thus, in the case of Leopoldville, when the provincial assembly met on June 18, in the absence of the Abako deputies to elect seven ministers, leaving three open, the following results were obtained:

Norbert Leta—	13	Sebastien Balongi—	5
Joseph Kulumba—	11	Pierre Mombele—	5
Basile Mabusa—	8	Antoine Gizenga—	4
Celestin Kalunga—	7		

Four others receiving less than four votes were eliminated, and these seven were named "ministers." The absurd possibilities opened by this procedure need not be elaborated.

4 *Congo 1960,* I, 162.

de facto rupture was complete, and the Abako provincial deputies refused to participate further in the assembly of what had been Leopoldville province, although the Abako Leopoldville provincial ministers remained in function until the formal termination of the original province in mid-1962.[5]

SUD-KASAI

The other initial provincial fracture occurred in Kasai, with the tragic exodus of the Baluba back to the ethnic homeland of Bakwanga and Gandajika, after the diaspora in the colonial period. It was not until the end of 1959 that the withdrawal of the Baluba from Lulua lands began, and only in March 1960 that South Kasai leaders began to think in terms of a regrouping of all Kasai Baluba with a distinct administrative homeland. The May elections took on the aspect of an anti-Baluba plebiscite in most parts of Kasai.[6] On June 3, Lumumba formed a *Front Commun* of all the provincial delegates except the Baluba deputies of MNC/K, and a decision was made to form a coalition excluding the Baluba. Although the operation of the voting procedure specified in the *Loi Fondamentale* for the constitution of provincial governments did give MNC/K three of the ten provincial ministries, in proportion to their strength in the assembly, the portfolios allocated to them were deemed minor.[7] On June 14, a formal decision was made by the Baluba deputies to secede from Kasai province; a telegram was sent to Brussels stating: ". . . Given factious majority realized against us by Lumumba including solely belliger-

[5] Diomi discredited himself in Bakongo milieu by remaining on as president of Leopoldville province after Kamitatu resigned to become central Minister of Interior. Although Diomi had been one of the three or four top Abako leaders before independence, he was offered no position in the Kongo Central government.

[6] See, for example, Merriam on the Basongye in this regard, *Congo: Background of Conflict*, pp. 173-94.

[7] The provincial president, who was elected in a separate ballot, allocated ministerial responsibilities among those elected. Ngalula demanded on behalf of MNC/K the posts of Interior and Finance, but neither of these requests was met. *Congo 1960*, I, 216-18.

ent Lulua tribe. . . [and] reactions of Baluba people throughout Congo, we demand modification of Article 7 of *Loi
Fondamentale* . . . before June 30 to permit us to form
separate provincial government directly attached to central
government by legal means."[8]

The same day, a South Kasai government was designated
by the MNC/K deputies,[9] headed by Ngalula. The final
provocation was the exclusion of the MNC/K from the central government formed by Lumumba. Then began a final
headlong flight of Kasai Baluba from other parts of the
province to the Bakwanga area, partly stimulated by the
MNC/K appeal for a rallying around the ethnic colors, and
partly forced by the explosive animosities they now confronted nearly everywhere in Kasai.

Lumumba told Parliament on September 7 that during
his July 11 Luluabourg visit he had urged a reforming of
the Kasai provincial government to give some satisfaction
to the Baluba; this was probably already too late, and
in any case it was not done. On July 26, an announcement
was made from Bakwanga that the "Mining Province"
would be officially proclaimed on July 30; however, it was
August 8 that a statement was issued announcing the
irrevocable decision:

". . . Considering the inability of the present government, just like the colonialist government before it, to
bring peace to Kasai;

"Given the total anarchy now reigning in the country,
which extinguishes any hope of solution . . .

"Given the assassination of several provincial deputies
of MNC/Kalonji and of M. Bienga, provincial deputy of
the *Parti du Peuple,* its ally;

"Considering especially the assassination of M. Kasanji,

[8] *Ibid.,* I, 218.
[9] Included in this bloc was one Muluba elected on a *Parti du Peuple*
ticket.

Senator and Bapende paramount chief, of M. Mualuanji, National Deputy and Tchokwe paramount chief;[10]

"Given the profound hatred and irreducible spirit of vengeance, irremedial consequence of eleven months of arson, pillaging, massacres, mutilations, hatred and vengeance created not only between the Baluba and Lulua, but also ... between their allies ...

"Declares in consequence that the division of Kasai ... is necessary at any cost; informs national and international opinion that, whatever the decision of the Congolese Parliament, the government of the 'Mining Province' is ready and will function at any moment."[11]

The ANC operations in South Kasai at the end of August, perceived by the Baluba as a veritable pogrom, completed the process of inculcating a sense of common ethnic purpose in the face of adversity. The organization of a Baluba province went forward with a remarkable *élan* in the final months of 1960. It was no doubt useful to be able to draw on the organizational resources of the diamond mining giant, *Minière du B.C.K.* (later *Minière du Bakwanga*, or Miba),[12] but what was achieved under Ngalula's leadership by the Baluba themselves was impressive. It is at this point fruitless to assign degrees of responsibility for the demise of Kasai province; more than any other, this partition was an imperative necessity by mid-1960.

[10] The two chiefs were slain at the Tshikapa airport as they deplaned in July 1960; both were favorable to the attachment of Tshikapa to Kalonji's Mining Province.

[11] *Courrier d'Afrique*, August 9, 1960, reprinted in *Congo 1960*, II 799-800.

[12] There were also some Belgian officers and other "mercenaries" fighting with the South Kasai gendarmery, although this "encadrement" was far less thorough than in Katanga. For some "I was there" mercenary accounts, see Michel Borri, *Nous . . . ces affreux* (Paris: Editions Galic, 1962); John Roberts, *My Congo Adventure* (London: Jarolds, 1963).

NORD-KATANGA

A third new province which bore an indisputable pedigree of necessity, at least when officially consecrated in 1962, was North Katanga. The causes here were more immediate; the Balubakat Cartel had no thought of separation until after the constitution of a homogeneous Conakat provincial government and the subsequent secession. It will be recalled that until the end of 1959, tensions in the South Katanga mining centers had been between the Kasaiens, especially Baluba, and the various Katanga ethnic groups. The very different political cleavage which developed in the December 1959 local elections, and especially 1960, produced for the first time a roughly north-south division. Further complicating the picture were the repercussions of political processes in the Kasai, where Lumumba had chosen to ally with the Lulua groups; this resulted in a painful conflict of loyalty for the Kasai Baluba in urban Katanga. Their own local contingencies pulled them toward the Sendwe Balubakat Cartel in the Katanga, while solidarity with the brethren in Luluabourg commanded an anti-Lumumba alliance with the Conakat.

Splitting the province also had the major disadvantage of withdrawing the poorer regions from the wealthy mining zones. North Katanga was well-represented in the population of Elisabethville, Jadotville, and Kolwezi, and thus had a considerable stake in preserving provincial unity. Finally, another ally of the Cartel, the Tshokwe party ATCAR, was not helped by partition; they lived in groups dispersed in Lunda territory, and could not be geographically excised from the Conakat-dominated zones.

The fury of the Balubakat began to rise when, despite a narrow plurality for the Cartel, the workings of the electoral system produced a slight lead for the Conakat. Like the Abako (and the Conakat), they had been convinced before the elections that ethnic arithmetic was in their favor. The resentment mounted when not only those elected

540

on individual lists but their MNC/K Cartel partners rallied to the Conakat. In this atmosphere of bitterness, it was impossible to negotiate an agreement on a provincial government; as with Leopoldville province, the provincial assembly met to elect the government in the absence of the alienated minority. However, unlike Leopoldville where in this situation only seven of the ten posts were filled, all the portfolios were distributed.[13] Two of the new ministers received only one vote, presumably their own, and three others had only three apiece. The Cartel reacted by announcing the formation of an autonomous "Baluba-Tshokwe" government in Leopoldville on June 21, although giving no details of the geographic scope; this was apparently a bargaining counter at this stage rather than a serious initiative.

The Balubakat did not at first respond to the announcement of secession. Although the many press reports predicting the imminent rallying of the Cartel to the solicitations of the Conakat[14] were no doubt exaggerated, it is clear that *sub rosa* contacts were taking place and that Sendwe did not want to burn the bridges immediately.[15] However, on July 27, a delegate of the Cartel told the Katanga assembly:

"In the name of all the members of the Cartel, we express our astonishment in noting that the government of Katanga, composed solely of the members of a single party and which we can term a puppet government, persists in proclaiming the Katanga independent. . . .

"If the disastrous consequences of this government con-

[13] The ambiguity of the "Baluba" notion should again be emphasized. The sundry populations of North Katanga loosely lumped under the Luba label were no more politically homogeneous than they were ethnically. Many Baluba Shankadi, in particular, under the influence of their powerful chiefs, were pro-Conakat. Two of the ministers elected in the Conakat government, Evariste Kimba (later Foreign Minister) and Valentin Ilunga (Justice), were Baluba.

[14] Tshombe on July 15 offered five portfolios and the vice-presidency to the Balubakat Cartel in an effort to rally them to the secession.

[15] Some of these are cited in *Congo 1960*, II, 725-29.

tinue to make themselves felt on our province, making martyrs of certain of the subjects and destroying their property, we will wind up dissolving the present government . . . Failing which, the Cartel will be obliged to form its own government of Northeast Katanga."[16]

By the end of August, the Balubakat zones of the north were in dissidence. In September, as the Katanga gendarmery took form, it had its baptism in action, undertaking a bloody campaign of reprisals and repression. On October 20, the constitution of a province of Lualaba was announced in Stanleyville, with Manona as its capital; the solemn proclamation declared:

". . . Given that Tshombe and his acolytes have delivered themselves with joyous heart to collective massacres of the majoritarian and convinced nationalist Baluba and Tshokwe populations . . .

"We decree that the Katanga will be divided into two parts, Northeast Katanga and South Katanga. This division is due to both political and social difficulties existing between the two forces in presence. . . .

"This province is composed of the following tribes: Baluba, Tshokwe, Babembe, Bahemba, Bazela, Basonge, Balubasania, Baholoholo, Balumotwa, covering 15 territories in three districts. . . ."[17]

In January 1961, a few hundred Baluba soldiers from the Stanleyville garrison reached Manono and consolidated the position of a handful of Balubakat leaders who, beginning in November 1960, had sought to organize a de facto administration. On January 30, 1961, ceremonies marking the official inauguration of the province were held in Manono, with Sendwe undertaking an inspection tour throughout the province in the first half of February. However, in March 1961, in the face of an imminent offensive

16 *Ibid.,* II, 730.
17 *Ibid.,* II, 780-81.

542

by the Katanga gendarmery, the Balubakat provincial government had only 164 soldiers. A desperate effort was made to compensate for the military weakness by the dubious experiment of distributing arms to the Balubakat youth. These became undisciplined, irregular bands, who were a constant menace to everyone within reach, beginning with the North Katanga government itself.[18] They shared responsibility with the Katanga gendarmery for the unbelievable atrocities perpetrated in this unhappy region from 1960-1962.[19]

At the end of March 1961, Manono fell to the Katanga gendarmes, and the North Katanga state momentarily went into eclipse. However, at the Coquilhatville Conference, its existence was recognized. In April and May 1961, strong Malay and Indian UN detachments occupied key positions in North Katanga and made it possible for the Balubakat to regroup. In November 1961, the ANC returned to North Katanga, and government offices were established in Albertville. The launching of a real administration can be dated from December 1961, when the area became financially reintegrated with Leopoldville, and civil servant salaries were again being paid by the central government.[20]

The central government chose the second anniversary of the Katanga secession, July 11, 1962, to promulgate North Katanga as the first of the new provinces, a fitting com-

[18] On March 15, North Katanga President Prosper Mwamba-Ilunga wrote to Gizenga, expressing his grave concern for the lack of discipline and misbehavior of the Balubakat youth groups. *Congo 1961*, p. 311.

[19] A glance at the nauseating photographs reproduced in the *White Book of the Katanga Government about the outlaw activities in some Baluba areas* (Elisabethville; 1961) is enlightening in this regard. The Katanga gendarmery, with its more efficient instruments of slaughter, obviously far surpassed the Balubakat youth in its total bag, if not in its capacity for cruelty; the Katanga *White Book* does not deal with this aspect of the tragedy of North Katanga. For the other side, see O'Brien, *To Katanga and Back*, pp. 140-56 and *passim*.

[20] Leclercq, "L'inflation congolaise," *Cahiers Economiques et Sociaux*, No. 1 (October 1962), p. 10.

mentary on its genesis. For the Balubakat itself, a new province was a move of desperation, which created more problems than it solved, and was reluctantly undertaken. For the rest of the Congo, North Katanga was essentially a reprisal against Tshombe's secession. Verhaegen's summary of North Katanga province is, as usual, apt:

"Historical analysis of the process of creation of the North Katanga province shows therefore that it was the result of preoccupations of a strategic character . . . and not a national consciousness preexistent or forged in the struggle for autonomy. It is nonetheless probable that the political and military events and efforts to establish new institutions which have marked the last two years constitute a positive factor in favor of the political viability of the new province, although one cannot be sure that it will be strong enough to compensate the existence of close bonds of complementarity between the north and south and the attraction for the North Katangan elites and populations of the economic, administrative, and intellectual centers of the South."[21]

Dialectic of Fragmentation

The example of these three splinter provinces was imitated in June 1960 by a number of then less important groups. In Leopoldville, the Abazi party, being unrepresented in the provincial government despite its having won two of the ninety seats in the assembly, threatened to set up a new province of North Kwilu.[22] In Equateur, there were the first threats of a Mongo province, as Unimo felt under-represented in its own homeland. Dericoyard on June 25 threatened in Parliament to reconstitute the Azande Empire in Orientale; Maniema felt cheated both at the na-

[21] Benoit Verhaegen, "Présentation morphologique des nouvelles provinces," *Etudes Congolaises,* IV, No. 24 (April 1963), 5.

[22] The *Alliance des Bayanzi* had the support of part of the Bayanzi ethnic group situated in Banningville territory.

tional and provincial level, and the Maniema autonomy cry was heard both in Leopoldville and Bukavu.

At this stage, only the Mongo threat in Equateur was really serious. On June 1, 1960, Bolikango succeeded in putting together a majority in the provincial assembly without Unimo. On June 9, Unimo cabled a warning to the Executive College: "If we do not obtain satisfaction [on the provincial government] . . . we demand before June 30 the separation of the Mongo and Ngombe districts into two distinct provinces. Equateur province is an entity fabricated by colonization to the disrespect of customs and traditions. No law imposes the maintenance of the Ngombe and Mongo in the same province after the departure of the Belgians."[23]

Two days later, armed Ngombe groups were seen in Coquilhatville, and the Ngombe-Mongo tension was at a peak. A temporary accord was reached, but was not respected during the assembly vote. The provincial institutions in Equateur had a brief period of relative success, but by 1961 had come apart.[24]

The next major phase in the fragmentation process came with the Tananarive Conference. The intervening months had been entirely dominated by the crisis which enveloped the country; at this point, only South Kasai had a genuinely functioning de facto administration, and North Katanga (Lualaba) a rudimentary one. Kongo Central, it will be recalled, was set up simultaneously with Tananarive in March 1961. An interesting principle of representation was adopted for participation at this meeting, stemming from the desire of the Katanga leadership who organized the

[23] *Congo 1960*, I, 167-68.

[24] Equateur President Laurent Eketebi made serious efforts to achieve harmony between the Mongo and Ngombe blocs, a task for which he was unusually well-suited, as his father was Ngombe, and his mother Mongo. However, he was not purely neutral; he ran as a Puna candidate (a mainly Ngombe party), and in 1961 began construction of a large home in Lisala, in the capital of Ngombe country. In 1963, he became president of Moyen-Congo.

conference to scrap the *Loi Fondamentale* as a source of legitimation. The conference was open to "de facto or de jure" leaders; this unusual formula left the door wide open to self-appointed leaders and provinces. The fact of physical presence in Tananarive established an a priori assumption of de facto existence.

There is a significant multiplier effect to note in the fragmentation process. The starting point is the old colonial province. The thin wedge of fission is entered by the strident demands of one group to separate—in the first instance, Kongo Central, South Kasai, and North Katanga. A disequilibrium is then created in what is left of the province; the remaining groups evaluate their political prospects in the new context, and some fear that it will operate to their disadvantage. With the door to separation thrown wide open by the ease of gaining recognition as a de facto authority, the temptation to use the opportunity for exit—which may not soon come again—is irresistible. A new equilibrium is not reached until the old province lies in at least three pieces—and in the case of Kasai, five.

An immediate result of the Tananarive Conference was to produce a new de facto state, the Kwango. In a small-scale *putsch* on the heels of Tananarive, all PSA militants in positions of authority and in general all natives of Kwilu district were expelled. This was carried out by the Bayaka followers of Albert Delvaux and, more important, their powerful paramount chief, the Kiamfu.[25]

Of the eleven "provinces" represented at Tananarive, two (Maniema and Orientale) were represented by dissidents who at that time exercised no visible authority in

[25] The Bayaka are the dominant tribe in the Kwango district; their ruling class is of Lunda origin, and the Kiamfu continues to pay symbolic obeisance to the Mwata Yamvo. It is widely believed in the Kwilu and Kwango that the influence of Katanga, transmitted through the traditional channels of Lunda aristocracy, was important, if not determinant, in provoking this coup. The Kiamfu had visited the court of Mwata Yamvo in February 1961.

their region. By the time of Coquilhatville, however, the process had gone much further; eighteen delegations were present, of whom four, purporting to represent zones controlled by Stanleyville, had dubious credentials (Orientale, Uele-Ituri, Maniema, Nord-Sankuru). A nineteenth delegation was present in the person of Bolikango, who incarnated the reluctant future province of Moyen-Congo. As can be seen from Table 29, the broad outlines of the future twenty-one provinces were clearly present at Coquilhatville; only one province represented there (Kwilu Septentrional) disappeared, and three others later emerged by the split of Uele and Ituri, North and Central Kivu, and East Katanga and Lualaba.

By the time of the Lovanium Parliament, three new provinces were thus established and functioning as de facto separate entities. Although the necessity was far from being universally accepted, it is difficult to see how Kwango or Maindombe could have been made to accept administration from Kikwit. In Equateur, despite the fervent opposition of Bolikango and Provincial President Eketebi, the Mongo demands for a separate province were irrevocable, and in this hypothesis Sudanic Ubangi insisted on separation from Ngombe Mongala. In Kivu, the aftermath of the Kashamura-Omari regimes produced an exodus of Maniema residents, mainly Bakusu, from Bukavu; as a consequence, pressure for separation in Maniema became irresistible as well.

Implementation: Law of April 27, 1962

Adoula, in his inaugural declaration August 2, 1961, pledged that the government would "take adequate measures permitting each region to administer itself according to its own profound aspirations" and would take immediate steps to initiate the constitutional revisions necessary for the legal accomplishment of this objective.[26] The legislative process was begun forthwith, but eight months of elephan-

[26] *Congo 1961*, p. 423.

tine labors were required to give birth to the inept law of
April 27, 1962. The unitarian Lumumbist block fought a
prolonged, rear-guard action against the measure, arguing
that the first problem was to eliminate the Katanga secession and anarchy elsewhere before discussing the division
of the present provinces.

TABLE 29

FRAGMENTATION FROM TANANARIVE TO FORMATION OF NEW PROVINCES

Former province	Tananarive	Coquilhatville	New provinces, 1962
Leopoldville	Kongo Central Kwango Leopoldville	Kongo Central Kwango Kwilu Lac Leopold II	Kongo Central Kwango Kwilu Lac Leopold II
Equateur	Mongo Equateur	Mongo Congo-Ubangi	Cuvette Centrale Ubangi Moyen Congo
Orientale	(Orientale)[a]	(Orientale) (Uele-Ituri)	Haut Congo Uele Ituri
Kivu	(Maniema)	(Maniema)	Maniema Nord-Kivu Kivu Central
Katanga	Katanga	Katanga Nord-Katanga	Katanga Oriental Lualaba Nord-Katanga
Kasai	Sud-Kasai Nord-Kasai Lomami[b]	Sud-Kasai Nord-Kasai (Nord-Sankuru) Unité Kasaienne Lomami	Sud-Kasai Kasai Central Sankuru Unité Kasaienne Lomami

[a] Those in parentheses were represented by delegations in exile from their regi‹
[b] Lomami also includes parts of Kivu and Katanga provinces.

The problem of defining criteria and procedures was
complex, in the face of the welter of conflicting claims
of political figures purporting to speak on behalf of one
or another group. The ethnic factor was generally advanced
as the guide to partition, but one immediately encountered

all the ambiguities of this concept. It is perhaps clear what the Bakongo group is, and its will to constitute itself into a separate political entity was manifest; however, where the Mongo community begins and ends is a subject of endless dispute amongst anthropologists, with significant variations between Mongophiles and Mongophobes. These disputes derived from the diffuseness of the notion of Mongohood at the margin where Mongo cultural zones blend into surrounding influences. Further, in many areas, such as the Kwilu and Kasai, precolonial migration patterns produced a mosaic of peoples of infinite intricacy, which all the modern techniques of gerrymander could not unscramble.

In the legislative debates, arithmetic was the central issue, for want of a better one. A minimum population requirement seemed the only relatively objective criterion available for determining the scope of fragmentation, presuming that the integrity of the colonial census figures was accepted. At the Leopoldville Round Table, in January and February, 1961, when this issue was first discussed, a minimum population of 300,000 was suggested. In the initial parliamentary debates, the Chamber of Representatives, where the Lumumbist bloc was most influential, proposed 1,200,000. This was patently unrealistic, as it would have excluded even the imperative cases of Kongo Central, South Kasai, and North Katanga. The Senate proposed 500,000.[27]

The final solution, promulgated as the law of April 27, set three prerequisites:

1) A population of 700,000;
2) Economic "viability"; and
3) A petition submitted by two-thirds of the provincial and national deputies from the region included in the putative province.

There was, however, one important escape clause, which

[27] "Les nouvelles provinces," *Etudes Congolaises*, II, No. 8 (October 1962), 29-30.

rendered the minimum population criterion meaningless; a population of less than 700,000 was acceptable *"si les imperatifs politiques et sociaux l'exigent."* Thus in the last analysis the only real requirement was a petition from two-thirds of the deputies from the region. Any such group could concoct "imperative reasons" for ignoring the population minimum, and economic viability was indefinable and hence inapplicable.

The first new province, as mentioned above, was North Katanga, approved by Parliament on July 11, 1962. A few days thereafter, South Kasai and Kongo Central followed, and then in a sudden rush at the end of July and beginning of August, thirteen other petitions were approved. This left behind only those forlorn fragments from which everyone had broken away: Moyen-Congo (Lisala); Haut-Congo (Stanleyville);[28] Kivu Central (Bukavu); and South Katanga. Moyen-Congo, Haut-Congo, and Kivu Central were approved in early 1963. With the splitting of South Katanga into Lualaba and Katanga Oriental in May and June, 1963, the process appeared to have come to an end.

A festering problem created by the establishment of new provinces is a string of disputed territories which have been directly administered by the central government since 1962. The areas involved are considerable: seven full territories and a number of lesser fragments are claimed by two or more provinces and are legally subject to a referendum; well over half a million persons inhabit these zones. The very factor which has made them open to dispute makes the referendum solution difficult to apply. The population tends to be bitterly divided concerning which province to join. Given the ethnic character of a number of the provinces, both sides fear that an unfavorable decision would

---

[28] In the case of Stanleyville, and to a lesser extent Moyen-Congo, the refusal to submit a petition was an expression of protest at the whole process of creating new provinces. However, by the end of July 1962, the MNC/L and Puna deputies joined the others in voting the creation of the proposed provinces.

make the losers a helpless alien minority. Not until 1964 was the first of the referenda held, and by the end of that year most were still unscheduled. Further, the problem is not confined to areas designated as disputed. Almost every province has some border zone where small groups are discontent with their present provincial affiliation.

Profile of New Provinces

In the public debate over new provinces, it was frequently suggested that they are essentially "tribal." Table 30 makes clear the inadequacy of this formulation; only eight provinces are clearly homogeneous in this respect, with four others partially so. A more accurate hypothesis is that ethnic tensions played a major role in provoking the dislocation of the old provinces and that the demands for ethnic provinces of a few large, highly self-conscious groups (Bakongo, Mongo, Kasai Baluba) were instrumental in triggering the dialectic of fragmentation described earlier. However, large areas of the country are made up of groups too small to sustain a strong ethnic nationalism, or they form such an inextricable mosaic with other groups as to be able to claim no territorial base. In these areas, a joint impetus toward separation might emerge from shared fears of domination by large, expansive groups. Unité Kasaienne is an example; the basis for the claim to provincehood was distrust both of Kasai Baluba and Lulua on the part of the numerous, mostly small tribal communities—Bushong, Bakete, Bashilele, some Bapende, some Tshokwe, and several others. But the important fact is that creation of new provinces did not eliminate the necessity for different ethnic groups in a majority of cases to find formulas for cooperative coexistence within shared modern institutions.

Indeed, the obverse of the hypothesis that new provinces were spawned by "tribalism" is at least as true; the creation of new provinces sharply reinforced ethnic self-awareness. Ethnicity, as argued in Chapter XI, is, and always

TABLE 30
Profile of New Provinces[29]

Province	1 Ethnic homogeneity	2 Party homogeneity	3 Administrative continuity	4 Strong traditional structures	5 Major economic resources	6 Incipient fragmentation	7 Stable institutions	8 Major disorders since 1962	Old Province
Kongo Central	yes	yes	yes	no	yes	no	yes	no	Leopoldville
Kwango	yes	yes	yes	yes	no	no	some	yes	
Kwilu	no	some	yes	no	yes	no	yes	yes	
Lac Leopold II	no	no	yes	no	no	yes	no	yes	
Cuvette Centrale	yes	yes	no	no	some	no	yes	some	Equateur
Moyen-Congo	yes	yes	some	no	some	yes	some	yes	
Ubangi	no	yes	yes	no	no	no	yes	no	
Haut-Congo	no	yes	yes	no	some	no	no	some	Orientale
Kibali-Ituri	no	yes	yes	some	no	no	yes	no	
Uele	some	no	yes	yes	yes	some	yes	no	
Kivu-Central	some	no	yes	yes	some	yes	no	some	Kivu
Maniema	some	some	some	no	yes	yes	no	yes	
Nord-Kivu	no	yes	yes	no	no	some	some	yes	
Katanga Oriental	no	yes	some	yes	yes	no	some	yes	Katanga
Lualaba	no	no	yes	yes	yes	some	some	yes	
Nord-Katanga	some	some	some	some	some	some	some	yes	

							Kasai
Lomami	yes	yes	no	some	no	no	yes	no
Luluabourg	yes	yes	no	some	no	no	no	yes
Sankuru	yes	yes	yes	no	some	no	no	yes
Sud-Kasai	yes	yes	no	some	yes	no	yes	yes
Unité Kasaienne	no	some	no	some	some	some	some	yes

KEY TO TABLE:
1. Refers to existence of a clearly dominant ethnic group.
2. Primary referent is the 1960 election, although subsequent developments have been taken into account.
3. Refers to coincidence of present provincial boundaries with those of one (or two) colonial administrative districts.
4. Self-explanatory.
5. Primarily based on existence of a major, exploited mineral resource, or a developed, commercial, export agriculture.
6. Refers to existence of an important zone not well-integrated into present provincial institutions.
7. Based on the existence of a continuous, reasonably effective provincial government of unquestioned legitimacy, in at least the major part of the province.
8. Determined by the occurrence of serious violence from whatever cause, including that in disputed territories claimed by the province.

[29] A word of caution is necessary in the interpretation of the information presented in the table. Each classification contains a host of ambiguities. For example, Kwango is considered as ethnically homogeneous because the Bayaka are the politically dominant group and their traditional system is the motor force in Kwango politics. There are, however, a number of other groups—the Tshokwe in Kahemba, the Basuku in Feshi, the Bapalende. Bambala, and Bangongo in Kenge, and so on. Haunt-Congo is rated politically homogeneous, based on the MNC/L sweep in 1960; however, the MNC/L is now in fragments, and new parties of undetermined significance have mushroomed forth in Stanleyville. There is obviously the problem of the marginal case when complex issues are reduced to three possible responses. This summary has only approximate validity, and should not be pushed further than that. Calculations are based on data through June 1964.

has been, a dynamic, not a static social phenomenon. It is situational in its response to the group perception of political facts confronting it. To cite one example, we might examine the responses of the Warega (Balega) group in Kivu to the unfolding political situation since 1960. The Warega are a cultural entity which has had no recent centralized structures, but through the vitality of its ritual leaders, the *Bami,* it retained through the colonial period considerable cultural cohesion.[30] The Warega had long been split administratively between Maniema and Sud-Kivu districts. Politically, they rallied mainly to an ethnic party, the *Union des Warega* (Unerga). They advanced no claim for an administrative entity of their own; well-represented in the Bukavu population, they had a considerable stake in the retention of Kivu as it was.

The Warega were entirely hostile to the creation of the new provinces of Maniema and Kivu-Central. Up to this time they occupied a comfortable, though not paramount niche in a province sufficiently plural so that no one ethnic group was dominant. The new provinces posed a grave threat; not only were the Warega to be split into two different units, with a provincial and not just a district barrier between them, but each of the new provinces would place them in the role of a subordinate minority to a clearly predominant group—the Bakusu in Maniema, the Bashi in Kivu Central. This engendered a sharp surge of Warega militance in the assertion of their ethnic identity; special delegations were sent to Leopoldville to demand the regrouping of the Warega in a single province. A Lovanium mission studying new provinces in early 1963 reported strong ten-

[30] Biebuyck, "La société kumu face au Kitawala," *Zaïre,* XI, No. 1 (January 1957), 37-38. He suggests this as one reason that Kitawala, very strong in the neighboring Bakumu tribe with whom the Warega had a joking relationship, did not take root amongst them. On the Warega, see also Commandant Delhaise, *Les Warega* (Brussels: Institut International de Bibliographie, 1909).

sions in the Warega territories of Shabunda and Fizi.[31] Even though there was a single ethnic party, political behavior in 1960 was relatively diffuse, with the Maniema Warega somewhat attracted to MNC/L, and the mountain and lake Warega more drawn into the vortex of Bukavu political competition. But an altered political situation which posed a direct threat to the Warega ethnic community as such resulted in an immediate upsurge in ethnic solidarity and awareness.

Another important dimension of the ethnicity phenomenon which seemed to lend an ethnic character to new provinces is the tendency of conflict to acquire an ethnic vocabulary. One example is the Kivu case. If closely examined, the shifting political combinations in Bukavu leading up to the scission of the province were much more complicated than a simple tribal rivalry between the mountain Bashi and Maniema Bakusu. Yet as tension grew in 1961, the dissensions were with increasing frequency described in these terms. MNC/Lumumba, for example, was referred to in the press as "MNC/Bakusu." From the ethnic lexicon there is a feedback into the arena of conflict, as the rank and file tend to relate themselves to the issue through the prism of ethnicity. Thus, although neither Kashamura nor Omari were Bakusu, and the son of Bashi paramount chief Alexandre Kabare served in these governments, the Kashamura-Omari regime acquired a "Bakusu" label; when

[31] The drama at an individual level can be illustrated by the situation of a Murega student at Lovanium, who was well-known for his ardent nationalist views, and who had been attracted to the Lumumbist program, despite the fact that Unerga was a "moderate" party which opposed MNC/L in Maniema. But with the crisis arising, he was called upon by the Warega elders as "their university student" to draft for them the petitions for Leopoldville to protect the ethnic group from the threatened insecurity of subordinate status. To refuse this task, although it might be said to be in the cause of "tribalism," would have been to secede from the ethnic and kinship system, a rupture with one's own which few would dare make.

it was overturned, many Bakusu residents in Bukavu fled to their Maniema homeland.

A somewhat different example of this phenomenon is the fate of Kwilu province, where what began as a leadership rivalry degenerated by the end of 1963 into a desperate regional-ethnic insurrection. One may affirm with certainty that the origins of the Kamitatu-Gizenga dispute were not ethnic, although Gizenga is a Mupende and Kamitatu a Mungongo. Yet the existence of the split at the top produced a polarization about each of the two dominant personalities, which even at the leadership level had an ethnic character. Kamitatu's chief lieutenants, such as Felicien Kimvay and Raphael Kinkie, were drawn mainly from the Bambala and Bangongo groups, while Gizenga's principal spokesmen, such as Gabriel Yumbu and Pierre Mulele, came from the Bapende and Bambundu in Gungu and Idiofa territories in southern Kwilu.[32] The perception of conflict at the mass level is translated almost completely into ethnic

[32] Some authorities suggest that the Bapende and Bambundu are closely related, at least in their chiefly lineages; the contemporary political alliance of the two may be confirmation of this hypothesis. Both have migrated relatively recently from Angola; the Bapende have retained in their oral traditions a clear record of an exodus from the Luanda region to escape the depredations of the Portugese. Both tribes have a strong sense of unity, incarnated in a particularly developed ancestor cult, and in the Bapende case expressed through a famous set of masks. Occupation of their areas was late, and traditional elders were long hostile to the intrusion of modernity; symptomatic of this is the very low number of conversions to Christianity, especially among the Bapende. G. Weekx, writing in 1937, notes that the Bambala had at that date far outdistanced other Kwilu tribes in adaptation to modernization; "La peuplade des Ambundu (District du Kwango)," Congo, 18th yr., T. I., No. 4 (April 1937), pp. 353-73; T. II, No. 1 (June 1937), pp. 13-35; T. II, No. 2 (July 1937), pp. 150-66. On this subject, see also J. Van Rompsey, "Les Oblats au Congo," Bulletin de l'Union Missionnaire du Clergé, No. 144 (October 1961), pp. 230-35; M. Plancquaert, Les Jaga et les Bayaka du Kwango (Brussels: ARSOM, Sci. Mor. & Pol., T. III, fasc. 1, 1932); G. L. Haveaux, La tradition historique des Bapende orientaux (Brussels: ARSOM, Sci. Mor. & Pol., T. XXXVII, fasc. 1, 1954). It was these two ethnic groups that took part in the Mulelist uprising, beginning in September 1963.

terms, which makes it at once comprehensible at the village level, and by the same token insoluble. From this perspective, the policy disagreements between the Kamitatu and Gizenga wings in Leopoldville, or different options in external alliances, were too remote to be understood. But when it is possible to describe the conflict as one of Bambala versus Bapende, then it comes within cognitive reach of the village and gives the peasant a sense of urgent personal involvement in the conflict. At the same time, perceived in these terms, the conflict is insoluble. And yet, were the rivalry at the leadership level resolved, much of the tension at the base could quickly disappear.

In six provinces, an interesting effort is being made by the leadership consciously to exploit and manipulate ethnic nationalism as a means of legitimation of provincial institutions. (Kongo Central—Bakongo; Cuvette Centrale—Mongo; Moyen-Congo—Ngombe; Sud-Kasai—Baluba; Luluabourg—Lulua; Lomami—Basongye.) Only in Kongo Central can it be said that tribal awareness has historic roots. In the other cases, ethnic self-consciousness has only recently developed to an important degree. For example, in Cuvette Centrale, the patrons of Mongo nationalism are a group of intellectuals, who in the 1950's began openly to reassert Mongo cultural values to distinguish themselves from the so-called "Bangala" in Leopoldville. A sense of active Mongohood crystallized somewhat later in Coquilhatville when, in two successive municipal elections in 1958 and 1959, the Ngombe through superior cohesion managed to win the burgomastership of the African commune. Thereafter, the feeling of being shortchanged in the provincial government gave the group fresh impetus. A Mongo congress was held in Boende in January 1961 and set forth a platform for Mongo political unification. With the establishment of Cuvette Centrale, the mechanism of the state became available for the propagation of Mongo ideals. Coquilhatville in 1963 was filled with giant posters

557

sounding the clarion call of ethnic unity. This was, in fact, the first time in history that any large part of the Mongo community had enjoyed a centralized organization.

Ethnic homogeneity is, however, no guarantee of political stability. It is a unity fed to an important degree by antipathy or fear toward external groups; once the threat from outside is removed, new sources of division become apparent. Even among the Bakongo, there are important subgroups which can form the basis for cleavage in the community. For example, in the early years of the Abako, before Kasavubu took over, the organization was accused of being entirely dominated by Bantandu, a Bakongo subgroup. The split between Kasavubu and Daniel Kanza in 1960 found the latter drawing most of his support from the Manianga subgroup in Luozi territory, his own region of origin. And in 1963, there were some mutterings that the Bayombe were now over-represented in Abako leadership, with both Kasavubu and Provincial President Moanda from this branch of the Bakongo family.

A more dramatic example lies in the tragic difficulties encountered by Sankuru. This province is inhabited by the Batetela and very closely related groups of the Mongo culture cluster. A part of the Batetela had come into cultural contact with the Arab bands penetrating from the East at approximately the same time as the Free State was being established. These, many under the command of Ngongo Lutete, subsequently rallied to the Free State, and were then used to help pacify other parts of what is now Sankuru. They were settled in village outposts scattered through the area, with the surrounding land awarded them by a grateful colonial administration in return for their services against the Arabs and in securing the submission of their own non-Arabized fellows. Their contact with both Arab and Free State tended to dispose them to early utilization of such opportunities of access to modernity as came available; a large part of the Batetela elite come from this group. Their differentiation from other Sankuru Batetela was, however, little visible during the colonial period, and when the 1960 election campaign came, the district was virtually unanimous for Lumumba and MNC/L.

Suddenly, this ethnic distinction erupted to the surface when the Sankuru provincial government was formed. Abbey Athanase Ndjadi, who had served as district commissioner in the area since 1961, opposed the candidacy of André Diamusumbu for the Sankuru presidency. Diamusumbu appeared to be elected by an 8-7 vote, but the opposition argued that the legal definition of a majority was one half plus one. Accordingly, the required vote would be 8½; 8 votes were not enough for election.[33] Ndjadi, from the "Arabized" group, moved with his supporters from the Sankuru capital of Lodja to Lusambo and set up a rival government in late 1962. Diamusumbu, from the non-Arabized group, adopted an increasingly aggressive attitude; in early 1963, he began openly denouncing the "arabisés" as domestic colonialists who had exploited their fellows. In May, armed attacks on the Arabized groups living in Lodja resulted in a number of casualties. During a visit in June 1963, the writer found Lodja a tense and unhappy place. Many of the better houses in this small town of roughly 10,000 lay in ruins. By some reports, they had been destroyed by the marauding bands; others indicated that many were burned by the owners themselves, as they fled from Lodja to the greater security of Lusambo.

The role of urban conflicts in the creation of new prov-

[33] This summary does not do full justice to the juridicial ingenuity involved in this dispute. Other arguments included the right to vote of a deputy whose name had been accidentally omitted from the required official ordinance from the Chief of State convening the new provincial assembly, and a *suppléant* member who was a presumptive replacement for a deputy who had become "incompatible." See B. Verhaegen, "La province du Sankuru," *Etudes Congolaises,* V, No. 7 (August-September, 1963), 22-36; *Courrier d'Afrique,* October 17, 1963; January 22, February 14, 1964.

inces has been crucial; 12 of the 21 new provinces can be directly traced to this factor, without counting the "multiplier effect". By 1962, serious ethnic tensions had surfaced in all the former capitals. In Coquilhatville, Bukavu, Elisabethville, and Luluabourg, the ethnic group(s) which believed that they had proprietary rights because of the geographic location of the city in their areas have taken over full control. In Stanleyville, where the Lokele and affiliated people had in the person of Bernard Salumu tended to assert an aggressive leadership in the city, if tempered by the anti-tribal ideology of Lumumbism in its vocabulary and symbols, some outlying groups simply deserted; some of those remaining formed an anti-Lokele party, the *Cartel des Cultivateurs*.[34] In Stanleyville and Bukavu, the respective exodus of the Azande[35] and the Bakusu marks the end of the former capital as a pole of attraction for the intellectual elements in the ethnic community. On a much larger scale, the same is true for Luluabourg. The riposte to exclusion in the old provincial capital is withdrawal and reorientation around a new one.

Another hypothesis advanced to explain the new provinces is that they are "one-party provinces."[36] It is true that in 13 of the 21 there is a single dominant party, with four other marginal cases. A major qualification to this is that in no less than three (or four) of the new provinces (Haut-Congo, Kibali-Ituri, Sankuru, and to some extent Maniema), MNC/L is the single party; here it would be

[34] The name is more poignant than would appear at first glance; the Lokele are a fishing people.

[35] Verhaegen, "Présentation morphologique des nouvelles provinces," *loc. cit.*, p. 18. The Azande never represented a large part of the Stanleyville populace; the UNESCO study of Stanleyville cites the figure of 1.6% (*Social Implications of Industrialization and Urbanization*, p. 265). Even those few hundred, which no doubt constitute a selective migration and mainly occupied high status positions, can be of real significance as the intellectual group thereby ceases to look to Stanleyville as a pole of attraction.

[36] Biebuyck suggested this in a paper presented to the American Society for African Culture, Washington, D. C., April 12, 1963.

arguable that rather than the parties shaping the provinces, the latter have consecrated the disintegration of a once potent and supra-ethnic party. In six, the parties were an expression of a strong sense of ethnic identity (Kongo Central, Sud-Kasai, Luluabourg, Kwango, Moyen-Congo, and Lomami). In reality, the ethnic and political party criteria overlap, and it is difficult even in analytical terms to disentangle them.

It is interesting to note the importance of the preexisting administrative divisions in shaping the new provinces. The first striking fact that emerges is that in only one case (Lomami) has a new province been established which straddles old privincial boundaries.[37] This can in some instances be explained by a coincidence of provincial frontiers with ethnic boundaries, but the more salient phenomenon is the number of important ethnic groups, divided for the purposes of colonial administration, who have remained so in the reorganized Congo. To cite only the more important cases, the Mongo (in the extended sense, to borrow Vanderkerken's dichotomy)[38] were split into five provinces, with some in every one but Katanga. The most recent split of the Mongo community occurred during the provincial reorganization of 1933, when the Mongo-Nkundo of Lac Leopold II were detached from Equateur and placed under Leopoldville jurisdiction. The closely related Batetela and Bakusu were split between Kivu and Kasai. The Basongye were divided between Kasai, Kivu, and Katanga, and the Bapende between Kasai and Leopoldville.

Although provincial boundaries underwent major revision in 1935, they have remained stable since that time,

[37] Excluding a very tiny sliver of Moyen-Congo, drawn from former Leopoldville province.

[38] In his classic *L'Ethnie Mongo*, Vanderkerken suggests that there is a Mongo heartland in the central basin, mainly in Equateur, where the sense of Mongohood is particularly sharp. In a broader area, there is an indisputable cultural relationship and a common recognition of descent from the single ancestor Mongo, but a less pronounced identity with the Mongo community.

whereas districts and territories have been constantly in flux. Intra-provincial migration was not encouraged; the provincial capital served as the primary pole of attraction for the young, the educated, and the ambitious. Thus the Otetela would migrate to Luluabourg, while his Mukusu cousin across the river would be drawn to Kindu or Bukavu. Subsequently, in 1959-1960, the province became a key echelon of political organization.

Within three provinces (Leopoldville, Orientale, and Kivu), the new provinces correspond closely to the former district division, with the Kongo Central and Uele provinces each covering two former districts.[39] In the case of the PSA, the district had served as the basic unit of party organization, so that it was natural that the new province should be coterminous with it. In cases such as Kwango and Kongo Central, the former district(s) coincided roughly with a dominant ethnic grouping. In still other cases, such as Lac Leopold II and Kivu Central, the groups inhabiting the new province find themselves clinging to the former district *faute de mieux*. It may be suggested that the former administrative units served as starting points for the fragmentation process. If there are strong reasons to redraw the lines, ethnic or political, this is done. Otherwise, the force of inertia operates in favor of retention of what is familiar.

The six provinces where traditional structures are important will be interesting laboratories in the coming years. In the case of Kwango and Uele, and to a lesser extent Kasai Central, the modern system seems to be undergoing a fusion with traditional structures. In the Kwango, the Kiamfu's preeminence leaves no doubt, especially given the weakness of modern development in the region. His numerous sons and relatives are encountered throughout the administration. In Uele, four of the eleven ministers in 1963

[39] In the Uele case, the two districts had been one from 1932-1956.

were sons of important Azande chiefs. The Minister of Agriculture had no fewer than sixteen relatives in the Uele assembly.[40] In Kasai Central, three of the eleven ministers were members of the family of Lulua paramount chief Kalamba.[41] The new provinces, where they coincide with centralized traditional systems, will clearly reinforce the political role of the chiefs.

Implications of Fragmentation

The new provinces have begun operation with varied success; in general, the most successful to date are those which broke away from the old provinces. In these the new capital suddenly has expanded administrative and political functions; the population which is dominant has a new outlet for its energies. The slowest to organize have been those which became provinces in spite of themselves: Moyen-Congo, Haut-Congo, Kivu Central, Katanga Oriental, and Lualaba. Here the leadership suddenly found itself with sharply narrowed horizons; cities such as Stanleyville, Bukavu, and Luluabourg, which had waxed fat and prosperous while providing administrative and auxiliary commercial services to a vast area of some 2,000,000 people, suddenly found themselves virtual backwaters. In a number of cases, the threat of further fragmentation is clearly present.

The wistful hopes of restoring the old provinces which have been expressed in most of the former capitals, especially Elisabethville and Bukavu, do not seem likely to materialize, with the possible exception of Katanga. New provincial institutions have rapidly created their own clientele. The administrative dismantlement was complete,

[40] Report of the Lovanium mission to study the new provinces.
[41] Ibid.; the three in question are President François Luakabwanga, former Kasai President Barthèlemy Mukenge, and Emery Wafwana. It will be recalled that Kalamba's claim to paramountcy is recent, and was founded upon the shrewd use of a European alliance in the 1880's; it is far from being universally accepted.

and reunification would no longer be an easy matter. Even the compromise of maintaining certain common services at the old provincial capital is viewed with disfavor by those in the newly created capitals; they fear that these services would be too subject to the influence of the provincial authorities situated at the old capitals. Katanga is excepted because of the strong attraction of the great urban centers of Elisabethville, Jadotville, and Kolwezi for both workers and elite from all of former Katanga province. Even in this case, where circumstances are particularly favorable, no concrete headway toward reunification had been made a year after termination of the secession.

By the end of 1963, three provinces had experienced peaceful changes of leadership, following prescribed legal methods (Kwango, Nord-Katanga, and Unité Kasaienne). In two cases, crises developed which required prolonged central intervention (Sankuru and Maniema), while brief interventions occurred in three other cases (Haut-Congo, Luluabourg, and Cuvette Centrale). However, in fourteen provinces the same government remained in power throughout the period and, in varying degrees, some stability had been achieved. For the most part, constitutional requirements of regular meetings of the new provincial assemblies (composed of the same deputies elected to serve in the original provinces) were met. The first serious assessment of the functioning of the new provinces, made by a Lovanium fact-finding team of social scientists in early 1963, was basically favorable:

". . . It seems that we should place our confidence in the movement which has begun; it is in any case irreversible.

"We do not pretend that the present provincial frontiers are definitively fixed; it is even probable that some entities which are not capable of survival will attach themselves to others.

"Nonetheless, the new provinces do have as common advantages:

a) An assembly more representative of public opinion.
b) Frequently, a government of technicians which is better able to know the situation of the province.
c) A regional pride to defend.
d) A more limited area.
e) An imperfect yet better realized ethnic cohesion."[42]

To this may be added the observation that the new provinces also have been constituted (excepting the leftover fragments) as a willing act of community by a large majority of the elected representatives of the region. This provision of the law of April 27, 1962, was scrupulously respected. Whatever may have been the role of ambitious politicians in the stimulation of some provinces, whatever may be the disrepute in which deputies were held by the population at large, this act seems nonetheless as representative an enactment of the will of the population as is likely under present circumstances.

The handicap of organizing new administrative structures from scratch has been overwhelming; for a long time to come, the real means of executing policy possessed by these provinces will be limited. The invaluable statistical and administrative infrastructure at the provincial echelon bequeathed by Belgium has been rendered nearly worthless. Political programs postulating radical transformation will have to be adjourned until tomorrow; on the other hand, there is every reason to suppose that the minimal governmental functions of preserving order, maintaining basic services, and arbitrating conflicts through the judicial system can be accomplished.

To win the loyalties of the population, the new entities will have to emerge as at least the centers which provide those services which the population has come to expect from government. Luckily for the newly established governments, these are not large; the rural mass does not yet

[42] These conclusions coincide with those of the writer formed during a visit to a number of new provinces in June-July, 1963.

have revolutionary expectations. The regional centers which are the new capitals, like the provinces which they serve, have been much less cosmopolitan in their population recruitment. So far, they have been spared the sharp tensions which tore apart the old provincial capitals. A second major prerequisite for success will be accommodation of the social tensions of modernization as the new capitals expand to fulfill their enlarged roles.

In any case, the establishment of new provinces has profoundly transformed the nature of the political system. The full implications of this reconstruction will only slowly become clear; they are certain to be substantial. The deliberate use of ethnic pride in several key provinces may well succeed in legitimating the province at the cost of further complicating the task of developing meaningful loyalties to the polity as a whole. Political party organization in the future will have to depart from the new provincial units. More efficient provinces may in the short run further weaken the central government. The Congo with twenty-one provinces is a very different kind of political system than it might have been with six.

Year	Leopoldville	Equateur	Orientale	Kivu	Katanga	Kasai
1960						
July	Kamitatu (PSA)	Eketebi (Puna)	Finant (MNC/L) Badjoko (MNC/L) Manzikala (MNC/L)	Miruho (Cerea)	Tshombe (Conakat)	Mukenge (UNC) / S. Kasai Kalonji (MNC/L)
1961 January				Kashamura (Cerea) Omari (MNC/L) ILLEGAL	Lualaba (N. Kat.) Ilunga (Balubakat)	
April	Kongo Central Moanda (Abako)	Central Intervention Omari				
July	Diomi (Abako)	Eketebi	Losala (MNC/L)	Kiruho		Lubaya (UNC)
October						
1962 January						
March		Manzikala/Losala Central govt. recognizes Manzikala		Cent. intervention Mayamba, Anany & Weregemere	Cent. intervention	Cent. intervention Mukenge / Kazadi (MNC/K)
July						

567

TABLE 3
LEADERSHIP AND STABILIT

Province	Dominant party[a]	Dissident parties	Major ethnic groups[b]
Kongo Central	Abako	Alco UDEA PNCP	BAKONGO
Kwango	Luka		BAYAKA
Kwilu	PSA/K	PSA/G PRA (ex-Abazi)	Bambala, Bangongo, Bayanzi, Bapende, Bambundu
Lac Leopold II		Unilac RDA (ex-RDLK)	Nkundo-Mongo, Baboma Basakata, Bateke, etc.
Cuvette Centrale	Unimo	MNC/L	MONGO
Ubangi	Meda		NGWAKA Mongwandi, Mbandja
Moyen-Congo	Puna	Unida PDC	NGOMBE Budja, Bobangi
Uele	(non-party)	MNC/L	AZANDE Babua, Mangbetu
Kibali-Ituri	MNC/L		Alur, Lugbara, Bale, etc
Haut-Congo	MNC/L	Cartel des Cultivateurs	Lokele, Topoke, Bakum
Maniema	MNC/L		BAKUSU Warega
Nord-Kivu	CEREA		Banande, Banyanga, Bahunde, Bahavu
Kivu Central	CEREA	Unerga, MNC/L	BASHI Warega, Watutsi
Nord-Katanga	PPC- Balubakat	Conakat	BALUBA Batumbwe, Baluba-Her
Katanga Oriental	Conakat	PANAF, ADA	Batabwa, Basanga, Baushi, etc.

568

ug	Oct	Jan	Apr	Jul	Oct
. Moanda ——————————————————————————→					
. Pashi ————————————————————→ P. Masikita ——→					
. Leta ——————————————————————————→					
Koumorico ————————————————————————→					
Engulu ——————————→ state of exception			Engulu ——————→		
Zondomyo ————————————————————————→					
tral administration ——————→ L. Eketebi ————————→					
Mambaya ——————————————————————————→					
Manzikala ——————————————————————————→					
tral administration ———————————→ G. Grenfell ———————→ P. Isombuma					
Kisanga ——————————————————→ state of exception					
Moley ——————————————————————————→					
ral administration ——————————————→ S. Malago————————→					
Iwamba-Ilunga ——————————————→ J. Sendwe ———→					
ssion ————————→ central administration ——→ E. Bulundwe ———————→					

TABLE 32 (*continued*)

Province	Dominant party[a]	Dissident parties	Major ethnic groups[b]
Lualaba	Conakat	Atcar	LUNDA Tshokwe
Sud-Kasai	RPL (ex-MNC/K)		BALUBA
Luluabourg	UNC	UDA	LULUA
Unité Kasaienne	PADENA (ex-COAKA)		Bakete, Bapende, Tshokw Bashilele, Bushong
Sankuru	MNC/L	PDC	BATETELA
Lomami	MUB		BASONGYE

[a] For a more detailed analysis of parties, following a somewhat different classifi
tion, see J.-C. Willame, "L'évolution des partis politiques au Congo," *Etudes C*
golaises, V, No. 10 (December 1963), facing p. 40.

[b] Ethnic groups indicated in capital letters form either a majority or are s
stantially the most numerous in the province.

Aug	Oct	Jan	Apr	Jul	Oct

ecession ⟶ central administration ⟶ D. Diur ⟶

. Ngalula ⟶

. Luakabwanga ⟶ A. Lubaya
Luakabwanga ⟶

. Kamanga ⟶ F. Mingambengele ⟶

. Diamasumbu ⟶ state of exception ⟶
A. Ndjadi
dissident government

. Manono ⟶

CHAPTER XIX

Conclusions

Wɪᴛʜ the coerced return of Katanga to the national community in January 1963, the Congo disappeared for a few months from the front pages of the world's newspapers. Five turbulent years after the Leopoldville riots which set the country careening toward independence, the patterns of the post-colonial political process were beginning to become visible. From the immense confusion of 1960 an equilibrium of sorts was emerging, if we include in this concept important vectors of disorder and instability. The purpose of this study has been to contribute toward an understanding of this equilibrium through an examination of the colonial society, the dialectic of decolonization, and the elements in the political system as they have operated in the environment of independence and breakdown.

Belgium had constructed in Africa a colonial state which stood out by the thoroughness of its organization, the formidable accretion of power through an interlocking alliance of state, church, and capital, and the ambition of its economic and social objectives. The very strength of the system as a colonial structure, and its steadfast refusal to face effectively the problem of political adaptation until it began to disintegrate, made an ordered transfer of power peculiarly difficult. A colonizer who suddenly lost the profound conviction of the righteousness of his policy was confronted with a revolution by the colonized which lacked both structure and ideology. Total colonialism was replaced by total independence virtually overnight, yet the very completeness of the victory of the colonized had as its concomitant an impotence which emptied success of its substance.

The final decolonization formula prescribed a wholly African set of political institutions paralleling a completely

European-run bureaucratic establishment, and backed by a European-officered army. Under the best of circumstances, this arrangement could hardly have been a stable one. It is difficult to imagine a European bureaucracy charged with implementing the program of radical African nationalism which by and large triumphed in the 1960 elections. Belgium's failure to take any serious steps toward opening access to positions of administrative responsibility to Congolese remains one of the weakest points of the Belgian case.

The Congolese nationalist response to Belgian colonial rule must be viewed in the context of the unusual society which had been created by the confrontation of Belgian and African. The character of the African elite was heavily determined by the bureaucratic nature of colonial society. Excepting those who were drawn into the clergy, the path to modern status lay necessarily through service as a clerk either in the administration or in one of the large colonial corporations. African commercial enterprise met with obstacles, beginning with the effective exclusion of Congolese from land ownership.

The new elite grew up in a number of regional centers with virtually no contact among themselves on a national scale until the Brussels Exposition in 1958. Certain ethnic groups which were favored by early availability of modernization opportunities, and adaptability to the challenges of modernity, were heavily represented in the elite—in particular the Bakongo, Kasai Baluba, and Bangala. The elite had no opportunity for overseas travel, and was sealed off with considerable effectiveness from the mainstream of African thought until the eve of independence.

At the level of the mass, the salient feature was the profound impact of the colonial system in its three-pronged penetration of traditional society by state, company, and mission. On a purely administrative level, the bureaucratic network established in the countryside was, by African

573

standards, very dense. The strong emphasis not only on government but on production which dates from the ivory and rubber days of the Free State culminated in the ambitious *paysannat* scheme, bound especially to the production of cotton. Thus the forces of modernization were felt not merely by the large numbers who migrated to the urban centers, although the Congo stands out in tropical Africa by the level of urbanization. Nearly every villager was proselytized by the local catechists, vaccinated by the medical service, poked and prodded by the omnipresent agricultural officers, taxed and put to work on the roads by his sector chief on behalf of the administration.

Thus, when the message of nationalism reached the village, it found a ready audience. Wrenching a population loose from its traditional moorings is unlikely to win popularity in the best of circumstances; until the last years the colonial administration maintained a harsh discipline and brooked no dissent from the program of progress which it defined. The nationalist political leaders found it possible to mobilize overnight their rural constituencies when suddenly the articulation of the manifold resentments and frustrations became possible. It was, however, a social mobilization resting on precarious foundations, as the elite and the mass had very different conceptions of the content of independence. The elite proposed to take over the management of the system and operate it more effectively; from the campaign oratory the mass had understood that the benefits of modernity—schools and tractors—could be redoubled, and the constraints—taxes and agricultural officers—eliminated.

The historic sequence in the emergence of the nationalist expression is of great importance. The precursor of nationalism was an ethnic awakening which took place in several parts of the Congo, most notably among the Bakongo. The crescendo of ethnic tensions in several of the Congo's largest centers, especially Leopoldville, Luluabourg, Jadot-

ville, and Elisabethville, contributed heavily to a new assertion of ethnic identity; the tendency of social status and
ethnic group to overlap made an explosive mixture. The refusal of the colonial administration to tolerate African political movements until after the first elections had diverted
the ablest leadership and organizational energies into tribal
associations. The first movement openly to espouse nationalist views was the Bakongo association, Abako.

The disabilities of the nationalist movement were thus
several. The regional elites lacked the mutual confidence
and respect which come of common political action and
long acquaintance. The collapse of colonial resistance
eliminated any compelling need for united action. In addition the urban elections, conducted without parties, had
catalyzed the latent ethnic polarization of the most important cities. The existing pattern of group behavior was
largely through the ethnic association; this was a logical
starting point for political organization. And the later en-
tries on the political score were confronted with a dialectic
begun by the emergence of the Abako as the *avant-garde*
of militant nationalism. As they could not join it because
of its exclusive character, they formed new movements
which tended in turn to be regional or ethnic in nature.

The agreed formula for decolonization lasted less than
a week. Within a fortnight, the Congolese government
found itself without an army, without its European cadres,
and without its wealthiest province. And by September,
the constitutional framework had collapsed as well. Africa's
most revolutionary decolonization was followed by its most
radical Africanization. The transfer of power into the hands
of the Congolese was complete indeed, equalled only by
the utter lack of means to execute any decision. The intervention of the United Nations in a new role as a sort of
"colonial surrogate without colonial authority" froze the
situation and set limits to disorder and external intervention. Over the next thirty months, legitimacy and unity

were painfully restored to the country, culminating in the reduction of the Katanga secession in January 1963. In the meanwhile, important transformations had occurred in the nature and structure of the political system.

Political parties and representative institutions were a major casualty of breakdown. Party activity in the country-side ceased from 1960 to 1963. Party cards were no longer sold, meetings no longer held, branches quietly ceased operating. The leadership had been absorbed into the ministries, national and provincial, the legislatures, or the administration. In the competition for power, especially at the national level, the mass base was no longer relevant. Maneuvering and combinations formed within the elite, with a significant dosage of external influences, were the essence of the political process in Leopoldville. Until the possibility of new elections emerged in 1963, there was little interest in maintaining party structures, except as parliamentary caucus groups.

Parliament and the provincial assemblies gravely impaired their potential role in July 1960 by quintupling their own salaries. As an institution with no roots in the polity, the representative bodies could ill afford the stigma of profiteering. Their steadfast refusal to vote any austerity provisions which would touch their own exorbitant privileges confirmed the popular animus toward the "Honorables." When Parliament was finally indefinitely adjourned in September 1963, hardly a voice was raised in protest.

The mass initially reacted by withdrawing into cynicism and alienation. "Politician" is a pejorative term which means he who has usurped all the material benefits of independence. Not only did the mass find the electoral promises of an earthly paradise without work or taxes unfulfilled but independence meant a sharp drop in real wages and standard of living. Jobs were difficult to find, and agricultural produce hard to market. The mood of alienation was symbolized by a trade union appeal for a general strike against the privileged class in 1962.

The dangers of the situation were clearly shown by the rapid spread of the insurrection initiated by Pierre Mulele in September 1963 in the Bapende and Bambundu zones of southern Kwilu. Mulele's alleged Chinese associations gave to the revolt the appearance of an ideological character which it clearly did not possess at the mass level. The ethnic content of the movement was important; the prolonged imprisonment of Mupende leader Gizenga and the widespread belief in Bapende-Bambundu circles that "Bambala" were monopolizing provincial power in Kwilu catalyzed alienation and at the same time gave the movement an exclusivist character which limited its scope. However, the hopeless adventure of challenging the ANC with the rudimentary weapons available in the village would hardly be credible without the additional sense of victimization by an independence which, seen from the village, appeared to give wealth to the "politician" and impoverishment to the countryside. Although this particular uprising has remained circumscribed, rural alienation and urban unemployment offer reserve armies of rebellion to other regional leaders who succeed in fusing local grievances with generalized discontent. The irony of the situation is that Mulelism offers no real solutions to the difficulties it exploits.

The elements which have emerged strongest from breakdown were precisely those upon which the colonizer had grounded his rule and his hopes for a successful decolonization—the bureaucracy and the army—although obviously in a very different context. The new Congolese territorial officers gradually asserted their authority in the countryside; this is by no means as far-reaching as that enjoyed by the colonial mandarins, but in the absence in many areas of an organized competitive group, it is nonetheless relatively effective. The new administrators have internalized the norms and values of the colonial bureaucracy. There is a technocratic orientation, a distaste for politics as mere trouble-making, an acceptance of administrative efficiency as the prime measurement of success.

Since September 1960, the reborn ANC has been a major arbiter of every political crisis. A new officer corps is evolving, which is bound to play a determining role in the future of the country. The demerits of military involvement in politics are well-known; in the Congo, the ANC exacts a heavy tribute from the state in the form of excessive salaries and unnecessary size. It has been responsible for a number of deplorable atrocities. Yet to its credit are some positive features. Both its officer corps and its units are ethnically integrated to a degree which is true of no other functioning institution in the Congo. The ANC has a genuinely national outlook, and a stake in the preservation of the unity of the Congo which is a precious asset during these early years when the very survival of the political community as a single entity is far from assured. The deployment of the ANC about the countryside in its gendarmery role is one of the few trump cards held by the central government in its desire to place some limits on regional autonomy, in the interests of the community as a whole.

An appropriate areal distribution of power has been a major preoccupation since the Leopoldville riots added urgency to decolonization. Even the limited federalism of the *Loi Fondamentale* was truly viable only if supported by informal political structures which could give it content. The failure of a single, uncontested leader and party to develop in the pre-independence period was crucial. The community was confronted with separatist aspirations at both its poles: the one deriving from a militant ethnic self-awareness, the other from the fusion of an economically rooted European movement and the ethnic frictions of the Katanga mining centers. The effective breakdown of the colonial tradition of highly centralized administration and the disintegration of the colonial provinces rendered essential a painful reconstruction of the whole community on new bases. This has been achieved at the high price of immediate loss of efficiency and the invalidation of much of the administrative legacy of Belgian rule. The process is irreversible, however, and eventually may amortize the administrative cost in producing a governmental framework which can more easily obtain a concensus for its operation.

At the same time, the creation of new provinces has entirely transformed the nature of the political system. Ethnic identity has been recognized as a legitimate basis for modern institutions, and in several cases it is being deliberately developed to gain sanction for provincial authority. In other cases, the splitting of the old provinces has created units which come within the ambit of traditional systems, and has considerably enhanced their role. Reemergent political party organization is most effective at the level of the new province. A national party, whether pro- or antigovernmental, can probably succeed in the near future only as an alliance of provincial groups. A wide range of once-central functions silently devolved upon the provinces during the period of central breakdown. Although many new provinces are not functioning well, provincialization of power is a crucial dimension of the emergent political system.

One of the many paradoxes of the Congo is the survival of constitutional norms simultaneous with the discrediting of constitutional forms. The elite's acceptance of the values of Western democracy is nearly as complete as it was at the Brussels Round Table. In the absence of effective national parties, the problem of legitimating the central structures of the state is very serious. Although few will defend the performance of the first Parliament, nearly all want parliamentary government. Military rule would be unpopular, unless sanctioned by a broad spectrum of the political leadership. But Parliament as now constituted delays the application of vital decisions, such as devaluation and austerity, without effectively playing the role of guardian of the public interest. The inevitable result is an increased reliance on the efficiency of the private sector. The widespread acceptance of democratic values is an asset which should be harnessed to national construction. Just how this can be done within a constitutional framework is not yet clear.

The temptation to yield to facile cynicism in analysis of the Congolese political system is strong, but would give an unjust conclusion. The shortcomings, which are patent, tend to obscure the very real achievements. In 1960, many dire forecasts were made of a decline to subsistence; 1963 figures belie the prophets of doom and despair, and a balanced budget and record exports may be within reach in 1964. Beside the frailty of some individuals, one must set the remarkable capacity displayed by the Adoulas and Kamitatus. The venality of a few has overshadowed the dedicated labors of many. The agricultural officer at Kikwit who created on his own initiative and without budgetary support a vast truck garden to help feed the town and absorb its unemployed; the medical assistant at Banningville who kept a hospital functioning on a shoestring; the teachers in Lodja who carried on with their instruction despite months without pay—these also are part of the Congo mosaic.

By the end of 1962, the solidity of the country's economic and social infra-structure was clear. Damage was surprisingly small; 1963 saw a renewed growth both in export production and local industries. Church and company had survived intact. The importance of these two structures as bastions of stability cannot be underestimated. The Church, on its side, helped maintain much of the educational system which represents the future hope of the country, beginning with Lovanium University.[1] The giant corporations are enclaves which rely very little upon government services, beyond maintenance of order. In addition, they perform many of the functions, such as road maintenance, which would normally be the domain of the local government.

Finally, one should not underestimate the value of the intense political education which has been taking place since 1960. The greatest sin imputed to the colonizer was the lack of preparation for the independent exercise of political responsibility. This apprenticeship, however painful it has proved on some occasions, has been going forward at a rapid pace.

In sum, the unusual formula of decolonization, the bureaucratic, fragmented nationalism, and the tumults of independence have combined to produce a political system as unique as its colonial predecessor. The Congo has the resources and the infrastructure to achieve stability and prosperity; indeed, in mid-1963 these seemed within reach. But the sad events of 1964 proved how fragile the political structure remained; catastrophe on a grand scale and renewed fragmentation, perhaps permanent, are also very real possibilities. Ramifying external participation which rapidly grew after UN military withdrawal make internal cleavages more difficult to bridge. Yet elite consensus on aims and methods is an absolute prerequisite to facing the elemental challenge of mass alienation. Solutions remain possible, but there is no inevitability to progress.

---

[1] A visit to any small center is a revealing experience in this regard. Take, for example, the town of Lisala, an important regional trading center on the Congo River. The visitor in 1962 found that the only place to obtain food was at the mission. If a car broke down, the only place it could be repaired was at the mission garage. The only meat locally available came from the mission cattle herds. The only place where bricks could be baked, or concrete poured, was in the workshops of the mission.

Epilogue

THE MONTHS following Katanga's coerced return to the national community had been a period of relative optimism in the Congo. Against the obvious shortcomings could be credited a clear improvement in performance of government at all levels, a return to pre-independence production levels in many key commodities, the preservation of the social and economic infrastructure, and a serious possibility of ending chronic budget and foreign exchange deficits. But 1964 was to produce a chain of revolts, culminating in the re-establishment of a rebel base in Stanleyville from August to November, which shook the fragile structure to its foundations. These insurrections, which produced a terrifying display of violence, the decimation of the civil service in whole regions, and grotesque atrocities, were far more profound in their effects than the 1960 disorders. This volume had been completed when the insurgency burst forth in its full dimensions; it is much too early to put forward the full account of the revolts, but an interim assessment does seem pertinent as a postscript to our study of the politics of independence.[1]

The rebellions represented a new phase in the pattern of opposition politics observable since the overthrow of the Lumumba government;[2] the core areas of insurrection were the peak ones of MNC-L (Maniema-Sankuru-Stanleyville triangle) and PSA-Gizenga strength (southeastern Kwilu). But as the revolts unfolded, some familiar themes in Congolese politics also became clear. Only superficially could these events be considered a single movement; on

[1] This analysis is based in good part upon the major Congolese newspapers, *Courrier d' Afrique; Le Progrès, L'Etoile du Congo; Essor du Katanga; La Presse Africaine* (Bukavu); *Le Martyr* (published August-November 1964 in Stanleyville). Other sources include *Etudes Congolaises; Travaux Africains* (CRISP); *Remarques Congolaises et Africaines; Cahiers Economiques et Sociaux* (IRES).
[2] *Supra,* pp. 372-76.

close examination, the rebellion dissolved into a series of revolts, strongly influenced by local contingencies, bound together by a shifting coalition of leaders, certain common grievances on the part of the population, and common external support. Fragmentation and factionalism were pronounced among those asserting the leadership of uprisings, even during the period of spectacular success by insurgent groups.

The Kwilu Phase: Village Revolution

By mid-1963, some elements in the opposition groupings had concluded that only a coup d'etat or an armed insurrection could succeed. In July, Pierre Mulele returned to Kwilu, ostensibly to take up an offer of a provincial government portfolio, as a symbol of reconciliation of the Kamitatu and Gizenga wings of PSA.

Mulele had served as minister of Education in the short-lived Lumumba government, and Ambassador to Cairo for the Gizenga government in Stanleyville; he did not return to the Congo after the Lovanium reconciliation, but travelled widely, presumably with some external financial support. His itinerary included a visit to China of undetermined length, although perhaps no more than two months. Even before, Mulele had been one of the most ideologically oriented nationalists in the Lumumba camp; although there is no evidence to support the view that he became a Communist, the Marxist-Leninist interpretation of Congolese independence—stressing the pre-emption of all benefits by a "national bourgeoisie" in coalition with neo-colonial and imperialist forces, and particularly Maoist strategy and tactics for guerilla warfare—blended well into his own perceptions.

Shortly after his arrival in Kwilu, he requested permission to "visit relatives" in his home area in Bambundu country, in Idiofa and Gungu territories. By September 1963, Mulele had organized a series of camps in the forest, where both rudimentary guerilla tactics, and a religio-political ideology was taught to young men from the rural villages. A "second independence" was the goal, whereby the un-filled promises of the first would at last be realized. A "class struggle" was necessary, to eliminate the "rétardataires" and "réactionnaires" (politicians in power, civil servants, teachers, soldiers, and policemen), who had supplanted the colonizer, but continued the same "system," operating hand-in-glove with the forces of neo-colonialism in the theft of the country's wealth. When the people of the villages had vanquished their exploiters, a new regime would be built, where all would work, and share in the fruits of their labor. Mulelism was a message addressed to the village; their way of life, and their mentality was held to be supe-rior to that of the rootless men of the city.

Mingled with the simplified peasant Marxism was a per-sistent religious theme, which had clear continuities with syncretic sects which had periodically swept the area since the 1930's. Mulele himself became a charismatic figure, with supernatural powers. He was believed to be omnipres-ent, and could transform himself into an animal, or a bird to travel long distances. He was also invulnerable; he fre-quently demonstrated this by firing blank bullets at him-self. This political use of witchcraft was highly successful; his followers marched fearlessly into battle, convinced that "Mulele mai" (Mulele water) rendered them immune to bullets. The obvious material fact of the death of hundreds of rebel warriors simply was attributed to their inadequate faith in Mulele and his powers.[3]

Mulele's initial efforts were concentrated in Bambundu and Bapende areas, where the Gizenga wing of PSA had

[3] The first and still classic study of the phenomenon of witchcraft in Africa is E. E. Evans-Pritchard, *Witchcraft, Oracles and Magic among the Azande* (Oxford: Clarendon Press, 1937). Its believers do not generalize from a single failure; the explanation for inefficacy of witchcraft in a given contingency can easily be supplied from within the system.

drawn its strength. Although the Mulele appeal was apparently not explicitly ethnic, implicitly this aspect was present, both from his own ethnic identification as a Munbundu, closely associated with Mupende Gizenga, and the fact that the "exploiting class" running the provincial government was seen as "Bambala" (meaning generally the several ethnic groups of the north and west). Although subsequently efforts were made to expand beyond the original base, and some success was achieved among several neighboring groups, especially the Bading[4], the marked Bambundu-Bapende character of the movement diminished its appeal to others.

By October 1963, rumors of Mulele's activity began to circulate, and the Kwilu government offered 500,000 francs reward for his capture. In December, a nervous provincial leadership asked army intervention to cope with possible guerilla activity; the following month, the uprising began in earnest, with attacks on administrative posts, mission stations, palm oil installations, and persons, Congolese and expatriate, identified in Mulele doctrine as members of the "exploiting class." For three months, Mulelist bands virtually eliminated government authority in Idiofa and Gungu territories; several times, ANC units were routed by village warriors armed only with spears, machetes, and bows and arrows. Government forces gradually regained a tenuous control over towns and communications routes, and Mulele disappeared. Village disaffection remained, however, and thus rebel bands could reform in the forest at any moment.[5]

[4] The Bading had been the major participants in an uprising caused by a religious sect, Mpeve, in 1962.

[5] On the Kwilu uprising, see especially A.-R. Ilunga and B. Kalonji, "Les évenéments du Kwilu," *Etudes Congolaises*, Vol. VI, No. 3 (March, 1964); J. C. William and B. Verhaegen, "Les provinces du Congo: structure et fonctionnement. 1. Kwilu-Luluabourg-Nord-Katanga-Ubangi," *Cahiers Economiques et Sociaux* (May, 1964); Bernardin Diaka's interview in *Courrier d'Afrique,* January 6, 1964. The Centre de Recherches Sociologiques in Leopoldville is now undertaking a thorough study of the Kwilu uprising.

Emergence of the CNL[6]

The formation of the *Conseil National de Liberation* (CNL) on October 3, 1963, was precipitated by two events; five days earlier, President Kasavubu had dissolved Parliament, arguing that it had failed in its mission to produce a permanent constitution for the Congo. A handful of opposition personalities, no longer protected by parliamentary immunity from arrest, chose to cross the river to Brazzaville. This in turn had become possible because six weeks earlier, on August 15, Abbé Fulbert Youlou had been overthrown; Youlou would certainly not have offered the same sanctuary for conspiracy which the Massemba-Debat government subsequently afforded.

The CNL from the outset was beset by factionalism, feuding over personalities, leadership, tactics, sources of external support, and goals. The majority of the members were from PSA/G and MNC/L; however, participation of neither of these groups was complete. In the MNC/L case in particular, only a fragment of the 1960 leadership went over. It will be recalled that some MNC/L members were still in the Adoula cabinet. Others, led by Senator Antoine Kiwewa, remained in legal opposition; this group organized a national MNC/L congress in Leopoldville in April 1964, which denounced the CNL. Finally, still others held provincial office in Kibali-Ituri, Haut Congo, Maniema and Sankuru.

The major factional leaders in the CNL were:

1. CHRISTOPHE GBENYE: A Mubua from the Buta area (Uele) and related by marriage to his arch-rival, Sûreté chief Nendaka, Gbenye was Minister of Interior in the first Lumumba government, and held the same office in Gizenga's Stanleyville regime. He claimed to have succeeded to the presidency of MNC/L following Lumum-

---

[6] Initially the CNL entitled itself "Comité National de Liberation;" later, the word "Comité" was dropped in favor of "Conseil."

ba's assassination, and thus to be the legitimate successor to Congolese leadership. Gbenye was initally head of the CNL but his title was quickly contested by other groups.

2. EGIDE BOCHELEY-DAVIDSON: Also a Mubua, from near Aketa (Uele), Bocheley-Davidson had been a second ranking MNC/L figure in 1960. His rivalry with Gbenye was a constant motif of CNL politics.

3. GABRIEL YUMBU, THOMAS MUKWIDI, SYLVAIN KAMA: This trio represented the PSA/G faction in the CNL. They tended to ally with Bocheley-Davidson against Gbenye; at the same time, they expressed reservations in the early phases of the Kwilu uprising about Mulele's tactics, and his presumed Chinese associations. Neither were they anxious to see Gizenga resume his leadership role; when the latter was released from his 30 month imprisonment by Tshombe in July 1964, they declined either to invite him over to assume a top CNL post in Brazzaville, or to join the new Lumumbist party proclaimed by Gizenga in Leopoldville, under his own leadership, after his release.

4. ANDRÉ LUBAYA: A Lulua, who had presided over Kasai province during the first half of 1962, prior to its dismantlement, he had played a key role in negotiating the Lulua-Lumumba alliance in 1960. His party, the UDA, had strong support in Luluabourg, and in some parts of Luluabourg province, and his energies since creation of new provinces had been primarily directed at overthrowing the Luakabwanga provincial regime. He was subsequently taken into the Tshombe government in July 1964; however, he brought no one else with him.

5. GASTON SOUMIALOT: Born at the point of confluence of Basongye and Bakusu cultures, he was district commissioner in Maniema in early 1961, then as a minister in Omari's provincial regime in Kivu during the Stanleyville period. Subsequently, he had travelled widely in Nord-Katanga, Maniema, Kivu Central, Lomami, and Haut Congo, seeking support for a rebirth of MNC/L under his

leadership. Unlike most of the other CNL leaders, he had been constantly preoccupied with rural organization, rather than political maneuvering in Leopoldville.

In addition to these major actors, other lesser figures moved in and out of the CNL entourage. The Kalonji faction of the Sud-Kasai Baluba participated sporadically until the "Mulopwe" himself returned to power as Minister of Agriculture in the Tshombe government. The Kanza family circulated on the CNL fringes, and Thomas Kanza subsequently became Stanleyville "Minister of Foreign Affairs" in August 1964; he brought to the movement extensive contacts in African diplomatic milieux, developed while Stanleyville representative at the UN in 1960-1961, and subsequently as Adoula's Ambassador to London in 1962-1963. In addition to his international constituency, Kanza enjoyed considerable prestige in university circles. A larger number of persons had sporadic contacts with one or another CNL faction; their numbers tended to expand or contract according to the fortunes of the CNL at any given moment.

Insurgency in Leopoldville

Initially, the CNL appeared to concentrate its efforts on an overthrow of the regime in Leopoldville itself. In November, a coup attempt, aimed at assassinating key members of the Binza Group, very nearly succeeded; Mobutu and Nendaka were both kidnapped, and escaped death only when the operation was betrayed at the last minute. A second such plot, aimed at Kasavubu, Adoula, and others, was uncovered in April. In May 1964 a campaign of urban terrorism was launched, with commando squads crossing from Brazzaville armed with plastic and simple explosives. These efforts, however, failed; the CNL leaders lacked support in the Leopoldville population, as Lumumba had in 1960. This, plus the factionalism of the CNL, made relatively simple the task of riddling the group with informers, and resulted in the capture of many of the commando squads as soon as they landed on the Leopold-ville side.

The CNL was permitted to organize at least two training camps in Congo-Brazzaville, one at Gamboma, near the Congo-Leopoldville river town of Bolobo, and a second at Impfondo, on the Ubangi River (dividing the two Congos) about 120 miles from Coquilhatville. However, these camps do not seem to have had large numbers in residence. The Gamboma base was used to launch a raid into Congolese territory, led by "Colonel" Vital Pakassa and Michel Mongali, which briefly captured Bolobo and Mushie in early June 1964.[7]

Soumialot and the Eastern Front

In February 1964 elements of the CNL set off on a new tack, with Gaston Soumialot opening an "eastern section" in Bujumbura. In May, a "second front" was established, with an uprising by Bafulero villagers in the Uvira region (Kivu Central) on the Burundi border. Initially, the Bafulero revolt seemed primarily attributable to local grievances; the leader, Moussa Marandura, had not only been excluded from Simon Malago's provincial government, but also harbored a long-standing grudge against Bafulero Mwami Henri Simba, whom he had for years hoped to supplant as chief. The crucial results of this episode was that a few hundred Bafulero, with some assistance from Watutsi refugees from Rwanda, succeeded in inflicting a humiliating defeat on two ANC battalions, and driving government forces from the Ruzizi plain. Burundi now

---

[7] Pakassa was a former ANC officer, closely associated with Gizenga, who had been expelled from the army for indiscipline and alleged complicity in the Kindu massacre of 13 Italian aviators in November 1961. Mongali had served in the first Adoula government, and subsequently rallied to the CNL; he had a local following in the Lac Leopold II area. Bolobo was disputed by Moyen Congo and Lac Leopold II, and had been the scene of acute ethnic tensions generated by this rivalry since 1963. Mushie, in Lac Leopold II, was approximately 75 miles by land, or 150 by river from Bolobo.

joined Congo-Brazzaville in permitting CNL operations to be conducted from its territory. We may note in passing that the government of Pierre Ngendandumwe was forced out of office by the Burundi parliament on March 30, to be replaced by Albin Nyamoya on April 4.

The ANC had been badly shaken by its difficulties in Kwilu, and its humiliation on the Ruzizi plain added to the demoralization. The limitations of the army as a fighting force became clear—of the ANC's twenty battalions, only about half a dozen were reliably led and moderately trained. Some of the elite units had to be retained in Leopoldville itself, and others were required to garrison the southern Katanga towns, with Katanga gendarmes still at large, and a mercenary-gendarme group poised across the border in Angola. Most of the reserve was committed to the campaign in Kwilu; the remaining units were likely to flee even before poorly armed insurgent groups.

Factional Rivalry in Nord-Katanga

The focus of attention then shifted to the battered province of Nord-Katanga. A bitter factional fight extending back to 1960 had plagued this region, which had also endured the murderous campaigns of the Katanga gendarmes, Stanleyville-based ANC units, and irregular youth bands from 1960-1962. Although Sendwe had initially been undisputed Balubakat leader, power had tended to pass into the hands of lieutenants who were more directly involved in the military phases of the struggle against the Tshombe regime, in particular Prosper Mwamba Ilunga. Until 1963, Ilunga had been provincial president, while Sendwe's role had primarily been at the central level. However, when the latter lost his Leopoldville ministry at the end of 1962, he redirected his ambitions to the provincial scene, and managed in August 1963 to supplant Ilunga. Ilunga never accepted his defeat, and by March 1964 managed a counter-coup in the provincial assembly, placing

590

one of his associates, Fortunat Kabangi-Numbi, in the presidency. Sendwe, however, was able to persuade the central government by dint of ingenious juridical argumentation that his ouster had been illegal; he was then restored to power by the ANC in April. By then Albertville had become a powder keg; both groups began organizing and arming youth gangs, doing this in a situation where displacement of many persons from their homes by Lake Tanganyika floods and a huge influx of refugees from Elizabethville engendered explosive social pressures.

The anti-Sendwe faction then linked itself to Soumialot. A coup in late May, which very nearly succeeded, had some help from small bands coming down from Fizi-Uvira. A month later, the ANC was chased from Albertville, with a group of primarily Babembe warriors from Fizi (to the north) playing a key part; Sendwe was immediately assassinated. Soumialot then appeared in Albertville to proclaim it the seat of a provisional government for "liberated territories in the east"; at his side was Laurent Kabila, a North Katangan provincial assembly member and quondam university student in France, the only prominent Katanga figure in the CNL. In the month that followed, the ANC garrisons in much of Nord-Katanga simply disappeared, and for a brief period irregular bands pushed as far south as Baudouinville and Manono, and even seemed to threaten the military complex at Kamina in west central Nord-Katanga. The precise origins of the irregulars in Nord-Katanga is obscure; probably they were mainly "youth" elements who had operated in the 1960-1962 period, and had reformed when constituted authority suddenly disappeared. However, Soumialot lacked roots in Albertville, and was incapable of profiting from the short-lived triumph. Conditions rapidly became chaotic, and by the end of August 1964 much of Nord-Katanga had been retaken as easily as it had been lost.

591

Olenga and the "People's Liberation Army"

Meanwhile, in southern Maniema a new force was gathering. Under the direction of "General" Nicholas Olenga, a "People's Liberation Army" was recruited, primarily from small towns and villages. The ideological content of the appeal is less well documented in this instance than in that of Kindu. However, this area was Lumumba's home region, and the devotion to his memory was particularly keen; it had been strongly mobilized politically in 1960. A succession of inept provincial governments in Kindu were a logical target for resentment; exploitive politicians and soldiers, and their American and Belgian allies could easily seem the betrayers of the Lumumbist message. However, the "class struggle" doctrines of Mulele were less visible; the cleavage was between "nationalists" (or "Lumumbists") and "counter-revolutionaries." In Soumialot's first message to Stanleyville after its capture, he declared: "Those whom we must combat are not those who have a beautiful car, or a handsome house, or a privileged social position they have won through many sacrifices. Those we must combat, by all the means at our disposal, are the Counter-Revolutionaries, those for whom clear proof exists that they have betrayed the cause for which Lumumba died. For those we will have not the slightest pity."[8]

Olenga himself was a Mukusu, from near Kibombo. He had been a clerk in Bukavu before 1960; in the national elections, he had been associated with the PNP. He became an associate of Soumialot's during the Kashamura-Omari regime in 1961 in Kivu, and had been unemployed in Bukavu since that time. He lacks the relative sophistication and international experience of Mulele; however, he did succeed in forming a nucleus of "simbas" (lions, as his troops were popularly known) which had far more military success than the Kwilu groups. His army was almost entirely

[8] *Le Martyr*, Stanleyville, August 6, 1964.

officered by Batetela-Bakusu, including a number of ex-ANC soldiers.[9]

The utilization of magic was even more pronounced here than in Kwilu. The simbas underwent initiation rites, presumably an eclectic borrowing from secret societies known in the region, and were protected in battle by "dawa" (medicine, or in this case a remedy against bullets). They were accompanied in battle by witchdoctors, charged with maintaining the efficacy of the magic. The simbas marched into Stanleyville, having shed European clothing, in single files, each headed by an unarmed man bearing a palm frond. And, when thus armed the simbas took Stanleyville with very few casualties, who was to say that dawa had not been effective? MNC/L in 1960 had been organized from the city out, and its style of operation bore an urban imprint. The "People's Liberation Army" campaign in 1964 was a conquest of the city by the country, and rural themes tended to predominate.

The simbas demonstrated on a number of occasions a kind of austere discipline. Certain types of activity, such as sexual intercourse, were held to result in loss of invulnerability. In many cases, simba commanders dealt with complaints against their troops by summarily executing the offending simba. However, dispensations could be purchased from the unit witchdoctor, and simba austerity was a highly relative concept. The simbas (like the ANC itself) were highly susceptible to rumors, or distorted versions of real events. Expatriates, or Congolese suspected of central government sympathies, were deemed responsible for the occasional air raids on rebel-held towns (particularly Kindu), and a wave of retaliation usually followed these events,

---

[9] Senior ANC officers distrusted the "Stanleyville element" in the army, and may well have quietly discharged a number of soldiers recruited in this area. Most ANC recruits are drawn from rural areas, like the simbas.

based on a belief that "thousands" of "nationalists" had perished.

In late July, the "People's Liberation Army" began its drive, beginning with Kasongo, and moving up the Lualaba valley to Kindu, Ponthierville, and arriving in Stanleyville on August 4. On their way, the simbas confiscated whatever vehicles they could find, in the hands of traders, companies, or abandoned by the army. Until Stanleyville, there was no resistance from the ANC; the capital of Lumumbism was taken after two days of sporadic fighting. The psychological shock of the fall of Stanleyville very nearly led to the collapse of Leopoldville itself. Many ANC defected to the simbas, and the conspicuous panic of the remaining troops rendered them worse than uselss. In Uele, local partisans (but not the ANC) fought briefly against armed groups from Stanleyville in the capital city of Paulis. In Kibali-Ituri and Sankuru, there was no resistance at all. By the beginning of September, at the high water mark of the rebellion, Stanleyville units had reached Boende in Cuvette Centrale, Lisala in Moyen-Congo, and Yakoma in Ubangi. Parts of Lomami, Nord-Kivu and Kivu Central also were lost to the central government. Bukavu was the scene of a bitter battle at the end of August; here, ANC units were pinned back against a peninsula in Lake Kivu with no retreat possible. Under the able command of Colonel Leonard Mulamba, with the assistance of newly recruited Katanga gendarmes, and armed irregulars of both Kabare and Ngweshi Bashi, the ANC enjoyed one of its rare triumphs.

"People's Republic" in Stanleyville

Once Stanleyville had been occupied, a "People's Republic of the Congo" was proclaimed, with Gbenye as its head; efforts were immediately made to relaunch MNC/L and its ancillary organizations. What stands out about the three and a half months of "revolutionary" government is its erratic course, and the almost complete turnover of leadership which had occurred since 1960. The new men in Stanleyville were far less educated than the first generation of 1960; for example, the commander of the Stanleyville detachment, "Colonel" Joseph Opepe, spoke little French, indicating a rural background and only brief primary school training. There were no less than three "governments" for Stanleyville itself during this period. The first was dominated by Alphonse Kingis and Victor Benanga. The former was a Kitawala leader, who had briefly served as Stanleyville burgomaster in 1961; however, he offended the Gizenga government by leading a gang to smash the religious statuary in front of the Stanleyville cathedral, and was dismissed. Benanga, aged 25, had been head of Bernard Salumu's "goon squads" during the latter's tenure as "boss" of Stanleyville in 1960-1962. Kingis and Benanga initiated a reign of terror; during their rule the first wave public executions of "counter-revolutionaries" took place.

One of the rare rebel leaders exhibiting serious interest in the practical problems of administering Stanleyville was Francois Sabiti, who eventually achieved some responsibility. He had been a minister in the first Orientale government, and had been suspected of moderation then. His uncle, Mabe Sabiti, was chief of the "arabise" quarter of Stanleyville.[10] However, a Sabiti was helpless to control the many atrocities of self-appointed vigilantes who roamed the town. Indeed, in the last phase of the rebel regime, Mabe Sabiti himself was assassinated.

The victims of "nationalist" vengeance were primarily

[10] The "arabisés" are the descendents of those who had formed part of Tippo Tip's retinue when he established his base at Stanley Falls in the late 1880's. Most of these had been captured or otherwise recruited in Maniema and were of Bakusu stock; however, they took on the dress and to a certain extent the religion of their Arab masters, and remained a distinct community when the handful of Zanzibar Arabs withdrew by 1894.

older civil servants, families of persons having collaborated with the Adoula government, captured ANC soldiers, and generally anyone who had become "americainisé." The full list will probably never be known, but there can be no doubt that these atrocities were on a large scale; the population, often including the expatriates, was summoned to observe. As the regime neared its end, the executions became more brutal, often involving disembowellment of the victims so that the liver and other organs could be consumed by the executioners, or drenching with gasoline to set them aflame.

Similar scenes were enacted in Kindu, Boende, Kongolo, Bunia, Buta, Bumba, and Paulis, and no doubt other smaller centers to a lesser degree. In Kindu and Paulis, the toll seems to have been particularly severe, with estimates running about 3000 in each case; in the latter case, the capable Uele provincial president, Pierre Mambaya, was slaughtered. An estimate of 20,000 Congolese executed by rebel groups is conservative.

The overall campaign of the "People's Republic" was primarily directed by Soumialot, Gbenye, and Olenga. Beginning with the establishment of the Stanleyville base, the stress was placed upon the "People's Republic" title, with MNC/L as its political base; the CNL designation tended to drop from current vocabulary. This in part reflected the hope that international recognition might be secured for Stanleyville as the legal government for the Congo from radical African states and perhaps the Soviet block or China (although the latter would have been of relatively small value unless accompanied by some African recognition). Another factor was the small part played by most of the CNL cliques in Brazzaville in the military successes of Olenga's simbas; significantly, although Gbenye was summoned from Brazzaville to head the People's Republic, the government proclaimed by Soumialot did not include members of the Bocheley-Davidson-Mukwidi-

Yumbu faction, or Gizenga. The latter group responded by announcing their own new "Popular Proletarian Movement of the Masses"; Gbenye was entirely excluded, and Soumialot was accorded only a second-ranking position. At the OAU emergency meeting in Addis Ababa in early September 1964, summoned to deal with the Congo situation, Bocheley-Davidson told reporters that he had "never heard of Gbenye," although "it was possible" that he was one of the members.[11]

Toward Recapture of Stanleyville

Confronted with the imminent collapse of its army, the newly designated government of Moise Tshombe chose some desperate expedients. The preceding Adoula government had been trying for several months to persuade some African states to send troops to assist with internal security when the final UN troop units were withdrawn on June 30, 1964.[12] Several governments were sympathetic in principle, but unhappy about the possibility of involving troops in Congolese internal rivalries. None, however, would risk the stigma of helping Tshombe. He then put his old Katanga gendarmes back into uniform, and recruited somewhat over 400 white mercenaries, mainly in Rhodesia and South Africa. Tshombe also obtained American assistance in supplying logistical air transport, and facilitating the acquisition of a small number of combat aircraft; he then hired Cuban exile pilots to fly the latter.

By mid-September, the Stanleyville drive had run out of steam. While it was expanding, new simbas could easily be recruited as the bands advanced. Opposition groups sent emissaries to contact rebel groups, to negotiate their participation in a movement which seemed to promise removal of those currently holding power. However, participation

[11] *Courrier d'Afrique,* September 17, 1964.

[12] The UN forces had been whittled to a skeleton force, mainly in southern Katanga, for a number of months before; UN troops had taken no part in the Kwilu hostilities.

in these outlying areas was far more superficial than it had been in the Stanleyville-Maniema-Sankuru triangle. When the reformed ANC columns, with a handful of mercenaries attached, began pushing back toward Stanleyville, they met as little resistance as had the simbas beforehand.

The whole phase came to a nightmarish close on November 24, when US-airlifted Belgian paratroopers dropped on Stanleyville to forestall rebel threats to massacre all expatriates if the ANC advance on Stanleyville were not halted; a few hours afterwards, the ANC itself arrived. The bulk of those held as hostages in Stanleyville itself were saved, but a European toll of more than 200 lives is likely when the final returns are in. Although the paratroopers caused very few casualties, the mercenary-ANC columns exacted their own reprisals on the roads back to Stanleyville. It is impossible even to guess at these casualties.

The Insurrection Assessed

The difference between this period and the Lumumbist rule in Stanleyville in 1960-1961 must be underlined. In the first phase, Stanleyville provided relatively effective administration, and the social and economic life of the area continued largely unimpaired. Although MNC/L had achieved in the spring of 1960 an impressive rural organization, which continued longer than party organization in most other areas after independence, its leadership was drawn from the urban elite. This time, however, Stanleyville was captured by rural troops. The insurrection was directed against many who had worn the MNC/L label in 1960.

By a curious paradox, the revolution carried out in the name of radical social progress has created the objective conditions for retrogression. The decimation of an elite, the destruction of administrative and economic structures, even though colonial in origin, has deprived large regions of the necessary instruments of social change. There is no al-

ternative in the Congo to the administrative framework bequeathed by the colonial state; it no doubt can and should
be gradually adapted, but cannot be totally replaced by a
political party or any other structure. There is further no alternative to an expatriate contribution in the economic and
educational sphere in the next decade; but the uprising
leaves in its wake conditions of physical insecurity unlikely
to ameliorate in the near future, and recruitment of expatriates for this zone will be extremely difficult. The cost of
the uprising will be borne above all by the people of the
areas affected, who will be deprived of opportunities for
social advance which will probably continue to be available
in other zones, especially the Lower Congo and southern
Katanga.

The fragmented character of the uprisings also stands
out. Mulele's Bambundu-Bapende strategy was both a
profound success in his home area and a failure in being
unable to expand significantly beyond; his campaign was
initiated without the cooperation of most of those subsequently rallying to the CNL. The Leopoldville terrorism,
and Bolobo-Mushie expeditions were mounted by CNL-
Brazzaville, as raids from a foreign sanctuary, rather than
internal uprisings. The Ruzizi plain was conquered by the
Bafulero for their own reasons, however convenient this
proved to be for Soumialot in Bujumbura. In Nord-Katanga, the CNL was merely superficially allied with one
side of a bitter factional dispute internal to the province.
Only with the formation of Olenga's Batetela-Bakusu-led
Army and the march on Stanleyville did one see emerge a
relatively coherent core to the insurgency—and even when
triumph seemed almost within grasp CNL-Brazzaville was
busily pursuing its own factious ends.

Should one seek out the hidden conspiratorial hand from
the outside in this dreary sequence of events? This study
has elsewhere not systematically dealt with this dimension of Congolese politics, important though it has been at

several junctures; we make only passing reference to this question here, although it is deserving of further exploration. Certainly the United States, and to a lesser extent Belgium, had been heavily committed to support of the Adoula government, as the best prospect for unity and stability in the Congo. After initial reluctance, this support was also accorded to Tshombe, and even increased, through air support, provision of aircraft, and tacit acceptance of the mercenary recruitment. The more militant African states became increasingly reserved toward the Adoula government, and totally hostile to the successor Tshombe. The latter's assumed role in Lumumba's death predisposed radical states toward sympathy with the CNL cause. Their violent antipathy toward Tshombe made Leopoldville unwilling to accept OAU mediation. Following upon the Stanleyville paratrooper operation, Algeria and the UAR announced that they intended to supply the remaining rebels with arms and men, adding another new dimension to the situation.

More uncertain is the role of the Soviet Union and China. Certainly both had been contacted by the CNL at various stages, and various Congolese had visited both countries. In the early stages, the Soviet Union had a monopoly of access to the Congo, but suffered humiliating reverses in 1960, and again in 1963 when its embassy staff was expelled in summary fashion. Gbenye in the first phases of the CNL seems to have been in touch with the Soviets, and captured correspondence in November 1963 included a letter from him warning the Russians of Chinese influence over Mulele. The Russians have expressed moral support for the CNL, and probably have contributed some funds. However, their role does not seem to have been very pronounced.

The establishment of diplomatic relations by China with Congo-Brazzaville and Burundi in early 1964 introduced an important new factor; both embassies had staffs far larger than routine diplomatic activity in small African states would seem to require. Soumialot and Kabila were in frequent and conspicuous contact with the Chinese embassy in Bujumbura. Some Chinese (and other Soviet bloc) arms were put on display in Leopoldville in December 1964, said to have been captured in Stanleyville; however, the quantities were not large. The likelihood is strong that some financial assistance to some CNL elements was provided. The Chinese were doubtless generous with advice on guerilla warfare tactics. It is possible that they perceived the movement as a genuine peasant revolt against "imperialism" and its instruments at the rural mass level. It seems unlikely that they could have had any illusions about the Marxist-Leninist commitment of "national bourgeois" leaders like Gbenye and Soumialot. However, perhaps the liquidation of some "imperialist positions" was all that was anticipated at this stage; the next phase would then need await the development of a truly revolutionary leadership.

Whatever the answer to these riddles may be, the profound transformation of the Congolese polity is not open to doubt. The revolution without revolutionaries of 1960 had been superficial by contrast, and the community had largely adjusted to its new circumstances. The insurrection of 1964, which destroyed the means for social change in the name of radical progress, again transformed the environment in large areas, but with recovery far less certain.

XX

Note on Methodological Assumptions

XXXXXXXXXXXXXXXXXXXXXXXXXXXXXXXXXXXXXXXXXXXXXXXXXX

IN RECENT years political scientists have devoted considerable energy to the quest for a theoretical framework for
the comparative study of political systems in under-developed areas. The most ambitious of these was the Al-
mond-Coleman volume, *The Politics of the Developing
Areas*.[1] While this work is without doubt an important
contribution to the task of theory-building, and there can
be hardly any quarrel with the case made for a functional
approach to the analysis of emerging political systems, the
particular model evolved does not seem to this writer to
have advanced us very far toward the effectively "proba-
bilistic theory of the polity" which is stated to be the goal.[2]
Successful application of a conceptual scheme such as
that developed by Almond presumes the existence of an
agreed upon body of data which, at least in the case of the
Congo, does not yet exist. The aggregation of areas of
ignorance, partial knowledge, or even misinformation can
only produce misleading results. This study is presented
on a much lower level and aspires only to contribute toward
filling some of the gaps in basic information. No particular
model of political change has been adopted as a frame for
the ordering of material, as none yet evolved, in this opinion, provides a felicitous scheme for scaling the significance
of the multifold facts pressing for the attention of the
student of Congo politics.

In recent years, there has been a rapid growth in the
use of quantitative methods in social science research. The
advent of the computer age has made possible a broad

[1] Gabriel A. Almond and James S. Coleman, *The Politics of the
Developing Areas* (Princeton: Princeton University Press, 1960).

[2] *Ibid.*, pp. 58-64. It should be added that the authors do not claim
to have done anything more than contribute toward the eventual
realization of this goal, which they clearly have accomplished.

range of new applications and stimulated the search for approaches to the study of politics which lend themselves to statistical and mathematical formulation. It is not surprising that this has been most fruitful in fields such as voting behavior where the mechanism of tallying ballots, added to the sophisticated schemes of scientific sample surveys, produce a body of raw material expressed in numbers. Here one approaches possession of quantitative tools of the level which the price system affords the economist for the study of economic behavior.

Unfortunately, very little material of this nature is available for the analysis of politics in the Congo. There were municipal elections in three urban centers in 1957, then in four others in 1958, nation-wide elections in December 1959 and May 1960, and further local balloting in 1963. The total environment within which these took place was in such rapid evolution that the figures are not susceptible to meaningful comparison at any rigorous level. Further, the complete, detailed electoral figures for the most relevant balloting, that of May 1960, have not yet been made generally available.[3] Legislative behavior, another area of real advance in the study of Western political systems,

[3] Verhaegen has recently obtained the complete breakdown (these are on deposit coded on computer cards at Massachusetts Institute of Technology), giving tallies more complete than those published to date, which gave only totals for the very large electoral *circonscriptions* used, the district in the case of seats in the national Chamber of Representatives, and the territory in respect to the provincial assemblies. A district is on the average three to four times the size of Belgium, and a territory is equivalent in area to three-fourths of the metropolitan power. It can be easily seen that these figures do not constitute a very discriminating set of analytical tools. In addition, the figures on preferential votes have not been released; by virtue of an unusual electoral procedure, the voter was enabled to indicate a preferential vote for an individual while voting on a party list, instead of merely accepting the ordering decided upon by the political party as the customary norms of a multi-member district, proportional representation system would appear to dictate. On the basis of these figures for the Kwilu, Weiss has been able to draw some surprising and important conclusions in his forthcoming PSA study.

603

likewise is not providing at the moment any very meaningful quantitative data in the Congo, and, in the absence of any clear notion of the function of representative institutions in the Congolese political system, does not seem an immediately fruitful avenue of research. Further, roll call votes are not recorded; only the debates are preserved. Sampling techniques may eventually yield some important political data,[4] but these are only beginning to be applied in African post-independence situations.

It is pointless to underestimate the enormous obstacles which stand in the way of sampling procedures (and political research in general). Political sensitivities impose taboos on inquiry into a wide range of phenomena of first importance; systematic interviewing on subjects of this nature is very difficult for the overseas researcher to perform, and Congolese researchers and assistants find it hard to establish a minimum situation of rapport and confidence outside their own regions or ethnic groups.[5] This type of research is little understood or valued outside the narrow confines of the university community. African scholars will clearly play a leading role in expanding the understanding

[4] INEP in Leopoldville and the *Centre d'Etudes Politiques* at Lovanium University have some interesting projects in this line, to be conducted with the aid of their students. However, these are at very preliminary stages of formulation at present.

[5] See in this regard the most interesting *Mémoire* submitted to the *Ecole Sociale de Louvain* by André Bo-Boliko, *Le comportement des travailleurs manuels congolais devant leurs rémunérations* (Louvain: mimeographed, 1958), pp. 8-10. Bo-Boliko is now head of the largest trade union, the *Union des Travailleurs Congolais,* a keenly intelligent observer, and certainly "modern" in outlook. He found, however, that the only basis on which he could organize his study was through restricting his field of observation to workers in Nioki and those from Kutu territory, in which Nioki is situated, in Leopoldville. He, or at least his family, was personally known or recognizable to his respondents, which enable him to overcome the suspicions that he was a spy for the colonial administration or the company, or both. While the colonial government could no longer be suspected of being the deus ex machina behind the research project, there is no lack of forces, internal and external, which could easily replace it as the object of suspicion.

of the Congolese political process and applying new quantitative techniques; even when the trickle now emerging from the universities becomes a stream, however, the aforementioned barriers will impose serious limits on the type of data which can be collected.[6]

Quantitative analysis by Belgian scholars in the pre-independence period was largely restricted to the sociological field, especially urbanization studies,[7] in large part because political studies were not encouraged by the colonial administration.[8] While it would be an exaggeration to argue that devotees of quantitative research in politics are confronted with a *tabula rasa,* it would be impossible to maintain that analysis can rest in any large part on available materials, or that the likelihood for improvement of the situation in the near future is very great.[9]

[6] One may refer to the case of the first Congolese to join the academic staff at Lovanium University; his doctoral thesis, in political science, has been directed to the problem of under-administration in African countries excluding the Congo, to avoid any accidental trespass into sensitive domains.

[7] Among those worthy of note are the works of André Lux, "Luluabourg, migrations, accroissement et urbanisation de sa population congolaise," *Zaïre,* XII (1958); L. Baeck, "Une société rurale en transition: étude socio-économique de la région de Thysville," *Zaïre,* XI (February 1957), 115-86, and "Léopoldville, phénomène urbain africain," *Zaïre,* X (June 1956), 613-36; the Stanleyville studies of V. P. Pons and Pierre Clement in the UNESCO-sponsored study by the International African Institute, *Social Implications of Industrialization and Urbanization South of the Sahara* (UNESCO: 1956); Jacques Denis, *Le phénomène urbain en Afrique centrale* (Brussels: ARSOM, Sci. Mor, et Pol., N.S., T. XIX, fasc. 1, 1958); Paul Minon, *Katuba: Etude quantitative d'une communauté urbaine africaine* (Liège: Institut de Sociologie, 1960); P. Caprasse, *Leaders africains en milieu urbain* (Elisabethville: CEPSI, 1959).

[8] James S. Coleman, "Research in Africa in European Centers," *African Studies Bulletin,* II (August 1959), 9-12.

[9] Some interesting innovations in manipulation of quantitative techniques are displayed in the various publications of Paul Raymaekers dealing with social problems in Leopoldville. Among those which have already appeared, one may mention "matériaux pour une étude sociologique de la jeunesse africaine du milieu extra-coutumier de Léopoldville," *Notes et Documents,* Institut de Recherches Economiques et Sociales de l'Université Lovanium, I (August 1960); "Le

Quantification has sometimes been proposed at a somewhat different level, involving reducing abstraction to mathematical expression. Karl Deutsch has suggested that the discipline is becoming divided between those who see themselves as "social scientists, studying political behavior by quantitative and experimental methods," and revolting against the heavy hand of those "rooted most deeply in the humanistic literary and historical tradition of scholarship and judgment," and relying upon "political intuition and historical narrative."[10] The former method seems unlikely to give decisive help in the effort to understand the phenomena which concern this study. There seems, in fact, no escape from the requirement of adequate application of "political intuition," whether or not it is filtered through an intellectually elegant analytical scheme with numerical accoutrements. At this stage, one may walk more swiftly through the thickets of Congolese politics if one first unbuckles cumbersome methodologies. Or to amend the metaphor, the forest must first be cleared before the heavy machinery can be brought in to cultivate.

It is, of course, impossible to explore unaided the complex polity of the Congo, with its intricately interacting traditional and modern systems and tensions born of uneven distribution of agonies and rewards of modernization. Especially indispensable is the assistance of the anthropologist. In the early years, the great bulk of this work was done by missionaries and administrators and was influenced, particularly in the case of the latter, by the prac-

squatting à Léopoldville," *Bulletin de l'Institut Interafricain du Travail,* Brazzaville, VIII (November 1961), 22-53; and the forthcoming "Prédélinquance et délinquance juvénile à Léopoldville."

[10] "Toward an Inventory of Basic Trends and Patterns in Comparative and International Politics," *American Political Science Review,* LIV (March 1960), 35. See also Deutsch's *Nationalism and Social Communication* (New York: MIT Press and Wiley, 1953). A more recent, massive effort in this line is found in Arthur S. Banks and Robert B. Textor, *A Cross-Polity Survey* (Cambridge, Mass.: MIT Press, 1963).

tical requirements of their respective institutions. Only since World War II has there emerged a school of anthropology in close touch with the state of research in other countries and deeply concerned with moving beyond the statics of traditional anthropological study to a dynamic understanding of the acculturative process.[11] Nonetheless, there remains a paradoxical poverty of ethnographic material which attempts to deal with social change under the impact of the colonial experience, amidst a wealth of descriptive information about the peoples contained with the Congo's frontiers.[12]

At the present stage of knowledge, then, the primary challenge to the student of Congolese politics remains the basic task of providing a conceptual framework adequate to order the mass of disparate data available. Change and flux are the crucial dimensions of emergent patterns of politics; yet these are the very vectors which have been least successfully assimilated into the new "behavioral mood" of American political science, as one of its leading practitioners freely concedes.[13] The very nature of the Congolese political community is not entirely defined. Both colonization and decolonization created profound disequilibria in the evolution of Congolese society. In this environment, the task of seeking comprehension of the dynamic would seem to merit priority over rigorous analysis of the static.

There is obviously no single pathway to enlarged understanding of Congolese or African political processes. These remarks are not intended as general methodological prescriptions directed at all research on African politics; they

[11] The ablest Belgian representatives of the postwar generation dealing with Congolese data are Daniel Biebuyck and Jan Vansina.

[12] A major recent exception to this general rule is Alvin W. Wolfe, *In the Ngombe Tradition* (Evanston, Ill.: Northwestern University Press, 1961).

[13] See Robert A. Dahl's admirable self-assessment in "The Behavioral Approach," *American Political Science Review*, LV, No. 4 (December 1961), 763-72.

are simply an effort to make explicit the assumptions and premises which underlie the present work.[14]

[14] On the general subject of defining a methodology for the study of Congolese politics, see the interesting article by B. Verhaegen and L. Monnier, "Problèmes concrets et concepts de science politique en Afrique. Application au Bas-Congo," *Cahiers Economiques et Sociaux,* Université Lovanium, No. 4 (June 1963) pp. 79-96.

THE appended bibliography includes not only works bearing directly on the study but those providing a historical and ethnographic framework for comprehending the phenomena which have been the concern of this work. The selection has not been rigorous, and the quality of the material listed is uneven. However, there has been no attempt to catalogue completely the rash of writing about the Congo since 1959, much of which bears the mark of hasty production. For this, the reader is referred to the excellent and virtually complete list by Dominique Ryelandt, published as a supplement to *Etudes Congolaises* in 1963.

Bibliographies

For many purposes, students of Congo politics will find that René Lemarchand's "Selective Bibliographical Survey for the Study of Politics in the Former Belgian Congo," *American Political Science Review*, LIV, No. 3 (September 1960), 715-28, and Catherine Hoskyns' "Sources for a Study of the Congo since Independence," *Journal of Modern African Studies*, I, No. 3 (September 1963), 373-82, supplemented by Ryelandt's contribution cited above will suffice. For an exhaustive set of bibliographies on all subjects, see the series produced by T. Heyse, assisted by J. Berlage, *Bibliographie du Congo Belge et du Ruanda-Urundi, 1939-1951*, in *Cahiers Belges et Congolais*, Nos. 4-22 (Brussels: 1953). For the early period, see A. J. Wauters, *Bibliographie du Congo, 1880-1885* (Brussels: 1895). The Musée Royal d'Afrique Centrale publishes an annual ethnographic bibliography listings; see also the excellent bibliographies for Katanga edited by Olga Boone and published as *Carte ethnique du Congo: Quart sud-est* (Tervuren, Belgium: Musée Royal de l'Afrique Centrale, 1961). Jean Berlage's *Repertoire de la presse du Congo Belge et du Ruanda-*

Urundi (Brussels: 1955), and J. M. Van Bol's *La presse quotidienne au Congo Belge* (Brussels: 1959). For materials on the Katanga, see M. Walraet's *Bibliographie du Katanga* (Brussels: ARSOM, Sci. Mor. et Pol., N.S., T. XXXII, 1958).

Zaïre and *Africa* have thorough coverage of Congo materials in their regular bibliographic sections. Happily, since independence, *Etudes Congolaises* is carrying on the excellent bibliographic work done before independence by other journals.

Books and Articles

I. EUROPEAN PENETRATION AND BELGIAN
COLONIAL ADMINISTRATION

BOOKS

Anet, H. and R. *Vers l'avenir*. Leopoldville: Conseil Protestant du Congo, 1929. Report of Jubilee Conference of Protestant Missions in Congo, and Missionary Conference in West Africa, Leopoldville, September 15-23, 1928.

Arnot, Frederick S. *Garenganze; or, Seven Years Pioneer Mission Work in Central Africa*. London: James E. Hawkins, 1889.

Baumer, Guy. *Les centres indigènes extracoutumiers au Congo Belge*. Paris: Editions Domat-Montchrestien, 1939.

Bentley, W. Holman. *Pioneering on the Congo*. 2 vols. New York: Fleming H. Revell Co., 1900.

Brausch, Georges. *Belgian Administration in the Congo*. London: Institute of Race Relations, 1961.

Buell, Raymond Leslie. *The Native Problem in Africa*. 2 vols. New York: Macmillan Co., 1928.

Burrows, Guy. *The Curse of Central Africa*. London: R. A. Everett & Co., 1903.

Cameron, Verney L. *Across Africa*. New York: Harper & Bros., 1877.

Cattier, Félicien. *Etude sur la situation de l'Etat Indépendant du Congo*. 2d ed. Brussels: Vve. F. Larcier, 1906.

Ceulemans, R. P. P. *La question arabe et le Congo (1883-*

1892). Brussels: ARSOM, Sci. Mor. et Pol., N.S., T. XXII, fasc. 1, 1959.

Le Congo Belge. 2 vols. Brussels: Inforcongo, 1958.

Le Congo. Documents 1956. Brussels: de Linie, 1957.

Congo 1885-1960. Positions socialistes. Brussels: Institut Vandervelde, n. d. [1960?].

Conrad, Joseph. *Heart of Darkness.* New York: Dell Books, 1960.

Coquilhat, Camille. *Sur le Haut-Congo.* Paris: J. Lebegue et Cie., 1888.

Cornet, René J. *La bataille du rail.* Brussels: Editions L. Cuypers, 1947.

———. *Katanga.* Brussels: Editions L. Cuypers, 1946.

———. *Maniema le pays des mangeurs d'hommes.* Brussels: Editions L. Cuypers, 1952.

———. *Terre Katangaise.* Brussels: 1955.

Cornevin, Robert. *Histoire du Congo-Leo.* Paris: Editions Berger-Levrault, 1963.

Crawford, D. *Thinking Black.* 2d ed. London: Morgan & Scott, Ltd., 1914.

Daye, Pierre. *Problèmes congolais.* Brussels: Les Ecrits, 1943.

de Bauw, A. *Le Katanga.* Brussels: Veuve Ferd. Larcier, 1920.

de Hemptinne, J. *Le gouvernement du Congo Belge. Projet de réorganisation administrative.* Brussels: Librairie Dewit, 1920.

———. *La politique des missions protestantes au Congo.* Elisabethville: Editions de l'Essor du Congo, 1929.

———. *Un tournant de notre politique indigène.* Elisabethville: Editions de la Revue Juridique du Congo Belge, 1935.

Dehoux, Emile. *L'effort de paix du Congo Belge.* Brussels: Robert Stoops, 1946.

Delcommune, Alexandre. *L'avenir du Congo Belge menacé.* 2 vols. Brussels: Office de Publicité, 1921.

————. *Vingt années de vie africaine.* 2 vols. Brussels: Vve. Ferdinand Larcier, 1922.

Dellicour, F. *Les propos d'un colonial belge.* Brussels: M. Weissenbruch, n. d. (1956).

Denuit, D. *Le Congo champion de la Belgique en guerre.* Brussels: Editions Frans van Belle, n. d. (1946?).

De Thier, F. M. *Singatini: Contribution à l'historique de Stanleyville.* Stanleyville: 1959.

Dettes de guerre. Elisabethville: Editions de l'Essor du Congo, 1945.

Deuxième Section de l'Etat-Major de la Force Publique. *La Force Publique de sa naissance à 1914.* Brussels: ARSOM, Sci. Mor. et Pol., T. XXVII, 1952.

Doucy, Arthur, and Feldheim, Pierre. *Problèmes du travail et politique sociale au Congo Belge.* Brussels: Editions de la Librairie Encyclopédique, 1952.

Durieux, André. *Institutions politiques, administratives et juridiques du Congo Belge et du Ruanda-Urundi.* 4th ed. Brussels: Editions Bieleveld, 1957.

Encyclopédie du Congo Belge. 3 vols. Brussels: Editions Bieleveld, 1953.

Fox-Bourne, H. R. *Civilisation in Congoland.* London: P. S. King & Son, 1903.

Franck, Louis. *Le Congo Belge.* 2 vols. Brussels: La Renaissance du Livre, 1930.

Gelders, V. *Quelques aspects de l'évolution des colonies en 1938.* Brussels: ARSOM, Sci. Mor. et Pol., T. IX, fasc. 4, 1941.

Gilbert, O-P. *L'empire du silence.* Brussels: Les Editions du Peuple, 1947.

Grévisse, F. *La grande pitié des juridictions indigènes.* Brussels: ARSOM, Sci. Mor. et Pol., T. XIX, fasc. 3, 1949.

Hailey, Lord. *An African Survey.* revised. London: Oxford University Press, 1957.

Haines, C. Grove (ed.). *Africa Today.* Baltimore: Johns Hopkins Press, 1955.

Halewyck de Heusch, Michel. *Les institutions politiques et administratives des pays africains soumis à l'autorité de la Belgique.* Brussels: Etablissements Généraux d'Imprimerie, 1934.

Heyse, Th. *Congo Belge et Ruanda-Urundi. Notes de droit public et commentaires de la Charte Coloniale.* 2 vols. Brussels: G. Van Campenhout, 1952-54.

Hinde, Sidney L. *The Fall of the Congo Arabs.* New York: Thomas Whittaker, 1897.

Hostelet, Georges. *L'oeuvre civilisatrice de la Belgique au Congo de 1885 à 1953.* 2 vols. Brussels: ARSOM, Sci. Mor. et Pol., T. XXXIII; T. XXXVII, fasc. 2, 1954.

————. *Le problème politique capital au Congo et en Afrique noire.* Brussels: Institut de Sociologie Solvay, 1959.

Jentgen, P. *Les pouvoirs des Secrétaires Généraux FF du Ministère des Colonies pendant l'occupation.* Brussels: ARSOM, Sci. Mor. et Pol., T. XIV, fasc. 4, 1946.

Johnston, Sir Harry. *George Grenfell and the Congo.* 2 vols. London: Hutchison & Co., 1908.

Keith, Arthur Berriedale. *The Belgian Congo and the Berlin Act.* Oxford: Clarendon Press, 1919.

Lejeune-Choquet, Adolphe. *Histoire militaire du Congo.* Brussels: Maison d'Edition Alfred Castaigne, 1906.

Livre Blanc: Apport scientifique de la Belgique au développement de l'Afrique centrale. 3 vols. Brussels: ARSOM, 1962-1963.

Louwers, O. *L'Article 73 de la Charte et l'anticolonialisme de l'Organisation des Nations Unies.* Brussels: ARSOM, Sci. Mor. et Pol., T. XXIX, fasc. 2, 1952.

————. *Le problème financier et le problème économique au Congo Belge en 1932.* Brussels: ARSOM, Sci. Mor. et Pol., T. III, fasc. 2, 1933.

Magotte, J. *Les circonscriptions indigènes.* La Louvière: Imprimerie Louviéroise, n. d. (1952).

Mair, L. P. *Native Policies in Africa.* London: George Rutledge & Sons, Ltd., 1936.

Malengreau, Guy. *Vers un paysannat indigène*. Brussels: ARSOM, Sci. Mor. et Pol., T. XIX, fasc. 2, 1949.

Marvel, Tom. *The New Congo*. London: Macdonald, 1949.

Masoin, Fritz. *Histoire de l'Etat Indépendant du Congo*. 2 vols. Namur: Imprimerie Pecard-Balon, 1912-1913.

Michiels, A., and Laude, N. *Congo Belge et Ruanda-Urundi*. 18th ed. of *Notre Colonie*. Brussels: L'Edition Universelle, 1958.

Mille, Pierre. *Au Congo Belge*. Paris: Armand Colin, 1899.

Morel, Edmund D. *King Leopold's Rule in Africa*. New York: Funk and Wagnalls Co., 1905.

———. *Red Rubber*. London: T. F. Unwin, 1906.

Objectivité sur mésure. Brussels: E. Vandenbussche, 1955.

Parisis, Albert. *Les finances communales et urbaines au Congo Belge*. Brussels: ARSOM, Sci. Mor. et Pol., N. S., T. XXV, fasc. 1, 1960.

Paulus, Jean-Pierre. *Droit public du Congo Belge*. Brussels: Institut de Sociologie Solvay, 1959.

Roeykens, R. P. A. *Léopold II et l'Afrique, 1885-1880*. Brussels: ARSOM, N. S., T. XIV, fasc. 2, 1958.

Ryckmans, Pierre. *Dominer pour servir*. Brussels: Edition Universelle, 1948.

———. *Etapes et jalons*. Brussels: Maison Ferdinand Larcier, 1946.

———. *La politique coloniale*. Brussels: Les Editions Rex, 1934.

Salkin, Paul. *L'Afrique centrale dans cent ans*. Paris: Payot, 1926.

———. *Etudes africaines*. Brussels: Vve. Ferdinand Larcier 1920.

Scheyven, Raymond. *Et le Congo?* Brussels: n. d. (1957).

Slade, Ruth M. *English-Speaking Missions in the Congo Independent State (1878-1908)*. Brussels: ARSOM, Sci. Mor. et Pol., N. S., T. XVI, fasc. 2, 1959.

———. *King Leopold's Congo*. London: Institute of Race Relations, 1962.

Smith, H. Sutton. *Yakusu*. London: Marshall Brothers, n.d. (1912?).

Sourdillat Jacques. *Les chefferies au Congo Belge*. Paris: Editions Domat-Montchrestien, 1940.

Stanley, Henry M. *The Congo and the Founding of its Free State*. 2 vols. London: Sampson, Low, Marston, Searle, & Rivington, 1885.

———. *Through the Dark Continent*. 2 vols. New York: Harper & Bros., 1878.

Stengers, Jean. *Belgique et Congo: L'élaboration de la Charte Coloniale*. Brussels: La Renaissance du Livre, 1963.

———. *Combien le Congo a-t-il coûté à la Belgique?* Brussels: ARSOM, Sci. Mor. et Pol., N. S., T. XI, fasc. 1, 1957.

Stenmans, Alain. *La reprise du Congo par la Belgique*. Brussels: Editions Techniques et Scientifiques, 1949.

Stillman, Calvin W. *Africa in the Modern World*. Chicago: University of Chicago Press, 1955.

Vanderkerken, G. *La politique coloniale belge*. Antwerp: Editions Zaïre, 1943.

Vandervelde, E. *La Belgique et le Congo*. Paris: Félix Alcan, 1911.

Van Iseghem, André. *A propos d'un projet de réorganisation administrative du gouvernement du Congo Belge*. Brussels: Hayez, 1920.

Vermeulen, V. *Déficiences et dangers de notre politique indigène*. Brussels: 1952.

Verner, Samuel P. *Pioneering in Central Africa*. Richmond, Va.: Presbyterian Committee of Publication, 1903.

Wauters, A. J. *L'Etat Indépendant du Congo*. Brussels: Librairie Falk Fils, 1899.

———. *Histoire politique du Congo Belge*. Brussels: Pierre Van Fleteren, 1911.

ARTICLES

Congo. 10th yr., T. II, No. 2, (July, 1929). (Special issue on "politique indigène).

de Hemptinne, J. "La politique indigène du gouvernement belge," *Congo*, 9th yr., T. II, No. 3 (October 1928), pp. 359-74.

Durieux, André. "La réorganisation du Ministère des Colonies," *Zaïre*, I, No. 3 (March 1947), 271-79.

Engels, A. "A propos de chefferies indigènes," *Congo*, 3rd yr., T. I, (January 1922), pp. 1-10.

Lotar, L. "L'immatriculation et l'ordre économique," *Congo*, 7th yr., T. I, No. 1 (January 1926), pp. 32-36.

Marzorati, A. "Le problème judiciaire au Congo Belge," *Bull. Séances*, ARSOM (1932), pp. 43-59.

"Mutineries au Congo Belge," *Bulletin Militaire*, No. 21 (March 1947), pp. 20-84.

Rubbens, A. "Le colour-bar au Congo Belge," *Zaïre* (May 1949), pp. 503-14.

Ryckbost, J. "La liberté syndicale et la grève en droit congolais," *Zaïre*, XIII, No. 3 (1959), 227-42.

Southall, A. W. "Belgian and British Administration in Alurland," *Zaïre*, VIII, No. 5 (May 1954), 467-86.

Vandewalle, F. A. "Mutineries au Congo Belge," *Zaïre*, XI, No. 5 (May 1957), 487-514.

Van Wing, J. "Le Congo déraille," *Bull. Séances*, ARSOM (1951), pp. 609-26.

―――――. "La Formation d'une élite noire au Congo Belge," *Bulletin Militaire*, No. 24 (August 1947), pp. 71-86.

II. ECONOMIC AND SOCIAL BACKGROUND

BOOKS

Bezy, Fernand. *Principes pour l'orientation du développement économique au Congo*. Leopoldville: Editions de l'Université, 1959.

―――――. *Problèmes structurels de l'économie congolaise*. Louvain: Institut de Recherches Economiques et Sociales, 1957.

Braekman, E. M. *Histoire du Protestantisme au Congo*. Brussels: Librairie des Eclaireurs Unionistes, 1961.

BIBLIOGRAPHY

Brixhe, A. *Le coton au Congo Belge.* 3rd ed. Brussels: Ministère des Colonies, 1958.

Carbonnelle, C., and Kirschen, E. S. *L'économie des deux Uélés.* Brussels: Editions Cemubac, 1961.

Choprix, Guy. *La naissance d'une ville. Etude géographique de Paulis, (1934-1957).* Brussels: Edition Cemubac, 1961.

CRISP. *Morphologie des groupes financiers.* Brussels: 1962.

Fédération des Entreprises Congolaises. *L'économie congolaise à la veille de l'indépendance.* Brussels: 1960.

Heyse, Th. *Grandes lignes du régime des terres du Congo Belge et du Ruanda-Urundi.* Brussels: ARSOM, Sci. Mor. et Pol., T. XV, fasc. 1, 1947.

Joye, Pierre, and Lewin, Rosine. *Les trusts au Congo.* Brussels: Société Populaire d'Editions, 1961.

Lefebvre, Jacques. *Structures économiques du Congo Belge et du Ruanda-Urundi.* Brussels: Editions de Treurenberg, 1955.

Malengreau, Guy. *Les droits fonciers coutumiers chez les indigènes du Congo Belge.* Brussels: ARSOM, Sci. Mor. et Pol., T. XV, fasc. 2, 1947.

Moutoulle, L. *Politique sociale de l'Union Minière du Haut Katanga.* Brussels: ARSOM, Sci. Mor. et Pol., T. XIV, fasc. 3, 1946.

Poupart, R. *Facteurs de productivité de la main-d'oeuvre autochtone à Elisabethville.* Brussels: Editions de l'Institut de Sociologie Solvay, 1960.

Robert, Maurice. *Contribution à la géographie du Katanga.* Brussels: ARSOM, Sci. Nat. et Med., T. XXIV, fasc. 3, 1954.

Sohier, A. *Traité élémentaire de droit coutumier du Congo Belge.* 2d ed. Brussels: Maison F. Larcier, 1954.

Tempels, R. P. Placide. *La philosophie bantoue.* Paris: Présence Africaine, 1949.

Terlinden, Charles, Cornet, Rene J., and Walraet, Marcel. *Comité Spécial du Katanga.* Brussels: Edition L. Cuypers, 1950.

Union Minière du Haut Katanga. 1906-1956. 2d ed. Brussels: L. Cuypers, 1956.

Van de Walde, Marcel W. *Economie belge et Congo Belge*. Doctoral thesis, University of Nancy (France), 1936-1937.

Van de Walle, B. *Essai d'une planification de l'économie agricole congolaise*. INEAC, Série Technique No. 61, 1960.

Vers la promotion de l'économie indigène. Brussels: Institut de Sociologie Solvay, 1956.

Wigny, Pierre. *Ten Year Plan for the Economic and Social Development of the Belgian Congo*. New York: Belgian Government Information Office, 1950.

ARTICLES

Beckers, Henri. "Le Fonds du Bien-Etre Indigène," *Zaïre*, V, No. 8 (October 1951), 787-812.

Boelaert, E. "Faut-il créer des réserves pour les indigènes?" *Zaïre*, IX, No. 2 (February 1955), 133-42.

———. "Les trois fictions du droit foncier congolais," *Zaïre*, XI, No. 4 (April 1957), 399-427.

Brausch, G. "L'action en Afrique belge de l'Institut de Sociologie Solvay," *Problèmes d'Afrique Centrale*, No. 41, 3rd quarter (1958), pp. 160-64.

Doutreloux, Albert. "Note sur le domaine foncier au Mayumbe," *Zaïre*, XIII, No. 5 (1959), 499-508.

Huybrechts, A. "La conjoncture congolaise en 1956," *Zaïre*, XI, No. 3 (March 1957), pp. 273-95.

———. "L'économie congolaise en 1959," *Zaïre*, XIII, No. 8 (1959), 843-59.

———. "La situation économique du Congo Belge en 1958," *Zaïre*, XIII, No. 2 (1959).

Koenen, G. "Missionerend Belgie," *Kerk en Missie*, No. 117 (January 1955), pp. 8-23.

Leclercq, H. "Principes pour l'orientation d'une politique fiscale au Congo Belge," *Zaïre*, XIII, No. 5 (1959), 451-97.

Leplae, E. "L'avenir de l'agriculture congolaise, conformément au discours du Duc de Brabant," *Congo*, 18th yr., T. I, No. 3 (March 1937), pp. 233-86.

――――. "La colonisation agricole belge au Congo," *Bulletin Agricole du Congo Belge*, IX, Nos. 1-4 (March-December, 1918), 3-28.

――――. "Histoire et développement des cultures obligatoires de coton et de riz au Congo Belge de 1917 à 1933," *Congo*, 14th yr., T. I, No. 5 (May 1933), pp. 645-753.

――――. "Notes au sujet du développement de l'agriculture du Congo Belge," *Bulletin Agricole du Congo Belge*, VIII, Nos. 1-2 (March-June, 1917), pp. 3-39; Nos. 3-4 (September-December, 1917), pp. 171-217.

――――. "Résultats obtenus au Congo Belge par les cultures obligatoires alimentaires et industrielles," *Zaïre*, I, No. 2 (February 1947), 115-40.

Malengreau, Guy. "De l'accession des indigènes à la propriété foncière individuelle du code civil," *Zaïre*, I, No. 3 (March 1947), 235-70; No. 4 (April 1947), pp. 399-434.

Peeters, G. "L'agriculture congolaise et ses problèmes," *Zaïre*, XI, No. 5 (May 1958), 451-77.

Romanuik, A. "Evolution et perspectives démographiques de la population au Congo," *Zaïre*, XIII, No. 6 (1959), 563-626.

Solow, Herbert. "The Congo is in Business," *Fortune*, XLVI, No. 5 (November 1952), 106-14, 172-82.

III. ETHNOGRAPHIC BACKGROUND AND SOCIAL CHANGE

BOOKS

Abel, Armand. *Les musulmans noirs du Maniema*. Brussels: Centre pour l'Etude des Problèmes du Monde Musulman Contemporain, 1960.

Anciaux, Leon. *Le problème musulman dans l'Afrique belge*. Brussels: ARSOM, Sci. Mor. et Pol., T. XVIII, fasc. 2, 1949.

Andersson, Efraim. *Messianic Popular Movements in the Lower Congo*. Upsala, Sweden: Studia Ethnographica Upsaliensia XIV, 1958.

Balandier, Georges. *Sociologie actuelle de l'Afrique noire.* Paris: Presses Universitaires de France, 1955.

———. *Sociologie des Brazzavilles noires.* Paris: Librairie Armand Colin, 1955.

Baxter, P. T. W., and Butt, Audrey. *The Azande and Related Peoples of the Anglo-Egyptian Sudan and Belgian Congo.* London: International African Institute, 1953.

Boone, O. and Maes, J. *Les peuplades du Congo Belge.* Brussels: Imprimerie Veuve Monnem, 1935.

Burssens, H. *Les peuplades de l'entre Congo-Ubangi.* Tervuren, Belgium: Annales du Musée Royal du Congo Belge, Monographies Ethnographiques, Vol. IV, 1958.

Capelle, Emmanuel. *La cité indigène de Léopoldville.* Leopoldville: Centre d'Etudes Sociales Africaines, 1947.

Colle, R. P. *Les Baluba.* 2 vols. Brussels: Institut International de Bibliographie, 1913.

Cunnison, Ian. *The Luapula Peoples of Northern Rhodesia.* Manchester: Manchester University Press, 1959.

Cuvelier, Mgr. J. *L'Ancien Royaume de Congo.* Bruges, Belgium: Desclee de Brouwer, 1946.

Cuvelier, Mgr. J., and Jadin, L. *L'ancien Congo d'après les archives romaines (1518-1640).* Brussels: ARSOM, T. XXXVI, fasc. 2, 1954.

de Beaucorps, R. *Les Bayansi du Bas-Kwilu.* Louvain, Belgium: Editions de l'Aucam, 1933.

———. *L'évolution économique chez les Basongo de la Luniungu et de la Goberi.* Brussels: ARSOM, Sci. Mor. et Pol., T. XX, fasc. 4, 1951.

de Cleene, N. *Introduction à l'ethnographie du Congo Belge et du Ruanda-Urundi.* Antwerp: Editions de Sikkel, 1957.

de Jonghe, Ed. *Les formes d'asservissement dans les sociétés indigènes du Congo Belge.* Brussels: ARSOM, Sci. Mor. et Pol., T. XIX, fasc. 1, 1949.

Delhaise, Commandant. *Les Warega.* Brussels: Institut International de Bibliographie, 1909.

Denis, Jacques. *Le phénomène urbain en Afrique centrale.*

Brussels: ARSOM, Sci. Mor. et Pol., N. S., T. XIX, fasc. 1, 1958.

Denis, Paul. *Histoire des Mangbetu et des Matshaga jusqu'à l'arrivée des belges.* Tervuren, Belgium: Musée Royal de l'Afrique Centrale, Archives d'Ethnographie, No. 2, 1961.

de Thier, Franz M. *Le centre extra-coutumier de Coquilhat-ville.* Brussels: Institut de Sociologie Solvay, Etudes coloniales, fasc. 2, 1956.

Domont, J. M. *Le prise de conscience de l'individu en milieu rural Kongo.* Brussels: ARSOM, Sci. Mor. et Pol., N. S., T. XIII, fasc. 1, 1957.

Douglas, Mary. *The Lele of the Kasai.* New York: Oxford University Press, 1963.

Epstein, A. L. *Politics in an Urban African Community.* Manchester: Manchester University Press, 1958.

Evans-Pritchard, E. E. *Witchcraft, Oracles and Magic among the Azande.* Oxford: Clarendon Press, 1937.

Gilis, Charles-André. *Kimbangu: Fondateur d'Eglise.* Brussels: Librairie Encyclopédique, 1960.

Grévisse, F. *Le centre extra-coutumier d'Elisabethville.* Brussels: ARSOM, Sci. Mor. et Pol., T. XXI, 1951.

Halkin, Joseph. *Les Ababua.* Brussels: Institut International de Bibliographie, 1911.

Haveaux, G. L. *La tradition historique des Bapende orientaux.* Brussels: ARSOM, Sci. Mor. et Pol., T. XXXVII, fasc. 1, 1954.

Hilton-Simpson, M. W. *Land and Peoples of the Kasai.* London: Constable & Co., 1911.

Hulstaert, G. *Carte linguistique du Congo Belge.* Brussels: ARSOM, Sci. Mor. et Pol., T. XIX, fasc. 5, 1950.

———. *Les Mongo: Aperçu général.* Tervuren, Belgium: Musée Royal de l'Afrique Centrale, Archives d'Ethnographie, No. 5, 1961.

Hutereau, A. *Histoire des peuplades de l'Uélé et de l'Ubangi.* Brussels: Bibliotheque Congo, n.d. (1919?).

International African Institute. *Social Implications of In-*

dustrialization and Urbanization South of the Sahara. UNESCO: 1956.

Laman, Karl. *The Kongo I.* Upsala, Sweden: Studia Ethnographica Upsaliensia, IV, 1953.

Lotar, R. P. L. *La grande chronique du Bomu.* Brussels: ARSOM, Sci. Mor. et Pol., T. IX, fasc. 3, 1940.

————. *La grande chronique de l'Ubangi.* Brussels: ARSOM, Sci. Mor. et Pol., T. VII, fasc. 2, 1937.

————. *La grande chronique de l'Uélé.* Brussels: ARSOM, Sci. Mor. et Pol., T. XIV, fasc. 1, 1946.

Masson, Paul. *Trois siècles chez les Bashi.* Tervuren, Belgium: Musée Royal de l'Afrique Centrale, Archives d'Ethnographie, No. 1, 1960.

McCullogh, Merran. *The Southern Lunda and Related Peoples.* London: International African Institute, 1951.

Mertens, R. P. Joseph. *Les Badzing de la Kamtsha.* Brussels: ARSOM, Sci. Mor. et Pol., T. IV, fasc. 1, 1935.

————. *Les chefs couronnés chez les Bakongo Orientaux.* Brussels: Sci. Mor. et Pol., T. XI, fasc. 1, 1942.

Minon, Paul. *Katuba. Etude quantitative d'une communauté urbaine africaine.* Liège: Travaux de l'Institut de Sociologie de la Faculté de Droit de Liège, 1960.

Mitchell, J. Clyde. *The Kalela Dance.* Manchester: Manchester University Press, 1956.

Moeller, A. *Les grandes lignes des migrations des Bantous de la Province Orientale du Congo Belge.* Brussels: ARSOM, Sci. Mor. et Pol., T. VI, 1936.

Nicolai, H., and Jacques, J. *La transformation des paysages congolais par le chemin de fer. L'exemple du B.C.K.* Brussels: ARSOM, Sci. Nat. et Med., T. XXIV, fasc. 1, 1954.

Pigafetta, Filippo. *A Report of the Kingdom of Congo.* Translated by Margarite Hutchison. London: John Murray, 1881.

Plancquaert, M. *Les Jaga et les Bayaka du Kwango.* Brussels: ARSOM, Sci. Mor. et Pol., T. III, fasc. 1, 1932.

――――. *Les sociétés secrètes chez les Bayaka.* Louvain: Bibliothèque Congo, 1930.

Schmitz, Robert. *Les Baholoholo.* Brussels: Institut International de Bibliographie, 1912.

Soret, Marcel. *Les Kongo Nord-Occidentaux.* Paris: Presses Universitaires de France, 1959.

Southall, Aidan (ed.). *Social Change in Modern Africa.* New York: Oxford University Press, 1961.

Torday, E., and Joyce, T. A. *Notes ethnographiques sur les peuples communément appelés Bakuba, ainsi que sur les peuplades apparentées. Les Bushongo.* Brussels: Ministère des Colonies, 1911.

――――. *Notes ethnographiques sur les populations habitant les bassins du Kasai et du Kwango Oriental.* Brussels: Ministère des Colonies, 1922.

Vanderkerken, Georges *L'ethnie Mongo.* 2 vols. Brussels: ARSOM, Sci. Mor. et Pol., T. XIII, fasc. 1 and 2, 1944.

――――. *Les sociétés bantoues du Congo Belge.* Brussels: Etablissements Emile Bruylant, 1920.

Van Geluwe, H. *Les Bira et les peuplades limitrophes.* Tervuren, Belgium: Annales du Musée Royal du Congo Belge, 1956.

Van Overbergh, Cyr. *Les Bangala.* Brussels: Institut International de Bibliographie, 1907.

――――. *Les Basonge.* Brussels: Institut International de Bibliographie, 1908.

――――. *Les Mayombe.* Brussels: Institut International de Bibliographie, 1907.

Vansina, J. *Les tribus Ba-Kuba et les peuplades apparantées.* Tervuren, Belgium: Annales du Musée Royal du Congo Belge, 1954.

Van Wing, J. *Etudes Bakongo.* 2d ed. Brussels: Desclée de Brouwer, 1959.

Van Zandijcke, A. *Pages de l'histoire du Kasayi.* Namur, Belgium: Collection Lavigerie, 1953.

Verbeken, Auguste. *Contribution à la géographie historique du Katanga et de régions voisines.* Brussels: ARSOM, Sci. Mor. et Pol., T. XXXVI, fasc. 1, 1954.

———. *Msiri.* Brussels: Editions L. Cuypers, 1956.

———. *La révolte des Batetela en 1895.* Brussels: ARSOM, Sci. Mor. et Pol., N. S., T. VII, fasc. 4, 1958.

Verhulpen, Edmond. *Baluba et Balubaisés du Katanga.* Antwerp: Editions de l'Avenir Belge, 1936.

Weeks, John H. *Among Congo Cannibals.* London: Seeley, Service, & Co., 1913.

———. *Among the Primitive Bakongo.* London: Seeley, Service, & Co., 1914.

Weydert, Jean. *Les Balubas chez eux.* Mimeo, 1938.

Wolfe, Alvin W. *In the Ngombe Tradition.* Evanston, Ill.: Northwestern University Press, 1961.

ARTICLES

"A propos du problème du milieu rural congolais," *Bulletin du CEPSI,* No. 36 (March 1957), pp. 141-89.

Baeck, L. "Léopoldville, phénomène urbain africain," *Zaïre,* X, No. 6 (June 1956), 613-36.

———. "Une société rurale en transition: étude socio-économique de la région de Thysville," *Zaïre,* XI, No. 2 (February 1957), 115-86.

Bailleul, H. "Les Bayaka," *Zaïre,* XIII, No. 8 (1959), 823-41.

Balandier, Georges. "Messianismes et nationalismes en Afrique noire," *Cahiers Internationaux de Sociologie,* XIV (1953), 41-65.

———. "Structures sociales traditionelles et changements économiques," *Cahiers d'Etudes Africaines,* I (January 1960), 1-14.

Benoit, J. "Contribution à l'étude de la population active d'Elisabethville," *Problèmes Sociaux Congolais,* No. 54 (September 1961), pp. 5-53.

Bertrand, A. "La fin de la puissance Azande," *Bull Séances,* ARSOM (1943), pp. 264-83.

Biebuyck, D. "Fondements de l'organisation politique des

Lunda du Mwaanlayaav en territoire de Kapanga," *Zaïre,* XI, No. 8 (October 1957), 787-817.

——. "La société kumu face au Kitawala," *Zaïre,* XI, No. 1 (January 1957), 7-40.

Boelaert, R. P. E. "Vers un état Mongo?" *Bull. Séances,* ARSOM (1961), pp. 382-91.

Bogearts, H. "Un aspect de la structure sociale chez les Bakwa Luntu," *Zaïre,* V, No. 6 (June 1951), 563-610.

Boulanger, A. "Evolution économique d'un milieu rural au District de Kabinda," *Bulletin du CEPSI,* No. 36 (March 1957), pp. 52-85.

Burton, W. F. P. "The Country of the Baluba in Central Katanga," *The Geographical Journal,* LXX, No. 4 (October 1927), 321-42.

——. "The Secret Societies of Lubaland, Congo Belge," *Bantu Studies,* IV, No. 4 (December 1930), 217-50.

Comhaire, J. "Une decade d'évolution en territoire d'Oshwe," *Zaïre,* VII, No. 3 (March 1953), 255-63.

——. "Sociétés secrètes et mouvements prophétiques au Congo Belge," *Africa,* XXV, No. 1 (January 1955), 54-59.

Cunnison, Ian. "A Watchtower Assembly in Central Africa," *International Review of Missions,* XL, No. 160 (October 1951), 456-69.

Daubechies, Mgr. "Le Kitawala," *Tendances du Temps,* 19th yr., No. 58 (1961), pp. 5-18.

de Bus de Warnaffe, Ch. "Le mouvement pan-nègre aux Etats-Unis et ailleurs," *Congo,* 3rd yr., T. I, No. 5 (May 1922), pp. 713-27.

de Cleene, N. "Les chefs indigènes au Mayombe," *Africa,* VIII, No. 1 (January 1935), 63-75.

——. "Individu et collectivité dans l'évolution économique du Mayombe," *Bull. Séances,* ARSOM (1938), pp. 63-74.

de Clercq A. "L'attitude des Baluba vis-à-vis de la pénétration des idées européennes," *Bull. Séances,* ARSOM (1931), pp. 46-51.

de Hemptinne, J. "Les 'mangeurs de cuivre' du Katanga,"

Congo, 7th yr., T. I, No. 3 (March 1926), pp. 371-403.

de Heusch, L. "Autorité et prestige dans la société tatela," *Zaïre*, VIII, No. 10 (1954), 1011-27.

de Jonghe, Ed. "Formations récentes de sociétés secrètes au Congo Belge," *Africa*, IX, No. 1 (January 1936), 56-65.

Denis, Jacques. "Notes sur le degré de stabilisation des citadins de Léopoldville," *Bulletin du CEPSI*, No. 33 (1956), pp. 151-63.

Dhanis, E. Récrutements de main d'oeuvre chez les Bayaka," *Zaïre*, VII, No. 5 (May 1953), 489-96.

Douglas, Mary. "Age Status among the Lele," *Zaïre*, XIII, No. 4 (1959), 386-413.

———. "The Pattern of Residence among the Lele," *Zaïre*, XI, No. 8 (October 1957), 819-43.

Duysters, Leon. "Histoire des Aluunda," *Problèmes d'Afrique Centrale*, No. 40, 2d quarter (1958), pp. 75-98.

Evans-Pritchard, E. E. "An Historical Introduction to a Study of Zande Society," *African Studies*, XVII, No. 1 (1958), 1-15.

———. "The Zande Royal Court," *Zaïre*, XI, No. 4 (April 1957), 361-89; No. 5 (May 1957), 493-511; No. 7 (July 1957), 687-713.

"L'évolution politique du Congo Belge et les autorités indigènes," *Problèmes d'Afrique Centrale*, No. 43, 1st quarter (1959).

Gluckman, Max. "Tribalism in Modern British Central Africa," *Cahiers d'Etudes Africaines*, I (January 1960), 55-70.

Grévisse, F. "Les Bayeke," *Bulletin des Juridictions Indigènes et du Droit Coutumier Congolais*, V, Nos. 1-8 (January-February, 1937, to March-April, 1938).

———. "Notes ethnographiques relatives à quelques populations autochtones du Haut-Katanga industriel," *Bulletin du CEPSI*, Nos. 32-36 (March 1956 to June 1957).

———. "Du pouvoir législatif dans les sociétés indigènes," *Bulletin du CEPSI*, No. 8 (1949), pp. 6-82.

Harlow, Vincent. "Tribalism in Africa," *Journal of African Administration*, VII, No. 1 (January 1955), 17-20.

Jadin, Louis. "Le Congo et la secte des Antoniens," *Bulletin de l'Institut Historique Belge de Rome*, fasc. 33 (1961), pp. 411-601.

Lux, André. "Luluabourg. Migrations, accroissement et urbanisation de sa population congolaise," *Zaïre*, XII, Nos. 7, 8 (1958).

Malengreau, Guy. "La situation actuelle des indigènes du Congo Belge," *Bull. Séances*, ARSOM (1947), pp. 216-28.

Maquet, Jacques J. "The Modern Evolution of African Populations in the Belgian Congo," *Africa*, XIX, No. 4 (October 1949), 265-72.

Marzorati, A. F. G. "The Political Organization and the Evolution of African Society in the Belgian Congo," *African Affairs*, LIII, No. 210 (January 1954).

Mercier, Paul. "Remarques sur la signification du 'tribalisme' actuel en Afrique noire," *Cahiers Internationaux de Sociologie*, XXXI (1961), 61-80.

Merriam, Alan P. "The Concept of Culture Clusters Applied to the Belgian Congo," *Southwestern Journal of Anthropology*, XV, No. 4 (Winter 1959), 373-95.

Minon, Paul. "Quelques aspects de l'évolution récente du centre extracoutumier d'Elisabethville," *Bulletin du CEPSI*, No. 36 (March 1957) pp. 5-51.

Moeller, A. "L'adaptation des sociétés indigènes de la Province Orientale à la situation crée par la colonisation," *Bull. Séances*, ARSOM (1931), pp. 52-66.

Raymaekers, Paul. "L'Eglise de Jésus-Christ sur la terre par le prophète Simon Kibangu," *Zaïre*, XIII, No. 7 (1959).

Roland, Dom Hadelin. "Résumé de l'histoire ancienne du Katanga," *Problèmes Sociaux Congolais*, No. 61 (June 1963), pp. 3-41.

Samain, A. "Les Basonge," *Congo*, 5th yr., T. I., No. 1 (January 1924), pp. 48-52.

Torday, E. "The Influence of the Kingdom of Kongo on Central Africa," *Africa*, I, No. 2 (April 1928), 157-69.

Vanderkerken, Georges. "La structure des sociétés indigènes et quelques problèmes de politique indigène," *Bull. Séances*, ARSOM (1932), pp. 291-312.

Vansina, J. "L'Etat Kuba dans le cadre des institutions politiques africaines," *Zaïre*, XI, No. 5 (May 1957), 485-92.

————. "Long-Distance Trade Routes in Central Africa," *Journal of African History*, III, No. 3 (1962), 375-90.

————. "Notes sur l'origine du Royaume du Kongo," *Journal of African History*, IV, No. 1 (1963), 33-38.

Van Wing, J. "Le Kibanguisme vu par un témoin," *Zaïre*, XII, No. 6 (1958), 563-618.

Viccars, John D. "Witchcraft in Bolobo, Belgian Congo," *Africa*, XIX, No. 3 (July 1949), 220-29.

Weekx, G. "La peuplade des Ambundu (District du Kwango)," *Congo*, 18th yr., T. I, No. 4 (April 1937), pp. 353-73; T. II, No. 1 (June 1937), pp. 13-35; T. II, No. 2 (July 1937), pp. 150-66.

IV. DECOLONIZATION AND INDEPENDENCE

BOOKS

L'Afrique belge devant son avenir. Louvain: 1957.

Artigue, Pierre. *Qui sont les leaders congolais?* 2d ed., Brussels: Editions Europe-Afrique, 1961.

Baeck, Louis and François, Christian. *Analyse économique de situation et étude du commerce extérieur du Congo: Evolution au cours de l'année 1960 et du 1er trimestre 1961.* Leopoldville: Institut de Recherches Economiques et Sociales, Université Lovanium, May 1961 (mimeo).

Biebuyck, Daniel, and Douglas, Mary. *Congo Tribes and Parties.* London: Royal Anthropological Institute, 1961.

Borri, Michel. *Nous . . . ces affreux.* Paris: Editions Galic, 1962.

Buchman, Jean. *L'Afrique noire indépendante.* Paris: Librairie Gale de Droit et de Jurisprudence, 1962.

Caprasse, P. *Leaders africains en milieu urbain.* Elisabethville: Centre d'Etudes des Problèmes Sociaux Indigènes, 1959.

Chomé, Jules. *La crise congolaise.* Brussels: Editions de Remarques Congolaises, 1960.

————. *Le drame de Luluabourg.* Brussels: Editions de Remarques Congolaises, 1959.

————. *Le gouvernement congolais et l'O.N.U.: Un paradoxe tragique.* Brussels: Editions de Remarques Congolaises, 1961.

————. *Indépendance congolaise: pacifique conquête.* Brussels: Editions de Remarques Congolaises, 1960.

————. *M. Lumumba et le communisme.* Brussels: Editions de Remarques Congolaises, 1961.

————. *La passion de Simon Kimbangu.* 2d ed. Brussels: Les Amis de Présence Africaine, 1959.

Compte rendu des journées interuniversitaires d'études coloniales. Brussels: Institut de Sociologie Solvay, 1952.

Coppens, Paul. *Anticipations congolaises.* Brussels: Editions Techniques et Scientifiques, 1956.

CRISP. *ABAKO 1950-1960.* Brussels: 1963.

————. *Congo 1959.* Brussels: 1960.

————. *Congo 1962.* Brussels: 1963.

————. *Parti Solidaire Africain (P.S.A.).* Brussels: 1963.

Davister, Pierre. *Katanga, enjeu du monde.* Brussels: Editions Europe-Afrique, 1960.

Davister, Pierre, and Toussaint, Philippe. *Croisettes et casques bleus.* Brussels: Editions Actuelles, 1962.

de Backer, M. C. C. *Notes pour servir à l'étude des "Groupements Politiques" à Léopoldville.* 3 vols. Brussels: Inforcongo, 1959.

Demany, Fernand. *S.O.S. Congo.* Brussels: Editions Labor, 1959.

Depage, Henri. *Contribution à l'élaboration d'une doctrine visant à la promotion des indigènes du Congo Belge.* Brussels: ARSOM, Sci. Mor. et Pol., N. S., T. V, fasc. 2, 1955.

De Vos, Pierre. *Vie et mort de Lumumba.* Paris. Calmann-Levy, 1961.

Dinant, Georges. *L'O.N.U. face à la crise congolaise.* Brussels: Editions Remarques Congolaises, 1962.

Dugauquier, D. P. *Congo Cauldron.* London: Jarrold's, 1961.

Dumont, Georges H. *La table ronde belgo-congolaise.* Paris: Editions Universitaires, 1961.

Durieux, André. *Nationalité et citoyenneté.* Brussels: ARSOM, Sci. Mor. et Pol., N. S., T. XXIII, fasc. 2, 1959.

————. *Le problème juridique des dettes du Congo Belge et l'Etat du Congo.* Brussels: ARSOM, Sci. Mor. et Pol., N. S., T. XXVII, fasc. 3, 1961.

————. *Souveraineté et communauté belgo-congolaise.* Brussels: ARSOM, Sci. Mor. et Pol., N. S., T. XVIII, fasc. 2, 1959.

Fedacol. *L'opinion publique coloniale devant l'assimilation des indigènes.* Brussels: mimeographed, 1951.

Ganshof van der Meersch, W. J. *Fin de la souveraineté belge au Congo.* Brussels: Institut Royal des Relations Internationales, 1963.

————. *Le droit electoral au Congo Belge.* Brussels: Etablissements Emile Bruylant, 1958.

Gérard-Libois, J. *Sécession au Katanga.* Brussels: 1963.

Gérard-Libois, J., and Verhaegen, Benoit. *Congo 1960.* 2 vols. Brussels: CRISP, 1961.

Gilis, Charles-André. *Kasa-Vubu au coeur du drame congolais.* Brussels: Editions Europe-Afrique, 1964.

Grootaert, J. E. A. *La réforme judiciaire au Congo après l'indépendance.* Leopoldville: L'Institut pour la Formation Politique Générale Accélérée, 1960.

Henri, Pierre, and Marres, Jacques. *L'Etat belge responsable en droit du désastre congolais?* Brussels: Editions R. R. Windfohr, n.d. (1961).

Hoskyns, Catherine. *The Congo: a Chronology of Events, January, 1960-December, 1961.* London: Royal Institute of International Affairs, 1962.

Houart, Pierre. *Les événements du Congo.* Brussels: Centre de Documentation Internationale, 1961.

———. *La pénétration communiste au Congo.* Brussels: Centre de Documentation Internationale, 1960.

Institut Belge de Science Politique. *L'avenir politique du Congo Belge.* Brussels: Editions de la Librairie Encyclopédique, 1959.

INCIDI. *Staff Problems in Tropical and Subtropical Countries.* Brussels: 1961.

J. K. (Van der Dussen). *André Ryckmans.* Brussels: Charles Dessart, 1961.

Kalanda, Mabika. *Baluba et Lulua. Une ethnie à la recherche d'un nouvel équilibre.* Brussels: Editions de Remarques Congolaises, 1959.

Kanza, Thomas R. *Tot ou tard. . . .* Brussels: Le Livre Africain, 1959.

Labrique, Jean. *Congo politique.* Leopoldville: Editions de l'Avenir, 1957.

Lanciney, Christian. *Les héros sont affreux.* Brussels: Charles Dessart, 1962.

Legum, Colin. *Congo Disaster.* Baltimore: Penguin Books, 1961.

Lumumba, Patrice. *Le Congo, terre d'avenir, est-il menacé?* Brussels: Office de Publicité, 1961.

Marres, Jacques, and de Vos, Pierre. *L'équinoxe de janvier.* Brussels: Editions Euraforient, 1959.

Merlier, Michel. *Le Congo de la colonisation belge à l'indépendance.* Paris: François Maspero, 1962.

Merriam, Alan P. *Congo: Background of Conflict.* Evanston, Ill.: Northwestern University Press, 1961.

Michel, Serge. *Uhuru Lumumba.* Paris: René Julliard, 1962.

Monheim, Francis. *Mobutu, l'homme seul.* Brussels: Editions Actuelles, 1962.

———. *Le problème des cadres au Congo.* Brussels: n.d. (1960?).

———. *Réponse à Pierre de Vos au sujet de "Vie et Mort de Lumumba."* Brussels: 1961.

631

Mosmans, Guy. *L'Eglise à l'heure de l'Afrique.* Tournai, Belgium: Castleman, 1961.

Niedergang, Marcel. *Tempête sur le Congo.* Paris: Librairie Plon, 1960.

O'Brien, Conor Cruise. *To Katanga and Back.* New York: Simon & Schuster, 1962.

Perin, François. *Les institutions politiques du Congo indépendant.* Leopoldville: Institut Politique Congolais, 1960.

Pevée, Albert. *Place aux noirs.* Brussels: Editions Europe-Afrique, 1960.

Poupart, R. *Première esquisse de l'évolution du syndicalisme au Congo.* Brussels: Editions de l'Institut de Sociologie Solvay, 1960.

Ribeaud, Paul. *Adieu Congo.* Paris: La Table Ronde, 1961.

Roberts, John. *My Congo Adventure.* London: Jarrold's, 1963.

Rouch, Jane. *En cage avec Lumumba.* Paris: Les Editions du Temps, 1961.

Sépulchre, Jean. *Propos sur le Congo politique de demain: Autonomie et fédéralisme.* Elisabethville: Editions de l'Essor du Congo, 1958.

Slade, Ruth. *The Belgian Congo.* London: Institute of Race Relations, 1960.

Stenmans, A. *Les premiers mois de la République du Congo.* Brussels: ARSOM, Sci. Mor. et Pol., N. S., T. XXV, fasc. 3, 1961.

Trinquier, Roger, et al. *Notre guerre au Katanga.* Paris: Editions de la Pensée Moderne, 1963.

Union des Travailleurs Congolais. *Les salaires au Congo.* Leopoldville: 1960.

Van Bilsen, A. A. J. *L'indépendance du Congo.* Brussels: Casterman, 1962.

———. *Vers l'indépendance du Congo et du Ruanda-Urundi.* Brussels: 1958.

Van Langenhove, Fernand. *Consciences tribales et natio-*

nales en Afrique noire. Brussels: Institut Royal des Relations Internationales, 1960.

Van Lierde, Jean (ed.). *La pensée politique de Patrice Lumumba.* Brussels: Editions Amis de Présence Africaine, 1963.

Van Reyn, Paul. *Le Congo politique.* Brussels: Editions Europe-Afrique, 1960.

Van Zeeland, Paul. *Impressions de voyage au Congo.* Brussels: 1959.

Verhaegen, Benoit. *Congo 1961.* Brussels: CRISP, 1962.

Wauters, Arthur. *Le monde communiste et la crise du Congo Belge.* Brussels: Editions de l'Institut de Sociologie Solvay, 1961.

Wauthion, R. *Le Congo Belge à un tournant.* Brussels: ARSOM, Sci. Mor. et Pol., N. S., T. XVII, fasc. 3, 1959.

ARTICLES

Bustin, Edouard. "The Congo," in Gwendolyn Carter (ed.), *Five African States.* Ithaca, N. Y.: Cornell University Press, 1963.

C. P. "La commission constitutionelle à Luluabourg," *Etudes Congolaises,* VI, No. 1 (January 1964), 22-30.

Clement, Pierre. "Patrice Lumumba (Stanleyville, 1952-1953)," *Présence Africaine,* No. 40 (1st quarter, 1962), pp. 57-78.

Crowley, Daniel J. "Politics and Tribalism in the Katanga," *Western Political Quarterly,* XVI, No. 1 (March 1963), 68-78.

de Bethune, E., and Wembi, A. "Le problème de la sous-administration dans les pays d'Afrique noire indépendante," *Civilisations,* XII, No. 4 (1962), 446-56.

Domont, J-M. "Prélude à la démocratisation des institutions politiques congolaises," *Problèmes d'Afrique Centrale,* No. 39 (1st quarter, 1958), pp. 3-19.

Doucy, A. "Réflexions sur la situation politique au Congo," *Socialisme,* No. 44 (March 1961), pp. 153-61.

————. "Sociologie coloniale et réformes de structure au Congo Belge," *Revue de l'Université Libre de Bruxelles,* Nos. 2-3 (January-April, 1957), pp. 212-29.

Dupriez, Gérard. "Les rémunérations dans l'ancienne province de Léopoldville," *Cahiers Economiques et Sociaux,* Université Lovanium, No. 2 (December 1962), pp. 3-74.

Dupriez, Pierre. "Transformations dans la structure des exportations de la République du Congo depuis l'indépendance," *Cahiers Economiques et Sociaux,* Université Lovanium, No. 3 (March 1963), pp. 3-58.

Durieux, A. "La Belgique et le Congo Belge," *Zaïre,* VII, No. 4 (April 1953), 339-79.

François, C. "Les balances des paiements de la République du Congo et du Katanga 1960-1962," *Cahiers Economiques et Sociaux,* Université Lovanium, Nos. 5-6 (December 1963), pp. 54-90.

G. M. "Les syndicats et la politique congolaise," *Etudes Congolaises,* VI, No. 2 (February 1964), 19-26.

Gérard-Libois, J. "L'assistance technique belge et la République du Congo," *Etudes Congolaises,* II, No. 3 (1962), 1-11.

————. "L'avant-project de Constitution pour la République du Congo," *Etudes Congolaises,* III, No. 10 (1962), 1-27.

————. "Les structures du Congo et le Plan Thant," *Etudes Congolaises,* III, No. 8 (October 1962), 1-16.

Glinne, E. "Le pourquoi de l'affaire katangaise," *Présence Africaine,* (June-September, 1960), pp. 49-63.

Herman, Fernand. "La situation économique du Congo au cours du premier semestre 1963," *Etudes Congolaises,* V, No. 7 (August-September, 1963), 1-21.

————. "La Situation économique et financière au Congo au 30 juillet 1962," *Etudes Congolaises,* III, No. 8 (October 1962), 1-27.

————. "Situation économique et financière de la République du Congo au cours du premier trimestre 1961," *Etudes Congolaises,* I, No. 2 (May-June, 1961), 15-25.

————. "La situation économique et financière de la République du Congo au cours du second trimestre 1961," *Etudes Congolaises,* I, No. 4 (September 1961), 13-24.

————. "La situation économique et financière du Congo en 1962," *Etudes Congolaises,* IV, No. 3 (March 1963), 1-27.

Hoffmann, Stanley. "In Search of a Thread: The UN in the Congo Labyrinth," *International Organization,* XVI, No. 2 (Spring 1962), 331-61.

Ilunga, A-R., and Kalonji, B. "Les événements du Kwilu," *Etudes Congolaises,* VI, No. 3 (March 1964), 1-21.

Kalanda, A. "Quelques réflexions à propos de la déclaration gouvernmentale sur le Congo," *Présence Africaine* (June-July, 1959), pp. 102-13.

Jesman, Maj. Czeslaw. "Background to Events in the Congo," *African Affairs,* LX (July 1961), 383-91.

Leclercq, Hugues. "L'inflation congolaise," *Cahiers Economiques et Sociaux,* Université Lovanium, No. 1 (October 1962), pp. 3-40.

Lemarchand, René. "The Bases of Nationalism among the Bakongo," *Africa,* XXXI, No. 4 (October 1961), 344-54.

————. "The Limits of Self-Determination: Katanga," *American Political Science Review,* LVI, No. 2 (June 1962), 404-16.

Lopez-Alverez, Luis. "Les congolais et leurs tuteurs," *Esprit* (November 1961), pp. 538-46.

Malengreau, Guy. "Le Congo à la croisée des chemins," *Revue Nouvelle,* V, No. 1 (January 1947), 3-18; No. 2 (February 1947), 95-108.

————. "La formation politique des Congolais," *Problèmes d'Afrique Centrale,* No. 14 (1951), pp. 269-78.

————. "Political Evolution in the Belgian Congo," *Journal of African Administration,* VI, No. 4 (October 1954), 160-66.

Mazrui, Ali Al'Amin. "Edmund Burke and Reflections on the Revolution in the Congo," *Comparative Studies in*

Society and History, V, No. 2 (January 1963), pp. 121-33.

Mendiaux, Edouard. "Le Comité National du Kivu," *Zaïre,* X, No. 6 (October 1956), 803-13; No. 9 (November 1956), 927-64.

———. "Pour une révision de la Charte Coloniale," *Zaïre,* XI, Nos. 9-10 (November-December, 1957), 1031-51.

Monheim, Francis, "Léopoldville en juin 1959," *Revue Générale Belge* (July 1959), pp. 29-46.

M(onnier), L. C. "Le Congrès de l'Abako," *Etudes Congolaises,* V, No. 8 (October 1963), 34-41.

"Les nouvelles provinces," *Etudes Congolaises,* III, No. 8 (October 1962), 26-36.

Paulus, Jean-Pierre. "Pour un fédéralisme congolais," *Terre d'Europe,* No. 9 (March 1959).

Perin, François. "La crise congolaise et les institutions africaines," *Civilisations,* XI, No. 3 (1961), 281-95.

"La province de Maindombe ou du Lac Léopold II," *Etudes Congolaises,* IV, No. 3 (March 1963), 28-32.

"Quelques notes sur le contentieux belgo-congolais," *Etudes Congolaises,* III, No. 4 (1962), 30-36.

Rae, Marcellin. "Note d'histoire et de droit coutumier sur le litige Lulua-Baluba avant le 30 juin 1960," *Bull. Séances* ARSOM (1961), pp. 366-76.

Rubbens, A. "La confusion politique au Katanga," *Revue Nouvelle,* T. XXVIII, No. 10 (October 1958), pp. 308-13.

———. "La consultation populaire du 22 décembre 1957 à Elisabethville," *Bulletin du CEPSI,* No. 42 (September 1958), pp. 77-81.

———. "La décolonisation du droit et de l'organisation judiciaire dans la République de Congo," *Bull. Séances* ARSOM (1961), pp. 798-808.

———. "Political Awakening in the Belgian Congo." *Civilisations,* X, No. 1 (1960), 63-76.

———. "La politique congolaise. Jouer le jeu," *Revue Nouvelle,* T. XXVII, No. 1 (January 15, 1958), pp. 59-65.

Sohier, A. "La politique d'intégration," *Zaïre,* V, No. 9 (November 1951), 899-928.

——. "Le statut des congolais civilisés," *Zaïre,* IV, No. 7 (July 1950), 815-22.

Sohier, J. "Problèmes d'organisation judiciaire dans l'Etat du Katanga," *Publications de l'Université de l'Etat à Elisabethville,* I (July 1961).

Stengers, Jean. "Notre nouvelle politique congolaise," *Le Flambeau,* 42d yr., Nos. 7-8 (September-October, 1959), pp. 453-76; Nos. 9-10 (November-December, 1959), pp. 637-61.

"Traitements, grèves, et politique d'austérité," *Etudes Congolaises,* II, No. 5 (1962), 1-32.

Van Lierde, Jean. "Patrice Lumumba leader et ami," *Présence Africaine* (1st quarter, 1961), pp. 112-19.

Verhaegen, B. "Autour de la décolonisation," *Présence Africaine,* No. 23, (December 1958-January 1959), pp. 97-106.

——. "Présentation morphologique des nouvelles provinces," *Etudes Congolaises,* IV, No. 4 (1963), 1-25.

——. "La province du Sankuru," *Etudes Congolaises,* V, No. 7 (August-September, 1963), 22-36.

"Why Belgium Quit the Congo," *Fortune,* LXII, No. 5 (November 1960), 129-31, 258-82.

W(illame), J.-C. "L'enseignment, les syndicats et le gouvernement," *Etudes Congolaises,* V, No. 9 (November 1963), 1-10.

——. "L'évolution des partis politiques au Congo," *Etudes Congolaises,* V, No. 10 (December 1963), 37-43.

Willame, J.-C. "Mise en place des nouvelles institutions provinciales au Congo," *Cahiers Economiques et Sociaux,* Université Lovanium, No. 4 (June 1963), pp. 97-111.

W(illame), J.-C. "La province de l'Ubangi," *Etudes Congolaises,* V, No. 9 (November 1963), 11-16.

Young, M. Crawford. "The Congo Begins to Stir," *Africa Report,* Vol. 8, No. 9 (October 1963), pp. 9-13.

―――. "Congo Political Parties Revisited," *Africa Report,* Vol. 8, No. 1 (January 1963), pp. 14-20.

Unpublished Studies

Bo-Boliko, André. "Le comportement des travailleurs manuels congolais devant leurs rémunérations." Mémoire. Ecole Sociale de Louvain, 1958. Mimeographed.

Kalanda, Auguste. "Organisation des Villes au Congo Belge." Mémoire de Licence en Sciences Politiques et Administratives. Université Lovanium, 1958.

Kisuka, Gustave. "La consultation populaire du 14 décembre 1958 à Ndjili." Seminar paper. Université Lovanium, 1959.

Madrandele, F. "Essai d'interprétation du résultat de la consultation de 1958 à Matete." Seminar paper. Université Lovanium, 1959.

―――. "Les parastataux au Congo." Mémoire en Sciences Politiques et Administratives. Université Lovanium, 1960.

Tshibangu, André. "La technique de nomination dans le statut des villes." Mémoire de Licence en Sciences Politiques et Administratives. Université Lovanium, 1958.

Tshiswaka, Theodore. "Salaires et budgets familiaux des travailleurs de la Minière du Beceka à Bakwanga." Mémoire, Ecole Sociale de Louvain, 1958. Mimeographed.

Wembi, Antoine. "Influence de l'organisation administrative coutumière chez les Atetela. Mémoire de Licence en Sciences Politiques et Administratives Université Lovanium, 1961.

Periodicals

The following select list of periodicals devoted mainly to the Congo includes only the most important, frequently consulted journals.

Bulletin de CEPSI, 1946—Beginning in 1957, renamed *Problèmes Sociaux Congolais.*

Bulletin des Séances, ARSOM, 1931—

Congo, 1920-1939.

Courrier Africain (CRISP), 1959-1961. Beginning in 1962, this irregular newsletter was renamed *Travaux Africains.*
Etudes Congolaises, 1961–
Problèmes d'Afrique Centrale, 1946-1959.
Remarques Congolaises, 1959–
La Voix du Congolais, 1945-1959.
Zaïre, 1947–

Newspapers

Excluding Belgian and Congolese newspapers, the most useful reporting on Congo affairs has been done by *Le Monde, The Times* (London), *The Observer* (London), *Economist* (London), and the *New York Times.* The list below includes the Belgian and Congolese newspapers which have been most frequently consulted. The Flemish language press is not included, although some of the Flemish papers, especially *Standaard* (Brussels), have had some quite good Congo reporting. Belgium has no single newspaper of historical record equivalent to the *New York Times, The Times* (London), or *Le Monde.* Of the French language press, *La Libre Belgique* and *Le Soir* are the most influential; both are very conservative.

I. Belgium
  La Cité (Catholic)
  Dernière Heure
  Drapeau Rouge (Communist)
  Echo de la Bourse (financial)
  La Libre Belgique (Catholic)
  Le Peuple (Socialist)
  Pourquoi Pas? (Liberal weekly)
  Le Soir (Liberal)
II. Congo
  A. Pre-independence African press.
    Notre Kongo
    Kongo Dieto
    Kongo dia Ngunga

Congo
L'Indépendance
L'Echo de Stanleyville
Uhuru
La Voix du Peuple
Emancipation
Solidarité Africaine
La Nation Congolaise
La Liberté
Kimbanguisme
Kongo Ya Sika
Nsango Na Kobikisa
La Vérité
La Phare
La Voix du Katanga

B. Post-independence. (Only those newspapers which appeared with some degree of regularity are included here.)

   1. Leopoldville
     *_Courrier d'Afrique_
     *_Présence Congolaise_
     Le Progrès
     Réalités Africaines
     L'Etoile du Congo

   2. Coquilhatville
     Alerte
     Manono

   3. Stanleyville
     Uhuru

   4. Bukavu
     Actualités du Kivu
     La Presse Africaine
     Dignité Nouvelle
     La Vérité

   5. Elisabethville

* Published before 1960.

*Essor du Katanga (formerly Essor du Congo)
*Echo du Katanga
La Voix du Katanga
6. Luluabourg
Le Batisseur

Documentary Sources

For study of the colonial system in the Congo, the following are the primary documentary sources:

Loi sur le gouvernement du Congo Belge (Charte Coloniale, 1908).

Loi fondamentale relative aux structures du Congo, 1960. (Found in Documents Parlementaires, Chambre des Représentants, no. 489, March 31, 1960, pp. 1-44.)

Piron, Pierre, and Devos, J. Codes et Lois du Congo Belge. 4 vols. Brussels: F. Larcier, 1959.

Bulletin Officiel du Congo Belge (decrees); Bulletin Administratif (ordinances), replaced in 1960 by Moniteur Congolais.

Annales Parlementaires. Chambre des Représentants.

Annales Parlementaires. Sénat de Belgique.

Rapports Annuels sur l'Administration du Congo Belge, présentés aux Chambres Législatives.

Conseil Colonial. Compte-Rendus Analytiques.

Conseil de Gouvernement. Compte-Rendus Analytiques.

Conseils de Province. Compte-Rendus Analytiques.

Discours d'Ouverture des Gouverneurs-Généraux aux Conseils de Gouvernement.

Bulletin mensuel des statistiques générales du Congo.

For the period since independence, documentary sources are much more fragmentary. Yet when all the different materials are put together, the sum total is impressive in its quantity, and in some cases in its quality. Statistical material is far more difficult to collect, but with some ingenious methodology and able personnel, such agencies as the

* Published before 1960.

Conseil Monétaire, and the *Institut des Recherches Eco-nomiques et Sociales* at the *Université Lovanium* have issued an impressive collection.

The official gazette is the *Moniteur Congolais* (and *Moniteur Katangais*). There are proceedings of the national Parliament and the provincial assemblies, although only the former have been published even in part; the rest are only in mimeographed form. An excellent chronology of events is prepared monthly by Louis Mandala, and appears in *Etudes Congolaises.* The *Conseil Monétaire* publishes regular statistical bulletins. The annual reports of the major companies, especially the *Société Générale,* provide some economic insights. The Ministry of Information has maintained a press service, *Congo Presse,* with voluminous releases; the semi-official *Agence Congolaise de Presse* also has had an enormous output. One of the most valuable sources is the thorough documentation issued by the United Nations and the various specialized agencies (WHO, FAO, UNESCO, etc.).

A short list of other documentary sources consulted is appended:

Annuaire Catholique. 1960-1961. Brussels: 1961.

Chambre des Représentants, session 1958-1959, *Document Parlementaire 100/3,* March 27, 1959. Commission parlementaire chargée de faire une enquête sur les événements qui se sont produits à Léopoldville en janvier 1959. Rapport.

Chronique de Politique Etrangère. "La crise congolaise," XIII, Nos. 4-6 (July-November, 1960); "Evolution de la crise congolaise," XIV, Nos. 5-6 (September-November, 1961); "L'O.N.U. et le Congo," XV, Nos. 4-6 (July-November, 1962).

The Congo. A Report of the Commission of Enquiry appointed by the Congo Free State Government. G. P. Putnam's Sons: 1906.

Congo Belge. Section Documentation, Bureau Archives.

BIBLIOGRAPHY

Documents relatif à l'ancien District du Kivu 1900-1922.
Leopoldville. 1959. Mimeographed.

Congo Belge. Service des Archives. *Documents pour servir à l'étude du milieu (histoire).* Part I. Ville de Léopoldville. Leopoldville: 1959.

Congo July 1960—Evidence. Brussels: 1960.

Economic Round Table Conference, Brussels, April-May, 1960. *Proceedings and Documents.* Mimeographed.

Gevaerts, Frans. *Vade Mecum à l'usage du Service Territorial.* 1953.

Guebels, L. *Relation complète des travaux de la Commission Permanente pour la Protection des Indigènes au Congo Belge.* Elisabethville: Centre d'Etudes des Problèmes Sociaux Indigènes, 1953.

Livre blanc du gouvernement katangais sur les événements de septembre et décembre 1961. Elisabethville: 1962.

Manifeste des universitaires congolais. 1961.

Ministère des Colonies. *Recueil à l'usage des fonctionnaires et des agents du Service Territorial au Congo Belge.* 5th ed., Brussels: 1930.

Ministère du Congo Belge et du Ruanda-Urundi. *Annuaire Officiel.* 35th ed. Brussels: 1959.

Munongo, Godefroid. *Comment est né le nationalisme katangais.* Elisabethville: June 16, 1962. Mimeographed.

Organisation des Conseils de Territoire, Conseils de Province. Leopoldville: Congo-Presse, 1959.

Province du Kasai. Administration de la Sureté. *Activité Kalamba et Association Lulua-Frères.* Bulletin d'Information, February 2, 1958.

Province Orientale. *Politique indigène: Instructions.* 1923.

Rapport du Groupe de Travail pour l'étude du problème politique au Congo Belge. Brussels: Inforcongo, 1959.

La réforme de l'enseignement: Mission pédagogique Coulon-Deneyn-Renson. Brussels: 1954.

Renseignments sur la population du territoire du Mweka située sur la rive droite de la Rivière Lubudi (Région de

Misumba) avec project de réorganisation politique. A. Lambert, Administrateur du Territoire, 1959. Mimeographed.

République du Congo. *Documentation technique du gouvernement concernant les résolutions de Coquilhatville.* Leopoldville: 1961.

République du Congo. *Les entretiens Adoula-Tshombe.* Leopoldville: 1962.

République du Congo. Ministère des Affaires Etrangères. *De Léopoldville à Lagos.* Leopoldville: 1962.

République du Congo. Ministère des Affaires Etrangères. *La Province du Katanga et l'indépendance congolaise.* Leopoldville: 1961.

Round Table Conference, Brussels, January-February, 1960. *Proceedings and Documents.* Mimeographed.

Scheyven, R. and de Schryver, A. *Message des Ministres du Congo Belge et du Ruanda-Urundi aux agents belges de l'Administration d'Afrique.* April 26, 1960.

Sénat de Belgique. *Rapport de la Mission Sénatoriale au Congo et dans les territoires sous tutelle belge.* 1947.

Tshombe, Moise. *Discours prononcé par le Président du Katanga à l'occasion de la fête du 11 juillet, 1962.* Elisabethville: 1962.

United States Congress. House of Representatives. Committee on Foreign Affairs. *Staff Memorandum on the Republic of the Congo.* Committee Print. August 24, 1960.

Ville de Léopoldville. *Consultation du 8 décembre 1957.* Leopoldville: 1958. Mimeographed.

Ville de Léopoldville. *Organisation des Villes—Documentation Conseils C. E. C. Matete-Ndjili.* Leopoldville: 1958.

White Book of the Katanga Government about the outlaw activities in some Baluba areas. Elisabethville: 1961.

Index

Abako, 117, 118, 119, 120-21, 156, 159, 192, 234, 247, 255, 266, 275, 294, 298, 299, 300-302, 304-306, 367, 378-79, 381-82, 504-12, 558, 568, 575; burgomasters, 125-26; Cartel, 159, 172, 513-14; 1956 Manifesto, 505

Abazi, 544

ABIR, 218

ABL, 383

Académie Royale des Sciences d'Outre Mer (ARSOM), 23

Action Socialiste, 296-97

Adoula, Cyril, 116, 174, 322, 338, 341, 343, 346, 362, 364, 375, 386, 388-89, 394, 455-58, 467-68, 547

ADA, 568

AFAC, 97, 178

Afrique Equatoriale Française, 477

Afrique Occidentale Française, 477

Afro-Asian Peoples' Solidarity Conference, March, 1964, 345

Agoyo, 347

Air Congo, 401

Albert, see royal family

Alco, 375, 382, 568

Alexander, General, 448

Algeria, 439

Almond, Gabriel, 582

alumni associations, 291-92

Alur, 133n, 568

Alves, Jean-Baptiste, 168n

Anany, Jerome, 346, 381, 384, 459, 567

Andhra, 533

Anekonzapa, 346

Angola, 255

Ankole, 480

Anversoise, 218

APIC, 97, 216, 267, 291, 313, 325, 436

Arabs, 559-60; wars 1892-94, 441

Argentina, 478n

Armée de Libération Nationale, 439

Armée Nationale Congolaise, 122, 438-52, 455-63, 577-78. See also Force Publique

Arthéon, General, 49

Association des Anciens Elèves des Frères Chrétiens (AS-SANEF), 292

Association des Anciens Elèves des Pères de Scheut (AD-APES), 292

Association des Baluba, 493, 497

Association des Classes Moyennes Africaines (ACMAF), 44, 202

Association des Immatriculés, 87

Assoreco, 427

Asumani, 347

ATCAR, 302, 540, 570

Avungara, 190

Azande, 190-91, 254, 282, 442, 521, 544, 560, 563, 568

Azikiwe, 272n, 387

Babadet, 368n

Babembe, 542

Baboma, 568

Babua, 282, 345, 386, 568

Badjoko, Charles, 379, 567

Badibanga, 348

Baganda, 189

Bahemba, 542

Baholoholo, 542

Bahunde, 568

Bakasai, 246

Bakete, 265, 551, 570

Bakongo, 108, 181, 185, 189, 217, 228, 239-40, 244, 246-47, 255, 256, 257, 270, 284-86, 293, 325, 557-58, 568, 573, 575, 576; separatism, 504-12

Bakuba, 135-36, 260, 261-63, 265

645

Bakumu, 253, 255, 287, 568
Bakusu, 122, 186, 521, 547, 548, 554-56, 560, 561-62, 568. *See also* Batetela
Bakutu, 212
Bakwanga, 331
Balandier, 189, 197, 247, 257, 270
Balumotwa, 542
Bale, 568
Baluba, 234, 241-42, 246, 264, 269, 270, 301, 325, 352, 493n, 501, 557, 568, 570; burgomasters, 126-27; Hemba, 493n, 568; Kasai, 121-22, 124, 192, 241, 251, 256, 258-61, 269, 294, 491-92, 493n, 520, 537, 573; Shankadi, 132n, 193, 241, 282, 493n
Balubakat, 193, 194, 300, 302, 304, 305, 335, 367, 375, 429, 452, 498, 502, 513; Cartel, 302, 429, 502, 503n, 504, 540-44; youth, 543
Balubasania, 542
Bamba, Emmanuel, 346, 391n
Bambala, 556-57, 568
Bambundu, 345, 382, 556, 568, 577
Bami of Rwanda and Burundi, 83
Banana, 154
Banande, 568
Bandibu, 240
Bangala, 108, 234, 240, 242-45, 246, 247, 249-50, 255, 269, 325, 442, 505, 506, 557, 573
Bangala, Mme, 428
Bangongo, 556, 568
Bannerman, Charles, 279
Bantandu, 240, 558
Banyamwezi, 186
Banyanga, 568
Bapende, 268, 269n, 377, 551, 561, 556-57, 568, 570, 577
Baptist Missionary Society, 257
Basakata, 568
Basanga, 568

Bas-Congo, 153, 229, 319, 403, 432-33, 535
Bashi, 123, 192, 255, 282, 554-55, 568
Bashilele, 287, 551, 570
Basoga, 189
Basongye, 122, 246, 250-52, 542, 557, 561, 570
Batabwa, 568
Batetela, 246, 558-59, 561-62, 570; Batetela-Bakusu, 248, 442, 467
Batumbwe, 568
Baudouin, *see* royal family
Baushi, 568
Bayaka, 120, 192, 209-10, 247, 282, 325, 546, 568
Bayanzi, 568
Bayeke, 192, 501
Bazela, 542
Bayombe, 558
BCK railroad, 18, 208, 260, 262
Beatrice, prophetess, 285
Belgo-Congolese Community, 45-47, 52-57, 277
Bemba, 240
Bena Kanyoka, 121, 570
Biebuyck, Daniel, 245, 253
Bienga, 538
Binda, 348
Binza Group, 379-80, 389, 469
Bisukiro, Marcel, 198, 301, 304, 346, 364n
Bizala, 347
black bourgeoisie, 43-45
Bloc Démocratique National, 361
Bobangi, 256, 568
Bo-Boliko, André, 210, 211-12, 213, 226-27
Bobozo, General Louis, 449, 459, 461
Bocheley-Davidson, Egide, 345
Boelaert, Father R. P. E., 46n, 130, 248, 249, 266, 268
Bokonga, 346
Bolamba, Antoine-Roger, 249, 280, 328n, 400

Bolela, 347
Bolikango, Jean, 120, 173, 245, 292, 304, 347, 389, 400, 505, 547
Bolobo, 257n
Bolya, Paul, 120, 249, 304, 347, 348
Boma, 146, 196, 199, 257, 480, 482
Bomans, 153-54
Bomboko, Justin, 147n, 178, 304, 313, 326, 346, 380, 386, 488n
Bouvier, Mme. P., 488n
boyeries, 91
boys, 196, 209
Brausch, Georges, 30, 44n, 103, 129
Brazil, 478n
Brazzaville, 35, 255, 257, 280, 345
Brussels, 146-52; exposition, 281, 573; Round Table Conference, 59, 155-61, 171-78, 278, 298, 300, 310, 313, 325n, 343, 385, 498, 512, 513-17, 535
Buchmann, Jean, 276, 359
Budja, 245, 282, 383-84, 568
Buell, Raymond Leslie, 10-11
Buganda, 133n, 478, 480
Buisseret, Auguste, 44, 96, 103, 143, 147, 149, 162, 188, 202, 216, 400, 494n, 498
Bukavu, 88, 90, 207, 209, 210, 255, 382-83, 429, 555-56
Bula Matari, 98n
Bula, Vital, 360
Bulundwe, E. 569
Bumba (Moyen-Congo), 383-84
Bunche, Ralph, 324-25, 341
Bunyoro, 480
Burma, 439,478
Bushong, 262, 551, 570
Buta, 187

cabinet, 408-11
Cambier, 484n
Cameron, 259
Camus, Mwissa, 255

Caprasse, G., 36, 194-95, 241, 254, 293, 387
Cardoso, 347, 415
Carte du Mérite Civique, 77-79, 84
Cartel des Cultivateurs, 560, 568
Cartel Katangais, see Balubakat Cartel
Cataractes, 403
catechists, 196
Centre d'Etudes des Problèmes Sociaux Indigènes (CEPSI), 42, 43, 67-68
Centre extra-coutumier (CEC), 70, 90, 107, 135, 293
Centre de Recherche et d'-Information Socio-Politiques (CRISP), 4n
Cercle St. Benoit, 292
cercles des évolués, 291-92
Cerea, 297, 301, 302, 304, 375, 383, 568
Chad, 477
Charlier, Colonel, 463
Charte Coloniale, 75
chefferie, 13—32
chiefs, 184-95
church, see missions
circonscriptions indigènes, 42, 66, 130-34, 135-38, 431-35
cité européene, 111
cité indigène, 90, 107-08, 111
cité suburbaine, 111
cité urbaine, 111
Coaka, 375
cobalt, 222
Coleman, James, 40n, 582
Colin, 347
Collard, 155, 160
Collège des Commissaires, 329-30, 332-33, 410, 467
collège permanente, 137
color bar, see discrimination
Cominière, 151n
Comité National du Kivu (CNKi), 64
Comité National de Libération (CNL), 345, 377

Comité Spécial du Katanga (CSK), 45, 64, 89, 482
comité urbain, 107, 110, 116
Commission for the Protection of Natives, 26-28, 38, 76, 77, 188, 219
Compagnie des Batetela, 293
Compagnie du Congo pour le Commerce et l'Industrie (CCCI), 18, 282
Compagnie Cotonnière Congolaise, 18
Compagnie du Katanga, 482
Compagnie Pastorale du Lomami, 18, 190
companies, 14-18, 150-52
Concordat of 1906, 13
Confédération des Associations Tribales du Katanga (Conakat), 193, 278, 298, 300, 302, 429, 453-54, 493-504, 512-13, 514-15, 540-41, 568, 570
Confédération des Syndicats Chrétiens (CSC-Catholic), 65
Confédération des Syndicats Libres du Congo (CSLC), 349
Congo, 279
Congo Free State, 15, 36, 48, 60, 217-18, 241, 282, 480
Congo River, 209
Conscience Africaine, 297, 505; 1956 manifesto, 46, 165, 297
conseil de cité, 116
Conseil Colonial, 20, 23-26, 99-100, 111, 166
Conseils d'enterprise, 62
Conseil de Gouvernement, 23, 28-30, 78-81, 111, 146, 166
Conseil de Législation, 166
consultations, see elections
contrat d'emploi, 65, 99, 100
contrat de travail, 65, 99, 100
Convention Peoples' Party (CPP), 306, 372
Coppens, Professor Paul, 488
Copperbelt, 237
Coquilhat, Camille, 242-43
Coquilhatville, 195, 210, 255, 265, 267, 427; Round Table Conference, 207, 337, 524-25, 543, 547
Cornélis, Henri, 49, 168, 401
cotton, 222, 223-27
councils, territorial, 169, 170
Courrier d'Afrique, 36, 117, 325
courts, 130, 420-23
Crèvecoeur, Major, 452
CSC, 291n
Cultivation, compulsory, 11, 66-67, 223, 224, 230, 435
Cuvette Centrale, 382, 384, 548, 552, 564, 568

Dahomey, 439
d'Aspremont-Lynden, Count, 50, 56, 521
Davister, Pierre, 496
Dayal, 447, 523n
de Bauw, A., 483
debt, public, 65
de Bruyne, Edgard, 149
Declarations of January 13, 1959, 37, 49, 151, 152, 155, 166-67, 278, 298, 507
de Cleene, N., 24n, 25
decolonization, French and British, 35
Decoster, A., 498
Decree of July 24, 1918, 101
Decree of Nov. 23, 1931, (centre extra-coutumier), 70
Decree of Feb. 10, 1933, 92
Decree of Dec. 5, 1933 (circonscriptions indigènes), 11n, 66, 67, 130-31
Decree of Feb. 10, 1953 (African land rights), 85
Decree of June 30, 1954, 99
Decree of Dec. 29, 1955, 11n
Decree of March 26, 1957 (statut des villes), 42, 106-17
Decree of May 10, 1957 (circonscriptions indigènes reform), 11n, 42, 106, 128-39, 437
Decree of Dec. 2, 1957, 105

Decree of May, 8, 1958 (judicial reform), 101
Decree of Oct. 13, 1959 (statut des villes reform), 169
Defawe, O., 80
de Hemptinne, Mgr. Jean, 4n, 27, 82, 103, 129, 130, 189, 223, 483
de Jonghe, E., 243
Delport, 49
Delvaux, Albert, 198, 326, 346-48, 546
de Meulemeester, 130, 481, 484n
Dendale commune, 125, 426-27
Depage, Henri, 43
depression, economic, 220-22
Dequae, André, 49, 146, 149
Dequenne report, 270n
Dericoyard, J. P., 82, 346-47, 505, 506n, 544
de Rop, E. P. A., 248-49, 266
desegregation, 87-105
de Schrijver, Auguste, 59, 149, 151, 158, 159, 160, 162, 171, 172, 173, 178, 401, 497
Deutsch, Karl, 586
development, economic and social, 61-65
de Vleeschauwer, Baron Albert, 149, 223
de Wilde, L. O. J., 25
Dhanis column, 283
Diaka, Bernardin, 377n
Damusumbu, André, 346, 559, 571
Dinanga, General Floribert, 454-55
Diomi, Gaston, 126n, 146, 280n, 304, 403, 509, 537n, 567
direct rule, 128-29
discrimination, 52, 87-105
Diur, D., 571
Doucy, Professor Arthur, 156, 488, 498
Douglas, Mary, 245
Dumont, René, 358

Echo du Katanga, 498

L'Eclaireur de la Côte d'Ivoire, 279
Ecole Nationale de Droit et d'Administration (ENDA), 423
economic decline, 140-41
economic round table, 152
Edindali, André-Marie, 167
education, see schools
Eketebi, L., 403, 547, 567, 569
elections, 112-24; 1957, 491; 1958; 123-24; 1959, 182, 298; 1960, 302-06
Elias, T. O., 344, 526, 530
Elisabethville, 88, 107, 112, 118, 121-23, 194, 195, 201, 205, 207, 210, 240, 246, 254, 265, 267, 300, 331, 429-30, 564, 575
elite, bureaucratic, 195-201
employment, 205-09
Engulu, L., 569
Epikilipikili, 287
Epstein, A. L., 237
Equateur, 217, 242, 535, 561
Essor du Congo, 82, 484, (after Katanga secession Essor du Katanga), 336
évolués, 196
Eyskens, Gaston, 49, 326n, 342

Farnana, Panda, 274n
Fédération des Associations de Colons du Congo et du Ruanda-Urundi (Fedacol), 44, 486
Fédération de Baluba-Central Kasai au Katanga (Fegebaceka), 491-92, 498
Fédération de l'Equateur et du Lac Léo (Fedequalac), 120n, 246, 249
Fédération Générale des Travailleurs Kongolais (FGTK), 325, 349
Fédération Générale des Travailleurs Belges (FGTB-Socialist), 65, 291n
Fédération Kasaienne (Fedeka), 202, 292, 429, 493

Fédération Kasaienne de Léopold-ville (Fedekaleo), 120n
Fédération Kwango-Kwiloise, 120n
Fédération Kwangolaise, 292
finance, public, 517-22
Finant, Joseph, 331n, 567
fin de terme settlements, 75, 441
Fonds d'Avance, 127
Fonds du Bien-Etre Indigène (FBI), 62, 64
Force Publique, 50, 182, 243, 280, 282-84, 309, 314-19, 320, 321. *See also* Armée Nationale Congolaise
Forescom, 211
Forminière, 17, 205, 211, 353
foyers sociaux, 61
Franck, Louis, 14, 21, 68, 128, 129, 147, 187, 220
front commun, 160, 161, 171, 172, 173, 175
Front National Congolais (Fron-aco), 375

Gabon, 439, 477
Gallikoko, 260
Gandajika, 226
Ganshof van der Meersch, W. J., 49, 149, 312, 466
Garveyite movement, 1n
La Gauche, 145
Gbenye, Christophe, 198, 304, 328n, 345, 346, 364n, 375, 376-77, 379, 386-87, 466, 468-69
gendarmery, Katanga, 452-54; South Kasai, 454-55
Genge, André, 384
Géomines, 18
Gérard-Libois, Jean, 497-98
Gilson, A., 155
Gizenga, Antoine, 198, 301, 304, 319n, 328n, 330, 333, 336, 338, 339, 375, 386, 389-90, 451, 455, 456, 457, 556, 557, 577
Gluckman, Max, 237

Godding, Robert, 33, 149
gold, 222
Graeybeck, Lode, 149
Grandry, 484n
Greeks, 201
Grenfell, George, 26, 257, 569
Grévisse, F., 67n, 126, 224, 246
Groupe Marzorati, 23
Groupe de Travail, 37-38, 46, 52, 55, 56, 127, 138, 148n, 162, 166, 171, 277, 444-45
Guèye, Lamine, 430
Guinea, 417
Gullion, Edmund, 341

Habran, 484n
Hammarskjold, Dag, 324, 448
Handlin, Oscar, 235
Harlow, Vincent, 237-39
Hausa, 479
Haut-Congo, 550, 560, 564, 568
Heenen, Gaston, 484
Henniquiau, Colonel, 446, 447
Henroteaux, Leopold, 126
Hilton-Simpson, M. W., 241
Hougardy, Senator, 310
Houphouet-Boigny, 387
Housiaux, 162
Hulstaert, G., 248, 266

Ibanche, 260
Ibo, 479
Idzumbuir, Théo, 401, 415
Ileo, Joseph, 178, 249, 326, 338, 347, 394, 467
Ilunga, Tshibinda, 501n
Ilunga, Valentin, 198, 304, 346, 541n, 567
immatriculation 27, 75-87
India, 478
indirect rule, 68-69, 128, 130-34, 189n
Indonesia, 439, 476
Institut National pour l'Etude Agronomique au Congo Belge (INEAC), 64n, 68

Institut pour la Recherche Scientifique en Afrique Centrale (IRSAC), 64n
Institut de Sociologie Solvay, 488, 498
International Labor Organization, 99
International Monetary Fund (IMF), 334
Isombuma, P., 569
Ituri, 548
ivory, 218, 282
Ivory Coast, 477

Jadotville, 88, 107, 118, 121-23, 195, 207, 210, 265, 267, 564, 574-75
Janssens, General E., 50, 309, 316, 444
Jehovah's Witnesses, 252
Jungers, Governor-General, 81, 84

Kabangi, Alois, 198, 251, 347-48
Kabare, Albert, 192
Kabare, Mwami Alexandre, 132n, 383, 555
Kabinda, 382
Kabongo, Boniface, 193, 493n
Kalamba, 187
Kalamba, Sylvestre-Mangole, 187n, 294, 404, 563
Kalanda, Auguste (Mabika), 107n, 116, 120, 258, 346, 394, 401
Kalenda, Mathieu, 168n
Kalonji, Albert, 178, 192, 269, 301, 304, 352, 387, 388, 393-96, 454, 455, 567
Kalonji, Isaac, 202, 280
Kama, Sylvain, 346
Kamanga, G., 198, 347, 571
Kamina, 154, 312
Kamitatu, Cléophas, 301, 304, 347, 375, 386, 387-93, 403, 469, 537n, 556-57, 567
Kandolo, Damien, 380, 469n

Kanyoka, 246
Kanza, Daniel, 148, 172n, 178, 301, 304, 425, 558
Kanza, Thomas, 94, 198, 280, 415
Kasai, 44
Kasai, 185, 217, 561; Central, 548, 562-63; South, 336, 352, 535, 537-39, 548, 549, 550, 553, 561, 570
Kasanji, 538
Kasavubu, 125, 148, 165, 172, 178, 182, 199, 229, 275, 277n, 304, 312, 314, 317, 318, 319, 322, 326, 328, 329, 330, 344, 366, 379, 386, 387, 388, 390-93, 426, 447, 455, 467, 495, 505, 509, 558
Kashamura, Anicet, 192, 198, 229, 301, 304, 328n, 331, 347, 349, 404, 429, 452, 567; Kashamura-Omari regime, 353, 547, 555
Kashemwa, 346
Kasongo, Joseph, 376, 379
Kasongo, Julian, 400, 447
Kasongo Nyembo, Emmanuel Ndaie, 132n, 193, 269, 454, 493n, 500, 501n
Katanga, 82, 90, 110, 185, 226, 229, 293, 309, 335, 337, 354, 561, 572, 576; Kyanana, 500; North, 434, 535, 540-44, 548, 549, 550, 552, 564, 568; Oriental, 548, 550, 552, 568; secession, 340-43; separatism, 481-90; South, 550
Kazadi, 346, 567
Kehleko, Dominique, 368, 373n, 387
Keita, Modibo, 387
Kenya, 439, 476
Kiamfu Panzu-Fumubulu, 192, 546, 562
Kibali-Ituri, 552, 560, 568
Kikongo, 244, 246
Kikwit, 382, 408, 547
Kilo-Moto, 205
Kilson, Martin, 230

Kimba, Evariste, 494, 541n
Kimbangu, Simon, 286
Kimbanguism, 247, 252, 284-86, 391
Kimvay, Félicien, 363, 556
Kini, E., 168
Kinkie, Raphael, 556
Kinshasa, 426
Kisanga, H., 569
Kisantu, 192; Congress 1959, 508, 511, 512-13
Kisolokele, Charles, 346, 348, 392n
Kitawala, 252-53
Kitenge, Gabriel, 296
Kitona, 154, 312; accords, 342, 526
Kittani, General, 449
Kivu, 90, 185, 229, 353, 561, 562; Central, 548, 550, 552, 562, 568; North 548, 552, 568; South, 554
Kiwewa, Antoine, 379
Kolwezi, 88, 207, 210, 265, 564
Kongo Central, 510, 535-37, 545, 548, 549, 550, 552, 561, 562, 568
Kongo dia Ngunga, 466n
Korea, South, 439
Koumorico, Victor, 280n, 569
Kupa, François, 368
Kwango, 192, 209, 255, 408, 546, 547, 548, 552, 561, 562, 564, 568
Kwilu, 153, 229, 408, 433, 544, 548, 552, 568, 577
Kyoka movement, 285

Labrique, Jean, 55
labor, 1920's shortage, 220; forced, 219
Lac Leopold II, 211, 217, 552, 561, 562, 568
landownership, African, 44-45, 66, 89-92, 227-29
language policy, 146
Laos, 439

Lassiry, Gabriel, 379
Laude, N., 24n, 25
Law of April 27, 1962 (new provinces), 565
Lebughe, Pierre, 346
Lefèvre, Théo, 342
Lens, 484n
Leplae, Edmond, 66
Leopold II, III, *see* royal family
Leopoldville, 88, 89, 90, 107, 110, 112, 146-52, 186, 195, 199, 201, 207, 208, 209, 217, 234, 245, 247, 255, 256, 257, 267, 269, 277, 300, 312, 325, 331-33, 354, 362, 425-27, 562, 574; 1957 elections, 118, 119-21; Round Table Conference, 337, 375, 522, 549
Le Roye, L., 24n, 25, 32
Leta, N., 569
Lever plantations, 220
Liberals, 17n, 141-45, 297, 498
Liboke lya Bangala, 120n, 245, 249
La Libre Belgique, 121, 171
Lihau, Marcel, 344, 346, 526
Lingala, 242, 244, 246
Liongo, Maximilien, 168n
Lippens, Maurice, 16, 484
Lisala, 245, 433, 567
Livingstone, 259
Lobobangi, 244
Lodja, 559; 1960 congress, 122n, 404
Loi Fondamentale, 51, 56, 176-78, 179, 326-27, 330, 337, 338, 343, 359, 367, 369, 380, 411, 515-17, 526-27, 530, 537-38, 546, 578
Lokele, 255, 256, 257n, 428, 560, 568
Lomami, 251, 548, 553, 561, 570
Lomami-Tshibamba, Paul, 275
Lopes, A., 167
Losso, Leonard, 459
Louwers, O., 25
Lozi, 240

Luakabwanga, François, 369, 563, 571
Lualaba, 331, 542, 548, 550, 552, 567, 570
Luanghy, Pascal, 122
Luapula, 186
Lubaya, André, 369, 377, 567, 571
Luebo, 260
Lugard, Lord, 235
Lugbara, 568
Luka, 381n, 426, 427, 568
Lulua, 124, 187, 234, 246, 254, 255, 258, 259n, 264, 265, 270, 493n, 557, 570; dispute with Baluba, 153; Frères, 124, 246, 265, 294-95, 466
Luluabourg, 207, 210, 251, 255, 256, 258, 264, 265, 267, 270, 277, 282, 325, 331, 561, 564, 570, 574; Congress, 278, 496; constitutional commission, 385, 531
Lumanza, 348
Lumbala, Jacques, 328n
Lumpungu II, 251
Lumumba, Patrice, 47, 86, 90, 100, 115, 122, 173, 182, 198, 229, 277, 280n, 295, 300, 301, 304, 309, 314-15, 316, 317, 318, 319, 322-25, 326, 328, 329, 330, 332, 346, 360, 388, 403, 447, 466, 467, 495, 537-38
Lunda, 186, 189, 192, 194, 269, 501, 540, 570
Lundula, General Victor, 122, 280n, 339, 446, 450, 455, 456, 457, 458, 459
Lusambo, 241, 258, 559
Lutula, 198, 346, 347

Maboti, Joseph, 346
Mackenzie, W. J. M., 35
Macquet, Jacques, 162
Madimba, 181
Maertens, Colonel, 446

Magotte, J., 69
Mahamba, Alexandre, 198, 347
Maindombe, 547, 548
Malago, Simon, 364n, 569
Malaya, 478
Malengreau, Guy, 33, 69, 81, 92, 224
Malimba, Paul, 504n
Mambaya, Pierre, 94n, 569
Mandi, André, 415
Mangbetu, 568
Manianga, 240, 558
Maniema, 153, 185, 186, 218, 226, 283-84, 339, 354, 404, 407, 535, 544-45, 547-48, 553, 554, 560, 564, 568
Mannoni, O., 59
Manono, Dominique, 251, 571
Manzikala, Jean Foster, 369, 376, 567, 569
Maquet, M., 25
Marlière, Colonel, 446, 450
Marxism, 213
Masena, 198, 346
Masikita, Pierre, 348, 569
Masons, 141
Massa, Jacques, 347, 381
Massaut, 484n
Mata Buike, 242-43
Matadi, 207, 208, 210, 217, 257, 317
Mathieu, 484n
Mayamba, Arthur, 567
Maus, A., 84
Mayombe, 240, 247
Mbandja, 568
Mbeka, Joseph, 346, 347, 415
Mbochi, 270
Mbuyi, 198, 347
medical services, 12, 62
Médie, Pierre, 364
Mercier, Paul, 239
Merriam, Alan P., 234
messianic movements, 3n, 284-88
Mexico, 478n
Michel, Serge, 325n
militias, private, 229
Mingambengele, F., 571

Minière du Bakwanga (ex-Formi-nière), 336, 539
mining, 15-16, 354
Mining Province, 538-39
Miruho, Jean, 331, 404, 457, 567
missions, 12-14, 148-50, 325
Mitchell, J. Clyde, 237, 240
Moanda, Vital, 558, 567, 569
Mobutu, General Joseph, 329, 330, 332, 339, 345, 380, 386, 446, 447, 448, 449-50, 455, 456, 457, 458, 459, 467, 468
Moeller de Laddersous, 130, 481
Moley, Benezet, 569
Mongali, Michel, 347
Mongo, 123, 130, 244, 246, 247-50, 255, 266, 325, 403, 404, 544, 545, 549, 557-58, 561, 568, Nhundo-Mongo, 248, 568
Mongwandi, 568
Mopipi, 346
Mosmans, Guy, 150
Moumié, Félix, 325n
Mouvement de l'Evolution Démocratique Africaine (MEDA), 381n, 568
Mouvement National Congolais (MNC), 38, 278, 297; Kalonji, 159, 300, 302, 304, 367, 511, 537-38, 570; Lumumba, 158, 159, 192, 299, 300, 302, 304, 306, 367, 368, 372-75, 375-76, 379, 383, 404, 560-61, 568, 570
Mouvement de Regroupement des Populations Kongolaises, 508
Mouvement de Résistance Bakongo, 507
Mouvement de l'Unité Basong(y)e (MUB), 251, 375, 381n, 570
Moyen-Congo, 245, 548, 550, 552, 561, 568
Mpadi, Simon, 286
Mpolo, Maurice, 198, 331, 347
Msiri, 186, 192, 499, 502n

Mudingayi, S., 167
Mualuanji, 539
Muké, General 453, 458, 459
Mukendi, Albert, 346
Mukenge, Barthélemy, 369, 404, 563, 567
Mukwidi, Thomas, 346
Mulamba, Colonel Leonard, 459
Mulele, Pierre, 198, 347, 377, 382, 459, 556, 577
mulopwe, 192, 395, 396n. See also Kalonji, Albert
Mungamba, Ferdinand, 348
Munongo, Antoine, see Mwenda-Munongo, Antoine
Munongo, Bernard, 193
Munongo, Godefroid, 186, 193, 304, 335, 430, 492
Mushiete, Paul, 415
Mushili, Gaston, 189n
mutinies, 282-84; Batetela, 441-42; Luluabourg, 77, 274, 442; 1960, 315-17
Mutombo, Pania, 251
Mutombo-Mukulu, 493n, 500
Muzungu, Christophe, 466, 467
Mwamba, Rémy, 198, 229, 328n, 346
Mwamba-Ilunga, Prosper, 193, 569
Mwami, see Kabare, Mwami Alexandre
Mwana Lesa, 287
Mwata Yamvo Ditende Yawa Nawezi, 132n, 186, 187-90, 191, 192, 194, 269, 500, 501n
Mwenda-Mukanda-Bantou, Odilon, 193
Mwenda-Munongo, Antoine, 83, 94n, 193, 500

nation-building, 5-6
nationalism, 234; Flemish, 129, 145-46, 266n, 267-68
Ndele, Albert, 334, 336, 380, 386
Ndjadi, Abbé Athanase, 559, 571
Ndjoku, Eugène, 249, 304
Nendaka, Victor, 204, 301, 332,

345, 364, 380, 386, 387, 467, 468-69
Ngaliema, 257n
Ngalula, Joseph, 116, 270, 336, 347, 382, 394, 396, 537n, 538, 539, 571
Ngiri-Ngiri, 426
Ngoie, Venant, 127n
Ngombe, 123, 245, 383-84, 545, 547, 557, 568
Ngongo Lutete, 186, 251, 558
Ngoni, 240
Nguvulu, Alphonse, 346
Ngwaka, 568
Ngwenza, 198, 347
Ngyese, 347
Niger, 477
Nigeria, 232, 303, 479, 533
Nioki, 211-12
Njoku, 403
Nkayi, Pascal, 198, 346
Nkokolo, Colonel, 314, 447, 449
Nkrumah, 309, 387, 476
Notre Kongo, 506
Nouvelle Anvers, 196, 242
Nussbaumer, José, 346, 467
Nyembo, Albert 346
Nyerere, Julius, 360, 387
Nyim, 260, 265
Nyirenda, Toma, 287
Nzeza, Simon, 148, 509
Nzeza-Nlandu, Edmond, 266, 466n

Office des Cités Africaines, 62, 90
Okito, Joseph, 47, 331
Olympio, Sylvanus, 439
Omari, Adrien, 404n, 429, 567
Omari, Antoine, 82, 192, 404-05, 567
Opangault, Jacques, 509
Orban, P. 25
Orientale, 153, 185, 226, 547, 548, 562

Paelinck, J., 269

Pakassa, Colonel, 456, 457n
Pakistan, 439
Palm oil, 221-22
Panaf, 568
parastatal structures, 63-64
paritary representation, 46, 110, 164n
parliament, 318-19, 322, 326-28, 337-40, 359-70, 547
Parti Démocratique Congolais (PDC), 381, 383, 384, 568, 570
Parti Démocratique de la Côte d' Ivoire, 236-37
Parti Démocratique de Guinée (PDG), 306, 311, 372, 417
Parti Démocratique National (Padena), 381n, 570. *See also* Coaka
Parti de la Liberté et du Progrès, 17n. *See also* Liberals
Parti National du Progrès (PNP), 167, 192, 300, 302, 304
Parti National Lumumbiste (Panalu), 375
Parti du Peuple (PP), 511
Parti Progressiste Congolais-Balubakat, 381n, 382, 568
Parti Social Chrétien (PSC), 17n, 141-45, 297
Parti Socialiste Belge (PSB), 17n, 21-22, 141-45, 297, 498
Parti Solidaire Africain (PSA), 159, 192, 246, 298, 299, 300, 301, 302, 304, 306, 375-76, 381, 382-83, 511, 562; Gizenga: 345, 379, 568; Kamitatu, 379, 568
Pashi, A., 569
paternalism, 59-72
paysannat indigène, 48, 68, 91, 224, 230, 574
Pene Misenga, Omari, 167
Pères Blancs, 199
Pères de Scheut, 269
Périn, Professor François, 176
Périn, Mme. François, 488n, 498
Pétillon, Léon, 36, 37, 38, 42, 48,

69, 106, 147-48, 149, 151, 162, 169
Pinzi, Arthur, 126n, 318, 346
Puati, Major Jacques, 461
Platonism, 10
PNCP, 382, 568
PNF, 427
Poigneux, F, 25
Pointe-Noire, 255
police, provincial, 463-65. *See also* gendarmery
Pons, 210
population, decline, 27; European expansion, 88, 93
portage, 217, 219, 285
Port Francqui, 260, 330
Portuguese, 201
pouvoirs concédants, 64
PRA, 568
Présence Africaine, 277
Présence Congolaise, 325
priests, African, 76, 198-99
Problèmes d'Afrique Centrale, 191
promenade militaire, 462
Puna, 302, 304, 375, 381n, 382, 383-84, 568
Punga, 287
Pye, Lucien, 438, 440

Quinze, 279

race relations, 73-105
Rae arbitration commission, 153n
Rassemblement Démocratique Africain (RDA), 381, 568
Rassemblement des Démocrats du Congo (Radeco), 381
Rassemblement Katangais, 494
Rassemblement du Peuple Luba (RPL), 381n, 382, 570. *See also* Mouvement National Congolais, Kalonji
Reco, 364n
recruitment, colonial, 20-21
refugees, 335
Renkin, Jules, 147
research, colonial, 22-23

revolts, 281-84
Rhodesia, Northern, 252
Rhodesia, Southern, 476
Rhodes-Livingstone Institute, 237
riots, 288-90; Luluabourg, 289; Matadi, 289; Leopoldville, 4, 58, 151, 152, 156, 228, 239, 266, 278, 289-90, 490, 504, 578; Stanleyville, 173n, 290n, 300
Robert, M., 25
Roberto, Holden, 508n
Robeson, Mrs. Paul, 275
Robinson, Kenneth, 36
Rolin, Senator, 174
Romanuik, A., 210
Rome Conference of Negro Artists and Writers, 280
Rouch, Jean, 240
royal family, 47-52; Albert, 48, 286; Baudouin, 48, 50, 52, 53, 58, 73, 151, 177, 183, 326n, 497; Leopold II, 48, 326, 482, 501; Leopold III, 48, 89, 91
Rubbens, Antoine, 39, 78-79, 84, 85, 88, 145, 296, 422, 489-90
rubber, 218, 222, 223, 282
Rudahindwa, Edmond, 198, 347, 364n
rural exodus, 209-10
Rutaganda, 192
Rwanda, 232
Rwanda-Burundi, 37
Ryckmans, André, 55, 164, 181, 319, 398
Ryckmans, Pierre, 33, 34n, 36, 60, 162, 230

Sabena airlines, 401
Saintraint, Antoine, 181
Salkin, Paul, 3
Salamu, Bernard, 427-29, 430, 560
Sandoa, 194
Sangara, Hubert, 168n, 401
Sankuru, 226, 287, 331, 339, 407, 548, 553, 558-59, 560, 564, 570; North, 547

San Salvador, 247, 285, 286
Sapwe, Pius, 429
Sawaba party (Niger), 374
Scheyven, Louis, 152n
Scheyven, Raymond, 49, 149, 152n, 155, 176
Schoeller, 123, 126, 153, 498, 511
schools, 13, 143-44, 148, 187-88, 229
sectors, 130, 131-32
Senate mission (1947), 93
Sendwe, Jason, 193, 304, 364-65, 382, 493, 497, 569
secession, 1959 attempt, 158; Katanga, 317-19; South Kasai, 324
Sépulchre, Jean, 55, 82, 484, 486, 488, 489, 490
settlers, 45, 486-87
Shils, Edmond, 440
Sita, Alphonse, 400
slave trade, 218-19
Société des Amis de Kasongo Nyembo et Kabongo, 293
Société des Basong(y)e et Tshofe, 293
Société de Crédit aux Classes Moyennes, 410
Société Générale, 17, 51, 190, 211, 503
Sohier, A., 20, 24n, 25, 81; Commission, 79-80
Le Soir, 171
Songolo, Alphonse, 198, 331n, 346
Soudan, 477
Soumialot, Gaston, 404-05
Southall, Aiden, 212, 270
Soviet Union, 308-09, 324
Spaak, Paul-Henri, 342
Spitaels-Evrard, Mme., 488n
Spitaels, Guy, 488n
Stanley, Henry, 242-43, 257n, 501
Stanley Pool, 186
Stanleyville, 88, 192, 195, 207, 209, 210, 216, 255, 277, 325,

330, 331-33, 335-36, 375, 427-29, 560
statut des villes, see Decrees of March 26, 1957, and Oct. 13, 1959
statut unique, 97, 182, 200, 402, 411-12
Stenmans, Alain, 510
strikes, 239
Sudan, 332, 439
Sundkler, B. C. M., 252
super-tribalism, 240-42
Sûreté, 202, 465-70
Swahili, 244
Symétain, 205

Tananarive Round Table, 337, 522-24, 545-46
Tanganyika, 186, 439
Tanganyika African National Union (TANU), 306, 311
Ten Year Plan, 229
Thirty Year Plan, 22, 36, 276
Thys, Albert, 482, 502
Thysville, 257, 286, 330
Tilkens, 484; 1933 reform (centralization), 480
tin, 222
Topoke, 568
Torday-Joyce expedition, 241, 262
Toro, 480
Touré, Sékou, 212, 309
traders, 201
Treaty of Friendship and Technical Assistance, 56
Tshala-Muana, 346
Tshatshi, Major, 449, 459, 461
Tshibamba, Marcel, 347
Tshibangu, André, 401
Tshikapa, 353
Tshiluba, 269
Tshokwe, 190, 542, 551, 570
Tshombe, Moise, 172, 189n, 191, 194, 304, 335, 341, 364, 429, 452, 458, 494, 495, 500, 521-29, 567; family, 201-02

Tshuapa (Equateur), 319
tungsten, 222
tutelle administrative, 113-14, 127

Ubangi, 548, 552, 568
Ubangi-Chari, 477
UDEA, 382, 568
Uele, 190, 226, 548, 552, 562, 568; Uele-Ituri, 547, 548
Uganda, 191, 232, 303, 439, 478, 480
Uganda Peoples' Congress (UPC), 303
Uketuenge, 347
Unibat, 375
Unida, 384, 568
Unilac, 568
Unimo, 124, 250, 302, 304, 305, 367-68, 381n, 403, 488n, 544, 545, 568
unemployment, 141, 215-16, 492
Union des Anciens Elèves des Frères Maristes (UNELMA), 292
Union pour la Colonisation (Ucol), 485, 488; manifesto, 489
Union Congolaise, 296, 490n
Union Démocratique Africaine, 344, 570
Union Katangaise, 494, 497, 498
Union Minière, 17, 61, 205, 208, 477, 221, 503n
Union National Congolaise (UNC), 300, 375, 404, 570
Union des Populations Camerounaises (UPC), 325, 374
Union des Populations d'Angola, 508-09
Union des Républiques d'Afrique Centrale (URAC), 508
Union des Travailleurs Congolais (UTC), 325, 349, 365
Union des Warega (Unerga), 383, 554, 568
UNISCO, 292

United Nations, 7-8, 53, 59, 323, 330, 334-35, 336, 340-42, 344, 417, 452, 522, 526, 529, 575; Charter, 34
Unité Kasaienne, 381n, 548, 551, 553, 564, 570
University, Elisabethville, 94, 146, 498; Lovanium, 94, 96-97, 436, 581; Lovanium student letter, 97; 1961 manifesto, 195
Upper Volta, 477
uranium, 223
urbanization, 574
urban reform, see Decrees of March 26, 1957, and Oct. 13, 1959
urban workers, 204-16
U Thant Plan, 342, 458, 529

Valkenberg, 484n
Van Bilsen, A. A. J., 4, 22, 40, 53, 55, 58, 276, 392, 505
Van den Aberle, 162
Van de Putte, M., 24n, 25
Van der Dussen, Jean de Kestergat, 55n
Vanderkerken, Georges, 128, 248-49, 561
Van der Linden, F., 24n, 25
Van Hemelrijck, Maurice, 17, 48, 49, 50, 148, 149, 151, 155, 157, 158, 163, 400, 510
Vansina, Jan, 185
Van Wing, Father J., 20, 25, 150, 228, 249, 266, 285
Venezuela, 478n
Vermuelen, V., 129
Vietnam, South, 439
La Voix du Congolais, 77, 249, 400
Von Wissman, 187, 259

Wafwana, Emery, 563
wages and salaries, 205-06, 208, 213, 360-61

Waleffe, F. 24n, 25
Wallerstein, Immanuel, 236, 240
Wangermée, Major, 482, 484n
Warega, 383, 554-55, 568
Watutsi, 568
Weeks, John H., 244
Weregemere, Jean-Chrysastome, 301, 304, 346, 364, 567
West African Herald, 279
White Fathers, *see* Pères Blancs
Wigny, Pierre, 53, 81, 149, 521
Working Group, *see* Groupe de Travail

World War I, 219
World War II, 222-23

Yav, Joseph, 198, 346
Yoruba, 212, 479
Youlou, Abbé Fulbert, 508, 509
Yumbu, Gabriel, 556
Yumbu, Joseph, 400

Zanzibar, 232, 441
Zola, Emile, 363
Zolberg, Aristide, 236-37
Zondomyo, A., 569